ALSO BY GEOFFREY PERRET

NONFICTION
Days of Sadness, Years of Triumph
A Dream of Greatness
America in the Twenties
A Country Made by War
There's a War to Be Won
Winged Victory

FICTION
Executive Privilege

OLD
SOLDIERS
NEVER DIE

OLD
SOLDIERS
NEVER DIE

The Life of
Douglas MacArthur

GEOFFREY PERRET

ANDRE
DEUTSCH

First published in Great Britain in 1996 by
André Deutsch Limited
106 Great Russell Street
London WC1R 3LJ

CIP data for this title is available
from the British Library

ISBN 0 233 99002 X

Printed in the United States of America

This work is dedicated to
Albert P. Brewster—sailor,
Japanese linguist and friend.

Acknowledgments

Many people have helped me over the years that I thought about this book, researched it and finally wrote it. The person who gave me the most help of all, though, was undoubtedly Edward Boone, Jr., at the MacArthur Memorial and Archive in Norfolk, Virginia. Ed's knowledge of MacArthur's life is remarkable; his knowledge is matched only by his enthusiasm. I owe him a deep and abiding debt. Without him, this would have been a different, and inevitably much poorer, book.

There are others at the MacArthur Memorial and Archive whose assistance was also important, notably Colonel Lyman Hammond, Jim Zobel and Jeffrey Acosta.

I would like to thank Jeff Flannery of the Manuscript Division at the Library of Congress for helping me track down original materials and for many valuable suggestions on sources I ought to pursue. I was ably helped, once again, by Alan Aimone at West Point Special Collections, and by Suzanne Christoff of the West Point Archives. Herb Pankratz at the Eisenhower Library in Abilene, Kansas, and Dale Myers and Dwight Miller at the Herbert Hoover Library in West Branch, Iowa, deserve special thanks. So, too, does Dr. Richard Sommers, the archivist-historian at the U.S. Army Military History Institute, Carlisle Barracks. I must also express my thanks to the staff of the Hoover Institution at Stanford University; the Mudd Manuscript Library, Princeton; the Sterling Memorial Library, Yale; the Franklin D. Roosevelt Library in Hyde Park, New York; and the National Archives, in Washington.

I am deeply grateful to Professor David Horner of the Australian National

University, in Canberra, Australia, and James J. Halsema, of Glenmoore, Pennsylvania, for their valuable assistance, so cheerfully given. I benefited, as well, from extensive conversations with two acknowledged authorities on MacArthur, Professor Clayton D. James and Dr. Stanley Falk.

I would also like to express my appreciation to the following for permission to quote from copyrighted material that they control: Barbara Arnold, Isabella Baldwin, Clayton Byers, John S. D. Eisenhower, the MacArthur Memorial and Archive, and Yale University.

Finally, I have been fortunate yet again to have had the benefit of the editorial skills of Robert D. Loomis, a man too modest to permit me to say here what I really think of him.

Contents

N

North
Sea

ENGLAND

London

English
Channel

Calais
Boulogne

Cambrai

Soissons
Château-Thierry
Paris

Seine R.

Loire R.

F R A N C E

Ijmuiden
Amsterdam
Rotterdam
Scheldt
Estuary
Antwerp

Neder R.
Waal R.
Maas R.

THE
NETHERLANDS

Arnhem
Nijmegen

Ems R.

Rhine R.

Wilhelmshaven

BELGIUM
Brussels

Scheldt R.

Aachen
HUERTGEN
FOREST

Malmédy

Bastogne

Essen
Dusseldorf
Cologne
Bonn
Remagen

Ruhr R.

Frankfurt

Our R.

Sedan

Rheims
ARGONNE
FOREST

Verdun
Châlons-
Sur-Marne

Marne R.

Meuse R.

Côte-de-
Châtillon

LUX.
Luxembourg

Metz

Moder R.

Nancy
Lunéville

Strasbourg
Baccarat

Saône R.

Chaumont

Belfort

VOSGES MTS

BLACK FOREST

Zurich

SWITZERLAND

Bern

Kms
0   100
0   100
Miles

© 1995 A·Karl/J·Kemp

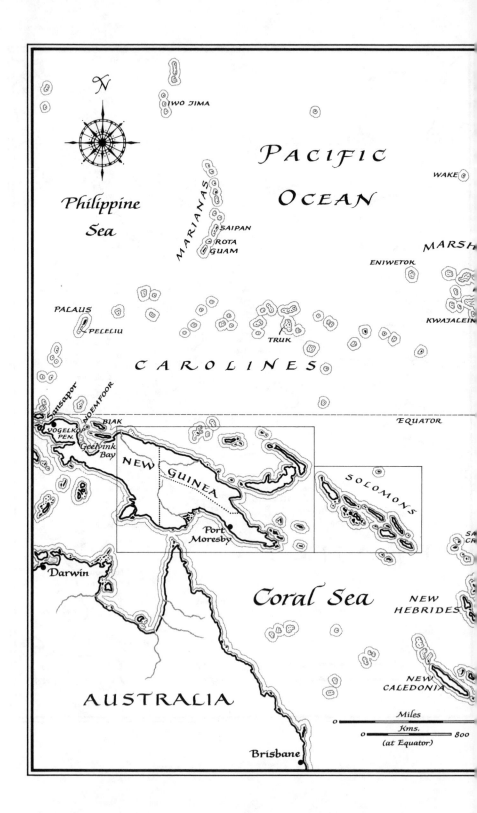

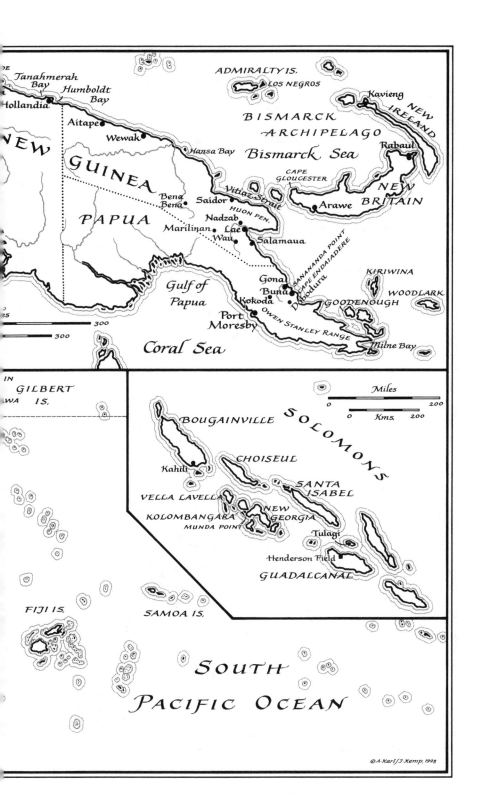

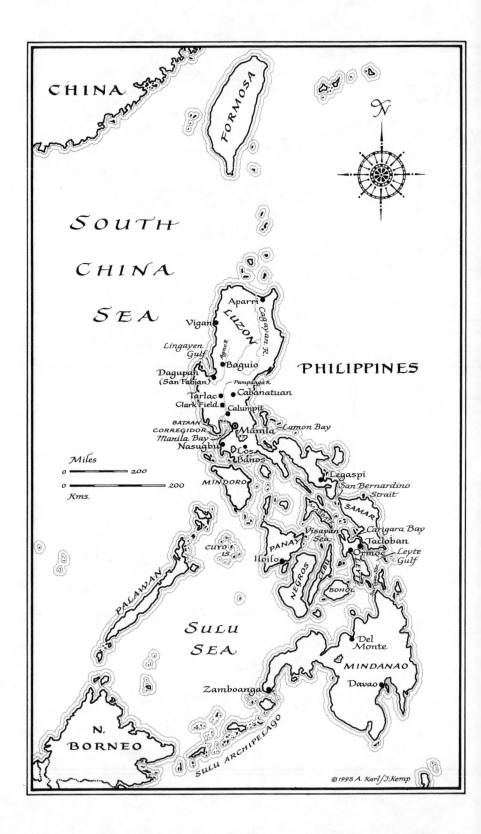

CHINA

FORMOSA

N

SOUTH

CHINA

SEA

Aparri

LUZON

Vigan

Cagayan R.

Lingayen
Gulf

Agno R.

Baguio

PHILIPPINES

Dagupan
(San Fabian)

Pampanga R.

Tarlac

Cabanatuan

Clark Field

Calumpit

BATAAN

Lamon Bay

CORREGIDOR

Manila

Manila Bay

Nasugbu

Los
Baños

Miles

0   200

0   200

Kms.

MINDORO

Legaspi

San Bernardino
Strait

SAMAR

CUYO
IS.

Visayan
Sea

Carigara Bay

Tacloban

PANAY

Ormoc

Leyte
Gulf

Iloilo

CEBU

PALAWAN

NEGROS

BOHOL

SULU

SEA

Del
Monte

MINDANAO

Zamboanga

Davao

N.
BORNEO

SULU ARCHIPELAGO

©1995 A. Karl / J. Kemp

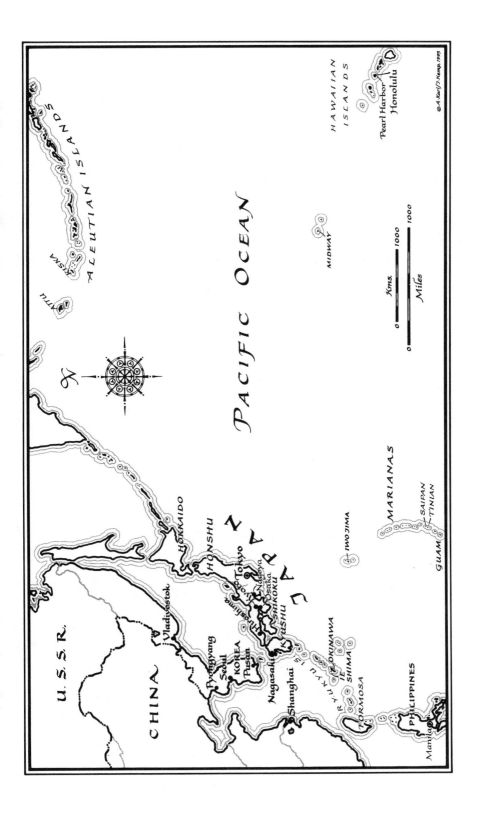

© A.Karl/J.Kemp 1995

OLD
SOLDIERS
NEVER DIE

The Sound of Bugles

Compared to both his peers and his predecessors, Douglas MacArthur was unique. From his birth at Little Rock Barracks, Arkansas, in 1880 to his death at Walter Reed Hospital eighty-four years later he never spent a day, or even an hour, outside the United States Army. Unlike the other five-star generals—Pershing, Marshall, Eisenhower, Bradley and Arnold—none of his formative years was passed in a civilian household, wondering what life in the military might be like. That military world was the whole of his existence from the time his mother clutched him as a baby to her breast. His first memory, he said, was "the sound of bugles."[1]

With an ancestry on his father's side that was almost entirely Scottish, MacArthur sprang from a people noted for excelling in two fields of endeavor—soldiering and the law. This inheritance was repeated on his mother's side. She came from Virginia, that other famous nursery of warriors and attorneys.

MacArthur's paternal grandfather, Arthur McArthur, born in Glasgow on January 26, 1817, considered himself a "double-distilled McArthur": Both his mother and father had the surname McArthur. Unfortunately, Arthur never knew his father, who had died ten days before the birth of his son. Born and reared in the lowlands of Scotland, this double-distilled McArthur convinced himself that the McArthurs had once been a clan in their own right, and a Highland clan too. There wasn't a scintilla of evidence to prove his case, but little romance clung to the Lowlands around dull, industrializing Glasgow. The romance, much improved on and sold to an enthralled nineteenth-century readership in the novels of Sir Walter

Scott, was all in the Highlands. And that, he felt, was where his forebears must really have come from, the land of purple braes, rocky crags, deep forests, fast-flowing salmon streams, picturesque castles and rousing tales of such warrior kings as Robert the Bruce and romantic figures like Bonnie Prince Charlie. Baby Douglas could count on being fed legends of heroic ancestors along with his mother's milk.

When he was seven years old, Arthur McArthur's mother remarried. In 1828, at the age of eleven, Arthur, his mother and stepfather emigrated to the United States, landing in New York. They soon moved to Uxbridge, Massachusetts. Ambitious, bright and interested in politics, young Arthur later returned to New York, became an ardent Democrat and, "by my own almost unaided efforts," gained the rudiments of a college education and went on to study law.[2] In 1841 he was admitted to the New York bar.

While studying in New York, he met, fell in love with and married a dark-eyed young woman from Springfield, Massachusetts, named Aurelia Belcher. She persuaded him to move to Springfield, where, in June 1845, their first child, a son, Arthur McArthur, Jr., was born. Four years later Arthur moved to Milwaukee, and there Aurelia bore him a second son, Frank.

Getting involved in the Democratic party, Arthur saw his career take wing. He became city attorney, and in November 1855 Arthur McArthur was elected lieutenant governor of Wisconsin. The next year the Democratic governor was briefly ousted while the state supreme court looked into allegations of ballot rigging in his election. For four days, while the court made up its collective mind, Arthur McArthur served as governor. The elected governor was eventually allowed to resume his post (although he turned out, once restored to office, to have palms that required periodic greasing), and Arthur returned to the lieutenant governorship.[3]

In 1857 McArthur was elected to a circuit judgeship, a position he held for twelve years. In the meantime the Republican party arose from the wreckage of normal political life, and the hapless, bitterly divided Democrats looked on like bemused spectators as Abraham Lincoln became President and the South seceded. In April 1861, a month after Lincoln's first inauguration, Confederate artillery opened fire on Fort Sumter, guarding the sea entrance to Charleston, South Carolina. The fort surrendered after two days of fierce bombardment. Lincoln called on the states to provide 75,000 militia. On May 3 he issued a second call. He wanted 42,000 volunteers to come to the aid of the Union and serve for three years. What he got instead was 230,000 men. Throughout the North there was a stampede to the colors. Men young and old, men who had never dreamed of giving up their lives as farmers, clerks and mechanics, were seized with a desire for soldiering and suppressing "the Rebellion." Adolescent students too, like Arthur McArthur, Jr., could think of nothing else; certainly of nothing more urgent, more interesting or more patriotic. When the 6th Volunteer Infantry Regiment paraded through Milwaukee in July 1861 on its way to the railroad station, Arthur, Jr., less than a month past his sixteenth birthday, went to every company commander—all ten of them—begging to be allowed to enlist in his company. "No, my boy," one of them told him bluntly. "You are not old enough and strong enough for a soldier. You would not last a month." Another, more sympathetic, said, "You would better be a scholar than a soldier, anyway."

"I propose to do both, sir," said Arthur, Jr.[4]

At home he talked nothing but war. Even before the South seceded, he was interested in going to Annapolis. One of his closest friends, living two houses away, was a lively youth named Charles King, the acknowledged leader of the neighborhood's teenage boys. King was about to go to West Point and would one day be famous as the leading writer on the Old Army in the Wild West. The judge's son suddenly wanted to don the Army blue too. Instead the judge sent him to a private military school, from where the boy might hope to go on to West Point. In May 1862, Arthur, Jr., visited the White House, accompanied by James R. Doolittle, senior senator from Wisconsin, and bearing a letter from the judge to Abraham Lincoln. "A desire to go into the military service of the country has become the absorbing object of his very existence," the judge had written. He vouched for his son's good health, keen intelligence and ardent patriotism. He urged the President "to give him a cadetship—a prize he treasures above every other earthly possession."[5]

Of the ten at large appointments in his gift, Lincoln had already awarded two to young men from Wisconsin, one of them being Charles King. And here was a Democratic supplicant asking for a third. The President allowed himself to be persuaded, but there were no vacancies for the class of 1866. The Adjutant General was ordered to award an at large appointment to Arthur McArthur, Jr., for the class of 1867, which would be enrolled in June 1863.[6]

That didn't satisfy young Arthur. The rebellion might be stamped out before the class of '67 graduated. It might even be over before he went to West Point, although Union Army failures in the first year of the fighting seemed to promise a protracted struggle. As his father had told the President, he was totally absorbed in ambitions of soldiering. The boy was determined to go to war.

He secured a commission in the newly formed 24th Volunteer Infantry Regiment. Arthur McArthur, Jr., was made a lieutenant and appointed regimental adjutant. Barely seventeen, he looked young for his age. The regiment's first muster-in roll, compiled in August 1862, gave his occupation accurately enough: He was a "Student." His height was given as five feet seven inches, his complexion was put down as "ruddy" and he was described as being of medium build. He was entered on the roll as "MacArthur" and retained that spelling of his name for the rest of his life.[7]

The officers and men of the 24th took his appointment as their first defeat. The colonel, Charles H. Larrabee, who would have to rely heavily on the adjutant in managing the regiment, was appalled. When the 24th formed for its first dress parade, the adolescent adjutant was almost laughably out of his depth. Just memorizing Army regulations would not turn a thin, pallid, softly spoken youth into an officer with command presence. Colonel Larrabee growled to his staff that he was going to demand the governor give him a fully grown man for an adjutant and get rid of that "white-faced, chicken-voiced boy" whose orders didn't carry much beyond the soldier standing nearest him on the parade ground. On that unpromising note, the military heritage of Douglas MacArthur began.[8]

The North would fight the war with forces that consisted of roughly 5 percent regular troops and 95 percent amateurs. The Regular Army wasn't broken up to provide a leavening of experience throughout the two million volunteers, state militia and draftees who fought the Union's battles. As a result, combat leadership was often placed in the eager but untried hands of officers who owed their rank to political pull or to election by the men they led. As for the men, unlike the sergeants in the Regular Army, they knew even less about war than the officers.

For the Union Army, the first year of the war was mainly a tale of defeats and retreats. In the spring of 1862, however, it went vigorously on the offensive, driving its forces deep into the Confederacy. Despite the colonel's objections, Lieutenant Arthur MacArthur retained his position as adjutant of the 24th Wisconsin and would soon find himself fighting for his life.

In September that year a Confederate army under Braxton Bragg sought to reverse recent Union advances by invading Kentucky. On October 8 Bragg's troops collided with the advancing forces of the Army of the Ohio, including Phil Sheridan's division. The division had recently been joined by the 24th Wisconsin. That day, outside Perryville, Kentucky, Arthur MacArthur got his first taste of battle and impressed his brigade commander with his "great coolness and presence of mind" in the midst of fierce fighting.[9]

At Christmas, Federal troops fought a ferocious four-day battle at Murfreesboro, twenty-five miles southeast of Nashville. The Union right was forced back and nearly enveloped. Sheridan's division was mauled. The 24th Wisconsin suffered heavily, losing nearly half the five hundred men it put into the battle. Neither Colonel Larrabee nor his second-in-command was present at Stones River. Command of the 24th devolved on a major and the adjutant. Both acquitted themselves heroically. Arthur MacArthur had finally won the respect of his regiment.[10]

In the summer of 1863 Arthur MacArthur, Jr., was ill with typhoid fever. His father came to visit him in hospital, then took him back to Milwaukee to recuperate. He rejoined the 24th Wisconsin, however, in time to partici-pate in its most dramatic battle. On September 19, 1863, the Confederates won what proved to be their last major victory. At Chickamauga Creek, outside Chattanooga, they brought a Union army to the brink of destruc-tion. The Federals pulled back into Chattanooga. Grant came and took command of the situation.

Northern troops had retreated so hastily they had abandoned the high ground that nearly surrounds the town. Chattanooga was virtually besieged. On November 24 Sherman seized the northern end of Mission-ary Ridge, which was the linchpin of the Confederate defenses. The next day Grant attacked, with Sheridan's division foremost in the advance. The troops had been ordered to seize the lowest line of trenches, which were expected to be lightly held. This line was swiftly overrun. Without orders, Union soldiers rushed onward to the second line, taking it in turn. Dis-charging the pent-up frustration of men who'd endured a prolonged siege, they headed irresistibly for the crest. It was a clear, sunny winter's day. "I watched their progress with intense interest," said Grant.[11]

Confederate resistance was light in most places, but not where the 24th Wisconsin advanced up the slope toward Missionary Ridge. Wisconsin men went down in droves, including the regimental color-bearer. Lieu-tenant Arthur MacArthur ran to the fallen man and seized the regimental color.[12] Climbing the slope had broken up the regiment's line, while mus-ket and artillery fire had torn large holes in it. For the 24th to continue to advance and fight as a unit, it needed to re-form its line. That was one rea-son for carrying regimental flags into battle. MacArthur led his regiment up Missionary Ridge.[13]

As Union troops approached the crest, yelling and shooting, the Con-federates pulled out and ran down the reverse slope of the ridge, pursued by Sheridan's soldiers. Family legend had it that a hero yet again, Arthur MacArthur, Jr., was recommended for the Medal of Honor by Sheridan. In truth the medal had just been created and only enlisted men and NCOs appeared eligible.[14] What he did get was a promotion. In January 1864, without his ever being a captain, the men of the 24th elected him to a major's oak leaves.[15]

The 24th Wisconsin meanwhile was advancing into Georgia as part of the 2d Volunteer Division. It would play an important role in William

Tecumseh Sherman's brilliant Atlanta campaign. In June 1864 MacArthur was entrusted with leading a reconnaissance in force as Sherman skirmished for Atlanta.

This is one of the most difficult of military operations. Reconnaissance in force missions are usually entrusted to fast-moving units composed of experienced troops. A successful reconnaissance in force requires luck, sound judgment and firm leadership. MacArthur's operation on this occasion unmasked strong Confederate defenses at Kennesaw Mountain on the approaches to Atlanta. His reconnaissance was cited after the war as a model of its kind in one of the most influential military texts in Army history. "The men of this regiment [the 24th Wisconsin] were instructed each to select a tree about 50 yards in front of the line and, at command, to run forward and halt behind the tree selected. The regiment thus pushing forward by a series of rushes, advanced three-fourths of the distance separating it from the enemy, developed his position and completely gained the object of the reconnaissance, with the loss of only two men killed and eleven wounded."[16]

Even so, Sherman proceeded to squander the intelligence harvest MacArthur had brought him. He did something completely uncharacteristic. He launched his troops, including the 24th Wisconsin, at the solidly entrenched Confederates. In the space of two hours he suffered three thousand casualties, with absolutely nothing to show for his losses. Among the wounded was nineteen-year-old Major Arthur MacArthur, whose life was saved by a packet of letters and a small Bible carried close to his heart.[17]

He soon recuperated, and at Jonesboro, Georgia, one day that summer he led a charge across an open field that sent Confederates fleeing from a bordering wood. On September 2 Sherman captured Atlanta. Later that fall he headed east, just as a Confederate army under the one-armed, one-legged John Bell Hood invaded Tennessee. Thirty-four thousand Union troops, including the 24th Wisconsin, were sent to Franklin and ordered to hold. On November 30 Hood's Confederates attacked, launching a stunning frontal assault. For five hours they had the Federals on the ropes, inflicting several thousand casualties, but suffering heavily in return.

The 24th Wisconsin fought a heroic rearguard action as the Federal lines buckled and other regiments pulled back toward Nashville. Major MacArthur led a counterattack that recaptured eight Union artillery pieces and the colors of one of the retreating regiments. He received two serious wounds, one in the chest and one in the leg, and was carried off the field of battle.[18] Federal casualties numbered twenty-five hundred, but Hood's exceeded six thousand.

The end of the war in April 1865 found MacArthur hunting down Confederate guerrillas operating around Blue Spring, Tennessee. Several weeks later MacArthur was promoted to lieutenant colonel. Still too young to vote, he now commanded a regiment and proceeded to lead it back to its home state. He was promoted once more, to colonel, and on July 4 led the 24th Wisconsin through Milwaukee in an Independence Day parade, walking with a slight limp, the result of his leg wound at Franklin. He had an uneven gait for the rest of his life.[19] Shortly afterward he returned to civilian life. Of the 1,150 original members of the 24th Wisconsin, barely 400 had survived the long struggle to save the Union.

The one and a half million men who'd served in the Union Army and survived the experience without being killed or crippled went back to their plows and workshops, their store counters and steel mills, their great adventure behind them. Having been soldiers for a part of their lives was enough to satisfy whatever patriotic urges and ideas of manly courage may have stirred their young selves. All but a handful had seen enough of military service. Yet for fifty years to come they would, through organizations such as the Grand Army of the Republic, dominate American life. They bored their families with their reminiscences, bought up the memoirs of their generals and in old age visited their former battlefields, where they embraced aged foes, who, like them, had kept their faded uniforms. Federal blue and Confederate butternut were sentimentally filmed in another age as skinny old men under big black hats, sporting white goatee beards, acting defiantly spry for Methuselahs.

Twenty-one-year-old Arthur MacArthur, Jr., however, found going to war had not satisfied the martial itch. Military service remained "the absorbing object of his very existence." He tried to settle down to being a student back in Milwaukee. For six months he studied law, but his heart wasn't in the dull mysteries of torts, estoppal and easements. He wanted to be back in Army blue, back as an officer, back with troops. He had applied for a commission in the Regular Army even before his return to Milwaukee.[20]

He sought to be commissioned as a captain but had to settle for something less. On February 23, 1866, he became a second lieutenant, with a promotion to first lieutenant next day in the 17th Infantry Regiment stationed at David's Island, a picturesque post in Long Island Sound. Feeling aggrieved that his war record was not getting the respect he felt it deserved, MacArthur continued to agitate for higher rank.[21] A certain prickliness where honor and what he considered his due were concerned became part of his legacy to his son Douglas. This lobbying effort was successful.[22] In September 1866 he was promoted to captain in the 36th Infantry Regiment, which was heading for Fort Kearney, Nebraska Territory. The regiment's main duty would be to protect the Union Pacific as the iron road snaked westward.

As the railroad advanced, so did the 36th Infantry. By the summer of 1867 MacArthur was in Wyoming Territory. His company was policing unruly frontier mining towns, patrolling the railroad and offering protection to emigrants heading down the Oregon Trail. Always a conscientious and capable officer, Captain MacArthur continued to feel aggrieved about his rank. He had plenty of company. Most former Regular Army officers who'd risen rapidly in the war had been forced to settle for something much less exalted in peacetime. Few, if any, liked it. MacArthur, feeling that he was really a colonel disguised as a captain, continued the tense correspondence with the War Department over his rank.[23]

He sought promotion with a brash and shameless ambition that might seem comical or pathetic were it not for the fact that overt lobbying was just about the only way an infantry officer could get promoted in the post–Civil War Army. He wasn't unique in his pleas. There were plenty of others like him. Nor was it simply a matter of status. Officers were paid considerably less after the war than they had received in wartime. Congress cut their pay to below the 1860 level.

The Union Pacific building west met up with the Central Pacific moving east at Promontory, Utah, in May 1869. With the great railroad completed, Congress cut Army appropriations. MacArthur remained a captain, but now he had no assignment. He went home that summer on leave while the War Department decided what to do with him.

Although the captain's fate remained in doubt, the judge's career was progressing splendidly. His wife had died during the Civil War. He remarried in January 1868 and later that year headed the American delegation to the Paris Exposition. Shortly after his return to the United States he quit the provincial purlieus of Milwaukee forever. He moved to Washington, to take up an appointment as a federal judge on the supreme court of the District of Columbia. Unhappily his second wife died soon after this.

The Army found a new assignment for Captain MacArthur, at the Cavalry Recruiting Rendezvous in the Bowery. It isn't likely that he enjoyed being a recruiting officer. The Regular Army was generally despised as the last legal refuge of men who were fit for nothing else. Discipline tended to be brutal, and desertion rates were high. For a line officer who had spent all his military service with troops, being stuck in New York signing up immigrants straight off the boat or trying to lure desperadoes from the streets of the Bowery can hardly have been a congenial form of service.

In September 1869 he was transferred out of New York, back to field service and the 13th Infantry Regiment at Fort Rawlins, in Utah Territory. He arrived to endure one of the coldest winters to freeze the high plains that century. The 13th was commanded by one of the more interesting figures in the Army, Colonel Philippe Régis de Trobriand, whose father had been a *général de brigade* in Napoleon's *Grande Armée.* He had studied law as a young man in Paris but never practiced it. He had become a journalist instead, a career choice that brought him the editorship of a French newspaper in New York before the Civil War. During the war he'd taken American citizenship and risen to become a brevet major general. After the war he wrote a classic account of his experiences, *Quatre Ans de Campagne à l'Armée du Potomac,* and was commissioned a colonel in the Regular Army.[24] In Utah he fought the Indians and tried to reason with the Mormons, neither of whom was willing to be told how to behave by politicians in Washington.

The life of the 13th Infantry in the early 1870s was like most field service—long periods of boredom punctuated by bouts of frenetic activity. There were periodic skirmishes that amounted to aggravated constabulary duty, but big fights were almost unknown after the 1860s.[25]

In 1874 MacArthur and Company K participated in a major expedition against the Sioux that ended with large numbers of Indians agreeing to move onto reservations.[26] Throughout the West the Indians were rapidly being penned in on some of the poorest land the United States possessed. When the 1874 campaign ended, the 13th Infantry got a new assignment. It was transferred to Louisiana. Having a French-speaking, French-born aristocrat for a commander (De Trobriand's father had been both a Bourbon count and a baron of the empire) may have inspired this move. At all events, the state was still under federal occupation, with a much-hated, Washington-imposed carpetbagger in the governor's chair, propped up with Army bayonets. The state legislature too was under Washington's control. When legislators opposed to the governor tried to take their seats in 1875, they were stopped by the 13th Infantry from entering the state capitol.

For Captain Arthur MacArthur, Jr., the high point of his time in Louisiana came when he attended a Mardi Gras ball in New Orleans in February 1875. There he met a tall brunette with expressive dark eyes and strong features, twenty-two-year-old Mary Pinkney Hardy of Norfolk, Virginia.

Her father was a prosperous commission merchant of old Virginia stock. During the Civil War the Hardy family had been displaced from its spacious home on the Elizabeth River to Baltimore, one northern city that was sympathetic to the South. There Mary, whose family nickname was Pinky, had attended a Catholic girls' school. The family was Episcopalian, but the gulf between upper-class Anglicanism and the Roman Church was pretty narrow. Her life appears to have been uneventful until, on a visit to New Orleans, she attended the same Mardi Gras ball as Captain MacArthur and both experienced what they remembered as "love at first sight."[27]

The course of true love did not promise to run smooth. Two of her brothers had attended Virginia Military Institute and fought for the Confederacy. Her entire family seems to have disapproved of Captain MacArthur. If he ever warmed to them, or they to him, no record of it survives.

The courtship was brief. The young couple married in Norfolk in May 1875. The captain was assigned to Washington, where he served as a staff officer on various Army boards. In the spring of 1876 Mary traveled down to Norfolk for the birth of her first child, Arthur III. Shortly afterward Captain MacArthur went back to Louisiana, to resume command of Company K, 13th Infantry.

The year 1877 saw the occupation of Louisiana draw to a close. The regiment was briefly deployed to western Pennsylvania, which was in the grip of a violent railroad strike. The breakneck industrialization that followed the Civil War brought numerous bloody struggles between business and labor. The Army was sent to intervene in many of these clashes, some of which were suppressed with deadly force.[28] Although the 13th didn't fire a shot in Pennsylvania, MacArthur, like most professional soldiers, probably found this kind of duty distasteful.

In 1878 the MacArthurs visited Connecticut, where Pinky's parents were on vacation. While there, a second child, Malcolm, was born. When the vacation ended, the captain, his wife and two infant sons returned to Louisiana and the 13th Infantry Regiment.

In 1879 the 13th was assigned to the former government arsenal at Little Rock Barracks, Arkansas. It was a fairly comfortable post as Army garrisons went, and MacArthur's duties weren't particularly heavy. Although not given much to socializing, he had become an enthusiastic Freemason and was warmly welcomed by the Grand Lodge of Arkansas in Little Rock, which awarded him its Fellowcraft degree.[29]

With a wife and two children to support, the issue of MacArthur's rank—and pay—was more pressing than ever. When he failed to move the War Department, the captain began urging the Senate to review his lowly position in the Army. This brought a stiff rebuke from the Adjutant General, with whom he was already quarreling about his place on the *Army Register.*[30]

While this acrimonious correspondence with the War Department rumbled on, a third son was born to the captain and his wife. Pinky gave birth to her last child, Douglas, in the Arsenal, a large redbrick structure, with two imposing octagonal towers, at Little Rock Barracks on January 26, 1880.

The Happiest Years

In 1880 two thirds of the Army's thirty thousand men were stationed west of the Mississippi, spread among 120 posts. Most of these were isolated garrisons, remote from any sizable town and occupied by a single infantry company. The soldiers of these outposts not only were far removed from the mainstream of American society but were almost like military orphans. It was a life of dull routine sustained by the pessimistic faith of soldiers down the ages—the certain knowledge that politics will fail and force will be needed—and by the somber rituals of military life. Every afternoon at five-thirty the entire company would assemble for retreat. The officers appeared in their frock coats, bedecked with red sashes, tasseled epaulets and gleaming swords. The men, chests pushed out, stomachs pulled in, were assembled in neat ranks, resplendent in spiked German-style helmets of black and gold. The post band of several buglers, a fiddler or two and a drummer pounded out the national anthem. The Stars and Stripes solemnly descended the flagstaff as the golden disk of the sun slid down the western horizon. A pack howitzer would be fired, its boom sending a shock wave through the little fort before spreading out to remind the yawning sky, the silent desert, the indifferent plains that these men were not really alone: They were simply the cutting edge of a great national adventure.

Such was the milieu in which the infant Douglas MacArthur grew up. Six months after his birth his father was ordered to take Company K to Fort Wingate, in northwestern New Mexico. There was a large Navajo reservation nearby. The main duty of the fifty officers and men of Company K was to keep the Navajos on the reservation and to protect them from marauding Apaches.

One of Douglas MacArthur's contemporaries, another Army brat, named Fiorello La Guardia, thought life at posts like this was "exceedingly unpleasant and undesirable for grownups but a paradise for a little boy."[1] There was the color and excitement of men in uniform, with big boots, clanking swords and gleaming leather holsters. There were ponies to be ridden and guns to be handled. Ever a soldier's son, MacArthur claimed he could shoot a gun before he could read, ride a horse before he could write his name.[2] At many posts there was a Christmas Eve wagon train that provided the high spot of the year for Army children. The lead wagon was driven by a soldier dressed as Santa Claus, and if he knew his business, the wagon train would come into view of the children crowded at the fort's main gate around midday on December 24.[3]

Pinky almost certainly found frontier life less entrancing than her youngest son. Before the 1870s few officers' wives had even seen a western fort. When Sherman became commanding general, he encouraged them to accompany their husbands. Their presence would go a long way in sustaining officers' morale. Nearly all had servants to help ease their burden, usually a black or Hispanic woman who would do the laundry and cleaning, help look after the children, do all the baking and tend the chickens or cows. The most prized servant of all, though, would be a Chinese girl.[4] What servants the MacArthurs had isn't known, but they would have had some.

With officers allowed to have their wives join them (a privilege not allowed enlisted men, who were recruited single and expected to stay that way) there were quite a few children at some of the western forts by the 1880s. Sherman had the War Department hire schoolteachers for them. One of the forts that got a school in 1882 was Fort Wingate. It occupied a large hospital tent at a corner of the parade ground. Douglas and Malcolm were too young to attend it, and even Arthur, aged six, may have been considered too young as well. The schoolteacher assigned to Fort Wingate, Edward Brown, brought a civilian's detached gaze to the military men he lived among, and Mr. Brown took careful note of the post commander. What struck him were Captain MacArthur's extraordinarily immaculate appearance and impeccable military bearing. These too became part of his legacy to Douglas.

The captain didn't socialize with his juniors, as other post commanders did, yet still got on well with all of them. The entire company, thought Brown, seemed to admire its commander, telling visitors and newcomers to the fort, "There goes a real soldier," when the captain appeared.[5]

Officers who liked the West tended to be amateur anthropologists, fascinated by Indian life, which still had a picturesque splendor, or they were men hooked on hunting and fishing, happy to find themselves in a sports-man's paradise. MacArthur was neither an anthropologist nor a hunter. He much preferred the company of a good book to the lure of the wild and doesn't seem to have been particularly interested in the colorful life of Native Americans before that life was utterly destroyed by the white man. After two years at Fort Wingate he'd had enough. The judge wrote to the President to request that Captain MacArthur be assigned as military attaché to China. Grant replied sympathetically but pointed out that for-eign service was a patronage matter and really in the gift of Congress, not the War Department.[6]

The captain, however, wouldn't be dissuaded. He wrote to Sherman, making the same request. Sherman acerbically responded that "half the Company officers are away on leave or duties non-military. . . ." Anyway, Sherman bluntly told him, there was "no such detail" as military attaché to China.[7] Captain MacArthur stayed on at Fort Wingate, but toward the end of year he was permitted to take his family on extended leave.

Some of it was spent in Norfolk, where, in the spring of 1883, all three of his sons came down with measles. Malcolm, the second child, died. This devastating loss only seemed to intensify Pinky's devotion to her sur-viving children.[8] The MacArthurs returned to Fort Wingate, and the cap-tain attempted to resume his correspondence with the War Department over his humble rank. The Adjutant General stiffly replied that the secre-tary of war "declines to reopen the subject."[9]

In February 1884 the MacArthurs finally escaped from Fort Wingate, only to be transferred to a place even more primitive: Fort Selden, an abandoned outpost in southeastern New Mexico. The arduous three-hundred-mile trek from Wingate to Selden provided Douglas MacArthur with his first clear childhood memories, trudging along beside Sergeant Peter Ripley at the head of the column, although at the age of four he couldn't have trudged far.[10]

The MacArthurs' new station consisted of a half dozen single-story adobe buildings, surrounded by an adobe wall six feet thick and roughly twelve feet high. Company K was to reactivate the post in response to a flare-up of Indian raids. Fort Selden offered much the same kind of life as Fort Wingate. Pinky probably considered it worse than wretched Wingate, yet she remained a proud figure, almost defiant in the face of hardship. Five feet ten in height, she was a striking figure, alert to everything around her. The daughter of an officer at Wingate remembered her as being "like a falcon. She was vivid, with a glancing quickness of movement." Seen from a child's perspective, Pinky had a formidable presence: "The angle and the light emphasised her swift poise and the imperious way she held her head."[11]

While his parents may not have liked it much, young Douglas nurtured only fond recollections of Fort Selden. In 1956 a tourist traveling through New Mexico came across its ruins—a few lumpy mounds of weather-worn adobe where the walls had once stood—and sent a postcard that portrayed them to MacArthur. He received a prompt reply that ran: "Thank you for sending me the Post Card showing the ruins of Fort Selden. I shall prize it always. I lived there for several years when a child—long, long ago."[12]

The Indian threat in southern New Mexico came from the fierce Chiricahua Apaches, led by Geronimo, who periodically raided settlements on the American side of the Rio Grande, then fled across the river into Mexico. Pursuing them was left largely to the cavalry, which never managed to catch them, but two cavalry officers, Henry W. Lawton and Charles B. Gatewood, went into Mexico and talked Geronimo into surrender. The United States would feed the Indians; Mexico would not. Like Sitting Bull, who'd fled to Canada after the Battle of the Little Bighorn, the prospect of regular rations for Indian women and children proved too strong for Geronimo to resist. The Indians' traditional economy had been so disrupted by settlements and conquest they could no longer feed themselves.

Meanwhile Captain MacArthur ran Fort Selden in his usual exemplary fashion. The department inspector general visited the post in September 1885. The company was "inspected and drilled in full dress . . . the military bearing and appearance of the troops was very fine." The captain, he discovered, had done more to provide comforts and amusements for his men than any other post commander he had visited. MacArthur, he concluded, was "an officer of more than ordinary ability. . . . The company and the post show evidence of intelligent, judicious and masterly supervision."[13]

The surrender of the Chiricahuas marked the end of the Indian wars in the Southwest. The 13th Infantry was dispersed; its ten companies were widely scattered. Company K drew the best assignment of all. It would go to Fort Leavenworth, Kansas, and serve as a demonstration unit at the Infantry and Cavalry School. In 1886, after twenty years of frustration and disappointment, Captain MacArthur stood at the turning point of his career.

In 1881 Sherman had ordered the establishment at Fort Leavenworth, Kansas, of a School of Application for Infantry and Cavalry that would offer a six-month course for line lieutenants. Besides meeting a clear need to get better-educated officers, such a school would act as a palliative to other pressures. As he confided to Sheridan, he was making a concession "to the everlasting demands of friends and families to have their boys escape company duty in the Indian country."[14]

Fort Leavenworth was sheer bliss compared to most Army bases out West. For one thing, the railroad reached it. For another, it was on the doorstep of a sizable town. It had its drawbacks, of course. Officer housing was still poor. Many houses lacked toilets and bathrooms. Even so, for families like the MacArthurs, arriving from remote garrisons, these shortcomings were no novelty. In recompense, there was an abundance of social life.[15]

Douglas and Arthur had until now been educated by their mother. At Fort Leavenworth they would finally go to school with other children. There was a grade school on the post run by two elderly spinster sisters, Laura and Julie Goodfellow. These charming old maids educated scores, possibly hundreds, of boys who grew up to be Army officers. When they reached the eighth grade, the Goodfellows' pupils moved on to attend the Leavenworth public schools. Douglas spent two years at the Goodfellow school but was, by his own admission, not the least bit studious.[16]

The Misses Goodfellow strove to provide children with an education in the social graces. At least once a month there was an afternoon dance at the post Hop Room, in Pope Hall. The 6th Infantry band provided the music, and the Fort Leavenworth commandant, Colonel Alexander M. McCook, would stop by. "When the dance ended, Colonel McCook made the boys escort their girl partners to their seats, bow and either retire or sit by the girl until the next dance began. Politeness and courtesy were strictly enforced. . . ."[17] Boys who were too shy or too recalcitrant to invite a girl to dance were forced to waltz with the colonel and dance a girl's steps.

The Hop Room provided Douglas and his big brother, Arthur, with a chance to practice in miniature those rituals that were an essential part of Victorian social life. It was an aspect of their education that doubtless reinforced what their well-bred mother had already taught them. Throughout life Douglas MacArthur brought to routine courtesies the easy grace of someone who has absorbed them when young.

At other times the MacArthur boys were free to enjoy the typically boisterous games of male children, such as prisoner's base. Being younger and smaller is always a handicap to a boy, and having your mother keep you dressed in skirts until you are eight years old probably doesn't help.[18] Yet Douglas's fiercely competitive nature was apparent even then. He was a remarkably determined and speedy little athlete.[19]

Fort Leavenworth offered even more diversions for a boy than did the frontier posts. Nearly every afternoon there was a full-dress parade, which Captain MacArthur often commanded. Douglas particularly enjoyed watching the cavalry drill. He also loved going out to watch the artillery batteries practice their booming art on the live-fire range.[20]

There was a single-track railroad called the Dummy Line that ran from the post into the nearby town of Leavenworth. On the other side of the town, where the line ended, was the Old Soldiers' Home. Children from the fort would go out there, or be taken there, to meet the colorful pensioners who still dressed in the Army blue uniforms of the Civil War, with dark blue fatigue caps sporting their old corps badges. Enthralled children would listen to them recall Gettysburg and Antietam, Shiloh and Nashville, or even battles of the Mexican War.

At Fort Leavenworth, Captain MacArthur had the pleasure of working for someone whose esteem he already enjoyed. As a brevet major general in the Civil War, McCook had commanded the Union left wing at Perryville and the right wing at Stones River. He knew how well the 24th Wisconsin and its boy adjutant had acquitted themselves in close combat.

McCook, who'd arrived at Leavenworth only a few months ahead of MacArthur, was one of the military progressives of the 1880s. With the Indian wars at an end, the Army had no clear mission to fulfill. The War Department tried to carve out a role in coastal defense and a large coast artillery branch was under development. Few people in Congress or the War Department, though, took the prospect of invasion seriously. Nor did the Navy appreciate the soldiers' sudden interest in defending the coast.

With its traditional role dwindling and no clear vision of what lay ahead, the Army was gradually turning into a sclerotic bureaucracy sustained more by habit than belief. It was getting gray and set in its antiquated ways. Little new blood was coming in, and promotion was glacially slow. What promotions there were tended to go to officers in the Corps of Engineers, who spent most of their time on civilian projects such as rivers and harbors. It was almost impossible for a line officer to get promoted, as Captain MacArthur had found, unless someone retired or died. Just about the only way to get ahead was to transfer out of the line, to one of the bureaus, such as the Quartermaster General's department or the Adjutant General's Office.

What the Army's progressives wanted to do was create a combat-ready force, and Leavenworth was a good place to begin. When McCook arrived, the school was running remedial classes for lieutenants who could barely read and struggled with basic math. The new commandant demanded higher standards, better-prepared students and an end to remedial education. He imposed a six-day working week on Leavenworth students, broadened the curriculum, introduced more tactical training and put a heavy workload on the instructors. "A disciplinarian, perhaps even a martinet,"[21] McCook turned Leavenworth into something more than a refuge from remote garrisons. There was an emphasis on problem solving and mastering the challenges inherent in a field command. It was no longer a place for officers seeking a paid vacation.

The McCook regime was probably meat and drink to a thoughtful, conscientious workaholic like Captain MacArthur. One thing is certain: He made a powerful impression on the commandant. McCook became his mentor and patron, opening the doors that finally got him out of the line. In December 1887 the inspector general of the Department of the Missouri, Major George H. Burton, announced his retirement. McCook tried to get MacArthur, still a fairly junior captain, appointed as Burton's successor. Burton, who'd praised MacArthur's "masterly supervision" of Fort Selden two years earlier, also recommended him.[22]

This effort failed, but it drew MacArthur to the attention of the new Adjutant General of the Army, Brigadier General John C. Kelton, another reformer. There would soon be a vacancy for an assistant adjutant general, with the rank of major. Would MacArthur be a suitable candidate? Kelton wanted to know. McCook replied that MacArthur was "beyond question the most distinguished Captain in the Army of the United States."[23]

The judge lobbied the secretary of war on behalf of his son in Washington. He also had printed a twenty-two-page pamphlet that was crammed with glowing testimonials from high-ranking officers and powerful politicians. Embedded within it was a two-page statement that damned "the vicious method of making selections for the staff" even while trying to exploit it.[24]

Congress regarded the sixty to seventy staff jobs that junior line officers could transfer into as patronage cases. There was no way to obtain one without political influence, and competition was keen for the handful that became vacant each year.[25] The efforts of Colonel McCook and Judge McArthur ultimately paid off. On July 1, 1889, Captain MacArthur was ordered to report to Washington, to assume the position of assistant adjutant general. With his new post went a promotion to major and a substantial increase in pay.

One of the pleasures of moving to Washington was the presence there of the judge and his third wife. Judge McArthur had retired from the bench in 1888, but he was still decidedly active. He was president of the board of regents of the National University and president of the Washington Humane Society. He provided wonderful company for his grandson Douglas, with whom he felicitously shared a birthday. Many years later Douglas MacArthur recalled him as "A large handsome man of fine presence, genial disposition and marked charm of manner. . . . It was he who taught me to play cards, including the game of poker. The last hand I ever played with him I held four queens and bet every chip I had. I can still feel the shock when he laid down four kings. And I have never forgotten his words, 'My dear boy, nothing is sure in this life.' "[26]

Major MacArthur's first year in the Adjutant General's Office was a busy one as he tackled two issues in which he had a strong personal interest. One was reforming the promotion system so that merit would count for as much as seniority. In framing the legislation that brought this about, he won the praise of Kelton and most of the reform-minded officers of the Army. "It places you," said Kelton, "at the head of the military reformers of the Department, where I look for you always to be found."[27] It was a brilliant start for the most junior of the sixteen assistant adjutants general on Kelton's staff.

Firmly ensconced within the AGO, MacArthur turned his attention to the second matter that preyed on his mind: He felt he deserved the Medal of Honor for his heroic leadership that September day when he led the 24th Wisconsin up Missionary Ridge under Grant's admiring eye. He found a loophole in the law that justified awarding the medal to officers. He collected witness statements attesting to his heroism in three battles and recommended himself for the award. A board of officers was convened, and the coveted medal, the only decoration for bravery in the Army's gift, was finally his. He was cited for his actions on Missionary Ridge.[28]

For Arthur MacArthur 1889 was turning into an *annus mirabilis*—a year of miracles—because besides getting a promotion, an assignment to Washington and the Medal of Honor, he was awarded his law degree, from the judge's own National University. He had done a lot of catching up.

What came after was nearly a decade of routine staff work. By comparison with that first hectic year in Washington it may have seemed anticlimactic, but MacArthur remained as diligent a soldier as ever. He continued to receive laudatory efficiency reports, and his evenings were spent as they had been out West—reading. He was, as he had promised to be, both a soldier and a scholar. In 1890, he recorded, he had read widely in political theory, studied American colonial and revolutionary history, improved his knowledge of constitutional law and made "quite an extensive examination into the civilization and institutions of China."[29]

Douglas found Washington dull after the daily excitements and diversions of life out West. Enrolled at a grade school on Massachusetts Avenue, he plodded through three years of formal schooling dressed in a plaid tweed suit and tie. He was a good teacher's worst-case scenario: the bright child who is too bored or too easily distracted to excel. He was an average student, no better or worse than most.

After four years in Washington, Major MacArthur was transferred to the headquarters of the Department of Texas, at Fort Sam Houston, on the outskirts of San Antonio. In Texas he would continue to do the ordinary staff work of an assistant adjutant general, which was concerned mainly with personnel matters and record keeping. The work hadn't changed, even if the location had.

Douglas was delighted to return to the West. He probably expected to roam and play as he had done before, with few constraints and little study, a life of shooting and riding and having fun, of hanging out with soldiers and listening to stories of Injun fighting. To his shock, his father enrolled him in a private school that had just been opened by an Episcopal bishop, the Right Reverend J. S. Johnston, Doctor of Divinity.

The school's prospectus promised that West Texas Military Academy would be a kind of Phillips Andover combined with the Moody Bible Institute, a place "unsurpassed in intellectual standing and moral tone." No one would have guessed it from the surroundings. The school occupied a site "part grass and part dirt, in good weather. All mud in rainy weather," according to one of its alums. It stood on Government Hill, next to the Fort Sam boundary.[30]

Originally limited to a single large wooden building surrounded by wasteland, WTMA stood conveniently near the entrance to Fort Sam and provided what amounted to both junior high school and high school education, but its students were "cadets" and wore uniforms of West Point gray. For many parents the emphasis on the military virtues of obedience and discipline provided much of the new school's appeal, maybe even most of it. Boys whom other schools had given up on as too unruly and intractable were shipped there from as far away as New York. Douglas was enrolled—maybe enlisted is a better word—in the equivalent of the ninth grade of the founding class, which numbered forty-nine.[31]

He went to his new school equipped with a Bible, the Book of Common Prayer, a hymnbook, a collection of new collars, six linen napkins and a silver napkin ring. The academy was an academic hybrid that offered a regimen which couldn't have been bettered had Major MacArthur designed it himself: half New England prep school, offering Latin and mandatory chapel, half southern military school, offering infantry drill.[32]

For some unknown reason Douglas MacArthur, well established by this time as an indifferent student, was suddenly sparked into intellectual effort. The most likely explanation is that one of the teachers there, whose name is lost to history, ignited his imagination. He may have been liberated too by the absence of his brother. Arthur had enrolled at Annapolis. Douglas now got all of his parents' attention. He was no longer living in the shadow of the remarkably bright and ambitious Arthur.

MacArthur's own will to win was formidable, even at this early age. Pinky had tended this flame carefully. Douglas had been spirited since childhood, and his mother did not simply encourage his competitive instincts; she sharpened them to a cutting edge. Once he started something, he had to see it through to success, no matter what. For instance, there was the summer when he was thirteen and she took him to Norfolk with her. He decided to earn some pocket money while he was there by selling newspapers. The streets of downtown Norfolk already had plenty of lads trying to sell newspapers on street corners. They did not appreciate the extra competition. He came home that evening looking sheepish, and his bundle of newspapers was intact, still bound up with twine. "Douglas, why didn't you sell any of the papers?" asked his mother. "Well," he replied disconsolately, "the other boys wouldn't let me." Pinky was a soldier's wife, and no son of hers was going to be permitted to accept defeat. She told him sternly, "Tomorrow you have to go out again and sell all your papers. Don't come home until you have." Douglas returned to the grandparents' mansion the next evening looking as if he'd been in a train wreck. His clothes were ripped, he had a black eye, dried blood caked his nostrils and mouth, his knuckles were red and raw, but every newspaper had been sold.[33]

Once he settled down to studying, MacArthur rapidly overtook all his classmates at WTMA. The hidden pleasures of thought, ideas and knowledge exploded the excitement of learning in his burgeoning mind, changing the youngest MacArthur as it changes all who experience it. By the end of his freshman year he was the academy's star pupil. Nor was he a dreary bookworm, the kind of adolescent Gradgrind who is tolerated by his peers but stands no chance of ever being accepted as one of the guys. He was a skilled and enthusiastic tennis player. He was also a superb horseman, and in 1896 he and a friend from WTMA spent the summer riding in the Rockies, the highlight being a ride to the summit of Pikes Peak.[34]

In his junior year the straight A student was a substitute end on the football team and shortstop-manager on the baseball team. Fulfilled intellectually and reveling in the physical vigor of young manhood, he enjoyed those four years in San Antonio immensely.[35]

Besides being brainy and athletic, he possessed the priceless gift of friendship. He grew up in an age when young men had Emerson quoted at them by their parents: "The only way to have a friend is to be one." Douglas had a knack for doing just that. When a fellow student, Charles H. Quinn, grew discouraged during an important exam and threw his paper into the wastebasket in despair, MacArthur fished it out, signed Quinn's name to it and handed the paper in. To his amazement, Quinn learned he had passed and went on to study engineering at Purdue.[36]

No school run by a bishop was going to neglect the spiritual side of life. Every morning, in fair weather or foul, the boys of WTMA trooped several blocks to St. Paul's Memorial Church to begin the day with half an hour of praying, hymn singing and inspirational homilies in the manner that upper-middle-class WASP families considered essential to the upbringing of young Christian gentlemen. At the typical age of fourteen Douglas MacArthur was confirmed in the Episcopalian faith.

The social side of a boy's development wasn't neglected either. The academy had a close association with the local Episcopalian girls' school,

St. Mary's Hall. Douglas dated several of the belles of St. Mary's, proving himself a regular fellow in this department too. Inherently shy, he never let that keep him away from young women.

They also gave him opportunities to display his courage. One afternoon he and a classmate went cycling in Brackenridge Park with three girls. They came to a rickety suspension bridge about a hundred feet long crossing a river. The bridge looked as if it were close to collapse, and the girls wanted to turn back. Douglas announced, "Well, if it will hold me, it will hold you," and walked across the swaying bridge, pushing his bike. The rest followed suit, one at a time.[37]

In his junior year he applied to President Grover Cleveland for an at large appointment to the West Point class entering in June 1897, the month he expected to graduate from WTMA. From before Douglas could even walk, his father had him headed for the Plain, the famous West Point parade ground. According to Peyton March, "He told me that he started Douglas towards West Point the day he was born."[38]

At Fort Sam the major invited young officers who had recently graduated from the Military Academy to come over for dinner and talk to Douglas about their alma mater. The judge and the major together massed the heavy artillery. The young man's application was supported by the commanding general of the Department of Texas and the commanding general at Fort Sam, by Senator John L. Mitchell of Wisconsin, four governors, two bishops, two representatives and Senator Redfield Proctor of Vermont. Proctor was chairman of the Senate Military Affairs Committee and a former secretary of war.

Despite all this firepower, Cleveland turned him down.[39] The MacArthurs had changed their political affiliations from the Democratic party over to the Republicans during the Civil War. Cleveland, the first Democratic President since 1860, probably didn't feel he owed them much.

In the long term, this rejection was probably the best thing that could have happened. At sixteen Douglas was too young to get the most out of West Point and not sufficiently well prepared academically to be number one in his class or to be made First Captain. The most he might have managed would have been to graduate in the upper half of his class. More likely, he would have suffered the fate of most of those who entered very young—washed out at the end of his first year. Even so, it seems safe to assume that Douglas MacArthur was deeply disappointed. Later that summer came a second blow. In August 1896 the judge died while on vacation in Atlantic City.

Showing tremendous self-control and tenacity, Douglas refused to allow these emotional upsets to deflect him. He continued to lead his school in scholarship, academics and drill. He was top sergeant of the Crack Squad, the school's drill team. He showed promise as an actor, holding his class-mates spellbound with his recital of poems such as "Casey at the Bat."[40] His fourth year saw him appointed first sergeant of Company A. He also became quarterback of the football team. A fellow player, Garahl Walker, thought he was too light. He weighed less than 150 pounds and had a slen-der build. "The scrimmages were hard on him. You could see his lips turn blue, but he would get up and fight it again."[41] Under him, the team won every game, and nobody scored a point against it. It was at West Texas that he won his first medals, for football, and he cherished them for the rest of his life.[42]

In June 1897 Douglas was valedictorian of the first class to graduate from WTMA. That made him, in effect, the first person to graduate from WTMA, a distinction of which he remained proud for the rest of his life.[43] MacArthur had a compulsion to be first in everything he did. It was not enough to be among the best. He had to be the best there ever was or the first there ever was, preferably both. Young Douglas received the highest academic honor Bishop Johnston could bestow—the Academy Gold Medal. He also won the school's Silver Medal for his first noted feat of public speaking. Having enthralled his classmates with his ability to recite poetry, he was a lead-pipe cinch to win the school's elocution contest orga-nized in his senior year. He won easily with his dramatic reading of "The Fight of the Privateer General Armstrong," by J. J. Roche. It was the kind of blood-and-guts, flag-waving tale lapped up by young men in every gen-eration. MacArthur's academic average was as close to perfect as was pos-sible in an age when no good school allowed there could be any such a thing as the perfect student. There was always something to strive for, even if you were the best. Douglas left West Texas Military Academy with a four-year grade average of 96.67.

He still hoped to go to West Point. He applied for an at large appoint-ment from Cleveland's successor, President William McKinley. Outstand-ing student that he was, he was turned down yet again. He would have to find another way in.

At this point an old friend of the judge's, Congressman Theobald Otjen, invited him to sit the competitive exam that Otjen would hold in the spring of 1898. The family was due to leave San Antonio anyway. Douglas's father had recently been promoted to lieutenant colonel and assigned to the Department of the Dakotas, whose headquarters were in St. Paul. Douglas and his mother would move to Milwaukee, where Douglas could establish residency in Otjen's district while preparing for Otjen's exam. In the fall of 1897 Mrs. MacArthur and her youngest son moved into a large, comfortable Milwaukee hotel, the Plankinton House. Lieutenant Colonel MacArthur commuted from St. Paul on the weekends to join them.

Although he was, in effect, a high school graduate, Douglas enrolled at the West Side High School, where he received intensive tutoring. Each morning he walked the two miles across town to the high school. He was usually the first student to arrive. Each evening he walked back to the hotel. The school rigged up a small laboratory where he could perform scientific experiments that were outside its usual curriculum. The principal, "Mac" McLanagan, took a strong personal interest in young MacArthur and gave him personal tuition. He was getting the benefits of what amounted to the first year of college. He was likely to need it. Some West Point applicants were college graduates. Most of those who succeeded had at least a year of college behind them.

Douglas probably felt that this was his last chance to get into West Point. "I never worked harder in my life."[44] He doesn't appear to have sought distractions. They came anyway. One night the section of the hotel where he and his mother lived caught on fire. They escaped with their lives but reached the street sooty, their faces smudged black.[45]

An even more tumultuous distraction was the sinking of the battleship *Maine* in the harbor at Havana in February 1898. Over the next two months public opinion, whipped up by a jingoistic press and fanned into flame by irresponsible politicians, clamored for war. There was no serious investigation into the loss of the *Maine* at the time. It was probably doomed by a major design flaw that put the coal bunkers too close to the ammunition bays. A victim, that is, of poor naval architecture, not Spanish villainy.[46] As Douglas MacArthur headed into the home stretch for the West Point exam, "Remember the *Maine!*" was brayed from soapboxes, was emblazoned on peppermint lozenges dissolving in the mouths of schoolchildren, was sung in vaudeville theaters to tacky martial airs, appeared in large, strident letters on storefronts and bobbed along the street on badges pinned to every patriotic lapel. Any youth hoping to pursue a military career yet forced to maintain his concentration in this atmosphere needed an iron will.

On April 20 Congress authorized the President to go to war to liberate Cuba from Spain. Three weeks later Douglas MacArthur took Congressman Otjen's exam. He was too nervous to sleep the night before it. He showed up at the Milwaukee city hall feeling ready to throw up, but Pinky was there to put steel into his backbone: "Doug, you'll win if you don't lose your nerve."[47]

A committee of three Milwaukee school principals had drawn up the exam. When they graded the candidates' papers, one stood out from the rest. The committee wrote to Otjen on June 7, informing him that Douglas MacArthur had come out top. "He is a young man of remarkable ability and mental power." His score was 93.3 percent.[48] The young man who came second hadn't even broken 80. MacArthur drew a lasting lesson from this experience: the crucial importance of careful preparation in getting something you want.

There were hurdles still to be overcome. There was some criticism in the local press that Congressman Otjen's winner was not a true son of Milwaukee. There were Democratic complaints that Douglas was a carpetbagger. The city's leading Republican newspapers, the *Milwaukee Journal* and the *Evening Wisconsin,* rallied loyally to his support.[49]

Certainly Douglas MacArthur's connections with the city were tenuous. They were destined to remain so. But his exam performance was too impressive to ignore. As a former governor of Wisconsin and onetime mayor of Milwaukee, George W. Peck, observed, "A boy with his attainments ought to belong somewhere and I am sure he would be a credit to Wisconsin."[50] While the Army as a whole was held in some disesteem, West Point itself was admired as a great national institution. In some midwestern towns there would be a parade, speeches and a civic send-off at the train station for young men when they set off for the academy. Otjen's best candidate by far had won.

The controversy soon died down, but he was not yet in the clear. For one thing, there was a small question mark over his health. Douglas suffered from a slight spinal curvature, but that was responding well to treatment. Intensely curious, he even turned his visits to the young doctor who treated him, Franz Pfister, into tutorials, picking Dr. Pfister's brain for information on anatomy, physiology and biology. Much impressed, the doctor regretted young MacArthur was so keen on a military career. "He would have made a great physician or surgeon," thought Pfister wistfully.[51]

The back problem was not going to keep MacArthur out of West Point, but there was still something that could: the challenging West Point entrance exam that all candidates had to take. Exams arranged by congressmen did not in themselves get a young man into West Point. They merely helped the congressman decide whom he would appoint. After that, however, came an even more rigorous examination that was organized by the academy. Those entering in June took it in the early spring each year. Douglas and his mother remained at the Plankinton so he could continue his studies at West Side High School.

He arrived at the granite gray "monastery on the Hudson" in the spring of 1899 primed for success. Had Cleveland given him an appointment three years earlier, the chances are fifty-fifty that he would have failed the entrance exam or not lasted beyond a few months at the Point. That was the fate of nearly all seventeen-year-old cadets. Even if they were bright enough intellectually, they weren't yet tough enough to take the searching test of character and competitiveness that four years at West Point demanded. Now, though, thanks to West Side High's work on his intellect and Pinky's work on the other parts, he was as ready as any young man who ever rode the New York Central Railroad up the banks of the Hudson to tackle the entrance exam.

3

The Corps, and the Corps, and the Corps

When the United States went to war with Spain in April 1898, Lieutenant Colonel Arthur MacArthur was assigned as chief of staff of the III Corps, at Chickamauga, barely ten miles from the brightest scene of his military career, Missionary Ridge. He had no intention of spending the new war as a staff officer, however. MacArthur asked for command of a brigade of volunteer infantry. While his application was pending, the Navy scored the first American victory of the war. On May 1 Commodore George Dewey sailed into Manila Bay and bombarded the obsolescent Spanish fleet into submission. One month later MacArthur was promoted to brigadier general of volunteers and shortly thereafter found himself heading for Manila.

Meanwhile Douglas MacArthur, having taken Congressman Otjen's exam, was suddenly seized by the same emotions that had played such a powerful part in his father's youth. He was so anxious to get into the Army in wartime he was ready to give up a place at West Point. His father urged him not to do it, reassuring him with the soldier's pessimistic creed that there were going to be more wars.[1]

In April 1899 Douglas and his mother traveled to Highland Falls, New York, the small, unprepossessing town that stands right at the gates of West Point. They moved into the West Point Hotel, located near Trophy Point. With Brigadier General MacArthur in the Philippines and her eldest son, Arthur, recently graduated from Annapolis and assigned to sea duty, Pinky had no home to call her own. She and the general did not own property anywhere. On Douglas's West Point registration form he gave his address as "War Department, Washington, D.C." His mother faced a clear choice:

life in a Washington hotel on her own or life in a hotel at West Point with the chance to see Douglas every day.[2]

Given that limited range of possibilities, she was happy to move into the West Point Hotel. This decrepit three-story structure with a view of the Plain was denounced in 1901 by the academy's Board of Visitors as "a mere hut."[3] It was unsanitary, uncomfortable and badly decayed. But none of that mattered much to her. The hotel was the only accommodation open to civilians that stood within the West Point grounds. Directly across the Plain, barely a hundred yards away, stood the cadet barracks. The hotel itself was off limits to cadets, unless they had a special pass, and that could usually be obtained only during a brief parental visit.

With Mrs. MacArthur in residence, her son got a special pass only on weekends. On occasion he took a chance—"ran it out," in cadet slang—and went into the hotel. One winter's day he took his classmate George Cocheu with him to the hotel. While they sat in the back parlor chatting with Douglas's mother, the superintendent arrived to call on Mrs. MacArthur. With every exit but the front door sealed for the winter, MacArthur and Cocheu had to escape via the coal chute.[4]

There was another proud cadet mother in residence at the West Point Hotel, Mrs. Fred Grant. Her husband, a brigadier general, was serving in the Philippines with Arthur MacArthur. Her son, Ulysses S. Grant III, was the grandson of the former President and an intelligent, ambitious youngster much like Douglas MacArthur and just as determined to live up to the famous name he bore.

In the 1890s there were about 250 appointments to the Military Academy each year. Most were what was known as direct appointments, but there was a steadily increasing percentage who, like Douglas MacArthur, secured their appointments by coming out top in a competitive exam.

While it was theoretically possible to get the entrance exam waived, virtually everyone accepted by West Point took it, including Douglas MacArthur. This was the biggest hurdle of all. He spent three months in Highland Falls prepping for it. Passing West Point's entrance exam was not a foregone conclusion for anyone. The aspirants were lodged during the three-day examination period in a part of the barracks known as Beast Barracks. They were taught how to stand at attention and address an officer. This was their introduction to military discipline, even though they were still civilians.[5]

The West Point entrance exam was famous for its difficulty.[6] About 200 out of the 250 appointees could be expected to show up and take the entrance exam. Most would have had a year or two of college, yet only 75 percent would pass it. Douglas MacArthur's entering class numbered 143 cadets.

If they made it through the next four years, they would not receive a bachelor's degree. All they would get was a diploma issued by the academy. Each graduate would also be commissioned a second lieutenant in the Army. Until recently there had been no obligation to accept a commission, despite the fact that West Point's raison d'être was to produce officers.[7] Starting with the class of 1897, all West Point appointees had to promise to serve a minimum of four years in the Army after graduation.

Douglas MacArthur was a typical West Point cadet of his generation—the product of an upper-middle-class, white, Anglo-Saxon Protestant family. What made him unusual was that his father was an Army officer.[8] Establishing a legal residence in a given congressional district while pursuing a peripatetic military career was so problematic that few officers even attempted to secure appointments for their sons.

During his time as a cadet Douglas was paid five hundred dollars a year, more or less what a skilled worker of the time earned. He had to remain within the limits of West Point almost the entire four years. He could ride a horse for a distance of up to six miles away, but he could not stop, dismount or speak to anyone. Or he might take a boat trip on the Hudson, but he couldn't tie up to the shore or talk to anyone on another boat. At the end of two years he would receive a ten-week leave, then would return for two more cloistered years. The West Point system created a sense of isolation that made it easier to model youthful clay into the kind of Army officer the Academic Board believed the country needed.

Douglas MacArthur was luckier than most cadets. The West Point Hotel stood within the academy grounds. He would have an outsider to talk to, to confide in, to turn to for advice. He was able to meet his mother most afternoons at a bench outside the hotel for half an hour. Cadets got used to seeing mother and son walking around Trophy Point deep in conversation. On days when he could not leave the area of his barracks, Pinky crossed the Plain and paced up and down the sidewalk outside the barracks with Douglas.[9]

Lodged in the West Point Hotel, Mrs. MacArthur and Mrs. Grant provided company for each other and a cheering section for their respective sons, who were locked in a keen competition to see which of them would come out on top in West Point's unique approach to a young man's education.

New cadets were known as plebes. They were issued uniforms and remained in Beast Barracks for three weeks, learning how to salute, how to drill and how to keep their quarters clean, learning too about hazing. It was the illicit privilege and dubious pleasure of the class ahead of theirs (the yearlings) and the senior class to make them miserable. So miserable, in fact, that some plebes would quit in despair or disgust.

At the end of three weeks they were issued tents and marched off to the summer encampment. There they erected their tents and moved in, two plebes per tent, and slept on a wooden floor. In camp each day began with drummers and fifers marching through at five-thirty each morning, tootling and beating assembly. The plebes were marched to breakfast, marched back, then changed into short white jackets, white trousers and white helmets for the ritual of guard mounting. Most of the day was occupied like this, with formality, discipline and hurried changes of uniform. Behind the orderly, military façade a minor melodrama was unfolding. Hazing was brutal and dangerous. It could even prove fatal.[10]

For Douglas MacArthur, being the son of a famous Army officer made him a prime target. Some of the southerners seemed determined to make him pay for his father's part in the Atlanta campaign. Other upperclassmen simply disliked him because his father was famous throughout the Army. As one of his classmates said, "He was a marked man."[11]

West Point did not encourage hazing, but it was a practice that was tacitly accepted by the Academic Board and the Association of Graduates as part of the toughening and weeding that turned boys into men and cadets into officers.[12] Tactical officers, who were in charge of cadet discipline, turned a blind eye to it. One of the most feared and disliked tacs in recent memory, John J. Pershing, had left West Point shortly before MacArthur arrived. As an upperclassman Pershing (USMA 1886) had been an enthusiastic tormentor of plebes, dreaming up new forms of humiliation for them.[13] When he returned to the Point in 1897 as a tactical officer, it was too much to expect someone like Pershing to do anything to discourage hazing, even though it was in clear violation of the academy's own regulations. "I hope the day will never come," he told a friend, "when hazing is abolished."[14]

West Point hardly seemed serious about putting a stop to it. The regulations that made hazing illegal provided for punishing the victim along with his tormentor if official intervention became necessary.[15] Several months before MacArthur's arrival the superintendent, Colonel A. L. Mills, issued a stern rebuke to cadets who had been involved in recent hazing incidents. Mills, a cavalryman who had won the Medal of Honor and lost an eye fighting in Cuba, also felt moved to observe that "the motives animating the Cadets concerned therein arose from the praiseworthy desire to free the Academy of unworthy members. . . ."[16]

Most of what plebes endured was more childish than vicious. They had to address insects as equals. When dessert was served, they might be ordered to shout out "the number of days until June." MacArthur was forced to recite (probably to his poker-faced delight) his father's exploits at Stones River and Missionary Ridge. Plebes had to expect that in the middle of the night they were going to be dragged feet first out of their tents while still half asleep. They had to chew on dirty rags. They had to beg to go to the bathhouse, a charade that could drag on interminably.

For many plebes, hazing also involved being beaten up. Yearlings pretended to take offense at a plebe's appearance or his tone of voice; anything would do. Challenged to a fight, he had little choice but to accept. If he didn't, he'd be called a coward and given the silent treatment, even by other plebes, and from there on it was only a matter of days or weeks before he quit West Point. The fights were bare knuckle affairs, which usually ended in knockouts. MacArthur served on the Plebe Fight Commission, which tried to coach those unfortunates who were challenged to put 'em up.[17] It was a rare, and lucky, plebe who won a fight. His reward for doing so was another fight, against someone even tougher, until he *was* knocked out.[18]

West Point wasn't unique in its acceptance of hazing; far from it. A young man who had tried and failed to get into West Point, George C. Marshall, had enrolled at the Virginia Military Institute in 1897. Shortly after arriving there, he was forced to squat over a naked bayonet until his knees buckled. He narrowly averted a truly horrifying injury. What he was left with instead was a large gash on his buttocks and an embarrassing souvenir for the rest of his life.[19]

Nor was this kind of brutality limited to military schools. It was practiced in fraternity houses, especially at the best all-male colleges. Nor was it uniquely American. The English novelist Thomas Hughes's most famous work, *Tom Brown's School Days,* provided a chilling account of the cruelty that was an accepted part of student life at a famous English public (i.e., private) school, Rugby, in the 1850s. It was the love of a good fight that animated the hearts of students such as Tom Brown. "After all," Tom decided one day, "what would life be like without fighting, I should like to know! From the cradle to the grave, fighting, rightly understood, is the business, the real, highest, honestest business of every son of man."

MacArthur didn't get involved in any bare knuckle fights at West Point, but he didn't escape lightly. He was hazed as rigorously as any plebe in his class. One night he was ordered to perform "spread eagles" over broken glass for an hour. This involved standing on his toes, extending his arms over his head, squatting over the broken glass, rising slightly, bringing his arms down and flapping them like wings, squatting again, before rising on his toes and starting over. In between "eagling," he was also forced to hang by his fingertips from a stretcher for long periods. By his reckoning, he performed more than two hundred spread eagles before his legs gave way and he fainted. Revived, he staggered back to his tent. His appearance shocked his tentmate, Frederick Cunningham. MacArthur collapsed again.

He had no control over his legs, which were wildly agitated. He asked for a blanket to be put under them, so the upperclassmen wouldn't hear his feet striking the ground, and told Cunningham to put a blanket in his mouth if he started to cry out in pain.[20]

The commandant, Lieutenant Colonel Otto Hein, evidently heard that this kind of hazing was still going on. He wanted those upperclassmen who were cadet officers to sign a statement saying that they had reported every instance of hazing that came to their attention, as the regulations required. All refused to sign; all lost their stripes.[21]

The worst hazing took place in Beast Barracks, but summer camp could also be an ordeal, as MacArthur had found. He toughed it out, but some plebes had had enough. One of those who left during summer camp was MacArthur's tentmate.[22]

When the camp broke up and the Corps of Cadets moved back into barracks, they faced an uncomfortable life. Virtually every West Point building was in an appalling condition. Some cadets thrilled to the decrepit structures. "As we lived, so did Jefferson Davis, Class of 1828, Robert E. Lee of 1829 . . . Ulysses S. Grant of 1843, George B. McClellan of 1846; Philip H. Sheridan of 1853; J. E. B. Stuart of 1854 . . ." wrote an entranced member of the class of 1898, Conrad S. Babcock.[23] It would be surprising if MacArthur, with his romantic view of military life and profound interest in military history, weren't as moved as Babcock.

Nonetheless this picturesque squalor, haunted though it was by the shades of great soldiers, guaranteed an existence that was in some ways comparable to the life of the poor in the big-city slums of the time. Cadets lived two to a room. Once they installed their uniforms, rifles and sabers, it was hardly possible for both men to stand at the same time. There was no running water. Cadets were required to visit the bathhouse "at least once a week" and take a bath.[24] Each morning they fetched water for washing in a five-gallon metal bucket. In the winter, as they carried it upstairs, water inevitably slopped onto the iron stairwells, adding ice to the hazards of running downstairs in the darkness for roll call at 6:00 A.M.

There was no electricity in the cadet barracks. Lighting was provided by gas lamps. Each room had a fireplace, but open fires weren't allowed. Heating was provided by steam radiators. The fireplace was used mainly for smoking cigarettes; a cadet stood in the grate and poked his head into the chimney while he indulged in this severely forbidden pleasure.

MacArthur got a lucky break when summer camp ended. One of the upperclassmen, Arthur P. S. Hyde, was looking for a roommate. He was so impressed with MacArthur's dignified bearing throughout Beast Barracks that he asked MacArthur if he'd like to share a room during the coming year. MacArthur consulted his mother, then accepted Hyde's offer.[25]

Because Hyde was in his fourth year, he was allowed to keep his light on until eleven. During their first three years cadets had lights out at ten. An extra hour of light meant an extra hour to study. No small advantage to a cadet whose ambition was plainly "to come One." But the biggest advantage of all was probably MacArthur's phenomenal memory. There is strictly no such thing as a photographic memory, but MacArthur had what would pass for a good imitation. His powers of recall were astounding and remained so for most of his life.[26]

When MacArthur joined it, the Corps of Cadets had fewer than 350 members, organized in a battalion of four companies, lettered A through D. He was assigned to A Company, the most demoralized, unhappy collection of young men at West Point. For the past two years its tactical officer had been Lieutenant John J. Pershing. He had taken a perfectly ordinary group of cadets and made them hate him. They called him Lord God Almighty. Pershing's methods amounted to a caricature of leadership and a living definition of the martinet. For some reason, being a tac brought out all the worst elements in his nature. The best thing that had ever happened to Company A was Pershing's departure two months before MacArthur arrived.[27]

He remained with the company until graduation. During those four years his life was to be governed by Army Regulations, the Regulations of the U.S. Military Academy, the Corps of Cadets Regulations (known as the Blue Book, on account of its pale blue binding) and recitation room regulations.

Most cadets rose at 5:30, to be dressed in time for roll call at 6:00. MacArthur was one of those who rose at 5:00 A.M., when lights were allowed to go on, and did some studying first. Ahead lay a day of military rituals, drill and seven hours of classes.

The instructors were not really teachers. They were recent graduates— usually lieutenants and captains—and they did little to encourage their students. Fear of failure was expected to provide all the incentive necessary. Nor did they explain much. They hadn't been exposed to much explanation themselves. They taught from assigned texts and graded students on assignments from those texts every day. The slavish adherence to textbooks was also a wonderful cover for incompetence. French was one of the major subjects all cadets had to study, but not one of the instructors could speak the language fluently. The head of the modern languages department couldn't speak it at all.[28]

To a degree that was probably unique, West Point cadets were self-educated. They were expected to come to the recitation room prepared to stand in front of a blackboard, pointer in hand, and recite their answers to whatever questions the instructor had assigned them to study at the previous class. Recitation was a formal presentation ritualized to the nth degree. The way they stood at the blackboard, even the angle at which they held the pointer, was prescribed by the recitation room regulations.[29] Such an austere, impersonal teaching environment did nothing to stimulate curiosity or sharpen the wits. Nor did it bear much relationship to the way things were done in the world beyond the Plain or to the challenges facing Army officers in command of troops. "West Point," thought one of MacArthur's classmates, "made human turnips out of perfectly good young men."[30]

Any ambitious cadet nonetheless had to take the system seriously, especially if, like MacArthur, he intended to become one of the Five. The top five men in each class went into the Army Register with a star next to their names and the accolade "Distinguished Graduate." No officer could have a better start to his career.

The subjects that counted were mathematics, chemistry and physics (which was divided into what was termed "chemical physics" and a course called "Natural and Experimental Philosophy"). How a cadet performed in these three subjects established his status among his classmates and would go a long way to determining how far he would go in the Army.[31] Math counted most of all. It was at the pinnacle of the intellectual pecking order, reflecting the strong French influence on the Military Academy before the Civil War. More time was devoted to math than any other academic subject.[32] The surest way of getting on course to be one of the Five was to do well in math. Of the 134 cadets remaining in MacArthur's class by June 1900, he stood first in math, first in English, first in drill regulations and first on the Order of General Merit. Ulysses S. Grant III was in second place.

Pinky, however, had suffered a setback. A well-known sculptor had been commissioned to create a statue of male beauty modeled after a West Point cadet. Pinky did not deign to push the merits of her handsome, slender son on the sculptor, assuming that the artistic eye was bound to fall on Douglas and perceive how splendidly he stood out from the rest. Unfortunately Mrs. Grant extolled the beauties of young Ulysses to the visitor so convincingly that it was his youthful form rather than Douglas's that was granted immortality in bronze.[33]

A year after entering West Point it was MacArthur's turn, if he chose, to humiliate and haze the new class of plebes. This was one cadet opportunity he allowed to pass him by. He devoted himself instead to the usual summer camp rituals. One day he drilled a squad of plebes under the critical gaze of one of the tacs, Captain Edmund M. Blake. After a while Blake turned to the cadet captain of A Company, Charles Burnett, and declared, "There's the finest drill master I have ever seen."[34]

When summer camp ended, the "new makes" were announced. MacArthur's faultless military bearing and mastery of the drill regulations had been rewarded. The tactical officers had chosen him to be the senior corporal of A Company, which was the highest rank a yearling could hold.

At about the same time a political storm broke over West Point, threatening to bring the wrath of Congress down on the academy. One Oscar Lyle Booz died at his home in Bristol, Pennsylvania. Booz had been a plebe back in June 1898. Challenged to a bare knuckle fight, he quit after one round. That made him a coward in the eyes of most cadets. When summer camp ended, he refused to satisfy his tormentors by doing what they considered the right thing—namely, quitting this gray granite shrine. His tormentors would not quit either. They forced poor Booz to drink huge amounts of Tabasco sauce at every meal.

His grades suffered from the perpetual hazing, and halfway into his first term, he resigned. Booz died of tuberculosis in the fall of 1900. His family blamed the tuberculosis on the consumption of more than a gallon of Tabasco sauce.[35] This was a medical impossibility, but when the story broke in the press, President McKinley demanded that West Point conduct an inquiry. At the end of December MacArthur was interrogated by a board of officers.

They were intent on extracting from him the names of those who had hazed him in Beast Barracks. At this moment, as at other critical times in his life, he wanted to vomit. Outwardly self-possessed, MacArthur was a deeply emotional man. The poise he showed under pressure was the refinement of a powerful will exerted on raging emotions. And now he was in one of the worst quandaries of his young life. If he did as ordered, he would incur the scorn of the entire corps. Yet if he refused to obey, he could be dismissed from West Point.

During a recess in the inquiry his mother sent him a note, in rhyming couplets. Part of it ran:

> Like mother, like son, is saying so true.
> The world will judge largely of mother by you.[36]

With this encouragement, he declined to give all the names demanded. He named only those cadets who had already admitted their guilt or been expelled. He made a fervent plea not to be dismissed for refusing to cooperate as fully as the court demanded. He begged the court of inquiry to consider that he had been part of the Army since birth, that his father was even now fighting a campaign on behalf of the United States. The court recessed, he returned to his quarters and to his surprise and relief he was not recalled.

What MacArthur did not seem to appreciate was that he held a strong hand, stronger than most cadets could ever hope for. While his fellow cadets were free to jeer at him as "a tin soldier," the supe, the commandant and the Academic Board knew they had to handle him carefully. He was not just another cadet. His father was a major general by this time, one of the twelve most important men in the Army. The Academic Board operated in two ways: harsh and unforgiving toward most cadets, solicitous and flexible toward those whose fathers had powerful friends in Congress or the War Department. A young man with the right connections could get thrown out—quite a few were, in fact—and be back a few months later once the degree of daddy's pull had been demonstrated. In Douglas's case, there was no doubt about his father's connections and no need to test them. That was why he was given more leeway than most.[37]

The ordeal wasn't over, however. Congress launched its own investigation. It was inevitable that the press would take an interest in Cadet MacArthur as the son of a famous father, and journalists soon picked up rumors about what had happened to him in Beast Barracks. Called to testify before the congressional committee in January 1901, MacArthur tried to minimize his ordeal. "The hazing that I underwent was in no way more severe or more calculated to place me in a serious physical condition than has ordinarily taken place. I was not in any physical condition that would have tended to injure me at all." MacArthur denied that he had been delirious and called the convulsions in his legs "a case of exaggerated cramps."

He was repeatedly asked to name the cadets who had hazed him. Once more the only people he was prepared to identify were those who had already left West Point and those still there who had admitted their guilt.

He tried to deny that hazing involved cruelty but finally conceded that it did. Asked if he thought being subjected to cruelty was "part of the essential education of an Army officer," he replied, "I do not think it is essential; no, sir." Did he think subjecting other people to such treatment was part of the training of an Army officer? "I should say not; no, sir."

A week later the committee took testimony from his former tentmate Frederick Cunningham, who gave a graphic account of MacArthur "reeling into the tent," without any control over his legs. "I think if you saw him in the same condition in the street you would call them convulsions," said Cunningham. The aftermath, however, was that he'd borne his ordeal with such fortitude that "he'd got the bootlick on the whole corps." Meaning? "It means," Cunningham explained, "admiration for his plucky resistance . . . they were proud of him, and they would practically give him the glad hand after that." The hazing of MacArthur had ended right there.

In Cunningham's opinion, MacArthur might have brought the hazing to a halt much earlier if he had been willing to fight. Instead he'd tried to avoid that. "I believe the fact that his mother was at the post led him to put up with a lot more than he otherwise would have done."

The congressmen were puzzled. Just what offense had MacArthur committed that made him the object of this kind of treatment? "MacArthur's real offense," Cunningham answered, "was that he was the son of General MacArthur." Did that mean he was vain and flaunted his family connections in front of the other cadets? "No, sir. There was not a finer fellow in the class," said Cunningham.[38]

Shortly after these hearings, Congress voted on the academy's appropriations for the next fiscal year and included in the legislation a demand that the superintendent "effectively prevent the practice of hazing." There was a powerful, implicit threat in tying hazing to appropriations.[39]

With this kind of pressure on him, the superintendent bore down hard. Further antihazing regulations were added to the academy's rules. Behavior that even resembled hazing would not be permitted. Not even the conservative and stubborn Academic Board was going to risk the anger of Congress. The board was independent but not idiotic. The tacs too were under pressure to stamp it out.

The Corps of Cadets got a break from routine by marching in McKinley's inaugural parade in March, but when they returned to West Point, tensions were still rising. The academy was primed to ignite. The spark was an incident in the mess hall at supper on April 9, when one cadet threw part of his supper at another. It was an action that looked like hazing. The senior cadet at the table, Robert Ralston, did not report the incident. The tacs learned of it, and a week later Ralston, the lieutenant of E Company (the corps had gained two more companies in the fall of 1900), was summarily reduced to the lowest of cadet ranks, private second class, at the evening parade on April 16. The order that was read out rebuked him for "a lack of character."[40]

When the parade was dismissed, cadets refused to return to their barracks. They milled about on the Plain, screaming, "Hullabaloo, hullabaloo, son of a bitch, god damn!" and shouting class yells. Every class had one, such as "Coyak! Coyak! Siss, boom, roar. West Point, West Point, Nineteen-Four!" The protest wasn't against the crackdown on hazing. It was a reaction to the unfair personal criticism in an official order of a popular cadet officer. Virtually the whole Corps of Cadets was involved, including MacArthur. A bonfire was lit on the Plain; the reveille gun was dragged from Trophy Point over to the superintendent's house, loaded with stones for ammunition and trained on Mills's front door. The colonel was challenged to come out and face the wrath of the mob.[41]

The tacs managed to get the situation under control. Five first classmen were expelled; six more were suspended for a year. Dozens were sentenced to walk punishment tours. MacArthur, although he'd shown which side he was on, escaped punishment. No one could doubt, though, that the superintendent was serious about putting an end to hazing. Soldiers, however, are not lawyers. The rules the academy drew up to abolish hazing proved unworkable because they lacked a precise definition of the offense. For the next decade every cadet who was expelled for hazing was eventually reinstated, either by the president or by an act of Congress, because the way dictionaries defined "hazing" bore little resemblance to what actually happened at West Point. Hazing rumbled on into the twentieth century and did not really end until the academy began to admit women.[42]

In the spring of 1901 MacArthur made the West Point baseball team and with the rest of his teammates signed a pledge not to smoke or drink during the season.[43] He would have loved to play football, but at five feet ten and one-half inches and weighing 140 pounds, he was too lightly built to make it. He didn't even risk rejection by trying out. The captain of the baseball team, Stephen Abbot, acknowledged that he wasn't a brilliant baseball player, "but somehow he could manage to get on first. He'd outfox the pitcher, draw a base on balls or get a single or out run a bunt—and there he'd be on first."[44] In May, West Point played its first ever baseball game against the Naval Academy. The middies had the home field advantage, but Army won 4–3. Some of his classmates claimed MacArthur hit the first run in the game; others that he hit the final, winning run. There is no proof that he hit either. What mattered most was that he had made the team, and when the season ended, he was awarded his letter. For the rest of his life he wore long bathrobes of West Point gray with a huge dark blue *A* embroidered on the left breast. He wore these terry towel reminders of athletic glory days with such zeal they had to be replaced every two years.[45]

When the academic year drew to a close, he was again the number one student in the class of 1903, whose numbers had now fallen to 104 cadets. He maintained his first place in math once more and was in the top five in every subject but "Drawing," a name which obscured the fact that it was really a course in topographical engineering and mapmaking. Combining his academic work with his rating for conduct, he once again ranked first on the Order of General Merit.

Having completed two years at West Point, he packed for his ten-week leave. Adding to the excitement and anticipation was the prospect of seeing his father again. Major General Arthur MacArthur, Jr., was due to return that summer from the Philippines.

Brigadier General Arthur MacArthur, Jr., arrived in the Philippines in June 1898 with five thousand men. These reinforcements allowed the Army commander, Major General Wesley Merritt, to mount an attack on

Manila. The Spanish governor had no intention of putting up a real fight for the city. He sought nothing more than a skirmish that would satisfy the honor of his fifteen thousand soldiers. A mock battle was arranged, with live ammunition.

On the morning of August 13 Dewey's warships in Manila Bay bombarded Spanish positions for an hour. American troops then advanced. MacArthur's brigade unexpectedly ran into serious resistance. An artillery lieutenant named Peyton C. March distinguished himself in this action by leading a charge that failed, followed by a reconnaissance that succeeded. MacArthur recommended March for the Medal of Honor. This wasn't awarded, but the seeds of a close association between March and the MacArthurs had been sown.[46] During March's second tour of duty in the Philippines he served for a time as MacArthur's aide.

The smoke had barely cleared from the Battle of Manila when MacArthur learned that he had been promoted to major general of volunteers and given command of the 2d Division. Over the next six months he played a key role in suppressing the tens of thousands of Filipinos who saw the defeat of the Spanish as the best chance in five centuries to create an independent Philippines. They had not expected the United States to replace the Spanish.

During the fighting the officer who won MacArthur's esteem more than any other was the commander of the 20th Kansas Volunteer Infantry Regiment, a small but muscular colonel named Frederick Funston. MacArthur recommended Funston for the Medal of Honor, which was soon forthcoming. A strong bond developed between the two men. When Funston's son was born several years later, he named the child Arthur MacArthur.

MacArthur commanded his troops in the field from the back of a sturdy Filipino pony. The strong nerves he had shown under fire as a young man remained with him in late middle age, as did his Civil War luck. On one occasion a major standing next to him fell seriously wounded when insurgent bullets rained down around the division commander and his staff, raising puffs of dust at their feet. MacArthur was unscathed and unconcerned. The heat bothered him more than enemy fire. Like many soldiers in the Philippines, he wore his large campaign hat without a dent or a crease in it, to improve the flow of air around his head.[47] With his paunch, his round face, his pince-nez, his salt-and-pepper mustache all surmounted by a dome of a hat he looked more like the stereotypical professor than the stereotypical fighting general.

By 1900 the *insurrectos* were holed up in the jungle-clad mountains. The most important insurgent leader, Emilio Aguinaldo, had barely escaped being caught in December 1899 by a pursuit force commanded by Major Peyton March. The insurgent leaders acknowledged at last that they could not hope to defeat American troops in conventional battles. What ensued was a bitter guerrilla war with atrocities committed by both sides.

On May 5, 1900, MacArthur became military governor of the Philippines. For a month he was responsible for everything.[48] Yet even as he took command, a group of civilians who would assume most of the responsibility for government in the islands was setting sail from San Francisco. The secretary of war, Elihu Root, had chosen William Howard Taft, former solicitor general of the United States and presently a federal judge, to head the Philippine Commision. Taft, with his four fellow commissioners, arrived in Manila aboard the steamer *Hancock* on June 3. To the commission's surprise, MacArthur did not come to the dock to greet them. He sent one of his colonels instead. Taft, dressed in a sweat-stained and crumpled white linen suit, met MacArthur at the Malacañang Palace next day. The heat was overwhelming, and the three-hundred-pound Taft was a heavy sweater in any climate, but MacArthur's greeting was so frosty that, according to Taft, perspiration ceased.[49]

For a time Taft tried to get along with MacArthur, but there was a wide range of disagreements. As tension between the two men grew, Taft began ridiculing MacArthur unmercifully in his letters home. He reported to Root that MacArthur was "too slow and deliberate and timid." He informed his brother Charles P. Taft that the general was "weak," "a martinet" and "a small man in a large place." He portrayed MacArthur as a man whose sole virtue was a dogged kind of loyalty to his country, but without real ability.[50]

Meanwhile, MacArthur continued his preparations to take the war to the insurgents. Like Taft, he believed that America's strategic interests in the Pacific demanded retention of the Philippines. He also saw the spreading of American institutions as a good thing in itself. At the same time he was virtually alone in professing "almost unqualified" faith in the Filipinos themselves.[51] He mingled with Filipinos on equal terms in Manila's Masonic lodges and used his power to prevent them from being closed. In February 1901 he threw a ball at the Malacañang at which Filipinos and Americans met and enjoyed themselves without any hint of discrimination. His liberal attitude toward Filipinos and his strong interest in the archipelago became part of the MacArthur heritage handed on to his son.[52]

Taft considered the insurgency as good as over. MacArthur considered it had reached a point where, unless he acted swiftly, it would soon get out of control. He revived a Civil War directive known as General Orders 100, which gave his officers wide powers to crack down on the insurgency, powers that were often abused and sometimes used to justify torture.[53] The people of countless Filipino towns where insurgents found shelter were uprooted, placed in camps under Army guards and their homes burned down. "Dead lines" were instituted around areas which had been secured. Thereafter any armed Filipino found on the wrong side of a dead line could be considered engaged in terrorism and shot on sight.[54] MacArthur's strategy worked. The number of *insurrectos* seeking amnesty simply soared. Army officers were also authorized to announce throughout the Philippines that Filipinos would be granted American citizenship once the fighting ceased. This was a powerful inducement, but one that the Supreme Court later invalidated.[55]

Aguinaldo, however, remained at large. Funston approached MacArthur with a daring plan to penetrate deep into *insurrecto* territory and capture the rebel leader. MacArthur gave his approval but told him, "Funston, this is a desperate undertaking. I fear that I shall never see you again."[56] In March 1901 Funston reappeared, with Aguinaldo as his prisoner. This was a devastating blow to the insurgents, especially to those in the northern Philippines. They never really recovered from it. Taft was invariably reluctant to credit the Army with achieving anything and belittled the importance of Aguinaldo's capture. Filipinos took a different view.[57]

On July 4 MacArthur got what he wanted most of all: out. On that day Taft became civil governor of the Philippines, and military rule in the islands ceased. Taft considered the insurrection over and was disappointed that McKinley hadn't already declared it so in his inaugural address. In fact, fighting continued in the northern Philippines for more than a year, and the struggle to control the southern Philippines kept the Army occupied for another decade. At all events, MacArthur was leaving. He would rejoin his wife and youngest son in Milwaukee.

During his first two years at West Point Douglas MacArthur had followed the war as closely as his schedule allowed. He was particularly proud of his father's role in pacifying the islands and often talked about it with his roommate Arthur Hyde. According to Hyde, "He often wondered if he would be as great a man as his father—and thought if hard work would make him so, he had a chance."[58] The only incident that seemed to upset him about General MacArthur's campaign to crush the Philippine insurrection was a newspaper account of a group of stark naked Igorots— one of the aboriginal tribes in the islands—charging an American patrol. The Igorots were armed only with bows and arrows. Forty of them were shot dead in this hopeless attack.[59]

Douglas's identification with his father was total. When he talked to his classmates, "His vivid imagination made him actually feel that he had gone up Missionary Ridge with his father's regiment in 1863," thought one of them.[60]

MacArthur had also absorbed his father's prickly sense of honor, leaving him overly sensitive to the least slight or discourtesy. He missed several of the weekly tests in math during his second year on account of illness. To his horror, on his return from hospital he saw himself listed with the "goats" of the class and scheduled to take a special examination with them at nine the next morning to avoid being failed in the course. He went to see the instructor and pointed out that the grades he had scored on those math tests he had taken were so high that in effect, he already had a passing grade. Whatever happened, he was not going to be stigmatized by being lumped with the class goats. He demanded that his name be taken off the list. The instructor told him that he was challenging a direct order and that the rule required every cadet to take a certain number of math tests no matter how well he performed on some of them. "Sir," said MacArthur emphatically, "I will not take the test." Back in his room he told his classmate the same thing. "I know it is an order, but it is an unreasonable one. If my name is not removed from that list by nine o'clock tomorrow morning I will resign."

"But what will your father say?" asked his roommate.

"He will be terribly disappointed, but I believe he will see my attitude in the matter and approve my action."

At eight-fifty the next morning an orderly came to MacArthur's room and said his name had been removed from the list. He would not have to take the test.[61] Another victory for honor? Yes and no. While Douglas's protest was undoubtedly sincere, the instructor should have realized that General MacArthur would indeed approve his son's action. If anyone had to leave the academy as a result of this episode, it was as likely to be the instructor as the cadet. In any event, no sensible man would make an enemy of a general who held the Medal of Honor and was currently leading American forces to victory in the field over a math test for the goats of ought three. That was one equation even a dunce could work out.

When Douglas returned to West Point in September, he faced the new academic year as cadet sergeant of A Company. Such appointments carried a fair burden of responsibility. Both as a cadet noncom and as a cadet officer he was charged with maintaining company discipline, but unlike some, he didn't curry favor with the tacs by handing out demerits freely. "He didn't bother with trivial offenses," said one of his A Company classmates.[62]

On occasion he would overlook serious offenses—serious, that is, to the faculty. Even as a cadet MacArthur was noted for his remarkable independence of thought and action despite the severe constraints of the West Point system. One night, for example, he was making an inspection of the barracks when he opened a door and looked down at the upturned faces of half a dozen startled cadets, caught in flagrante while humiliatingly on their knees, gambling with dice. Looming over them, he gravely intoned, "Gentlemen, I must ask you not to study so hard. If you do you will soon be seeing *spots* before your eyes."[63]

There was also the famous incident when a cannon from Trophy Point was found on the roof of the West Academic Building. The cannon weighed close to a ton, and getting it across the Plain in the middle of the night without creating noise, then hauling it up four flights of stairs and onto the roof were an organizational feat that left the professors bewildered. They could not figure out how it had been done, but there was only one cadet who was considered both smart enough and daring enough to mastermind this unprecedented prank: MacArthur.[64]

That fall he also took over as manager of the football team. If he couldn't play, he would be involved in some other way. Football was a passion that stuck with him throughout life, enhanced rather than diminished by the frustration of pacing the sidelines instead of a getting a grip on the pigskin.

The demands of managing the team may have been one reason why his grades fell this year. He slipped from first place to fourth on the Order of General Merit, which factored in such nonacademic matters as a cadet's ability to perform infantry drill and the number of demerits he had incurred. Being late to a formation or to class was the principal source of MacArthur's demerits. His dusting also got him into trouble.[65]

When the new cadet officers were announced, MacArthur was appointed captain of A Company. An even greater accolade was his appointment as First Captain of the Corps of Cadets, the highest honor a cadet might aspire to. This went not only, or even mainly, to those who led their class academically. It was awarded to the cadet whose military bearing and interest in soldiering had most impressed the supe, the com and the tacs. Pershing had stood little above the midpoint in his class but been First Captain. So had a noted cavalryman, Jonathan Wainwright.

Most cadets took a mocking attitude toward what they called tin soldiers. Deriding what the faculty admires is considered cool by students everywhere. MacArthur stood out not only in his love of soldiering but in his tremendous military bearing. Little more than a youth, he already looked like a man born to command.[66]

Despite the slight dip in his grades, he was almost certain to be one of the five "distinguished graduates" of his class. Nevertheless in his final year he studied as hard as he had ever done. Nearly all cadets were intelligent young men, but down the decades the roster of those who'd been dismissed for academic deficiencies was a mile long. What counted as much as brains was the ability to concentrate. MacArthur's intellectual concentration was formidable.[67]

It wasn't all study, of course. In the fall of 1902 he was best man at his brother Arthur's wedding. Arthur was off to a promising beginning as a naval officer. He would become a pioneer in the dangerous new technology of submarine warfare. His bride was the daughter of an admiral.

MacArthur returned to the academy and the delights of the social life open to cadets in their final year. His interest in young women was part of the growing legend. Handsome, charming and the son of a famous man, he was probably as much pursued as pursuer. He was reputedly engaged to eight young women at the same time, breaking the former academy record of seven.

This seems to be a story garbled by the passage of time, however. It is hardly credible that MacArthur handed out eight engagement rings, met eight sets of parents, introduced eight girls to Pinky as future daughters-in-law and talked about eight wedding days. What is likely is that he was dating eight girls at the same time. If the record was seven, he would go for eight; had it been fifty, he would have somehow managed to date fifty-one. Even so, he laughed off the story of eight engagements. "I have never been so hotly engaged by the enemy!" he protested.[68]

One of the eight young ladies was seen kissing him on Flirtation Walk—a partly screened path with a breathtaking view of the Hudson—when one of the tacs appeared. MacArthur braced himself for a fistful of demerits, but the tac merely grinned and said, "Congratulations, Mister MacArthur!"[69]

He was not, it is fair to say, the only Adonis around. He had competition from one of his cadet friends, Grayson Mallet-Prevost Murphy, a millionaire's son from New York. In February 1903 MacArthur had a blind date to a cadet "hop" with a young woman from Brooklyn, Bess Follansbee. He was, she told her diary, "a splendid dancer" and had a "very bright, pleasant manner." Even so, she contrived to dance even more with Grayson Murphy, who was "extremely handsome." Next day MacArthur and two of his classmates "ran it out" to the West Point Hotel. While they sat around a cast-iron potbellied stove, Mrs. MacArthur, who was on a visit, came in and warned them that an officer was entering the hotel. MacArthur and his friends grabbed their overcoats and hid downstairs until the officer departed. No coal scuttle this time.[70]

When the final grades were posted at the end of May, he again stood at the top of his class, which now numbered 93 survivors, out of the 143 at the beginning. He had achieved a rare double, of being First Captain and also the number one man in his class. He was not the only cadet, or the first, to achieve this distinction. Nor did he have the highest grades ever recorded at West Point. Changes in the curriculum over time make it impossible to compare the top graduates from one era with the outstanding graduates from another era. What is striking is that virtually all the number one men at West Point have sunk rapidly into oblivion. MacArthur himself decided later in life that in itself it was an honor that did not mean much, "except that some people don't like it."[71]

The question before him now was which branch would commission him. The top ten students in each class could choose, and nearly all chose the Corps of Engineers. The area of study in which MacArthur had his poorest grades was engineering. It didn't seem to interest him much. Besides, he wanted to be a field soldier, to be like his father, and serve in a combat arm. Before he set off for West Point, his heart had been fixed on joining the cavalry, the most glamorous soldiers in the Army. He would join the men with big boots, flashing swords and spirited horses whose color and dash had enlivened the dull Army posts of his childhood.[72]

But it was now evident the days of the horse cavalry were numbered. His preference had shifted to the infantry. His father talked him out of it. Promotion in the infantry is slow, the general said—how well he knew! Peacetime promotions go to the engineers. When war comes, you will be able to transfer to the infantry, and you will go to war with a higher rank than if you had been with the infantry from the beginning.[73] Douglas took a commission in the Corps of Engineers.

On June 11, 1903, the secretary of war, Elihu Root, awarded the diplomas. As one of the Army's senior generals Arthur MacArthur was invited to sit in the front row of the assemblage of proud parents. He chose instead to sit modestly at the back. As the number one man Douglas received the first diploma from Root, then made his way to where his parents sat. He smiled down at his mother, who, moved to tears, was dabbing her eyes, then handed the diploma to his father, who, had it not been for going to war in 1862, would have entered West Point in 1863.[74] A circle closed. The achievement of the son helped complete the ambitions of the father.

4

A Tragic Joke

The proud wearer of the shiny gold bars of a second lieutenant, Douglas MacArthur knew exactly what he wanted: assignment to the Philippines. Many of his classmates wanted the same thing.[1] For a young officer eager to advance in his profession in wartime the best thing he can do is get to the front. To MacArthur's delight, he was ordered to proceed to Manila.

His father now commanded the Department of the Pacific, with head-quarters in San Francisco. Douglas spent two months with his parents at Fort Mason before embarking for the Philippines. It was an enjoyable summer in a beautiful city, enlivened by the escape of a military prisoner on a work detail at the fort. Armed with a scythe, the prisoner went into hiding. Armed with a revolver, Lieutenant MacArthur found him in the bushes and made him a prisoner again.[2]

Stopping by his father's office one day, MacArthur was introduced to Captain John J. Pershing, freshly arrived from Manila.[3] Pershing was probably the best-known junior officer in the Army. He had made a name for himself in Cuba, commanding black cavalrymen in the charge up San Juan Hill alongside Roosevelt's Rough Riders. During the past year he had waged a successful and highly publicized campaign on the island of Mindanao against the Moros, fierce Muslim warriors who were considered the most ferocious tribe in the Philippines.[4] Pershing's ramrod bearing, steely gaze and confidence-inspiring jaw created almost a caricature of nature's soldier. He left Lieutenant MacArthur slightly awestruck. At the same time, Pershing noted, "I was favorably impressed by the manly, efficient appearance of the second lieutenant."[5]

Assigned to the 3d Engineer Battalion, MacArthur sailed for Manila in September aboard the transport *Sherman*. His brother Arthur was in command of the destroyer USS *Henderson* and had just returned from Japan. Arthur was at the dock to bid Douglas farewell. The two brothers were exceptionally close, despite—maybe because of—the fact that they had not seen much of each other since Arthur's departure for Annapolis ten years earlier. It was an intensely emotional parting for both of them.[6]

Douglas had the company of nearly a dozen of his classmates during the leisurely five-and-a-half-week voyage to Manila. When he arrived in the islands, he discovered that the enervating heat and humidity meant drilling before the sun came up. The day's work was done mainly between breakfast and noon. Lunch was followed by a siesta until 4:00 P.M. Then came the ceremony of retreat. Fastidious officers such as MacArthur changed their uniforms four times a day and took three showers.[7] But MacArthur was not simply fastidious; he attached enormous importance to appearances. If he could not do something stylishly, he chose not to do it at all. Many young officers stationed in and around Manila went into the city most evenings to enjoy themselves. MacArthur went out only if he could afford a carriage and driver to take him into town and return him to his quarters. And when MacArthur was out on the town, he wore his best white uniform.[8]

The heat and the easy ways of Philippine life were a challenge. A young man with a long-standing interest in girls, MacArthur was sorely tempted by some of the Filipinas he met. It was hard to resist what he called "the moonbeam delicacy of the Philippines' lovely women."[9] No white officer could date them without risking his career. It was inevitable that some would take a chance. There was said to be a defiant jingle that ran, "Roses are red, violets are blue/My girl's brown, what's it to you?" Pershing, for example, was a notorious womanizer, and when he was stationed in the Philippines, he fathered two children—a boy and a girl—by a Filipina. The girl was said to bear an amazing resemblance to her father.[10]

We can be fairly sure, though, that Pinky and the general had given their sons firm instructions on the subject of self-control, instructions that the bishop and WTMA had done their best to reinforce. MacArthur's physical armor against all that moonbeam delicacy consisted of a full-length mirror. He bought the mirror and installed it in his quarters. When the testosterone storms raged and nature seemed about to get on top of nurture, he stood in front of the mirror and gave young Second Lieutenant MacArthur a stern dressing-down, like an irate tactical officer back at the Point dealing with some incorrigibly horny cadet.[11]

Still, sexual urges continued to plague him. There were various diversions available to a young Army officer, such as playing polo or going hunting on the game-rich Bataan Peninsula. There were tennis courts, squash courts and a billiard room at the Army and Navy Club. But what Lieutenant MacArthur enjoyed more than any of these was going to the Manila Opera House with his classmate William Rose. There they feasted their eager eyes on the delectable form and wildly agitated legs of a gorgeous young singer called Tamanti as she tore at her hair, rolled her flashing eyes, bit her lip and sang her heart out as poor, mad Lucia di Lammermoor. He could then write home and tell Pinky and the general about the highly cultural way he was spending his free time, but it was little Tamanti's half-naked body that went spinning through his dreams.[12]

Lieutenant MacArthur spent his first few months working on construction projects in the southern islands. He supervised the building of piers, for example, at Tacloban, near to where he would set foot once more in the Philippines on October 20, 1944. One of the great thrills of the Second World War for him would be to see those piers still standing forty years later, like old friends awaiting his return.[13]

While working on the island of Guimaris in November 1903, he was ambushed by a pair of *insurrectos*. One opened fire with his rifle, putting a bullet through the top of MacArthur's campaign hat. Before he could fire again, MacArthur drew his revolver and shot both men dead. The construction foreman, an Army sergeant, rushed to the scene, looked at the two men, eyed the hole in the hat, saluted and pronounced in a strong Irish brogue, "Begging the lieutenant's pardon, but the rest of the lieutenant's life is pure velvet!" It was a story that MacArthur loved to tell and seems to have told to nearly everyone he knew. How true it was, who can say? He would not have invented a shooting scrape, so it's a safe bet that someone took a shot at MacArthur and missed, in which case he almost certainly shot back. But whether he actually killed anyone is open to doubt.[14]

In the spring of 1904 MacArthur took his examination for promotion to first lieutenant. The senior officer on the promotion board, a colonel, posed a problem for him to solve: How would he defend a harbor threatened by a combined naval and ground assault? MacArthur explained how he would deploy his forces. The colonel then reduced his forces to almost nothing. What would he do now?

Two things, MacArthur replied. "First, I'd round up all the sign painters in the community and put them to work making signs reading BEWARE— THIS HARBOR IS MINED. I'd float these signs out to the harbor mouth. After that I'd get down on my knees and pray. Then I'd go out and fight like hell."[15]

Promoted to first lieutenant, MacArthur was assigned as assistant to the chief engineering officer in Manila. Busy as he seems to have been, his heart even now probably wasn't entirely with the engineers. He found the time to write a pamphlet on reconnaissance for the Philippine Constabulary, the paramilitary police force created by Taft. It was manned by Filipinos under American officers, and its motto was "To be outnumbered, always—To be outfought, never."[16] The head of the constabulary, Captain James G. Harbord, was so pleased with MacArthur's contribution that he took the young author to dinner at the Army and Navy Club in Manila.

The white, three-story building was one of the most splendid structures in Manila. It had a breathtaking view of Manila Bay and stood in three acres luxuriant with flame trees, magnificent palms and bougainvill ea bushes that looked like living fountains sending out huge cascades of brilliant tropical flowers that covered great swaths of the lawn.[17] The night Harbord took MacArthur to dinner, he introduced the lieutenant to two young Filipino lawyers named Manuel Quezon and Sergio Osmeña. Quezon had been Aguinaldo's aide, but following Aguinaldo's capture by Funston, Quezon had abandoned the insurrection as a lost cause.[18] Like Osmeña, he had enrolled in law school, to prepare for a life in politics, agitating ceaselessly for his country's independence. Both Quezon and Osmeña were destined to become major figures in MacArthur's life, and he in theirs.

The principal threat to American troops in the Philippines no longer came from the Moros or the *insurrectos*. It came from malaria. A year after arriving in the island MacArthur was sweating and shaking with malarial fevers. To add to his torments, he was also suffering from that other scourge of the tropics, ringworm. He was sent home in October 1904 to recover. He returned to the United States, sharing a cabin aboard the troop transport *Thomas* with his friend and classmate Bill Rose.[19]

MacArthur's year in the Philippines had brought excellent efficiency reports from the engineering officers he had worked for. He was assigned to the district engineer's office in San Francisco. The malaria continued to sap his strength, and his eyes started to trouble him. His health remained fragile for a long time, but his superiors ensured his duties were comparatively light. During his first year in San Francisco the only task he took much interest in was an assignment for several months to the California Debris Commission. The commission was charged with clearing up the environmental mess created by placer mining in the foothills of the Sierra Nevada.

MacArthur covered the mine country on horseback under thrillingly blue skies, his lungs filled with the intoxicating air of the mountains. This was the best medicine any doctor could have prescribed. The pine-clad slopes, the half-empty gold towns, the sparkling streams and screaming eagles echoed the life of the Old West. MacArthur regained health and vitality by wrapping himself tightly in a nostalgic cloak of memories of an idyllic childhood out on the frontier.

In December 1903 General Arthur MacArthur visited Hawaii on an inspection tour. It would have been a routine event had he not spoken unguardedly about the ambitions of imperial Germany to a pair of National Guard officers. The general was worried about the way large numbers of Germans were emigrating to South America, where they were making such political inroads that Germany could soon pose a challenge to the Monroe Doctrine. The Germans also had ambitions in the Pacific. He didn't spell them out, but he didn't have to. Politically aware people knew that one important reason for the American annexation of Hawaii and the occupation of the Philippines had been to prevent the Germans from grabbing them. All in all, Arthur MacArthur thought a war between the United States and Germany was inevitable. One of the Guard officers passed on these remarks to a journalist, and they soon spread from Hawaii to the mainland.[20]

What stirred up the biggest furor were the aspersions MacArthur had cast on the loyalties of German-Americans. German-American associations protested vehemently to the White House and the War Department. Roosevelt rebuked MacArthur, and one of the first things Taft had to do on becoming secretary of war in March 1904 was seek an explanation from MacArthur as to what exactly he had said.[21]

This tempest soon passed, pushed aside by the rapidly escalating Russo-Japanese War, which had begun in February 1904. An ambitious, expansionist Japan maneuvered Russia into a war over which of them would dominate Korea. The Japanese sailed into the Korea Bay, landed an army in the Chinese province of Liaoning and fought their way south to the major Russian military base in the area, at Port Arthur, and besieged it.

The sudden emergence of Japan as a potential great power could not be ignored. In December 1904 Arthur MacArthur, with his long-standing interest in the Far East, requested assignment as an observer. He said that he hoped to witness at least one major battle and to study the field organization of the Japanese Army.[22] His request was granted, but by then Port Arthur was on the verge of surrender.

He would be assigned temporarily as an American military attaché in Tokyo. The permanent attaché would be none other than Captain Pershing.[23] The MacArthurs and the Pershings set sail together for Tokyo. In the meantime Douglas too requested assignment as a war observer, but his lack of rank and experience counted heavily against him. He was turned down.

From Tokyo General MacArthur was able to travel at last to China. He arrived in Mukden shortly after it fell to the Japanese but returned to Japan without witnessing any battles. In September his aide Captain Parker West was ordered to return home. His place would be taken by Lieutenant MacArthur. The general had gotten around the problem of his son's disqualifications as a war observer by having him appointed his aide.[24]

General MacArthur does not appear to have seen any of the combat in the Russo-Japanese War, which had turned into something of a laboratory for military experiments. Nearly fifty Western military observers had been attached to the opposing forces—seventeen from the United States alone.[25] Japanese supremacy at sea controlled the course of the war and nullified many of the advantages the Russians should have enjoyed.

There were many lessons to be learned from this war, the most important being the difference that light machine guns made.[26] Neither side possessed many of these weapons, but their effects were devastating for infantry caught in the open. In short, Manchuria was a harbinger of what the First World War would bring, but despite the plethora of military observers there and the accuracy of their reports, its lessons were largely ignored by Western armies.

One of the American observers was General MacArthur's former protégé Captain Peyton C. March, whose report concentrated on the Japanese use of artillery. He thought it was excellent.[27] In October 1905 he returned to Japan, where he may have met up with his former mentor. When General MacArthur returned to the United States from the Philippines in 1901, he had tried to get March appointed commandant at West Point. March didn't get the appointment, but his career was clearly on the rise. He had been one of the first officers appointed to the General Staff when it was created in 1903.

Douglas MacArthur arrived in Yokohama at the end of October. Three days later he and his father set off on their inspection tour. For the general, it was probably a dream come true. His interest in the Far East had only deepened and broadened over the years. He shared the vision of William H. Seward, who, as Lincoln's secretary of state, had negotiated the purchase of Alaska. Seward had justified his action to a skeptical Congress and national press by claiming, "The Pacific coast will be the chief theatre of events in the great hereafter." And MacArthur, during his three years in the Philippines, had a standing order with a bookseller in Hong Kong to send him a copy of every new book published on the Far East.[28]

The general, his son and his wife set off on their trip in early November 1905, first visiting Japanese military bases. From Japan they journeyed to Singapore, where the British were creating their greatest military outpost in the Far East. The MacArthurs went north to inspect garrisons farther inland before setting off for Java in the Dutch East Indies. After returning to Singapore for Christmas with the British, they traveled to Burma and early in the New Year took a ship to Calcutta.

The British Army in India was probably the epitome of British soldiering at this time. It attracted many of the best officers the British possessed. Its standards were high, and the turbulent North-west Frontier provided a low-intensity conflict where, as in the Philippines, junior officers could learn their trade under fire but with a reasonable chance of surviving and passing on what they had learned to others. During their two months in India the MacArthurs made an inspection of the North-west Frontier.

In March 1906 they arrived back in Singapore. From there they visited Siam (now Thailand), the only Southeast Asian country to escape foreign occupation. At a state banquet the lights went out, and the quick-thinking Lieutenant MacArthur saved the situation by replacing a fuse. The king was prepared to decorate him for this prompt action, but he politely declined it. News that he had been given a medal for replacing a fuse would do nothing for his career.[29]

From Siam the MacArthurs moved on to China. During their two months there they visited the German naval base at Tsingtao, a place later even more famous for its beer. They inspected Chinese garrisons in the last twilit days of the Manchu dynasty. Soldiering had long been despised among the Chinese, and now, desperate to prop up their crumbling regime, the Manchu rulers had invited the Japanese Army to provide instructors. Blind people clinging to the back of a tiger.

In June 1906 the trip ended where it began, in Yokohama. The general and his son discussed the Russo-Japanese War with some of the senior Japanese Army commanders. These talks only cemented the impressions they had already gained of the inevitable rise of Japan as a major military power.

This eight-month tour provided Douglas MacArthur with one of the most formative influences of his life. He gained from it a conviction that while colonial rule provided law and order in underdeveloped countries, it did so only at the cost of blocking the educational development of the people and blighting their hopes of a higher standard of living. Above all, though, he now shared his father's vision of an Asia that would one day be so populous and rich that the existence of the United States itself would eventually depend more on its relationship with the Far East then on its old ties of blood and belief with Europe.[30]

The Spanish-American War and the Philippine insurrection gave Congress and the public the best view they had had since the Civil War of the strengths and weaknesses of the Army. There were no disastrous shortcomings, but there were many serious faults. There were many elderly majors and lieutenant colonels, for example, who proved to be unfit. They were unceremoniously pushed into long-overdue retirement when Elihu Root became secretary of war.[31]

The Army needed a major overhaul, and Root was just the man to tackle it. As he started down the long, stony road toward creating an American General Staff, he established the Army War College, in 1901. Two years later, the commandant of the War College, Samuel B. M. Young, was sworn in as the Army's first Chief of Staff, and the General Staff was established. Young was an able officer who had served with distinction in the Philippines under MacArthur.[32]

To sharpen the "brain of the Army," Root reformed the Army's school system. Before 1900 officers like the studious General MacArthur and his well-read son were rare. Army officers were notorious for their lack of formal education.[33] Root set up schools for junior officers at nearly every large Army garrison in the continental United States. The existing Infantry and Cavalry School at Fort Leavenworth was upgraded. It became the General Service and Staff College, where potential staff officers were trained. Root's educational reforms set the Army on a path that over the next twenty years saw a proliferation of professional schools for soldiers. By 1940 American generals would be better educated, in terms of formal schooling, than their counterparts in business or politics.[34]

When Root stepped down as secretary of war in 1904, Roosevelt summoned Taft from the Philippines to take Root's place. For Major General Arthur MacArthur, who was hoping to crown his career by becoming Chief of Staff, Taft's appointment was a crushing blow.

All lieutenants were expected to enroll at the garrison schools that Root had created. They would follow a two-year course, and those who did best in these schools were selected to attend the schools of application for their branches of the Army. In the fall of 1906, however, MacArthur, who had never even been enrolled in a garrison school, was ordered to Washington Barracks, where he would attend the Engineer School. This assignment put him several years ahead of all of his West Point classmates who had gone into the Engineers.

He was also made an assistant to the President's military aide, at Roosevelt's request. His duties weren't particularly time-consuming. He merely helped out at dinners and receptions held at the White House. Proximity to the glamorous, exciting Teddy nevertheless thrilled him, and Roosevelt's interest in the lieutenant's opinions flattered an already healthy ego.

One day Roosevelt hurriedly called a meeting of the Cabinet, hoping that by acting quickly, he could keep the meeting secret. Washington being as leaky then as now, the doors had hardly closed on the Cabinet Room before reporters started flocking to the White House. When Roosevelt emerged from the Cabinet Room, they were waiting to pounce, bombarding him with questions he was not yet ready to answer. As he blustered in his best Teddy style, getting redder and redder in the face, a servant appeared carrying a tray loaded with coffee and sandwiches for the Cabinet members. MacArthur, taking in the scene, put out his foot, tripping the servant. The huge silver tray fell to the ground, sending sandwiches flying and hot coffee splashing over the reporters. In the confusion Roosevelt vanished, back into the Cabinet Room. When he reemerged later, he had a statement prepared to give to the reporters, and that was the end of the affair. Except for one small detail. The next time he saw MacArthur, he told him, "Lieutenant, you're a great diplomat. You ought to be an ambassador!"[35]

While pursuing the Engineer School curriculum, MacArthur was required to complete the garrison school course as well, but as that had been designed for part-time study, it seemed a manageable burden. He spent two months in the summer of 1907 studying the garrison school texts; then, in August, he got a new assignment. He was ordered to report to the district engineer in Milwaukee, Major William V. Judson.

This posting reunited MacArthur with his parents. His father, lacking an assignment, had returned to his home city to write his memoirs. The general and Pinky had rented a large, three-story house on North Marshall Avenue with a porch that ran around all four sides. The back porch had a fine view over Lake Michigan. Every late afternoon, when the weather was good, neighborhood children watched as the maid brought out a large silver tray with tea and cookies, followed by Mrs. MacArthur. Large and stately, she invariably dressed in a high-necked white dress with a gold watch pinned near the collar. For half an hour or so the MacArthurs took tea together and gazed at the lake as the sun went down.[36]

Major Judson was an 1888 graduate of West Point, a classmate of Peyton March's. Third in his class, Judson had gone into the engineers and had since pursued a successful and varied career. Judson's work in Wisconsin was typical of Corps of Engineer assignments in the Midwest—developing rivers and harbors. While MacArthur was happy to be assigned to Milwaukee, working on wharves and docks was a potential setback. If he excelled in this work, he might have trouble escaping from it. Rivers and harbors were the corps's bread and butter and the basis of its pull in Congress. For a young officer who longed to command troops, however, working on the waterways was a muffled death knell. Among line officers, engineers were considered notoriously unsuited for command assignments.[37] And where is the advantage in leading the race for promotion if it only takes you deeper into a blind alley?

MacArthur was further distracted by falling in love. This was not another passing attachment to a pretty girl. No, the lieutenant was in love at last, and with someone he could be proud to take home to meet his parents. She was a well-educated, widely traveled young woman with a millionaire father. Her name was Fanniebelle Van Dyke Stuart of New York, currently visiting Milwaukee, and he was so completely bewitched he asked her to marry him.

MacArthur courted her for months, sending her page after tormented page of Hallmark-type poetry, but without the excuse that they'd been written by somebody else. Miss Stuart, however, seemed unmoved by his ability to crank out rhyming couplets by the yard and not as thrilled as she might be by the attentions of the handsome lieutenant with impeccable military bearing. Nor was she greatly impressed by his family. The MacArthurs were big time in Milwaukee, but they would not cut much of a dash on Park Avenue or the Champs-Élysées.

MacArthur's versifying turned bittersweet. Writing in a neat, mature hand that bore little resemblance to the ornate, rounded and startlingly clear handwriting of his youth (which was almost an exact copy of his mother's), he poured out his aching heart onto the engineer office stationery. By way of Corps of Engineers Form 38 he plaintively told the adored Miss Stuart,

> I live in a little house of dreams,
> In the land that cannot be,
> The country of the fair desire,
> That I shall never see.[38]

And, shortly after this, came a cry of frustration:

> Fair Gotham girl,
> With life a whirl
> Of dance and fancy free,
> 'Tis thee I love
> All things above.
> Why cans't thou not love me?

Shortly after this Miss Stuart returned to New York. He continued to write but conceded despairingly, "Love hath no power o'er spirits such as thine." MacArthur played his last card, asking her to marry him, and composed a twenty-seven-page drama in verse. He offered it, he told her, "in the spirit of fair play." His purpose was to provide an insight into what life as an Army wife might be like if she consented to be his. The poem begins with a blissfully happy picture of a devoted young couple blessed with two lovely children—sons named Malcolm and Arthur. War breaks out, and the husband, an infantry colonel, is summoned to the front. His wife bravely but tearfully urges him to go:

> Our cause is so holy, so just and so true—
> Thank God! I can give a defender like you!
> For home and for children, for freedom, for bread—
> For the house of our God—for the graves of our dead . . .
> I grudge you not, Douglas—die, rather than yield,
> And, like the heroes of old, come home on your shield.

Douglas and his wife, the beautiful "Fan," embrace passionately; then he mounts his horse and rides off to the war. Whether it was a good idea to woo a woman with scenes of battle is open to question:

> The wail of the bugles—the roll of the drums—
> The musket's sharp crack—the artillery's roar—
> The flashing of bayonets dripping with gore—
> The moans of the dying—the horror, the dread,
> The ghastliness gathering over the dead. . . .

Our hero is brought home seriously wounded. The devoted Fan nurses him back to health. The war continues, growing ever more dreadful, until it eventually reaches the peaceful valley where they live. Douglas returns to his regiment and leads it into a ferocious battle. The war he describes does not sound like the war as the Union experienced it and his father fought it. Strangely—or maybe not so strangely—it sounds more like the Civil War the South endured, war as his mother would have heard about it from her brothers, especially the battles in the Shenandoah. The enemy is repulsed at appalling cost, but Douglas dies heroically, leaving Fan widowed. She bears her immeasurable grief nobly, sustained by the pride she feels for her brave soldier husband and faces a long, bleak widowhood without regrets.

This twenty-seven-page poem is so fatalistic it suggests strongly that MacArthur knew that his fight for Fan's heart was as doomed as the battle he describes, leaving Douglas dying in a valiant but hopeless struggle. He knew he was fighting in a losing cause. The elusive Fan provided an opportunity, all the same, to express yearnings and fears that troubled his soul, furnished his imagination, inflamed his spirit. Beneath the dross of the poems lies the kernel of the force that drove MacArthur on: an unquenchable thirst for adventure.

In April 1908 he wrote his last known letter to her. The versifying itch was still upon him. It began "Love is at best a tragic joke—Begun in flames and ends in smoke." Attached was a brief message of farewell, wishing her all the best for the future. As for himself, he expected his life to go on much as before, "unless some day out there in the jungle a Moro bolo or a snub-nosed forty-five changes it all—into still waters and silence."[39]

No one would guess from this correspondence that the lieutenant was an engineer working on dull rivers, banal harbors, a life of dredging sludge and building levees, putting in wharves and talking about dams. But the bullet through his campaign hat and two dead men in the jungle—maybe—excused what in other circumstances would have been juvenile posturing. In his imagination MacArthur was a leader of men, a young colonel doomed to an early but glorious death and, like many a romantic hero, suffering from unrequited love. The engineering work was not truly real to him. He *was* a hero, if only so far in his dreams.

These poems, we should remember, were not the effusions of a nine-teen-year-old plebe. They were penned by a man of twenty-eight who had traveled more widely than most and conversed with presidents and kings. They tell us a lot about the way he saw the world and his own place in it. To MacArthur, real soldiering was a romance, a real life was an adventure, and real love hurt.

Not surprisingly Major Judson discovered that the lieutenant's mind was not on his duties. MacArthur was so bowled over by Fan he did not even pretend it was. When he was ordered away from Milwaukee in the late fall of 1907 to supervise a project at Manitowoc, some sixty miles north of the city, he protested vigorously, but Judson would not back down. When the two officers went up to Manitowoc and checked into the town's only hotel, MacArthur was taken to the hostelry's finest room, while Judson was given something small and gloomy. Judson was dismayed to find that in Wisconsin the name MacArthur counted for more than his major's oak leaves. This trip only added to the strain on their already crumbling relationship.[40] MacArthur was not confined to Mani-towoc for long. When winter weather shut down operations in the field, he returned to Milwaukee and the big house on North Marshall Avenue.

Even before his doomed passion for Miss Stuart reached its inevitable conclusion, MacArthur began seeking a new assignment, away from Jud-son, away from rivers and harbors. What he had in mind was an assignment to Panama, where that modern engineering marvel the Panama Canal was currently under construction. Here was a project worthy of his talents, an enterprise as mighty as building the Pyramids. To his shock, he discovered the War Department intended to send him back to West Point as an instructor. He argued against this assignment too.[41] In the end he and the War Department settled for a return to the 3d Engineer Battalion, presently stationed at Fort Leavenworth. At least he would part company with Major Judson.

Leavenworth at this time revolved around the Army Service Schools, constituting the School of the Line, which took the most outstanding graduates of the garrison schools; the Army Staff College, which took the top 50 percent of the graduates of the School of the Line; and the Army Signal School. The 3d Engineers provided demonstration troops for the two schools. If the schools wanted to see how one of their bright ideas would work if actually put into practice, they used the engineer troops as guinea pigs.

Lieutenant MacArthur was given command of Company K, by common agreement the worst outfit on the post. Over the next year he flattered and cajoled the best performance he could from his men, creating challenges that they could tackle successfully, thereby imbuing them with the confidence and self-esteem that would eventually enable them to excel at even more demanding tasks. There was a small lake at Leavenworth, and MacArthur used it to teach his men to build pontoon bridges faster than any other company in the Army. Under his leadership Company K became one of the best outfits at the post.

MacArthur's duties also involved going to Fort Riley to give lectures at the Mounted School. He talked about what engineering could do for the cavalry. Before he went to West Point, he had wanted to be a cavalryman, and he delighted in the time he spent at Fort Riley. Cavalrymen were a close-knit fraternity, the most glamorous, preening, strutting soldiers the Army possessed and not easily impressed. They liked MacArthur, though; he was a handsome bird of their own lustrous feather. He got not one but two highly commendatory letters for his work at the Mounted School.[42]

Until now MacArthur had received uniformly good efficiency reports. The engineer officer he had worked under in California in 1906 had found him "exceptionally bright and attentive to his duties." The commandant at the Engineer School in 1907 had found he showed "peculiar fitness for detail as an instructor."[43] When the commander of the 3d Battalion, Major Thomas H. Rees, submitted his efficiency report on the lieutenant for the year 1908, he praised MacArthur highly as an instructor, lauded the way he handled the enlisted men of Company K and recommended him, one of the most junior officers in the Army, for assignment to the General Staff.[44]

After MacArthur left Milwaukee, however, Judson filed a damning efficiency report, assessing his attention to duty as being only "fair." He went on to accuse MacArthur of "lacking zeal in learning" and being "absent from the office during office hours more than I thought proper. . . . I am of the opinion that Lieutenant MacArthur did not conduct himself in a way to meet commendation, and that his duties were not performed in a satisfactory manner."[45]

Every criticism Judson made was right on the money. During MacArthur's Milwaukee assignment engineering work was the last thing he cared about. He put his energies into wooing Fan. Rivers and harbors got whatever was left over, which wasn't much. He was stung by this efficiency report and probably frightened. A report as damning as this could kill his career. He wrote a lengthy rebuttal, disputing Judson's claims. Above all, MacArthur said, "I feel keenly the ineradicable blemish Major Judson has seen fit to place upon my military record."

The chief of engineers endorsed Judson's report. It meant, in effect, that he believed Judson's criticisms and disbelieved MacArthur's rebuttal. In desperation MacArthur unwisely demanded that other officers under whom he had served be asked to offer their appraisals. Most confirmed what they had already written about him, but the one whose opinions carried the greatest weight, the commandant at the Engineer School, who had earlier praised MacArthur, now placed on record a letter asserting that "Lieutenant MacArthur seemed to take but little interest in the work" and claimed he had done the bare minimum needed to avoid failing the course.[46]

Besides the appalling implications they had for his career prospects, these reports rocked his self-esteem. For the first time in his life he was staring at a beast he had never met before: total failure. His mother grew alarmed, and without telling him what she had in mind, she wrote to Edward H. Harriman, the president of the Union Pacific Railroad, in April 1909. Would the railroad be interested, she wanted to know, in her son? She reminded Harriman that they had met at a dinner in Tokyo and recalled his observation to her that "first class men are always in demand." She extolled Douglas's abilities and told Harriman, "Frankly, I would like to see my son filling a place promising more of a future than the Army does."

This was a breathtaking remark coming from a woman whose husband was then a lieutenant general. It indicates that within the MacArthur household Douglas's prospects were considered pretty bleak.[47] If the lieutenant was interested, the railroad was not an outlandish choice. On the contrary. Almost all the nineteenth-century railroads had been built under the supervision of West Point graduates who had been commissioned in the Corps of Engineers.

One of Harriman's executives went to Leavenworth to interview the lieutenant, who was amazed and appalled when he learned what maternal solicitude had wrought. He was, reported the executive, "much surprised and a little annoyed . . . it is evidently a case where the mother wants to get her son out of the army, and not where the son is figuring on getting out himself."[48]

MacArthur rebounded from the setback Judson's efficiency report had inflicted in his own way. Just as he had distinguished himself in the Philippines by writing a pamphlet, so now he turned his hand to writing another one, titled "Military Demolitions." Illustrated with photographs that featured the lieutenant at work, it revealed just what kind of engineering interested him. He had boasted to the visitor from the Union Pacific that his company held the world's record for constructing pontoon bridges, and the pamphlet was devoted to what later became known as combat engineering. "Demolitions," it stated with relish, "may have to be carried out in the presence and under fire of the enemy." Like his father, he loved to startle with unusual words. The general had flummoxed the Philippine Commission early on with the word "mediatize." The lieutenant threw "demolate" into his pamphlet. The essence of what it had to offer was highly practical, however. It offered a quick and dirty guide to the best and fastest way to destroy a bridge (if wood, burn; if stone, blow up; if chain, ax), destroy railroad tracks, block roads and slow the enemy's advance.[49]

The commandant at Fort Leavenworth adopted the pamphlet for use in all the Army Service Schools. More important still, the chief of engineers praised the lieutenant's pamphlet as a valuable contribution.[50] At a single bound MacArthur had, within the space of six months, reversed the shocking setback of Judson's critical efficiency report.

MacArthur was glad to be back at Leavenworth, where he had first gone to school and whose every vista—except, possibly, the grim military prison—evoked happy childhood memories. He had a small two-room suite in a building known as the Rookery, which was home to a score of bachelor officers. Like bachelors anywhere, they partied together, formed friendships and diverted themselves with amusements such as poker. At weekends they made trips into Leavenworth or visited Kansas City, thirty miles away.

He may have stopped dating for a while following Fan's rejection, but at Leavenworth it is certain that he courted at least one young woman, Janet Clark, daughter of an Army captain. Her younger brother, Mark, was a tall, dark and handsome youngster eager to go to West Point and make a name for himself as a soldier. The entire family doted on Lieutenant MacArthur. "We knew he was a brilliant, fine man," said Mark Clark.[51]

Apart from taking Janet Clark dancing, MacArthur's chief amusements were polo and baseball. He kept his own polo pony and played on the engineers' team.[52] There were horse races and athletic contests. He not only played on the Fort Leavenworth baseball team but managed it too. The secret of the team's success was its way of wining and dining visiting teams so well that when the time came to "Play ball!" the sober Leavenworth players stood an excellent chance of thrashing their inebriated guests.[53]

As a lieutenant he lacked the rank to become an instructor at the Army Service Schools, where there were only two exceptions to this rule. The more important of the two was George C. Marshall, who had graduated first in the School of the Line class of 1907, then gone on to attend the Army Staff College. Nearly all his classmates were senior to him, and some had already served on the General Staff, but he more than held his own. When his class graduated in June 1908, Marshall was considered so outstanding that the rule that only captains and above could serve as instructors was waived. The other exception was Lieutenant Walter Krueger, who, like Marshall, was making his way in the Army without the West Point ring. How much contact there was between MacArthur and Marshall isn't clear, but what is certain is that there was no particular rapport between them.[54]

In 1910 much of the Engineer School course was transferred to Leavenworth. MacArthur would have been involved ensuring that this transfer went smoothly and evidently succeeded. He was recommended for a captain's bars and traveled to New York to take the required exam. The senior engineer officer at Leavenworth extolled his "ability, study, energy and originality."[55] In February 1911 MacArthur was promoted to captain, became adjutant of the 3d Engineers and was appointed an instructor in the Army Service Schools. Later that year he was finally allowed to go to Panama and marvel at the magnificent new canal.

Shortly after his return, while on temporary duty in Texas, he came close to being killed at Fort Sam Houston. One of his former baseball teammates at Leavenworth, Captain Benjamin D. "Benny" Foulois, was a pioneer aviator, only the second man to become an Army pilot. Several of MacArthur's classmates had gone into the Aviation Section, and one, Tom Selfridge, had the unhappy distinction in 1909 of becoming the first person ever to perish in an air crash.

From March to July 1911 MacArthur was assigned to what was known as the Maneuver Division at Fort Sam. The Army had no permanent combat divisions, at a time when all other major powers were organizing their armies around them. Even China had one. There was trouble on the Mexican border that summer, and the Army seized on it to set up an experiment that would allow it to figure out just how a division operated. A temporary maneuver division was spatchcocked together at Fort Sam out of a variety of units drawn from all over the United States.

MacArthur returned to San Antonio in a kind of romantic reverie. He visited the West Texas Military Academy campus once more and discovered it was now a large and thriving institution. He also learned one of the most painful lessons that human beings have to absorb: Don't go back. The WTMA cadets laughed at him, mocking his battered campaign hat, and could not have cared less that he had been the top man in the founding class even had they known it. One evening he decided to go take a look at his former home, in the moonlight. That seemed more romantic than visiting it in the day. This trip down memory lane crashed abruptly when a young woman came out onto the porch, took him for a drunken prowler and threatened to call the guard.[56]

Foulois, like the many other aviation pioneers, was eager to prove that the airplane had a place in war. He was trying to impress this on the field artillery by buzzing a gun battery and scattering its horses when he discovered that he was heading straight toward a row of tents occupied by the 3d Engineers. As he wrestled with the controls, "I failed to see a horse and buggy standing directly ahead. I still had enough momentum to swerve slightly, but not enough to avert a collision. For a split second the horse and the pilot glared at each other, then the horse reared up on his hind legs, upset the buggy and galloped off to join the artillery horses. . . ." Foulois crash-landed, chagrined but unhurt, next to the wrecked buggy.

The shaken buggy owner picked himself up from the dirt, bellowing indignantly. Foulois, staggering from his crumpled airplane, shouted back. "The battle of words ceased when a commanding voice boomed out, 'Benny, what's going on over there?'

"Turning around angrily, I saw the soldierly figure of Douglas MacArthur. He was standing at the entrance to the tent which would have been torn to ribbons had I not swerved to avoid it. 'Doug, I either had to mow down your tent or this man's horse and buggy,' I replied."

MacArthur took a good look at the wreckage, turned to Foulois and remarked, "Benny, speaking as a disinterested bystander, I'd say you made the right decision."[57]

When the maneuver season ended, MacArthur returned to Leavenworth. He continued to receive good efficiency reports, but when you read between the lines, one thing was clear: He was not a heart-and-soul engineer. Nor did he like being an instructor in the Army Service Schools. One standard question on the report asked if an officer had shown "peculiar fitness" for his current assignment. The post commander at Leavenworth in 1912 was not alone in reporting "Has shown no peculiar fitness for details." Whatever excitement there might have been in mastering his Leavenworth assignment, it had worn pretty thin. He was ready, more than ready, to move on.[58]

When Major General Arthur MacArthur returned to the United States in the summer of 1906, he assumed command of the Pacific Division, the successor to his old Department of the Pacific. His headquarters were still in San Francisco, a city shaken and charred in the earthquake that April.

Half the city had burned down. The Army had shipped two cavalry regiments to San Francisco to maintain law and order. It established a large tent city in Golden Gate Park to provide shelter for thousands of people who had found themselves suddenly homeless, took over the provision of essential services and fed the needy.

MacArthur arrived just as the Army was handing control of the city back to local politicians. When the Army's role ended, so did MacArthur's. He was occupying a place too small for a man with three stars and found the incongruity embarrassing. Lieutenant general was the highest rank an officer might aspire to. The result was a poignant correspondence with Taft over what he might do, but there was really no assignment available that called for someone with experience as broad and deep as his.

He made his final important contribution to the Army in February 1907, when he established the Musketry School at Monterey.[59] This was the forerunner of the later Infantry School at Fort Benning. One month later he was ordered to return to Milwaukee, take two clerks with him, rent an office and write up a report on his extended travels in the Far East.[60] It was an anticlimactic ending to a remarkable military career.

In June 1909 General MacArthur reached his sixty-fourth birthday, the Army's mandatory retirement age. He issued a statement that proudly proclaimed, "I have received from my country every high honor it can bestow on a soldier, except the privilege of dying for my country at the head of its men."[61] His statement masked his deep disappointment at having been passed over for Chief of Staff. Not only had fate denied him a soldier's most glorious end, death in battle—and not for want of providing fate with the opportunity—but Taft had denied him the chance to be professional head of the Army.

After an active life of command and adventure, Arthur MacArthur found the narrow purlieus of Milwaukee and days of enforced idleness hard to bear. His health suffered. His one consolation was the chance to meet regularly with his old comrades-in-arms, the ninety or so survivors of the 24th Volunteer Infantry Regiment. On the evening of September 5, 1912, he attended the regiment's fiftieth anniversary reunion, held at the University Building in downtown Milwaukee. The weather was ferociously hot, and he was unwell, but he couldn't disappoint his friends. MacArthur began to speak about the regiment's reconnaissance in force outside Atlanta. Suddenly he faltered. "Comrades, I am too weak to go on." He collapsed into a chair. The regimental doctor examined him. The general was dying, felled by a massive stroke.

Placing him on the floor, the other old soldiers knelt around him and recited the Lord's Prayer. When they had finished praying, the adjutant took the Stars and Stripes standing near the podium and placed it over MacArthur's corpse. Then the adjutant too collapsed and died, another stroke victim.[62]

Mrs. MacArthur had been ill for some months before this shattering blow. Her condition rapidly worsened. Douglas, who was due for reassignment after four years at Fort Leavenworth, applied for Judson's former post, commanding the Milwaukee engineer district, so he could be near her. His modest rank, to say nothing of his indifference to rivers and harbors, ruled that out.

For Douglas, as for his mother, the death of his father created a wound that never healed. As those who have been bereaved know, time does not heal all wounds. It merely makes even the most grievous loss bearable. He missed his father keenly for the rest of his life. Wherever he went, he carried a framed photograph of the general's round face. Those bland, slightly pompous features looked back at him from a bedside table for the next fifty years.

Mrs. MacArthur sought treatment at Johns Hopkins, in Baltimore. Captain MacArthur was given a Washington posting so he could see her regularly and help take care of her. The present Chief of Staff, Leonard Wood, had begun his Army career as a surgeon out on the frontier and had served under Arthur MacArthur at Fort Wingate. He felt the Army owed a debt to the general for his long and distinguished service.

Douglas MacArthur took up his duties at the War Department in the late fall of 1912. There was no General Staff vacancy for him to fill. Instead he held down a miscellaneous desk that handled anything the General Staff wasn't organized to respond to. For a time Wood kept him in Washington by making him superintendent of the gray, clifflike pile of the War, State and Navy Building next to the White House. And when his efficiency reports were filed for 1912, there was a contribution from the Chief of Staff himself. Wood noted that the captain was "A particularly intelligent and efficient officer."[63] MacArthur was on the inside track and moving up fast.

Woodwork

In early 1913, as Pinky's health improved, she rented a house in northwest Washington, bought a new Cadillac and hired a black chauffeur. Douglas availed himself of the car and chauffeur to court a young lady in Maryland, but his mind remained on his career rather than romance.[1]

MacArthur found himself working under the direction of one of the most singular figures in the history of the Army, a man whose temperament and ideas were much like his own. There would be traces of Leonard Wood in much that MacArthur did and said for the next fifty years. Thirty years earlier, with the parchment of his Harvard Medical School diploma still stiff and white, young Dr. Wood had joined the Army as a contract surgeon. On the expedition to capture Geronimo in 1890 he was the only man to finish the campaign with the Medal of Honor.[2] Shortly afterward he was assigned to the White House as President McKinley's doctor. In 1898 Wood and the assistant secretary of the navy, Theodore Roosevelt, created the Rough Riders. On a hot day that summer they rode together up San Juan Hill. When the war ended, McKinley made Wood a brigadier general in the Regular Army and military governor of Cuba. In July 1910 Taft appointed him Chief of Staff, knowing that it would please Roosevelt to see a friend and fellow Republican running the Army.

Wood was an imposing hulk of a man: tall, blond, with an abundant but disciplined mustache, the piercing gaze of a blue-eyed hawk, a barrel chest and a trim stomach, flat testimony to the corsetiere's art.[3] He was not a school-made staff officer, or a West Pointer, but an outlander, resented by much of the Army as a "political" general, rather than a real one. Wood was a reformer and a visionary. Almost his first public pronouncement on becoming Chief of Staff was that "Sooner or later the aeroplane will be the greatest factor of the century in world affairs."[4] The Army at the time owned exactly one airplane.

His force consisted of approximately ninety thousand officers and men scattered among more than fifty bases in the United States and overseas. Line regiments were at less than half their authorized strength. There was no modern artillery and few machine guns. The one thing the Army was not prepared to do was fight. Wood made it his mission to turn the Army into an effective, modern fighting force.

Before he could do that, however, he had to assert his authority over the purely administrative bureaus that presently dominated it, such as the Adjutant General's Office, the Ordnance Corps, the Quartermaster General and so on. The generals who ran the bureaus refused to accept that Wood had any right to tell them what to do.

MacArthur was but one of the many reform-minded young officers to whom Wood was an inspiration. He seemed to be as well endowed with moral courage as physical bravery. When congressmen bleated about his plans to shut down surplus Army posts, he was philosophical about it. "Game fish run in troubled waters." He shrugged off virulent press attacks with equanimity: "Public men must expect public abuse."

While Wood was trying to re-create the Army, he kept Captain MacArthur busy monitoring the Army's biggest new construction project, the fortification of Hawaii. The islands were presently commanded by Arthur MacArthur's devoted friend and admirer Brigadier General Funston. Captain MacArthur of the engineers became the General Staff's project officer for the creation of Hawaii's defenses. These involved constructing permanent barracks, sewers, roads, wharves, hospitals, railroad sidings and coastal artillery sites. The present garrison of seventy-four hundred men would be more than doubled. The cost of the project was seven million dollars, a lot of money for the Army at the time.[5] MacArthur also kept track of the progress of river and harbor projects on behalf of the General Staff.[6]

And all the time MacArthur was studying Wood. The captain was no longer the plastic material of youth but a man in his early thirties. Yet he was still open to the influence of strong figures, and with his father gone Wood offered a role model who was in many ways an extension of his father's pronounced virtues and weaknesses. Wood was fearlessly, sometimes recklessly, outspoken. He was obviously ambitious and had risen without the aid of a West Point ring. He was openly Republican in his political beliefs. He was generous to his friends, hated his enemies with a passion, had tremendous self-confidence, developed a singular personality that seemed pompous and overbearing to some people yet helped spread his fame—and he held the Medal of Honor. It would be too much to claim that MacArthur patterned his personality on that of Leonard Wood. Nevertheless there were elements within his character that Wood's behavior was sure to sanction and encourage.

Wood's way of dealing with hostile politicians was to make his pitch over their heads, to the people. For that he needed the support of the press. Senior officers tended to be suspicious of newspapermen and contemptuous of newspapers. Wood, however, welcomed them openly. Every day he met with the journalists assigned to the War Department and tried to give them something they could turn into a story.[7] Among the journalists close to Wood was John Callan O'Laughlin, one of Roosevelt's friends. O'Laughlin was military correspondent of the *Chicago Tribune* and wise in the ways of Washington. He had been an undersecretary of state in the closing days of the Roosevelt administration. Wood consulted O'Laughlin on how the War Department should handle the press in time of war.[8]

In the course of these discussions MacArthur met O'Laughlin, and a new interest developed. Included in Leonard Wood's diary for March 1914 is a five-page, single-spaced document titled "Regulations Concerning Correspondents with the United States Army in the Field." The style of its prose makes it almost certain that MacArthur wrote it.[9] This document has to be seen as a marker that when the chance came, he, like Wood, intended to advance both his career and the cause he believed in, a stronger Army, by making friends with the media.

Wood's overriding objective was to get the Army ready for war. In 1912 he had the General Staff draw up a plan to organize the Army into three infantry divisions and a cavalry division. When a political crisis erupted in Mexico in February 1913, Secretary of War Henry Stimson was able to assure Taft that he could send an entire division to Texas City "with only a single order," and he did so.[10]

A month later Taft handed over the White House to Woodrow Wilson, who was expected to fire Wood. Instead Wilson kept Wood, a man of openly Republican sympathies, as his Army Chief of Staff. The new President also supported Wood's latest venture: summer training camps, where college students could acquire the rudiments of drilling and marksmanship. Two camps were opened that summer, at Gettysburg and Monterey. Both were considered successes. Under Wood's energetic direction the Army was gradually improving its ability to fight, but there was no obvious place where it might be put to the test, with one exception—Mexico.

Wilson became President in March 1913, only weeks after a coup d'état plunged Mexico into political turmoil. To American dismay, General Victoriano Huerta seized control of the government. Numerous atrocities had been attributed to Huerta and his followers. An outraged Wilson withheld recognition of the new Mexican government, but Germany decided to supply Huerta with the arms he needed to defeat his rivals for power. A German ship carrying 260 machine guns and 15 million rounds of ammunition set sail for Veracruz.

The Navy was ordered to prevent the ship from docking. A small naval task force, including a battalion of marines, took station outside the harbor. On April 9, 1914, a party of marines went ashore to collect supplies and were arrested. Admiral Frank F. Fletcher, in command of the naval force, demanded their release, an apology and a twenty-one-gun salute to Old Glory. The marines were set free before nightfall, and an apology was forthcoming from the local Mexican commander, but no boom of saluting Mexican artillery was heard. Wilson backed up the demand for a salute. Huerta ordered one fired . . . if the Americans replied with a twenty-one-gun salute to the Mexican flag. Exasperated, Wilson ordered Fletcher to occupy Veracruz and seize the customs house.[11]

The Navy lacked the manpower to seize and hold a city of forty thousand people. The Army would have to take control of Veracruz. Wood's four divisions contained forty-three thousand combat troops, but they were widely scattered across the United States in small units. However, the General Staff had drawn up a plan in the fall of 1913 to ship one brigade to Veracruz on short notice, with the rest of its parent division later. And if necessary, the entire force of four divisions could be deployed to Mexico within weeks as a field army.[12]

The Navy went ahead and seized the customshouse. What Wilson had assumed would be a routine operation triggered a fierce house-to-house fight with Huertistas and Mexican nationalists. Eighteen marines were killed, and nearly fifty wounded. Mexican casualties ran into the hundreds.[13]

Two weeks after the initial Veracruz incident, Funston set sail from Galveston with the 5th Brigade of the 2d Infantry Division. His four-thousand-man brigade was reinforced with thirty-three hundred marines. There had still been no salutation to the American flag, and war with Mexico seemed almost inevitable.

Meanwhile back in Washington Wood had stepped down as Chief of Staff and been designated to command the field army. His plan was to lead his army from Veracruz to Mexico City, much as Winfield Scott had done in 1848 to conquer a peace. While the United States and Mexico hovered on the brink of war, Wood decided he needed an advance man on the scene to keep abreast of a rapidly evolving situation. He sent Captain MacArthur, who arrived in Veracruz on May 1 aboard the battleship *Nebraska*.

MacArthur was under orders "to obtain through reconnaissance and other means . . . all possible information which would be of value in connection with possible operations" by the field army that Wood was preparing to bring south.[14] Funston's brigade expected to serve as the spearhead of Wood's advance, yet it was so hampered by Funston's orders from Wilson that it couldn't conduct reconnaissance behind the Mexican lines and determine what the route to Mexico City was like or where the bulk of Huerta's troops was concentrated.

The brigade was also in a poor position to move for want of railroad engines. There were hundreds of boxcars available in Veracruz, but few locomotives, and as American trains operated on a different gauge, there was no point in shipping locomotives down from the United States. MacArthur decided to tackle both Wood's needs and Funston's. He would penetrate deep behind the Mexican lines and bring back some locomotives. Bribing several Mexican railroad workers to take him to Alvarado, forty miles away, on a handcar, MacArthur set off on his self-assigned mission.

In the report he sent to Wood he described an adventure that reads like a movie script. He and his Mexican helpers reached Alvarado on a misty night. There they found three large and powerful locomotives, but were accosted by five armed men. MacArthur and his companions engaged in a brief and successful firefight and got away with the three engines. Farther down the line, however, the handcar that he was riding was charged by fifteen mounted guerrillas. After a fierce exchange of gunfire he shot his way out of trouble, but three bullets went through his clothes without touching him. As he neared the American line there was yet another shooting scrape—and another victory for MacArthur's little band. He got another bullet through his clothes, but this one too did not even scratch him. MacArthur made his way back to Veracruz by pony and handcar, followed by his three Mexicans driving the three big pullers.[15]

How much of this story is strictly true and how much is embellishment is impossible to say, but there is no doubt that he really did go behind the Mexican lines and return with three locomotives. That in itself was an astonishing feat. The claim of having to shoot his way out, however, seems to have been calculated to help bring him the Medal of Honor, as we shall see.

MacArthur, like much of the Army, still expected that Wood would soon arrive to command the army in the field and wrote to him on May 7, only hours after his return, to tell him that while Funston was a competent commander, "I miss the inspiration, my dear General, of your own clear-cut, decisive methods. I hope sincerely that affairs will shape themselves so that you will shortly take the field for the campaign which, if death does not call you, can have but one ending—the White House." He made only a cursory, if vivid, reference to his daring mission behind Mexican lines. His complete report was written some months later.[16]

Life in the field brought out a different side to MacArthur. He began to dress in an extravagant, eye-catching style that screamed, "Look at me!" The most noticeable thing about him was not just his good looks but his determination to be noticed. He had arrived at West Point wearing a huge Stetson, as if he had just traveled from Texas, not Milwaukee. Over time his choice of headgear would provide a chapter on fashion in itself. In Veracruz he wore a slightly battered campaign hat. Nothing much to interpret there. But below that he wore his captain's bars sideways on his shirt collar, a cardigan that stretched to his knees, a brightly colored large silk cravat around his neck, and stuck in his mouth was a pipe. He had taken the relaxation of dress regulations in the field and run with them until he scored what seemed to him like a touchdown. Here, then, was the emergence of another MacArthur, the peacock strutting among pigeons.[17]

The American occupation of Veracruz turned into a Mexican standoff: The American side wouldn't budge; neither would the Huertistas. Wilson had decided against going to war. As public attention shifted elsewhere, to the outbreak of war in Europe, the occupation of Veracruz was quietly phased out. The Germans now had need of all the machine guns and ammunition they could produce.

Wood's prospective mission of leading an army into Mexico ended that summer. His new assignment was commanding the Department of the East, with headquarters in New York. He intended to continue his campaign for American preparedness, all the more so now that Europe was engulfed in war.

Two officers on the Veracruz expedition had recommended MacArthur for the Medal of Honor. Wood did so too. When MacArthur returned to Washington in September, he finally made a detailed report of his reconnaissance–cum–railroad heist, and there cannot be much doubt that he hoped it would lead to the Big Medal. He may even have felt confident it would come his way. It had certainly found its way onto the breasts of a lot of other people. The Navy and Marine Corps awarded fifty-five Medals of Honor for the two-day brawl around the Veracruz customshouse—the largest number ever given for a single engagement. Even Admiral Fletcher, who had remained aboard his flagship during the combat, got one.[18]

There can't be much doubt that MacArthur wanted the Medal of Honor, and wanted it badly. The fact that his father had won one was both a source of pride and a crushing responsibility for a soldier son. To be considered anywhere near as good as his father, it was essential that he win one too. There were going to be problems, though. Even if all he said in his report was true, there was a lack of eyewitnesses, other than the Mexicans, and men who have been bribed into betraying their trust are not what most people would consider reliable witnesses.

Funston was asked for his views and sent back mixed signals. The fact that MacArthur had arrived in Veracruz as something of a free agent while he, Funston, had been staked to the ground still rankled more than six months later. He wrote that while from a personal standpoint he considered MacArthur's feat heroic enough to justify the award, "Captain MacArthur was not a member of my command at the time and I had no knowledge [of his reconnaissance]. . . . I do not consider this the occasion to enter into a discussion of the advisability of this enterprise [which has] been undertaken without the knowledge of the commanding general on the ground [i.e., Funston]. . . . However, it must be presumed that Captain MacArthur was acting in good faith. . . ."[19]

The three-man Army decorations board decided not to grant the award. One member felt the requirement for incontestable independent proof shouldn't be ignored. The other two felt that giving the medal to an officer who was not acting under the local commander's orders would only encourage other staff officers to undertake similar ventures on their own initiative, "possibly interfering with the commander's plans with reference to the enemy."[20]

MacArthur was bitter in rejection. His emotional nature flared up and reached out to singe the men who had wounded him. In an angry memorandum to the new Chief of Staff, Major General Hugh L. Scott, he said he was "incensed" at the decision. He damned the board's "rigid narrowmindedness and lack of imagination."[21]

The board's decision was nevertheless upheld, unanimously, by a review panel consisting of Scott, the assistant chief of staff, Major General Tasker H. Bliss, and the assistant secretary of war, Henry Breckinridge. MacArthur's outburst probably made their task easier.

While he brooded on this injustice, as he saw it, the broad outlines of his character were clear. The personal legend that he was creating out of a romantic nature, his attraction to the nineteenth-century great man style as he had seen it practiced first by his father, later by Leonard Wood, his Victorian vision of himself as the fearless man of action thrust into the scene of great events, had produced a creation that already set him apart from other Army officers without making him unique.

Consider this description: "He is always playing a part—an heroic part. And he is himself his most astonished spectator. He sees himself moving through the smoke of battle—triumphant, terrible, his brow clothed in thunder, his legions looking to him for victory, and not looking in vain. He thinks of Napoleon; he thinks of his great ancestor. Thus did they bear themselves; thus, in this rugged and most awful crisis will they bear themselves. It is not make-believe, it is not insincerity; it is that in that fervid and picturesque imagination there are always great deeds afoot with himself cast by destiny in the Agamemnon role." MacArthur? No, a description of Winston Churchill published in 1913.[22]

Neither the Wilson administration nor the Army was, in 1915, attempting to draw military lessons from the war that was ravaging Europe. Major Johnson Hagood, a former aide to Leonard Wood and a friend of Douglas MacArthur's, returned from the Philippines that spring and asked a General Staff officer how many people the War Department had assigned to monitor the war. "One half of one man. I myself am assigned to that job, but half my time is devoted to routine duties."[23]

When the President learned that the General Staff was drawing up plans for war, Wilson sent for Tasker Bliss, the head of the planning section. "Trembling with rage," Wilson ordered him to desist. Bliss mildly pointed out that military planning was what the law required the General Staff to do.[24]

Came the fall, with the election only a year away, Wilson suddenly changed his mind on preparedness. If the United States were pushed to the brink of intervention—or worse, suppose it were pushed over it?—he would be vulnerable to the charge of having left his country unready for war. There was already a growing public mood toward preparedness. With one mighty bound Woodrow the politician vaulted to the head of the marching column.

This shift did not, however, save his secretary of war, Lindley Garrison, who had been urging greater preparedness. Garrison had taken up the cudgels on behalf of the four-hundred-thousand-man Army reserve that Wood had demanded several years earlier. Called to testify on behalf of Garrison's proposal, Wood was unenthusiastic. Too little, too late, he intoned. Should be two million men now. Garrison didn't get his four hundred thousand reservists. What Congress did instead was to take up Wood's earlier proposal to federalize the National Guard and train it up to Regular Army standards, which was what the General Staff still wanted.

As officers like MacArthur were well aware, if the United States went to war, the best thing to do with the Regular Army was to break it up, to have its officers and NCOs train the millions of volunteers, draftees and national guardsmen who would have to do most of the fighting. The Regular Army was too small, its experience too valuable, to be plunged straight into combat, only to be destroyed in a heroic and hopeless battle to the death. By federalizing the Guard, the government would provide the Army with a large pool of manpower from which divisions could be created, while volunteers or draftees were being trained to be formed into even more divisions.

Garrison resigned. His replacement as secretary of war was a former journalist and mayor of Cleveland, Newton D. Baker. A few years earlier

Baker had been a prominent member of various pacifist organizations. A tiny man with pince-nez, he could hardly see over his desk when standing next to it and seemed lost perched on the large chair behind it. He was a curious choice for the War Department, but he assured the press that he had no doubts about his new job. "I love peace," he acknowledged. "So much so that I would fight for it."[25]

While the General Staff was gratified to see the National Guard federalized, it was still trying to get the size of the Regular Army doubled, to 220,000 men. One of the officers working on that objective was MacArthur, who had been promoted to major in December 1915. When Baker became secretary in March 1916, MacArthur was courting and cajoling the senior Republican on the House Military Affairs Committee, Congressman Julius Kahn, to push through a substantial increase.[26]

Baker gave him an extra assignment: Improve the War Department's relations with the press. A Bureau of Information was created, and MacArthur, as the man who had shown an interest in press relations while working for Leonard Wood, was the logical choice. He soon made plain his conviction that if America went to war, the government and the military should have a strict censorship policy. The press, he claimed, represented two dangers: First, it might betray military secrets, undermining Army operations; second, it could demoralize the American people by inaccurate or biased reporting.[27]

Despite his belief that the press should be carefully controlled in time of war, MacArthur got on well with journalists. He enjoyed his new job and reported to Wood later that year, "I am working very hard with my newspaper men."[28]

He was also looking after his mother. He and Pinky moved into the Ontario, one of Washington's most desirable residences. More than half the Ontario's apartments were occupied by people on the District's *Elite List*. It was the kind of address that would have impressed all but the most blasé young women MacArthur dated, and he dated quite a few.[29]

While the General Staff wrestled with the problems of preparing for a big war, Mexico continued to distract the Wilson administration like a sore that wouldn't heal. In March 1916, two days after Baker became secretary of war, Pancho Villa attacked the town of Columbus, New Mexico, under cover of darkness and killed eighteen Americans, including half a dozen soldiers.[30]

A punitive expedition was organized under Brigadier General John J. Pershing. Ten thousand troops and eight Army airplanes went into northern Mexico to bring Villa and his force of approximately one thousand men to book. The Mexican government demanded that Pershing leave, and at Parrizal on June 21 he ran into a force of entrenched Mexican government troops.

The Americans charged. Twelve were killed and ten were wounded. The United States was once again in danger of sliding into a war with Mexico.[31] The entire National Guard, which consisted of roughly one hundred thousand men, was placed on the border that summer. Pershing continued his perambulations until January 1917, when Wilson, having been reelected, ordered him to come home.[32]

While Pershing was in hot pursuit of Villa, Congress was considering the National Defense Act of 1916, the capstone on Wilson's preparedness campaign. This was really a Navy bill. Wilson didn't think much of the muddy Army, which had marched through his native state of Georgia and left an unfortunate reputation behind, but he positively loved the clean and glamorous Navy. The 1916 act aimed to create a two-ocean navy, with a huge fleet of battleships in the Atlantic and a force of battle cruisers patrolling the Pacific. The Army got the crumbs. The Regular Army would be increased to 165,000 men.[33] Yet as 1916 drew to a close, the General Staff calculated that if America entered the war, it would need an army of 3 million men if the United States were to play a decisive role.[34] The only way such numbers could be raised was by conscription.

On the evening of February 19, 1917, Funston, commanding the Department of the South, with headquarters at Fort Sam Houston, was sitting in an armchair in the lobby of one of San Antonio's finest hotels awaiting the dinner gong when he slumped over, dead from a heart attack at the age of fifty-two. The telegram that announced his death was delivered several hours later to MacArthur, who had drawn the graveyard shift on the General Staff that night. This was a stunning development. It had been taken for granted that if an American army were sent to France, Funston would command it. He had commanded at Veracruz, and been Pershing's commander during the Villa chase. He was the obvious choice.

Baker was hosting a dinner for the President that night. MacArthur went to the secretary's house, but the butler refused to let him enter the dining room. MacArthur elbowed his way past the butler, hoping to have a word privately with Baker, but Wilson caught sight of him. "Come in, Major, and tell us all the news." The President was, despite his stern, professorial visage, a highly sociable and fun-loving man. "There are no secrets here." The dinner guests broke into applause, as if the major were part of the entertainment.

"Sir," declared MacArthur, clicking his heels together and saluting, "I regret to report that General Funston has just died!"[35]

The gathering broke up instantly. Wilson asked, "Newton, who will take over the Army now?"

Baker evaded the question, turning instead to MacArthur. "Whom do you think the Army would choose, Major?"

According to MacArthur's memoirs, his reply was: "I cannot, of course, speak for the Army, but for myself, the choice would be Pershing or Peyton March." Baker, on the other hand, distinctly recalled his suggesting March and not mentioning Pershing at all, and Baker's version is the more plausible of the two. At the time MacArthur had to confront this question Peyton March was, like the recently deceased Funston, a protégé of General Arthur MacArthur's. Pershing, on the other hand, was simply an officer the MacArthur family knew and liked but had never been close to. It was the 1930s, as we shall see, before Douglas MacArthur and John J. Pershing became good friends. Until then their relationship was often a difficult one. That later friendship may have influenced MacArthur's recollection of his reply to Baker's question.[36]

As Baker and Wilson considered who should command the Army, events in the war were about to take a dramatic turn. The German high command had decided to resume unrestricted submarine warfare, the one thing that was certain to bring American intervention. But the Germans were gambling that a U-boat offensive would allow them to win the war before the United States could train an army and ship it to France. The evening of April 2 Wilson went to Congress and asked for a declaration of war. Returned to the White House, he put his head on the huge table in the Cabinet Room, blubbering that he had never believed in neutrality.[37]

The administration hoped it would only have to send a token division to France, but the Army had no such illusions. It had a draft act ready to send to Congress, but it "bristled with bayonets," in the words of Major Hugh Johnson, one of MacArthur's West Point classmates and an officer on the General Staff.[38] It put conscription firmly under military control, something that public opinion wasn't likely to tolerate. The bill was rewritten to put selective service in the hands of civilian draft boards and require potential draftees to register themselves with their local boards.

Even so, the bill had to be sold to the country if it was going to be passed. Responsibility for selling the draft law fell squarely on the shoulders of Major MacArthur. His careful cultivation of the press for the past two years finally paid off. The country's newspapers produced resounding editorials in favor of the draft. The bill sailed through Congress six weeks after the American declaration of war. A short time later twenty-nine Washington correspondents put their signatures to an encomium that praised MacArthur for his brilliant handling of the press.[39]

It would be a year yet before any sizable number of draftees would be ready to go overseas. Many senior officers believed that the Regular Army alone would have to do whatever fighting was necessary, while the National Guard remained at home and kept watch on the borders. MacArthur considered this stupid but felt unable to do much about it. He argued that the

Guard would have to go to France but was warned that if he persisted in this way, he would remain a major for a long, long time. A staff study calling for sending the Regular Army to France and keeping the Guard at home came to his desk. He endorsed it, adding a weary note that he was doing so only because he recognized the futility of trying to change it.

The document went to Baker. The secretary sent for MacArthur. Sunk into the big chair and puffing on his pipe, Baker looked up and said he had just read his equivocal endorsement. Before MacArthur could reply, he stood up. "I agree with you," he said. Here, at last, was a secretary of war who understood what General Staff officers such as Major MacArthur had been frustratingly, vainly attempting to explain for the best part of a decade.

He collected his hat and took MacArthur next door, to the White House, to present his case to the President. The secretary and the major gave Wilson a tutorial that lasted more than an hour. The President listened carefully and was finally convinced. The Guard would go to war. The Regular Army would be broken up, not destroyed. Its experience and knowledge would be shared, not squandered.[40]

Even so, MacArthur was itching to get into the war. He could not bear the thought of spending it tied to a desk in Washington. His destiny was no longer here, but there—somewhere among the trenches and dugouts, the squalor and the mud and the imagined glories of battle. When several journalists he knew came to see him one day, he remarked as they strolled through the War, State and Navy Building, "You see all these generals in the offices along this corridor? Well, in a few months not one of them will be here. Younger men will be in their places. War is a young man's game."

One of the reporters asked him, "And are you going to stay here and occupy one of these important positions on the General Staff?"

"Oh, no," he replied. "The real promotions will go to the men who go to France."[41]

Shortly after this Baker asked what would be the best way to get the Guard into the war. The only two extant Guard divisions were from New York and Pennsylvania, and a dozen more were planned. Whichever division went to France first, it would create jealousy in other states. If only, Baker mused aloud, we had a division with men from every state. MacArthur responded that it might be possible to create such a division out of units not already committed. Major General William A. Mann, the head of the Militia Bureau, and MacArthur made a quick survey of the units available, and MacArthur returned to Baker with an enthusiastic answer. Such a division not only was feasible but would "stretch like a rainbow across the United States"—an elegant expression of a clever idea. Baker was delighted.[42] The 42d Division thereby not only came into existence but was born with a ready-made nickname, the Rainbow.

Baker chose Mann to command it. Mann, who at sixty-three was "stout and inert, but a politician always," looked like a ridiculous choice for a combat command, but for its chief of staff, the division would have Douglas MacArthur.[43] Baker offered him a colonelcy and assumed he would prefer to have it as an officer in the Engineer Corps rather than in the General Staff Corps. Here, at last, was the chance to realize one of his oldest, deepest ambitions. He would, he told Baker, prefer a commission in the infantry.

One wish stated, one wish granted. He would go to war a colonel of infantry, a commander of fighting men. That was how he had imagined it in his long, melodramatic poem to Fanniebelle Stuart. And now part of the poem had, by a roundabout, unpredictable course, come to life. He would have his chance to realize the rest: the wounds, the heroism, the anguish, the self-sacrificing dream of the eternal soldier.

6

Soldier's Soldier

A month after war was declared, Leonard Wood asked for a command in the force going overseas, even if it was only a division. His outspoken criticisms of Wilson, however—including a speech in which he had thundered, "We have no leadership in Washington!"—ruined any chance of that. Wilson did not trust him, and Baker considered Wood "the most insubordinate general in the Army."[1]

Command of the American Expeditionary Forces (AEF) went instead to Major General John J. Pershing, a man whom stars seemed to fall on. In 1906 he was only a captain and getting old for such a humble rank when Theodore Roosevelt dramatically promoted him over the heads of 862 officers who were senior to him to become the youngest brigadier general in the Army. Having the chairman of the Senate Military Affairs Committee, Senator Francis Warren, for his father-in-law helped too.

In May 1917, with Funston dead, Wood persona non grata, the other major generals of the Army too old or too ill to go to war and Peyton March still only a colonel, Pershing was the only real choice to command the force being raised to fight in Europe.[2] He sailed for France in June 1917.

Leonard Wood was doomed to sit out the war, frustrated and indignant. MacArthur, however, did not forget him. He wrote to Wood from Camp Mills, Long Island, in August 1917, days after becoming a colonel, to console his former mentor. "I have believed in the past, and am more convinced by recent events, that the day will come when you will be the Hope of the nation, and when that day comes you will find me fighting behind you as I always have in the past. . . ."[3]

The Rainbow Division would contain Guard units from twenty-six states and the District of Columbia. It took time to put it together. All the combat units had to mount recruitment drives to grow to the size the division required. Once the units were up to strength, or sufficiently close to it, they had to be shipped to Camp Mills, outside Hempstead, Long Island. The division wasn't in shape to begin training until September.

MacArthur used his War Department connections to provide the 42d with some of the most promising officers in the Army. He got nearly a dozen of his West Point friends and acquaintances assigned to the division staff, including Colonel Robert E. Wood, who had made a big reputation for himself on the Panama Canal project, and his classmate Grayson Mallet-Prevost Murphy, who had resigned his commission in 1907 in favor of investment banking. Ten years later Murphy was one of the richest men in America and a leading figure in the American Red Cross. MacArthur also acquired an able young Boston lawyer, Hugh Ogden, to be the division's judge advocate, a famously efficient major named John De Witt to serve as G-1, and a promising young VMI graduate, Captain Thomas Handy, to serve as the division commander's aide. There were also quite a few officers who had once served under his father in the Philippines, including the commander of the 84th Infantry Brigade, Brigadier General Robert A. Brown, and the commander of the division's artillery brigade, Colonel Charles P. Summerall, a well-known and intimidating former First Captain at West Point. MacArthur provided the 42d with what was probably the best staff that any division took overseas.[4]

Some of the Rainbow regiments brought excellent officers of their own to the division. Major William Donovan of the Fighting 69th was an outstanding lawyer from Buffalo who had distinguished himself commanding a cavalry troop on the Mexican border in the summer of 1916.

The great weaknesses in the 42d's leadership were, as was true of nearly every American division sent to France in 1917, at the very top and down among the junior officers. The division commander, William Mann, was essentially a political appointee, too powerful to ignore, too weak to keep and too unfit for frontline service. The problem lower down was the large numbers of inexperienced officers who desperately needed training themselves before they could train their men.

MacArthur spent that summer as the ultimate workaholic. He pulled every string within reach to give the Rainbow everything from competent staff officers to boots and shelter halves. Wilson's neglect of preparedness had squandered the most valuable asset a nation going to war can possess: time. The United States declared war lacking an arms industry capable of equipping the mass army now being formed. Being one of the first divisions to be activated and having MacArthur devote all his influence and energy to the task, the 42d would depart as well equipped as it could hope to be.

To its dismay, the Rainbow did not have the honor of being the first Guard division shipped to France. That distinction went to the 26th Yankee Division, raised in New England and commanded by Clarence Edwards, one of the first officers assigned to the General Staff. Edwards had pull, and it paid off.

The 42d was eager to reach France, and an American government under pressure from the Allies to ship divisions overseas and have them finish their training when they got there was just as eager to see it depart. Before it set sail, MacArthur took care of one final detail. He rounded up dozens of priests from the parishes of Brooklyn and trucked them out to Camp Mills so that every man in the division would have the chance to take the sacraments before going to meet his fate on some foreign field whose name he would probably never be able to pronounce properly.[5]

When the Rainbow started shipping out in October, its various battalions and regiments were split among half a dozen convoys. The 42d's units reached their destination piecemeal. MacArthur was among the first to depart, sailing aboard a former Hamburg-America Line vessel that had been renamed the *Covington*. At one point on the fourteen-day journey from Hoboken to St.-Nazaire there was a U-boat scare, but someone had informed him—wrongly—that his brother, Captain Arthur MacArthur, was out there somewhere in command of the cruiser U.S.S. *Chattanooga* protecting the convoy. That thought gave him much comfort. In fact, however, his brother and the cruiser *Chattanooga* were back in Groton, Connecticut.[6]

The officers and men of the Rainbow arrived in France to be treated to one of the wettest, coldest winters the hardy French had endured for a century. In early 1918 they were gradually reassembled as a division. At this point they couldn't have fought their way out of a wet paper bag. They were not even half trained. Hardly a man among them, including Colonel MacArthur, knew anything much about modern war. They would get some more training from the French, but the Germans would provide most of what they learned.

Pershing had arrived in France in June 1917 and become a cadet again, filling notebooks with what the British and French had to tell him about their tactics and the Germans'. How was a meeting engagement handled? A delaying action? A general retreat?[7]

When it came to organizing American divisions, the French advised that the right size would be a formation of seventeen thousand men. Anything bigger would be too unwieldy to manage effectively in combat. It wouldn't be able to maneuver under fire or respond quickly to a change in plan.[8] Ignoring this advice, Pershing demanded the creation of divisions of twenty-eight thousand men. He believed these huge formations would have more staying power in combat and would carry the mass needed to break through German lines. He had been to Manchuria and managed to miss the most important lesson of the Russo-Japanese War: Massed infantry attacks against modern quick-firing artillery and light machine guns achieved little except to run up a huge butcher's bill.

Pershing's failure to learn that lesson had serious consequences for the AEF. It meant that Pershing created divisions that were top-heavy in infantry and handicapped by a crucial lack of firepower. It was the kind of organizational mistake that cost a lot of men their lives, their sight or their limbs. Although nearly twice the size of French or British infantry divisions, Pershing's divisions did not have twice as much artillery.

Of the four American divisions in France by 1918—the 1st, the 2d, the 26th and the 42d—only the Rainbow was at full strength. The others were, on average, seven thousand men short. Brigadier General Fox Conner, Pershing's chief of operations, proposed turning the 42d into a replacement division and stripping it to bring the 1st, 2d and 26th up to full strength.[9]

The Rainbow's first battle was a fight for survival. Mann was about to be fired and sent home, so he was not much help in this struggle. The challenge of winning it fell on MacArthur, but one colonel against the massed battalion of generals at Pershing's headquarters carried no weight. He went over their heads, with a telegram to the secretary of war: PERSHING INTENDS CHOP UP RAINBOW DIVISION FOR REPLACEMENTS STOP MEANS RUIN OF CRACK DIVISION TRAINED TO WORK AS TEAM AND DESTROY MORALE OF TROOPS PROUD OF BEING RAINBOW MEN STOP URGE PROMPT ACTION TO SAVE THE DIVISION SPONSORED BY PRESIDENT WILSON HIMSELF MACARTHUR.[10] MacArthur won his first battle in France, but at the cost of alienating the AEF staff and annoying Pershing.

Mann was, inevitably, sent home. His replacement was a field artillery officer, Major General Charles Menoher, one of Pershing's West Point classmates. Having been spared being broken up and used as replacements, the Rainbow was raided anyway. It had arrived fully supplied with everything but its artillery. MacArthur could only watch in dismay and frustration as the supplies and equipment he had spent many hours scrounging for were parceled out by AEF headquarters at Chaumont to other, less enterprising divisions.[11]

The American portion of the Western Front covered the mountains and forests of northeastern France. It was here that the 42d Division was reassembled in a "quiet sector" around Lunéville, a walled town at the foot of the Vosges Mountains.[12] A quiet sector was one where the lines were a mile or two apart, where there was no objective on either side that was likely to tempt the other into a major attack, where patrols and raids occasionally broke the tedium but only the sporadic growling of the guns hinted at the profound killing power of modern war. The Lunéville sector would provide the 42d with its finishing school. When the Rainbow moved in, the *Drachen*—German gray observation balloons—rose from the lines opposite to get a good look at the newcomers.

Assigned to the French VII Corps, the Rainbow spent the first few months of 1918 absorbing the most important lesson the French had to teach— namely, how the infantry and artillery had to fight as a team. In attack or defense, it was combined arms that brought the best results. Besides teaching the 42d Division, the French were carrying out raids and patrols.[13]

The objective of most raids was to seize prisoners for interrogation. When he learned that the Chasseurs Alpins were planning a raid for February 20, MacArthur insisted on going along. The division advocate general, Major Hugh Ogden, noticed MacArthur and Menoher departing in a hurry at midday. At 2:00 P.M. the heavy artillery began firing.

The raid was scheduled for that night. MacArthur daubed his face with mud, declined the offer of a trench knife and armed himself with a swagger stick in one hand and a pair of wire cutters in the other. When the order was given, he went over the top with the French. The raiding party slithered and squirmed through the mud of no-man's-land, then cut its way through the German wire. From time to time German flares shot into the night sky, fizzing and sizzling, throwing off gobbets of chemical fire as they slowly descended, casting a cold white light over no-man's-land that forced the raiders to freeze. To move was to die. Between the flares, the thump! of exploding grenades, the fatal chatter of machine guns, the earthquaking explosions of artillery fire, the raiding party snipped its way through to the German trenches, threw a grenade and, when it exploded, jumped into the enemy positions.[14]

Men struggled and grunted in the darkness, stabbing each other in brutal hand-to-hand fights, pressing handguns against each other's heads or ribs, having to guess in an instant which they should do: kill the man or take him prisoner. A German colonel rushed from his dugout, and MacArthur poked him in the back with his swagger stick. The German instantly put up his hands.[15]

In close combat an hour passes like a minute. The raid probably seemed over to MacArthur almost as soon as it began. The raiders scrambled back to their lines with a fine bag of prisoners, including the German colonel. Ogden noted in his diary:

We had a merry bombardment all the afternoon. The 155s boomed out, the 75s pitched in, and the planes flew around like mad. The General came back for dinner and told me there was a little push on. . . .

MacArthur did not come back until midnight. With the crazy exuberance of youth he pushed on beyond the batteries and out into the front line of the infantry assaulting column.

He walked about 25 miles altogether and footed it back to headquarters. We were scared to death, fearing something had happened to him. He walked in at breakfast and planted in the middle of the table a German steel helmet he had (peaceably?) acquired from a prisoner. He ought to stay back here and not do such crazy stunts. He is too valuable to risk dodging barrages. He said the German artillery barrage was perfect. They laid down a line of shell at five yard intervals as straight as a ruler across the map. The French took a lot of prisoners. . . . The men were not striking, old and stunted Bavarian Landwehr.[16]

One of the Rainbow's officers asked MacArthur why he had taken such risks. Surely they were not part of a chief of staff's duties? "It's all in the game," said MacArthur. After the raid concluded, he visited a French field hospital, to learn how the French handled their wounded, then went and sat in on the interrogation of the Germans taken prisoner. By dawn he had studied the raid from just about every possible angle.[17]

The commander of the VII Corps, General Georges de Bazalaire, promptly awarded MacArthur the Croix de Guerre for his part in the raid. This was the French style—decorations awarded quickly and liberally. It was a tradition that went back to Napoleon. The AEF was more conservative and bureaucratic, but in due course MacArthur received his first Silver Star for this raid, on Menoher's enthusiastic recommendation.[18]

The Germans too made raids. On March 4 they struck the 168th Infantry Regiment a sharp blow. Two days later the French delivered their reply. MacArthur went along once again, this time being mentioned in dispatches and cited for "advancing coolly under fire of the enemy, in order to follow at close range the movements of our troops."[19]

The German riposte was to rake the Fighting 69th, the division's famous infantry regiment recruited mainly from Irish neighborhoods in New York City, with a prolonged artillery barrage. The regiment suffered nearly a hundred casualties, with nothing to show for it. The tempo was picking up.

The 42d Division struck back with a battalion from the 168th Infantry, an Iowa regiment, on March 9. The French laid down an artillery barrage at dusk, to silence the German guns, and MacArthur and a French staff major appeared at the command post (CP) of an infantry company preparing to go over the top. The Frenchman talked to the Americans as they prepared to go into their first real fight. He was impressed by their eagerness and turned to MacArthur. "They conduct themselves like veterans," he said. "I have never seen better morale."

MacArthur was deeply moved. The 168th had served in the 2d Division in the Philippines under his father. He said to the Americans standing around him, "Is it any wonder my father was so proud of this regiment?"[20] When the order came for the Iowans to go over the top, he stripped off his overcoat, threw it on a bush, pocketed his colonel's insignia and led them over the top.[21]

This was the moment when faith—in himself, in these men—was put to the test that matters above all others among soldiers. "You never really know about men until a time like that," he said later. "You never know what's inside of them. I thought I knew what was inside our men, but, after all, they were not really professional. They had been National Guardsmen. None of them had ever been under fire.

"And then, there we were—ready to go. When the time arrived, I climbed out and started forward, and for a dozen terrible seconds, as I went forward, I felt they weren't following me. But then, without turning around, I knew how wrong I was to doubt even for an instant. In a moment they were all around me . . . ahead of me. I'll never forget that." It was the most intensely satisfying emotional experience of the time he spent in combat.[22]

They followed him even though he had removed his insignia of rank and advanced in a sweater and cap. No helmet. Few men realized just who he was, so they called him "Buddy" or "Say you." The raiders struck the first line of German trenches, only to find much of it deserted. One portion, however, which formed a salient, was crammed with machine guns, which soon took a toll on the raiders. MacArthur's role in the brief, bloody fight to wipe out the machine-gun nest brought him a recommendation for the Distinguished Service Cross.

The inspector general from Pershing's headquarters at Chaumont, Major General A. W. Brewster, paid a visit to the division to explain the AEF policy on decorations. He reported back to Chaumont that although MacArthur was a staff officer, he had gone on the March 9 raid "to inspire confidence and I am informed this result was obtained . . . he well merits the DSC." The decoration was approved.[23]

So far MacArthur had been unscathed, but on March 11 he was caught in a German gas attack and hospitalized. While he insisted that his soldiers wear their gas masks, he never wore his. He needed hospital treatment for two weeks but had recovered sufficiently to greet Newton Baker when he visited the 42d on March 19. Baker attended the funeral service of a dead Rainbow soldier, and MacArthur triumphantly gave the secretary of war the spiked German helmet he had taken on his first raid. Baker gallantly sent the helmet on to Mrs. MacArthur.[24]

Most nights MacArthur stayed in the division command post, directing the fighting by telephone. German artillery batteries barked throughout the night, and raiding parties probed the division's defenses. The 42d's judge advocate general, Hugh Ogden, wrote in his diary that as the reports were phoned into division headquarters,

> Colonel MacArthur sits there, perfectly cool, and puts all these reports together. Is it a little evening strafing or an artillery prelude to a raid? Will MacArthur sit and do nothing, not waste his powder, or will he let them have it, and if so, where and how? Pretty soon, when he has had twenty or thirty reports from all along the Front and he has made up his mind what is up, he will act. He will say, "Tell so and so to give them 155s in such and such a place every thirty seconds. Give them 75s on such and such a place every ten seconds for fifteen minutes. Give them gas on such and such a place." And inside of a minute our batteries are pounding away, giving just what he orders. You might close your eyes and say if he was a doctor he, in exactly the same impersonal tone, would be saying, "Give him one of these pills every hour until relieved, and two spoonfuls of this on going to bed."[25]

Besides the dramas of raids made and thwarted, the 42d was still struggling to fight off the depredations of AEF headquarters. There was a minuscule pool of able officers in France, and the Rainbow seemed to have more than its fair share. During its first six months overseas it saw many of the best officers MacArthur had found for it transferred. When Pershing organized his first corps headquarters, the 42d was stripped of eight of its best staff officers, from its chief surgeon to its quartermaster. One of the eight, Colonel Robert E. Wood, was soon on his way to Washington, to become acting Quartermaster General of the Army.

MacArthur fought to prevent the hemorrhage of talent from dooming his beloved division to mediocrity. Chaumont twice tried to transfer William Donovan to be an instructor at the Field Officers' School. MacArthur blocked it both times. When a third attempt was made, Donovan pleaded in person to be allowed to remain with his battalion in the 69th. MacArthur said, "Let's go, Bill. Don't let them get you away from the Line. Fighting men are the real soldiers." That was an article of faith with MacArthur, one from which he never deviated. No matter how high a man might go as a staff officer, no matter how greatly he might excel in one of the branches like Ordnance or Signals, he would always be slightly incomplete as a soldier. To understand how MacArthur judged other men, it is important to remember that. He took Donovan to Chaumont, and together they made a personal appeal to Pershing to leave Donovan where he was. For once Pershing relented.[26]

The Rainbow had a powerful sense of its uniqueness, and while Menoher was competent, he was also colorless. MacArthur's distinctive personality seemed to fit the 42d Division perfectly, and Menoher never got in his way. As division chief of staff MacArthur was expected to function as Menoher's chief problem solver. And after the sun went down and the guns on either side of the front reached out to probe the other's defenses, MacArthur drew up a midnight bulletin that summarized the day's events.

To the French, *le style, c'est l'homme,* and MacArthur by this time had certainly developed his own *style,* especially in the way he dressed. Like other successful commanders, including his hero, Napoleon, he ensured that he stood out on the field of battle, as if personal leadership were still what mattered most, as if men had to be able to see him to be reassured, as if this were still the nineteenth century, when a commander was expected to rally his troops in the open field. Even Ulysses Grant, plain, simple, brilliant Grant, had his own style of dress—a private's blouse with a general's stars. Patton too made sure he looked different. No one else, though, did it with MacArthur's panache.

He took the grommet out of his cap, making it look shapeless and jaunty. He wore a thick turtleneck sweater and purple muffler seven feet long that Pinky had knitted for him as protection against the coldness and dampness of the trenches. He strode through the incessant mud of the marlaceous, war-torn fields of France in shiny, calf-hugging boots. He did not carry a weapon. Instead his large, powerful hands clenched a riding crop or a swagger stick, which he periodically flicked at his cavalry boots as he walked as if he were riding a horse. To look at him, you might think he was a nonchalant, aristocratic British infantry officer, rather than an American. Like British officers, he refused to wear a helmet, except when it rained. He justified his highly individualistic garb by claiming that it made it easier for people who had to find him in a hurry, such as couriers and scouts. But a divisional chief of staff was not expected to be hard to find. All you normally had to do was go to the division's headquarters.

MacArthur had a dream of himself—all adventurous spirits do—and in his dream he was always the man of action, always at the heart of events. That was not a choice, the kind of decision that another man might make in becoming a dentist or a stockbroker. He had been summoned by destiny, marked out by a mysterious and unmovable power to live such a life, to be such a man. It was in his birth, his blood, his stars. That was why he never had to fear death or wounds on the field of battle. "All of Germany cannot fabricate the shell that will kill me," he said. It was not a boast; it was not bravado. Thus armed he went into battle as calmly as the business executive entering his office at 9:00 A.M. When he got there, he rallied other men to the grim business of killing.

He carried within him the fire that ignites the latent courage in other men. As the son of an infantry company commander he had been studying the most difficult and most rewarding part of soldiering, combat leadership, since he was in ringlets and dresses. MacArthur had absorbed rule number one almost with the first breath he had drawn: Take care of your men. "He was a soldier's soldier," one of them recalled some years later. "He was natural and friendly, though he insisted on the attitude of a soldier from all of us. His first thought was always for the soldier, looking out for supplies, trying to check frozen feet and trench foot, getting hot food to them in the line and taking care of everything. I was near him for a year and a half and he never did anything wrong as a soldier."[27]

MacArthur won the enduring loyalty of those who had even fleeting contact with him, such as Al Ettinger, a dispatch rider with the 69th. One stormy night Ettinger was ordered to take some papers to MacArthur. After a hair-raising ride along dark, muddy roads and coming off his bike a dozen times to avoid careering trucks and marching men, Ettinger was taken to see MacArthur covered in dirt, bleeding from various cuts, looking pathetic in a uniform that was torn in half a dozen places. MacArthur ignored all that. He thanked Ettinger for the dispatches, then shook his hand, grasped him by the shoulder and told him, "Ettinger, you are a good soldier." The bedraggled messenger nearly wept.

MacArthur turned to one of the NCOs present and told him, "Go find my cook and see that Ettinger gets a shower and a hot meal. I mean a good meal. Then have the supply sergeant draw a new clothing issue for him and find him a bunk to stay overnight. He'll not return to regimental HQ until after daylight, and then only if the weather has cleared."[28]

MacArthur made regular visits to the front lines to see the situation for himself. He was tickled with delight one day when he stopped by a company and asked if the men had seen the colonel who commanded the regiment. No, they said, they had not. How about the battalion commander then? Nor him either, they replied. Then one man shouted out, "But we've seen you!"[29]

Leadership did mean not only being seen by the troops but sharing the dangers and hardships. High-ranking officers were famous throughout the AEF for giving each other gallantry awards, and the soldiers mocked them for it by singing,

> *The general got the Croix de Guerre, parlez-vous,*
> *The general got the Croix de Guerre, parlez-vous,*
> *The general got the Croix de Guerre,*
> *The son of a bitch was never there,*
> *Hinky dinky parlez-vous.*

No soldier in the 42d, however, is on record as having doubted MacArthur's courage or questioned any of his decorations. He never showed or expressed fear. Even as he went about his staff duties, he courted danger. On one occasion he had his driver take him up to the front line in a staff car, which was raked by German machine-gun fire. Neither he nor the driver was scratched, although the car was a mess.[30]

His conviction that the real soldiers were the fighting men did not really square with his role as a divisional chief of staff. The famous chaplain of the 69th Infantry, Father Francis Duffy, observed in his diary in May 1918: "Our Chief of Staff chafes at his own task of directing instead of fighting, and he has pushed himself into raids and forays in which some older heads think, he had no business to be. His admirers say that his personal boldness has a very valuable result in helping give confidence to them [and] Menoher approves in secret of these madnesses. . . ."[31]

One officer who almost certainly did not approve was Pershing. Nineteenth-century battlefields were fairly small, as anyone who has visited them knows. The modern battlefield was often so big no one man could see more than a piece of it. Besides, military organization had become much more complicated. As Pershing rightly put it, "The days for brigadier generals to rush forward in the firing line waving their hats and yelling 'Come on boys!' are in actual warfare at least a thing of the past."[32]

The French nevertheless thought MacArthur was wonderful. As a rule French commanders had strong reservations about their American counterparts, whose courage was rarely in question but whose skills were always subject to doubt.[33] MacArthur, however, was a *beau sabreur,* charismatic, fearless, with terrific dress sense, the kind of soldier the French readily give their hearts to. When Pershing's inspector general visited VII Corps headquarters, he spoke to De Bazalaire and his staff about MacArthur. "French generals," reported the IG, "said that he was an officer of great capacity and a brilliant soldier."[34]

He read French easily and could converse, if haltingly, with the French in their own language. That spring Pershing's staff had each division make a survey of language skills. MacArthur led the 42d with his knowledge of French, Spanish, German and Italian. His shyness, however, made him seem unsociable at times, a trait that endured throughout his life. He organized a club for French and American officers yet never went there. He also arranged a dinner at Lunéville's best hotel for sixty French officers from the VII Corps. The dinner was a great success, but he stopped by only for a minute, to look in on what he had wrought, confirmed that all was going well, then departed with a smile.[35]

As spring 1918 approached, the Rainbow stood, as it sensed, on the verge of big battles, even though it was still only half trained. The collapse of the Russian Front in the winter of 1917 allowed the Germans to move nearly a million men to the Western Front.

Field Marshal Erich von Ludendorff intended to thrust a wedge between the British and French and seize the Channel ports. This would allow him to crush the Allied left flank, then roll up the center. The Germans brought up elite units under cover of darkness, hiding them in woods and houses during the day. Instead of unleashing prolonged artillery bombardments, the new German tactic was to penetrate the main line of resistance, not smash it. In ten days the Germans advanced forty miles, inflicted three hundred thousand casualties and brought the British Fifth Army to the edge of the abyss. A gap opened up between the British and French.

Marshal Ferdinand Foch was named the Supreme Allied Commander and given complete control over strategy. Pershing hurried to Foch's field headquarters and, rising to the desperate call of the hour, achieved the best French utterance of his life: *"Infanterie, artillerie, aviation—tout ce que nous avons est à vous. Disposez-en comme il vous plaira!"* (Everything we have is yours. Use it any way you wish!)[36]

In this crisis the four American divisions in France were pitched into battle without completing their training. The 42d relieved a French division at Baccarat, ten miles east of Lunéville, after it suddenly decamped to take part in the huge battle raging northwest of Paris.

Menoher was an aggressive commander. With a domain of his own, he soon showed a strong will to dominate it. He used his artillery lavishly, as an artillery officer might be expected to do, firing up to thirty thousand rounds a day in a sector that had seen few heavy bombardments in three years. MacArthur meanwhile was organizing raids and patrols virtually every day, every night. Menoher had decided to conquer no-man's-land, the space between the lines.[37] The Rainbow's soldiers gave neither the Germans nor themselves much rest. The division suffered two thousand casualties during its four months in Lorraine, most of them in the Baccarat area.

By June, Ludendorff's armies had reached the valley of the Marne, putting them on a direct road to Paris. Here was one of the most serious crises of the war. The Rainbow Division was ordered to head for Châlons-sur-Marne and join the battle to stop Ludendorff from reaching Paris.

Pershing came to visit the division the day it moved out and lost his temper. Many American officers had been impressed by the immaculate appearance of British troops in France. The British ran a spit-and-polish army even in the trenches. The officers may have been casually attired, but the troops, even the horses, looked ready for the parade ground. The French, by contrast, had an army that was like a French house or apartment: not much to look at from the street but likely to be beautiful once you got inside it.[38]

Pershing was outraged. "This division is a disgrace," he railed. "The men are poorly disciplined and they are not properly trained. The whole outfit is just about the worst I have seen. MacArthur, I am going to hold you personally responsible for getting discipline and order into this division. . . . I won't stand for this!" This would have been an amazing outburst in front of any division. It was universally accepted that it was the division commander who had primary responsibility for a division, and if the division failed, he would be fired. The Rainbow was different. The 42d took its style from MacArthur, and Pershing knew it. MacArthur was indifferent to spit and polish; so was the Rainbow. MacArthur dressed much as he pleased; so did the men of the Rainbow. Given the casual style of both MacArthur and the French, it was almost inevitable that the 42d looked more like a French division than a British one.

Pershing represented an older, narrower faith. He believed in an immaculate appearance and strict military bearing even at the front. His attitude rubbed off on other officers, such as Patton, who took Pershing as their role model. Patton demanded that his men go into combat in World War II wearing ties and with every button on their uniforms buttoned. MacArthur represented the future of combat soldiering, and Pershing upheld the past. In the U.S. Army of the next war, the Quartermaster Corps would strive to devise clothing that would keep men warm and dry in surroundings of utter discomfort. Before MacArthur's military career ended, he would command men who wore field jackets and combat fatigues that were designed to be almost shapeless and comfortable. For now, though, about all MacArthur could do was bark, "Yes, sir!" before Pershing stalked away.[39]

A stern disciplinarian, immaculate in appearance, holding himself so erect, Pershing seemed almost a stage parody of the modern general rather than the real thing. He was a formidable figure, the more so when he was angry. MacArthur admired him as a wonderful example of soldierly virtues but did not share all of them. Pershing, for example, could take criticism right on his big, strong chin, but the least slight cut MacArthur to the depths of his soul. It isn't hard to guess how deeply hurt and humiliated he felt at being publicly rebuked by a man he admired so much. On this chastened note Colonel MacArthur and the 42d Division set off for Châlons-sur-Marne and their first real battle of the war.

7

The Dominant Feature

The Germans were holding a strong position north of the champagne city of Rheims, with a long, narrow salient that extended nearly all the way to the Marne River—the traditional invader's route to Paris. Caesar had once passed this way; so had Attila the Hun. The Germans too had been here before, in 1914, only to be halted tantalizingly short of their goal. Their latest drive toward Paris had been stopped just a few miles from the Marne at Château-Thierry, by French and American troops.

Ludendorff planned a do-or-die offensive to capture Paris and win the war before the four million American troops presently being trained in the United States could land in France. His preparations, however, were no secret. German prisoners taken at the end of June talked of a coming offensive in Champagne. French and American aviators, including Billy Mitchell, monitored the buildup well before the blow fell. Several hundred thousand troops, including the 42d Division, were moved toward Rheims to meet the German attack.[1]

As the intelligence picture developed, MacArthur became convinced that the crucial moment of the war had arrived. Everything was on the line, for both sides. Two engineer officers visiting division headquarters found him pacing up and down, his mind racing. After greeting them warmly, he said, "I want to tell you something. The Germans are going to win or lose the war within ninety days."[2]

While these events were unfolding, Pinky was following the course of the war by tracing Douglas's movements across France. Whenever he left one place to move to another, he wrote to let her know where he had been.

As one of the most glamorous figures in the AEF her son was a magnet for American war correspondents and appeared regularly in the newspapers back home. Ever since the Veracruz expedition, Pinky had kept a large scrapbook of press clippings that related Douglas's exploits. World War I kept her busy cutting and pasting.[3]

Before leaving the Baccarat sector, Douglas wrote and let her know that Menoher had recommended him for a star. Mrs. MacArthur, as brazen as ever in her efforts to get Douglas promoted, proceeded to write an imploring letter to Newton Baker on June 7. Pinky told him how deeply gratified she was by Menoher's praise of her son: "Even if my boy fails to win promotion, I shall always feel that he has made good."[4] All the same, he had proved himself an outstanding combat soldier. She urged Baker to follow through on Menoher's recommendation.

Baker replied, "I am sure you know my personal affection for Colonel MacArthur too well to doubt where the dictates of my heart would lead me if I were free to follow them, or, indeed, where the dictates of my judgment would lead, for I greatly admire his soldierly qualities."[5] Baker did not say so, but Pershing had not endorsed Menoher's recommendation. Nor had he objected to it. He had simply ignored it.

Baker forwarded Pinky's passionate missive to Pershing for his consideration. Pinky was taking no chances, though. On receiving Baker's reply, she wrote a second letter, this time to Pershing, begging him for a star. She said she understood that nearly a hundred officers would soon become generals and reminded Pershing that Douglas had been top of his class at West Point. She leaned heavily on the fact that he had spent two years working directly under the secretary of war. Douglas had shown himself to be a highly capable officer, she pointed out, yet others who were junior to him were already brigadier generals. So was one of his West Point classmates, Hugh Johnson, who had graduated far below Douglas. She concluded with a little emotional blackmail: "I feel I am placing my entire life, as it were, in your hands. . . ."[6]

Such a plea would surely have been wasted on Pershing so soon after the incident at Baccarat, but a higher power was about to intervene. Peyton C. March had recently become Chief of Staff. He may well have been Mrs. MacArthur's source of information that a large number of stars was about to become available, although the figure of one hundred was far too high. March had asked AEF headquarters for the names of officers deserving promotion. Pershing promptly sent in a list of nearly fifty people, many of them members of the AEF staff. March added MacArthur's name to the list and removed five of the people Pershing had recommended. The amended list was duly approved by the Senate, creating four major generals and forty-three brigadier generals.

On a scorching hot afternoon, June 26, to be precise, a private named Pat Robinson, a man who would one day be a war correspondent and well-known sportswriter, went looking for MacArthur. A telegram had just arrived from Washington and been decoded by the division's intelligence officer, Colonel Nobel B. Judah. Robinson found MacArthur, saluted, and said, "Colonel Judah's compliments to Colonel . . . pardon me, sir, I mean, *General* MacArthur."

MacArthur smiled, saluted and said, "Thank you very much, Robinson."[7]

Pinky's letter arrived at Chaumont after the news of MacArthur's promotion came through, so her efforts—described by most MacArthur biographers as being decisive—were academic. Pershing had gotten 90 percent of the promotions he had asked for, but he was outraged over the five recommendations March had turned down, even though March had already given him a complete, and well-reasoned, explanation for amending the list.[8] At thirty-eight MacArthur was by far the youngest general in the AEF, and would remain so until October, when two thirty-five-year-olds, Lesley J. McNair and Pelham D. Glassford, became brigadiers.

Not even Pershing would have denied that MacArthur deserved his star. Rather, he preferred to reward his officers in his own time and in his own way. The deed, though, was done and could only add to the tension between Black Jack and MacArthur. And, incensed at March's handling of promotions, Pershing tried to get the Army Chief of Staff fired. For once Baker declined to oblige him.[9]

Unaware that it was March who had made him a general, MacArthur wrote a warm letter to Pershing. "I thank you very sincerely for promoting me to brigade rank," he began. "To be recognized by you in such generous measure is an inspiration." He recalled the admiration and affection that both his father and mother had had for him. MacArthur concluded, "May you go on and up to the mighty destiny a grateful country owes you."[10] He either knew or, more likely anticipated, the way Pershing's mind would turn once the war ended.

Although he was now a general, MacArthur intended to continue as a chief of staff and as a combat soldier. Being a divisional chief of staff would never be as glamorous or exciting as leading men in battle, yet it posed its own leadership challenges. And, said Tom Handy, later a four-star general and Marshall's right-hand man in World War II, "Boy, was he a leader! He was taking ordinary people and getting first class work out of them." Chaumont had liberally raided the 42d Division to provide a staff for the I Corps headquarters that Pershing established as a prelude to creating an American army in France. MacArthur warned Pershing's staff that they were going to be disappointed. "Well, they took the people that MacArthur told them they didn't want and some of them were relieved in two or three months. They were turning out first class work under MacArthur. But that was MacArthur, it wasn't this individual."[11]

July 1918 found the 42d Division digging in around Souain, a small town southeast of Rheims, to meet the impending German offensive. The Rainbow was assigned to the French XXI Corps, which in turn was assigned to the French Fourth Army, commanded by General Henri Gouraud.

At forty-six, Gouraud was the youngest army commander in France. With his red beard and awesome reputation as a fighting soldier, he seemed like a character out of *Beau Geste*. Known in the French press as *le lion d'Afrique,* he walked with a severe limp, the result of a serious hip wound in Algeria. Commanding the French corps that fought at Gallipoli, he had left an arm there. His empty left sleeve, pinned to a jacket pocket, was a decoration in itself. Gouraud wore his general's kepi at a jaunty angle that insouciantly conveyed a fearless nature and a young man's delight in field soldiering. Smiling, alert and courageous, vivacious in manner despite the constant pain of his wounds, he captivated MacArthur.[12]

On July 7 Gouraud issued a clarion call to his Franco-American army. "We may be attacked at any moment. You all know that a defensive battle was never fought under more favorable conditions. You will fight on terrain that you have transformed into a redoubtable fortress. . . . The bombardment will be terrible. You will stand it without weakening. The assault will be fierce. . . . In your breasts beat the brave and strong hearts of free men. None shall look to the rear; none shall yield a step. . . . Each shall have but one thought, to kill, to kill plenty. . . . Your General says to you, 'You will break this assault and it will be a glorious day.' "[13]

A thoroughly professional soldier, Gouraud made meticulous preparations to meet the impending German attack. By July 11 French military intelligence knew the axis of advance, the approximate size of the German force involved, the width of the attack and that it would come in the next few days.[14] The Germans were planning to launch their offensive at midnight on Bastille Day, July 14, hoping to catch the party-loving French while they were still joyfully inebriated. German artillery would lay down a heavy artillery bombardment starting at midnight, with the infantry assault to be launched at 4:00 A.M. on July 15.

The afternoon of Bastille Day, showers swept the Rheims area. To their delight, a huge, shimmering rainbow hung in the air in front of the 42d Division's men, like God's promise written in Crayola. When night fell, Gouraud had his artillery put down short, intense barrages to cover two raids into the German lines. The raiders brought back twenty-seven prisoners, including an officer. German prisoners were an interrogator's dream. Suggest that maybe the German Army wasn't quite as superb as some people claimed and German soldiers were likely to boast their heads off, telling their captors everything their unit had done or intended to do.[15] Gouraud soon learned that tonight was the night. The telephone soon rang in the 42d Division headquarters with a message from the Fifth Army: "François 570, François 570. Good luck."

At 11:30 P.M., with German infantry from more than twenty divisions crowded tensely in their assembly areas waiting for the battle to begin, more than twenty-five hundred French and American guns, the combined firepower of three armies, split the night sky. A metallic Niagara of high explosive and gas shells rained down on German troops, inflicting serious losses. At four minutes after midnight the Germans nonetheless began their bombardment. The infantry assault was launched, only slightly delayed, at 4:30. Red flares soon showed above Gouraud's first line of trenches. By dawn the Germans had reached the 42d Division's strongpoints.

The fighting was fierce, with heavy losses on both sides. It was whites-of-their-eyes shooting and hand-to-hand combat. The enemy broke through in one part of the Rainbow's sector, but those Germans who advanced to the main line of resistance were disorganized and demoralized, having been terribly mauled by the artillery. Gouraud rushed troops forward from the reserve and quickly contained the penetration at Souain.

MacArthur took a look at some of the prisoners being brought back and was unimpressed. The enemy was thoroughly demoralized. It had been a good day for his division, and for him: Menoher awarded him another Silver Star, and Gouraud recommended him to be made a commander of the *Légion d'Honneur.* But the sight of men in their death throes dulled the romance of war. It was never, he said, the same for him again.[16] The Rainbow Division had won its first major victory, at a cost of sixteen hundred casualties.

The Germans made no advance on July 16. Fighting died down while the German high command tried to decide what to do next. A lull fell over the battlefield the following day, and at midnight MacArthur began his bulletin, "The day of the 17th was relatively quiet."[17] Some hours earlier Ludendorff had decided to pull back east of Rheims and try to hold the ground he still held west of the city.

On July 19 Gouraud's Fourth Army held its Bastille Day celebration, five days late, but with a famous victory to toast. The German threat to Paris had been ended. From here on the Allies would do all the attacking, the Germans all the retreating.

The French had been preparing a counteroffensive against the Germans weeks before Ludendorff's pincers movement around Rheims. Foch had chosen to wait for the storm to blow itself out before attacking. A week after the German assault, French and American divisions struck the Germans west of Rheims.

The 42d was redeployed to take part in this offensive, assigned now to the French Sixth Army, under General Jean Marie Joseph Degoutte, a man who was unpopular with American soldiers. Degoutte had neither Gouraud's charm nor his ability. He was a conventional soldier, a dour, earnest figure with an unhappy reputation for squandering men's lives.[18]

Forced back from the Marne, the Germans were assumed to be in full retreat toward the Ourcq River, which isn't much of a river in midsummer, just a slow-moving creek that isn't wide, deep or even pretty. The challenge the Ourcq posed to advancing Allied troops was the steep banks on both sides, banks that were well within range of German machine guns and mortars on the line of low hills beyond.

The 42d Division advanced on the Ourcq without its artillery, which would take several days to catch up. Degoutte, convinced the Germans were still retreating, ordered the 42d to cross the river at night, without artillery prepping and without firing a shot. There was not a moment to lose, he claimed. He wanted the Americans to make a surprise attack and fall on the retreating Germans with bayonets just before dawn. This was the kind of stalking rifleman warfare that Pershing claimed Americans excelled at.

The crossing was scheduled for the night of July 28, but firefights broke out along the river throughout the day. When darkness fell, the Rainbow's regiments, crossing on planks that spanned the narrow stream, had barely started crawling up the opposite bank when they came under fierce mortar and machine-gun fire. MacArthur began his midnight bulletin with a single graphic expression: "A day of fierce infantry fighting." He had himself been out under fire to rally the troops and won his third Silver Star. Far from retreating, the Germans had dug in along the high ground overlooking the Ourcq. Degoutte had guessed wrong, and the Rainbow was paying in blood for its lack of artillery support.[19]

As reports filtered into division headquarters, MacArthur was astonished to discover the Rainbow was now fighting four German divisions, one of them the excellent but half-strength 4th Prussian Guards Division. The 42d thus found itself heavily committed on both sides of the river in a battle that was more intense than anything its troops had ever encountered.[20]

The division's artillery raced to the scene and deployed. In the confusion the commander of the Rainbow's 84th Infantry Brigade, Robert A. Brown, twice countermanded MacArthur's orders for artillery support, thinking some of his most advanced units were at risk of being struck by friendly fire. Menoher fired Brown and gave MacArthur command of the 84th Brigade.[21]

The situation was so fluid that MacArthur did not officially take command of the brigade for another couple of days, but while he continued to function as division chief of staff and still penned the midnight bulletins, MacArthur was also leading his men into battle. During the struggle to drive the Germans away from the Ourcq he was marching at the head of the 84th Brigade at night, dressed in an overcoat and helmet as protection against the unseasonal cold and rain. He was probably the only general to lead American soldiers into combat this way in the entire war. It just wasn't done like that anymore. But it was the way his father had led the 24th Wisconsin.[22]

On August 1 the Germans abruptly disengaged. The 42d, which had suffered a thousand casualties a day since the battle began, was in a severely weakened state but had reached its objective. MacArthur, however, jumped onto the running board of a field ambulance heading into the small town of Sergy, which had just fallen to the Rainbow. A quick look around Sergy convinced him the enemy was retreating in disorder. Exhausted and nearly crippled, the Rainbow had just won a major battle. What it had to do now, MacArthur had no doubt, was summon the last dregs of energy, invest in its hard-won success and pursue the beaten foe.[23]

MacArthur hurried back to division headquarters to see Menoher and explained the situation to him. Menoher was torn between doing what his brilliant, persuasive chief of staff wanted and following the orders from Degoutte's headquarters. He could not give MacArthur the order he asked but told him he would not stand in his way either.

The division held a four-kilometer front. It stood there panting, bleeding profusely, ready to drop. MacArthur raced the whole four kilometers on foot, going from regiment to regiment, urging, pleading, smiling, being charming, begging for one last push. The men knew the 4th Division was coming forward even now to relieve them. Why should they go a step farther, lose another man? They had done all that corps and army headquarters had asked of them.

If, though, MacArthur could get one regiment to move, the others would follow. He concentrated on the Fighting 69th, commanded by Colonel Frank McCoy, prayed over by Father Francis P. Duffy and its fighting spirit exemplified by William Donovan. MacArthur explained the situation to McCoy and his staff, concluding, "It's up to you, McCoy."

The colonel called Captain Martin Meaney, who was standing nearby. Meaney commanded the regiment's 3d Battalion, now at less than half strength, and asked him how he felt about MacArthur's request. "My men are few and they are tired," said Meaney, "but they are willing to go anywhere they are ordered and they will consider an order to advance as a compliment." Minutes later the 3d Battalion began to move forward, setting the entire division in motion.

"By God, McCoy," said MacArthur, "it takes the Irish when you want a hard thing done!"[24]

For the next two days the Rainbows pushed the Germans back, forcing them to abandon the Marne salient. Menoher was thrilled. As he described it to Pershing, "In advance of orders [from corps or army headquarters] and without delay he galvanized the entire division into a prompt pursuit which soon brought it on the very heels of the enemy and gained entire possession of the great massif [i.e., the ridge] of the Forêt de Vesles. . . . General MacArthur personally instructed each of the infantry regiments of the divisions, moving across the entire divisional front of four kilometers and swung the artillery and supporting arms into immediate accompaniment despite a terrain which hardly offered a road."[25] Menoher awarded him his fourth Silver Star.

The division pushed itself forward five miles over the next two days. By then the 42d was played out. On August 3 it was relieved by the 4th Division. In a week of fighting it had suffered sixty-five hundred casualties and gained seven miles. The rifle companies, which, as always, had borne the brunt of the losses, were reduced to the size of platoons.[26]

While the battle raged, MacArthur received orders to return to the United States. March and Baker were both well aware that he wanted a combat command. They sought to arrange that by giving him command of a brigade in the 11th Infantry Division, which was still in Maryland, in training. Events on the battlefield had overtaken their plans and brought MacArthur command of the 84th Brigade. Menoher protested to Chaumont that MacArthur should stay where he was. It was not too hard to get the War Department to agree.[27]

The Rainbow headquarters staff presented MacArthur with an enduring gift to mark his departure as chief of staff now that he had a brigade to command. It was a gold cigarette case, with an inscription probably unique in the history of American staff officers. It read, "To the bravest of the brave."[28]

The attitude of the troops toward their new brigade commander was equally awestruck. Although Menoher was on his way to becoming one of the most successful division commanders of the AEF, the Rainbow seemed more an expression of MacArthur's personality than his. The story went around of an officer from Chaumont searching for MacArthur along a road one night in heavy rain and coming across a bedraggled private. "Would you know General MacArthur if you saw him?" asked the officer. "Hell, sir," said the private, incredulous at the ignorance of some people, "everybody knows General MacArthur."[29]

Pershing demanded that enlisted men know the names of their brigade, division and corps commanders. Shortly after MacArthur got command of the 84th Brigade, Menoher asked a young soldier from Alabama if he knew the name of his brigade commander. "General MacArthur, sir," the soldier replied. And what kind of a general, asked Menoher, was he?, expecting the soldier to say, "A brigadier general."

But the young man thought hard for a minute; then a smile lit up his face. "Well, I'll tell you, by God, he's a piss cutter!"[30]

Pershing had held out staunchly for an independent American army and, despite intense political pressure from the British and French, had finally gotten his way. It was his greatest achievement and one that won the admiration of every American soldier. When it came into being that August, he was so proud of his creation that he took personal command of the First Army. It was huge: fourteen divisions, with an average strength of twenty-five thousand men, plus more than a hundred thousand support troops, mainly French, to keep it supplied and maintained.

Confidence rising, Pershing now ended British and French instruction. He poured scorn on what his allies had to teach. "At this stage of the game," he decided, "they are behind the times." He was convinced that the trench system was about to collapse, ushering in a war of maneuver.[31] His army would fight his way, although had he truly had his own way, Pershing would have fought the war with horses. He requested two cavalry divisions be raised in the United States and sent to France. March rejected this bizarre proposition, unable to see what horses and saber charges would achieve against machine guns and quick-firing light artillery.[32]

Pershing proposed to unleash the First Army's five hundred thousand men against the St.-Mihiel salient, which cut the railroad line between Paris and Nancy and deprived France of some of its best iron mines. It also provided an excellent assembly area for German armies attacking Verdun and helped secure the German hold on the city of Metz, one of France's leading industrial centers.

Pershing intended to employ virtually the entire force available to him. It was an odd way to prove the merits of maneuver warfare. Putting two thousand men to the square mile into battle was something no British, French or German commander would have dreamed of doing. This would produce such bunching up that if German artillery line proved to be strong and alert, the casualty list would be enormous. The gossip at Chaumont, MacArthur told one of the 42d's officers, was that taking St.-Mihiel could cost seventy-five thousand American dead and wounded.[33]

While the 42d prepared for this offensive, MacArthur decided to give all the men of his brigade a few days' leave in Paris. For many this could be the last chance they would ever have to enjoy themselves. But Pershing, who treated ordinary soldiers as mere "bodies" to be expended like cartridges, did not believe in leave for enlisted men, except maybe for a couple of days in whichever miserable little village or war-ravaged town they happened to find themselves in. When MacArthur's men tried to make their way to Paris, they were stopped at gunpoint by MPs and sent back to the brigade. They were outraged at Pershing, but more devoted than ever to their commander.[34]

Despite the 42d's superb performance so far, Pershing still did not think much of the Rainbow. Like most regulars, he tended, anyway, to look with disdain on National Guard divisions. On September 7 he visited both the 1st and the 42d to distribute medals. MacArthur and Donovan received DSCs from him on this occasion. That evening Pershing noted in his diary, "The ceremony at the 1st Division was very good. That at the 42nd was very badly organized."[35]

The St.-Mihiel attack was set for 5:00 A.M. on September 12. MacArthur wasn't expected to take part. He was ill with the flu on September 10 and seemed too weak to stand. Even so, he swore he would lead his men into the coming battle.

Pershing's plan called for a minimal artillery preparation, hoping yet again to catch the enemy by surprise. This news horrified the troops, and the 42d's artillery officers agreed with them that it was a bad idea. The chances of catching the Germans by surprise were nil. MacArthur drew up his own plan, which included ample artillery support for his brigade, and did not inform Chaumont of what he had done. "It's sometimes the order that you don't obey that makes you famous," he told an admiring artillery colonel.[36]

The evening of September 11 Newton Baker visited Chaumont. He wanted to be present when the First Army made its combat debut. Was there anything he could do to help? he asked. Only one thing, said Pershing: "Pray for fog." When the troops jumped off at 5:00 A.M., a comforting blanket of fog covered the St.-Mihiel salient.[37] That, though, was all the comfort they got. Heavy rains had fallen for the past two weeks. The troops sloshed and slithered as they advanced into a sea of mud.

The aim of the converging attacks from south and west was to drive in the shoulders of the salient and trap the Germans before they could retreat. The only trouble with this design was that the Germans were already pulling out. Their numbers had been reduced to twenty-three thousand men, and only two days before the First Army lunged into the fog they had received orders to withdraw.

MacArthur's fever looked as if it would keep him out of this attack. But no, he gave instructions that four orderlies would carry him into the battle, if necessary on a stretcher. When the bullets flew, he would be there to hear the shrill music of incoming fire playing artillery arpeggios. As zero hour drew near, he summoned the strength to visit his Alabama regiment, the 167th Infantry, and as the artillery bombardment unfolded, he changed into the clothing of an enlisted man, picked up a rifle and bayonet and led Company B over the top when the whistle blew. He personally led the entire division in the attack.[38]

Pershing's First Army advanced swiftly. It enjoyed overwhelming superiority in every department. The troops were supported by an air force of nearly fifteen hundred airplanes, most of them French, but commanded by Billy Mitchell, and an American tank brigade of thirty Renaults under Colonel George S. Patton, Jr. The afternoon of September 12 Patton led his tanks forward.

"I walked right along the line of one brigade," Patton wrote to his wife some hours later. "They were all in shell holes except the general, Douglas MacArthur, who was standing on a little hill. . . . I joined him and the creeping barrage came along toward us. . . . I think each one wanted to leave but each hated to say so, so we let it come over us." When a shell exploded nearby, throwing dirt on them, Patton remained erect but flinched. "Don't worry, Colonel," said MacArthur wryly. "You never hear the one that gets you." MacArthur's combat performance this day brought him his fifth Silver Star and Patton's enduring respect. He told his family MacArthur was "the bravest man I ever met."[39]

For the Germans, what had begun as an orderly pullout was turning into a rout. Germans surrendered eagerly to almost any American officer they could find. Some surrendered to MacArthur. Patton too was slowed down by Germans eager to shout "*Kamerade!*" at him and be marched into captivity. The battle had, to all intents and purposes, been won. Metz was only fourteen miles away. MacArthur made a command reconnaissance, accompanied only by his aide, and reached the outskirts of the city. It seemed evident to him that Metz, for two centuries one of the most heavily fortified places on earth, had been left virtually defenseless. He returned and exhorted Menoher to allow his brigade to make a lightning strike and seize the city, but that was way beyond Menoher's powers.

MacArthur hurried to Pershing's headquarters. From Metz, he argued, the Allied armies could drive into central Germany. He promised to take it within forty-eight hours. "The President would make you a field marshal," he said. "And I think you'll agree that I would have earned a second star."

Pershing wouldn't consider it. He wasn't about to take any risks. Not the most articulate of men, and certainly in no mood to debate someone as eloquent as MacArthur, he bellowed, "Get out! And stay out."

Leaving Chaumont in disgust, MacArthur remarked bitterly to his adjutant, Captain Walter Wolf, "I made a mistake. I should have taken Metz and *then* asked his permission!"[40]

MacArthur remained angry for years afterward at what he considered a major strategic blunder, but in all probability the 84th would have taken Metz only to be destroyed in the counterattack the Germans would have mounted. The First Army lacked the agility and the logistics to take and hold so great a prize.[41]

By September 16 the St.-Mihiel operation was virtually over. It had gone more smoothly than anyone had imagined. The British military historian Sir Basil Liddell Hart joked that St.-Mihiel was "the sector where the Americans relieved the Germans."[42] The cost had been seven thousand casualties, of which the 42d had suffered twelve hundred.

In the two weeks following the clearing of the St.-Mihiel salient five hundred thousand troops were moved sixty miles to the east, into the Meuse-Argonne area. Other divisions arrived to join them. Pershing found himself with a million-man army for his next offensive, of whom 85 percent were Americans.

Having created this huge force, Pershing was looking for a strategic objective his troops could take. He and his staff decided to aim for the Sedan-Mezières-Carignan railroad line. Severing it would paralyze the German Army's lateral communications for half the length of the Western Front. To do that, however, they would first have to break through the defenses of the Kriemhilde Stellung, a dense network of prepared killing grounds the Germans had created between the Meuse River and the Argonne Forest.

The terrain was a formidable obstacle in itself—"a natural fortress," said Hunter Liggett, commanding the I Corps, "beside which the Wilderness in which Grant fought Lee was a park."[43] The main German line was based in part on trenches, but for most of the front their position rested on possession of hundreds of machine-gun nests sited on the high ground. Behind these positions were hundreds of mortar pits. In front of them were dense barriers of barbed wire up to twenty-five feet in depth.

In some places there were concrete pillboxes, a development that was fairly new. These were World War II defenses, about to be attacked with World War I tools. Although the Kriemhilde Stellung was manned by second-rate German divisions, even they would be able to put up a fierce defensive fight. Having acquired monopoly rights to all the best high ground, they had made the most of it.

The First Army's sole advantage was in numbers. The attackers would outnumber the defenders by about six to one. In artillery they had a superiority of ten to one. They had hundreds of tanks and nearly a thousand airplanes.

The key to the Kriemhilde Stellung was a collection of hills known as the Romagne Heights. Pershing planned to thrust around both sides of the

Romagne Heights on the first day of his attack, isolate the hills and then reduce them. The few divisions still resting around St.-Mihiel, such as the 42d, mounted a diversionary attack to bluff the Germans into thinking the main American onslaught would be made in that sector. MacArthur accompanied at least one raiding party and won his sixth Silver Star.

Pershing's Meuse-Argonne offensive began early on September 26. The attacking force walked into a buzz saw. Woefully inexperienced, crammed into a narrow twenty-five-mile front, the Americans got nowhere. Dazed troops milled around in confusion, desperate for leadership. Thousands of men simply fled to the rear. When his flanking movement failed, Pershing resorted to brutal frontal attacks. All he could think of now was to push more men into the fight, take even heavier losses and hope something would give before the First Army was bled into defeat. He noted grimly in his diary, "There is no course except to fight it out." No brave talk there of outmaneuvering the enemy and forcing him into the open.[44]

On October 11 and ill with the flu that was sweeping like an epidemic through his divisions, Pershing turned the First Army over to Hunter Liggett. The offensive would be reinforced with several experienced and rested divisions, including the 42d. The Rainbow was assigned to the V Corps, commanded by Major General Charles P. Summerall, the able artillery officer who had come to France in command of the division's artillery brigade. Like MacArthur and Pershing, Summerall had been First Captain of his West Point class. A hard-driving, overbearing, impatient commander in the Pershing mold, he had been in France little more than a month before he was taken away from the Rainbow's artillery and given command of the 1st Division. In its early battles he had driven his division into combat "with the fierceness of a fanatic." In the Meuse-Argonne offensive the relentless way he pushed his troops forward in doomed assault bled his division white and forced Pershing to pull the Big Red One out of the line but brought Summerall promotion to a corps command.[45]

If the Romagne Heights was the key to the Kriemhilde Stellung, the key to the Romagne was a low hill mass known as the Côte de Châtillon. On the evening of October 11 the 42d relieved the 1st Division on the lower slopes of the Romagne Heights, which were littered with decomposing corpses.[46] The Germans welcomed the Rainbows with a barrage of gas. MacArthur was caught again without a gas mask and needed medical treatment.

Despite inhaling even more gas the next day and spending much of his time lying down and vomiting, MacArthur nonetheless intended to lead his brigade's attack on the Côte de Châtillon, which rose abruptly, dark and distinctive, like a volcanic island, several hundred feet above yellow-ing fields that in peacetime grew poor-quality wheat fit only for feeding to animals. It was a natural strongpoint. The evening of October 13 Summerall came to visit the 84th Brigade, ate a hurried, midnight supper and, as he was departing, said to MacArthur in the brusque style for which he was well known and widely disliked, "Give me Châtillon or a list of five thousand casualties!"

When it came to melodramatics, MacArthur could outperform anyone in the Army, maybe even in France, despite potential competition from Sarah Bernhardt. "If this brigade does not capture Châtillon," he told Summerall, "you can publish a casualty list of the entire brigade, with the brigade commander's name at the top." Summerall, who managed to intimidate most of his subordinates, was so taken aback he seemed about to burst into tears. He walked out of the CP unable to trust himself to say another word.[47]

Rumor quickly circulated among the men that MacArthur had promised to take the hill or take 100 percent casualties. One soldier was reported to have turned to his buddy on hearing this and said, "Generous son of a bitch, ain't he?" But this did not shake the men's confidence in MacArthur, knowing that he intended to be a casualty too.[48] What did upset them was learning that the plan was to attack just before dawn and try to take Châtillon by stealth, at bayonet point. The ghastly Ourcq experience was still strong in their memories. Officers and men alike bitterly protested, and MacArthur changed his plan. The brigade would make a conventional frontal attack in daylight behind a rolling artillery barrage.[49]

At six the next morning the 42d advanced toward the Côte de Châtillon through steady rain. MacArthur had quit his sickbed, still vomiting, to direct operations from his command post. Within a few hours, however, the attack was in deep trouble. He left the CP and placed himself at the head of his brigade. Like his father before him, he would have the chance to win glory leading his men in a desperate uphill assault. Death seemed incomparably preferable at that moment to failure.

The brigade to MacArthur's left, the 83d, soon fell behind and hastily entrenched when it came under flanking fire. Even so, with MacArthur personally leading his men forward, the 84th pressed on, taking terrible losses. He remarked to an infantryman standing near him as the troops scrambled out of their trenches to attack the German lines, "If this is good, I'm in it. And if it's bad, I'm in it, too."[50] By nightfall one of his regiments had managed to reach the crest of one of the Côte's hills, but its hold on the crest was agonizingly precarious.

The Rainbow tried to press forward next morning to the highest point of the Romagne Heights, Hill 288, but the 83d Brigade hardly moved on MacArthur's left, and the 32d Division, on his right, was stopped by a counterattack. The farther he advanced, the more dangerously exposed his flanks were.

MacArthur returned for a short time to his command post, where he found two journalists waiting. One of them noticed a hole in the left sleeve of his sweater where a machine-gun bullet had recently passed through. "When did brigadier generals get to be expendable?" he asked. MacArthur grinned, looking slightly embarrassed. "Well, there are times when even general officers have to be expendable," he replied. "Come on inside and we'll rustle some coffee."[51]

After his visitors had left, MacArthur returned to his frontline positions, rallied his men and led yet another assault on Hill 288. The 84th Brigade made five frontal assaults that day on the hill, every one of them in vain. There were 230 machine-gun nests on the Côte de Châtillon, most of them in pillboxes. It seemed almost impossible to move without being shot. Each time an attack was thrown back MacArthur rallied his men, revived their spirits and led them up the hill again. Men fell all around him, dead, dying or wounded. Yet other than his centimetric brush with injury when the machine-gun bullet passed through his left sleeve, he emerged from this ferocious battle unscathed. He seemed, as some Rainbow men said, "bullet-proof."[52]

By nightfall on October 15 the attempt to storm the Romagne Heights was once again on the point of failure. Furious, Summerall fired the commander of the 83d Brigade and the commander of the 165th Infantry Regiment. He refused to listen to officers who tried to explain what the situation was. He didn't care, didn't want to know. All he was interested in was results. He directly ordered MacArthur to take the Côte de Châtillon by nightfall on the sixteenth. MacArthur sent back the same message as before: The 84th would take its objective or be destroyed in the attempt, and that included the brigade commander.[53]

There were reports from aviators and from patrols of a place where the dense German wire thinned out. MacArthur made a command reconnaissance before most attacks. He had a habit of walking the battlefield by night, often alone, looking for weak spots in the enemy's defenses.[54] After organizing a night patrol to locate the reported thin spot in the wire, he went along with it. Crawling like insects over the darkened landscape, the patrol probed the German flanks. Suddenly the troops came under a fierce artillery barrage. Men rolled into shallow craters reeking of gas. When the barrage lifted, MacArthur slithered from shell hole to shell hole, whispering to each man to follow him; he would lead them back to the Rainbow's lines. He shook each soldier he spoke to, assuming that he, like him, was totally exhausted and, given a chance to lie down, had fallen asleep.

MacArthur gradually came to a horrifying realization: Each and every one was stone dead.

He alone had been spared. Why? It made no sense. To have survived this deluge of artillery fire without so much as a scratch had to be destiny. Or, for a devout Christian, God's will. He had been spared by the protection of the divine, the all-powerful; nothing less. No other explanation made sense. MacArthur crawled back to the 84th's lines humbled, awestruck, but exalted too. "It was God," he said. "He led me by the hand, the way he led Joshua."[55]

In the phantasmagorical light of bursting shells, MacArthur had glimpsed where the wire, normally twenty feet deep, thinned out to something that men with wire cutters could snip through fairly quickly. It wasn't much, but it could provide a way to outflank the enemy.

Next morning something rare happened in the Meuse-Argonne offensive. Instead of launching yet another futile frontal assault, American troops maneuvered. On October 16 MacArthur led most of his brigade forward under strong artillery and machine-gun support, to pin the Germans down on one flank, while a battalion of Iowa infantrymen, led by Major Lloyd D. Ross, worked their way around the other flank, got through the wire and hit the Germans from the rear.[56]

By nightfall the enemy position on the Romagne Heights was unraveling faster than MacArthur's sweater, as German troops, unnerved at being attacked from behind, surrendered freely or simply fled in the direction of Germany. The 42d drove nearly a mile beyond the enemy's main line of resistance before coming to an exhausted halt. MacArthur sent a message to Chaumont: "I have taken Hill 288." Then he fell into an exhausted, merciful sleep and did not awaken for sixteen hours.

Taking its objective had cost the Rainbow more than four thousand casualties—roughly one third of the division's riflemen at the beginning of the battle. In some of the infantry battalions of MacArthur's brigade losses in the space of three desperate days came to 80 percent; in effect, these battalions had been wiped out. Nonetheless the Kriemhilde Stellung had been breached. Nothing could now stop the First Army from reaching the Sedan-Mezières-Carignan railroad line.[57] The shattered, battered 42d remained on top of its prize, nursing its wounds, while the fighting moved on.

For MacArthur, there could hardly have been a greater success. The day after the Côte fell Pershing sent a telegram to the War Department recommending him to be promoted to major general.[58] Menoher was awed by what had happened on the Côte de Châtillon. He reported to Summerall that it was only "the indomitable resolution and ferocious courage of these two officers [MacArthur and Ross] in rallying their broken lines time and again, in re-forming the attack and leading their men that saved the day. Without them the German line would not have been broken. On a field where courage was the rule their heroism was the dominant feature. I regard their efforts as among the most remarkable of the war." He too urged MacArthur's promotion to major general and shortly after this put both MacArthur and Ross in for the DSC.[59]

MacArthur had equaled—in some ways excelled—his father's feat on Missionary Ridge. Yet the memory of it would haunt him for the rest of his life. He could never speak about the Côte de Châtillon without a fierce struggle to control his emotions.[60]

The 42d Division remained out of the line for two weeks, to rest, refit and receive replacements. On October 30 it moved out, to take part in the final push toward Sedan. The Meuse-Argonne offensive was close to its strategic goal. The British and French, meanwhile, were making huge advances in Flanders and Picardy. The German Army was in retreat along most of the Western Front.

On November 5, with Sedan almost in sight, MacArthur, making yet another reconnaissance, was briefly detained at gunpoint by troops of the 1st Division, who saw a strange figure in an English coat, a purple muffler more than six feet long, a parody of an American officer's cap and carrying a riding crop. He claimed to be an American officer, but they wanted to check him out first. Maybe he was a German spy. Fortunately a 1st Division officer who was nearby knew MacArthur and vouched for him. The story went around and gave everybody a good laugh. Everybody but MacArthur, that is. He never had much of a sense of humor when it came to himself and, whenever the story came up after the war, strenuously denied that he had ever been held for questioning, even briefly.[61]

That same day Pershing's chief of operations, Colonel George C. Marshall, wrote an order that began, "General Pershing desires that the honor of entering Sedan should fall to American troops." It concluded, "Boundaries will not be considered as binding."[62] The result was a land rush. Marshall's intention was to have American troops move into the area in front of the slowly advancing French Fourth Army. Instead the 1st Division cut across in front of the 84th Brigade, which MacArthur was pushing pell-mell toward Sedan.

In the midst of these developments, Menoher left the Rainbow to assume command of a corps. MacArthur got command of the division and his seventh Silver Star. He also had a problem to resolve with the French as well as with the Big Red One. The French were outraged by the American dash for Sedan. The city had a symbolic importance to French soldiers that few Americans understood. It had been the fall of Sedan to the Germans in 1870 that had brought France's defeat and the loss of Alsace-

Lorraine. The French hinted very strongly that if necessary, they would fire on American troops who tried to beat them into the city. Marshall's ill-advised message was soon withdrawn. At 11:00 A.M. on November 11, when the Armistice came into effect, the French were in Sedan and MacArthur was on the heights overlooking the city.

The AEF did some things well and more than a few things badly. One of the worst was its handling of decorations. They were handed out parsimoniously and slowly. Many soldiers had to wait for years to get their medals, something that took the shine off most of them. To some degree the fault lay with the War Department's glacial bureaucracy, but the grudging policy on medals was also a reflection of Pershing's attitude. He didn't believe in them. A soldier did his job, won the esteem of his fellows and the gratitude of his country, and that should be reward enough. It certainly was for him.

It was nowhere near enough, though, for thousands of soldiers, including MacArthur and Patton. Recommended for the DSC after being severely wounded in the posterior during the Meuse-Argonne offensive, Patton was half convinced he wouldn't get his medal, in which case he intended to resign from the Army.[63]

Despite his own beliefs, Pershing realized that a country that had sent two million men overseas and suffered a hundred thousand casualties needed heroes. He had every headquarters reexamine its DSC awards to see which of them could be upgraded to a Medal of Honor. Some 6,039 DSCs were awarded (out of 14,000 recommendations). The review of DSCs went on for years. One such review brought Eddie Rickenbacker a Medal of Honor as late as 1930. Pershing assigned a member of his staff to visit the divisions and advise them on what Chaumont was looking for.

When Pershing's directive reached the 42d Division, a board of Rainbow officers submitted a list of nine people, with MacArthur's name at the top. He was probably the only general in the AEF to be recommended for the Medal of Honor, yet he was also a fairly obvious choice, being one of only 111 people to hold the DSC with an oak leaf cluster. The officers who had drawn up the list stated categorically that of all nine Medal of Honor recommendations from the Rainbow, his performance on the Côte de Châtillon was the most outstanding feat of arms in the division's history. Pershing's adviser agreed with them.

The board's members were therefore incredulous and outraged when Pershing bluntly rejected this recommendation and granted the medal to six other people on the list. Pershing stated flatly that MacArthur had not met the standard of heroism required. That was simply absurd. There was hardly an officer in France who had shown greater valor or more effective combat leadership. The 42d Division protested vehemently against the decision, but in vain.[64]

Pershing had already shown that the reward he thought appropriate for MacArthur's heroic feat at the Côte de Châtillon was a promotion to major general. He was a miser, anyway, when it came to granting the Medal of Honor. It was Pershing who established the modern criteria for the Army's award of the medal, and they are far more demanding than those required by the Navy or Air Force. Only four—out of a total of ninety-five— Medals of Honor were approved by the AEF before the Armistice. Pershing's attitude was that if it went to anyone, it should go to the enlisted men and junior officers who did nearly all the fighting. It would hardly encourage ordinary soldiers to fight hard if they believed the top awards were handed out by generals to other generals. Besides, showing great courage and inspired leadership under fire was exactly what a general was expected to do.

And, finally, there was nothing in the report to show that MacArthur had killed anyone on the Côte de Châtillon. Pershing set a lot of store by infantry soldiering at its most intense and individualistic, where the warrior actually gets blood on his hands.[65]

To give MacArthur the medal would have tested Pershing to the limits of his simple faith. It is just possible that he might have relented had MacArthur been killed, but the living MacArthur stood no chance at all. Not one general officer in the AEF received the Medal of Honor, and when Newton Baker tried to make an exception and give one to Pershing, Black Jack flatly refused to consider it.[66]

Despite the assertions by some MacArthur biographers, such as Frazier Hunt, of a MacArthur-Pershing feud, there is no evidence of malice or pettiness in Pershing's refusal to grant MacArthur the Medal of Honor. He was, by his lights, acting on principle. The result was an injustice all the same. The entire 42d Division knew it, and so did MacArthur. He had to settle for other accolades instead. There were plenty to choose from. Nearly every officer or enlisted man who had any contact with him during World War I thought he was simply wonderful. They were fulsome in their praise. Typical was Newton Baker's judgment: "He was the greatest American field commander produced by the war."[67]

As for MacArthur's creation, the 42d Division, it had proved itself to be one of the finest units the Army sent to France. A critical study of the AEF published in 1992 examined the records of every division. Weighing up such factors as the number of days in combat, the amount of ground taken against enemy fire, the number of prisoners captured and decorations awarded, the Rainbow was the second most effective division in Pershing's command. Only the 2d Division, which was half Regular Army and half Marine Corps, did better.[68] MacArthur's creation, the easygoing Rainbow Division, could never compare with Pershing's creation, the 1st Division, when it came to saluting or organizing a ceremony. It was an abysmal failure in the spit-and-polish department. The Rainbows could not salute worth a damn and cared less what they looked like. The only thing they did superbly was fight.

8

Bon!

The 42d was among the nine American divisions assigned to occupation duty, and in December it deployed to the area around Coblenz. Most Rainbow soldiers were billeted in German homes. There was little friction between them and their dragooned hosts, and living in warm houses, sleeping in comfortable beds, eating food that had been properly cooked and not being shot at were blissful. Even so, like troops throughout the AEF, nearly all were counting the days until they were sent home and discharged.[1]

Less than two weeks after the Armistice, MacArthur had to give up command of the Rainbow to Major General Charles A. Flagler, his former battalion commander at Leavenworth. He might have held on to the division had his second star come through, but that wasn't going to happen. The day after the Armistice, March had put a block on promotions. There would be no more stars awarded while the War Department got to grips with demobilization. MacArthur returned to commanding the 84th Brigade.[2]

He was forced to spend much of the winter of 1918–19 in bed. Being gassed and spending long periods in the trenches had left MacArthur with a lifelong susceptibility to coughs, colds, influenza and infections of the throat and chest. He came down with throat ulcers in December 1918. In January he was felled by *la grippe*—the French term for flu. Then, in February, he had a bout of diphtheria.[3]

In the midst of these ailments, one of the country's best-known and most respected journalists, William Allen White of Emporia, Kansas, visited the division. White had met Arthur MacArthur several times but was unacquainted with the son. "I had never before met so vivid, so captivating, so magnetic a man," White recalled years later. "His staff adored him, his men worshipped him, and he seemed to be entirely without vanity. . . . He wore a ragged brown sweater and civilian pants—nothing more.

"He was greatly against the order prohibiting fraternization. He said the order only hurt the boys. In one little town of a thousand people, the boys had rigged up a Christmas tree in the town hall. They had dressed it beautifully and were solemnly having a stag dance, while outside looking in at the windows were two hundred girls. The General danced with a sergeant to show his good will. . . ." MacArthur was also, White thought, "much too handsome."[4]

By the time Pershing came to inspect the division, on March 16, 1919, MacArthur had thrown off the ills of winter. Never a believer in "eyewash," he spared his men as much of the spit-and-polish routine as he could. Pershing was once again appalled at the Rainbow's showing. "The matériel of the artillery and transportation had not been turned out and only the personnel of the units were there . . . [and] while the personnel of the 42nd Division was good, it did not compare with that of the three divisions [2d, 4th and 32d] which I have already inspected in the Third Army. The men were not so well set up physically and their clothing showed lack of proper care. . . . I learned also that the venereal rate in this division is higher than in any other combatant unit."[5]

During his visit, Pershing pinned the Distinguished Service Medal on MacArthur. This gave MacArthur an unusual distinction: He held both the DSC and the DSM, the highest decoration given to staff officers. There were a few others in the AEF who shared this double. Patton was one; William Donovan another.

Shortly after this MacArthur received another tribute, this time from General Gouraud. The U.S. military attaché in London, Lieutenant Colonel Samuel L. H. Slocum, was visiting France when he happened to meet Gouraud, who asked if he knew Douglas MacArthur. Slocum replied that he did indeed know MacArthur. Gouraud then said, "I consider General MacArthur to be one of the finest and bravest soldiers I have ever served with." Slocum was so moved by this encounter that he informed the Adjutant General and recommended that Gouraud's remark be entered in MacArthur's official record, his 201 File.[6]

In April 1919 the 42d received orders to head for Brest and St.-Nazaire. The division was going home. The men of the Fighting 69th paraded down Fifth Avenue and were given an ecstatic welcome home. That night the senior officers of the division were fêted at a ball in the Waldorf-Astoria. MacArthur stepped onto the dance floor with a young lady but did not progress far with his waltzing before an assistant manager rushed onto the floor and pointed accusingly at the general's spurs. "Sir," he protested, "you may not dance in spurs. You might injure the dance floor!"

MacArthur looked at him hard. "Do you know who I am?" Meaning, do you know I am the most highly decorated American soldier of the war?

The assistant manager replied, "Yes, sir. I do. But I must request you leave the dance floor and remove your spurs." MacArthur took his date by the arm and walked out of the hotel without another word, but swearing to himself never to set foot, spurred or unspurred, in the Waldorf again.[7]

Shortly after this, his father's old friend Peyton March summoned him to Washington and told him, "Douglas, things are in great confusion at West Point. The Academy is forty years behind the times." During the past winter March had tried to convince the Academic Board at West Point that reform was needed, but the board and the present superintendent had adamantly rejected March's ideas. The secretary of war, on the other hand, enthusiastically supported March.

"We want you to go up there and revitalize and revamp the academy. It has been too parochial in the past. I want to broaden it and graduate more cadets into the Army."

MacArthur was taken aback. "I'm not an educator. I'm a field soldier," he protested. "Besides, there are so many of my old professors there. I can't do it."

"You can do it," March reassured him. What he seems to have been counting on was MacArthur's youth, his idealism, his intelligence and his *lack* of teaching experience. MacArthur had no vested interest in defending old habits or ideas. Rather, he would be keen to learn what the newest ideas were and apply them . . . if he could.[8]

MacArthur would soon have realized too that in giving him this appointment, March was protecting something that interested both of them. These days wartime generals were being unceremoniously reduced to their permanent ranks almost every week—and MacArthur's permanent rank was major. March had given MacArthur his first star and was now making sure that Douglas held on to it.

When the United States declared war on Germany, 50 percent of the Regular Army's 5,000 officers were West Point graduates. By the time the war ended, West Pointers amounted to a mere 1.5 percent of the officer corps. All the same, they provided three fourths of the 480 generals. The academy's contribution to the war effort was immense, yet this unique institution was in danger of being destroyed. The officer shortage that afflicted the wartime Army was so acute that a sixty-nine-year-old retired colonel named Samuel E. Tillman had been recalled to active duty, given a star and installed as superintendent.

In the frantic push to create officers, West Point became little more than the forerunner of the modern Officers Candidate School. The class of 1918 was graduated in August 1917; the class of 1919, in June 1918; the classes of 1920 and 1921, in November 1918. A special plebe class that was exempted from the normal entrance requirements was enrolled that same month and graduated in June 1919.

The traditions on which the academy was built, the core of memory, habit and beliefs that was as granitic as the rock on which West Point is built, seemed in danger of being washed away. What continuity existed reposed mainly in the Academic Board, which consisted of the superintendent, the commandant of cadets and the heads of the departments of instruction. In these turbulent times the board more than ever felt itself the guardian of a sacred trust in defending West Point's traditional values and methods. Tillman's parting shot as he handed West Point over to MacArthur was a statement that "the Academic Board's influence should not be diminished or its conclusions disregarded."[9]

MacArthur looked like no general the members of the Academic Board had ever seen or imagined. For one thing, he was amazingly young, at thirty-nine, to be superintendent. He was the second youngest since Sylvanus Thayer. Only Colonel Thomas H. Ruger, a Civil War hero who had been appointed supe in 1871 at the age of thirty-eight, had been younger. They knew MacArthur had returned from France with more gallantry awards than any other soldier in the AEF, yet he did not wear a single ribbon on his chest. He dressed in a short overcoat and faded puttees that were lashed to his skinny shanks by curling, war-weary leather straps. He carried a riding crop, and when cadets saluted him, with the usual solemnity of cadets, he replied with a nonchalant elevation of the riding crop to the peak of his shapeless, grommetless cap. As he walked, MacArthur tilted his head back; that gave him the excellent posture that led people to describe him as being six feet tall, although he stood little more than five feet ten inches. The angle of his head raised his nose to an arrogant plane that seemed to bring his gaze to the permanent contemplation of distant horizons.[10]

In discussions with his staff, MacArthur expressed his approval with an emphatic *"Bon!"* He treated staff members like his family, never scolding, never rebuking, looking to them for emotional support as well as the execution of his directives. He sat on the desk of his adjutant William Ganoe while talking to him—a typical MacArthur trait. The hallmark of the MacArthur style was high seriousness of purpose combined with a studied informality of manner.

He believed he had a mission in life, and the summons to West Point was no more than partial fulfillment of what amounted to a high calling.

The sense of mission was not limited, unlike that of most soldiers, whose creed is the romantic call of duty, sacrifice, personal honor. Gifted, and at times cursed, with the imagination of an artist and the temperament of an intellectual, he was a paradox even to those who worked most closely with him. "A complete contradiction," said a baffled Ganoe. "He commanded without commanding. He was both a patrician and a plebeian."[11]

MacArthur spent little time in his office. He arrived there around 11:00 each morning and dealt with his mail. Between noon and 1:00 P.M. he held a meeting with his staff and saw members of the various departments. He took a two-hour lunch break, which permitted him to nap. Then he returned to his office for another two hours and went home to mother at 5:00 P.M. At least once a week he had an evening meeting with the Academic Board.

He made it clear to his staff that he considered most paperwork unnecessary. After MacArthur had replied to a letter, he was likely to throw it away. A report might go through several drafts, but only the final version was saved; the rest went into the garbage. On one occasion, when illness kept him in bed for a few days, MacArthur called an officer and told him to bring over any papers that needed his signature. He had a clear idea of what he wanted. "Bring over the papers that are going to win or lose the next war," said MacArthur. "You sign the others."[12]

MacArthur was forever trying to penetrate the surface of things, to seek out a premise on which he could base or justify his actions. Tradition, habits and convention meant little to him. On the contrary, he loved to challenge them. "Fudge the regulations," he would say. "They're sometimes made to be broken for the good of the whole."[13]

When he turned his powerful mind to what was wrong with West Point, he decided March was right. It needed major surgery. "My assumption of the command of the United States Military Academy synchronized with the ending of an epoch in the life of this Institution," he reported at the end of his first year as superintendent. In private, he called conditions at West Point "chaotic."[14]

West Point had been founded on the assumption that future wars would be fought largely by small, professional armies, led by officers who relied on rigid discipline and brutal punishments to control men in battle. Its role was to produce officers capable of leading such armies. That limited view of its function had survived despite the Civil War, which had half the United States fighting the other half. MacArthur was determined that it would not also survive World War I.

Wars in the twentieth century were going to be titanic struggles, and the armies that modern nations fielded were not going to be composed of professional soldiers. As in the war just ended, these armies would consist of amateurs, of fresh-faced young men torn from factory and farm, classroom and office. What's more, many of them were, in MacArthur's experience, intelligent and quick-witted. They bore no resemblance to the traditional cannon fodder of professional armies for centuries past. The old, brutal methods of leadership would not work with them or be accepted by a modern society. A new kind of officer was needed, "a type possessing all the cardinal military virtues of yore, but possessing an intimate understanding of the mechanics of human feelings, a comprehensive grasp of world and national affairs and a liberalization of conception which amounts to a change in his psychology of command."[15]

Obvious as such conclusions seemed to him, to March, to Baker, they were anathema to the twelve-man Academic Board, which saw nothing fundamentally wrong with West Point. Drawn almost entirely from senior faculty members, the board was a powerful obstacle. MacArthur had only one vote on it and only two allies: the youthful commandant of cadets, Colonel Robert M. Danford, a wartime brigadier general whom he had known when they were cadets together, and the head of the English department, Colonel Lucius Holt, the only faculty member with a Ph.D. and by reputation the best teacher at the academy.[16]

Some board members openly showed their disdain when MacArthur arrived in 1919. One elderly professor constantly interrupted him during one of his first board meetings, until MacArthur's patience ran out. He slapped the table in front of him. "Sit down, sir!" said MacArthur. "I'm talking!" The man sat down, red in the face. Board members treated him with more respect after that, but they never really relented in their opposition to MacArthur and his reforming zeal.[17]

Until now the superintendent had usually seen his role as implementing the board's policies. Here was MacArthur, demanding that they implement his. No politician, and not much of a diplomat, he stood little chance of getting the board's cooperation in this lurch into the unknown. The members of the board were not the dim-witted, obstinate fools he sometimes liked to portray. He put them down daily, indirectly insulted their intelligence and told everyone who was half willing to listen how much he despised them. In the small, closed world of a college setting, almost everything he said would have gotten back to them. They were realists, though, and the fact that he was backed by the Chief of Staff and the secretary of war forced them to moderate their opposition no matter how much they resented his youth, his informality and his impatience. Both sides needed to find common ground.

MacArthur, unable to get root-and-branch reform, settled for a wide range of incremental changes that ultimately paved the way for other, future superintendents with reform on their minds. Study of the Civil War ended; study of the World War was introduced in its place. The internal-combustion engine entered the curriculum for the first time. The use of slide rules was finally permitted. There would be less teaching of topography and more instruction in French. A history department would be created, under Colonel Holt, who had written several books on European history as well as a textbook on English poets. The one new course MacArthur got the board to accept combined the study of government with that of economics. This was its sole concession to the rise of social sciences, the great academic growth industry of the twenties.

Instructors would still, as in the past, be drawn almost entirely from recent graduates of the academy, but MacArthur demanded that every instructor spend a month each year at a civilian college or university, studying modern teaching methods. Educational reform was not limited to the classroom. MacArthur was determined to lower the walls between West Point and the world beyond the Plain. Every cadet was now expected to read a daily newspaper as part of the English course. Cadets also got five dollars of their monthly pay of fifty dollars in cash, to spend how they pleased. Formerly cadets never handled cash until they left the academy. Upperclassmen, moreover, were given leaves that allowed them the chance to spend occasional days in New York City. And to improve their ability to express themselves, cadets were required to write poetry.

Having learned to dance while young, MacArthur believed firmly in dancing as an essential part of an officer's training. All cadets were required to learn how to waltz and do the two-step. Faculty wives and daughters served as female partners, and MacArthur hired a professional dancing instructor. "Dancing is one of the accomplishments no man should fail to possess," he pronounced, but he admitted that even he found the proliferation of new dances a challenge. At weekends august Cullum Hall shook with the sounds of jazz bands pounding out "Yes, We Have No Bananas" and other popular hits, while flappers in cloche hats showed bemused cadets how to do the camel walk and the toddle.[18]

Summer camp, a largely social event, was abolished. This annual treat for the faculty was a reenactment of a military encampment around the time of the War of 1812. It involved much formality, fancy dress, white wigs, white gloves, evening hops and a lot of fife-and-drum music. He got rid of all that. He even had the site of the summer camp razed, as if it bred pestilence. Cadets under MacArthur were sent to Camp Dix, New Jersey, for basic infantry training under Regular Army instructors each summer to become real soldiers, not ornamental figures.

For all the new emphasis on the practical and the modern, MacArthur did not tamper with West Point's belief in leadership. What he did do was to allow the cadets to rate one another on their ability to lead other men.

These ratings were no longer the exclusive province of the tacs. It was leadership, which is an expression of a person's character, not something acquired from a book, that justified the existence of West Point. That was the one point on which MacArthur and even his most disgruntled critics on the Academic Board agreed.

He had arrived at West Point in June 1919 determined to maintain the image he had of himself as a field soldier. He was not going to be seduced by the ease of a superintendent's life. West Point provided him with a big house, a good salary, a staff of servants and dinner on gold plates. The luxuriousness of his present surroundings jarred painfully with the memory of what he and his men had endured in France. So he had an Army cot set up in the basement. And there he shivered some nights, wrapped in a couple of blankets.

After a while, however, the charm of enforced hardship faded. And one day he had some New York sportswriters to lunch. They dined on the gold plates and were much impressed. He showed them the cot in the basement. They were even more impressed. A week or so later the cook reported a gold plate was missing. The supe's quarters were turned upside down. No gold plate. MacArthur wrote to the sportswriters, the last people to dine with him, to see if they could cast light on the mystery. One of them mischievously replied that if MacArthur had slept in the basement several times a week, as he claimed, he would have found the missing plate. It was between the two blankets piled on the cot, where the writer had hidden it.[19]

When MacArthur became superintendent, the Corps of Cadets was a motley bunch. Some were not even dressed in cadet gray but in regulation GI uniforms, an outward and visible symbol of an institution that had lost its way. Tradition lingered chiefly in hazing and in discipline. Hazing had recently cost one cadet his life. On New Year's Day 1919 Cadet Stephen M. Bird, hazed unmercifully by upperclassmen for writing poetry, had killed himself.[20]

Discipline was of the same mind-bogglingly petty variety common when MacArthur had been a cadet. There were strict rules on the consumption of tobacco, for example. The one brand of tobacco on sale in the cadet canteen was Bull Durham, suitable only for making cigarettes, but cigarettes were outlawed. Students had to smoke their Bull Durham in pipes and only in their rooms at designated hours.[21]

Never much concerned for spit and polish, MacArthur allowed the standards of appearance to drop. One old grad, Colonel Conrad S. Babcock, visiting his son was shocked. The bugle and drum corps, a band of approximately twenty enlisted men who provided music at the academy and marched the cadets to their meals, was "the worst looking collection of soldiers I had seen." During Babcock's own days as a cadet the bugle and drum corps had been "almost as snappy as the Corps of Cadets." It was exactly the kind of thing that MacArthur did not care about, and old grads did.[22]

One of the first things MacArthur did was tackle the hazing scandal. He still felt bitter about his own experience. "I was hazed more brutally than some members of my class," he told his adjutant, Major Ganoe. "The animosity engendered in me against some of the hazers, who seemed to delight in being cruel, can never be erased. It's a sad result for them and me."[23]

He had a group of upperclassmen meet with him to talk about hazing. He shook hands with each one instead of saluting, offered them cigarettes and patted them on the arm. Most were charmed, but at least one thought it all an obvious act and doubted the new supe's sincerity.[24] MacArthur asked the upperclassmen to act as a committee and draw up a code of conduct that would curb hazing.

Soon after he arrived, he was persuaded, with deep reluctance, to allow a cadet newspaper to be published. There were student newspapers at many of the better colleges those days. It seemed a liberal thing to do, and it was bound to be popular with the cadets, so he went along with it. A weekly paper, called *The Bray,* was soon in operation, but after only a few issues it ran a letter that criticized MacArthur for his policy on hazing.

Nothing affected MacArthur like being attacked in print. He was highly strung and overly sensitive, and the least criticism stung and burned like a bullwhip's lash, doubly so when it was inflicted publicly. His troublesome pride, his prickly self-esteem, seemed to burst in an outpouring of rage and unassuageable pain. *The Bray* had hardly been distributed before tactical officers were out seizing every copy they could find. The confiscated papers were burned, *The Bray* was put out of business and MacArthur had Major Archibald V. Arnold, the officer assigned to censor *The Bray,* immediately reassigned to a post far from West Point.[25]

Meanwhile the antihazing committee was at work producing a pamphlet that condemned such dangerous practices as forcing plebes to do splits over naked bayonets. It also outlawed fistfights. Lesser forms of hazing were still permitted, if only by implication. The new code was adopted and, to a considerable degree, implemented, but MacArthur still wasn't satisfied. The committee had not gone far enough. Unable to get his way by persuasion, he shut down Beast Barracks. Tactical officers assumed complete responsibility for the plebe's first three weeks as a cadet.

MacArthur decided to build on what the First Class Committee had done by having the cadets form an Honor Committee, one that would formalize the existing honor code and enforce it. The code, which banned lying, cheating and stealing, dated back a century, to Sylvanus Thayer. Until now it had been enforced by the tacs. MacArthur put it firmly in the hands of the most outstanding cadets in each class. He and Danford also tackled the pettiness that passed for discipline. They got rid of much of it, which was better for both the cadets and the tacs, even if it did nothing for the blood pressure of most Academic Board members.

MacArthur was never truly popular with the Corps of Cadets, mainly because he took such a strong line on hazing. Cadets still tended to think hazing was a legitimate way of weeding out those young men unfit to become officers. MacArthur probably regretted his unpopularity, but he wasn't at West Point to be liked. He was there to help get these men ready for the next war. One day three cadets came to him and protested that they were being unjustly punished. The tacs had inflicted on them three months' confinement to their rooms and a huge number of punishment tours (which consisted of walking stiffly for hours in a small area wearing full-dress uniform and carrying a rifle) for an offense they swore they had not committed. They demanded a court-martial to establish the truth of the matter, which they were certain would prove their innocence.

MacArthur's response was "War with Japan is inevitable." He proceeded to explain why. And when it came, he went on to tell them, the United States was going to need all the professionally trained officers it could find. How well West Point fulfilled its mission in producing able officers was likely to determine the outcome of the war. The three cadets thanked him for his time and walked their punishment tours without another word of complaint.[26]

Part of the MacArthur mystery was his aloofness. At times he seemed to cultivate distance as a way of adding to the personal legend he was creating, and distance lends enchantment . . . sometimes. It can also be misunderstood. Many of the officers at West Point were baffled and irritated by his aloofness. His lack of sociability seemed a form of snobbery, as if no one were good enough to mix with him.

He chose to live as his father had done. Arthur MacArthur had not mixed with his brother officers. He had chosen, instead, to spend his free time on reading and thinking, not on bourbon, poker and small talk. The son, like the father, had no casual conversation in him. Despite his artistic temperament and his intellectual abilities, Douglas MacArthur's hinterland was broad, so far as intellectual interests went, but in other respects it was narrow. He had no love of or interest in art or literature, in science or technology, in economics or philosophy. His interest in books was limited to works of nonfiction that might help him in his career. He was a military Mr. Gradgrind. He liked to ride horses, and he played a good game of tennis, but these activities were utilitarian: They helped him keep fit. His sole diversion was football.

MacArthur had arrived at West Point as a cadet with a passionate love of the game but was too light to play it at the college level. When he returned as superintendent, he brought that same passion with him, along with an insight into why it mattered: He had found the first principle, the underlying reality. When he was deeply moved by what he was saying, MacArthur tended to pace his office floor and address the wall. On one occasion he revealed to Ganoe why he felt football was vital to the education of cadets.

"Over there," he intoned in his mellifluous, stage actor's voice, "I became convinced that the men who had taken part in organized sports made the best soldiers. They were the most dependable, hardy, courageous officers I had. Men who had contended physically against other human beings under rules of a game were the readiest to accept and enforce discipline. They were outstanding. . . . I propose, therefore, to obtain for the Academy athletes, those who have had bodily contact, especially football."[27]

One fall day in 1920, when he was watching the football team practice, MacArthur went over to Coach Charles Daly and said he had an idea for a pass play. The players crowded around, and MacArthur told them to line up as they normally did, only he would take the position of the right end. He took five long strides down the field, turned to the left and took another fifteen strides, stopped and carved an X in the turf with his right heel. "This spot is where the pass should be thrown to."

The players looked in bemusement at one another, cast despairing glances at Coach Daly and stared at the X in disbelief. The supe was talking through his hat. Anybody who knew the first thing about football knew you threw to the runner, not to some stupid spot. And it is true, that was what everybody knew back then. Half a century later, of course, the ball was often thrown to the spot, not to the man.[28]

One night in the spring of 1922, when the baseball team unexpectedly defeated a powerful Navy nine, the cadets paraded around the Plain at midnight in their pajamas. Half a dozen or so were beating drums. The cadets bawled West Point fight songs, yelled their class yells and built a huge bonfire on the edge of the Plain. The tacs were noticeable by their absence.

Next morning a grim-faced MacArthur summoned the commandant, Robert Danford, to his office. "Well, that was quite a party last night," said MacArthur.

All Danford dared do was agree with him. "Yes, sir. Quite a party."

MacArthur thought for a moment. "How many of them did you skin?" Meaning, how many have been punished?

Danford could not contain himself any longer. "Not a damn one!" he declared, bracing himself for a dressing-down.

MacArthur slapped his desk hard. "Good!" he responded. The two men stared at each other for a moment. "You, know, Com," said MacArthur, "I could hardly resist the impulse to get out there with them."

"Me neither," said Danford.[29]

During MacArthur's tenure as superintendent the football team was good only against weak teams. And like any big-league owner, he knew what to do to make his team better: get a new coach. He hoped to get rid of Daly, but only if he could replace him with somebody better. The man he had in mind was a young coach who had just been hired by Notre Dame, named Knute Rockne. To MacArthur's disappointment, Rockne chose to stay on at Notre Dame and see what he could do for *that* school's mediocre football team.[30]

MacArthur showed up at nearly every practice session for the academy's baseball and football teams. One day when a young athlete named Earl Blaik confessed he had trouble hitting a curveball, MacArthur stripped off his blouse and showed him how it was done. Besides attending the practice sessions, MacArthur, fascinated by every aspect of the game, spent hours talking football with the coaching staff. He sought vicariously the only prize that had eluded him as a cadet, gridiron glory.[31]

He had ambitious plans to rebuild West Point. Many of its buildings were cramped, gloomy and unsuitable for either instruction or accommodation. During the war, he grumbled to Danford, the Army had spent billions, but the War Department must have been in a trance—"Not one penny came to West Point."[32] The 1920s saw huge football stadiums spring up at many of the country's best colleges and universities, and part of MacArthur's building plan called for a fifty-thousand-seat football stadium. To his intense disappointment, and that of countless Army football fans, he did not get it.

MacArthur's lasting athletic monument at West Point was not a stadium but the creation of a system of intramural athletics. When he become supe, the academy competed in just three sports: football, baseball and basketball. What he wanted was to increase the range of competitive sports to seventeen and require that every cadet would have to participate in at least one of them. The present system of physical training was run by the master of the sword, Lieutenant Colonel Herman Koehler, and it was outmoded. Such athletic competitions as existed were voluntary. A national gymnastics champion in his youth, Koehler was "a Teuton of commanding presence, impressive physique and wonderful grace of movement." This stentor possessed a voice so powerful he could bark, "Hong Kong!" and be heard two miles away. Koehler was one of the most admired officers at the academy, but the physical education program that he ran consisted mainly of calisthenics and bored most cadets rigid.[33]

MacArthur succeeded in selling mandatory, intramural athletics to Koehler. He was aided and abetted too by the academy's chaplain, Clayton Wheat, who was himself an enthusiastic sports fan. For a century Sunday observance had been sacrosanct at West Point. Nothing happened on a Sunday that was not connected in some way with hymns and prayers. Many a chaplain would have resisted MacArthur's plans, but Wheat supported the idea of intramural athletics on Sunday afternoons with a zeal that matched the superintendent's own.

The Academic Board grumbled, and cadets moaned about "intermurder," but the program was well established by 1922. MacArthur memorialized his creed, and his contribution, by having two lines of blank verse that he had composed chiseled over the entrance to the gymnasium:

> On the fields of friendly strife are sown the seeds that
> Upon other fields and other days will bear the fruits of victory.[34]

In September 1921 a party of Army officers drove up to West Point for the day and took some female friends from New York with them. One of them, a divorcée named Louise Cromwell Brooks, was introduced to MacArthur. The world seemed to open up at his feet, and he fell into the abyss like a bird shot from a tree. He was instantly, hopelessly, totally infatuated with this short, moon-faced thirty-one-year-old who had lustrous brown eyes and a vivacious manner.[35]

Louise Brooks was one of the world's richest heiresses, but that was not the secret of the spell she cast. No, Louise would have bewitched him if she had been working behind a counter at Macy's. She was one of those women who are more than the sum of their parts, which, taken individually, don't seem anything special. She was no great beauty and not particularly bright. What Louise had, though, was a power that other women might envy even more than her money: She simply radiated sexual excitement. MacArthur had known many women in his forty-one years, but never one who exerted such a spell or aroused him so.

Louise's father, Oliver E. Cromwell, was a millionaire businessman who claimed direct descent from England's lord protector, Oliver Cromwell. Her stepfather, Edward T. Stotesbury, was a J. P. Morgan partner and one of the richest men in the world. His fortune was estimated at $150 million, making him the equivalent of a 1990s billionaire.

Lively, wayward and completely spoiled, Louise had married a Baltimore businessman, Walter J. Brooks II, back in 1911. Brooks was reputedly a pompous, self-important character. Louise, who had no intention of living in any man's shadow, belittled him in public.[36] All the same, she did her wifely duty and bore him two children—Walter III and Louise II.

The superrich and dynastically pretentious Brookses had homes in various fashionable places, and after the United States had entered the World War, they used their Paris apartment to entertain American officers of the right class and rank. Louise thereby met Pershing. Black Jack was the Army's most notorious swordsman, and it was inevitable that once these two magnets came within range of their force fields they would end up in bed together. When the shooting stopped, Louise gave Pershing a simple choice: Marry her or no more fun in bed. Pershing was by this time tiring of Louise. He had recently started an affair with a twenty-year-old Romanian girl who had asked if she could paint his portrait. He was ready to move on, and his response to Louise's crude attempt at sexual blackmail was a brutal put-down. "Louise," he told her, "marrying you would be like buying a book for somebody else to read." Then he walked out of her boudoir for good.[37]

She soon rebounded from the collapse of the affair with Pershing, but Black Jack had given her a taste for men in uniform. She seduced Britain's glamorous, famous and handsome young admiral Sir David Beatty and helped bring his marriage to an end.[38] She also dated a British brigadier, results unknown. For a time she allowed herself to be squired around Washington by Senator Walter E. Edge of New Jersey, but if he was a typical senator, he was probably as boring and self-important as Walter Brooks, from whom she had decided to get a divorce. Marriage was cramping her style.

After Pershing's return to the United States, he and Louise apparently decided to be friends, now their days as lovers were over. He was trying to get himself the Republican presidential nomination, and being a widower, he needed a hostess. Louise volunteered to help him out, for old times' sake. To keep herself amused, she also started dating Pershing's handsome aide and captain of the Army polo team, Colonel John G. Quekemeyer. The colonel, who was thirty-eight and, much like MacArthur, had never married and was still living with his mother, was completely smitten. Quekemeyer hoped to marry her, and Louise had not tried to dissuade him. So far as Pershing was concerned, the two of them were practically engaged, and he was delighted, because he looked on "Queck" as being almost a son. It may seem strange that he would be happy to see his protégé marry his former mistress, but among the sophisticated such developments are not unknown. Besides, Louise was rich.

It was at this point that she met MacArthur. She felt as strongly attracted to him as he did to her and invited him to come and visit her in New York, where she had a huge suite at the Ritz-Carlton. MacArthur was too busy wrangling with the Academic Board to get away, but he invited her to come back to West Point for the first football game of the season, against Yale, several weeks later.

Army lost to Yale, but for once MacArthur's mind wasn't on the game; it was only on Louise. When the final whistle blew, he proposed marriage, and Louise instantly accepted his proposal. For both of them, their first meeting had been "love at first sight." Given the course and ultimate fate of their marriage, however, it seems clear that what really had happened was something most people would recognize as overwhelming, irresistible lust. Had they been prepared to acknowledge to themselves what aroused them so furiously, they could have had an affair. Huge egotists that both were, they concocted a thrilling fable for their passions and placed themselves far above what mere mortals know. MacArthur and Louise convinced themselves that theirs was one of the greatest love stories of all time and had to be part of the mysterious workings of fate.

Louise returned to New York after the game, leaving MacArthur both ecstatic and stunned.[39] Over the next few months he wrote to her several times each week, telling her constantly that compared to her, nothing else seemed to matter much any longer.[40]

Pinky has always been portrayed as disapproving of Louise. In fact, Pinky took a liking to her from the start, despite Louise's divorced state and two small children. Perhaps Louise's fabulous wealth exerted a charm all its own. "She says to tell you," MacArthur wrote Louise, "that she keeps your room ready at all times and the door is on the latch," so Louise could come and go as she pleased. Even so, Louise was at first wary of MacArthur's mother. Would she really welcome the idea of her adored son marrying a divorced woman? MacArthur reassured her: "Mother loves you dearly. . . ."[41]

Having decided to get married, they could not yet set a date for the ceremony. Louise wanted to wait until Walter Brooks had made a financial settlement that secured the future of little Louise and little Walter. Her divorce had come through a year earlier, but negotiations over trust funds for the children were protracted. In the meantime MacArthur remained in a reverie. "Was ever such a romance in all this world before!" he wrote to Louise. "Some great destiny is involved in our union. . . ."[42]

In late November 1921 Pinky had a heart attack. She was rushed to New York for surgery but remained desperately ill for ten days and was not expected to survive. Her attending physician, Dr. Norman Scott, remained close to her hospital bed throughout this time. On each of those ten days Mrs. Scott received a dozen long-stemmed American Beauty roses from MacArthur, with a note expressing his gratitude that Dr. Scott was devoting so much time to Pinky and saying how much he appreciated the sacrifice this entailed for the doctor, his wife and their son.[43]

By the time Pinky pulled through it was January 1922. The financial settlement had finally been agreed on for Louise's children. MacArthur and

Louise decided to marry on Valentine's Day, February 14, at her mother's seafront mansion in Palm Beach. Pinky was still too weak to travel, but she told journalists the wedding of Douglas and Louise "will be lovely." Among her gifts to Louise was one of her most precious possessions—the scrapbook that she had kept for years of newspaper and magazine cuttings about Douglas. It was for Louise to look after now.[44]

For the wedding MacArthur wore white and Louise wore apricot. The ceremony was held in the salon, which was decorated with the flags of West Point and the Rainbow Division. There were red, white and blue ribbons and an improvised altar heaped with flowers and palms. Chaplain Clayton Wheat conducted the ceremony, and Louise's brother, Jimmy Cromwell, dressed in his uniform as a Marine captain, was her best man. The wedding was immortalized in a newspaper headline that read MARS MARRIES MILLIONS.[45]

The morning after the wedding a blissful Louise appeared for breakfast, declaring rapturously to Jimmy Cromwell, "He may be a general in the Army, but he's a buck private in the boudoir." This has usually been interpreted as a put-down when in fact it was exactly the opposite. It was, thought her brother, "the finest compliment he had ever heard a woman pay to a man." MacArthur evidently made love with the directness and unrestrained enthusiasm of the lower orders.[46]

The path to the altar had not been entirely smooth, however. Pershing was angry. William Manchester claims MacArthur had "stolen his girl" when he had done nothing of the kind. Pershing's love interest those days was his Romanian mistress, Michelline Resco.[47] What outraged him was the way Louise had dumped Quekemeyer. He tried to talk Louise into changing her mind but failed.

In November 1921, only days after Louise broke her unofficial, unannounced engagement to Quekemeyer, Pershing wrote to MacArthur "to advise you that at the end of the present school year you will be available for a tour of service beyond the limits of the United States."[48] Although there was no fixed term for a superintendent's tenure, MacArthur's predecessors had usually had roughly four years in this assignment. He had been assured when he accepted the assignment that he would remain at the academy for four years. Pershing had instituted a rule on overseas service that looked as if it were written with one person in mind: MacArthur. No officer had ever been sent abroad under this rule until now. And if MacArthur did go abroad, it would almost certainly be to either Panama or the Philippines, neither one of which was going to have much appeal to Louise, who much preferred life on the New York–Paris axis to whatever charms hot, disease-ridden and impoverished countries had to offer. What Pershing intended, MacArthur told Louise, was to make her feel "intimidated and frightened into regretting that you engaged to marry me."[49]

Protest, however, achieved nothing. MacArthur was heading for the Philippines, and his new bride would be going with him. He reconciled himself to the prospect with the thought that he had changed his alma mater forever, that his reforms had struck such deep roots nothing would be the same again. "On the ashes of Old West Point I have built a New West Point—strong, virile and enduring."[50]

MacArthur's assignment as superintendent ended on June 30, 1922. Next day Pershing wrote MacArthur's efficiency report. He rated him merely "above average" on his performance at West Point and for knowledge of his profession. In the Army, "above average" means mediocre. Of the forty-six brigadier generals in the Army, Pershing rated MacArthur thirty-eighth. Such a rating was hardly credible. Most of the thirty-six brigadiers Pershing rated higher were obscure paper shufflers who would be retired in the next few years, unheralded and unmissed. Pershing conceded that MacArthur was "A very able young officer with a fine war record for courage," but that did not seem to count for much in Pershing's present state of mind. He had once recommended MacArthur to be a major general and had protested to the War Department when MacArthur was denied a second star. Yet now, he said, MacArthur did not deserve promotion to major general. Pershing concluded with the kind of personal remark that hardly ever appears in efficiency reports: "Has an exalted opinion of himself." It would be impossible to deny the truth of this observation, but for it to appear in an official document is remarkable. It only shows how angry Pershing still was over what his former mistress had done to his favorite aide. He might have consoled himself with the thought, however, that as virtually every man whom Louise had so far gotten involved with ended up regretting it, MacArthur stood little chance of avoiding the same melancholy fate.[51]

9

Americans Don't Quit

The arrival of an Army transport in Manila was always a colorful, exciting event. The Philippine Constabulary band was at dockside, playing a medley of patriotic airs, martial tunes and popular songs of the day. Scores of beribboned officers crowded the quayside to welcome the newcomers and meet up with old friends. Dozens of officers' wives gathered, swathed in white muslin and cool white duck. There were screaming Filipino laundry-men, the *lavanderes,* jostling one another in noisy competition to sign up new customers. Big black carabao, the hairless water buffalo of Southeast Asia, stood placidly between the shafts of huge carts, endlessly chewing their cud. Dozens of Filipino taxis—small carriages called *calesas*—drawn by sturdy, pint-size ponies, provided daubs of red and gold, vivid blue and brilliant green to the hectic scene, while mango sellers and papaya hawkers held up their wares and cried the merits of fresh fruit. And everywhere, embracing everyone like a steaming cloak, was the heat—stunning, ener-vating, inescapable. Arrival at the Manila dock was grand opera in a Turk-ish bath.

Ships from the United States did not come in every day. The transport *Logan,* on which the MacArthurs sailed in September 1922, made this voyage only four times a year. It took a month to sail from San Francisco to Manila and another month to sail back.

More than a hundred officers and about forty Army wives were aboard the *Logan* with the MacArthurs and Louise's children, Walter and Louise. Sixteen of the officers were newlyweds, accompanied by their brides. Louise managed to alienate them and nearly all her other fellow passengers before the ship even set sail. When the *Logan* took on baggage in San Francisco, the MacArthurs' luggage went aboard first. After all, the general was the highest-ranking officer on this sailing. Louise filled the baggage hold with so many trunks, hatboxes and suitcases that no one else could take more than one trunk. The MacArthurs also put several cars aboard ship, taking up all the space available for automobiles, leaving no room for anyone else to take a car.[1]

The longueurs of life aboard ship on an extended voyage are usually relieved by an endless round of social events, but given this spoiled brat beginning, Louise probably had a pretty lonely voyage. As for MacArthur, he remained as aloof at sea as he did on dry land. The other officers aboard had little contact with him.[2]

Many officers and their wives loved assignment to the Philippines. The work was not particularly demanding, there were opportunities to travel, docile English-speaking servants could be hired for a pittance and there was a busy social scene. The MacArthurs, on the other hand, seethed at this posting.

There was no assignment open in the Philippines for a one-star general. That only advertised to the entire Army that Pershing had, in effect, fired MacArthur from West Point. The Philippine Department tried to create a slot for him by establishing a phantom command called the Military District of Manila. As there were only five hundred American troops assigned to the city, it was not a post for a general.[3] The duties that went with the new Military District were so footling they could only bore or irritate him. MacArthur ran the departmental rifle competition, for example, a job that could as well have been be done by a lieutenant.[4]

His new posting was not without its compensations, however. The Spanish had built a large wall around the old city in the seventeenth century. In places the wall, called the Intramuros, was up to fifty feet thick, and on top of one stretch of it stood a picturesque building known as 1 Calle Victoria, formerly the headquarters of the Philippine Constabulary. There was a charming small garden to be enjoyed and wonderful views of the city on one side, while the blue expanse of Manila Bay shimmered on the other. One of MacArthur's West Point classmates at departmental headquarters, Major Robert C. Richardson, arranged to have "the House on the Wall" turned over to him.[5]

MacArthur seemed to delight too in his stepchildren, especially young Walter. He had ample free time to teach the youngster to ride, and the two of them seem to have become fairly close.[6] Louise, meanwhile, continued to antagonize the other Army wives. There was, for example, the lace imbroglio. French nuns ran a convent which took in abandoned baby girls and trained them to be lacemakers. The convent girls produced lace that was considered the finest souvenir an Army wife could bring back from the Philippines. Louise, unlike the others, didn't want some of it; she wanted all of it. Shortly after arriving in Manila, she contracted for the entire output for the next two years.

Whatever she did, she did in her own way. Besides hiring several female servants, she employed five young male Filipinos and dressed them in livery. They wore navy blue uniforms, with a bright red "MacA" on the breast surrounded by a large red circle, and black chauffeurs' caps. They seemed almost like soldiers, carrying themselves with a grave, straight-backed military air.[7]

It was probably inevitable that Louise, lacking friends or, so far as one can tell, any interest in other women, became lonely and bored. She involved herself in some of the charitable activities that were common to women of her class, but these don't seem to have provided much satisfaction. She was not one of nature's social workers. Seeking to relieve the old ennui, she got herself into uniform and became a part-time policewoman and made at least one arrest. She collared a miscreant who was maltreating a horse.[8]

Louise also occupied herself by redecorating the House on the Wall in what probably seemed to her the height of modernity. She painted all the interior walls black and had expensive silver ornaments hanging from them.[9]

The MacArthurs rented a small house on the beach at Pasay, about ten miles from Manila, where they could spend the weekends together. They did little socializing, apart from going to dinner every couple of months or so with the governor-general, MacArthur's former mentor and old friend Leonard Wood. Louise complained bitterly to Wood about the way Pershing had banished MacArthur from a job he loved and sent him into the wilderness, wasting his talents and blighting his prospects. Wood agreed it was all terrifically unjust, but there was nothing he could do about it.[10]

The tedious business of living in Manila was relieved for Louise by a sudden return to the United States in early 1923, after Pinky fell seriously ill. MacArthur, Louise and the children returned half expecting she would not pull through, but the old lady survived yet again.

MacArthur took advantage of his return to seek another assignment. Neither he nor Louise—especially not Louise—wanted to go back to Manila. MacArthur personally took up his case with the secretary of war, John Weeks, who was sympathetic but not about to have a clash with Pershing, whom he respected immensely. All the same, he did not want the Army to lose MacArthur. He assured him his time would come. In the meantime, he said, "Don't ever be tempted to leave the service."[11]

Having failed to get Weeks to intervene and end his banishment, MacArthur could think of only one address left to try. He encouraged

Louise to get her immensely rich and influential stepfather, Edward T. Stotesbury, to discuss it with President Calvin Coolidge.[12] But this did no good either. They were going back to the Philippines.

It was a move that placed new strains on their marriage. MacArthur's indifference to mingling with other people grated on Louise's intense sociability. The affairs he did go out for, such as the boxing matches and Masonic meetings, either did not appeal to her or did not allow women. What made matters even worse was the fact that it was really he who had a social life, without seeking one, and Louise, who craved one, was left pining for company. MacArthur was elected president of the Manila Army and Navy Club; that meant he had to host dinners at the club regularly. He also organized a party for Spanish-American War veterans who had served under his father. Before his time as president ended, MacArthur installed a handsome oil portrait of his father in the room where the club held its board meetings.[13]

He also infuriated Louise with his insistence on punctuality. She had probably never been on time for anything in her pampered life. The planet Louise had only one inhabitant—herself. One evening, when she was still at her dressing table and making them late for a dinner engagement, he stood behind her, his arms folded, urging her to hurry up. He looked, she thought irritably, "just like Napoleon." She grabbed a hand mirror, jumped up and smashed it over his head.[14]

Shortly after he returned to Manila in June 1923, MacArthur was assigned to command a brigade in the recently created Philippine Division. This was a watershed in his life, for he now turned his mind to trying to devise a way to defend the Philippines. The General Staff had studied the subject for twenty years and had never been convinced it could be done. The most trenchant review of the subject before World War I was undertaken by the chief of engineers, who suggested that "a colossal military blunder was made in 1898 in taking the Philippines from Spain." He concluded starkly: "The Philippines are indefensible against any strong Oriental power by any land force we can maintain there."[15]

Despite this fact, American politicians were not prepared to let the Philippines go. The result was that the Army felt it had to support government policy by assuming responsibility to defend the islands, yet the Navy felt free to plan on steaming back to Hawaii as fast as its boilers could propel it if the Japanese ever landed troops on Philippine soil.[16]

When MacArthur was reunited with his old friend and mentor Leonard Wood, they began looking for ways to defend the islands. Here were two of the most "can-do" officers in the Army. They felt bound by their honor as men and as officers to find a way to implement American policy, even if on the face of it that policy looked impossible. The United States would never maintain enough American troops in the Philippines to defend them. That was the heart of the problem. Wood had wrestled with the problem of Philippine defense since his time as Chief of Staff. It had become something of a personal crusade.[17]

Wood hit on what he thought was the answer: Why not train an army of Filipinos by creating a Swiss-style system of reservists? Once properly armed and trained, such a force could make any invasion of the archipelago so costly it wouldn't be worth taking the Philippines. No one, after all, has tried in five hundred years to conquer Switzerland, even though it is a small, strategically placed country surrounded by powerful neighbors with a habit of going to war with one another.[18]

Nothing was done for the time being to put Wood's idea into practice, but it was an idea that MacArthur never forgot and would one day actually try to put into effect. What he did instead was try to imagine what would happen if the Japanese did attack. The key strategic asset for them would be Manila Bay. Control of the bay rested on possession of the Bataan Peninsula and the small island off its southern tip, Corregidor. MacArthur had surveyed much of Bataan twenty years earlier. Now he walked and rode the mountainous, jungle-clad terrain of Bataan, mapping its defensive possibilities. If war came, this was where it would have to be fought.[19]

The commander of the Philippine Department, Major General George W. Read, admired the way MacArthur devoted himself to this new, self-assigned task. On MacArthur's efficiency report, Read rated him first out of the thirty-five brigadier generals known to him personally.[20]

A year after becoming commander of the Military District of Manila, MacArthur finally got a real job. The War Department had organized its two regiments of Filipino Scouts and its sole American infantry regiment in the archipelago, the 31st, into a new combat force, called the Philippine Division. As divisions went, this one was tiny—only seven thousand men, roughly one fourth the size of a U.S. infantry division at full strength. The division was organized into two brigades, and MacArthur was given command of one of them.

He was delighted to be back with troops. Even though there were doubts about the utility of the Philippine Division, he liked Filipinos, trusted them and treated them exactly as he did everyone else: relaxed and informal with the few he chose to mix with, aloof and distant from the rest. He had renewed his acquaintance with Manuel Quezon, who had risen in recent years to become one of the most influential figures in Philippine politics, which revolved around a single issue: independence. He met with Quezon regularly.

MacArthur's attitudes were remarkably enlightened for an Army officer of his generation. Wood was much more typical. He would never speak to a Filipino about official business unless another white man was present. MacArthur treated the Filipino leaders he knew with unfeigned respect and was persuaded that the islands deserved their independence. Wood, by contrast, precipitated a political crisis by trying to run the Philippines without the support of Filipino politicians and argued strenuously that independence was impossible for many years to come.[21]

Although it symbolized a joint commitment to defense of the archipelago, the Philippine Division was not free from the undercurrents of tension that existed in nearly all American-Filipino relationships. The Scouts, who constituted two thirds of the division's strength, were paid much less than the troops of the 31st Infantry Regiment. In July 1924 they mutinied over the inequality in pay, allowances and pensions. More than two hundred Scouts were arrested. Most were duly convicted and dishonorably discharged. Shortly after this MacArthur was given command of the division, presumably because his liberal, antiracist views were widely known among Filipino soldiers.[22]

The division commander, Major General Omar Bundy, rated MacArthur second out of the twenty-five brigadier generals of his acquaintance on his efficiency report. This rating, combined with Read's, made a strong case for promoting MacArthur to major general. Nor had Pinky's pen run dry. At about this time she wrote a gushing letter to Pershing: "Won't you . . . give me some assurance that you will give my Boy his well earned promotion . . ."[23]

Wood took up the cause by writing directly to the secretary of war in May 1924: "I invite your attention to his many excellent qualities and his qualifications for promotion." The fact remained, however, that MacArthur stood no chance of promotion while Pershing remained Chief of Staff. On the other hand, on September 13, 1924, Pershing would reach his sixty-fourth birthday and, by law, be retired from active duty. John Weeks assured Wood that MacArthur's promotion was more or less assured—"his turn will come in the early future."[24]

Sure enough, ten days after Pershing stepped down as Chief of Staff, his successor, John L. Hines, announced that MacArthur's name would go to the Senate for promotion to major general in January 1925. At the age of forty-four he would be the youngest of the Army's twenty-one major generals. It was a stunning coup de théâtre, as if the gods had banished him to Manila only in order to provide the setting for a triumphant return.

In January 1925 the MacArthurs sailed for home aboard the Army transport *Thomas,* accompanied by five Filipino servants. And Louise had done it again. The inmates of Bilibid Prison were famous for their excellent handmade furniture. Louise had furnished 1 Calle Victoria with many fine examples of Bilibid craftsmanship. She loaded up the baggage hold of the

Thomas with her trunks and hatboxes, her pile of lace, her furniture and her automobiles. The other Army wives aboard ship returned home seething, laceless, servantless again, limited to one trunk, and with their own Filipino furniture piled up back on the dock.[25]

Much as Arthur MacArthur, Jr., had taken advantage of his assignment to the War Department in 1889 to assert his claim to the Medal of Honor, so Douglas's return from the Philippines as a two-star general brought yet another attempt to win a decoration for his exploits at Veracruz in 1914. There was no chance of getting a Medal of Honor—although he almost certainly felt entitled to one—but the wartime creation of the Distinguished Service Cross and the Distinguished Service Medal opened up new possibilities. He asked for, and got, a review of his case. He probably felt he had a good chance. After all, Funston was dead, and his own record in France had shown beyond any doubt that he was one of the bravest soldiers in the Army.

MacArthur had what might be considered a medal fixation. To a considerable extent, it was nothing but a craving common to his profession. Much as CEOs expect to be well paid for their efforts and writers or artists seek immortality as their due, so career officers are likely to want all the ribbons, awards, medals and badges that they feel they have earned.

A chestful of decorations, even if rarely worn, is the sine qua non of the successful soldier and parades his career in a shorthand that even a skeptical congressman can read. Given the largeness of his personality, however, and the dazzling course of his career, MacArthur's appetite for decorations seemed trivial, almost demeaning. He simply had to have them. The obsessive spirit that he brought to trophy hunting made him seem a smaller man than he was, not a grander one.

At all events, MacArthur was turned down again. The Decoration Board rejected his claim in language that was as blunt as could be and resolved the Veracruz question forever: "Extraordinary heroism not displayed; duty not considered one of great responsibility and exceptional merit not displayed. Not sufficient gallantry in action displayed."[26]

He moved to Atlanta in May to assume command of the IV Corps area. Shortly after this, MacArthur and his staff attended services at an Episcopal church one Sunday morning. MacArthur felt slightly apprehensive, wondering what kind of reception he would receive. His father's role in the Atlanta campaign was well known, but he hoped that Georgians would also recall that all six uncles on his mother's side had fought for the Confederacy.

When he and his staff entered the church, heads turned, whispers passed from pew to pew and three quarters of the congregation got up and walked out of the cathedral. He was outraged and sent a telegram to the War

Department beseeching that his tour of duty in Georgia be terminated forthwith. After a mercifully short stay in Atlanta, the MacArthurs were able to move to Baltimore, where he took command of the III Corps. Louise's estate, Rainbow Hill, was only a twenty-minute drive from the city.[27]

Hardly had he settled in as commander of the III Corps before he was summoned to serve on the court-martial of Brigadier General Billy Mitchell. This flamboyant airman was an old friend of MacArthur's. Mitchell was from Milwaukee, and for a time MacArthur had dated one of Mitchell's sisters back in 1905, but it was not until World War I that Billy and Douglas became friends when they both were serving in the War Department.

In some respects, they were much alike. Mitchell, for example, dressed according to his own tastes, not the Quartermaster General's. He liked to wear a sharply cut jacket of his own design, gleaming cavalry boots and a British officer's "pink" breeches, the whole adorned with numerous silver stars and gilded propellers. When Pershing became Chief of Staff, he had installed Charles Menoher, the former commander of the Rainbow Division, as chief of the Air Service. Mitchell, the assistant chief, resented Menoher's appointment, as did nearly every Army pilot. Menoher was a despised "kiwi"—the only officer in the Air Service who could not fly an airplane. Why Pershing imagined the Air Service would accept him is a mystery. Before long Mitchell delivered a "him or me" ultimatum to the secretary of war. Rather than lose Mitchell, who was adored throughout the Air Service, the secretary asked Menoher to resign.[28]

Difficult, temperamental and visionary, Mitchell was notoriously outspoken. Following several major air disasters, the excitable Mitchell had publicly excoriated the War Department and the Navy for "the incompetency, criminal negligence and almost treasonable administration of the national defense."[29] The Army responded by charging him with the Old Mother Hubbard article of war, the one that covered everything—"conduct prejudicial to good order and discipline."

Even close friends and admirers, such as Lieutenant Colonel Henry "Hap" Arnold, knew he was guilty as charged. Mitchell probably realized it too, but he intended to turn his trial into a showcase presentation of the need for the Air Service to be given its independence from the Army.

The court-martial board consisted of six major generals, including Charles P. Summerall and MacArthur, plus five brigadier generals, one of whom, Frank McCoy, was a Pershing protégé and considered a potential Chief of Staff. The court convened in a dingy old warehouse, with seats for only about a hundred people, and was filled every day. Half the spectators were reporters. The other half were young women in short skirts, cloche hats and plenty of lipstick, one of whom was Louise

MacArthur. She had little recorded interest in airpower, but quite a lot of interest in being seen. Besides, Washington was still a dull southern town, not remotely like the rich, cosmopolitan and beautiful city it became half a century later. Billy Mitchell's trial was one of the most exciting things to happen there between the world wars.

Throughout the seven weeks it lasted, MacArthur said not a word in public. Instead he spent each session gazing adoringly at his wife, while Louise smiled radiantly back over the bouquet of fresh flowers she carried each day.[30]

Billy Mitchell's conviction was inevitable. He was sentenced to five years' suspension from active duty, with loss of pay and allowances. There was a legend that MacArthur alone had voted for Mitchell's acquittal. This seems unlikely, and MacArthur never made such a claim. What he did say, twenty years later, was that he had prevented Mitchell from the ultimate disgrace, being dismissed from the service, and that may well be true. Even so, he probably could not have achieved that on his own, but rumor had it that two other court-martial members were similarly determined to save Mitchell's career. True or not, it made little difference, because Mitchell resigned his commission. He spent the rest of his life as a civilian, free to agitate for air independence, strategic bombardment and stronger defenses in the Pacific.[31]

In February 1926 one of Louise's former lovers, Colonel John G. Quekemeyer (whom she had dated when he was an aide to Pershing), died suddenly. He was about to begin an assignment as commandant of cadets at West Point when he died. Louise sent a bouquet of white orchids and a letter of condolence to the grief-stricken Pershing, who had loved Quekemeyer like a son.[32]

By this time the tensions within her second marriage had brought it close to the breaking point. As Louise advanced into middle age, she became increasingly fat. Her sexual allure was fading fast. Besides, marriages based on sex rather than mutual devotion rarely hold up over the long haul, and the MacArthur marriage was no exception. MacArthur was losing interest in sex with his wife, just as she tried to get him to leave the Army. Her stepfather was one of J. P. Morgan's partners and in a position to bring him into the fabled House of Morgan at a level where riches were guaranteed.[33]

The allure of Army life can hardly ever be conveyed to people whose world revolves around money and possessions, comfort and purchased pleasures. It is doubtful that MacArthur even tried, but in 1927 he delivered a speech that made clear to anyone willing to listen the value he placed on his profession and his infinite contempt for the world that

Louise admired. Addressing the Reserve Officers Association's annual convention, he said the nation was deeply indebted to the military, because "from Magna Carta to the present time there is little in our institutions worth having or worth perpetuating that has not been achieved for us by armed men." The greatest danger that Western civilization now faced, he added, was not the barbarism of war but a new, more insidious menace: "the barbarism of ostentatious splendor."[34]

That summer Louise moved to New York, leaving MacArthur to live at Rainbow Hill, where he put up a flagpole. It may have been the last erection of his marriage to Louise. At about the same time the president of the U.S. Olympic Committee died unexpectedly, creating a minor crisis in American athletics. The Olympic Games, which would be held in Amsterdam in 1928, were less than a year away. MacArthur's renown as a promoter of amateur athletics and his prominence brought him the presidency of the committee and the chance to take the U.S. team to the Netherlands.

He had always loved meeting with coaches, attending practice sessions, talking up the character-building nature of athletics and encouraging the young. So much so that despite his continuing responsibilities as a corps commander and his new assignment with the Olympic Committee, he organized the Regular Army football team that in the fall of 1927 defeated the Marine Corps' team, to Summerall's delight.[35]

The Olympic assignment was made for him, and he reveled in it. He got high on every success, took every defeat to heart. There were minidramas and crises almost every day, and he overcame them all. The American sprint champion, Charley Paddock—"World's Fastest Human"—was under investigation for accepting money and thereby violating his status as an amateur and his right to run in the Olympics. When MacArthur insisted on taking Paddock, some members of the Amateur Athletics Union protested, and one of them resigned from the AAU over the Paddock case after the ship carrying the team to Holland set sail. When he heard of the furor raging at home, MacArthur sent back an angry cable that read, "We won't stand for sniping from the rear."[36]

He led the team as it paraded during the opening ceremony, dined with Queen Wilhelmina of Holland and fussed over his athletes like a mother hen. The main thing, though, was to win, to bring back medals. No one believed in medals more than MacArthur. And when the American boxing team manager withdrew his fighters from the competition in protest after an outrageously bad decision, MacArthur ordered them to fight their remaining bouts. He told them sternly, "Americans do not quit."[37] In the end he had the profound satisfaction of seeing the Olympic team he took to Holland dominate the games. It set seven world records and seventeen

Olympic records and returned home with twice as many medals as any other nation. He gave every member of the team a gold charm as a token of his appreciation for his or her efforts.[38]

On his return MacArthur wrote the committee's official report to President Coolidge. It began, "In undertaking this difficult task, I recall the passage in Plutarch, wherein Themistocles, being asked whether he would rather be an Achilles or a Homer, replied, 'Which would you rather be, a conqueror in the Olympic Games or the crier who proclaims who are the conquerors?' And indeed to portray adequately the vividness and brilliance of that great spectacle would be worthy even of the pen of Homer himself. No words of mine can even remotely portray such great moments. . . ." But that did not stop him from trying.

This fustian drivel ran on at excruciating length, before grinding to a poetic and overblown halt:

> To set the cause above renown,
> To love the game beyond the prize,
> To honor, as you strike him down,
> The foe that comes with fearless eyes.
> To count the life of battle good,
> And dear the land that gave you birth,
> And dearer yet the Brotherhood
> That binds the brave of all the Earth.[39]

MacArthur's father had been a master of this kind of ponderous rodomontade, and look what that had done for his career! It could only irritate Coolidge, though. In its exaggeration, its constant straining for effect, its self-important air, it represented much that Coolidge, a plain-speaking, simple-living New England Puritan, loathed.[40]

MacArthur was not home long before he was on his way to Manila once again. His assignment this time was to command the Philippine Department. The estrangement from Louise was irreparable. She would remain in New York to live the kind of life of ostentatious splendor that she considered normal.[41]

Six months after his departure Louise headed for Reno and filed for divorce. MacArthur's first name was entered on her divorce petition as "Donald," and the reason given for filing was "failure to support." The whole thing sounded like a joke. Louise brushed aside press stories that her marriage had ended rancorously. Nonsense, she declared. "I have the greatest admiration and respect for General MacArthur. We part as friends."[42] Some friends. Louise spent the rest of her life looking for ways to belittle MacArthur and hold him up to scorn. She was a bitter woman, and MacArthur had not heard the last of her.

Leonard Wood had died in 1927, leaving American relations with the islands in a vexed condition. He had improved the Philippines' finances but achieved nothing that furthered the Jones Act. This legislation, which dated back to the Wilson administration, had promised the Philippines their independence once the Filipinos had shown they had a capacity for stable, democratic government. Wood's attitude toward Filipino politicians was that they could never exercise power responsibly.

Manuel Quezon had loathed the racist Wood and journeyed to Washington after Wood's death to urge Coolidge to appoint Henry L. Stimson the next governor-general. Stimson, who had been Taft's secretary of war, was the kind of well-bred, high-minded, patrician colonialist that the Filipino elite could get along with, unlike the brash and temperamental Wood. Coolidge gave the appointment to Stimson.

By the time MacArthur returned to the Philippines in October 1928 Stimson had already made his mark. He mingled freely with Filipinos and never offended their racial sensibilities. He encouraged Filipino political life but refused to consider independence. He and Quezon agreed in private on something less—dominion status, comparable to the relationship between Britain and Canada—but in public Quezon continued to call for complete independence.[43]

With Coolidge declining to run for reelection that fall, the front-runner for the Republican nomination was his secretary of commerce, Herbert Hoover. Pershing nonetheless had fantastic hopes of being chosen as the compromise candidate if Hoover's bid failed. His campaign manager was the publisher of the *Army and Navy Journal,* MacArthur's friend and admirer John Callan O'Laughlin. To boost Pershing's chances, O'Laughlin wrote a short hagiographic excuse of a biography, but the book sank like a stone, an ominous indication of Black Jack's doomed hopes. With Pershing out of the frame, O'Laughlin's attention began shifting toward MacArthur as a presidential possibility.[44]

MacArthur meanwhile was trying to make some sense of his responsibilities as commander of the Philippine Department. The existing Orange Plan was, he told Johnson Hagood, commanding general of the Philippine Division, simply "rotten." The Army's commitment to stay and fight in case of invasion was unrealistic, given the Navy's intention to pull out. The only solution MacArthur could see to the fundamental flaw in the Orange Plan, which had the Army and the Navy heading in opposite directions, was Leonard Wood's proposal to arm and train hundreds of thousands of Filipinos. A force that size could make invasion too costly to be worth the attempt. Yet it could not be implemented without political progress toward independence.[45]

MacArthur won the loyalty and admiration of strong-minded officers like Hagood by doing whatever he could to advance their careers. When Hagood was ordered to return home and take what amounted to a colonel's job, MacArthur told him not to do it. Instead, he said, demand to see the Chief of Staff, to tell him you want a corps. He will refuse to see you, so demand to see the secretary of war. He, too, will refuse to see you. Then insist on seeing the President. At that point they will give you a corps, because there is a major cover-up going on in the War Department concerning a high-ranking officer, and the last thing they are going to risk right now is a congressional investigation into how it is running its affairs. In the event, MacArthur was proved right. Hagood got command of the VII Corps, with headquarters in Omaha.[46]

In February 1929 President-elect Hoover chose Stimson to be his secretary of state. MacArthur may well have had hopes of succeeding him as governor-general. During his comparatively brief working relationship with Stimson, they did not get along well. His disagreements with Wood over the future of the Philippines and how to deal with the Philippine elite were managed within the context of a deeply rooted friendship. His disagreements with Stimson, on the other hand, brought out the fundamental antipathy in their personalities. MacArthur did not like Stimson, but Stimson positively disliked MacArthur.[47]

There was press speculation that MacArthur coveted the governor-generalship—speculation that was probably inspired by O'Laughlin, with or without MacArthur's explicit approval. "According to close friends," *The New York Times* reported, "General MacArthur has his eyes on the White House for eight or twelve years hence, via a successful administration as Governor General for four years, followed by a cabinet post, either as Secretary of State or Secretary of War."[48] Whatever hopes he may or may not have had, the governor-generalship did not come his way.

What he got instead was an offer from Hoover to be chief of engineers. The devastating Mississippi floods of 1927 had created an economic and political crisis in a dozen states. Taming the Mississippi was the biggest engineering project since building the Panama Canal. It was a project in which Hoover, having organized the relief mission for the hundreds of thousands of flood victims, had a strong interest. He saw the offer to make MacArthur the chief engineer as an accolade. Running the project was an administrative and political challenge, not a hands-on engineering assignment. To his mind, MacArthur was "the ideal man."[49]

Rivers and harbors, however, were work that MacArthur had tried to shun as a young engineer. To have it thrust on him now would create an existential crisis. He was not a mere administrator, no matter how exalted, but a high-ranking commander, a leader of fighting men, with a fistful of medals to prove it, even if he had been denied all he deserved.

"I feel a great mistake would be made in my detail as Chief of Engineers," he cabled Summerall. "I do not possess the technical qualifications for such a highly specialized position. Moreover, the fundamental reorganization of the Philippine Department which is now taking place, including new war plans and projects, which, in effect, provide for the first time an adequate defense policy for the Philippine Islands, requires my presence here for at least another year."[50]

This rejection was certain to annoy Hoover and was likely to prove fatal to MacArthur's hopes of becoming Chief of Staff. Engineer officers almost never got command of troops, and being Chief of Staff was the ultimate command assignment in the Army. If he was ever going to realize his ambitions, MacArthur had to turn Hoover down. The best he could do now was hope that even if Hoover did not make him Chief of Staff, some other president might.

Summerall would be retired on grounds of age no later than March 1931. By a strange demographic and promotional conjunction, MacArthur, although the youngest major general in the Army, would by then be the senior major general with at least four years left to serve on active duty by the time Summerall stepped down. Yet seniority was no assurance of becoming Chief of Staff, especially now that he had antagonized the President.[51]

Hoover was not going to be starved of strong candidates. The Army had created half a dozen major generals in 1925. Although MacArthur's appointment was the first among them, he ranked the highly regarded former deputy chief of staff, Dennis Nolan, by just one day and the present deputy chief, Fox Conner, by six months. Nor did he have much seniority over the highly esteemed president of the War College, William D. Connor, and even less over Johnson Hagood.

Much could depend on the preference of the secretary of war, who was now a colorful, handsome, rich young lawyer from Oklahoma, Patrick J. Hurley. Hurley identified strongly with the young major generals who were coming to the top of the Army, but he had never met MacArthur. His executive assistant, Brigadier General George Van Horn Moseley, however, was a strong MacArthur advocate and pitched the absent MacArthur's candidacy strongly. Hurley had his doubts, however.[52]

When he traveled to Cedar Rapids, Iowa, for Wood's funeral, he met and was impressed by the local commander, Johnson Hagood. Hurley later traveled to Omaha to sound out the VII Corps commander on who should be Chief of Staff, expecting Hagood to make a case for himself. Instead Hagood extolled MacArthur. But wasn't MacArthur vain? Pompous?

Intolerant of his superiors' wishes? Overbearing toward civilians? Hagood brushed all that aside. MacArthur, he said, was "the ablest man and the best soldier" in the Army.[53]

Hoover was meanwhile getting a similar ear bashing on the merits of Douglas MacArthur. His military aide, Colonel Campbell Hodges, was one of MacArthur's West Point classmates and extolled his abilities freely to the President. So too did former Chief of Staff Peyton March.[54]

The publisher Roy Howard, whose Scripps-Howard newspaper chain promoted the progressive Republicanism that Hoover had done much to create, was a regular visitor to the White House. Every time he called he lobbied strongly for MacArthur's appointment as Chief of Staff, but the President still held it against MacArthur that he had declined appointment as chief engineer.[55]

Summerall may or may not have been pushing MacArthur. What is certain is that there was plenty of sentiment in favor of Nolan on the General Staff. As for Pershing, he was still hostile to MacArthur. So hostile that even though Hurley was seriously ill, he went to Hurley's sickbed to try to persuade him not to make MacArthur Chief of Staff. He urged the appointment of Frank McCoy instead.[56] In sickness as in health, however, Hurley would not budge. He was sticking with MacArthur.

Pershing would not be deterred. He played his last card and asked to see the President. Pershing made a direct appeal to Hoover to appoint anyone but MacArthur. Hoover himself remained reluctant to give the assignment to MacArthur, and he suggested to Hurley that it would be a good idea to look for a compromise candidate. Even under this pressure, Hurley still stood up for MacArthur's appointment.[57] So too did Howard, whose newspaper chain was the only section of the press that Hoover could rely on. The strong support of Hurley and Howard made MacArthur by far the strongest candidate.

In August 1930 MacArthur was summoned home, to become Chief of Staff. At the age of fifty he had reached the summit of one of the world's most competitive professions.[58] The news, when it came, took him by surprise. He had never expected Hoover to make him Chief of Staff. He accepted the assignment with "many misgivings" but was excited nonetheless. The one prize to escape his father was his. It would have been strange if MacArthur did not wish, at least once, that his father were still alive to share his son's triumph.[59]

10

D'Artagnan of the Army

The sentiment that Charles P. Summerall was most likely to instill in other people was fear. He had never gone beyond the unreconstructed leadership style learned at West Point in his youth, which consisted of a bullying manner and an unbreakable will. Summerall drove men, rather than lead them. The result was a General Staff that was demoralized and embittered.[1]

The tense, unhappy atmosphere in the War Department lifted almost from the moment MacArthur was sworn in as Chief of Staff in November 1930. The surgeon general of the Army, Merritte Ireland, went to meet the new chief and was bowled over. Under Summerall, nobody had dared speak freely. But MacArthur was eager for debate and discussion, he informed former Chief of Staff John L. Hines, who had gone out to command the Philippine Department. The atmosphere had altered completely, virtually overnight. Laughter was heard once again, trust had returned, people now enjoyed their work. "We have come into a very sane administration of the Army," thought Ireland. He was on the verge of retirement but couldn't help envying the officer who would serve under the new Chief of Staff.[2]

MacArthur's greatest challenge would be to maintain the Army as a viable fighting force capable of rapid expansion in time of war. In the fall of 1930 the American economy was on the edge of a massive slump. The Wall Street stock market crash of October 1929 had triggered an unavoidable recession. The downturn in the economy, with its inevitable rise in unemployment, terrified millions of consumers. Many ordinary people were heavily in debt after the spending spree of the 1920s. They stopped buying anything but groceries, stopped borrowing and stopped investing throughout 1930. That was all it took to tip the economy into the slump that became known as the Great Depression.

Hoover had been applying the screws to government spending even before the crash and sought large savings from the War Department. A Quaker by upbringing and a renowned proponent of efficiency, he reduced the War Department's share of government spending in 1930 to only 7.5 percent, barely half what it had been before World War I. This was also a time when pacifism was in the ascendant. The 1928 Kellogg-Briand Pact was hyped by politicians as a giant step toward abolishing war, and ordinary people desperately wanted to believe them. The zeitgeist was all in favor of the disarmers.[3]

MacArthur knew his biggest challenge would be the fight to save the Army from dying the death of a thousand budget cuts in this era of inflated hopes of lasting peace. Even before leaving the Philippines, he issued a call for an increase in armed forces pay.[4] MacArthur would also have to tackle, head-on, the rising tide of pacifism and antimilitarism as they threatened the viability of the Army. The natural craving for a world at peace was sourly turning in the early 1930s into a revulsion against anything and everything connected with the military, as if arms caused wars, rather than wars that caused arms.

When he was sworn in as Chief of Staff on November 21, the press hailed him as "dashing and debonair . . . the D'Artagnan of the Army." Republican newspapers praised his good looks, paraded his medals and wished him well. Pro-Democratic newspapers reserved their judgment.[5]

In his new assignment MacArthur tried to create a kind of family, or "general's household," around himself. He called it "my gang." He had old friends assigned as his aides and assistants. Some were West Point classmates, like Charles F. Severson. Others were people with whom he had served before. Childless, divorced and to the world at large an aloof figure, he craved companionship.

One thing was certain: MacArthur did not have to live alone any longer. Despite her heart problems, Pinky had survived and would be able to move with him into Quarters Number One at Fort Myer, across the Potomac from Washington. MacArthur had worried about her constantly during his time in the Philippines. He had regularly requested of a friend in Washington, "Go and see my mother and write and tell me exactly how she is."[6]

The decade just past had been a hard one for Pinky. Douglas was abroad much of the time, and her eldest son, Arthur, had died suddenly in December 1923 when his appendix burst, bringing to a tragic end a promising career. Arthur was a naval captain at the time of his death and was married to an admiral's daughter, Mary McCalla. He had become one of the Navy's leading authorities on modern submarines and seemed certain to rise to high command in his chosen service. Handsome and debonair, highly intelligent and ambitious, he was much like his brother Douglas. Arthur's death turned his wife and his mother into close friends, despite the wide difference in their ages. Pinky lived with Mary for much of the seven years between Arthur's death and Douglas's swearing in as Chief of Staff.

The old lady's devotion to her son, and his equal devotion to her, were legendary. He told acquaintances that he owed everything he had ever achieved to his parents, but especially to Pinky. "My mother raised my father from a lieutenant's bar to a lieutenant general's three stars. She had a much earlier start with me than with him, and she had so improved with practice that she made me a general, with four stars."[7]

Some writers claimed that whenever MacArthur left the house and Pinky decided the weather looked unpromising, she would hurry to the front door of Quarters Number One before MacArthur got into his chauffeur-driven car. Standing on the porch, she called out, "Dougeee—did you remember to take your overshoes?"[8]

To the intense disappointment of many officers' wives who wanted to get a good look at one of the most famous women in the Army, MacArthur announced shortly after he became Chief of Staff that Mrs. MacArthur would not be receiving callers. Calling was, to many military wives, almost as important as breathing. *No* callers? Even if one had to allow for Pinky's advanced age and poor health, this was a setback, but there it was.

Only one woman had the nerve to try scaling this barrier to sociability: Bea Patton, the wife of George Patton. Like her husband, she was not going to be deterred by a formidable front. She went over to Quarters Number One with her teenaged daughter, Ruth-Ellen, and a calling card, with one corner turned down to indicate it had been delivered by her own fair hand and not dropped off by a servant.

When Mrs. Patton rang the bell, a Filipino houseboy appeared at the front door and asked if she wanted to come inside. She stepped into the hall but did so only to hand him her calling card. Pinky appeared from deep shadows at the back of the hall and said airily, "Since you are within, you may remain."

Lieutenant General Arthur MacArthur had been dead for twenty years, but Pinky was dressed entirely in black and wore dark glasses, which hid her eyes. She took her unexpected visitors into the sitting room, and when Mrs. Patton explained who she was, Pinky replied, "Ah, yes. Your husband's grandfather was a colonel in the Twenty-second Virginia, I believe. He was killed at Cedar Creek." She summoned the houseboy and told him to fetch her jewel case.

The houseboy returned carrying a box the size of a child's coffin. Pinky rummaged in it for a while, then pulled out a brooch that was set with an unusual smooth pale stone. She handed it to Ruth-Ellen. "Young lady, do you know what this is?" Ruth-Ellen had to confess she hadn't the faintest idea.

"It is," said Pinky, "a piece of my brother's skull. He was wounded in the head at Antietam and sent the bone splinters back to his sisters. We had them mounted into brooches." MacArthur came by his flair for self-dramatizing honestly; he'd inherited it from his mother.[9]

Happy as he was to be living with Pinky once again, he needed, like most people, to be in love before he could feel he was fully alive. His love interest now, though, was far removed from the world of Louise and a long way from what his mother would have approved. One evening in April 1930 while he was attending the fights at Manila's Olympic Stadium, his gaze had been arrested by a lovely sixteen-year-old Eurasian girl named Isabel Rosario Cooper. Glances were exchanged, and there was evidently a promise there worth exploring. MacArthur scribbled a note and told his aide Captain Thomas Jefferson Davis to take it over to Isabel.

MacArthur's adolescent mistress had a Scottish father and a Filipina mother. Her modest talents for singing and dancing enabled her to earn a living as a chorus girl in vaudeville shows and circuses. Before long she was entertaining MacArthur regularly and serving him a drink of her own invention, a "Douglas," consisting of crushed mangoes, Spanish brandy and ice.[10]

Given his romantic nature, MacArthur could not help craving love as much as sex. He did not want one or the other; he had an overwhelming need for both. Before long he was swearing his devotion to Isabel. When the summons to Washington came, there was only one thing to do: She had to go to America. He told her the few months they had known each other were the happiest time of his life. But it was too risky for them to travel together. A sex scandal could ruin his career. She would simply have to follow him on a later ship. He bought her a ticket, and on September 19, 1930, he stood at the rail of the ship taking him back to the United States, staring intently at the petite teenager in a bright green dress waving furiously from the dock. Sick at heart with fear that he might never see her again, he stared at her until she disappeared from view.

MacArthur spent much of the voyage thinking of nothing but Isabel. He wrote to his "Darling One" and "My Baby Girl" regularly, sometimes twice a day. He mailed letters to her at each port where he stopped. In Shanghai he bought her a fur coat. MacArthur worried that Isabel might simply be taking him for a ride. What was to stop her from making a fool of him and simply turn in the ticket he had given her for a cash refund? He was also afraid that even if she held on to the ticket, she might forget to catch the ship. She was not, it seems, particularly bright. He was afraid too of what might happen if she did catch the ship and, like him, get off in Singapore. The city seemed to him to be crawling with pimps and white slavers. A sexy sixteen-year-old without much common sense was tempting prey. The world of chorines merges imperceptibly into the demimonde, and Isabel had already had at least one brush with that kind of danger.[11]

MacArthur was tormented not only by his fears that Isabel would not reach America but by a consuming sexual desire. He told her in his letters how much he missed her, especially at night when he went to bed. Memories of her "deep lips and soft body" taunted him and left him panting and sweating with lust. He declared that their love united them forever, in this world and the next. If anything should happen to her, he swore, he would simply die.

As it turned out, Isabel caught her ship, eluded the white slavers of Singapore and arrived as scheduled at Pier 9 in Jersey City in early December. MacArthur installed her in an apartment in Georgetown. He gave her the fur coat, a jade and diamond ring, an allowance, a chauffeur-driven car, a large collection of lingerie and a few furtive hours of Daddy's time whenever his busy schedule and Pinky's needs allowed.

Being the secret mistress of a famous, powerful man is probably pretty boring. Isabel had no friends of her own, no real life of her own. The relationship with MacArthur was under constant strain. His fear that one of his enemies might learn of this affair made her a prisoner, yet no lively teenager can be happy in confinement. Far from being a pair of lovers hopelessly and deliriously lost in the thrill of romance, they were an absurdly mismatched couple locked into a stultifying affair that was based entirely on agitating the bedsprings. This relationship was as doomed as his sex-based marriage to Louise.

In the fall of 1931 MacArthur traveled to Europe to watch various armies on maneuvers and to pick up some handsome foreign decorations. His letters and postcards to Isabel were signed "Globetrotter." Nothing could have better pointed up his freedom to roam and her gilded cage. When he returned, there were almost certainly some angry scenes and harsh words, because she wrung a major concession from him: The next time he went abroad, she would do so too.

As a peace offering he moved her into a much fancier place—a suite in the prestigious Chastleton Hotel, on Sixteenth Street NW. Isabel seems to have wanted to elevate her status from kept woman to something more in keeping with her new address, because she began calling herself Mrs. Isabel Cooper.

When MacArthur returned to Europe for more maneuvers and medals in the fall of 1932, Isabel set off on a vacation of her own. She headed for Havana. MacArthur was terrified at the thought of this sexy, now eighteen-year-old girl enjoying herself in what was considered *the* sin city of the

Western Hemisphere. He swore that nothing could separate them in the future but death. It was an impossible promise. He must have known that, and so, in all likelihood, did Isabel. Their affair was heading straight for the rocks, and this risible pledge proved it. The only question was when.[12]

As MacArthur sought to create a "family" around himself in the War Department, his attention was soon drawn to the talents of an affable young major named Dwight D. Eisenhower, who was serving as executive assistant to Assistant Secretary Frederick H. Payne. Eisenhower had graduated first in his class at the Command and General Staff School in 1926. That success had put him on the track for a Washington assignment.

This was a development that had surprised his West Point classmates. Ike had graduated from the academy in 1915 in the middle of his class. A star running back until he wrecked his knee, Eisenhower had been a mediocre student in every academic subject but one. He had excelled only in English—the subject that MacArthur considered the most important of all to a professional soldier's advancement. Eisenhower could write a report, a letter, a memo that was lucid, well organized and effective.

He had helped Pershing write his memoirs and had written most of the official guide published by the American Battlefields and Monuments Commission under the title *American Armies and Battlefields in France,* a work that has since become a major source on AEF combat operations. Returning to Washington to work for the assistant secretary of war, Eisenhower studied the problems of economic mobilization until he became an authority on the subject. He wrote some of the Army's basic guidelines.[13]

Once MacArthur was aware of this talented major in the office down the hall, he borrowed him from Payne for important writing assignments, such as the Chief of Staff's annual report. He was so impressed with Ike's work on the 1931 report that he placed a glowing letter in Eisenhower's 201 File. "I desire to place on official record this special commendation for excellent work of a highly important nature," it ran. "You not only accepted this assignment willingly, performing it in addition to your regular duties in the office of the Assistant Secretary of War, but you gave me a most acceptable solution within a minimum of time. . . .

"I write this special commendation so that you may fully realize that your outstanding talents and your ability to perform these highly important missions are fully appreciated."[14]

Such fulsome praise from a Chief of Staff was almost unheard of. When Ike took this home to show Mamie, she was astounded. A few days later Ike recorded in his diary, "Mamie had it framed!!!"[15]

While employing his pen on behalf of the government, Eisenhower was also recording his impressions of the people he worked for. He did not think much of Hurley: "Affable but rather petulant. . . . His interests seem almost wholly political . . . meticulous as to details of dress and personal appearance . . . a 'dandy'. . . I do not believe he will go higher in the political world although he is very ambitious. . . . He is not big enough to go higher."

MacArthur, on the other hand, was highly esteemed:

Essentially a romantic figure . . . positive in his convictions—a genius at giving concise and clear instructions . . . his interests are almost exclusively military. He apparently avoids social duties as far as possible— and does not seek the limelight except in things connected with the Army and the War Department. Magnetic and extremely likable . . . has assured me that I am one of the people earmarked for his "gang."

In my opinion, he has the capacity to undertake successfully any position in government. He has a reserved dignity—but he is most animated in conversation on subjects interesting him. . . . He is impulsive—able, even brilliant—quick—tenacious of his views and extremely self-confident.[16]

MacArthur continued to fight what amounted to a losing battle over the Army's budget. As the slump deepened, millions were thrown out of work. The jobless rate reached 20 percent in 1932 and continued to rise. Hoover launched a wide range of initiatives to counteract the Depression, but was trapped in the conventional economic wisdom that had him applying poison to the problem in the confident belief that it was medicine. Although he had been secretary of commerce, he was as economically naïve as the men selling apples on street corners. Hoover believed that the way to get the economy back on its feet was to achieve a balanced budget. If more money had to go on public works to create jobs, less money would have to be spent on something else—such as the military. The idea that the right response to an economic downturn was to borrow money and increase government spending to check the downward spiral of decline was unthinkable and probably immoral.

Hoover slashed spending on the military but increased it for almost everything else. In July 1932 Army salaries were cut by 10 percent. This was unwelcome but manageable for officers above the rank of major. For junior officers and enlisted men it brought a severe cut in their already modest living standards. As publisher of the *Army and Navy Journal,* John Callan O'Laughlin heard countless stories of the hardship being inflicted as the Budget Bureau cut, cut and cut again. O'Laughlin wrote to MacArthur to tell him the fight over the 1932 budget was "one of the most serious crises since the Civil War."[17]

It was not only money that was at issue. The chairman of the House Appropriations subcommittee, Congressman Ross Collins of Mississippi, clashed repeatedly with MacArthur over the kind of military the United States should have. The general believed people won wars, while Collins believed wars were won by superior matériel. The way to pay for modern tanks and planes was to reduce military manpower and stop wasting money on salaries. Collins had written a clause into the Army's budget that would impose a reduction of two thousand officers. MacArthur responded with an open letter to the House minority leader that strongly defended the General Staff's emphasis on men over matériel.

"An army can live on short rations," MacArthur conceded. "It can be insufficiently clothed and housed, it can even be poorly armed and equipped, but in action it is doomed to destruction without the trained and adequate leadership of officers. An efficient and sufficient Corps of Officers means the difference between victory and defeat."[18]

He concluded by pointing out that the Army was hardly gobbling up the nation's wealth. It was presently less than half the size projected under the 1920 National Defense Act and "Among the armies of the world it ranks 16th in strength. . . ." The House nevertheless approved Collins's officer reduction measure.

MacArthur fought back. He talked to Colonel Ernest Graves, an astute officer on the staff of the chief of engineers. The Corps of Engineers was currently engaged in one of the biggest engineering projects in American history, trying to tame the Mississippi River. This was a project that was important to a dozen states. MacArthur urged Graves to lobby the senators from those states to reject the officer reduction bill when it came up in the Senate. This political effort paid off. The Senate rejected the bill, but MacArthur had made an implacable enemy of Ross Collins. It was a victory that would come back to haunt him.[19]

Collins's next economy measure was a proposal to end retirement pay for officers who had income from other sources amounting to more than ten thousand dollars a year. There was a suggestion too that the special pension of eighteen thousand dollars that Congress had voted for Pershing should be eliminated. MacArthur fought zealously to defend existing pension rules and went out of his way to justify Pershing's money. It hardly compared, he pointed out, with the five-hundred-thousand-dollar trust fund that the British government had established for Douglas Haig in reward for his services in World War I, plus a hereditary peerage and a generous pension. Collins's attacks on the Army's retirees were quietly abandoned.[20]

MacArthur's heartfelt defense of Pershing marked a watershed in their relationship. Black Jack wrote to MacArthur: "Please allow me to send you my warmest congratulations upon the way you have succeeded in overcoming opposition in Congress to the Army. . . . And may I also express my appreciation for the way you have defended the Retired List and especially your reference to me."[21]

MacArthur's second year as Chief of Staff ended on a note of alarm. His efforts to save the Army from the budget slashers had accomplished little but slow the process of decline. It had done nothing to alter direction. The Army's strength fell in 1932 to 130,000 enlisted men and 12,000 officers. In his annual report he said flatly that this was "below the point of safety."

MacArthur left no record to show that the thought ever actually occurred to him, but the situation had become so desperate under Hoover that even he, lifelong Republican that he was, may have had one of those blinding three-in-the-morning epiphanies, the kind that can jolt someone awake in a cold sweat and feeling slightly nauseated, that the best thing for the Army, as for the country, might be a different president.[22]

MacArthur dearly wanted to make the Army bigger. If it got much smaller, it would be more of a constabulary than a real fighting force. At the present time it was only half the size authorized by the 1920 National Defense Act, but Congress would not finance any expansion. MacArthur increasingly devoted his efforts to improving on what the Army already possessed. The War Department had been authorized to operate three army headquarters but had never established even one. Instead the Army within the United States was organized into nine corps. As a step toward war readiness and better training, MacArthur pushed through the creation of four field army headquarters, covering the West Coast, the Great Lakes, the Northeast and the Southeast. Once they were established, he insisted that they hold regular command post exercises and field maneuvers. In time of war these four headquarters would be available to train citizen armies and take them overseas.[23]

He was so committed to the four-army plan that he put his own ambition to one side. The present corps commanders were two-star generals. So too were the three army commanders they reported to. The General Staff argued, rightly, that this was an anomalous situation. As things stood, divisions, corps and armies were all under the command of two-star generals. The sensible thing to do was to promote the corps commanders to three stars and the army commanders to four.

This posed a dilemma for MacArthur. At the present time there was only one four-star general, and he was it. As Chief of Staff he was a temporary full general. But when he stepped down or retired, he would revert to being a major general again. If, however, he accepted the General Staff's recommendation, he might be portrayed in Congress as looking out for his own interests rather than the Army's interests. Some congressmen, such as Ross

Collins, were almost certain to claim he had pushed for army commanders to have four stars so that he could assume command of an army when he ceased to be Chief of Staff. That way he could hold on to his four-star rank. To avoid that kind of accusation, he turned down the recommendation from the General Staff, but the result was four very unhappy army commanders.[24]

One of the most complicated organizational problems MacArthur faced was what to do about tanks. The Army had taken a keen interest in the Experimental Mechanized Force that the British created in the late 1920s. A handful of American officers made a strong case for something similar in the United States. They persuaded Summerall and his last directive as Chief of Staff read: "Assemble that mechanized force now."[25]

A small force of light tanks, armored cars and truck-towed artillery was organized at Fort Eustis, Virginia, and began trying to work out the tactics of armored warfare. Known officially as the 7th Cavalry Brigade (Mechanized), it was no potent weapon of war, but it created considerable interest all the same. The infantry wanted to get its hands on tanks. After all, it had been tanks that created the huge rents in the German defenses that allowed British and French armies to break through in the closing stages of World War I.

The horse cavalry meanwhile looked enviously and apprehensively at the tank experiments. The commander of the mechanized brigade, Colonel Adna Romanza Chaffee, urged MacArthur to assign his force to the cavalry. Chaffee was himself a horse soldier, as were many of the officers in the brigade. There were doubts within and without the Army over the future of horse cavalry, but some cavalry officers, such as George Patton, foresaw a future in which horses and tanks operated together![26]

At the same time, infantry was the basic arm of the Army, and MacArthur was an infantryman. He would not ignore the infantry's plea for armored support. In the end MacArthur gave tanks to both the infantry and the cavalry.[27]

A living, breathing challenge to the military's obsession with standardization, MacArthur continued to assert his individuality in the way he dressed. Something within him resisted, if not resented, the limits of uniforms. In 1926 the Army got rid of the World War I uniforms, which were high-necked with stiff collars. They were so obviously uncomfortable it took discipline to wear them. The old uniform was replaced with an open-necked jacket, a shirt with a soft collar and a black silk tie, just like a businessman. When MacArthur became Chief of Staff, he put his black tie away and started wearing a purple tie, cut from satin.[28]

He also turned his attention to reforming something that was literally close to his heart: medals. The Army had never had a sensible medal policy. He reformed it. The small silver star that was awarded to men whose bravery had been cited in official orders was better known as the "citation star" and was worn on the ribbon of the relevant campaign medal. MacArthur had it transformed into the modern Silver Star, a medal in its own right, ranking just below the Distinguished Service Cross among gallantry awards. The first Silver Star awarded went to him and was engraved "No. 1."[29]

He also got rid of the old, unprepossessing "wound stripe," a small bit of yellow cloth that was worn on the left sleeve. He revived the first American decoration, the Purple Heart, which Washington had created to reward military merit. The new Purple Heart could be awarded for merit, but most recipients would receive it in recognition of wounds, and the list of qualifying wounds placed being gassed ahead of all other categories. The very first Purple Heart awarded went to MacArthur, and on the back this medal too is inscribed "No. 1."[30]

By introducing these awards, the Army took a major step toward properly recognizing the courage and sacrifice of American soldiers. The Purple Heart in particular was prized. It was, and is, the decoration men want least, but the one that those who have it are inclined to value most.

The General Staff was unpopular with much of the Army and was regularly sniped at by some members of Congress. MacArthur bolstered its pride and boosted its status by designing a handsome green, black and gold badge for General Staff officers. In size and magnificence it seemed almost like the insignia of an exclusive European military order, the kind of bauble conferred in a palace by royalty.

MacArthur also amended the regulations on decorations so that all of them could be worn. He wore on his chest both his DSC ribbons, for instance, plus all seven Silver Star ribbons, plus both Purple Heart ribbons. In outright defiance of Army regulations, he wore one of his father's medals—the Philippine Campaign Medal from the days of the insurrection, not so much perhaps to wear an extra ribbon as to mingle his father's military glory with his own. He also continued to wear his two wound stripes.

His eight rows of ribbons, his General Staff badge and the rest made quite a display. Easy to mock, of course, but a harbinger of military shows yet to come. Half a century later that would be the look not only of American generals but of many officers and even senior NCOs—row upon row of ribbons, with badges below and badges above, stretching, it seemed, from clavicle to navel. The first among peacocks was far from the last.

Nothing in MacArthur's long military career was as controversial as his action in routing the Bonus Army and driving it out of Washington in July 1932. This clash did more harm to his reputation than anything else he ever did. It became a kind of folk tale that dressed in his fanciest uniform and riding a white horse down Pennsylvania Avenue at the head of heavily armed troops, he drove thousands of impoverished, unemployed demonstrators who were exercising their rights as citizens out of the capital at gunpoint and with the naked blades of bayonets. Hundreds of women and children were caught up in this melee, and they too were mercilessly teargassed and clubbed, their wretched hovels set ablaze by MacArthur's troops and their pathetic squatter camps razed. This affront to the nation's conscience was brought about because one man—Douglas MacArthur— was so arrogant, so bent on unleashing the power at his command on these defenseless, wretched people that he defied a direct order from the President not to allow his troops to enter the Bonus Army's camps. A general who could act with such brazen contempt for civilian authority and the rights of American citizens in the streets of their own capital city seemed to many liberals to be a threat to American government itself.

The legend of MacArthur the brutal and ruthless, of MacArthur the "man on horseback" merely awaiting his chance, of MacArthur the insubordinate general is well entrenched by now. Nor, at first blush, does it look like a legend. The two most authoritative scholarly accounts of what happened both go a long way toward sustaining it, even while correcting some of the details. MacArthur did not, for example, ride a white horse down Pennsylvania Avenue in July 1932. But even MacArthur's admirers, such as William Manchester, Frazier Hunt and Cornelius Ryan, have trouble defending his handling of the Bonus Army and are defensive about MacArthur's actions that day. However, the truth is more interesting than the legend, which bears almost no resemblance to what actually occurred.

What happened in Washington in July 1932 sprang directly from the Depression. The near collapse of the American economy wreaked unspeakable injustice and hardship on millions of people who had done nothing to deserve such a fate. Of all the groups that felt they had a special claim for help from the government, veterans of World War I were the most vocal and the most inclined to take direct action. Some 3.5 million veterans held Adjusted Compensation Certificates, which Congress had authorized in 1924 over strong objections from Coolidge. These certificates amounted to a bonus. The redemption value of the average certificate was one thousand dollars, which was payable on death of the holder or in 1945. Out of work and down on their luck, many veterans wanted their money now, and Congressman Wright Patman of Texas introduced legislation that would let them have it. In the spring of 1932 more than ten thousand veterans, calling themselves the Bonus Expeditionary Force, or BEF, headed for Washington, led by a former artillery sergeant in the AEF, Walter Waters. They intended to lobby Congress for passage of the Patman bill.

When this news reached the War Department, George Van Horn Moseley, the assistant chief of staff, advised MacArthur that the Army should have plans to maintain order in the streets. The Chief of Staff disagreed. The Army should not get involved. If there was any trouble, the District police would handle it.[31]

On its arrival in Washington, the BEF launched the biggest, longest-lasting demonstration that Capitol Hill had ever witnessed. Bonus Army marchers took up residence in half a dozen condemned buildings along Pennsylvania Avenue and set up squalid camps on wasteland. The biggest camp was on a swampy stretch of derelict ground alongside the Potomac known as Anacostia Flats.

The District's superintendent of police, Pelham D. Glassford, openly sympathized with the demonstrators. Glassford had been the youngest general in the AEF, winning his brigadier general's star at the age of thirty-four. Tall, handsome and cruising his domain on a huge motorcycle, he did all he could to make sure these men were fed regularly and received medical attention. Hoover too was moved by their plight. He wanted them out of the District, but that did not still his humanitarian impulses. He too ensured, if secretly, that the most urgent needs of the marchers were met, while praying that once the Patman bill was out of the way, the BEF would go back to where it came from.[32]

As more and more bonus marchers arrived, the mood of the protest became increasingly bellicose. MacArthur began to wonder whether the police really could maintain order if Patman's bill was rejected. He told Moseley to make preparations just in case the worst happened and the police called for the Army's assistance. Moseley moved half a dozen Renault tanks from Fort Meade, Maryland, down to Fort Myer and had extra troops brought into the Washington area.

The House passed Patman's bill, but the Senate turned it down. Some bonus marchers accepted the Veterans Administration's help in returning home, but most stayed on well into July. Tensions were rising sharply. Congress had adjourned for the summer, but more than five thousand bonus marchers remained in the District. More to the point, they refused to evacuate the buildings they were occupying along Pennsylvania Avenue. The squatters did not feel they were doing any harm. All the buildings were condemned. The main shopping district on Pennsylvania Avenue was being redeveloped. Demolishing these nineteenth-century buildings and erecting new, modern structures were a public works project aimed at creating hundreds of jobs. The project was falling behind schedule because of the occupation by bonus marchers. The demolition contractor was urging the government to remove them because he was losing money by this prolonged delay.[33]

The people occupying the buildings were warned they faced eviction, and most left peacefully. Waters meanwhile went to see Hurley, to ask if the Army had any tents to house them. When he entered the secretary of war's office the afternoon of July 26, he found Hurley seated at his desk and MacArthur pacing furiously. Hurley listened to what Waters had to say, then asked MacArthur, "Is there any tentage available?"

MacArthur's reply was a brusque "No."

Hurley proceeded to give Waters a long lecture, which was clearly intended to intimidate him and his followers into leaving Washington immediately. "We are interested only in getting you out of the District," he said sternly at one point, "and we have plenty of troops to put you out."

Waters refused to be browbeaten. He asked MacArthur, as one soldier to another, "If the troops should be called out against us, will the BEF be given the opportunity to form in columns, salvage their belongings, and retreat in orderly fashion?"

MacArthur stopped pacing and looked at Waters. "Yes, my friend, of course!"

To Waters that was a clear promise that even if the troops were put on the streets, "the evicting force would not drive us out like rats." It was a tiny crumb of comfort, but it was a lot more than Hurley was offering.[34]

On the morning of July 28 a small group of bonus marchers advancing under an American flag reclaimed one of the emptied buildings. The police moved to regain it at noon. Glassford took command on the spot, just as a scuffle broke out. He slumped to the ground, felled by a brick. A wartime Medal of Honor winner, police officer Edward G. Scott, stood over him, attempting to protect the fallen superintendent. Scott too went down, his skull fractured by a brick. The result of this fracas was six policemen hospitalized, two of them with serious injuries.

Two hours later there was a second outbreak of violence. This time one BEF member was shot dead and another suffered a bullet wound in a scuffle with the police. Senior police officers advised the District commissioners that the situation was about to get completely out of control. There were six hundred policemen confronting five thousand potential rioters.[35]

The commissioners informed MacArthur that troops were going to be needed and made a verbal request to Hoover to put the Army on the streets. Hoover rejected their request, telling them he would not accept it unless they put it in writing. They promptly sent a formal letter to the President stating that the police could no longer maintain law and order "except by the free use of firearms . . . however, the presence of Federal troops in some number will obviate the seriousness of the situation and result in far less violence and bloodshed."[36]

Hurley and MacArthur came to the Oval Office and urged Hoover to issue a proclamation of martial law. Hoover refused to consider it. He would not declare martial law, and he would not give the Army a free hand. The soldiers would operate in support of the police. He told MacArthur to restore order on the streets, herd the marchers back to Anacostia Flats and hold them there.

Troops of the 16th Infantry Brigade, commanded by Brigadier General Perry L. Miles, were soon moving into the District, crossing the Memorial Bridge from Fort Myer. Patton accompanied the armored contingent, consisting of the tanks that Moseley had brought from Fort Meade.

MacArthur, to Eisenhower's dismay, decided to oversee the operations in person. It was customary for Army officers working in Washington not to wear their uniforms most of the time. They were hoping to spare civilian sensibilities in this new, pacifistic, antimilitaristic age. Ike went home to change, and MacArthur sent his Filipino valet to Fort Myer to fetch a uniform. The valet returned with the fanciest outfit the general owned, the one with the chestful of ribbons and marksmanship badges.

In midafternoon MacArthur received written orders from Hurley: "The President has just now informed me that the civil government of the District of Columbia . . . is unable to maintain law and order in the District . . . proceed immediately to the scene of disorder. Cooperate fully with the District of Columbia police force which is now in charge. Surround the affected area and clear it without delay."[37]

MacArthur left the War Department and went to join General Miles, who was astonished when MacArthur appeared and told him he was going to supervise the operation. Miles had enjoyed a distinguished career and held both the DSC and the DSM; he was MacArthur's kind of soldier, a man who excelled in both combat and staff work. They had known each other for more than thirty years. MacArthur was not going to justify his actions to an aide, but he would explain them to a fellow general, at least, to a general like Miles. He said he had come at the suggestion of the President and the secretary of war, and he would "take the rap if there should be any unfavorable or critical repercussions." The two men got into Miles's staff car and headed down Pennsylvania Avenue.[38]

When they found Glassford, who had returned to the scene of disorder despite his injuries, MacArthur told him he had orders from Hoover "to drive the veterans out of the city. We are going to break the back of the BEF." Glassford, the friend of the bonus marchers, raised no objections. He and MacArthur went back a long way. Glassford was West Point '04 and had been assigned to Company A. For three years as a cadet he had followed MacArthur's orders. While MacArthur was ostensibly under

Glassford's orders now, the command relationship was really what it had been since their days together as cadets.[39]

The Army drove the bonus marchers off Capitol Hill with the free use of tear gas, the flat side of sabers and the menacing point of naked bayonets, driving them back toward Anacostia Flats. While this was happening, the head of the Secret Service White House detail, Edmund Starling, raised the question of what would happen to the women and children in the BEF's main camp. Surely the Army wasn't going to expose them to tear gas and bayonets? Hoover told Hurley not to allow the troops to cross the Anacostia bridge until the women and children had been removed.[40] The troops were not to cross the Anacostia bridge and force the evacuation of the camp.

Hurley in turn informed Moseley. "I left my office," Moseley recorded, "contacted General MacArthur, and as we walked away from the others, I delivered that message to him. He was very much annoyed at having his plans interfered with in any way until they were executed completely."[41]

This entry in Moseley's memoirs is the source of the story that MacArthur deliberately violated his orders in an arrogant and insubordinate act of disobedience. What is interesting is that none of the scholars who have relied on it has ever questioned its veracity, yet all have been learned men of liberal views. This is remarkable, considering the fact that Moseley was a vehement anti-Semite and a man whose political views were essentially those of a fascist. Moseley was an embarrassment to the Army. As Kenneth Crawford of *Newsweek* pointed out in 1939, "responsible Army leaders take Moseley seriously only as a menace to the prestige of the service."[42]

Moseley's claim that he delivered this message to MacArthur was flatly contradicted by three unimpeachable witnesses. All had good reputations for honesty, and neither had anything to gain by denying Moseley's story. One was the assistant secretary of war for air, F. Trubee Davison. The morning after the rout of the Bonus Army, Davison went into his office and found Frederick Payne there talking to Moseley. "Payne and Moseley were patting themselves on the back about the wonderful job they had done, and I said, 'What in the world have you fellows done that's so terrific?'

"They said, 'Well, the President wrote an order to MacArthur to stop at the Anacostia bridge.'" Then, they gleefully told Davison, they had made sure MacArthur never got it. "With the result that MacArthur and the whole force went across the bridge."[43]

Davison's story was corroborated by Eisenhower: "The President's message just didn't get to him."[44] Miles, too, insisted that MacArthur had received no such order.

Why, then, would Moseley lie in his memoirs? He repeatedly claimed that he admired MacArthur, and he no doubt did. Even so, in an unguarded moment he had told the truth to Davison and Payne. His memoirs were written, like most memoirs, to justify his life and work. He had his own reputation to defend, and it was always likely that Davison would talk. MacArthur too might rebut what he claimed. Moseley provided for that eventuality when he left his papers to the Library of Congress. Virtually everything was made available to researchers from the time of Moseley's death in 1960. The memoir, however, was embargoed for a further five years. After MacArthur's death in 1964, Moseley's devastating lie seemed safe forever.

When the troops reached the Anacostia bridge, night was falling fast. An emissary came out from the camp and asked MacArthur for enough time to evacuate the women and children. MacArthur readily agreed and had the troops stop for dinner. They did not move again for nearly two hours.

During that time Hoover heard almost nothing of what was happening out in the streets and began to wonder if MacArthur had received his order. He told Hurley to send another officer down there to repeat his earlier order. Because the President believed there was a risk of serious bloodshed if the troops advanced into the Anacostia Flats camp, he did not think such a movement should be attempted. The actual decision, however, was left to the general's discretion.

The message was given to a colonel, but Moseley told him to "get lost." The colonel took three hours to travel less than three miles. By the time he arrived at the Anacostia bridge, the soldiers had finished eating and were moving out. According to Miles, "General MacArthur sent back word that it was too late to abandon the operation. The troops were committed . . . and some had crossed the bridge already."[45]

As the troops closed on the entrance to the camp, the hundred or so bonus marchers who were still inside began setting fire to their crude shacks in rage and frustration. The soldiers stopped at the entrance, and Glassford's police took over. Miles and the troops who had cleared the BEF from Capitol Hill returned to Fort Myer, while MacArthur went back to the War Department and reported to Hurley. Several truckloads of troops who had been held in reserve were now brought forward and put under direct police orders. They entered the camp with the police and forced its evacuation.[46]

At 11:00 P.M. Hurley and MacArthur held a news conference. The Chief of Staff was still excited after the day's events. He boasted to the press that the Army had just saved the United States from "incipient revolution." An ardent Bonapartist, it is even possible that he saw himself reliving his hero's famous action in the streets of Paris when he had put down a rioting

mob with "a whiff of grapeshot" and saved an unpopular French government. Next morning, however, Hoover upbraided him. The President was
already one of the most unpopular men ever to occupy the White House.
The furor over the routing of the Bonus Army was certain to cost him the
forthcoming election. MacArthur felt that he had followed orders, exer-
cised the discretion the President had allowed him and done nothing
wrong. He offered to resign but pointedly made no apology.[47]

Hoover stoutly defended MacArthur's actions in public, and once his
anger had cooled, he privately said that everything MacArthur had done
had been within the scope of his instructions. Glassford, too, who was officially in charge of operations and on the scene despite his injury, praised
MacArthur's actions without reservation. He believed MacArthur's
actions were completely justified.[48]

Even so, the legend of MacArthur the brutal and insubordinate man on
horseback, the general who scourged the poor and unemployed and drove
them out of town at the point of naked bayonets, endures. Miles tried for
years to get MacArthur to write a book that would set the record straight,
but MacArthur always claimed he was too busy.[49] The truth is more likely
to be that he wanted the whole sorry business to dwindle into obscurity, but
that was never going to happen.

The rout of the Bonus Army did just what Hoover feared: It guaranteed
the election to the presidency of MacArthur's distant cousin Franklin
Delano Roosevelt.

The Noblest Development
of Mankind

As the Army's senior officer, General of the Armies John J. Pershing had been grand marshal of every inaugural parade since 1921, but in March 1933 he was too ill to ride. It would fall to MacArthur to lead the parade that greeted the new President. This news brought strong protests from some veterans, resentful of his treatment of the Bonus Army, but on a cold, rain-swept March afternoon MacArthur rode a magnificent bay stallion at the head of marching bands and parading troops down Pennsylvania Avenue for the inauguration of Franklin D. Roosevelt. It was photographs of MacArthur riding this white horse that inspired the legend that he had ridden at the head of the troops who drove the Bonus Army out of Washington.

New Dealers generally looked on MacArthur with suspicion, and some regarded him with loathing. His emotional speeches attacking pacifism alienated many liberals, who regarded the idealism that motivated the vast majority of pacifists as an ornament of a democratic society rather than a threat. Even his attacks on Communists antagonized people who were determined to resist any recurrence of the disgraceful Red Scare of the early 1920s. But it was really the rout of the Bonus Army that made MacArthur a great hate figure among Democrats. For years afterward prominent Democrats such as Eleanor Roosevelt continued to believe that the Army, on MacArthur's orders, had opened fire on the bonus marchers.[1]

The rumor in the corridors of the War Department in the weeks leading up to the inauguration was that one of the first things the new President was going to do was fire MacArthur and find a new Chief of Staff.[2]

Franklin Roosevelt, however, was in no hurry to fire MacArthur. He had more pressing business to deal with than looking for a new Chief of Staff. The new President appointed a former governor of Utah, George Dern, to be secretary of war. Dern was a mining engineer, a large, affable man with little political experience and no prior interest in military affairs. The fact that someone like Dern got this appointment indicated how little importance Roosevelt attached to the military at the start of his administration.

The most urgent issue facing the incoming New Deal was putting people to work. Roosevelt had hardly gotten himself behind the desk in the Oval Office before he was pressing Congress to create the Civilian Conservation Corps. The aim was to have at least 275,000 young men enrolled by July 1, 1933. Congress quickly passed the legislation, and the new administration, filled as it was with people who were suspicious of the military, was soon dismayed to discover that only the Army could implement a program on this scale in the time the President had set.

MacArthur gave the CCC all the help he could. There was an opportunity here to create goodwill for the Army within the new administration and the newly elected, Democratically controlled Congress. The most important action he took was to give the nine corps commanders the widest powers to set up and operate the camps in their corps areas. He would establish policy, but it was for the corps commanders to work out ways to implement it according to local conditions. By decentralizing the Army's role but making clear his strong support for the program MacArthur sped the creation of the CCC.[3]

On July 1 there were nearly three hundred thousand men enrolled. More than 80 percent were high school dropouts under the age of twenty-one and had never held a job in their young lives.[4] The Army clothed them, fed them and ran the camps along military lines. There was reveille at 6:00 A.M. and retreat at 5:00 P.M. Each camp numbered about two hundred enrollees, under the control of two officers and several enlisted men. Some officers found the whole program distasteful and considered it a waste of their time. When they ought to be training soldiers to fight, they were instead showing poorly educated youngsters how to plant trees, build small dams, erect lookout towers in the forests and fight forest fires. Other officers, however, found this the best school of leadership they could have hoped for. There was no military discipline in the CCC camps. There was nothing to stop the enrollees from refusing to work. They were free to leave at any time. It was for the Army to motivate them to work hard and like it.[5]

Once the camps were up and running, MacArthur wanted his officers back. There were twelve thousand officers in the Regular Army, and nearly 30 percent were assigned to CCC work. That situation, he warned Roosevelt, could not continue without harming national defense. The President reluctantly agreed. Within a year most of the officers working with the CCC were reservists.[6]

MacArthur's success with the Civilian Conservation Corps probably saved him from being replaced as Chief of Staff. The persistent rumors that Roosevelt was planning to relieve him were finally scotched in September 1933, when the War Department announced flatly that the President planned to retain MacArthur as Chief of Staff.[7]

Despite the evident success of the CCC, there was loud agitation in the liberal press to end the Army's involvement completely. Whether reservists or regulars, ran the refrain, Army officers would "militarize" these young men. MacArthur rejected such criticism out of hand.[8]

All the same, once the CCC had established itself as a popular success, he wanted to get some military advantage from it. The Army had no enlisted reserve worthy of the name. MacArthur proposed that those who came to the end of their one-year enrollments should be encouraged to sign up for membership in an Auxiliary Enlisted Reserve, which would provide them with six months of military training. This brought such an outcry in Congress that Dern, for once, was unwilling to support him, and the President wasted no time in letting it be known that he did not favor the idea. It died aborning.[9]

This furor was but one manifestation of the powerful tide of hostility to the military that was pervasive in the 1930s. And war being the business of the military meant, to many people in the 1930s, that there was something wrong with men who were attracted to the military life. These were exactly the kind of people who should not be entrusted with America's young.

MacArthur fought the antimilitary mood at every opportunity. He was even prepared to go where few politicians have ever dared and told the nation's clergymen they were in the wrong. He lectured them on the dangers of pacifism and traded biblical quote for biblical quote. His God was Christ militant, the deity who said he did not bring peace but a sword, rather than the more emollient Christ of the New Testament who recommended turning the other cheek.

Pacifist groups had for more than a decade been lobbying to end the compulsory Reserve Officers Training Corps in the nation's colleges. MacArthur poured scorn on those who opposed it. "This feature of our military preparation is frequently subjected to bitter attacks by radicals, pacifists, and the uninformed," he declared in 1934. But the ROTC was not an Army plot to warp young minds. "The law has required military instruction in our land grant colleges since the Civil War, and any militarizing effect on our people would have long ago been apparent." It was noteworthy too, he pointed out, that at the eighty-three colleges where the ROTC was compulsory, the overwhelming majority of faculty and students favored its retention. The agitation against it was centered on campuses where there was no ROTC or where it was voluntary.[10]

MacArthur's most famous challenge to campus pacifists had occurred when he went to receive an honorary degree at the University of Pittsburgh in June 1932. His presence stirred up such passions that the local police felt unable to maintain order without putting more than a hundred student activists under arrest the day of MacArthur's visit to prevent a riot. "Pacifism and its bedfellow, Communism, are all about us," he thundered. "In the theaters, newspapers and magazines, pulpits and lecture halls, schools and colleges, it hangs like a mist before the face of America. . . . Day by day this canker eats deeper into the body politic. . . .

"For the sentimentalism and emotionalism which have infected our country we should substitute hard common sense. Pacific habits do not insure peace. . . . Any nation that would keep its self-respect must be prepared to defend itself."[11]

Far from discouraging campus pacifism, such speeches probably only encouraged it, but the brief fuss over the "militarization" of the CCC soon died down, and the civilian director of the project, onetime machinists' union leader Robert Fechner, felt indebted to MacArthur's wholehearted efforts to make the program succeed. When MacArthur's tenure as Chief of Staff drew to a close, Fechner sent him a letter thanking him warmly. He told MacArthur how gratifying it had been to see "Your personal interest" in the CCC. "I know that your sympathetic interest was the main spring in the work that the Army has performed."[12]

MacArthur was sufficiently moved by this tribute to send something better than the flowery, empty note that people who flattered him usually received. He told Fechner frankly, "My work with the Civilian Conservation camps has been a real inspiration to me. It is a type of human reconstruction that has appealed to me more than I sometimes admit."[13]

Although MacArthur had managed to convince Roosevelt to keep him on as Chief of Staff, he was still bitterly disliked by many of the people around the President. He had an implacable antagonist in the new secretary of the interior, Harold Ickes, a former journalist with sharp wits and an even sharper tongue.

The interior secretary delighted in his nickname, the Old Curmudgeon. It had a bold ring to it, a strong hint that here was a man of integrity, a damn-your-eyes kind of colorful figure who spoke his own mind and sought the favor of no one. There was no doubting Ickes's devotion to public service. MacArthur, though, got under Ickes's skin, bringing out something a lot more vitriolic in him than mere irritability. Ickes hated MacArthur and couldn't contemplate him for a moment with an objective gaze. "MacArthur is the type of man," Ickes noted shortly after coming to Washington, "who thinks that when he gets to heaven God will step down from the great white throne and bow him into His vacant seat, and it gave me a great kick to have him in and break the news to him [that the Army wouldn't get large dollops of WPA money for new equipment]. . . . He gave me a lecture on the necessity for the little old peanut Army posts that we have scattered around the country."[14]

Ickes also antagonized MacArthur by his blatant empire building. He tried to get Roosevelt to transfer Arlington National Cemetery to the National Park Service. This would have denied the Army the responsibility, and honor, of burying its dead. Something like a gasp of pain and amazement came from the War Department. Dern protested strongly to the President that transferring Arlington to the Park Service "will deeply offend the sensibilities of the officers and enlisted personnel of the Army and Navy and will be openly resented by the veterans of our wars." And not even Ickes, he pointed out, was able to criticize the way the War Department had managed Arlington for the past sixty years. Roosevelt let Ickes have control of the Custis-Lee mansion overlooking the cemetery, but the graves remained in the Army's care.[15]

MacArthur had another powerful enemy in Congressman Ross Collins of Mississippi. Following the Democratic landslide of 1932, Collins had become the chairman of the House subcommittee that handled military appropriations. A sarcastic keep-the-niggers-in-their-place kind of southern Democrat, a man who never criticized a lynching but pandered instead to the deadly prejudices of his constituents, Collins was not exactly an advertisement for American democracy. Eisenhower was only one among many who loathed him. "Ross Collins," he recorded in his diary, "is either stupid or a shrewd charlatan."[16] From his new vantage point Collins was perfectly placed to make life hard for MacArthur.

Following Hoover's defeat, MacArthur had Dwight Eisenhower reassigned, away from the assistant secretary of war. Ike was now ensconced in a small room next to MacArthur's spacious office. The two men were separated only by a slatted door. MacArthur did not need to raise his voice to command the major's presence. Ike's new title was Senior Aide to the Chief of Staff. This made Ike a key member in the "family" that MacArthur was trying to create out of his colleagues.[17]

Eisenhower was clearly on the inside track of the Army establishment. He had become right-hand man to the Chief of Staff entirely on his abilities, which were great, and his ambition, which was equally outstanding.

No one rises within a profession as competitive as the military without a clear strategy for getting ahead.

During a tour of duty in Panama in the 1920s Ike once told an Army friend, Bradford G. Chynoweth, how it was done. "When I go to a new station I look to see who is the strongest and ablest man on the post. I forget my own ideas and do everything in my power to promote what *he* says is right." His approach, thought Chynoweth, was much like that of an actor accepting the role given him by a director.[18]

MacArthur still went home each day to have lunch with his mother, and he was home for dinner most evenings too. Isabel, meanwhile, was feeling increasingly neglected. Her globe-trotter was so busy in Washington, a lot busier than he had ever been in Manila, that she hardly saw him, or anyone else.

In 1933 she signed up for educational courses that would get her out of the Chastleton and give her a chance to meet people her own age. That was exactly what happened. She met a young law student. Interest in Daddy, already fading, grew pretty tenuous. When MacArthur realized that his Dimples was pursuing other interests than hanging around at home doing little more than apply nail polish and lipstick while awaiting the warrior's return, his mood grew ugly. In April 1934 their relationship finally broke up.

He saw Isabel for the last time in July, when he gave her some money and a steamer ticket to take her back to the Philippines. She had no intention of leaving, however. She cashed in the ticket and looked for a cheap place to live in Washington. By the end of September she was broke and demanded more money from MacArthur. Incensed, he scribbled an angry note to her that read, "From the Humane Society. Apply to your Father or Brother for any future help." To rub it in, MacArthur carefully cut six inches from the "Help—Women" classifieds in *The Washington Times*. The jobs on offer then were much like those advertised now—selling mediocre products door-to-door, slaving for peanuts as a home help, work as a beauty parlor trainee. Still, what else was Isabel qualified for?[19]

As MacArthur surely knew, he had taken a huge risk in bringing her to Washington. Dimples was a walking time bomb that could easily blow up in his face. And of course, that's exactly what happened.

MacArthur was despised by much of the liberal press. By far the most ferociously hostile journalist he ever encountered—and there were many outstanding contenders for that prize—was the columnist Drew Pearson, a man who was not particularly accurate in his reporting but had an uncanny ability to ferret out scandals and failures in government. Pearson loathed MacArthur as militarism incarnate. He used his newspaper column to attack MacArthur so vehemently that MacArthur was stung into striking back. It was to prove one of the biggest mistakes he ever made.

Roughly six weeks after sending his Humane Society note and the newspaper cutting to Isabel, MacArthur filed a libel suit against Drew Pearson. The "Washington Merry-Go-Round" column that Pearson wrote had for the past year regularly criticized MacArthur and held him up to scorn. The column accused him of being disloyal to Roosevelt and Dern, of pulling strings to get himself promoted, of being vain and incompetent. Pearson was not conjuring his stories out of thin air. He had a source— Louise.

A year after her divorce from MacArthur, she had married an English character actor named Lionel Atwill. The marriage, however, was not destined to last. Rumor had it that Atwill had acquired some Hollywood habits, including group sex. He was also reputed to be a cross-dresser. Locked into a bizarre marriage to a strange man, Louise became self-pitying and hugely fat. She looked ever deeper into the contents of bottles and, in Drew Pearson, found at least one person who would listen, fascinated, to her tales, especially those about MacArthur.

Pearson fed much of what she told him into his "Merry-Go-Round." The resulting concoction was a potent blend of one man's hatred and an unhappy woman's scorn. She told him, for example, that MacArthur was impotent. It was the kind of ludicrous lie that hurt people tell when drunk. She would raise a crooked finger, in a bony parody of a flaccid organ, and say, "This is Douglas's penis. He thinks it's just for peeing with!"[20]

What she said was partly true, but MacArthur was not impotent. As his letters to her show, in the first few years of their marriage there was tremendous sexual excitement in their relationship. His letters to her when they were apart were filled with sexual references and reminiscences. Their sex life involved a game in which he was a stud called Dapple and she was a mare called Apple, and their bed became "the stall" where Dapple mounted Apple. In the last years of their marriage, however, he had lost interest in sex with Louise. But she was hardly going to tell Pearson that.[21]

Louise made other claims too that were simply untrue. She claimed, for example, that it was she who had gotten MacArthur promoted to major general. She had achieved this feat simply by getting her fabulously rich stepfather, Edward T. Stotesbury, a major Republican party contributor, to use his influence with Coolidge's secretary of war, John Weeks. It was an absurd claim, but Pearson believed every word of it. The fact is, Stotesbury had had so little influence with Weeks he could not even get MacArthur's assignment changed so that he and Louise would not have to go back to the Philippines.

When MacArthur sued Pearson for $1.75 million, the most he could have hoped for was a settlement of $100,000 to $200,000. Juries awarded much lower damages then than they do now. A $100,000 judgment, however, would have been more than enough to put Pearson out of business. He was not a rich man, and his column had been running for only a couple of years. If he lost, the Merry-Go-Round would come to a screeching halt. Pearson, however, did not expect to lose. Louise hated MacArthur so much she would surely be happy to repeat her stories in court. Besides, her stories were true . . . weren't they?

When Pearson offered her the opportunity to repeat what she had told him in front of a jury, she was terrified. She absolutely refused to take the stand. Louise had always pretended to journalists that she remained on good terms with her former husband. To tell the truth now would have been to put the real Louise—the embittered, maudlin divorcée—on show. No chance. When she pulled the plug on Pearson, he was left staring into a bottomless pit papered with every dollar he had or might ever hope to have.[22]

Just as he began to despair, Ross Collins came to his rescue. It was like something out of Dickens. Collins tipped off Pearson that MacArthur had "a Chinese mistress" somewhere in Washington. If Pearson could track her down, she just might have something Pearson could use to fight off MacArthur's libel suit. Pearson and his partner, Robert Allen, immediately launched a frantic search for her. They discovered she had left the Chastleton. The love nest was empty. Isabel was not Chinese, but that aside, Washington in those days was much smaller than it is now and a lovely Eurasian teenager could be expected to be noticed.

Within a week Pearson had found Isabel. She had just what he needed—blackmail material: twenty-three letters, telegrams and postcards that faithfully charted the progress of the affair from early euphoria to venomous parting.[23] This correspondence was dynamite, but there was more.

Isabel, unlike Louise, was willing to take the witness stand. She was prepared to testify under oath that MacArthur had boasted, "Dern is a sleepy old fool and completely dependent on me," "Hoover was a weakling, but I finally put some backbone into him" and "I have surpassed my father's achievements." He was also, she said, in the habit of referring to Roosevelt as "that cripple in the White House." It is easy to believe MacArthur said such things. They sound exactly like the kind of boasting and attempts at cleverness that men indulge in just to impress women. Pearson's lawyer, Morris Ernst, interviewed Isabel, then informed MacArthur's lawyer that he not only had the letters and the postcards but also had Isabel's promise to testify. She was prepared to confirm many of Louise's stories under oath and had some additional stories to tell too.[24]

Isabel's price for handing over the letters, postcards and telegrams was fifteen thousand dollars. MacArthur's price was one dollar: In exchange for one dollar from Pearson, he would drop the libel suit. Affidavits and payments were exchanged between the parties, and as her part of the deal Isabel pledged never again to ask MacArthur for money.[25]

She married the law student a few months later but soon divorced him and moved to Hollywood, where she hoped to break into movies. Pearson lost sight of her. From time to time he met Harold Ickes, and they invariably traded stories about the man they loved to hate. Pearson and Ickes were so unbalanced on the subject of MacArthur they considered it possible that he had murdered Isabel and managed to hide the evidence of his crime.[26]

In fact, Isabel had dropped out of sight simply because her attempts to become famous got nowhere. She never got into the movies. She eked out a precarious living in low-paid jobs in Los Angeles until 1960, when she swallowed a fistful of barbiturates, ending her short, unhappy life at the age of forty-seven.[27]

The rumors that went around Washington about MacArthur and the women in his life—his mother, Louise, Isabel—only added to the fascination with the Chief of Staff. There had never been such a glamorous general in the history of the War Department. The personal legend was growing, and MacArthur, deliberately or not, encouraged it every day. He had installed a huge floor-to-ceiling mirror in his office and shamelessly preened before it even in front of visitors.

He seemed unable to think and sit at the same time. Whenever he started talking seriously about anything, he rose from his desk to pace up and down, thinking out loud, playing his sonorous voice like an orchestral instrument and clapping a hand on his chest in imitation of Napoleon. To the amazement of other officers in the War Department, he sometimes wore a silk kimono over his uniform and, clutching a Japanese fan in one hand, puffed relentlessly on a Lucky Strike wedged into a jeweled cigarette holder that he brandished in the other. Finding himself at the top of the Army seemed to have demolished whatever restraints might have once curbed his idiosyncratic behavior. As he stood on the summit of his profession, the rarefied atmosphere of success made him more eccentric than ever, more charismatic and more openly egotistical.[28]

To his enemies, he was a potential threat to the Republic, a leader in waiting for a military-fascist coup. The Depression dealt a devastating blow to faith in democratic government and encouraged political radicalism. Communists found this the only propitious period they ever enjoyed on American soil. Inevitably the political fevers of the 1930s that encouraged the growth of the extreme left also nurtured demagogues on the far right. People like Ickes and Pearson convinced themselves that MacArthur was itching to plant his gleaming boots inside the White House, in cahoots with the plutocrats of Wall Street. And according to Marine Corps two-time Medal of Honor winner Major General Smedley Darlington Butler, retired, that was exactly what was afoot.

In November 1934 Butler testified before the newly created House Un-American Activities Committee. He had been contacted, he told the agog congressmen, by a Wall Street bond salesman named Gerald McGuire, a onetime commander of the American Legion in Connecticut. McGuire wanted Butler to organize a military coup on behalf of the Street.

This was a strange choice, inasmuch as Butler had addressed rapturous Bonus Army rallies, been openly sympathetic to the marchers and run for the Senate on a pro-bonus ticket. He was not noted for being friendly toward Wall Street. *Au contraire.* In his old age he dismissed his thirty-two years as a marine as being no more than "a mercenary for capitalism." Butler had lost his Senate race but in a way that only endeared "Old Gimlet Eye" all the more to thousands of former doughboys.

McGuire and his associates informed Butler that three million dollars was available to finance a coup d'état. The money, they said, had been raised by Grayson Mallet-Prevost Murphy, who happened to be a big-time New York stockbroker as well as a close friend, West Point classmate and wartime companion of Douglas MacArthur. The plan was to have Butler raise an army of five hundred thousand veterans who would follow him in a new march on Washington. They would seize the government and install Hanford MacNider, former commander of the American Legion, in the White House. The veterans would get their reward in an even bigger bonus. As for the Wall Street plutocrats—who included J. P. Morgan—once they had overthrown Roosevelt and seized control of the government, they would put the United States back on the gold standard, thereby safeguarding the value of their millions. Butler knew MacNider and doubted that he would have anything to do with the scheme. Ah, said McGuire. That's easy. We'll get Douglas MacArthur to take MacNider's place.[29]

When the story broke, Murphy and McGuire denied everything. So did J. P. Morgan. MacArthur thought the plot was hilarious. He called Butler's testimony "the best laugh story of the year." Nevertheless the mood of the nation in the mid-1930s was grim. People were afraid of their own shadows. Without anything to support it beyond MacArthur's treatment of the Bonus Army, the idea took hold among many liberals that MacArthur was the fabled "man on horseback" who would one day try to overthrow democratic rule. It was an exaggerated, melodramatic and paranoid idea, worthy, indeed, of MacArthur's own imagination in its darker moods. Only, while he feared people on the left, those on the left feared him, and what united them both was that they were sometimes almost comically wrong in their assessments.

Even Roosevelt briefly entertained the notion of MacArthur as a potential military dictator. He told Rexford G. Tugwell, the head of his Brain Trust (a name originally applied to the General Staff), that MacArthur was "one of the two most dangerous men in the country." The other was the famous rabble-rousing, Democratic governor of Louisiana, Huey "Kingfish" Long.[30]

It was inevitable that MacArthur and Roosevelt would grate on each other. For one thing, Roosevelt had an interest in military matters that was unusual in a president. He considered himself his own expert in this field, capable of being his own secretary of war and his own secretary of the navy. He did not look to either Dern or MacArthur to advise him on the Army.

The real reason for the clash, though, was that here were two gigantic, overly inflated egos. As one General Staff officer who observed them in action ironically put it, "Each was a Hamlet . . . and there was no place on the stage for two Hamlets."[31]

MacArthur could only watch the Army's budget dwindle with something like anguish. Almost the first economy measure implemented by the New Deal was a cut in Army pay by 15 percent. This reduced a private on $21 a month to a poverty-level $17.85. Congress meanwhile was advancing yet another ploy to reduce the Army to a constabulary. An innocuous-looking clause added to the Army's appropriation bill for 1934 would allow the president to "furlough" every officer in the Army, if he so decided, and cut the number of enlisted personnel by twelve thousand. MacArthur immediately responded that he was "violently opposed" to any such measure.[32]

The prospects for the Army had never looked grimmer. Roosevelt, a former assistant secretary of the navy, seemed indifferent to the need to maintain a ground force capable of modern war. MacArthur pointedly informed the House Military Affairs Committee in April 1933 that the Army had shrunk to a point where the number of combat troops available was barely sixty thousand men—"Three times the size of the police force in New York City."[33]

The new administration had inherited Hoover's budget for fiscal year 1934. The Army had asked for $321 million. One of the last things Hoover did as president was slash that figure to $277 million. Roosevelt and the new director of the Budget Bureau, Lewis Douglas, proposed to reduce the Army's budget for fiscal year 1934 by a further $90 million.

MacArthur was alarmed. He let it be known that if this budget proposal was allowed to stand, he would resign his commission and would devote all his energies to campaigning across the country for a more reasonable figure. Dern strongly backed MacArthur. He threw down his own gauntlet by going on the radio to make a speech defending the current level of military expenditure.[34]

MacArthur demanded an appointment with Roosevelt but was told he could not have one. "Unless I have word that I can talk with President Roosevelt by one this afternoon," he replied, "I shall hand in my resignation as Chief of Staff at two and shall explain my reasons in full to the press associations at three."[35]

Roosevelt agreed to see him. Dern accompanied MacArthur to the meeting. The President turned his scorn on Dern, evidently nettled by the secretary of war's temerity in publicly criticizing the administration's policy. Tempers rose, and MacArthur's self-control, which was always on a taut thread, broke. He jumped in and, he later conceded, "I spoke recklessly. I said something to the general effect that when we lost the next war, and an American boy, lying in the mud with an enemy bayonet through his belly and an enemy foot on his dying throat, spat out his last curse, I wanted the name not to be MacArthur but Roosevelt."

MacArthur concluded the interview by declaring he was resigning as Chief of Staff and left the Oval Office. When he got outside, he was overcome by nausea. In what was—whether intended or not—a highly symbolic act, he vomited onto the White House steps.[36]

Roosevelt backed down, and Congress voted $280 million for the Army. Even so, this budget was a devastating blow. The burden of reductions fell on the training programs and the service schools, making the Army more unready than ever to fight or, more to the point, to teach other men how to fight.

Harold Ickes was meanwhile trying to force the Army to concentrate its men in 15 big posts and shut the remaining 195. It was an idea that Budget Director Lewis Douglas enthusiastically supported. MacArthur urged Dern to "set forth vigorous opposition" to the base closures. Congress too was reluctant to eliminate so many jobs in scores of districts. Roosevelt nevertheless shut 50 posts within the continental United States.[37]

Far from closing military bases, MacArthur wanted to modernize them, and he asked the WPA to provide most of the money. Ickes, as we have seen, got great pleasure from rejecting MacArthur's requests for money and ridiculed his efforts to keep Army bases open. Ickes did not foresee that in seven years the government would be struggling to create dozens of new posts and would reopen old bases to accommodate the millions of men who would need training under the 1940 draft law. MacArthur saw only too clearly what was coming; that helped account for the fervor of his attacks on pacifism. Eisenhower too saw it. William Randolph Hearst offered him twenty-five thousand dollars a year—six times as much as the

Army paid him—to resign his commission and become the Hearst chain's military correspondent. Convinced that there would be another world war around 1940, Ike turned him down. Other Army officers, such as George Marshall, took much the same view. The interior secretary's sheer hatred of MacArthur made him blind to the disaster ahead.

Despite Ickes's implacable hostility, MacArthur persistently tried to convince the WPA to provide the money needed to reequip the tank units and motorize the Army's three infantry divisions. Dern made a personal plea to Roosevelt for money to buy new tanks. In vain. The United States had exactly twelve modern tanks in 1933. That was all it was going to have for some time yet.[38]

"I have humiliated myself," MacArthur reflected bitterly. "I have almost licked the boots of some gentlemen to get funds for the motorization and mechanization of the Army."[39]

In 1934 the budget struggle loomed once more. Under the law, no government agency could ask Congress for more money than the Budget Bureau had requested. This clearly helped the executive branch to present its case with a single voice. It also gave Congress an excuse for not looking too deeply into the effects of budget decisions. When MacArthur came to testify for the Army's fiscal year 1935 budget, however, he waded right in like a man with nothing left to lose.

Brilliant speaker that he could be, this was a struggle that oratory would never win. Had MacArthur spoken with the tongue of an angel he could never convert an embittered antagonist like Ross Collins. While he had his admirers in Congress, they were likely to be Republicans and heavily outnumbered by his Democratic critics. Even the immaculate appearance and strict military bearing he presented on Capitol Hill were held against him. Lieutenant Colonel George Kenney overheard one member of the appropriations subcommittee remark to another, "Well, it's about time to go over and hear what the Dude has to say."[40]

And there was the time when Collins and other members of the House Appropriations subcommittee made what MacArthur considered insulting personal remarks while he was testifying before them. MacArthur's response to the least slight was always instantaneous and furious. Sensitive and highly strung by nature, he was a man more and more out of his time, the last Chief of Staff who was not a military manager but a warrior, a man who took his sense of honor from the yellowing pages of an ancient military code. Containing his rage but unable to pretend he had not heard what was said, MacArthur rose abruptly, collected his papers from the table in front of him and declared, "Gentlemen, you have insulted me. I in my profession am as high as you are in yours. When you are ready to apologize,

I shall return." He headed for the door. The committee called MacArthur back and offered an apology.[41]

When he testified for the fiscal year 1935 budget before the Senate Armed Services Committee, he said flatly that Congress could not escape its share of the blame for damaging national security. The senators bristled, but he persisted. The Budget Bureau sends its figures up here and you have to respond to them, he acknowledged, yet that does not relieve any of you of the responsibility the Constitution places on Congress for "raising and maintaining armies." He told them squarely, "You are not bound by budget figures." One senator was finally moved to agree, conceding that Congress had "hidden behind the petticoats of the Budget" for too long.[42]

The administration tried to rein MacArthur in and hinted it would put stricter limits on the Army's dealings with Congress, but short of ordering the Chief of Staff never to testify before Congress again—something clearly unconstitutional—there was not much Roosevelt could do, unless he was willing to fire him. MacArthur continued to lobby for a larger appropriation. The Budget Bureau had requested $289 million. MacArthur demanded $305 million.

Aside from the budget, he also asked repeatedly for $405 million in WPA money to reequip the Army with modern weapons. Its World War I equipment was already obsolescent. MacArthur's lobbying accomplished nothing. When Congress voted on the 1935 budget, it gave the Army $284 million—even less than the Budget Bureau had asked for and more than $20 million less than the War Department requested. It was a setback.

A year later, however, MacArthur made his arguments all over again, this time for the 1936 budget. What a difference a year makes. The international scene was becoming increasingly unstable, with the rise of nazism threatening the peace of Europe and Japan's renunciation of its disarmament treaty obligations acting as a prelude to more aggression in Asia.

The War Department had asked for $361 million, but the Budget Bureau slashed this request to $331 million before submitting it to Congress. MacArthur returned to Capitol Hill to urge that the Army's enlisted strength be raised from its present level of 125,000 to the 165,000 the General Staff considered a bare minimum. He pleaded for money to buy new equipment. Above all, he reminded Congress yet again that it did not have to accept the President's budget; it could vote whatever sum it wanted. He was asking it, in effect, to tell the White House that it was wrong on national security and MacArthur was right.

He had prepared his ground better this year than last. While Congress debated the budget, MacArthur was running a behind-the-scenes lobbying campaign. The American Legion had drawn up a questionnaire on national security. Every member of Congress received a copy, mailed by the veterans among his constituents, asking him pointedly just what his position was on strengthening the Army in these perilous times.[43]

Congress finally gave MacArthur what he asked for, and then some. It voted the War Department all the money it had originally asked for and threw in an extra $2 million, for a total of $363 million. MacArthur also got the authorization he had requested for another forty thousand enlisted men.[44]

It was a stunning payoff to a five-year campaign that had consisted largely of defeats and frustration, setbacks and failures. He, Dern and the General Staff rejoiced. "The change has come not too soon," MacArthur exultantly told congressmen as he expressed his gratitude. "The turn has at last been reached."[45]

It was a paradox, but despite penury and public scorn, morale in the War Department had probably never been higher in peacetime than it was from 1930 to 1935. Few people who worked there at the time were critical of MacArthur's performance as Chief of Staff, and the number who praised him is legion. Eisenhower was irritated by his refusal ever to admit that he had made a mistake, but apart from that, the comments of the Surgeon General of the Army, Merritte Ireland, were typical. Ireland wrote to former Chief of Staff John L. Hines: "MacArthur certainly has the faculty of getting people to work and keeping them happy."[46]

The view from the field was much the same. The most important command within the continental United States was the Third Army, with headquarters at Fort Sam Houston. The Third Army included the only two regular divisions with anything approaching the strength to function as divisions, the 2d Infantry and the 1st Cavalry. Its area encompassed half a dozen National Guard divisions and many Air Corps installations. Its commander, Major General Johnson Hagood, remarked flatly, "No man is perfect, unless it is Douglas MacArthur, whom I have never known to be wrong."[47]

Despite MacArthur's frequent clashes with the airmen, who were agitating for independence from the Army, the commanding general of the Air Corps, Benjamin Foulois, revered the Chief of Staff. They had been friends for a long time, and Foulois, the reader may recall, had saved MacArthur's life in 1911 by swerving a crashing plane away from his tent. "Aloof, yet understanding, military to the core, yet warmly human when you were alone with him, MacArthur was the kind of man you either deeply respected or hated with a passion. I not only respected him, I believed him to be possessed of almost godlike qualities."[48]

Morale was also sustained by the fact that even with a shrinking budget and dwindling military force the Army was animated by a spirit of reform.

The tougher the times, the stronger the commitment and the more resourceful the people who remained.

MacArthur also advanced the careers of many of the best young officers by opening up the Command and General Staff School at Fort Leavenworth to lieutenants. He revitalized the Army War College too, changing it from a place where elderly colonels spent a somnolent, pleasant year before retirement into a place where ambitious young captains and majors could demonstrate their ability for eventual high command.

When World War II came, the Army would have little trouble finding men who could handle divisions and corps in combat. The overwhelming majority of those given such commands succeeded, and nearly every single one had graduated from Benning and Leavenworth or Leavenworth and the War College.

MacArthur widened the search for leadership talent. Despite the agitation over compulsory ROTC, he managed to make the program more attractive than it had ever been. As a result, the number of ROTC graduates accepting Army commissions reached its interwar peak under MacArthur.[49] He also persuaded Congress to fund a program that allowed a thousand reserve officers each year to spend twelve months training with the Regular Army. At the end of the course the top 5 percent were offered regular commissions.

His other successes with Congress embraced that place on earth that mattered more to him than any other, his beloved West Point. He got millions appropriated for new construction, providing the next generation of cadets with more comfortable and functional quarters. He had tried as supe to get an increase in the size of the Corps of Cadets and failed. Now he succeeded. He wanted to double the number of cadets from the present 1,374. Congress would not go that far but authorized enlargement up to 1,960. It did something else too: It authorized the academy to grant bachelor's degrees. Every West Point graduate got a degree, all the way back to 1802—a typical MacArthur gesture.

Unable to get new tanks and artillery, he had more success with his efforts to reequip the infantry with the world's first practical semiautomatic rifle. In 1929 the Ordnance Board conducted firing tests involving a .30-caliber semiautomatic designed by John C. Garand and a .276 made by John D. Pedersen. The experiment involved shooting twenty anesthetized pigs. The fatal wounds were examined minutely, and it was found that the smaller bullets had done the most damage.

Garand was told by the Ordnance Board to drop the work he had been doing and turn out a .276-caliber weapon. A year later he had a new rifle designed to meet the new specification. It had fewer parts than the Pedersen rifle and would be easier and cheaper to manufacture.

This time twenty anesthetized goats were shot dead. The Goat Board confirmed the findings of the Pig Board: Small bullets were better. Garand perfected his new rifle. In 1932 the Ordnance Board felt that after twelve years of effort it had finally produced just what the Army needed: a reliable, rugged semiautomatic rifle that weighed only 8.5 pounds. A unanimous and enthusiastic recommendation went to the Chief of Staff that the Army should put Garand's rifle into mass production.

MacArthur was not an expert on firearms. Nor was he an enthusiastic hunter, unlike Marshall or Pershing. There was one field in which he was an expert, though, and that was infantry close combat. He wouldn't trust his life to a small bullet, no matter how many pigs or goats had died scientifically to prove its merits. MacArthur turned down the Ordnance Board recommendation cold and demanded it produce a .30-caliber semiautomatic rifle.[50]

Shortly before his tenure as Chief of Staff drew to a close, the Ordnance Board was able to report success. A few months later the Army officially adopted the Garand M-1. It represented the future of military rifles for the next thirty years.

While he pushed reforms throughout the Army, there was one area where MacArthur was not willing to attempt radical change, and that was in the recruitment and training of black soldiers. Of all the senior commanders of his generation, he is one of the few who could be said to have had a liberal and progressive approach to race. Certainly there was never the slightest hint of racism in his dealings with Filipinos or with the Japanese. Toward the end of his life Thurgood Marshall, in an interview with a reporter, claimed that MacArthur was "a racist." Marshall had visited Japan and Korea in 1950 on behalf of the NAACP's Legal Defense Fund. The reports he filed at the time, however, contain no such assertions. Nor does his correspondence. On the contrary, Marshall praised MacArthur for his openness and helpfulness. What he did criticize him for was the absence of black soldiers at GHQ and his slowness at integrating the units in Korea.[51]

The fact that MacArthur liked and trusted Filipinos showed that he did not preach equality but believed in it. For all his faults, racism was not one of them. Yet there were limits to what he found politic to do in the strictly segregated Army of the 1930s, which had numerous southerners in the officer corps, many of its largest installations in the South and a ludicrous belief among officers and NCOs that blacks would not fight and could not fight.[52]

In June 1933 MacArthur gave the graduation address at West Point. He floored the cadets with his appearance, including the purple satin tie. He spoke dramatically and directly to them. They had never experienced anything like it. Like most people, they expected important figures to bore them with long-winded speeches that were read out in a monotone from a sheaf of papers. But MacArthur, in all his singularity and good looks, stood before them like a man speaking from inspiration, not preparation. The freshness and directness were all part of the magic. He did not memorize his speeches in advance, but he rehearsed them carefully in front of the fifteen-foot mirror in his office. MacArthur had learned the technique from Leonard Wood, who hardly ever wrote out speeches in advance. Instead he jotted a few key words or phrases on the back of an envelope, just in case he needed a reminder. But on a good day MacArthur did not even bother to look at the envelope. This made it seem that he was speaking extemporaneously and from the heart. His technique allowed him to turn a speech into a performance, seize an audience by its emotions and squeeze it dry.[53]

So, on this June afternoon, periodically gripping and releasing the lectern before him, MacArthur stood under a wide awning that protected the assemblage of graduation day notables from the blazing sun. He addressed the cadets as "my dear young comrades-in-arms" and as soldiers preparing for the next war. MacArthur fervently intoned, "As the necessity of national defense is sacrificed in the name of economy, the United States presents a tempting spectacle. It is a spectacle that may ultimately lead to an alignment of the nations, which may lead to another World War, and that war would find a score of nations ready for the sack of America. . . .

"History has proved that nations once great, that neglected their national defense, are dust and ashes. Where are Rome and Carthage? Where Byzantium? Where Egypt, once so great a state? . . .

"It is my conviction that at this moment the Army's strength in personnel and matériel and its readiness for deployment are below the danger line."[54]

MacArthur's pessimistic view of history had much to nourish it as the 1930s dragged their frightening way toward the abyss. His historical sense combined with a conception of his calling that was fatalistic yet exalted. MacArthur had fashioned a creed for himself that was martial yet spiritual, combative but also consoling. And it was that faith in the religious nature of soldiering that provided both the vision of MacArthur the military reformer and the moral courage to fight to save the Army when public opinion, Congress and the President all seemed against him.

Being a soldier was not a job but a vocation, a calling as holy as that of the priesthood. Without being especially pious and without being a regular churchgoer, he never doubted that he had been summoned by the divine will. In his man-of-destiny moments he seemed to hear God calling to his chosen: Samson! Gideon! Joshua! MacArthur!

A young man named John Agnew, Jr., wrote to the Chief of Staff to ask whether the Army could provide him with a satisfying career. He got a two-page reply in which MacArthur pointed out, inevitably, that an Army officer would never earn more than a modest living and during the first years of his career could expect financial hardship. Moreover, "your liberty of action will be more limited than in civilian pursuits."

Besides its financial and other constraints, the profession of arms was exceptionally demanding. "Always you must be striving to increase your own ability to be of maximum value to your country in the event of war. You must learn to lead men and to control them efficiently under conditions involving hunger, exposure, privation and danger." The responsibilities of command in wartime were staggering, and the suppression of personal desires could be "irksome."

Yet despite the burdens and disadvantages of a soldier's life:

> A commission in the Army opens up to the young man an opportunity to serve in many stations throughout the United States and, at times, in the far corners of the earth . . . he is brought into contact with individuals from all walks of life. He must learn something of every subject that has a bearing on the safety of the country. Probably no other profession offers its followers wider opportunity for broad education and culture than does the military.
>
> In the commissioned ranks of the Army success depends solely upon ability and honest effort. . . . An efficient officer does not have a month-to-month or year-to-year job. He has a real life's work. . . . Beyond this he has little—but to many men it is more than sufficient.[55]

The ultimate expression of MacArthur's beliefs was offered for the first time, but not the last, on July 14, 1935. It was Bastille Day, seventeen years after the Rainbow's first big battle in the Champagne region under one-armed Henri Gouraud.

MacArthur used the occasion to warn yet again of the dangers of unpreparedness in a warlike world. "In the last 3,400 years only 268—less than one in thirteen—have been free from wars," he observed, and quoted Plato's observation that only the dead have seen the last of war. He told the Rainbow veterans what he had told the West Point cadets two years before: that rich nations that had lost their martial ardor were doomed to conquest by poorer but more warlike peoples.

The core of his speech, though, was MacArthur's tribute to the American soldier:

> The military code which he perpetuates has come down to us from even before the age of knighthood and chivalry. It embraces the highest moral law and will stand the test of any ethics or philosophies ever promulgated

for the uplift of mankind. Its requirements are for the things that are right, and its restraints are from the things that are wrong. Its observance will uplift everyone who comes under its influence.

The soldier, above all other men, is required to perform the highest act of religion—sacrifice. In battle and in the face of danger and death he discloses those divine attributes which his Maker gave him when He created man in his own image. No physical courage and brute instincts can take the place of the divine annunciation and spiritual uplift which will alone sustain him. However horrible the incidents of war may be, the soldier who is called upon to offer and give his life for his country is the noblest development of mankind.[56]

This passage, which he repeated in at least two other speeches during the next seven years, was the Apostle's Creed of MacArthurism, the essence of his militant faith.

The 1920s had seen fierce interservice rivalry between the Army and Navy, but when MacArthur became Chief of Staff, he enjoyed a rare stroke of luck. The commander in chief of the Navy was Admiral William Veazie Pratt, and he was one sailor who got on well with soldiers. Eventually Pratt became one of MacArthur's staunchest admirers.[57]

The most problematical interservice issue they had to tackle was one that had vexed relations between the Army and the Navy for a decade: Where did the air defense of America's coastline begin? Pratt's predecessors had wanted to create a large force of long-range patrol bombers operating from bases on land, a position that posed a challenge to the Air Corps's belief that it alone should operate long-range bombing aircraft. The Navy's job, as the Army conceived it, was to fight naval actions against enemy fleets with planes based on the fleet, not onshore.

The coastal defense issue was resolved quickly. Pratt was open to argument, and MacArthur was able to announce only two months after becoming Chief of Staff that henceforth "The naval air forces will be based on the fleet and move with it as an important element in performing the essential missions of the forces afloat. The Army air forces will be land based and employed as an element of the Army in carrying out its mission of defending the coasts."[58]

The other major problem that MacArthur wanted to take up with the Navy was football. The superintendent of the Naval Academy, Thomas C. Hart, had scrapped the annual Army-Navy game. The eligibility rules at Annapolis were much tougher than those at West Point. This was likely to put the middies at a disadvantage on the field of play, and Hart was not prepared to concede victory to the Army team year after year. The cancellation of the Army-Navy game was a serious matter to MacArthur, fully worthy of the Chief of Staff's attention. MacArthur spent ninety minutes on August 25, 1932, bending Hart's ear on the crucial military value of football. Rather than have MacArthur go over his head to Pratt, Hart caved in. That fall the Army-Navy series was resumed.[59]

A rich stockbroker friend of MacArthur's named Charlie Munn threw a party to mark the occasion. Festivities reached a climax when a dozen leggy chorines from the *George White Scandals* appeared. Half were dressed in Army uniforms, half in Navy uniforms, and portions of said garments had been cut away so that as the girls twirled and swayed, breasts and buttocks were revealed. And there, pirouetting in the middle of this feminine display was the Chief of Staff, enjoying one of his rare nights out.[60]

MacArthur's relationship with the Air Corps was a lot more problematical than any of his dealings with the Navy. Throughout his time as Chief of Staff, MacArthur had to battle against Air Corps officers who demanded independence from the Army and was berated by their powerful allies in Congress. He was not blind to the value of airpower. On the contrary, he saw it as a valuable contribution to a modern military force. Shortly after becoming Chief of Staff, MacArthur climbed into an airplane and, once aloft, shouted into a small microphone, "This proves that by using the airplane the commander of an army can lift the fog of war—the fog of war which in the past, because of hiding facts from him, has robbed him of victory or brought him unforeseen defeat."[61]

Many airmen sincerely believed that the General Staff was hostile to them and ignorant of airpower's potential. They were wrong, at least as far as MacArthur was concerned. He had freely acknowledged in a long memo to Hurley in 1931 that "aviation is an element of national strength which must be given a high priority." The Air Corps was presently trying to raise its strength to 1,800 planes. MacArthur recommended going much further, to give the Air Corps a minimum of 2,950 planes.[62]

What he *was* opposed to was giving the Air Corps an independent role, which would free it from its responsibilities as part of the combined arms team. He also refused to provide a separate promotion list for Air Corps officers. Promotion was glacially slow in the Army. By having a separate list, the airmen hoped they might be promoted faster. Flying pay already provided Air Corps pilots with a 50 percent supplement to their salaries. They could also earn even more money on top of this by flying more than the minimum number of hours the regulations required. Some airmen, such as Hap Arnold and Tooey Spaatz, earned more than MacArthur did, and they were only lieutenant colonels.[63]

MacArthur was infuriated and indignant that Congress, which was committed to enlarging the Air Corps even before he became Chief of Staff, insisted on doing so at the expense of the other combat arms. The infantry, artillery and cavalry looked on in alarm as, year by year, their budgets shrank in order to pay for the extra planes the Air Corps was allowed to buy.

MacArthur was virtually helpless. The airmen had a powerful friend in the chairman of the House Military Affairs Committee, John J. McSwain of South Carolina. They had also had a friend in Ross Collins. Secretary of War George Dern supported MacArthur in nearly every congressional struggle, but he was so ill much of the time that he could contribute little. McSwain continued to promote legislation that would have severed the air from the ground or given the airmen a separate promotion list, even at the risk of alienating every nonflier in the officer corps and driving many of them to resign from the Army in disgust. As Eisenhower groaned in a letter to the former assistant chief of staff George Van Horn Moseley in February 1934, "All our contacts with the Military Affairs Committee of the House this year have revolved around air problems."[64]

The Air Corps gave MacArthur another headache when it tried to fly the mails. When Roosevelt became President, there were questions in Congress and the White House about whether the airlines that were presently carrying airmail had secured their contracts without favoritism. Before the issue had been fully investigated, Roosevelt decided to cancel the airmail contracts. The assistant postmaster general, Harllee Branch, sent for Foulois at noon one Friday in February 1934 and asked him whether the Air Corps could carry the mails. Foulois, after a brief study of the challenge with a couple of his assistants and motivated by an excess of "can-do" spirit, gave Branch the answer he wanted.

About an hour later, just as Foulois was about to inform the assistant chief of staff of his conversation with Branch, "General MacArthur appeared. His face was flushed and I sensed immediately that I was precisely the man he was looking for and I was in trouble. 'Foulois,' he barked, 'a newsman has just told me that the President has released an Executive Order giving the Air Corps the job of flying the mail. What do you know about it?' "[65]

MacArthur was annoyed that Foulois should have committed the Army, and its prestige, to such a risky venture without at least talking to him about it first. Suppose the Air Corps was not up to this challenge? Still, there was no turning back now. He could only hope for the best and put the best face on it that he could. MacArthur called a press conference. "I have the utmost confidence that the Army will handle the mail in a magnificent way," he declared to a gaggle of hastily summoned reporters. "I believe it will illustrate again the Army's ability to adjust itself to requirements—as demonstrated by its organization of the CCC. This will be another example of the Army's preparedness to take every call in its stride."[66]

As he and everybody else was about to discover, the glamorous Air Corps, the only part of the military that Congress seemed to like, was in poor shape. It lacked the instruments to fly in bad weather, and its planes were not suited to carrying mail. Yet Foulois had committed his men to this venture without laying down any qualifications on this mission, had left himself no way out if it proved too tough and failed to foresee that it was going to end badly. Which it did.

There was severe winter weather across much of the United States in February 1934. Seven pilots perished in accidents in the course of training to carry the mails. As the death toll mounted, the press heaped the blame on the President. Once the operation was under way, however, the accident rate dropped sharply.[67]

Then, on the night of March 9, three more pilots were killed, bringing the total number of fatalities to ten. Next morning MacArthur was summoned to the White House. The President wanted to see him and General Foulois immediately. Shortly afterward they were ushered into Roosevelt's bedroom. Roosevelt was propped up in the famous Lincoln bed and without a word of greeting bitingly demanded to know, "General, when are these airmail killings going to stop?"

Foulois responded, "Only when airplanes stop flying, Mr. President."

That brusque reply infuriated Roosevelt. He tore into MacArthur and Foulois, berating them fiercely for ten minutes, using his talent for scorn and ridicule without restraint. MacArthur took it without saying a word. Roosevelt concluded by flourishing a letter he had written to Dern ordering— yes, *ordering*—that aviation accidents must cease at once! Then, with a lordly and disdainful wave of his hand, he dismissed the two somber-looking generals.[68]

Shortly afterward the arrival of spring weather cut the accident rate to almost nothing. Congress and the White House realized, belatedly, that the problem with the airmail was not favoritism but subsidies: Unless it was heavily subsidized, no airline would carry it. New contracts were issued— to the same carriers the administration had only a short while before pilloried as crooks with wings.

That summer the Air Corps managed to embarrass MacArthur all over again. Hap Arnold led six B-10 twin-engine bombers from Washington to Alaska and back. The flight was a publicity stunt to regild the Air Corps's tarnished escutcheon. The Alaska mission generated reams of favorable publicity, but Arnold could not resist taking his planes on a thousand-mile detour over open water between Juneau and Seattle, to bolster the airmen's claim that they could find and attack enemy fleets far out at sea. In so doing, they were spitting on MacArthur's deal with Pratt over coastal defense roles. MacArthur was incensed. Arnold and his fliers came home in clouds of headline glory, expecting to get the Distinguished Flying Crosses that Arnold had promised them. MacArthur made sure that neither Arnold nor anyone else got a medal for the Alaska flight.[69]

In an attempt to resolve his various disputes with the Air Corps, MacArthur had Dern organize an independent board of inquiry, headed by former Secretary of War Newton D. Baker. The Baker board would make a thorough investigation of America's aviation defense needs. After two months of deliberations the board recommended an increase in Air Corps strength to 2,320 planes, temporary promotions to circumvent the Hump, better training and plenty of it, no move toward independence but, instead, a reorganization of the Air Corps. For a decade or so various people had suggested putting all the Air Corps tactical units under a separate headquarters, which would report directly to the Chief of Staff. The chief of the Air Corps would be left to manage all the problems of recruitment, training, supply and maintenance. It was an idea that MacArthur already favored. And now the Baker board had endorsed it.[70]

MacArthur selected one of the most admired, charismatic figures in the Air Corps, Brigadier General Frank Andrews, to command the General Headquarters Air Force. He had no illusions that the creation of GHQ Air Force would dampen the airmen's push for independence from the Army. Andrews, in fact, was an ardent Mitchell man and used his new command to agitate for the development of four-engine bombers. What MacArthur had achieved was to ensure that airpower would become an integral part of a combined arms team. Here again he was being prescient. In the war to come the U.S. Army would achieve a battle-winning integration of planes, tanks, trucks, artillery and infantry in attack or defense that no other force in the world could even approximate, only envy.

While there was no fixed term for a Chief of Staff's appointment, it was assumed in the War Department that MacArthur would serve for four years at the most. In that case his tenure would end in November 1934. MacArthur, however, had no desire to step down. While the War Department buzzed with speculation about his successor and various MacArthur enemies agitated for a prompt replacement, several important admirers were lobbying the President to keep him on. Both Morris Sheppard, chairman of the Senate Military Affairs Committee, and Joseph Byrne, the House majority leader, urged Roosevelt to leave MacArthur where he was. Even more effective, in MacArthur's opinion, was a plea from Pershing to the President that the Chief of Staff be allowed to complete the reforms he had begun.[71]

MacArthur bolstered his case with a General Staff report that claimed that the German Army had performed so much better than the French because the average tenure of the German chief of staff had been thirteen years, while the French Army got a new chief every two or three years. Dern repeatedly urged Roosevelt to retain MacArthur and had a study made of the legal position.[72] MacArthur nonetheless expected he would be reassigned, wrote a personal farewell message to the Army and asked for the First Army, with headquarters on Governors Island, New York, for his next post. It was evident, though, that he found the thought of stepping down to a subordinate position repugnant. Meanwhile, "The Secretary of War directed a series of insistent recommendations to the President," according to Eisenhower.[73]

While Roosevelt was slowly making up his mind, the Chinese government, headed by Chiang Kai-shek, wanted to know if MacArthur would be willing to build up a Chinese army of five million men to fight the Japanese. MacArthur declined Chiang's offer. For one thing, he thought it would take twenty years to create a Chinese army capable of fighting the Japanese. For another, he had his eye on a job in the Philippines.[74]

Congress was about to pass the Tydings-McDuffie Act, which would turn the Philippines into a commonwealth, with its own constitution, its own president and a large degree of autonomy in its internal affairs. There were rumors that the present governor-general, Frank Murphy, would return to the United States to resume his political career once the commonwealth was created. MacArthur hoped to be appointed Murphy's successor.[75]

These hopes were dimmed, but not entirely killed off, when, after months of hesitation, Roosevelt finally announced on December 12 that MacArthur would remain where he was until a new Chief of Staff had been chosen. "I am doing this," Roosevelt declared, "in order to obtain the benefit of General MacArthur's experience in handling War Department legislation in the coming [congressional] session."[76]

MacArthur could expect another year or so as Chief of Staff. He would then become available for other employment. In the spring of 1935 he got two more offers, one from Manuel Quezon, the other from Roosevelt.

Congress had passed the Tydings-McDuffie Act. The Philippines could now count on becoming an independent country in 1946. Quezon would be inaugurated as first president of the Philippine Commonwealth in November 1935 and would steer it toward independence, with all the costs and dangers that involved. He was worried at the prospects facing his impoverished, underdeveloped country as it tried to fend off the attentions of a politically voracious and militaristic Japan.

In the summer of 1935 Quezon during a trip to the United States went to see MacArthur and asked him bluntly, "Do you think that the Philippines can be defended after they shall have become independent ten years hence?"

MacArthur's reply, as Quezon recalled it, was "I don't think so. I know the islands can be protected, provided, of course that you have the money which will be required." The figure he had in mind was five million dollars a year for ten years. The islands obviously could not afford to create a large modern army. Instead MacArthur proposed Leonard Wood's idea: a Swiss-style army reserve embracing hundreds of thousands of well-drilled young riflemen formed around a small regular army that would provide training to the reservists in peacetime, combat leadership in war. With that kind of defense, MacArthur concluded, "No nation will dare to attack you, for the cost of conquest will be more than the expected profit."[77] That, at least, is how Quezon recalled their meeting.

MacArthur's recollection was different: What mattered was time and money. Given enough of both, the Commonwealth could be defended. Given too little of either, it did not stand a chance. All of which was no more than common sense. Yet, according to Quezon, MacArthur had told him the Philippines could be defended on the cheap, which seems unlikely. One way or another, though, there was already a basic misunderstanding of what it would take to defend the Philippines.[78]

Quezon invited MacArthur to come to the Philippines and take on the task of building up the islands' defenses, but MacArthur still had hopes of succeeding Murphy. When the commonwealth came into existence, the governor-general would be replaced by a high commissioner. In September 1934 Roosevelt invited MacArthur to come up to Hyde Park for lunch, as if signaling the start of a new and closer relationship between them. Over lunch Roosevelt offered the high commissioner's post to MacArthur, who was thrilled and delighted at the prospect.

When he returned to Washington, he asked the Army's top lawyers what they thought. They told him bluntly that if he accepted Roosevelt's offer, he would have to retire from the Army. MacArthur disconsolately informed the President that he was "somewhat dismayed and nonplussed" to discover that he could not accept assignment as high commissioner and remain on the Army's active list.[79] He hoped the law could be changed, but for now, given a choice between ending his Army career and becoming the first high commissioner to the Philippines, he preferred to remain a soldier, a man of action. It was an inevitable choice, given his conviction that another war was coming.

He accepted Quezon's offer to become military adviser to the Philippine Commonwealth. Because the Philippines were still an American colony, their defense was an American responsibility. The Army, in effect, would lend him to the commonwealth government. There were Army officers on active duty currently working as advisers to nearly a dozen countries, such as Cuba and Nicaragua. These assignments were not much sought after by able officers. Being in a foreign country and working for a foreign government were not likely to help an officer advance in his career. If anything, being out of the Army's mainstream was likely to prove a handicap. The only way to encourage talented officers to take these assignments was to allow them to draw two salaries—one from the United States and one from whichever foreign government they worked for.

The existing legislation was amended to include the Philippines on the list of countries that could hire American officers to serve as their military advisers. MacArthur accordingly received a letter from the Adjutant General that specifically informed him that his contractual arrangements with the Philippines "are hereby approved by the Secretary of War." He negotiated a deal with Quezon that he would receive the rank of field marshal in the Philippine Army, be paid an annual salary of $18,000 and get $15,000 for expenses. While this was a big step up from his present $7,500 a year, it was only what the governor-general received.[80]

But there was more to come. The letter from the Adjutant General also allowed him to make extra financial arrangements with the commonwealth government. And, the letter explicitly declared, he did not have to clear these in advance with the War Department. "You are authorized to negotiate such changes in compensation and emoluments as may be mutually agreed upon at any time by you and the Commonwealth government. Such changes are hereby approved by the Secretary of War." This letter was written in MacArthur's office—possibly by MacArthur himself—and sent over to the Adjutant General for his signature. The result was a grant of authority to negotiate with Quezon that could not have been broader. There was no limit to the amount of money MacArthur could accept for his services.[81]

MacArthur expected to spend at least seven years in the Philippines. He persuaded Quezon to agree to pay him a commission of 46/100 of 1 percent of Philippine defense spending up to 1942, if his defense plans were accepted by the commonwealth government. As he and Quezon were talking of defense spending of roughly $5 million a year, MacArthur could therefore expect to receive a performance bonus of nearly $250,000 when his mission in the Philippines ended. He had every prospect when he did leave active duty of enjoying a well-padded retirement.[82]

12

Sir Boss

On October 1, 1935, MacArthur, accompanied by his eighty-two-year-old mother, his sister-in-law, Mary McCalla MacArthur, and his aides Dwight Eisenhower and Thomas Jefferson Davis, boarded a westbound train. They were heading for San Francisco to catch the SS *President Hoover.* The *Hoover* was going to be crammed to the gunwales with notables—including Vice President John Nance Garner and dozens of senators and representatives—all intent on seeing the Philippine Commonwealth launched and Quezon installed as the islands' first president.

Roosevelt had assured MacArthur that he would remain Chief of Staff until December, by which time a replacement would have been named and MacArthur would be free to start his work as military adviser. The day after the train carrying the MacArthur party headed west, however, Roosevelt appointed Malin Craig as MacArthur's successor, effective immediately.[1]

MacArthur was incensed. He had expected to travel to Manila and take part in the ceremonies as a four-star general. His travel orders explicitly stated, "He will stand relieved from duty on the General Staff and as Chief of Staff as of date Dec. 15, 1935."[2] The moment he ceased to be Chief of Staff, he reverted to being a mere major general. He felt betrayed. Roosevelt knew how important the matter of his rank was to him, and to break a promise in order to remind MacArthur of just who was the boss seemed calculated to wound. MacArthur ranted and raved in "an explosive denunciation of politics, bad manners, bad judgment, broken promises, arrogance, unconstitutionality, insensitivity, and the way the world had gone to hell," according to Eisenhower, but there was nothing he could do about it. He sent Craig, who was an old friend, his congratulations.[3]

This was a stressful time for MacArthur. Pinky was in poor health, and her condition was made worse by a broken arm. She was too ill even to leave her cabin aboard the *Hoover.* She continued to be nursed by Mary McCalla MacArthur, who was completely devoted to her, and was watched over by her anxious son, who rarely left her cabin in the daytime.[4]

Paradoxically, one of the happiest chapters in MacArthur's life began during this voyage: He met the woman who would become his second wife. A number of accounts have described Pinky's taking an immediate shine to petite, thirty-five-year-old Jean Faircloth from Murfreesboro, Tennessee, even that she introduced her to MacArthur. According to one biographer, Jean was "the indomitable old lady's last gift to her son."[5] In fact, they never met.

Jean was heading for Shanghai, to stay with some English friends. A well-heeled, well-traveled single woman, she had become acquainted with the captain of the *Hoover* on an earlier trip to the Far East. She and another female passenger were invited to dine at the captain's table, as was the notoriously crooked and colorful former mayor of Boston, James M. Curley. It was Curley who introduced Jean to MacArthur the evening before the *Hoover* arrived in Honolulu. After going ashore the next day, Jean returned to her cabin and found a large bouquet of flowers from MacArthur.

His routine aboard ship was to emerge only for breakfast. He took all his other meals with Pinky. From Honolulu to Manila Jean Faircloth did something she had not done for years: She got up early each morning, dressed and went to breakfast, instead of sleeping late and having breakfast in bed. MacArthur left the ship in Manila, and the *Hoover* steamed on to Shanghai, which was Jean's destination. By the time it reached Shanghai, however, she had changed her mind. She was not going to stay with her English friends after all. She headed straight back to Manila and checked into a hotel.[6]

Coming from Murfreesboro, Jean, like Pinky, knew what it was like to grow up in a town haunted by the Civil War. One of the biggest and bloodiest battles of the war had been fought at Stones River, just south of the town. Her ancestors included a number of Confederate veterans. She was active in the Daughters of the Confederacy and the Daughters of the American Revolution. The Faircloth family was one of the most prosperous in that part of Tennessee. Her father owned a flour mill, several bakeries and a large share of a local bank. When he died, her portion of his estate came to two hundred thousand dollars—roughly two million dollars in 1996 money. Never married, she had devoted her life since to having a good time, which involved a lot of travel to exotic places. In the course of her journeys she had met and become friendly with a number of Army families. She had, as MacArthur seems to have realized almost from the outset, all the makings of a good Army wife, although he later claimed he fell in love with Jean only when he discovered that she liked westerns almost as much as he did.

Little more than a month after reaching Manila, Pinky died. MacArthur was plunged into grief that shook him to his soul. He was too heartbroken even to face the press. It was Mary McCalla MacArthur who broke the news. "Mother MacArthur was a wonderful person," she declared. "She was the most generous and just person I have ever known and a real soldier."[7]

MacArthur took the death of his mother very hard and for a time found it almost impossible to come to terms with. He felt helpless for the first time in his life, and was left depressed for many months.[8]

Much has been made of MacArthur's relationship with his mother, as if it accounted for the flaws in his character. He was, beyond any doubt, a devoted son. After Pinky's death, he carried her walnut walking stick, which she had leaned on for the last decade of her life. He kept his mother's Bible beside his bedside and read a few pages from it each night, a reverent ritual honoring both the God that he prayed to and the mother he adored.

Her most enduring and important legacy to him was a profoundly emotional nature nourished by a melodramatic imagination. For MacArthur, anything worth feeling was worth feeling deeply, and it was honest emotion, freely expressed, that was the cement of real life, the stuff that held the bric-a-brac of daily existence together and gave it shape and meaning. His temperament was that of the poet, the artist, the thinker, as well as the man of action.

He was also, for all his singularity, a product of a particular time and place. The America in which MacArthur lived placed a high premium on motherhood. Franklin Roosevelt's relationship with his mother was at least as close as MacArthur's with Pinky, and maybe more so. When Franklin went to Harvard, his mother moved to Cambridge for the whole four years, compared with Pinky's two years at West Point. When Franklin got married, his mother moved into the house next door. There were times when an entire year would pass without MacArthur's even seeing his mother. Roosevelt could never make such a claim, or want to. While Louise blamed the failure of her marriage to MacArthur on "an interfering mother-in-law" but did not cite a single instance to support this assertion, there is abundant evidence that Roosevelt's mother made life miserable for Eleanor.[9]

The overwhelming role of mothers in the lives of their sons was denounced in a famous polemic by Philip Wylie in 1942. The curse that hung over American society, claimed Wylie, was "momism," which had produced a nation of neurotic, insecure, unhappy males. "Our land," Wylie observed, "subjectively mapped, would have more silver cords and apron strings crisscrossing it than railroads and telephone wires." If MacArthur was in some way a mama's boy, he was far from alone. There were millions like him.[10]

Certainly he felt incomplete without a woman in his life. He once remarked, "A general's life is loneliness," an observation hinting at both grandeur and misery.[11] Like many men who are deeply emotional by nature, he probably found the prospect of life without a woman to share it with almost intolerable. In Jean Faircloth, however, he had seen an excellent prospect of alleviating the loneliness his mother's death brought.

MacArthur kept Pinky's body in the Manila morgue until he could return with it to the United States and bury her next to his father at Arlington. In April 1937 he journeyed to Washington with Quezon and Pinky's casket. She was finally laid to rest. Pershing sent a floral tribute that touched MacArthur deeply.[12]

With Pinky buried at last, MacArthur traveled to New York, to meet up with Jean. Eighteen months after their first meeting, they were married in a brief ceremony at the Municipal Building. Bride and groom both wore brown. They emerged to face a horde of shouting, jostling reporters. All MacArthur would say was "This is for keeps." Then the couple headed for the Waldorf and a wedding breakfast of ham and eggs.[13]

It is claimed that when he returned to Manila, MacArthur, ignoring his fifty-seven years, gallantly carried his hundred-pound bride over the threshold of the air-conditioned penthouse apartment that had just been completed atop the Manila Hotel.[14] The seven-room apartment at the top of the six-story hotel provided the second-fanciest digs in the archipelago, outshone only by the Malacañang Palace, which was occupied by Quezon. If the story is true, then MacArthur would have carried Jean into the unprepossessing entrance hall, a modest foyer that gave little hint of the spacious, elegant apartment beyond. From the hall they would have passed into the drawing room, a large and imposing space ornamented with autographed photos of MacArthur's heroes, such as Pershing and Leonard Wood, in heavy silver frames. Like all the main rooms, the drawing room had a high ceiling and big windows, with venetian blinds and heavy silk brocade drapes.

The dining room offered views of Manila Bay on three sides. It featured a beamed ceiling from which, hanging pendulously and low over the twelve-place dining table, descended a huge, ugly chandelier carved from Philippine mahogany. However much it may have been a triumph of wood carving, the chandelier was a failure in the lighting department: It carried only a dozen candles. For everyday dining there was a breakfast room, in a style that might be termed Hollywood, but featuring a large silk screen embroidered with colorful wading birds, a motif that MacArthur particularly liked.

There were three bedrooms in the apartment. MacArthur took the smallest of the three, a modest room burdened with awful halfhearted Bauhaus furniture that groped for a contemporary feel but failed to grasp it. Jean had the largest bedroom, which featured a huge Louis XV–style dressing table and ornate gilded mirror. This was the only place in the apartment that had a photograph of MacArthur on display. For all his egotism, MacArthur could not stand to see photographs of himself. While other generals were likely to display photographs showing themselves with the President or receiving a decoration or handing out an award, there was nothing like that in the penthouse of the Manila Hotel. There was only the one small photo, easy to overlook, in Jean's bedroom.[15] The third bedroom, reserved for guests, was done in art deco. At least it was art deco as far as that style was understood in the Philippines.

The heart of the apartment was the library, where MacArthur kept his own books and his father's. Display cases preserved both the medals of father and son. On a small table were two red leather volumes tooled with gold leaf. One contained all of his father's orders, from his commission as a second lieutenant through to his retirement. The second volume, growing steadily thicker, contained all of MacArthur's orders.[16]

The library was expansive and restful. There were several large tables with freshly cut flowers. Some smaller tables bore lamps. There was a large, comfortable sofa and six silk-covered armchairs. At one end of the room stood his desk, and looming over the desk, on the wall behind, was a large painting of a naked, heroic male figure, with an angel standing slightly behind, seeming to give encouragement and guidance. The books were arranged on shelves that ran the length of the room, approximately thirty feet, on facing walls. In all, there were nearly two thousand volumes on display, to which MacArthur, who was a voracious reader, added regularly.

Ten months after the wedding, on February 21, 1938, Jean bore MacArthur a son, christened Arthur MacArthur. A friend, offering his congratulations, couldn't help remarking, "I didn't know you had it in you."

"Neither did I," MacArthur laughed, clearly delighted at becoming a father.[17]

The three of them soon settled into a harmonious family routine. Jean called MacArthur "Gin'ral" in her pronounced Tennessee accent. Her own pet name for him was Sir Boss, after the benevolent autocrat in *A Connecticut Yankee at King Arthur's Court*. He called her Ma'am, as if she were royalty. And the son, named Arthur IV, was known as Junior.

From his birth, MacArthur sought to instill in the child the ambition to be a soldier, go to West Point, maintain the tradition. Once Arthur could walk, he was taught to enter his father's room at seven-thirty each morning, salute, accept his father's salute, then march around the bedroom with the general, chanting "Boom! Boom! Boomity Boom!" with him. While MacArthur shaved with his old-fashioned straight razor, they would sing Army songs together, and that was fun. "The only person who appreciates my singing in the bathroom," MacArthur wryly observed to friends, "is Arthur."[18]

After shaving, MacArthur rubbed his head for a few minutes with a ring attached to the end of his comb, stimulating the scalp in a losing fight against baldness. As he approached sixty, his hair was thinning and receding. Toilette completed, he would give half an hour to sitting-up exercises before going to have breakfast with Jean. Young Arthur would spend most of the rest of the day with his Chinese amah, Ah Cheu.[19]

The apartment had a large terrace crowded with tropical plants, and before long it acquired a rubber wading pool for Arthur, in which small rubber toys floated like corpses. Two flagpoles rose from the roof of the penthouse, bearing the flags of the United States and the Philippine Commonwealth. A small terrace off the dining room overlooked the hotel swimming pool to the rear.

The views from the penthouse were magnificent, with a panoramic perspective on Manila Bay to the west while to the east could be seen the walled heart of old Manila, the Intramuros. At dusk, as the blazing red orb of the sun slipped into the bay and the skies above turned purple and gold, MacArthur liked to spend an hour or so pacing the terrace, deep in thought, avoiding the potted plants and the puddles around Arthur's pool, and swinging a watch chain with a small gold football attached to one end.[20]

Apart from the splendor of the penthouse apartment, MacArthur lived simply. He liked plain food, three times a day. His diet was unrelievedly bland and uninteresting. He did not drink coffee, and alcohol was limited to a single predinner gimlet, a cocktail of gin and lime juice. All was not middle-aged moderation, though: He smoked heavily, at least a pack a day. MacArthur owned a dozen cigarette holders, most of them carved from ivory, and used them. He was also an enthusiastic pipe smoker, and he nearly always had a large Filipino corona after dinner. All in all, he was a tobacco company's dream customer—smoked all the time, was completely, totally addicted to nicotine, but never got cancer.

MacArthur went to the movies most nights. Manila had six cinemas showing first-run feature films. If there was a good card on at the Olympic stadium, he would go to the fights. On the rare occasions when Jean did not go with him, to the movies or the fights, he had a general's privileges: he could always summon the company of his three aides, Eisenhower,

Ike's friend and West Point classmate Major James Ord, and Captain Thomas Jefferson Davis. Jean liked to dance, but MacArthur had stopped dancing after his first marriage ended. He had his aides dance with her in his place.[21]

He had almost no interest in parties or formal dinners. MacArthur visited the Masonic lodge for major ceremonies, including his own installation as a thirty-second-degree Mason. There were also social events involving Quezon or the high commissioner that had to be attended. He was away from home only one or two evenings a month. By and large MacArthur's private life in Manila in the late 1930s was tranquil to the point of dullness, which was exactly how he preferred it. The challenge of creating an army to defend the Philippines provided more than enough drama and tension to satisfy the man of action.

The Philippine archipelago covers an area the size of Great Britain but has a longer coastline to defend than the United States. The Navy considered it virtually impossible to hold on to the islands. It was the Army that cried up the strategic value of Manila Bay, mainly for political reasons; it was American policy to defend its possessions. The Navy was approaching the problem from a purely military perspective and decided, rightly, that Manila Bay had almost no strategic value at all. It would take a lot more to defend it successfully than it was worth in strictly military terms. Throughout the 1930s War Plan Orange envisaged a swift naval withdrawal from the Philippines in the event of war with Japan. That decision was confirmed in revisions to the plan in 1934 and again in 1936. It was a scenario that the Army's War Plans Division itself came to accept as virtually inevitable.[22]

There was no shortage of Army officers who agreed that the Navy's view was the right one. Major General Johnson Hagood, who knew the islands well and had commanded the Philippine Division in the 1920s, had told Hoover bluntly in 1930 that the Philippines could not be held against a Japanese attack. Corregidor, well prepared, well stocked with food, might hold out for six months or more, but all other American troops in the islands would only be captured or killed when war came.[23]

The legislation that paved the way to Philippine independence more or less wrote off the islands as any kind of bastion. Congress urged the President, "at the earliest possible date, to enter into negotiations with foreign powers with a view to conclusion of a treaty for the perpetual neutralization of the Philippine Islands. . . ." Roosevelt ignored this advice. Far from respecting neutrals and leaving them alone, the military clique that ran Japan increasingly looked on neutral nations as being friendless, defenseless and ripe for the picking.[24]

MacArthur dismissed the Navy's view as defeatism. He remained as committed to the defense of what he sometimes called "my second country" as his mentor Leonard Wood had been. As he told the officer who liaised between the military adviser's office and Quezon's office, Bonner Fellers, "I was in complete disagreement with the Orange Plan when I became Chief of Staff but I realized at once I would be wasting my time in trying to educate others to my point of view. I, therefore, short-circuited it by seeing the President personally and telling him that if mobilization became necessary during my tenure of office that my first step would be to send two divisions from the Atlantic coast to reinforce the Philippines . . . that I intended to defend every inch of those possessions and defend them successfully. This being the case, the Orange Plan was a completely useless document . . . the man who is in command at the time will be the man who will determine the main features of the campaign. If he is a big man he will pay no more attention to the stereotyped plans that may be filed in the dusty pigeon holes of the War Department than their merit warrants."[25]

This statement was nonsense. When MacArthur was Chief of Staff, the Army did not have two combat-ready divisions on the Atlantic coast available for shipment to the Philippines. The entire Army at the time consisted of three understrength divisions whose regiments were scattered widely over the United States. National Guard divisions were in even worse shape. And if "the man who is in command at the time" was intended to mean the Chief of Staff, this was nonsense too. The man in command would be the president, and it would be the president who would decide whether to make a fight for the Philippines or not.

MacArthur nevertheless was completely committed to creating a Philippine Army that would be able to defend the islands once they received their independence. He saw himself fulfilling an almost sacred mission. His father had begun arming Filipinos to defend their country. The great challenge now was to bring Arthur MacArthur's work to completion.[26]

In doing so, he was operating in something of a vacuum. The Army's organization in the Philippines consisted of a headquarters known as the Philippine Department, which was responsible for all U.S. Army forces in the archipelago. Nearly all the Army's ground combat elements had been organized in the 1920s into the Philippine Division, which consisted mostly of Philippine Scouts—enlisted Filipinos, that is, serving mainly under American officers.

MacArthur was not answerable to the the Philippine Department. He was answerable only to Quezon and the War Department. Nor was the Philippine Army that he was creating going to come under the Philippine Department. It was responsible only to the commonwealth government, but it was assumed that in time of war it would be federalized and become, in effect, a local reserve force to back up the Philippine Division.

MacArthur had no power over the Philippine Department or the Philippine Division. Nor did he command the Philippine Army. That was commanded by a Filipino general. All he could do was advise Quezon on what he thought ought to be done to prepare the islands' defenses.

The bedrock of his efforts was his faith in the Filipinos to produce first-class soldiers. Many American officers serving with the Philippine Scouts shared his confidence in them. It was an honor to be a Scout and competition for the chance to enlist was keen. "The Philippine Scouts were excellent soldiers, no question about it," said J. Lawton Collins, a Marshall protégé who served with them in the mid-1930s and became Army Chief of Staff twenty years later. William M. Hoge, who would go on to become a four-star general, was there at the same time and had the same opinion: "They were fine people, those Scouts. Crackerjacks."[27]

MacArthur never doubted that with such excellent human material he could create a Philippine Army that would give a good account of itself in defense of its homeland. He, Eisenhower, T. J. Davis and Jimmy Ord spent six months drawing up a detailed plan to create such an army at a price the commonwealth government could afford. It provided for a regular force of 920 officers and 10,000 enlisted men—less than a full division of troops. This tiny regular army would train 40,000 young men, aged eighteen to twenty-one, each year. In the meantime a Philippine military academy at Baguio would be established, providing the regular army with a steady supply of highly trained professional officers by the time independence was achieved. And each year the army would be able to organize another division for the First Reserve, giving the islands ten fully trained reserve divisions, comparable to National Guard divisions, by the time independence came. The reservists would be recalled for refresher training each year. The Philippine Army's ten divisions "must, of course, be such as to produce the essential qualities of mobility and fire power."[28] The price tag on MacArthur's plan was 160 million Philippine pesos, or $80 million.

A year later, however, MacArthur's staff had to take another look at the figures. They calculated the defense plan would now cost 210 million pesos, or $105 million. On this basis, MacArthur's commission or performance bonus of 46 cents for every $100 spent on defense by the commonwealth would amount to almost $500,000. This is a subject that will come up again because it resulted in one of the most controversial episodes in MacArthur's career.[29]

The Philippine government meanwhile had drawn up a national defense act that followed MacArthur's outline closely and, in many places, adopted or paraphrased what he had written. Quezon expected 80,000 Filipinos to register for military training. To his surprise and delight more than 150,000 young men came forward. The entire archipelago, it seemed to him, was ablaze with patriotic sentiments now that independence was on the horizon. Writing to an old friend, the publishing magnate Roy Howard, Quezon praised the "strength . . . will power . . . [and] determination" of the Filipinos.[30]

While many Americans, including Army and Navy officers, looked on the Philippines as being marginal at best to U.S. security and, at worst, a major liability, MacArthur believed as strongly as he had ever done that Asia was poised to shake the world and dominate it for centuries to come. He was not alone in this, of course. One of the most influential books of the 1890s, Charles Hall's *National Life and Character,* had said much the same thing, and said it so effectively that the United States, Australia, Canada and Great Britain had introduced laws to restrict the outflow of modern technology and the inflow of Asian immigrants. Hall, however, had pointed to the year 2000, not 1900, as the time when an Asia armed with modern technologies, ample foreign capital and a huge, hardworking but cheap labor force would arise to overshadow the West. Hall was giving a long-distance warning, and so was MacArthur. The first section of MacArthur's report on Philippine defense was titled "Economic Revolution in Eastern Asia" and confidently claimed that whatever happened henceforth in Europe or the Americas would amount to nothing but "colorful incidents," while the real drama of world history was played out on a very old but suddenly new stage as a rich and powerful Asia rose phoenixlike after a long period of decline.

Where MacArthur was wrong was in his belief that the Philippines had a geographical position that placed them at the very heart of these developments. He claimed the archipelago was, "in some important respects, the most important . . . section of the great and vaguely defined region known as the Far East."[31] Looking ahead to the growth of international air travel, he even persuaded himself that nearly all the major east-west air routes across the Pacific would have to pass through Luzon. He was, like most people in the era before jet travel, certain that the shortest distance between two points is a straight line. And it is, on a flat surface. On a spherical object such as the Earth the shortest distance for a long-haul flight is a curve, which is the way Pacific Rim air travel has developed.

While he exaggerated the strategic importance of the Philippines—"stretching," as he liked to say, "through sixteen degrees of latitude"—he minimized the possibility of any attempted invasion. In an address to a group of officers in August 1936 he pointed out that in his father's time it had taken a hundred thousand American soldiers three years to suppress only twenty thousand insurgents. So it was inconceivable that anyone would attempt to conquer the Philippines without landing at least three hundred thousand men on their shores. Yet a force that size that would require 1.5 million tons of shipping, more than any major trading nation—by implication, Japan—could spare without seriously harming its economy. He reinforced his point by citing the British example: "Never since modern armies have come into being with their enormous size and huge amounts of impedimenta has Great Britain been compelled to drive off a land attack from its shores." It was the sea that had really protected the British, not their navy. All the Royal Navy did was "increase the effectiveness" of the ocean as a barrier—news which would have surprised His Majesty's sailors had it come to their ears.

He played down the role of battle fleets even further, saying their function was to hold open lines of communication far from their home shores. Coastal defense could be entrusted to torpedo boats, supported by airpower, something for which there was no solid evidence whatever. No nation had ever done it or even attempted it.

The rugged terrain of the Philippines, much of which is covered by mountain and jungle, would also aid the defenders and hamper potential invaders. The country was heavily populated and well able to put hundreds of thousands of men into its defense. He was heartened too by the fate of the last major amphibious assault in military history, the attack on Gallipoli in 1916. The invading British, French and Australians were well armed with modern weapons yet suffered a comprehensive defeat at the hands of poorly equipped Turks, soldiers of "the sick man of Europe."[32]

Nor would a naval blockade starve the Philippines into submission. The islands were self-sufficient in food. Or so MacArthur believed. In fact, the population, already the fifteenth largest in the world, was fast outstripping the food supply.

MacArthur was convinced that his defense plan would transform the military security of the United States. "What I am doing is far more than merely accomplishing the security of the Philippine islands," he wrote to Frederick Payne, the former assistant secretary of war. "We are actually building up [the] fatally weak left wing of our Pacific defense. We have never secured our Navy base here and the Navy has never really been able to concentrate here. All this will be changed now. . . . Our real Pacific line should extend from Alaska to the Philippines. This would call for a naval base in Alaska. When this is accomplished, our line—Alaska, Philippines—will lie athwart every trade route in the Pacific and give us complete control of the Pacific problem. . . . The old defeatist line of Alaska, Hawaii and Panama, was in my opinion fatally defective . . . it pitched the potential battle areas on our own coast and, second, destroyed the maneuvering potentialities of the fleet. . . ." And to Dern he wrote that strong defenses in the Philippines "will give the United States a position of such mastery in the Pacific as to give pause to any forces of aggression."[33]

Returning to the islands in the summer of 1937 aboard the SS *President Coolidge* after burying his mother and marrying Jean, MacArthur gave an interview to a journalist on board. Asked if he believed a world war was imminent, he dismissed the idea. "I do not agree with those who predict an imminent war," he said. "The complete state of preparedness of practically all nations is the surest preventive of war."[34]

Yet even as the *Coolidge* was sailing into Manila Bay, the Japanese Army was launching an offensive in China that went far beyond any of the previous "incidents." By October the Japanese had besieged Nanking, and in December they took the city, murdering more than one hundred thousand people in one of the worst atrocities of the blood-soaked twentieth century. Tension rose dramatically throughout the Far East as the Japanese campaign in eastern China developed.

There were already worrying developments within the Philippines. There were up to forty thousand Japanese living in the archipelago, and the Japanese business community in the islands was raising money to help finance the Japanese Army's operations in China. The Japanese were also arming themselves and bribing local officials not to interfere. In October 1937 MacArthur's staff prepared a memo which spelled out the belief that the Philippines was already a target of Japanese military ambitions.[35]

When Quezon returned to the Philippines that fall, MacArthur warned him starkly of "the greatly increased risk, due to the continuous decline of national security throughout the world, of prematurely drawing the Philippine Islands into war. . . . As a result, I deem it essential to purchase without delay supplies and equipment originally planned by me for procurement at a later date."[36] As MacArthur was to discover, however, the sudden prospect of war would not stiffen Quezon's resolve. On the contrary, he began to doubt everything MacArthur was doing.

Quezon's entire political career was based on a simple, obvious idea: The Philippines must have their independence from the United States. Not that he necessarily meant it every time he demanded it. There were periods when he admitted, in private, that he, like most Republican politicians in the United States, did not think the islands were truly ready to stand on their own.[37] To the Philippine people, however, he was Mr. Independence. Nobody could outflank Don Manuel on this issue. Quezon liked to proclaim, "I would rather live under a government run like hell by Filipinos than under a government run like heaven by Americans."[38]

Despite remarks such as this, many of the American officials who knew him liked Don Manuel. As one high commissioner, Francis B. Sayre, described him, Quezon was "Always dramatic, charming beyond words to all whom he set out to win, impulsive, adroit, daring, ambitious, and he had out-manoevered [*sic*] every rival."[39] Quezon's lifestyle, however, was not one that the puritanical Sayre was ever likely to approve. It revolved around nightclubs, lavish parties, gambling casinos and free-spending habits. He cut a wide swath through the demimonde of chorus girls, starlets and hatcheck personnel, to the grief of his faithful and pious wife, Aurora, who could never be sure when dawn broke just where Manuel was and what he was doing. A confidential State Department memo on the Philippines said bluntly, "Mr. Quezon's primary interest is self-aggrandizement; his second concern is the welfare of the group of friends who assist him [and] are enriching themselves at the expense of the masses."[40]

He was also immensely vain. Quezon's official portrait, like most royal portraits, offered a highly romanticized version of the man as he imagined himself. It was, at first glance, a work of fiction, but fiction only hides the truth, it does not obliterate it. He was shown as being about forty-five, although when the portrait was painted, he was nearly sixty. He sprawled languidly in an armchair, and from the length of his legs the viewer would think he was a six-footer, although he was really about five feet five inches tall. The only accurate details were that he dressed like the Duke of Windsor and held a cigarette like Noël Coward. The statesman as lounge lizard.[41]

The people closest to Quezon were mainly American millionaires, the dozen or so rich businessmen who dominated commercial life in the islands. They posed no political threat to him and were, in his mind, the only source of truly independent advice he could count on. He took them yachting on his luxurious boat, the *Cassiana,* played poker and bridge with them and, after he became president, established the Union Club in Manila for them. This was the most exclusive establishment in the islands. It had only twenty-five members, consisting of Quezon and rich businessmen, most of them Americans. MacArthur did not qualify for membership.[42]

Although Quezon was godfather to MacArthur's son, Arthur, and despite the fact that MacArthur and Quezon had known each other a long time, the friendship between them was too strange, too problematical and too reliant on pretense to stand up well in a crisis. The mutual openness and trust, the underlying devotion and commitment in good times and bad that are the mark of the real thing, simply were not there. It is inconceivable that either man would have risked his career or his ambitions in defense of the other.[43]

Quezon got on well with Frank Murphy, the man who was governor-general of the Philippines when MacArthur became military adviser. Murphy had made a national reputation for himself in his heroic efforts to battle the worst effects of the Depression in Detroit, a city that scraped the bottom of the barrel of despair. His commitment to the unemployed, the unlucky and the suffering made the young redheaded mayor an inspiration to Roosevelt and other liberal Democrats when the New Deal was launched.

Murphy was both the last of the governors-general and the first of the high commissioners. Shortly before leaving the War Department in 1935, MacArthur had engaged in a protracted bureaucratic struggle to prevent Murphy from turning the post of high commissioner into an even more powerful office than that of governor-general. It was an issue that he took much more seriously than Quezon. Murphy's viceregal ambitions, MacArthur protested, were an affront to the Filipinos and an insult to Quezon as president of the commonwealth. MacArthur thought Quezon merited a twenty-one-gun salute at his inauguration. Murphy said he was entitled to no more than nineteen. After all, he wasn't a real head of state, while he, Murphy, representing Roosevelt, should get a twenty-one-gun salute. And at his inauguration nineteen was all Quezon got, and all that Murphy got too. MacArthur, though, was determined to have the last word, or boom, on the matter. After he reached the Philippines, he arranged for Quezon to get a twenty-one-gun salute on important occasions, but only within the grounds of the Malacañang Palace.[44]

When Murphy returned to the United States in the spring of 1936 to run in the Michigan gubernatorial race, MacArthur's hopes of being appointed high commissioner flared up again, like a peat fire that refuses to go out and simply smolders underground between eruptions. But first it would be necessary for the administration to persuade Congress to alter the present law that barred officers on the active list from holding the post. Murphy used his influence to put a block on that.

MacArthur managed to get himself elevated anyway. Following passage of the commonwealth's National Defense Act, he became a field marshal. Eisenhower tried to talk him out of it, unaware that the idea had originated with MacArthur, not with Quezon. Ike later learned, from Quezon, that this was one of the conditions MacArthur had set for his employment as military adviser.

The fancy new title, never borne before or since by an American citizen, was a challenge to MacArthur's highly, if not overly, developed dress sense. He conjured up an outfit that made him look like the headwaiter at an Army and Navy club—a white linen jacket of military cut, with a pair of black trousers. What set it apart was the pale blue fourragère of the infantry officer on the right shoulder and the large black, green and gold badge of the General Staff—which he had established while Chief of Staff—gleaming on the left breast. The outfit was crowned with a cap that sported a large American eagle. The design principle on which the cap was based was glittering; MacArthur was going to set a new American record for the amount of gold braid stitched onto a single piece of headgear. While the rest of the outfit was mediocre, the cap was a great success. He loved it. He treasured his field marshal's cap for the rest of his life. To complete the ensemble, Aurora Quezon formally presented him with the ultimate military fashion accessory, an eleven-ounce gold baton, in an elaborate ceremony on August 24, 1937, while Don Manuel read out MacArthur's commission as a field marshal. The hat, the baton, the trumpet blast of a title all carried Napoleonic echoes. He intended to be a great man, but in the nineteenth-century style.[45]

MacArthur's critics scoffed. Even some admirers were dismayed. And to Pershing, all this field marshal nonsense was just another manifestation of MacArthur's worst traits. Black Jack wrote to their mutual friend John Callan O'Laughlin deploring MacArthur's "rather boastful claims as to the soundness and efficiency of the organization proposed for the Philippine army," and "his appointment as Field Marshal of a State and an army, neither of which has, as yet, an independent existence, was more or less ridiculous."[46]

MacArthur got a withering blast of the scorn he'd aroused full in his face at a banquet in Washington during his 1937 trip to the United States. "I see we have the Field Marshal with us," observed Senator George Moses wryly. "Well, that reminds me of the U.S. Marines captain who went to help train one of those small foreign armies. And the little army made him a brigadier general and, of course, he was mighty proud of his new uniform.

"He, too, came back to Washington and got himself invited out to dinner with various Army and Navy officers. And he asked a Marine colonel how he should dress for the party—should he come as a captain of Marines or as a brigadier general of the other army?

"And the colonel said, 'In Washington, a brigadier general of an army such as yours eats in the kitchen.' "[47]

The diners erupted into howls of laughter—all, that is, save one. MacArthur, his face frozen into immobility, concentrated on the demanding task of tapping the ash from his cigar. It wasn't that he lacked a sense of humor. He had a fund of funny stories to tell and loved to hear other people being amusing. But his sense of humor was severely limited. MacArthur could never laugh at himself. A man of destiny does not do that, and probably can't.

Meanwhile the fact that he had designed a uniform befitting his exalted new rank was reported in American newspapers. He took the story as a personal affront and issued a vigorous denial: "I have never worn and never expect to wear any other than the uniform of the United States Army specifically prescribed for my rank and organization. My sensitiveness may be due partly to the veneration in which I hold the American uniform in which I have seen so many of my comrades in arms die and in which I, myself, was twice wounded on the battlefields of France."[48]

The claim that he had worn a regulation GI uniform in France may have brought a smile to the face of many a Rainbow veteran. He was also overlooking the purple tie. And these days, on those occasions when he donned his glittering field marshal's cap, he was hardly dressed like anyone else on active service in the American Army. All the same, and strange as it may seem, MacArthur probably believed every word of his denial was true.

The president of the commonwealth was thrilled by the first steps toward creating a citizen army, to the exclusion of almost all other government business. "I believe in him and his opinion I accept fully," said Quezon in January 1937.[49] Shortly after this Quezon and MacArthur sailed together for the United States. The new high commissioner, former Indiana Governor Paul V. McNutt, had invited them to attend his swearing-in ceremony, which would take place in Washington that spring. The President, said McNutt, would also like to talk to Quezon if the invitation proved acceptable.

Now was certainly a good time to go. There was a new Chief of Staff, Malin Craig, a new secretary of war, Harry H. Woodring, and a new head of the War Plans Division, Major General Stanley Embick. MacArthur and Quezon needed the support of all three if their efforts to create a Philippine Army were going to succeed. Even before it had trained its first soldiers, it was causing ripples of concern in both the War and State departments. For one thing, it complicated American efforts to pressure the Japanese to live up to their treaty obligations on disarmament. And for another, MacArthur and his staff were demanding men and equipment from the already undermanned and thinly stretched Philippine Department to train Quezon's troops. During his time as Chief of Staff MacArthur had begun construction of a huge tunnel under Malinta Hill on Corregidor. The tunnel would add to the defensive strength of that small island by improving its transportation and providing emergency shelter and a vast bombproof bunker for military supplies. As military adviser he pushed the tunnel project to completion, but the money for it came out of the budget of the Philippine Department.

Instead of treating the journey to Washington with the seriousness it deserved, Quezon turned it into a ten-month round-the-world ego trip. He took a huge entourage with him, numbering more than twenty cronies and political friends, all having a lavishly good time at other people's expense. He also encouraged the countries that he visited en route to treat him like a head of state. He got a twenty-one-gun salute in Canton. He got another twenty-one-gunner from the Imperial Japanese Navy when his ship sailed into Tokyo Bay, plus an interview with Emperor Hirohito, which MacArthur also attended. When his ship docked in Los Angeles, Don Manuel told the assembled press he had come to speed up the timetable of Philippine independence. The date he had in mind was 1938.

From Los Angeles he made a beeline for the bright lights of New York. Washington to him was a provincial backwater he would visit only when he started to feel bored. He had a wonderful time in New York, taking over Roseland when the mood struck him, going to parties, nightclubs and banquets. He was completely oblivious of the fact that his behavior was certain to be seen in Washington as a snub to the President. After a while Quezon began to wonder why he hadn't received an invitation to come to the White House.

MacArthur seems to have been as puzzled as Quezon, and that does not say much for MacArthur's own astuteness. He traveled to Washington to find out and was told that Roosevelt was too busy to see him and had no interest in meeting with Quezon. Two can play at the indifference game. Only then did MacArthur wake up and realize that he and Quezon had a crisis on their hands. He insisted on seeing the President and was offered five minutes of Roosevelt's time.

When they actually got down to talking, the meeting ran on for five hours. It was a battle of wills, with MacArthur insisting over and over that the President had to see Quezon. In the end Roosevelt grudgingly agreed to invite Quezon to lunch. Don Manuel duly arrived at the White House, but when he got there, he made a fool of himself by demanding independence in 1938. It was not a successful meeting, although Roosevelt can hardly have been surprised.

None of the problems that MacArthur and Quezon needed to resolve had been settled. And by antagonizing the President, they had undermined MacArthur's position. In effect, they had delivered themselves into the hands of their enemies, Harold Ickes and Frank Murphy. The Department of the Interior's Bureau of Insular Affairs had a major role in the administration of the Philippines, and Ickes believed that MacArthur had so much influence over Quezon that "he comes close to being a dictator."[50]

As for Murphy, he was completely opposed to MacArthur's defense plan. He did not have MacArthur's faith in Filipino loyalty to the United States. Like General Embick of the War Plans Division, he questioned the wisdom of providing tens of thousands of Filipinos with arms. The Philippine insurrection was only thirty years in the past. When MacArthur tried to get a large shipment of obsolescent rifles at a giveaway price from the War Department to equip the new Philippine Army, Murphy used his influence with Roosevelt to prevent the sale. Beyond that, though, he was convinced that MacArthur's defense plan was unworkable. "I haven't met an army officer in the Philippines or in Washington who shares his [MacArthur's] view that the Philippines are defensible," he wrote a friend in September 1936. The only thing to do with the Philippines, Murphy told Roosevelt, was to neutralize them.[51]

Neutrality, however, was an even less realistic idea than MacArthur's army of reservists. The neutrality fantasy was an intellectual refuge from the conundrum of how to defend a weak, impoverished country cursed by geography to lie in the path of the oncoming Japanese juggernaut. The Japanese did not want the Philippines as such. They wanted what lay beyond them, the mineral wealth of Southeast Asia—the rubber of Malaya, the oil of Borneo, the tin, the gems and the gold that a capricious fate had bestowed on others. The Philippines sat on the flank of the sea routes between Japan and the objects of its desire. To secure those routes, the archipelago would have to be occupied by the Japanese Army. The Philippines were cursed, not blessed, by geography. There was no more solution to the problem of defending the islands than there has ever been to that well-known European military problem, How do you defend Poland, trapped as it is between Germany and Russia?

The real difference between Murphy and MacArthur was that one thought it worth making the Japanese fight if they wanted to occupy the Philippines and the other, a high-minded pacifist, didn't. The President, who had the responsibility to resolve this issue, decided to settle it by relieving MacArthur. Roosevelt probably did not think the Philippines were worth defending anyway. He was a former assistant secretary of the navy and a believer in sea power and airpower, not armies. As the War Department discovered even after Pearl Harbor, Roosevelt was slow to grasp the need for ground forces.[52]

Bringing MacArthur home would stop the attempt to create a Philippine Army in its tracks, make the War, State and Interior departments happy and pave the way toward reshaping War Plan Orange so that the Navy view prevailed. General Embick, the head of the War Plans Division, believed the Navy view was right and the Army's part of the plan should be rewritten to harmonize with the Navy's intention of pulling out and fighting its way back at some unspecified later date. There was no point in leaving a garrison there to be trapped and ultimately to surrender.

While Roosevelt believed he had found the solution to the problem, Malin Craig strongly disagreed. Craig had known MacArthur since the days when they were both young officers working under Leonard Wood. He warned that if MacArthur was ordered to return, "the object which the President has in view of withdrawal will not be accomplished, as the present incumbent [MacArthur] will either retire or resign and continue in his present capacity. That would leave MacArthur free to press ahead with his plans, and the War Department would have less opportunity than ever to control him."[53] Roosevelt brushed aside Craig's warning.

In August 1937, shortly after MacArthur returned to Manila, he was informed that he was going to be recalled to the United States and given another assignment. Craig told him there was no point in trying to get the decision reversed—this one came right from the top.[54]

MacArthur responded with a bellow of outraged pride. "Your letter has amazed me," he cabled Craig. "The action suggested would constitute my summary relief. . . . Considering rank and position it can only be interpreted as constituting disciplinary action . . . my good name and professional reputation are threatened by the proposed action . . . almost forty years of loyal and devoted service should insure for me the same just treatment and reasonable consideration that our army has traditionally and rigidly observed towards even its rawest recruit."[55]

Roosevelt tried to mollify him, by offering him any command in the United States that interested him and telling him that world conditions were so worrying he needed MacArthur to be stationed close at hand so he could benefit from the general's advice.[56] MacArthur refused to be flattered into submission. "I find the thought repugnant of resuming to a subordinate command after having been military head of the Army," he wrote Craig. "It would be as though President Roosevelt were required to go back to his functions as Assistant Secretary of the Navy. It would not only be unsatisfactory to me but the reaction would be such as to make me an unsatisfactory subordinate commander." He ignored the fact that other former chiefs of staff, including his mentor Leonard Wood, had gone on to other assignments after descending from Olympus. He himself had once assumed that after his time as Chief of Staff ended, he would take on another command within the United States. To be recalled in this way was simply too embarrassing. It amounted to a public declaration that his mission to the Philippines had failed.

He requested instead that he be retired from the Army, but he also pointed out that in the event of war he would be as available for service on the retired list as he was on the active list. "I am convinced, however," he told Craig, "that the United States will not become involved in war during my day. The magnificent leadership of President Roosevelt practically assures against such a calamity."[57] Convinced as he still was that war was not far off, he did not intend to burn all his bridges. When the war came, he wanted to return to active duty and hold a major command once again. His compliment to Roosevelt, which Craig was almost certain to pass on, was a form of insurance. He applied to be retired from the Army as of December 31.

When old friends wrote and asked about his plans, he replied vaguely about returning to what he called "my ancestral home in Milwaukee." The Alonzo Cudworth American Legion Post Number 23 in that city excitedly offered him membership and anticipated his attendance at future meetings. He graciously accepted the offer of membership.[58] Friends and admirers throughout the Army meanwhile sent effusive, often touching tributes. They congratulated him on his magnificent career or simply expressed lasting gratitude at having known him and worked for him. Doubleday got his old friend Theodore Roosevelt, Jr., to contact him and ask if he planned to write his memoirs.[59]

As Craig had foreseen, however, Quezon asked MacArthur to stay on as military adviser. He could keep his salary, continue to live in the Manila Hotel and would still be entitled to his bonus of 46/100 of 1 percent of Philippine defense spending. It would be a long time, if ever, before he graced the distant portals of Alonzo Cudworth Post Number 23.

13

Great Men

The offices of the Philippine defense mission were housed in 1 Calle Victoria, the large and picturesque building known as the House on the Wall. On one side was the Intramuros, the collection of Spanish colonial buildings, mainly in stone, that was Spain's architectural legacy to Manila. On the other side, 1 Calle Victoria looked down on the former moat, now a nine-hole golf course. But the eye was drawn inevitably toward the sparkling waters of the bay beyond and, looming through the purple haze, the mountains of Bataan. There was a magical, nostalgic quality to 1 Calle Victoria for MacArthur. It was not simply a quaint and charming old building. Its associations with his father's three years in the Philippines made it part of the family legend. He called it the Cradle of Philippine Defense.

"Many a person," MacArthur wrote, "has turned away from the entrance, convinced that this headquarters is a private dwelling. At the entrance, the carved furniture, the tapestries, and the very oriental round door heighten that impression. Even at the head of the stairs doubt still assails the newcomer. Beige Chinese rugs, comfortable furniture, floor lamps and homelike knick knacks invite the entrant but fail to dispel his confusion. Slowly the conversation of busy officers and the clickety clack of the inevitable Army typewriter create the expected atmosphere."[1]

His office as military adviser was in the large, handsome room that had been his bedroom during his assignment as commander of the Military District of the Philippines. Like all the principal rooms in the building, it was spacious, with a high ceiling and a feeling of coolness and airiness. His office was, thought one visitor, "more like a formal drawing room than a soldier's office. There are old books and pictures, inlaid cabinets dating back to the Spanish occupation, a deep sofa and comfortable chairs, a beautiful Chinese screen and a huge Chippendale desk."[2] The only military element was a magnificent display of flags against one wall. MacArthur had collected flags for years. His military career could be read in his flag collection, including the bright banner of the Rainbow, almost as well as in his medals.

MacArthur was a clean-desk man. There was rarely anything on it other than the document he was presently dealing with, his tobacco pouch and a half dozen pencils. When anyone came to see him, MacArthur was likely to pace up and down while he talked, pausing only to line up the pencils now and again, like a student wrestling with a geometry problem.[3]

At various times during the day he would wander out of his office and visit members of his staff. He had a habit too of talking to the clerks, sitting on the edges of their desks and chatting about their families, their hobbies, whatever came to mind. The other side of the famous aloofness and lifelong shyness was that within the confines of his own headquarters MacArthur was relaxed, casual and friendly.

When MacArthur retired from active duty in December 1937, there were thirty-two officers and eight enlisted men assigned to the military adviser's office. The two senior officers on the staff, Majors Dwight Eisenhower and James Ord, received their normal Army pay plus an extra five hundred dollars a month from the Philippine government, virtually doubling their salaries. Other officers got at least an extra hundred dollars a month. When MacArthur retired, they all were reassigned to the Philippine Department. His role as military adviser was no longer an official U.S. Army position. Fortunately, however, Craig allowed them to continue working for MacArthur and to continue receiving extra payments from the commonwealth for their services. In effect, matters continued much as before.

However far away, MacArthur continued to follow Army football with an interest that sometimes verged on the obsessive. Old friends, such as John "Court House" Lee, destined to rise to four stars, sent him accounts of Army football games they had attended. Ike, on a trip to the United States in the summer of 1938, made sure to come back with the inside dope on the prospects for the impending football season. MacArthur corresponded with the West Point coach, William H. Wood, assuring him, "an almost lifetime experience with West Point football has given me a perspective that along certain lines of general principle might be of some assistance . . ." before stressing the importance of having a more varied offense, extolling the neglected art of kicking as an offensive weapon and expressing pleasure at the heftiness of the current squad. Wood, for his part, wrote regularly to keep the general up-to-date on developments.

Unfortunately there was not a lot of good news to report. The late 1930s saw Army football mired in difficult times. When Superintendent Garrison Davidson stepped down in June 1938, he sent MacArthur a brief note of apology that the Black Knights of the Hudson had been drably lackluster during his time as supe.[4]

MacArthur arrived at his office in the late morning, worked until about 1:00 P.M., took a long lunch break and a nap, before returning to the office for another hour or two in the late afternoon. In Dwight Eisenhower and James Ord he had, and knew he had, two of the best young officers in the Army. Ike accepted the Manila assignment on condition that he could take a friend, and the friend was Ord. They had been at West Point together, at Leavenworth together and had served in Washington together. Even if Ord had not been Ike's friend, however, the chances are that he would have gone to Manila with MacArthur anyway. When MacArthur accepted the offer of becoming Quezon's military adviser, he wanted a thorough study made into the defense problems of the Philippines. The General Staff was too busy with other projects to undertake it. So a committee of War College students was given the task, and Ord had chaired the committee.

The National Defense Plan for the Philippines was in large part shaped by Jimmy Ord. He brought to this challenge a number of advantages. Ord had been born in Mexico and spent much of his childhood there; he spoke Spanish fluently—a major benefit in dealing with the Filipino political class. He was also energetic, sociable and sophisticated. It was the extroverted Ord, not the introverted MacArthur, who dealt with the Philippine Assembly and lobbied its members on behalf of the defense plan. In fact, so far as Bill Hoge was concerned, "Ord was the best man in the entire outfit. . . . Ike did well but he didn't have the knowledge of things" that Ord possessed.[5]

His relationship with Eisenhower was essentially a brotherhood, as symbolized in the cable address they created for themselves: Telegrams sent to either one were transmitted to JIMIKE, Manila. Ord's presence certainly helped make the Philippine assignment, which Eisenhower had never sought, more endurable. What Eisenhower wanted more than anything else was service with troops, but MacArthur, determined to retain Ike's "flaming pen" for his own use, would not let him go.

This was a policy guaranteed to get under Ike's skin. The normal and proper pattern for an officer's career development in peacetime is staff-school-troops. Eisenhower had filled plenty of staff assignments and had attended four schools since World War I, but he had spent only six months with troops.

Nor was Eisenhower cut out temperamentally to be assigned to one man for much of his career. What MacArthur was creating in Manila was less a modern military staff than an eighteenth- or nineteenth-century general's "household." Its members were expected to owe a degree of personal loyalty to him that was at least as great as that they gave to the Army. He did not want people passing through 1 Calle Victoria for a couple of years as they moved from assignment to assignment. He was trying to form a military family, a happy coterie that would remain as long as he needed them. When Ord visited the United States in the summer of 1937 to try to get supplies and money from the War Department, word got back to MacArthur that Ord was talking about future assignments. MacArthur railed indignantly in front of his adjutant, Captain T. J. Davis, at the "conceited and self-centered attitudes" of some staff members.

If this was intended to bring forth declarations of loyalty, and it probably was, he could not have helped noticing that he did not get one from Eisenhower. "From the beginning of this venture," Ike recorded, "I've personally announced myself as ready and willing to go back to an assignment in the U.S. Army at any moment. The General knows this if he knows anything. . . ."[6]

The MacArthur management style owed nothing to the Army management style, which was fundamentally impersonal. MacArthur, however, was not a product of the Army school system. His brief experience with it, at the Engineer School, was of little relevance to his career as a commander anyway. He had not been to Leavenworth or the War College. He was not a modern staff officer. He created his own kind of staff and ran it in his own idiosyncratic way.

There were many officers who were products of the Army school system who, once drawn within the MacArthur magnetic field, nevertheless had absolutely no desire to wander off and orbit someone else for a while. Ike was the major exception to this pattern, yet ironically, he was the senior assistant and the staff member closest to MacArthur.

Shortly after being assigned an office next to MacArthur's in the War Department in 1933, Eisenhower had turned his mind to the subject of great men. Did they exist anymore? Clearly MacArthur believed they did. The birthday message he sent on Quezon's sixtieth birthday began grandiloquently: "The birthdays of great men mark the milestones of the world's progress. History is but the sum of their biographies."[7]

This was a nineteenth-century idea, promoted by philosophers and historians, such as Carlyle, Hegel and Nietzsche, but it was a view that was crumbling fast in the 1930s as writers and artists celebrated the ascendancy of the Common Man. Eisenhower, only ten years younger than MacArthur but a whole generation away in grasping the spirit of the age, decided on reflection: "There are no 'great men' as we understood that expression when we were shavers. The man whose brain is so all-embracing in its grasp of events, so infallible in its logic, and so swift in formulation of perfect decisions, is only a figment of the imagination." Unable, then, to look upon MacArthur as MacArthur looked upon himself, Ike really was not a good man to take to Manila. On the contrary, he was no longer the ambitious junior officer eager to rise by pleasing the boss and taking the boss's ideas as his guiding light. Eisenhower, blessed with a cool, objective approach to military problems, was by this time well aware of his own considerable abilities and willing to argue with MacArthur when he thought the general was wrong.[8]

Almost as soon as the National Defense Plan was ready to go to the Philippine Assembly, Eisenhower openly criticized MacArthur's intention to start training twenty thousand reservists once registration was under way and placing them in 128 training camps. The result was a heated argument.[9]

MacArthur's relationship with Eisenhower did not improve. Instead it grew worse. He convinced himself in the summer of 1936 that Roosevelt was going to lose the November election and rammed this news down the throats of his essentially apolitical staff. Yet what was the source of his unique insight into American politics that year? "Your weekly letters," he told the vehemently Republican John Callan O'Laughlin, publisher of the *Army and Navy Journal,* "provide the only reliable information here on the situation there." He was also convinced by the famous *Literary Digest* poll of its readers' voting intentions that predicted that Alf Landon, "the Kansas Sunflower," would defeat Roosevelt. MacArthur overlooked the fact that the *Digest* was available only by subscription and the people most likely to subscribe were middle-class Republicans.[10]

Ike advised him not to spread his prophecies of a Roosevelt defeat so widely and showed him letters from a well-informed friend in Abilene who said flatly that Landon could not even carry Kansas. MacArthur bawled him out furiously, ridiculing Ike's intelligence and telling him he was "fearful and small minded" for advising caution.[11]

As it turned out, Landon carried just two states: Maine and Vermont. Roosevelt buried him on election day. "Boy, did the General back pedal rapidly," wrote Ike in his diary. "I hear he rushed out to Quezon and 'took back' what he had said. . . . Accused the Lit. Digest of 'crookedness.' " MacArthur was afraid his prediction of a Roosevelt defeat would get back to the President, and it probably did.[12]

This episode strained MacArthur's and Ike's relationship, and in the summer of 1937 Ike dropped a heavy hint that he'd had enough. He told MacArthur that he would probably have to return to the United States for health reasons, an idea that took the general by surprise. There was nothing evidently wrong with Ike's health.[13] Shortly after this MacArthur tried to placate him by promoting him from senior adviser to chief of staff of the defense mission. This gave Eisenhower control over the staff, but it made no difference because of what happened next.

The political situation in the Far East was starting to spiral out of control. Quezon suddenly lost his earlier enthusiasm for MacArthur's defense plan. In a misguided attempt to revive it, MacArthur decided to bring forty thousand Filipino reservists to Manila and parade them through the city in early 1938 as marching proof of progress. He had the staff draw up plans but made one crucial mistake: He did not sound out Quezon in advance.

When Don Manuel heard about the planned parade, he was appalled. The commonwealth's finances were too tightly stretched to bring forty thousand men to Manila from all over the archipelago and keep them fed and housed outside the capital for a week. He told MacArthur not to do anything so absurd. MacArthur was famous for his loyalty to his subordinates. That was an important reason why he was so widely admired by Army officers.

All the same, one thing he was never good at was admitting that he personally had made a mistake. To accept personal responsibility now would be to embarrass himself in front of Quezon, just as Quezon was starting to question whether creating a Philippine Army was worthwhile. Rather than infuriate Quezon, MacArthur put all the blame for the parade plan onto Ike and Ord.

Staff officers get used to taking the blame for the general's mistakes, just as secretaries do in civilian life for an errant boss. But the way to do it is to talk it over with them first. MacArthur could not do that. His subordinates found themselves being blamed for something that MacArthur had told them to do, while he was brazenly telling Quezon that he had not ordered anyone to plan a parade.

This was a turning point in the seven-year MacArthur-Eisenhower relationship. "General, all you're saying is that I'm a liar, and I am *not* a liar," protested Ike when he learned what MacArthur had done. "So I'd like to go back to the United States right away."

MacArthur put his arm around Ike's shoulder. "It's just fun to see that Dutch temper take you over," he said lightly, treating the entire incident as a trifling matter, now that he'd pacified Quezon. "It's just a misunderstanding, and let's let it go at that." Ike later commented, "Never again were we on the same warm and cordial terms."[14] Eisenhower could still esteem MacArthur's military abilities, but the memory of MacArthur's conduct over the parade that never was rankled for years.

It seems to have been a watershed for Davis too. After Ike became a power in the Pentagon, he had Davis transferred, with Davis's enthusiastic agreement, to his own staff. Davis spent World War II as Eisenhower's adjutant, not MacArthur's.[15]

A month or so after the parade idea was dropped, Jimmy Ord was killed. He was a passenger in a plane flown by one of the fledgling Philippine Air Force pilots. The plane stalled at low level and crashed. The pilot survived, but Ord, who was thrown from the plane, died from his injuries.[16]

Quezon attended Ord's funeral. So did High Commissioner Paul McNutt. MacArthur was absent. Just as he was deeply religious but almost never went to church, so he could be eloquent over the deaths of young men in the service of their country but avoid their funerals. Physically fearless, he had a profound aversion to churches, funerals and hospitals. MacArthur always had a doctor among his aides, but he dreaded illness. He would not even watch a movie if he knew it contained a hospital scene.[17]

Ord's death was one of the most heartbreaking events of Eisenhower's life. What interest he had managed to retain in his present assignment seemed to evaporate. Shortly after this, he talked it over with Mamie and his son, John. Pacing up and down the living room, much like MacArthur, he said, "The only reason left for me to stay in this place is the extra money the Philippine government is giving me. Other than that, there's not much to keep me here."[18]

What he hadn't taken into account was Quezon. Ike had an office in the Malacañan and saw Quezon regularly. When Quezon heard that Ike was thinking of leaving, he turned all the force of his charm on the lieutenant colonel and pleaded with him not to jeopardize all that the defense mission had accomplished. Surely he owed it to the Filipino people to ask for a year's extension to his assignment? Reluctantly Ike did so.[19]

MacArthur was delighted. The efficiency reports he had placed in Eisenhower's 201 File were glowing. He gave him the highest rating possible, "Superior," and in the space allowed for personal comments, he wrote, "In time of war this officer should be promoted to general rank immediately."[20]

When Eisenhower requested an extended trip to the United States in the summer of 1938, to improve Mamie's health and to lobby the War Department for money and supplies, MacArthur agreed. Ord's replacement, Major Richard K. Sutherland, had recently arrived from China, where he was serving with the 15th Infantry Regiment, and would fill in for Ike while he was away.

During the three months that Eisenhower was gone, Sutherland proved himself to be a highly competent staff officer. The Yale-educated son of a senator from West Virginia, he had been to all the right schools: Benning, Leavenworth, the War College, as well as the French Army's École de Guerre. MacArthur had met Sutherland in 1932, when Sutherland was at the War College, and had specifically requested him for this assignment. He was soon convinced of the wisdom of his choice. "Sutherland has proven himself a real find," MacArthur wrote to a friend. "Concise, energetic and able, he has been invaluable in helping me clarify and crystallize the situation."[21]

When Eisenhower returned, however, he did not like Sutherland, and he would never like Sutherland. Few people did. The end, however, was in sight. Ike would be due to return to the United States in late 1939, once he had spent four years overseas. The only thing that would keep him in Manila beyond 1939 would be for him to ask for another extension and for MacArthur to endorse his request. He made no such request. In due course he got orders to return home.

"Mamie is counting the days until December 13," Ike wrote his old friend Leonard "Gee" Gerow in October. "She really wants to come home . . . as the day draws near, I must say I begin to share her impatience."[22]

Only John was sorry to leave Manila. He liked the school where he was enrolled and liked the colorful life that he saw all around him. Before leaving the Manila Hotel, he went up to the penthouse to say his farewells to the MacArthurs. Jean took him out to the terrace, where the general was pacing among the potted plants, hands clasped in Napoleonic style behind his back. "Immediately his theatrical impulses manifested themselves. He walked over and shook hands—in his typical fashion with his left hand on my right shoulder—and recited in detail the positions I had been elected to in my senior year . . . the general's memory, his charm and his ability to show interest in an inconsequential boy always impressed me and explained to a large degree how he was able to mesmerize any individual he wanted, including my recalcitrant Old Man."[23]

The general and Jean came to say goodbye aboard the ship that would take the Eisenhowers home. They seemed to part on reasonably friendly terms, with no evident indication of animosity. Yet one of the best-known MacArthur stories has him describing Ike as "the best clerk I ever had." And one of the best-known Eisenhower stories has him saying, "I studied dramatics for seven years under General MacArthur." Both stories are plausible, but no has ever provided a reliable source for either one. And there is good reason to doubt both of them. In later years MacArthur and Eisenhower remained in touch, writing to each other when there was no evident reason to do so except respect for each other's professional abilities. "Hostility between us has been exaggerated," Eisenhower told Clayton James. "After all, there must be a strong tie for two men to work so closely for seven years."[24]

The first year of training the Philippine Army's reservists produced a long catalog of failures and frustrations. The camps were not ready, nor were there enough competent officers to train the reservists or to ensure that the small stock of equipment available was maintained properly. Although the soldiering abilities of the well-established Philippine Scouts were respected by American officers, the leadership of the new Philippine Army left a lot to be desired.[25]

Forty thousand reservists were to be trained each year. The course consisted of five and a half months of basic and advanced infantry instruction. Besides offering rudimentary military instruction, the program gave many young Filipinos a basic education in literacy, with proper health care for the first time in their lives, with a balanced diet and a program that made them physically fit. At the end of that time, however, they went back to their villages and were soon as undernourished and physically soft as they had been before. In the opinion of one of the leading American experts on the Philippines, Evatt D. Hester, MacArthur's training program was doomed. Hester told Harold Ickes, "The only way to have an army remain fit in the Philippines is to have a standing army." MacArthur was trying to create a Swiss Army without the Swiss.[26]

Nevertheless, if only one person believed in it at this time, that man was MacArthur. His plan called for creating three divisions a year, each consisting of seventy-five hundred men. By 1946 the Philippines should be able to field a force of thirty reserve divisions, which he said was "the irreducible minimum" to ensure the new nation's defenses.[27] His strategy was one of "beach defense"—meeting the invaders as soon as they landed and were at their most vulnerable. With an army trained as he intended, up to the strength he intended, as well armed as he intended, he believed it would cost the Japanese at least five hundred thousand casualties and as much as five billion dollars to conquer the Philippines.

MacArthur's staff meanwhile struggled to scrounge arms for the nascent Philippine Army. They were able to get some matériel on loan from the War Department, but there was resistance in both the War and State departments to issuing weapons to tens of thousands of people whose political loyalties were uncertain. The biggest obstacle, though, was a widespread conviction among Army planners that MacArthur's plan was unrealistic. After talking to Major General Stanley Embick, the head of the War Plans Division, in July 1937, Jimmy Ord had concluded glumly, "I am thoroughly convinced that he has little confidence in our plan." Embick seemed to believe that all the equipment shipped to the Philippines was going to end up in enemy hands.[28]

MacArthur applied his own talents to enlisting assistance wherever he could find it. Quezon was hoping to harness the islands' hydroelectric potential to provide cheap energy, and a Philippine Power Development Corporation was established. The corporation brought two well-respected Army engineer officers from the United States, Captains Lucius D. Clay and Hugh J. "Pat" Casey, to supervise the construction of dams. MacArthur had an addition built onto 1 Calle Victoria to provide the engineers with offices. "My real purpose in having them here," he told his staff, "is that although they are paid by funds from the Power Development Corporation, I can use them to help us out whenever they are not busy at other work." As ploys go, this one worked like a charm.[29]

All he had to do was convince Clay and Casey to go along with it. "He gave Casey and me an hour talk on the Philippines," Clay wrote later. "On its economy, its politics, its relations with America—one of the most inspired talks I've ever heard." Casey was similarly impressed. He eventually joined MacArthur's staff and would stay with him throughout World War II.[30]

At about the same time that Clay and Casey arrived, Lieutenant Colonel William Hoge was sent out to command the 14th Engineer Regiment of the Philippine Department. Hoge, who would go on to have one of the most successful careers of the World War II Army (building the Alaska Highway, commanding the Engineer Special Brigade at Normandy, capturing the bridge at Remagen), was one of the few officers who disliked MacArthur. On their first meeting, what he saw was a man who was as pleasant as could be but essentially a windbag, "Always full of big ideas," but giving him no practical advice. When Hoge went to see him to talk about building a highway across Bataan to improve its defenses or about how to find more engineers for the Philippine Army, all MacArthur seemed to want to talk about was football or West Point, preferably both.[31]

The person who impressed Hoge was Eisenhower, and Ike talked him into becoming chief engineer of the Philippine Army. In the Philippines, American officers usually worked only until about 1:00 P.M. Hoge agreed to run the 14th Engineer Regiment in the mornings and spend his afternoons working for the Philippine Army. After hearing MacArthur's inspirational talk, Clay decided to do the same and assumed responsibility for supervising engineer training. They began with only five or six Filipino engineer officers. Hoge estimated that if MacArthur's plan were carried to fruition, the Philippine Army would need thirty-five hundred engineers by 1946. Where they were going to come from was a mystery. When Hoge left the Philippines in 1940, there were still fewer than one hundred engineer officers in the Philippine Army.[32]

The defense plan also called for creation of a miniature navy. This would consist of fifty torpedo boats, which MacArthur imagined swarming out to sink enemy troop transports steaming into Lingayen Gulf. The Navy was not interested in participating in his scheme, and when he tried to get it to produce torpedo boats for him, the Navy turned him down flat, saying to do so would be illegal.[33]

The only boats available were British, manufactured by Thorneycroft. When Eisenhower learned how much they would cost, he was "staggered." The price was $250,000 per boat. Fifty boats would come to $12.5 million, equivalent to the entire Philippine defense budget for more than eighteen months. That kind of money was not available.

MacArthur decided he needed his own naval expert. There was a personable Navy lieutenant who played golf with Ike, named Sid Huff. One day Huff had a heart attack while golfing. His career as an active-duty Navy officer collapsed on the links when he did. Huff returned home to recuperate. To his surprise, he received a message from MacArthur asking him to return to Manila and be his naval adviser. Huff reported to 1 Calle Victoria in December 1936 and got the treatment in MacArthur's well-flagged office—the pacing, the inspirational talk, the rearranging of the pencils. Then MacArthur came to the point. "I want a Filipino navy of motor torpedo boats, Sid. If I get the money, how many can you get built in ten years?"

Huff could only blurt out, "General, never in my life have I even seen a motor torpedo boat."

"That's all right," said MacArthur, "you will."[34]

Huff tackled the challenge with enthusiasm, striving to live up to the confidence that MacArthur had expressed in him. Huff set to work designing a cheap copy of the Thorneycroft boat, one that could be built in the Philippines out of local materials. Not one was ever finished.[35]

MacArthur's plan called for a Philippine Air Force of 250 planes, mainly fighters and trainers. The Air Corps assigned two officers to help him, and both were deeply impressed by MacArthur. One of them, Lieutenant Hugh Parker, was "simply amazed at the details MacArthur knew about Air Force training." Nonetheless pilot training posed enormous challenges in a country where few people had ever done so much as drive a car. MacArthur was expecting him to "get them off a carabao and into an airplane [but] they had very poor appreciation of speed, distance or anything mechanical."[36]

When Parker reported to 1 Calle Victoria, Ike told him how MacArthur worked. "He will never tell you to do anything he doesn't believe that you could do. So if he ever tells you to do anything, the answer is, 'Yes, sir. I'll try.' Or just, 'Yes, sir.' " Parker did as Eisenhower told him and thereby found himself shortly after this flying a small training plane for twelve hours through a typhoon to deliver serum to an isolated leper colony. Parker thought he was going to perish at any moment, but to his astonishment, he survived, much as MacArthur had evidently expected.[37]

Parker's superior, Lieutenant William Lee, scoffed at the idea of building up a fleet of patrol boats. Modern fighters cost fifty to sixty thousand dollars apiece and were far better weapons than PT boats against an invading force. When Lee, who was the argumentative type, raised such issues with Eisenhower, Ike would say, "Let's go see the old man." They would then have a session out on the terrace in the Manila Hotel or in the long, rectangular library, and while MacArthur paced and swung his gold watch chain with the football pendant, Lee made his argument. "Of course," he recalled, "you didn't get to talk much when you went to see MacArthur. He did the talking. And he called me 'Commodore' for some damned reason or other." Lee, who would become a brigadier general in World War II, never persuaded MacArthur that PT boats were useless, but remained convinced that "MacArthur was the greatest strategist we've ever had in this country."[38]

For the two and a half years that Paul V. McNutt was high commissioner, from January 1937 to July 1939, MacArthur had a friend and fellow thirty-second-degree Mason to turn to for support. McNutt had begun as a skeptic on Philippine defense but been converted to MacArthur's view that with enough money and equipment he could make the islands defensible by 1946.[39]

McNutt headed for home in July 1939 to seek the Democratic party's presidential nomination in 1940. It never occurred to him that Roosevelt would seek a third term. The handsome, capable McNutt vanished into the void. MacArthur meanwhile cabled Roosevelt's assistant Stephen Early that he would "be very glad to have [the President's] favorable consideration. . . . I believe I could render him and our country valuable service in this exposed outpost here [which] is the weakest link in our defense system." This was his convoluted way of saying he would like to be high commissioner.[40]

Nothing came of this. Roosevelt chose Francis B. Sayre to succeed McNutt. Sayre, a former lecturer at Harvard Law School, was married to Woodrow Wilson's youngest daughter, Jessie. He had also served as foreign affairs adviser to the king of Siam, the grandson of the one Yul Brynner later portrayed in *The King and I*. Sayre had returned to the United States to resume teaching at Harvard Law School, and in 1933 he was rewarded for his work as Roosevelt's foreign policy adviser during the 1932 campaign with the post of assistant secretary of state. He had not shown any great abilities in this role, and Roosevelt had doubts about making him high commissioner. Sayre was a shy, buttoned-up Boston Brahmin, hardly the kind to join Quezon, his acolytes and *poules de luxe* at the gaming tables or to take a trip on the presidential yacht and chow down on that Filipino delicacy the *balout*—the boiled egg, that is, of an about-to-hatch chick—a treat that left the diner with a mouthful of fine little feathers and crunching his way through a pair of tiny chicken feet. Roosevelt made the appointment anyway.

When Sayre arrived in Manila in the fall of 1939, he found himself dealing with a Quezon who was alarmed, at times panicky, at the menace of war. The optimistic reports he was receiving from MacArthur on the progress of the Philippine Army conflicted sharply with the pessimistic accounts he was getting from the more able Filipino commanders. It was increasingly clear to Quezon that with too few trained officers and virtually no modern weapons it would be a long time before the Philippines could be defended. Even ten years might not be enough. MacArthur, he grumbled bitterly, "has hoodwinked me."[41]

The way Germany had gobbled up Poland in less than a month looked like a terrifying portent of what the Japanese Army could do to the impoverished Philippines. In a speech that launched the commonwealth's new Department of National Defense, he said it had an impossible task. "Even though we armed every male citizen," Quezon lamented, the islands could not be defended. He made a public appeal to Roosevelt to negotiate neutralization treaties covering the Philippines.[42]

Shortly after this he confronted MacArthur with his doubts. What, he asked, will happen if we get our independence in 1946, have an army of three hundred thousand men in position and the Japanese decide to attack? MacArthur told him it would be possible to fight for six months, provided ammunition and other vital supplies continued to be imported. "And how could I import such supplies without a navy if the Japanese were attacking us?" asked Quezon in bewilderment.

MacArthur told him that he would have to hope that the British or some other naval power would decide to intervene and prevent any invasion. In that case, asked Quezon, "Why the necessity of maintaining and paying for an expensive army?" MacArthur had no clear answer to that.

And what about Mindanao? Quezon wanted to know. Mindanao was the largest island in the southern Philippines and only six hundred miles from Japanese bases on Palau. Did MacArthur's plan assure a strong defense of Mindanao? MacArthur conceded it did not. "What then would prevent Japan from seizing and occupying Mindanao indefinitely?" Again MacArthur could not give him any reassurance.[43]

Despite these conversations, MacArthur continued to make public statements that the defense plan was proceeding successfully and that the archipelago, all of it, could and would be defended. Quezon was appalled. MacArthur's public pronouncements were "fantastic," he told Sayre. They could mean only one thing: "General MacArthur is crazy."[44]

He asked Sayre to get MacArthur recalled to the United States. Sayre was willing—he was no admirer of MacArthur's—but he would not do it without a written request. Quezon was an experienced politician. He had no intention of leaving a documentary record that proved he had stabbed his military adviser in the back. He was stuck with his field marshal.[45]

Quezon did not have to see him, though. MacArthur was informed that from now on he would have to deal with the president's secretary, Jorge Vargas, that Quezon wanted no further contacts with him. If this insult was meant to force MacArthur to quit, it did not work. He persevered with this humiliating new arrangement but remarked pointedly to Vargas, "Jorge, some day your boss is going to want to see me more than I want to see him."[46]

These were difficult days for MacArthur. His relationship with Quezon was foundering, and he had disliked Sayre from the outset. Nothing that happened in 1940–41 inclined him to change his mind about the prissy and self-important lawyer that Roosevelt had shoved on to him. What made the situation even worse was that when McNutt departed, Roosevelt had transferred the Bureau of Insular Affairs from the War Department over to Harold Ickes and the Department of the Interior. So MacArthur had Ickes to deal with, if indirectly, through Sayre. Ickes was insisting that Sayre must oversee preparations for defending the Philippines.[47]

While Sayre was beyond peradventure Roosevelt's representative in the Philippines, he was one of the least qualified people in the history of the Republic to discharge such a responsibility. Sayre was a pacifist. Despite being a fit, healthy young man, Sayre had exploited his influence as President Wilson's son-in-law to avoid military service during World War I and worked for the YMCA instead. Even in 1940 he found war unthinkable. He convinced himself that despite the war ravaging Europe, there would be no war in the Pacific, and certainly no war involving America. MacArthur despised him, as did Quezon, who decided Sayre was just another polite, well-bred, highly educated racist.[48]

Where, then, was MacArthur to turn for assistance? Certainly not to the War Department. In June 1940 a group of well-placed Republicans who favored American intervention on the side of Great Britain convinced Roosevelt that the isolationist Harry Woodring would have to go. Roosevelt prevailed on Henry L. Stimson, no friend of MacArthur's, to be secretary of war.

George C. Marshall, the recently appointed Army Chief of Staff, wanted to help MacArthur if he could, but there was little he could do beyond telling Major General George Grunert, the new commander of the Philippine Department, to try to cooperate with him. Grunert resented having to help MacArthur's advisory mission and gave as little help as he could get away with.[49]

Eisenhower, now back in the United States and serving with troops, wrote MacArthur a long, informative letter in December 1940. He told his former boss and mentor that the War Department was so overwhelmed by the challenge of the first peacetime draft in American history it had little time to deal with the Philippines. Ike also noted that the training program the Army had adopted for its draftees looked as if it had been copied from MacArthur's program for creating a Philippine Army.[50]

MacArthur may have hoped, fleetingly, that he would have a sympathetic ear when, in October 1940, the Navy sent a new commander out to the Asiatic Fleet, Admiral Thomas Hart. Despite his four-star rank, Hart's "fleet" consisted of an unimpressive collection of obsolescent craft of dubious combat value. Hart himself joked, "All my ships are old enough to vote."[51]

The MacArthurs and the Harts had been acquainted for forty years. Tommy Hart had been a close friend of MacArthur's sailor brother, Arthur, and been a pallbearer at Arthur's funeral in 1923. Yet even here MacArthur found himself confronting a true disbeliever. Hart could sit back and look at MacArthur dispassionately as he paced and the flow of words, sometimes turning into a whisper so that you had to strain to hear them, sometimes so forcefully delivered they seemed to presage a storm about to break, poured from MacArthur like a strange and powerful music that threatened to sweep the least sentient listener along to a destination he had not intended to reach. Hart was one of the few who could resist, and also one of the few allowed to call him Douglas to his face. But as MacArthur gave Hart inspiring lectures on how he would defend the beaches, it seemed to the admiral that his grasp of how amphibious forces operated to overcome shore defenses was out-of-date and patchy. "Douglas knows a lot of things which are not so," Hart reflected shortly after arriving in the Philippines. "He is a very able and convincing talker—a combination which spells danger." Even so, Hart could not help admiring MacArthur's fighting spirit.[52]

With critics, skeptics and opponents wherever he turned, MacArthur had few illusions about what he had accomplished on behalf of two governments that seemed to him to be alike only in being ungrateful and unhelpful. In March 1940 he wrote to an old friend: "Conditions in the Far East are in a state of flux. A man would be a fool or a knave who pretended to predict with accuracy what the future holds. . . . I have been doing everything that I can during the last four years to strengthen this very weak outpost. . . . Much progress has been made but nothing compared to what I had visualized. . . ."[53]

After many conversations with MacArthur, Hart concluded in January 1941 that MacArthur had had enough. He felt MacArthur wanted "to duck out, because he doesn't appear too happy in the job," and only the large salary the commonwealth was paying kept him in the Philippines.[54]

There were newspaper stories shortly after this that Roosevelt was thinking of recalling Sayre. MacArthur swiftly sent a long letter to Stephen Early, almost begging to take Sayre's place. "I am writing to offer my services to the President in these monumentally momentous days," he began. He went on to assert that so far as the Philippine defense plan was concerned, "I have now completed everything along that line that is possible and I will probably close out my work with the Philippine Army within the year." He claimed that the Filipinos esteemed him, that he was "thoroughly familiar" with everything that was happening "from Vladivostok to Singapore" and had "a personal acquaintance with everyone of importance in the Orient." He closed with an unctuous hallelujah to Roosevelt as "our greatest statesman . . . our greatest military strategist."[55]

The newspapers were wrong about Sayre: He was not about to return to the United States. But MacArthur's efforts had not been wasted. He received a reassuring letter from his old friend Major General Edwin "Pa" Watson, Roosevelt's military aide: "The President asked me to write . . . he wished me to tell you that he wants you there in your military capacity rather than any other."[56]

The first encouraging word in a long, long time. MacArthur was overjoyed. He replied that he was "delighted that the President desires to utilize my services in a military rather than a civil capacity. This would naturally be my own choice. . . . I shall therefore plan to continue to develop the Philippine Army for an emergency. . . ."[57]

Shortly after this he wrote to Marshall to say that he planned to shut down the defense mission, because he expected the Philippine Army would soon be federalized and come directly under the War Department. Marshall wrote back on June 20 to tell him he was being premature, that there were no such plans. However, during discussions with Stimson "it was decided that your outstanding qualifications and vast experience in the Philippines make you the logical selection as the Army commander in the Far East should the situation approach a crisis."[58]

Back in December 1940, when everything was at a low ebb, a journalist from *Time,* Theodore White, had visited the Philippines. White had spent much of that year touring the Far East, talking to military commanders of all nations. When he arrived in the Philippines, he went straight to the Philippine Department's headquarters in Manila and was told by Grunert's press officer there was no point in seeing MacArthur. "He cuts no more ice in the U.S. Army than a corporal." White went to see him anyway.

Even though the general was approaching sixty-one and his hands trembled and his voice was squeaky when he grew emotional, he was still a spectacle of energy and determination. Age had not withered the MacArthur command presence. Nor was it affected by being dressed in a gray West Point bathrobe with a big blue *A* on the back and "his skinny shanks protruding as he paced."

MacArthur pointed, stabbed with his cigar, roared, pounded the furniture, brandished a pipe, poured out a deluge of statistics—manpower, firepower, mileages, tonnages, airpower, sea power—until White's mind reeled and he was left spellbound. Then he reminisced, paraded his almost unbelievable career in front of his visitor: the Army childhood, the years at West Point, killing the two Filipinos who had ambushed him, going behind the lines to rustle locomotives in Veracruz, the awesome battles on the Western Front, seizing the Côte de Châtillon, reforming West Point, saving the peacetime Army from destruction, trying to create an army for Quezon, and all of it was but a prelude to this hour. The greatest feats were just ahead.

"I am holding myself in readiness," he told White. "I will command the American expeditionary force in the Far East when war comes." He had no doubt war was coming. Japanese ambition made it inevitable. White had reached the same conclusion before arriving in Manila. They rejoiced that they had met, that there were at least two Americans, maybe only two Americans, who understood the peril that Japan now posed to the peace and security of the United States.

As the sun descended into Manila Bay and the interview drew to a close, MacArthur stopped his pacing and turned to face White. "It was destiny that brought us here, White, destiny! By God, it is destiny that brings me here now."[59]

14

The Army
of the Far East

MacArthur paced his terrace, navigating between the potted plants and Junior's vulcanized wading pool, deep in thought. Despite the gathering war clouds that cast long shadows across the western Pacific, there was no reason to believe that the Japanese military wanted to fight the United States. To do so would be suicidal. Japan's great challenge was China, not America. The Japanese Army had driven so deep into China that pulling out had now become unthinkable, yet it lacked the manpower and logistics to subjugate so vast a country. The Japanese military's solution to the Chinese dilemma was to seize the mineral wealth of Southeast Asia. That might enable Japan to create a war machine big enough and rich enough to realize the empire's political and military ambitions of dominating the Far East.

By invoking German help to put pressure on the Vichy government, the Japanese were allowed to move into French air and naval bases in Indochina in early July 1941. This gave them a strong military position in Southeast Asia from which they could grab much of what they wanted.

Roosevelt was not looking for a war in the Pacific, but the United States could not allow the Japanese a free hand to conquer the Far East. The President had already attempted to blunt Japanese expansion by imposing an embargo on the sale of scrap metal to the empire. Roosevelt's response to the move into Vietnam was to impose a total oil embargo, cutting off at a stroke Japan's principal source of petroleum.

MacArthur considered this a major blunder. The Japanese, he was convinced, would now feel they had to move into the Dutch East Indies, and fairly soon. The Japanese Navy faced the prospect of being beached when its reserves of fuel oil ran out sometime in the spring of 1942. The only alternative supply of oil was the oil fields of the Dutch East Indies. If the President was going to act in such a provocative way, he should have ensured the defenses of the Philippines first and then imposed the oil embargo. It was unlikely that the Japanese would try to seize the oil fields of Southeast Asia without first neutralizing the Philippines. By acting impulsively, Roosevelt was gambling with the security of the commonwealth.[1]

Stimson recognized the danger at once. He wrote to the President on July 25: "Due to the situation in the Far East all practical steps should be taken to increase the defensive strength of the Philippine islands. . . . One of the more urgent measures recommended is the calling into active service of the military forces of the Commonwealth of the Philippines. . . ."[2]

Two days later MacArthur was having breakfast when a courier from 1 Calle Victoria brought him two cables that had just been decoded. Both were marked "Urgent." One, from Marshall, read, "Effective this date there is hereby constituted a command designated as the United States Army Forces in the Far East." The new command would include the military forces of the commonwealth plus those of the Philippine Department. "You are hereby designated as the commanding general of the United States Army Forces in the Far East. . . . Orders calling you to active duty are being issued effective July 26, 1941." The second cable consisted of an executive order signed by Roosevelt federalizing the military forces of the Philippine Commonwealth.[3]

MacArthur sent for Sutherland, who was just teeing off for a game of golf in the former moat of the Intramuros before the sun made even golfing uncomfortable, to meet him at 1 Calle Victoria. When Sutherland arrived, MacArthur dictated General Order Number 1, formally activating USAFFE and accepting command.

He and Sutherland then set to work, looking for a way to integrate the various units now under MacArthur's command, ranging from raw native levies to highly trained American regulars, into a single force capable of fighting the Japanese. After several hours Sutherland looked up from the table where they sat and remarked, "You know, General, it adds up to an almost insurmountable task."

MacArthur, who was studying a map, glanced at Sutherland over his reading glasses. "These islands must and will be defended. I can but do my best," he said.[4]

All the same, he was excited to be back on active duty. When he went home, he told Jean, "I feel like an old dog in a new uniform."[5]

Word arrived next day that MacArthur had been promoted to lieutenant general. Sid Huff congratulated him on the extra star. MacArthur thanked him but remarked wryly, "It looks like I'm gradually catching up with myself."[6]

Although he now had a new and important assignment, MacArthur disliked the name United States Army Forces in the Far East. He would probably have preferred to be consulted about the designation of his new command. He personally called it the AFE—echoes, there, of the AEF—for the Army of the Far East.[7]

His command now included the Philippine Department. He had never received much cooperation from any of the three department commanders who had served in the Philippines during his time as military adviser. The present commander, Major General George Grunert, was an able, well-liked cavalryman, but his attitude toward MacArthur had always been cavalier. Now, though, MacArthur could plunder Grunert's staff to man 1 Calle Victoria, and instead of abolishing it, MacArthur decided to keep the department in being. He would use it to supervise training and handle routine administrative tasks while he got USAFFE up and running. As for Grunert, MacArthur had no plans to employ him.

Several days after the creation of USAFFE MacArthur issued General Order Number 2. This appointed Lieutenant Colonel Richard K. Sutherland chief of staff of the new headquarters. A short time later Sutherland was promoted to brigadier general, achieving his first star without ever having been a bird colonel. By the summer of 1941 Sutherland had been with MacArthur for three years, and the two of them worked well together. Sutherland was a strong-willed, tough-minded, highly intelligent man whose only ambition as a youth was soldiering. It was a desire that his father, a U.S. senator from West Virginia and later an associate justice of the Supreme Court, simply deplored. While it was well within his power to secure an appointment to West Point for his son, the senator refused to consider it. Sutherland went to Yale instead, but one of the first things he did on reaching New Haven was to join the Connecticut National Guard as a seventeen-year-old private.

On his graduation from Yale in 1916, the Guard commissioned him a second lieutenant. At the end of World War I Sutherland was awarded a regular commission. Since then he had attended all the major Army schools and served successfully with troops, but where he excelled was as a staff officer. Besides being quick-witted and ambitious, Sutherland was a workaholic, a man who put in sixteen-hour days without any sign of exhaustion and soaked up details like a gray-matter sponge. He had a brusque, abrasive manner and a sarcastic way of expressing himself. Some people were intimidated by him. Many simply disliked him. MacArthur had no particular fondness for Sutherland personally, but he had found him useful. Sutherland had much of Eisenhower's ability to translate MacArthur's wishes into plans and his thoughts into orders that were models of clarity. MacArthur credited himself with developing his chief of staff's talents. As he once told Quezon, "Sutherland has been thoroughly schooled by me."[8]

They did not necessarily spend much time together each day, but at twelve-thirty most afternoons they met in an anteroom off MacArthur's office. Slumped in a pair of armchairs facing each other, they listened to the main daily news broadcast. Then they would go into MacArthur's office to talk over whatever implications there might be in what they had heard for the military situation in the archipelago. After that MacArthur went home for lunch.[9]

MacArthur gave Sutherland a deputy chief of staff, a highly competent lieutenant colonel named Richard J. Marshall, an officer who was noted for remaining calm however intense the pressure. Always pleasant and reasonable, Marshall would serve as a valuable counterweight to the prickly and difficult Sutherland. He was the kind of officer MacArthur was always looking for but not always able to get assigned to him. Marshall, a Quartermaster Corps officer, was also a graduate of the Army Industrial College, Leavenworth and the War College. He was, that is, one of the most promising young officers in the Army. MacArthur kept a copy of the *Army Register* in his desk and kept track of people like Marshall. When the opportunity arose to request the services of such men, he put in a bid. He was lucky enough to get Marshall sent out to him in 1940 and made him his G-4, or supply officer, but promoting him to deputy chief of staff of USAFFE created a hole.

MacArthur sought to fill it by appointing Lieutenant Colonel Lewis Beebe, an officer serving with a Philippine Scouts regiment, to be USAFFE's G-4. Beebe, however, was an infantry officer who had graduated from Benning, Leavenworth and the War College. Supply is a fate that infantry officers normally dread, and Beebe, with no experience in this area, may not have been a good choice for this assignment.

Another officer on MacArthur's list was already in the Philippines. This was a captain named LeGrande A. Diller, who was serving on the staff of the Philippine Division. He got on the list because he played golf with Sutherland, and Sutherland, who was on the lookout for an aide for MacArthur, felt Diller had the right background: He had a degree in civil engineering but had taken his commission in the infantry, graduated from Benning and gone on to Leavenworth. MacArthur himself had a background in engineering but had transferred to the infantry at the first opportunity. When Sutherland told him that he had just found him a new aide, though, MacArthur was irritated. "I usually choose my own personal aides," he said. But once Sutherland had given him Diller's background, MacArthur added Diller's name to the list.

On July 28, 1941, Diller was summoned to meet Sutherland and was told he was being assigned to 1 Calle Victoria to handle MacArthur's appointments. Captain Diller had been in the Philippines for two years but had never even seen MacArthur. As Admiral Hart had noticed, there were parties in Manila all the time, but the MacArthurs never attended them. They did not even go to parties organized solely by the Army for its personnel. Hart tried to encourage MacArthur to socialize more, but without much success. MacArthur remained a remote figure to most Army officers living and working in Manila.[10]

He arrived at 1 Calle Victoria at 10:00 A.M. on July 28, dressed, as he normally did, in a white linen suit, a gray silk shirt, a gray silk tie, and two-tone black-and-white wing tips. He was, Diller recalled, "Tall, handsome, with a smile on his face and a spring in his step. . . . He said a cheery 'Good morning,' and went on into his office."[11]

Three days later MacArthur asked Diller to join his staff as an aide. Diller hesitated. Several months earlier the Navy and the War Department had ordered the dependents of American service personnel in the Philippines to return home. Jean and young Arthur had been exempted because MacArthur, as a retired officer, was not affected by it. Diller, however, had said goodbye to his wife in May, the sorrow of parting made bearable by knowing that his tour in the islands would end in a few months. If he accepted MacArthur's offer, his tour of duty in the Philippines would be extended. There was no knowing when he might see his wife again.

MacArthur could see the thoughts racing through Diller's mind. "Don't make up your mind now," he said casually. "Ask your friends, and talk it over with them. I think my stamp is still good."

Diller returned next day and told MacArthur he would accept the offer. MacArthur rose from his desk and walked over to Diller, took his hand and looked deep into his eyes. "You're a member of my family now."[12]

MacArthur's family also included one of the oddest figures in the Army, Charles A. Willoughby, who had been born in Germany to a German father and an American mother. Inclined to credit himself with an aristocratic pedigree and forever affecting what he believed were patrician airs, Willoughby, whose family name was Tscheppe-Weidenbach, had nevertheless been obliged to join the Army as a private, back in 1913. He had never been to college and had no influential friends to help him secure a commission. On becoming a soldier, he had shed his German moniker and assumed a solidly English-sounding name. He spoke with a strange accent that was partly Prussian, partly British and wore pince-nez on a silken cord.[13] For him, as for countless immigrants, the Army offered a chance to become an American. It also opened the way to a career. In 1916 Willoughby took a competitive exam for a commission and became a second lieutenant.

Despite the fact that his pantomime as a superior being excited widespread dislike among fellow officers, Willoughby was not without ability. He had an inquiring mind and a facile pen. He graduated from Benning, Leavenworth and the War College and in 1938 was promoted to lieutenant colonel on the same day as Sutherland. Willoughby had been head of the military history department at the Infantry School and had taught at Leavenworth as well. These experiences left him promoting two interesting claims. One was that 10 percent of the entire active list as of 1938 had taken his course. The second interesting claim he made was that everything he taught was based on the ideas that MacArthur had promoted while Chief of Staff and had summarized in his final report. Willoughby had written a book based on what he had learned from MacArthur and titled it *Maneuver in War.* In 1938 he more or less begged MacArthur for an assignment on his staff. This was at a time when most officers considered MacArthur's career over. Yet Willoughby's career was on the rise. So it had to be true devotion. Willoughby went on the list, but when he was sent to Manila, in 1939, he was assigned to the Philippine Department and made—to his bewilderment—Grunert's G-4. Following the establishment of USAFFE, MacArthur had Willoughby assigned to his headquarters and made him his G-2, or intelligence officer.[14]

Restored to active duty, MacArthur faced the future with equanimity, or claimed he did. As Diller was to discover, though, the more strongly MacArthur asserted his confidence about something, the more likely it was that he was still really thinking about it. That was the time to try to get him to consider other possibilities. On the other hand, it was when he seemed to be of two minds about something that he was disguising the fact that he had already decided what to do. "If he was low key and very quiet, there was no chance for argument."[15]

In his reply to the cable informing him that USAFFE had been created and that he was to command it, he had told Marshall: "I would like to assure you that I am confident of the successful accomplishment of the assigned mission."[16] He also wrote a letter to former Deputy Chief of Staff George Van Horn Moseley that summer, telling him, "I have every confidence that if war comes I can defend these islands."[17]

Did he believe all this? Probably not. What he really believed is likely to be what he had told Sutherland that first day back in harness: "I can but do my best." Had he expressed the least doubt or hesitation about defending the Philippines, however, the entire venture would have collapsed right there. His immediate strategy was to bluff the Japanese into not attacking the Philippines by proclaiming how strong the archipelago's defenses were. And while the Japanese paused, he would use the time gained to turn that bluff into firepower, turn make-believe defenses into real ones.

Shortly after USAFFE was activated, MacArthur wrote to an old friend in the United States, giving him a pessimistic assessment of the situation in the Far East. Everything now pointed to a war with Japan. It might begin at any time. "In World War I," MacArthur wrote, "I was brash and untrained. Since then, I have read everything I can get my hands on about war. This time, I am prepared."[18]

With the creation of USAFFE MacArthur was more or less liberated from Quezon and High Commissioner Francis Sayre, but that did not mean that either of these self-regarding figures was completely out of the frame. Blocked from any major role in military planning now that the Philippine Army had been federalized, Quezon began creating a fuss over civil defense. He had argued for the creation of a civil defense program some months earlier, but while he claimed the United States should pay for it, Sayre just as firmly disagreed. Accumulating emergency food supplies and building bomb shelters, he insisted, were "solely within the jurisdiction and powers of the Commonwealth government."[19]

Don Manuel, however, would not be convinced. Important things were happening, and he had to be center stage. Civil defense was his chosen platform. Becoming increasingly hysterical, he publicly declared that in the event of war Roosevelt and Sayre "ought to be hanged from lampposts" for blocking his civil defense program.[20]

MacArthur tried to stand aloof from this affray. His task was to create forces that could fight. From time to time Sayre nagged him, complaining about MacArthur's "utter lack of frankness" and his failure to cooperate as closely as he should with the high commissioner's office.[21] MacArthur indicated what he thought of Sayre by pointedly failing to attend a testimonial dinner given in the high commissioner's honor.

Now that MacArthur's standing as a powerful military figure had been restored he had regained Quezon's respect and was no longer treated like an unwelcome guest at Don Manuel's feast. Quezon's prospects too had been transformed. The constitution of the commonwealth allowed a six-year presidential term. Quezon had always insisted that he would not run again, but when the moment drew near, he changed his mind and was reelected. MacArthur sent a note of congratulations. "My love and affection for you is [sic] such that not even your immediate family can feel a greater surge of pride than that which animates me."[22]

Even before the activation of USAFFE, the Navy was planting mines at the entrances to the Philippines' principal ports and Manila was undergoing periodic blackout rehearsals. MacArthur's recall to active duty nonetheless charged the humid tropical air with kinetic electricity, the kind of electricity that is produced by movement. The pessimism and defeatism that had prevailed in Manila as the Japanese threat loomed larger were suddenly dispelled once it seemed that America would fight for the Philippines after all.[23]

Only the previous fall MacArthur had gloomily counseled Quezon that "the military forces maintained here by the United States are little more than token symbols of the sovereignty of the United States" and warned, "It is not beyond the bounds of possibility that a strategic abandonment may be planned by the American government."[24] In August 1941, however, all such anxieties were dispelled. The War Department reversed its long-standing inclination to write off the Philippines. Not because of MacArthur's oratory or warnings, but because the President wanted to make some kind of stand against Japanese expansion.

The question of what would happen to the Philippines had suddenly shot to the top of the War Department's agenda. What was the policy now: Pull out or fight? The least hint that the United States would not fight for the Philippines not only would encourage the Japanese but might even bring an invasion of the archipelago. The politics of the situation demanded a firm and well-publicized commitment to fight for the Philippines. On July 31 Marshall told his staff, "It is the policy of the United States to defend the Philippines," although nothing that was done to defend the islands would be allowed to impinge on policy in Europe, which was to keep Britain and the Soviet Union fighting.[25]

On August 9 MacArthur went down to the dockyard to see one of his ambitions cut loose. While an excited crowd applauded, Aurora Quezon wielded a bottle of champagne and launched the first of Sid Huff's locally manufactured PT boats. She christened it the *Q-112*. It joined the two British boats MacArthur had already purchased.[26]

Shortly after this a naval lieutenant named John D. Bulkeley arrived in Manila to take command of the six PT boats assigned to the Asiatic Fleet. MacArthur sent for him and asked Bulkeley to do him a big favor. Would he train the crews of the commonwealth's torpedo boats? Bulkeley agreed to do so, although given the need to train his own men, it was hard to see where he would find the time.[27]

On August 15 MacArthur held a conference at 1 Calle Victoria for all the senior American Army officers in the Philippines, including the commander of the Philippine Division, Brigadier General Jonathan Wainwright. He explained that he intended to fight for the whole of the Philippines. The current official strategy was still the plan outlined in War Plan Orange-3. This called for the Philippine Division to attempt to prevent an enemy landing on the beaches of Lingayen Gulf, but if that failed—and given the modest firepower and mobility of Wainwright's division, it surely would—the troops would then proceed to withdraw into Bataan and try to hold Manila Bay until the U.S. Navy could break through with reinforcements. The Navy's part of the plan called for a prompt withdrawal in a southerly direction when hostilities began but promised a return at some later, unspecified date.

Wainwright shared MacArthur's disdain for WPO-3. A tall, lean figure, Skinny Wainwright was a former cavalryman with a combative temperament. He walked these days with a heavy limp and a stout stick, the consequences of a bad fall from a spirited horse. Like MacArthur, Wainwright had been a First Captain at West Point, in 1906, and was one of the most colorful figures in the Army. He deplored WPO-3 as a defeatist document, with its dispiriting message that the Army would have to hunker down and wait to be rescued by the Navy. "Defense must be active, damn it, not passive! It must involve counterattacks," said Wainwright. Like MacArthur, he wanted to stop the Japanese from establishing a beachhead on Philippine soil.[28]

MacArthur explained how he proposed to defend the archipelago. He was going to call up 76,000 Philippine Army reservists and organize them into ten divisions. Bolstered by the Philippine Army's single division of regulars, which would be broken up to provide training and leadership to the rest, the commonwealth should be able to put roughly 85,000 men into beach defense by the end of November, with another 40,000 to be available for even more divisions in early 1942.

On September 5 Marshall cabled MacArthur that he was prepared to send him "a first class National Guard division of approximately eighteen thousand men" as soon as shipping could be found. MacArthur promptly cabled back that he would rather have more supplies to equip the forces he already commanded, plus a lot more planes and antiaircraft artillery. Marshall acceded to this request.[29]

One reason MacArthur turned down the division was that he lacked the facilities to train the men properly and to take care of their equipment. Also, as he would surely have known, there was at this time no such thing as a "first class National Guard division." Without exception, these divisions were poorly trained, badly equipped and commanded by elderly, out-of-shape officers. A Guard division would add to his problems, not solve them.

Airpower, on the other hand, was ripe with promise. The Air Corps had pushed the development of the B-17 with the claim that it could find and sink enemy invasion shipping hundreds of miles out to sea. If so, the Flying Fortress might make outposts such as Alaska, Hawaii, Panama and the Philippines invulnerable. Marshall and Stimson wanted to believe this, although no B-17 had ever bombed a maneuvering warship. However, one of the people closest to Marshall was Major General Frank Andrews, the first commander of GHQ Air Force. There was no more attractive figure in the AAF and no more persuasive advocate of the heavy bomber than Andrews. Yet only the RAF had used B-17s in combat, against targets in France, and the German Air Force had demolished them. At this point in its development the B-17 was essentially a training aircraft, not an effective weapon. It lacked tail guns, nose guns and self-sealing fuel tanks.[30]

MacArthur had always been an airpower skeptic. He was not hostile to air, but in his experience airmen had a habit of promising a lot more than they could deliver. And the commanding general of the Philippine Department's air units, Brigadier General Henry B. Clagett, justified his skepticism. Clagett was a notorious drunk, and Clagett's aide, Lester J. Maitland, was another one. When Clagett was not drying out in the hospital, he was out drinking with Maitland.[31] Fortunately Clagett's staff included a live-wire colonel named Harold H. George, a short and slender man who was a superb pilot and a fighter veteran of World War I. With the activation of USAFFE, Clagett's command became the basis of a new headquarters, Far Eastern Air Force, but MacArthur asked Washington for a new air commander. In the meantime George made a careful study of USAFFE's air needs.

The Japanese, George concluded in a report that he wrote but Clagett submitted, could bring 1,000 land-based bombers and nearly 1,000 fighters to bear on the Philippines. George thought the islands could be held despite this aerial armada, provided the United States had 272 heavy bombers, 162 dive-bombers or light bombers and 586 fighters ready for operations in the Philippines, as well as several hundred transport and observation planes. Given a standard reserve of 25 percent for planes that were being maintained or repaired, defending the Philippines would require approximately 1,500 combat aircraft. For USAFFE's air command, the Far Eastern Air Force, to operate on this scale, MacArthur would need fifty-six airfields.[32] In the early fall of 1941 he had fewer than 100 combat aircraft operating from seven sod strips. He soon had his engineers surveying potential airfield sites throughout the Philippines.

While MacArthur digested George's report, he was also entertaining an important visitor, Clare Boothe Luce, the wife of Henry Luce, owner and creator of *Time, Life* and *Fortune*. Henry Luce, the son of American missionaries to China, had a lifelong interest in the Far East. In February 1941 *Time* had run a long article on MacArthur and taken a skeptical view of his attempts to create a Philippine Army.[33] Luce had come to take a look for himself in July 1941, shortly before MacArthur's return to active duty, and remained skeptical.

Luce had dinner with Sayre and grilled the high commissioner half to death. When he went to see MacArthur, every question brought a forthright response, but Luce was irritated at the way MacArthur presented himself as the only man who could stop the Japanese from conquering all of Asia. When he got home, his wife, the beautiful and talented Clare Boothe, asked Luce what he made of MacArthur. "He's either a great fraud or a genius," muttered Luce. "Probably both."[34]

In September Luce sent his wife to Manila to write a profile of MacArthur for *Life*. MacArthur agreed to talk to her but wanted to see her article before it went to press. She agreed. He gave her his complete cooperation and assigned Diller to show her around Luzon, but it was Willoughby whom Mrs. Luce bedded. "Sir Charles" was left smitten for life, although for her he was just another diversion, like seeing the Malacañang. He gave her a copy of *Maneuver in War,* blissfully unaware that it was he who had been out-maneuvered.[35]

When MacArthur met Mrs. Luce, it was like pushing two magnets together. They would either be instantly, mutually repelled or instantly, powerfully attracted. She was charming, voluble, lovely; he was gallant, voluble, handsome. They took an instant liking to each other. Mrs. Luce's keen intelligence noted the whiteness of MacArthur's skin, indicating how little time he spent outdoors, his narrow, sloping shoulders, his trembling hands, surprisingly small for a man his size, and the way he combed his thinning black hair from left ear to right, across his head, in a losing struggle to conceal advancing baldness. What stood out most was the face, famous from a thousand photographs, but surprising all the same when seen in the flesh. It was "intellectual, aesthetic, rather than martial."

MacArthur saw in her a chance to arouse American public opinion to support him in his campaign to turn the Philippines into a strong redoubt. He turned all the power of his oratory on her. "We must foil the enemy," he intoned. "We stand on the eve of a great battle. . . . We must not spill our precious blood on foreign soil in vain, in vain!" And so on, for more than an hour, sometimes whispering, sometimes booming, but always passionate and heroic. He told her that all his plans were geared toward the spring of 1942. By then, he said, he would have "125,000 well-trained and fairly well-equipped Filipino soldiers" and if the Japanese attempted to land, he would advance to attack them.[36]

MacArthur believed that only the offensive is decisive in war, and he described his conception of an offensive strategy as "Hit 'em where they ain't," quoting a well-known baseball player of the World War I era, Wee Willie Keeler, who had a knack of getting base hits at critical moments in a game.

How, she asked, would he describe a defensive strategy?

"Defeat."[37]

He had no doubt, MacArthur told her, that he stood in the path of the Japanese, because geography had made the Philippines "the key that turns the lock that opens the door to the mastery of the Pacific," and "the man who holds a key, no matter what its special nature, from a strategic military opening to a boudoir door, is in a dangerous position," and right now, he held that key.[38]

She wanted to know what he thought of the war on the Eastern Front. On June 22 the Germans had launched a massive assault on the Soviet Union. By September they had penetrated five hundred miles and taken more than two million prisoners. It was generally taken for granted that the German Army would seize Moscow before the winter and knock the Soviet Union out of the war. MacArthur said flatly that the Germans would never be strong enough to take Moscow.[39]

Before leaving Manila, Mrs. Luce took some photographs of MacArthur on the wall outside his office. This part of the ancient rampart was a picturesque stretch of the Intramuros, with penile turrets in the Spanish colonial style rising from the corners. It made a perfect backdrop. MacArthur looked steely-eyed across Manila Bay, his piercing gaze fixed on the far horizon, as if daring the Japanese fleet to come into view.

Clare Luce kept her word and let him see her article before it was published. He objected to some of her personal observations about him. He was touchy, for example, about the way she described his hair. The piece was still so reverential in its attitude to MacArthur that it took extensive rewriting before *Life*'s editors considered it publishable.[40]

Besides giving Mrs. Luce an upbeat appraisal of his plan to defend the Philippines, he had also recently assured Marshall that "The Philippine Army units that have been called are now mobilizing in a most satisfactory manner and the whole program is progressing by leaps and bounds."[41]

In the light of later events, statements such as this would make him seem blind to the obvious realities around him. Yet the truth was that he had few, if any, illusions about the state of his command. In a long and revealing letter to George Grunert, written only two days before his letter to Marshall, he had said, "In my inspections to date I have found large groups of trainees and their officers standing around and doing nothing . . . there was a complete lack of decisiveness in instructional procedure. Some American officers were practically ignorant of what was going on, and a pall of inactivity was evident."[42]

Nor was Wainwright's Philippine Division, which provided the bulk of his regular troops, in good shape to fight, and he had admitted as much to Marshall: "I was disappointed in my inspection of the Philippine Division. Its training is adequate up to the battalion echelon, but little has been accomplished beyond that point."[43] In the summer of 1941 it consisted of ten thousand men, eight thousand of whom were Philippine Scouts. Wainwright considered his Scouts fine soldiers, but his division was only two thirds of its authorized strength and seriously deficient in artillery and vehicles. His immediate challenge was to bring his division up to strength and get his troops thoroughly trained.

Wainwright's fighting spirit nevertheless impressed MacArthur, who gave him two Philippine Army divisions to whip into shape along with his own Philippine Division. One day in late September MacArthur drove out to Fort McKinley in his big black Cadillac V-12 sedan, a red flag with three white stars fluttering on the front bumper, to see how the Philippine Division was coming along. He called Wainwright over to his car. "General Grunert is going to be returned to the States," said MacArthur. The Philippine Department would be abolished. "That will make you the senior field commander."

USAFFE's tactical units on Luzon had been split; half belonged to a North Luzon Force and half to a South Luzon Force. MacArthur offered Wainwright his choice of command. Already knowing the answer, Wainwright asked, "Where do you think the main danger is—the place where some distinction can be gained?" If the Japanese attempted to land, their main force would strike northern Luzon.

MacArthur replied, "The North Luzon Force, by all means." But he did not want to upset the current plan for divisional maneuvers, scheduled for December. So he told Wainwright, "For the time being I want you to stay with your division."[44]

The biggest challenge to MacArthur's hopes was the poor state of the infant Philippine Army. After three and a half years of existence, its instruction to date consisted almost entirely of individual training. There was little or no unit training to speak of. None of its divisions had done any divisional training. There had been no training at all in combined infantry-artillery tactics. The sole Philippine regular division had held maneuvers that summer, but without modern communications and an adequate supply of equipment, such exercises verged on farce.

The situation in the reserve divisions was incomparably worse. Most of the reservists lacked firearms. Many hobbled about for most of the summer, made semi-invalids by having to wear leather shoes for the first time in their lives. Others got tennis shoes, which fell apart after a couple of long marches. The rest remained barefoot.

Each Philippine division had several dozen American officers and a hundred or so American NCOs assigned to supervise their training. Most Filipinos did not speak English. They spoke obscure tribal languages that were incomprehensible even to other Filipinos. American officers assigned to Philippine divisions were shocked at the monumental challenges that confronted them.

MacArthur had no illusions about the Philippine Army. When Colonel Bradford G. Chynoweth arrived that fall to command the 61st Division of the Philippine Army, defending the Visayans, in the center of the archipelago, MacArthur sent for him. Chynoweth had worked on the General Staff in the early 1930s but rarely got so much as a glimpse of the Chief of Staff back then. Ushered into the flag-draped office in 1 Calle Victoria, he was soon under MacArthur's spell. MacArthur recalled that Chynoweth's father had served with his own father in the Philippines and said that his father had regarded Chynoweth's dad highly. Chynoweth was deeply moved. "The impact of his personality and his emotional powers took me completely by surprise and left me at his feet," wrote Chynoweth later. "I felt deeply that, come what might, we should all do our best under such a leader."

MacArthur told Chynoweth what to expect. The 61st Division was seriously deficient in equipment. "You will have to make do," MacArthur said, "because you cannot expect to get any more." Equally dismaying, MacArthur told him, "Your Filipino officers are not all that could be wished," because in the Philippine Army commissions were largely a matter of political or family connections. "I expect a Japanese attack sometime soon," he concluded, and wished Chynoweth well.[45]

The dilemma MacArthur faced was this: If he let it be known that he had no faith in the Philippine Army's ability to fight, he would be virtually inviting the Japanese to come in and take the archipelago. Yet it was American policy to defend the islands or at least Manila Bay. He had to find a role for the Filipinos. If MacArthur was going to use the Philippine Army at all, he had to have these troops fight where they stood. He lacked the logistics, the firepower and the mobility to do anything else with them, even had they been well trained. As things were, the most he could hope for was that despite being underequipped, undertrained and poorly led, these men might be willing to put up a fight for their home villages or provinces.

As Chynoweth discovered when he reached the Visayans, many were indeed eager to fight. He had only a couple of thousand old British Lee-Enfield rifles with which to arm them and then could provide only twenty rounds of ammunition per man for rifle training. Those who did not have rifles, he armed with bows and arrows and set them shooting at targets on a twenty-five-yard range. He gave his officers bolos, made sure they kept them sharp and had them practice ambushing Japanese troops on jungle trails to cut throats and capture rifles.[46]

Despite the present shortage of modern weaponry, the massive reinforcements the War Department had promised MacArthur seemed to make his aim of defending the Philippines begin to look feasible at last, provided he could win enough time to get his troops ready to fight. There were one hundred thousand tons of supplies on their way to him in November, with a further one million tons sitting on the docks of West Coast ports waiting for shipping to be found. As men and munitions started flowing in, he grew more impatient than ever with the Navy.[47]

MacArthur met regularly with Tommy Hart, the commander of the Asiatic Fleet, partly because Hart lived in the apartment below the Manila Hotel penthouse. The little sailor—he stood barely five feet four inches tall—held the rank of full admiral, so that despite the modest size of his grandiosely named "Asiatic Fleet," Hart still had one more star than MacArthur. "Small fleet, big admiral," MacArthur remarked cuttingly.[48] One day that fall he bluntly informed Hart that he did not consider himself bound by WPO-3, which was a joint Army-Navy plan. "I am not going to follow, or be bound in any way by whatever war plans have been evolved, agreed upon or approved," he remarked emphatically, punching his left palm with his right fist. "I am going to fight a glorious land war." Let the Japanese get ashore. "I will crush them."

Hart tried to interrupt, saying that he still intended to carry out his assigned role in the Orange War Plan and have the Asiatic Fleet withdraw to the Indian Ocean. MacArthur shrugged off Hart's caution. Whatever the Navy did, it was the ground battle that would decide the issue. "The Navy has its plans," said MacArthur, "the Army has its plans. We each have our own fields."[49]

At the end of October MacArthur and Hart received copies of the newest version of the overall U.S. war plan, Rainbow-5, which covered the entire world. The section dealing with the Philippines was almost exactly the same as WPO-3: The Navy would withdraw, and the Army would try to deny Manila Bay to the enemy. There was no indication of when the Navy would return. The implication was that USAFFE's role was that of a forlorn hope. Its destiny was to die as gloriously, but as slowly, as possible in a last-ditch stand.

MacArthur was indignant. He urged Marshall to revise Rainbow-5. MacArthur argued strongly that the creation of the Philippine Army made it possible at last to defend the archipelago, making the old Orange plans completely out-of-date.[50]

He also pointed to his growing air strength as another reason why the islands would soon be defensible. Even as he dictated his letter to Marshall, MacArthur was looking forward to the arrival of a new commander for Far Eastern Air Force. Clagett, and Maitland, had to go. They had done nothing to prepare FEAF for war, apart from digging slit trenches at Clark Field. Hap Arnold, commanding general of the Army Air Forces, had offered MacArthur a choice of three people. The one MacArthur chose was Major General Lewis Brereton, commander of the Third Air Force.

Brereton and his chief of staff, Colonel Francis M. Brady, arrived on November 3, bringing two communications for MacArthur. After taking his briefcase, containing the top secret messages, to 1 Calle Victoria for safekeeping, Brereton checked into the Manila Hotel and called the penthouse. MacArthur told him to come straight up.

He greeted Brereton in his bathrobe, leaving Brereton feeling slightly embarrassed at the thought that he'd just fished MacArthur out of his bath. MacArthur greeted him like an old friend and reminisced about the observation squadron that Brereton had commanded in 1918, when it had flown in support of the Rainbow Division.

This was no occasion for Brereton to speak his mind, to tell MacArthur he was worried that the development of FEAF was dangerously lopsided. That could wait, probably indefinitely. Brereton nonetheless felt strongly that B-17s were being rushed into the Philippines too fast. Defense should come before offense. Fighter groups with modern planes should be introduced first, and adequate airfields constructed. An early-warning net equipped with radar was essential too. Without proper base defense heavy bombers were sitting ducks. Brereton had argued the issue with Arnold and Marshall before leaving. They conceded that what they were doing amounted to "a calculated risk."[51]

The morning after his arrival in Manila, Brereton went to 1 Calle Victoria, collected his briefcase and handed MacArthur the two messages he had brought over. One was a letter from Marshall that told him Rainbow-5 was going to be revised so that MacArthur would be free to fight a land war, if he chose. The other was a memorandum from Arnold, which provided a long list of air reinforcements that would be shipped to the Philippines over the winter. MacArthur jumped up from his desk, excited, and hugged the startled Brereton.

"Lewis, you are as welcome as the flowers in May," said MacArthur. Then he turned to Sutherland. "Dick, they are going to give us everything we have asked for."[52]

Brereton turned his attention to getting airfields built to receive the expected influx of planes. He thought MacArthur's chief engineer officer, Colonel Hugh J. Casey, was doing a brilliant job of airfield construction.[53] Casey was one of the most recent, and most valuable, additions to MacArthur's "family." When his earlier tour to the Philippines had ended, in 1939, Casey had returned to the United States. Following the establishment of USAFFE MacArthur put in a request for Casey, who was glad to return to Manila and MacArthur.

When he arrived at 1 Calle Victoria in early October, MacArthur had greeted him like an old friend. Then he told Casey about the projected buildup of airpower he was aiming for. USAFFE urgently needed dozens of new airdromes, but he was sure Casey could create them in time. "This is your job, now you take care of it." That was MacArthur's way of getting things done: Give a man a large task and tell him you believe in him. Don't tell him how to do his job, but give him all the authority he needs to accomplish it.[54]

While Casey surveyed potential airfield sites in the central and southern Philippines, MacArthur had Brereton make a quick trip to the Netherlands East Indies and northern Australia to look at still more sites. The existing ferry route from the United States was too vulnerable to interdiction by the Japanese. A longer, more southerly route would provide additional security for the flow of the air reinforcements Arnold had promised.

While Casey and some of the other people on MacArthur's staff were responding with a sense of urgency to the impending crisis, still others seemed in a daze. Lewis Beebe, MacArthur's G-4, and his quartermaster, Colonel Charles Drake, were working hard, but trying to do everything by the book, as if this were still peacetime. Yet virtually every American officer whom Bradford Chynoweth had met in the Philippines took it for granted that war was about to break out. MacArthur's G-4 and quartermaster, however, would not ship supplies to units in the field until warehouses had been constructed. Ammunition was not shipped because there was a shortage of concrete shelters to store it safely. And so on.[55]

In one respect, MacArthur too was still acting as he did in peacetime. Despite the long days he was now putting in, he continued to take his usual keen interest in West Point football. The present superintendent, Brigadier General Robert Eichelberger, sent him newspaper accounts after every game and sometimes movie film. MacArthur continued to offer advice to the coach, Earl Blaik, who had been a cadet during MacArthur's superintendency and whom MacArthur had at one time tried to have assigned to his staff as an aide.[56]

With Casey rushing airfield construction and a large influx of planes in the pipeline, the air position seemed likely to improve spectacularly over the winter months. In aerial warfare nothing matters more than numbers. Yet the naval situation remained as problematical as ever, and MacArthur's relationship with Tommy Hart, already strained, was rapidly getting worse. The senior British commander at Singapore, Air Marshal Sir Robert Brooke-Popham, visited Manila to talk about the possibilities of joint action in the event of war with Japan. During some of MacArthur's longer perorations, the air marshal dozed off but probably didn't miss much.[57]

The British fleet at Singapore was without aircraft carriers, but the Royal Navy had hopes of operating in Philippine waters under MacArthur's air umbrella. MacArthur, however, had to rely in the first instance on the U.S.

Navy to defend the sea-lanes, and the piffling size of the Asiatic Fleet was a constant burr. Its obvious weakness was a signal a blind man could read that the Navy did not intend to fight for the archipelago.

MacArthur was also arguing with Hart over the control of aircraft operating over water. Hart felt that FEAF's air operations should be coordinated with the air patrols of the Asiatic Fleet. MacArthur took this as an attempt by the Navy to control FEAF and told Hart he did not intend to have his air arm directed by a naval force "of such combat inferiority as your Command."[58]

The evening after reading the messages Brereton had brought him, MacArthur had Jean call Hart and suggest that the general come down and have a word with Tommy, if that was okay. The admiral agreed. MacArthur appeared a short while later in his bathrobe. MacArthur was still excited about the promised reinforcements heading his way. Hart wrote, "After extolling the Big Show which he would, eventually, have, he said, 'Get yourself a real fleet, Tommy, then you will belong!' I listened to such patronizing talk . . ." Shortly after this Hart wrote his wife, "Douglas is, I think, no longer altogether sane . . . he may not have been for a long time."[59]

Despite the fact that he and MacArthur did not get on, some of MacArthur's fighting spirit was starting to rub off on the admiral. And while his fleet was small, it was also being reinforced. The recent arrival of twelve modern submarines had bolstered his force considerably, but he still had only two cruisers and thirteen destroyers. Encouraged by the growth of his fleet and, it seems, by MacArthur's constant needling, Hart informed the Chief of Naval Operations, Admiral Harold "Betty" Stark, in late October that he no longer planned to withdraw toward Singapore if the Japanese attacked. He would instead mount offensive operations, using Manila Bay as his base. The Navy Department chewed on this idea for more than three weeks, before finally telling Hart to stick to the provisions of Rainbow-5 and withdraw if the Japanese mounted an invasion.[60]

While the Navy was pondering Hart's proposal, the War Department was coming to the conclusion that war with Japan was virtually inevitable. In mid-November Marshall held an off-the-record background briefing for a handful of highly regarded journalists. "The U.S. is on the brink of war with the Japanese," said Marshall. "Under great secrecy, the U.S. is building up its strength in the Philippines. . . . MacArthur is unloading ships at night [and] is building airfields in the carefully guarded interior. . . . We are preparing for an offensive war against Japan, whereas the Japanese believe we are preparing only to defend the Philippines. . . . We have 35 Flying Fortresses there—the largest concentration anywhere in the world. . . .

"The last thing the U.S. wants is a war with Japan, which would divide our strength [but] if war with Japan does come, we'll fight mercilessly.

Flying Fortresses will be dispatched immediately to set the paper cities of Japan on fire." The B-17s did not have the range for a round trip from Luzon to Japan, but Marshall spoke confidently of the bombers flying on and landing in Vladivostok and seemed to expect they would then be refueled and bombed up by the Red Air Force before flying back to the Philippines, setting more paper cities on fire along the way. It was a notion that amounted to a total denial of reality. Stalin was bending himself into pretzel shapes to avoid giving the Japanese any excuse to attack the Soviet Union while it was fighting the Germans.

Nor was China a better prospect. There were no bomber airfields in China. They would have to be built, by hand, far inland, beyond the reach of advancing Japanese armies. They would need to be stocked with bombs and gasoline. As the AAF would one day discover, operating even one heavy group from China was a nightmare. Moreover, the B-17s available in 1941 were the C and D models: no tail guns, no nose guns, no self-sealing tanks. Marshall also confidently informed the busily scribbling journalists that the B-24, which was just going into mass production, would fly even higher than Japanese fighters, making it virtually immune to attack. As it turned out, a fully loaded B-24 flew several thousand feet lower than the B-17 and had no bottom turret, making it vulnerable to attacks from below. It would eventually take a force of more than a thousand B-29s to raze Japan's cities with fire. To expect a few inexperienced groups of B-17s to do the same thing was absurd.

Marshall was one of the greatest men ever to wear an American uniform, a visionary and an innovator, but he had one weakness: no understanding of airpower. Impressed by movies of the German Stuka, he had forced the AAF to buy a huge fleet of essentially useless A-24 dive-bombers, to the intense frustration of the Air Staff, whose members kept their mouths shut rather than get into a fight with him.

The reporters asked Marshall what the Navy would do. The answer was that the Navy was too heavily committed in the Atlantic to fight an offensive in the Pacific, but when they were not burning down paper cities, the B-17s were expected to sink enemy invasion fleets. No one believed in the B-17 more than Marshall.[61]

MacArthur, however, did not share Marshall's aviation fantasies. On the contrary, he knew they were nonsense, just as he knew the A-24 was rubbish. Shortly after Marshall's press conference, MacArthur was bluntly informed by the War Department that although B-17s would continue to be sent to him, he would have to start sending their pilots back to the United States. There was such a shortage of experienced bomber pilots in the AAF that it had too few instructors to get itself trained for war. Just who was going to fly Marshall's projected aerial onslaught against Japan was left unclear.[62]

Even so, on November 22, MacArthur received a message from Marshall telling him that because of the buildup of airpower in the Philippines, Rainbow-5 had been "modified . . . to include strong air operations," giving him the authority to fight for the archipelago in whatever way he thought best and authorizing offensive operations against the Japanese. He was free from the defensive posture of WPO-3.[63]

The tension that had been building all summer and fall seemed about to burst into something violent and terrible. Forty-eight hours after receiving Marshall's message, MacArthur telephoned Wainwright. "Jonathan, you'd better take command of that North Luzon Force now," he said. "Forget the maneuvers. How soon can you go?"

Wainwright left Fort McKinley immediately that day to assume command of the four Philippine Army divisions in northern Luzon. He would also have command of the 26th Cavalry Regiment, which comprised nearly eight hundred well-trained Philippine Scout cavalrymen. The North Luzon Force was responsible for the defense of an area that covered seventy-five hundred square miles, yet Wainwright possessed hardly a single truck to provide transportation for his far-flung troops. What mobility they had they were standing on or curry-combing. MacArthur told him, "You'll probably have until about April to train those troops."[64]

MacArthur had told Brereton much the same thing: The Japanese would not attack before spring 1942, at the end of the rainy season. Brereton, however, felt MacArthur's forecast "[m]ay have been more of a hope than a considered opinion."[65]

On November 27 the War Department informed the Army commanders in Hawaii and the Philippines, "Negotiations with Japan appear to be terminated . . . hostile action is possible at any moment. If hostilities cannot, repeat cannot, be avoided, the United States desires that Japan commit the first overt act . . . you are directed to undertake such reconnaissance as you deem necessary. . . ."[66]

On receipt of this message, MacArthur sent an alert to his field commanders, telling them, "Under existing circumstances it is not possible to predict the future actions of the Japanese." They were to "take necessary action to insure immediate readiness for any eventuality."[67]

The Navy Department had meanwhile sent a message to Hart that was even more blunt than the communication MacArthur had received. Hart was told starkly, "This is a war warning." The Navy Department assumed that war was inevitable and likely to occur at any moment.

MacArthur met with Hart and Sayre at the high commissioner's office to discuss the messages they had received. Hart seemed resigned to the impending disaster, but Sayre refused to believe even now that war was coming. MacArthur, however, was in a defiant mood as he strode up and down puffing on a big black cigar. The Japanese, he said confidently, would not attack before spring, and by then he would be able to defeat them.[68] Hart said little, but when he returned to his headquarters, he ordered his cruisers, including his flagship, to steam away from Luzon.

While Hart was placing his biggest ships out of harm's way, the admiral and MacArthur continued to bicker over long-distance air patrols. It took another three days before they reached an agreement. In the end they decided that Army planes would patrol northward from Luzon, toward Formosa, where the Japanese had dozens of airfields. The Navy assumed responsibility for long-distance patrols to the west and southwest of Luzon, in the direction of Indochina. In the meantime, both USAFFE and Hart's Asiatic Fleet increased antisabotage measures and brought their tactical units to a higher state of alert. MacArthur sent a cable to Marshall next day reporting, "Everything is in readiness for the conduct of a successful defense."[69]

On December 5 MacArthur held an off-the-record briefing for journalists. He told them what to expect if war broke out. For one thing, it would be the most heavily reported conflict in history, he said, and he intended to give the press all the help he could. "Regardless of the pressure on me," he assured them, "I plan to meet the press for half an hour daily and give you the progress of operations, change of lines and other information, rather than leave it to your own conjecture. I intend to take all of you who may want to take the risks, to the front, so you may see with your own eyes how the battle is progressing." It was reassuring and scary at the same time.[70]

Next day the commander of the British fleet at Singapore, Admiral Tom Phillips, flew into Manila to confer with Hart and MacArthur. He was hoping to get eight of Hart's thirteen destroyers sent to Singapore to defend his capital ships.

MacArthur told Phillips, "Admiral Hart and I operate in the closest cooperation. We are the oldest and dearest friends." Hart's aides nearly choked, trying not to laugh, while Hart maintained the composure of the Sphinx.[71] MacArthur told Phillips it would take him until April 1942 to make the Philippines strong enough to resist a Japanese attack, but he was confident he could do it. "The inability of an enemy to launch his air attacks on these islands is our greatest security. . . . The inability to bring not only air but mechanized and motorized elements leaves me with a complete sense of security."[72] Pure moonshine.

The truth of what he thought was not to be found in what he told Phillips. It was to be found in the abrupt cancellation of the division maneuvers he had planned for December. It was to be found in the message he sent to Wainwright, ordering the North Luzon Force to move into its beach defenses. It was to be found in the order he had given to FEAF for its pursuit squadrons. There had been Japanese flights over Luzon on several nights recently. On December 5 he gave orders that the next night intruder should be shot down.[73]

Far from being unimpressed by the Japanese air threat, he had given orders on December 1 for FEAF to move the B-17s based at Clark Field, seventy miles north of Manila, down to Del Monte, on the island of Mindanao. As he had recently explained to Marshall, the abundance of Japanese airfields on Formosa, three hundred miles north of Luzon, "indicate[s] that heavy bombers should be located south of the island of Luzon, where they are reasonably safe from attack, but from where, through partial utilization of auxiliary fields, they can deliver their own blows." He had hoped to base his B-17s in the central Philippines, but so far Casey had found few sites there that could be quickly turned into airfields. At the Del Monte pineapple plantation on Mindanao, however, Casey had put fifteen hundred men to work, and in just two weeks they transformed a small airstrip used by the company's lightplanes into a runway a mile long and capable of handling B-17s. Del Monte airfield, five hundred miles south of Clark, was well out of range of Japanese land-based bombers.[74]

On the other hand, the new airfield suffered a major drawback: no officers' club. Pilots could live with crude runways, but they demanded a minimum of comfort, and a club was the bottom line. They resisted going to Mindanao. Many were presently parading around in large, unkempt beards, in protest at being held in the Philippines beyond the expiration of their assigned tours of duty. The slovenliness of AAF officers at Clark came as a shock to airmen arriving from the United States that fall.[75] And Brereton was not a man to interfere. He ignored MacArthur's instruction to move the thirty-five B-17s of the 19th Bomb Group from Clark to Del Monte.

On December 4, however, Casey informed Sutherland that while Del Monte was now operable, not one heavy bomber had been sent south. Infuriated, Sutherland phoned Brereton's chief of staff and berated him freely. "Goddamnit!" he roared. "You know General MacArthur ordered those B-17s down to Mindanao. Why the hell aren't they down there? We want them moved."[76]

Brereton grudgingly sent sixteen of his heavy bombers down to Del Monte next day, but the rest remained at Clark. The pilots of the 27th Bomb Group, a dive-bombing outfit, were planning a big party at the Manila Hotel on Sunday night, December 7, in Brereton's honor, and the pilots of the 19th were expecting to join in the fun. The bespectacled, professorial-looking Brereton was one of the foremost party animals of the entire AAF. He would spend much of the coming war in pursuit of a good time and prove to be one of the most lackadaisical, underperforming

American generals of the war. Many people liked him personally, but his judgment was often disastrous. It was Brereton, for example, who pushed for and got the catastrophic low-level attack on Ploesti in August 1943. No one ever said he was a good combat commander. Brereton held half the 19th at Clark so it could honor him too. The revels were a huge success. The party did not break up until 2:00 A.M., although an admiral who dropped in alarmed Brereton by telling him the shooting might start at any minute. Brereton finally seemed to grasp that war really was at hand.[77]

On the brink of disaster, MacArthur continued his pacing, continued thinking, continued trying to fathom a situation rapidly spiraling out of control. He had gambled that he could turn his bluff into a reality and made claims he knew were not true. At least they were not true now, but in time . . . ? The evidence of what he really thought was not in what he said. It bounced against his right thigh as he paced. After receiving the war warning at the end of November, MacArthur had Sid Huff go and buy some bullets for his father's old two-shot derringer. MacArthur put the loaded gun in his pants pocket each morning and, taking it out each evening, slipped it under his pillow. He went to bed the night of December 7 armed, like a man already at war.

The telephone rang in MacArthur's apartment at 4:00 A.M., December 8. It was Sutherland, telling him that he must come to 1 Calle Victoria at once. The Japanese were attacking Pearl Harbor. MacArthur reached for his mother's Bible and read for a minute or two; then he prayed.[78]

While MacArthur dressed, Richard Marshall and MacArthur's signals intelligence officer, Colonel Spencer B. Akin, called the rest of the staff and told them the Japanese were attacking Pearl Harbor. Hawaii being nineteen hours behind Manila, it was still the morning of Sunday, December 7, in Honolulu when news of the attack reached Manila. There was no doubt that the Philippines would be hit soon.

While his staff made their way on foot through the predawn darkness to 1 Calle Victoria, MacArthur spoke to Brigadier General Leonard Gerow at the War Department. Gerow told him to expect an air attack soon. MacArthur held a brief meeting at 5:00 A.M., mainly to bring people up-to-date. There was little to tell so far, beyond the fact that the United States was now at war with Japan. There was a mood of astonishment throughout USAFFE headquarters. No one was surprised the Japanese had struck, but everyone, including MacArthur, was puzzled that the first blow had been aimed at Pearl Harbor. Why not at them? Why not at the Philippines?[79]

MacArthur soon had them too busy to worry about such questions, but no one would imagine that from previous biographies. This is surprising, because it is not difficult to reconstruct how he spent his first day at war.

There is a widespread belief, however, that MacArthur was taken by surprise. Even a writer as sympathetic to him as William Manchester could write in *American Caesar* that MacArthur was "in shock," paralyzed by "input overload." As we shall see, he was neither in shock nor overloaded.

There was also a story, widely quoted and widely believed, that MacArthur had promised Quezon that he would prevent the Philippines from being dragged into the war and therefore did nothing, for fear of provoking the Japanese. The source of this story is Cyrus L. Sulzberger, the foreign correspondent of *The New York Times,* who claims that Ike told him this, on the basis of something that Quezon had told Ike.[80] There is no corroboration for this from anyone else, there is no document that supports it and the story is completely implausible in light of the verifiable facts about MacArthur's attempts to prepare for war. It seems obvious that either Sulzberger misunderstood Ike or that Ike misunderstood Quezon. There is absolutely no reason to believe the story is true, and various reasons to believe it is false.

The moment MacArthur was recalled to active duty his obligations to Quezon came to an abrupt end. He was no longer military adviser to the commonwealth. He did not, as Eric Larrabee asserts in *Commander in Chief,* "wear two hats" and dither because he did not know which obligation—to the United States or the Philippines—had priority. At this point he had exactly one employer and acted accordingly.[81]

There are no real mysteries about what happened at 1 Calle Victoria on December 8. Mistakes were made, but they were nothing compared with the bad luck. Each officer on MacArthur's staff was plunged into a hectic, nerve-racking day, alerting USAFFE units, trying to round up transportation to move troops, giving orders for the distribution of ammunition, assigning the Philippine Department responsibility for handling food supplies, and so on through a thousand details now that war had begun.

At 6:30 A.M. Japanese Navy dive-bombers launched from an aircraft carrier off Mindanao attacked a seaplane tender and two PBY patrol planes in the harbor at Davao. At about the same time Japanese Army fighters flying from Formosa strafed a radio station at Aparri, the northernmost town on Luzon. At 7:15 Brereton arrived at 1 Calle Victoria. He said he wanted to use his bombers to hit back at the Japanese. MacArthur told him "Our role is defensive, but stand by for orders."[82]

MacArthur wanted a clearer picture of what the Japanese were doing before he used his bombers. The War Department had confirmed the attack on Pearl Harbor nearly three hours earlier but had not given him any instructions even though both the telephone and teletype links with Washington were working perfectly. And so far he had heard nothing of the dawn attacks on Aparri and Davao harbor. It would be another two hours before MacArthur would learn of these dawn raids. USAFFE had to rely on a system of field telephones for most of its communications beyond Manila. So far as he knew, the Japanese had yet to make a major move against USAFFE. He was not going to commit his most powerful weapon until he had a better picture of what the Japanese were doing.

At 8:50 Sutherland told MacArthur that Brereton was calling from FEAF headquarters, still asking permission to mount an attack, but he could not specify a single military target on Formosa for his bombers to strike. He simply hoped they might find some shipping to attack. MacArthur said, "Hold off for the present."[83]

At 9:30 MacArthur called Sayre and told him that it might be a good idea for the high commissioner to leave Manila and head for Baguio, the picturesque mountain town one hundred miles north of Manila, where Quezon was presently in residence.

Half an hour later, at 10:00 A.M., Brereton called Sutherland and told him reports were coming in that Baguio had just been bombed. Sutherland still would not allow him to order a bombing raid. Exasperated, Brereton told him bluntly that if the Japanese attacked Clark Field, where nineteen of his thirty-five B-17s were located, FEAF would be unable to undertake any offensive operation.

MacArthur called Sayre again and told him that maybe going to Baguio would not be a good idea after all. The high commissioner might as well stay in Manila.[84]

Confirmation finally arrived of the attacks on Davao and Aparri. At 10:14 A.M. MacArthur called Brereton and gave him permission to make a reconnaissance flight over Formosa. If the recon photos showed worthwhile targets, it would be possible to launch a B-17 strike in the late afternoon.

All but three of the B-17s at Clark were presently in the air. Brereton had ordered them to take off at dawn to avoid being caught in a sunrise attack, but they would soon start running low on fuel. They would have to land in an hour or two. Once they came down, Brereton intended to have them refueled and bombed up for an afternoon attack against airfields on Formosa or, lacking that, on Japanese shipping.

Shortly before 11:00, MacArthur told Sutherland to phone Brereton and get an account of all known enemy air operations in the past two hours. He was puzzled, like everyone else: Why had the Japanese not made a heavy air attack on Clark Field? Brereton was still unable to provide an answer.[85] The answer to this puzzle was weather. Fog over western Formosa at dawn had blanketed the airfields of the Japanese Navy's 11th Air Fleet. Over eastern Formosa, however, where the Japanese Army Air Force was based, the day had dawned clear. It was the short-range planes of the Japanese Army that had struck Aparri and Baguio. These were tactical raids. The strategic targets—namely, Clark Field and Iba Field—were south of Baguio and assigned to the longer-range planes of the Japanese Navy. When the fog lifted over western Formosa around 10:15 A.M., the 11th Air Fleet prepared to strike.[86]

The B-17s at Clark made it a strategic target. At Iba the main objective for enemy air action was the only working radar in the Philippines, an SCR-270 set that could track aircraft heading for Luzon. At 11:40 FEAF was informed that Iba was tracking a large formation of planes heading south over Lingayen Gulf.

At noon FEAF realized there were two groups incoming—one heading for Clark, the other for Iba. The commander of the 24th Pursuit Group at Clark Field, Major Orrin Grover, was ordered to intercept the planes heading for Clark. The sixteen B-17s that had spent most of the morning in the air had landed and were now being refueled. Given the obvious dangers, it is astonishing that Brereton's FEAF staff allowed all the bombers to land at the same time. They were such sitting ducks on the ground that the only sensible thing to do was to land a few at a time—with fighter cover over the field—refuel them, and get them back into the air before the next flight came down. Common sense, however, was lacking at FEAF that day.

To make matters worse, Grover seemed paralyzed by the crisis. While his pilots fumed, Grover dithered and procrastinated. When he finally found the nerve to act, he sent two of his three squadrons off to protect the shipping in Manila Bay. His third squadron was still on the ground at 12:35 P.M., just as ninety Japanese bombers and fighters appeared overhead. Within minutes every B-17 at Clark was destroyed or damaged. At Iba more than a hundred Japanese planes wiped out the radar station and shot down half a dozen P-40s that attempted to intercept them.[87]

While bombs were exploding on the runways of Clark Field, Lieutenant Howard W. Brown of the Signal Corps arrived at 1 Calle Victoria with a top secret message for MacArthur. The message was a Japanese communication that had been intercepted by U.S. Navy cryptographers and decoded. It said, in effect, that Japan was now at war with the United States and Great Britain. Sutherland read it and remarked sarcastically, "Very interesting and timely!"

MacArthur was on the telephone, getting the news from FEAF that Clark Field was under attack. He was outraged, and he kept Brown waiting for five minutes while he upbraided Brereton's chief of staff for keeping B-17s at Clark in defiance of his orders. After slamming down the phone, he noticed Brown, who stood transfixed and clutching a message. MacArthur took it from the lieutenant and read it quickly. The lieutenant apologetically explained that it had taken several hours to bring this important communication to USAFFE headquarters because of the cumbersome, bureaucratic system that was always followed in handling naval decrypts. MacArthur listened, expressionless, and made no comment, but when Brown had finished, he simply said, "Thank you, son."[88]

He dictated a number of messages to the War Department. In one he declared, "I am launching a heavy bombardment counter attack tomorrow morning of enemy airdromes in southern Formosa." In another he said he was turning his A-24 dive-bombers over to the Filipinos. Unlike Marshall, he considered them a waste of good aluminum. He seized this opportunity to get rid of them and demand something better.[89]

In the early afternoon Brereton arrived at 1 Calle Victoria flustered and upset. He insisted on seeing MacArthur. He had just had a telephone call from Arnold, said Brereton, and Arnold had angrily demanded to know "how in hell" the B-17s had been destroyed at Clark Field. Would MacArthur explain the situation to Arnold? "Don't worry, Lewis," MacArthur told him. "You go back and fight the war."[90]

Shortly after this MacArthur had a meeting with Hart. Both men were in a somber mood. MacArthur was frankly dismayed at the loss of planes and life. After Hart left, Sayre arrived. MacArthur read him a message from the War Department summarizing the attack on Pearl Harbor: the long list of ships sunk or disabled, the more than 100 airplanes destroyed, the heavy loss of life. And the Philippines too had suffered, he told Sayre. "Many of our own planes have been destroyed on the ground at Clark Field." The high commissioner left dazed, hardly able to believe war had come.[91]

By this time evening was nigh. MacArthur gave instructions that there would be only a partial blackout in Manila. As the British had discovered, a full blackout was itself a major hazard to life and limb, almost as dangerous as leaving all the lights on. Only if there was warning of an impending air attack, MacArthur said, should a full blackout be imposed.

At 6:00 P.M. MacArthur held a commanders' conference. It was a tense, somber occasion. Nothing but bad news, with every prospect of worse to come. After the meeting broke up, he called for his car and headed back to the Manila Hotel. His driver took him swiftly through the wet, deserted streets. It had been raining.

15

Times When
Men Must Die

MacArthur was incensed at the appalling performance of Brereton, Brady and the Far Eastern Air Force. Publicly he defended the airmen. He invariably shielded his subordinates from criticism by those he considered outsiders, including senior commanders in the War Department. When Arnold demanded to know what had happened at Clark Field, MacArthur replied blandly that FEAF had taken "every possible precaution . . . losses were due entirely to the overwhelming superiority of the enemy. . . . No unit could have done better. Their gallantry has been conspicuous, their efficiency good. . . . You may take pride in their conduct."[1] In private, however, he called Brereton and Brady "bumbling nincompoops" and looked for a way to get them out of the Philippines before they did any more damage.[2]

Almost as soon as the war ended, Brereton got his account of what had happened published as *The Brereton Diaries*. Few readers ever realized that the section dealing with the Philippines was not based on a diary at all but was written months, possibly years later. Its aim was to defend Brereton's reputation, and to a large extent it succeeded, despite its mendacity. In the course of researching a book on the World War II Army Air Forces, *Winged Victory,* I read more than a thousand interviews and debriefings of AAF officers. Dozens were by people who had served with Brereton. Not one thought he was a competent commander. Many were scathing about "Louie." He was indolent, self-indulgent and mediocre. Only the fact that he was an old crony of Arnold's saved his career from ending in disgrace. His so-called diary offers an undocumented, uncorroborated and implausible version of events in December 1941. This has proved no obstacle to its being used by two generations of writers and historians as if it were a reliable, contemporaneous account of air operations in the Philippines.[3]

In the days that followed the initial Japanese attack, Brereton's pursuit pilots took to the air, despite insuperable odds, to engage Japanese fighters. FEAF's remaining flyable B-17s were pitted against enemy shipping. As we now know, they inflicted little damage, but at the time it was believed they were striking powerful blows, and the courage of the bomber crews was inspiring. MacArthur demanded that FEAF issue prompt recommendations for DSCs and DFCs so that men could be decorated while the memory of their deeds was still bright.[4]

The rapidly dwindling force of B-17s consisted of C and D models that stood no chance against well-flown enemy fighters and were virtually useless against a moving target, such as a maneuvering warship. Even so, a B-17 pilot, Captain Colin Kelly, became the first American hero of the war. His plane was credited (mistakenly) with sinking the battleship *Haruna* on December 10, after which it was jumped by a swarm of Zeros. Bullets raking the fuel-filled wings turned his B-17 into a flaming torch. Kelly ordered the crew to bail out. He stayed with the burning plane until they had parachuted to safety, but he perished when the plane hit the water. MacArthur personally decorated Kelly's crew and awarded Kelly a posthumous DSC. "It gives me great pleasure to pin these decorations on your breasts," he told them, "where for all eyes and for all time they will be the symbol of the devotion, fortitude and courage with which you have fought for your country. It is my profound sorrow that Colin Kelly is not here. I do not know the dignity of Captain Kelly's birth, but I do know the glory of his death. He died unquestioning, uncomplaining, with faith in his heart and victory his end. God has taken him unto himself, a gallant soldier who did his duty."[5]

The mission on which Colin Kelly died was an antishipping strike against a Japanese landing at Aparri, on the northern coast of Luzon, where there was a crude airstrip. The Philippine Army troops posted on the beach simply fled. A second landing, at nearby Vigan, followed hard on the heels of the Japanese arrival at Aparri, but at Vigan there was no airstrip and not a single defender.

MacArthur's reaction to these landings was to play a waiting game. If he sent Wainwright's North Luzon Force to fight for Aparri and Vigan, they could be cut off when the Japanese main force landed, as he confidently expected, on the western side of Luzon, somewhere along the long, flat beaches of Lingayen Gulf. Aparri and Vigan were written off, but orders went out to commandeer the explosives held by mining companies operating in the mountains of northern Luzon and use them to blow the bridges and ferry docks on all the roads and rivers leading south.[6]

Having knocked out FEAF, the Japanese still had to neutralize the Navy. On December 11 they mounted a heavy air attack on the navy base at Cavite, seven miles south of downtown Manila. MacArthur was in his office, with the door open, when Sid Huff shouted to him that Japanese planes were heading for Manila Bay. He stepped onto the section of wall outside his office. Standing with hands on hips and feet wide apart, he watched as a large Japanese formation came across the bay from the northeast, flew directly overhead, dropped a few bombs on FEAF headquarters at Nichols Field, then flew on to unleash a torrent of ordnance on the docks, the workshops, the storage tanks, the power plant and the barracks of the 16th Naval District.[7]

Next day the Japanese landed three thousand men at Legaspi, at the southern end of Luzon, more than two hundred miles from Manila. MacArthur still made no major move. He explained what he was doing to puzzled journalists. "The basic principle of handling troops is to hold them intact until the enemy has committed himself in force." He was still waiting for the main landing, which Willoughby forecast would come around December 28.[8]

When the war began, a convoy of seven ships guarded by the cruiser *Pensacola* was southwest of Hawaii, heading for the Philippines. The convoy was bringing nearly five thousand troops, eighteen P-40s, fifty-two A-24s, twenty artillery pieces and thousands of tons of ammunition. Once the shooting began, the convoy was turned around and started steaming back toward Hawaii. On December 13, however, MacArthur got the cheering news from Marshall that the *Pensacola* convoy had been directed to resume its course for the Philippines, via northeastern Australia.

MacArthur went to see Hart. Would the Navy ensure the *Pensacola* convoy got through? Hart was all gloom and doom. MacArthur returned to 1 Calle Victoria in a grim mood and dashed off a long message to Marshall, complaining bitterly about Hart's pessimism: "He gave as his estimate of the situation that before the ships could reach here a complete blockade would be established. . . . He seemed to be of the opinion that the islands were ultimately doomed."

Throughout 1941 the United States had been discussing with the British the strategy to be pursued if America entered the war. The conclusion reached was that a strategic offensive would be mounted against Germany, while the United States would assume the strategic defensive in the Pacific. That decision, however, had not yet been confirmed, and MacArthur made a desperate bid that it not be. "If Japan ever captures these islands the difficulty of recapture is impossible of conception. If the Western Pacific is to be saved it will have to be saved here and now. . . . Every resource of the Democratic Allies in sea, air and land should be converged here immediately and overwhelmingly," he told Marshall. "The Philippine theatre of operations is the locus of victory or defeat and I urge a strategic review of the entire situation lest a fatal mistake be made." Marshall responded three days later that the President recognized the strategic importance of the Philippines and that all possible assistance would be sent there. Hart, however, still would not commit himself to bringing the convoy through to the Philippines.[9]

On December 16 the Japanese bombed the Manila docks. This attack was bound to jangle the nerves of an already tense city. To a background noise of ferocious detonations, MacArthur called Carlos Romulo, the editor and publisher of the *Manila Herald,* the Philippines' English-language newspaper, and ordered him to report for duty next day. Romulo arrived at USAFFE headquarters early on the morning of the seventeenth dressed in a borrowed uniform and wearing the insignia of a major in the Philippine Army reserve.

MacArthur greeted Romulo effusively. "Carlos, my boy, congratulations! But who made you that terrible uniform?" He told Romulo that he was going to be Diller's assistant. His job was to keep the people of Manila informed and to counter the rumors that were sweeping through the city. There were rumors of espionage, fifth columnists, thousands of Japanese paratroopers. "Keep 'em informed," MacArthur said, "but don't panic them. Always tell them the truth. People can stand the truth."[10]

MacArthur was also thinking about what he would do if the Japanese managed to get ashore in force and pose a strong ground threat to Manila. He would have little choice but to abandon the city. Provided he could deny the Japanese use of the bay, the city had no strategic importance.

He told Sid Huff to go see Quezon and Sayre and tell them to be ready to leave for Corregidor on four hours' notice.[11] Quezon was appalled. It had never occurred to him that he would have to leave Manila. He demanded to see MacArthur at the Manila Hotel.

That night the two of them met at the service entrance to the blacked-out ballroom. Had Quezon visited the penthouse, the whole city would have heard about it by morning. People were laughing, drinking, dancing, enjoying themselves on the other side of the service entrance door. MacArthur and Quezon stepped into the hotel garden and walked around the grounds in the dark, debating in whispers. Quezon could easily imagine how it would look: the politician who ran away and took refuge, leaving his people to suffer under a cruel and rapacious enemy. "I shall stay among my people," he insisted, "and suffer the same fate that may befall them."

"Mr. President, I expected that answer from such a gallant man as I know you to be," MacArthur replied. What was at stake, though, was not Quezon's personal safety but the continuity of the government of the Philippines if Manila fell to the enemy. "It is my duty to prevent you falling into the enemy's hands," he told Quezon. It was a duty, he implied, that he intended to fulfill.[12]

On December 20 the Japanese put troops ashore at Davao, on Mindanao. Later that night came reports of a large Japanese convoy heading for Lingayen Gulf. The reports were false, but the evening of December 21 the submarine *Stingray* tracked a convoy numbering at least eighty ships. This had to be the main force. Hart sent six submarines toward the gulf as the invasion fleet approached it in the early hours of December 22. By dawn Japanese landing barges laden with infantry were chugging toward the shore.

Ironically, one of the first messages to come in from Washington that morning announced MacArthur's promotion to full general. Hart phoned to offer his congratulations. MacArthur thanked him and remarked, "I'm glad to have my rightful rank back."

The defense of islands nearly always depends on control of the sealanes. The Navy's determination to pull out and not defend the Philippines meant that they were doomed, whatever MacArthur believed and whatever MacArthur did. That determination was so complete that Hart did not even bother to have Lingayen Gulf mined, even though it was as obvious to him as it was to MacArthur that this was where the main invasion fleet would drop anchor.

MacArthur did not raise the issue of mining. It is possible he did not even think about it, although he and his staff should have done so. What *did* bother him was the failure of Hart's submarines. The Asiatic Fleet's surface units had pulled out, but its submarine force—which numbered twenty-nine boats—was still operating in and around the Philippines. There were now more than eighty Japanese ships in Lingayen Gulf, but Hart's submarines had not sunk one of them. "What is the matter with your submarines, Tommy?" asked MacArthur, taunting and impatient.[13]

He went back to reading the intelligence reports and studying his maps. After a while he shook his head and said bitterly to Sutherland, "What a target this would have been for the submarines!"[14] MacArthur could not know that the submarines *were* attacking the Japanese transports, but their torpedoes had a magnetic exploder that had been developed when Hart commanded the Torpedo Station some years earlier and the exploder did not work. It would be another eighteen months before the Navy figured out why it was denting a dozen Japanese ships for every one that it sank.[15]

Frustrated and alarmed, MacArthur sent a message to the War Department asking for an aircraft carrier to steam within range of the Philippines and fly fighters to him. It was, as he probably knew, a hopeless request.

Throughout the day the telephone on his desk rang incessantly with commanders in the field sending in reports. In between receiving and sending messages he paced, his head slightly bowed, a worried expression on his face, which was becoming increasingly lined and gray. In the midst of these fresh alarms he came to a decision and remembered something. He drew up a proclamation declaring Manila an open city and had Sutherland call Corregidor to tell the commander there that USAFFE headquarters would be moving in.

MacArthur sent for Sid Huff and told him, "I've forgotten to buy Jean a Christmas present." He had no idea what she wanted, but Huff would think of something.

MacArthur had recently managed to get Huff, who was a retired naval officer, commissioned in the Army as lieutenant colonel. Undaunted by his new assignment, Huff returned several hours later carrying beautifully wrapped boxes tied up with ribbon, containing dresses and lingerie from stores that he knew Jean patronized. MacArthur took them home and told Jean to open them now: She would have no chance to do so on Christmas Eve.[16]

The next morning reports poured into USAFFE of Japanese troops pushing inland from the beaches of Lingayen Gulf. MacArthur sent a message to the War Department that was bleakly pessimistic yet defiant. He estimated the strength of the invasion force at eighty to one hundred thousand troops. "I have available on Luzon about 40,000 men in units partially equipped . . . this enormous tactical discrepancy will compel me to operate in delaying action . . . to final defensive position on Bataan to cover Corregidor. . . . I will evacuate the High Commissioner and the Government. I intend to hold Corregidor."[17]

The real strength of the Japanese main force, the Fourteenth Army, commanded by General Masaharu Homma, was half what MacArthur guessed. As for having only forty thousand troops on Luzon, MacArthur had about seventy thousand. But he had only forty thousand in a position to defend the ground between Lingayen Gulf and Manila. And while the figures he sent to Washington look misleading in retrospect, he was right about the essentials: He would have to fight a delaying action back to Bataan.

That afternoon, when word arrived that the Japanese had moved twenty miles inland and had reached the major highway heading south, MacArthur told Sutherland to send an order to all field commanders: "War Plan Orange 3 is in effect."

At first light on December 24, seven thousand Japanese troops started coming ashore at Lamon Bay, on the eastern coast of Luzon. MacArthur's forces were now caught in a huge pincers operation. The battle ahead would be to save them from destruction. Whatever faint hope there might have been of holding Manila was snuffed out. It would be difficult for trained troops to fight a battle on the open expanses of the central plain of

Luzon against an enemy that had air superiority and tanks. For his untrained Filipino levies, it was simply impossible. They would either run away or be slaughtered, accomplishing nothing. If he could get them dug in on the rugged terrain of Bataan, however, he could buy time while he pleaded with Washington for reinforcements. MacArthur informed Marshall that he would be moving his headquarters to Corregidor.

He telephoned Hart and told him the same thing. When USAFFE pulled out, Hart's staff would have no option but to do the same. Hart was indignant and demanded a personal conference. MacArthur said it would have to wait.[18]

Then he told Huff to go and inform Quezon and Sayre that they should be ready to catch an interisland steamer, the *Mayon,* at 2:00 P.M. It would take them to Corregidor.[19]

He sent for Brereton, and when Brereton arrived, he told him to move his headquarters to Australia. Brereton was astonished. He offered to remain and handle any job MacArthur wanted to give him. MacArthur did not tell him that he was seizing this opportunity to get rid of Brereton. During the past week he had tried to find a way to wash his hands of both Brereton and his chief of staff, Francis Brady. The only air commander MacArthur had any use for was Hal George, whom he had just promoted to brigadier general. He would keep George and send Brereton on his way.[20]

"No, Lewis," said MacArthur. "You go on south. You can do me more good with the bombers you have left and those you should be receiving there soon than you can here."

Still puzzling over what MacArthur was really up to, Brereton rose to leave. MacArthur extended his right hand. "I hope," he said, "that you will tell the people outside what we have done and protect my reputation as a fighter."

"General, your reputation will never need any protection," said Brereton.[21]

While MacArthur was preparing to leave on Christmas Eve, so was Jean. The USAFFE staff members going to Corregidor, including MacArthur, were allowed to take only one suitcase each. She packed a case with clothes and canned goods. Jean was about to depart when she was stricken at the thought of how much the general's mementos meant to him. She dashed back into the apartment, retrieved the gold baton, opened the display cases in the library and scooped up his medals, including Purple Heart Number 1, wrapping them in a towel that was brightly embroidered "Manila Hotel" along one side. Other treasured heirlooms, such as Arthur MacArthur's orders and decorations, were abandoned.[22]

The MacArthurs would travel to Corregidor aboard the *Don Esteban,* another interisland steamer. At 6:00 P.M., with the steamer due to sail in an hour, MacArthur walked out of his office and into Romulo's. News that MacArthur was leaving Manila and that Quezon had already departed— wearing a U.S. Army uniform and a steel helmet—had not been released. Standing next to Romulo's desk, MacArthur told him, sotto voce, that he was about to leave and would establish an advanced echelon of USAFFE on Corregidor. Richard J. Marshall, the deputy chief of staff, would remain behind for the time being. Romulo would stay in Manila too and handle the press. MacArthur gave him a sealed envelope, to be opened only when ordered to do so. Then MacArthur shook Romulo by the hand. "I'll be back, Carlos," he whispered fiercely.[23]

Returning to his office, he took a last look around and summoned Sergeant Paul Rogers, the clerk whose services he shared with Sutherland. His gaze was fixed on the magnificent display of flags along one wall, the banners that summarized in silk the story of one soldier's life. He stared for a moment at the last flag of all, a small red banner with the four white stars of a full general in the U.S. Army. Tied now to a staff, it occupied one corner of the room, separate from the row of flags against the wall. It was the flag that had streamed from the bumper of his car when he was Chief of Staff. He pointed to it. "Rogers, cut off that flag for me."

Rogers did not make a move. He was wondering where he would find a knife. MacArthur, irritated, repeated his command. "Rogers, cut it off."

Improvising a solution, the sergeant grasped the staff, untied the thongs, rolled up the flag and handed it to him. "Thank you," said MacArthur, tucking it under his arm.

He walked out to the anteroom, followed by Sutherland. "Well, Dick. I guess it's time to go. There isn't anything left to do here." They went down the steps and into the car that was waiting for them, drove out through the smoke-filled courtyard, where a large bonfire was being fed thousands of classified documents, and drove through the tunnel that penetrated the wall of the Intramuros below 1 Calle Victoria.[24]

When they reached the dock, Hart was waiting to talk to MacArthur. They walked along the waterfront for fifteen minutes, while Hart protested indignantly that MacArthur had not given him more than a few hours' notice to quit Manila. There was nothing, though, that could be done now. MacArthur had his own complaints to make about the performance of the Asiatic Fleet. They parted, never to meet again.[25]

The *Don Esteban* cast off a little after 7:00 P.M. to make the twenty-seven-mile journey across the bay to Corregidor. The scene as it drew away from the dock was phantasmagorical, beyond anything those aboard, except possibly MacArthur, had ever imagined. At the various Army and Navy installations in and around the city everything of potential military value to the Japanese was being put to the torch. There were fires all along the waterfront. At Cavite the oil storage tanks were ignited, creating billowing clouds of greasy black smoke ringed at the bottom with huge orange tongues of dancing flame.

Above, the night sky was clear and luminous with a thousand brilliant stars. It had been a hot day, and the temperature was still close to eighty degrees. Many of those aboard went out onto the forward deck to enjoy the evening breeze. As they gathered there, they broke feelingly into song. "Silent Night" and other Christmas carols rose into the air while receding into the distance, the fires of Manila winked and flickered along the stygian horizon.

MacArthur sat in the saloon, holding his head in his hands, sunk in deep, inexpressible grief.[26]

Corregidor is a tadpole-shaped island in Manila Bay nearly four miles long and only two miles south of the Bataan Peninsula. The western end is dominated by Malinta Hill, which contained a high and wide tunnel fifteen hundred yards long. It was MacArthur who had gotten Malinta Tunnel built. Construction began shortly after he became Chief of Staff and ended shortly after he left Washington for Manila. At the top of the hill was a small fort, with a parade ground, barracks and a half dozen houses for officers. Known as Topside, this was where the advanced echelon moved in. The MacArthurs were installed in a small but comfortable white house, and he and his staff set up their offices in one wing of a concrete barracks building.

There was regular contact with Manila, by both telephone and ferry, for a week, while the Japanese advanced slowly on Manila. They were still expecting to fight a huge battle on the central plain of Luzon. MacArthur's withdrawal into Bataan took them completely by surprise.

Two days after reaching Corregidor, MacArthur sent Sid Huff back to Manila, to the penthouse apartment. In the bedroom he would find MacArthur's old campaign hat and the Colt .45 he had carried in World War I. MacArthur wanted to carry them through this war too.[27]

That same day he sent a message to Romulo: He was to open the sealed envelope and release the contents to the press. The contents turned out to be the proclamation MacArthur had written on December 22 declaring Manila an open city.[28]

MacArthur's mood was buoyed when, on December 28, Marshall informed him "the President [has] personally directed the Navy to make every effort to support you. You can rest assured War Department will do all in its power to build up at top speed air power in Far East to completely dominate that region." An even more encouraging message arrived on December 29 from Roosevelt. The President's tone was upbeat; his words were emphatic: "I give to the people of the Philippines my solemn pledge that their freedom will be redeemed. . . . The entire resources in men and materials of the United States stand behind that pledge. . . . The United States Navy is following an intensive and well-planned campaign against Japanese forces which will result in positive assistance to the defense of the Philippine Islands." Journalists who inquired whether something had to be lost before it could be redeemed were assured by Roosevelt's press secretary that was *not* the President's meaning.[29]

Meanwhile Marshall sent MacArthur further messages promising aid. One said, "We are leaving no stone unturned to provide you with assistance." A follow-up cable informed him that a large force of bombers, fighters and ships was being deployed, to produce "an early superiority in the Southwestern Pacific. Our strength is to be concentrated and it should exert a decisive effect on Japanese shipping and force a withdrawal northward."[30]

During the course of December 29 MacArthur issued an order to commandeer rice supplies. His supply officer, Lewis Beebe, and the USAFFE quartermaster, Charles Drake, were still back at 1 Calle Victoria, rounding up barges and boats to ship food over to Bataan. The shortage of transportation made it difficult to build up supplies on Bataan in the limited time available. And while there was an abundance of food in Manila, MacArthur refused to allow Beebe and Drake to strip the city. He was not going to inflict starvation on the inhabitants of Manila to feed his troops over on Bataan.[31]

Shortly before noon on the twenty-ninth Japanese bombers flew over Corregidor. For three and a half hours they pounded Topside. MacArthur was standing out in the open when a salvo of bombs came whistling down. One blew up his house, but fortunately Jean and Arthur sheltered in the tunnel during air raids. As the earth heaved around them, MacArthur and his orderly, a Philippine Scout sergeant named Domingo Adversario, sprawled in a shallow ditch that ran beside a hedge. MacArthur refused to wear a helmet even in the heaviest bombardment. Sergeant Adversario took off his own helmet and held it over MacArthur's head. A piece of shrapnel sliced open the back of Adversario's hand. When they scrambled to their feet, MacArthur dressed the wound and later awarded the sergeant both the Purple Heart and the Silver Star.[32]

Next day Quezon was sworn in for the second time as president of the commonwealth. A small platform had been erected near the entrance to Malinta Tunnel, which now housed the headquarters of USAFFE. In a brief inaugural address Quezon quoted from Roosevelt's message, which he read as a promise of help. MacArthur made a brief speech praising Quezon. As his address drew to a close, his voice broke, and he did something he had never done before in public. His hard-won composure cracked and he began to weep openly. Tears coursing down his cheeks, MacArthur raised his gaze to the skies and pleaded, "From the grim shadow of the Valley of Death, oh merciful God, preserve this noble race!"[33]

Quezon was hardly sworn in before Roosevelt urged that he be evacuated and brought to the United States. MacArthur met briefly with Quezon every morning, but on this occasion he called a meeting that included Sutherland, Willoughby, Quezon and Sayre and read aloud the message from Roosevelt. Then he read out his proposed reply, saying evacuation would be too hazardous for Quezon to undertake. Quezon's War Cabinet, on the other hand, urged him to try to get out if he could.

On New Year's Day, with the Japanese poised to enter Manila, MacArthur had the rear echelon of the USAFFE staff move to Corregidor. He now had his entire military family safe on the Rock.

In his first week on Corregidor, MacArthur's greatest challenge had been managing the withdrawal of his North Luzon Force and his South Luzon Force into Bataan. If the North Luzon Force retreated south to Bataan too quickly, the South Luzon Force, moving north, could be blocked from entering Bataan by the Japanese troops pursuing the retreating Wainwright and would be annihilated.

MacArthur's strategy of withdrawal was to have Casey's engineer troops build defensive positions for his troops to fall back to and hold just long enough to make the Japanese pause and regroup for a frontal assault. During the pause the engineers would create another line of defenses about ten miles back. Just before the Japanese attacked his frontline positions, MacArthur ordered a withdrawal to the new defensive position in the rear. When the Japanese blow landed, it struck nothing. Wainwright did this five times as his North Luzon Force retreated across the central plain of Luzon and covered the move into Bataan by the South Luzon Force.

It is a truism of ground warfare down the ages that the hardest military maneuver of all is a fighting withdrawal. The retreat into Bataan became one of the classic operations studied in detail by postwar students at the Command and General Staff School.

On January 2 MacArthur told Quezon that the withdrawal would be completed soon without major losses of either manpower or matériel. That same day, however, the Japanese moved into Manila. A huge Rising Sun flag was hoisted above the penthouse of the Manila Hotel. MacArthur could see it, through his binoculars, much as General Homma, the new occupant of his apartment, probably intended.[34]

There was a large vase in the entrance hall of the apartment that had been given to his father by the emperor of Japan in 1905, with an inscription in Japanese to that effect. MacArthur chuckled at the thought of Homma encountering the vase. "I wonder if he bows?"[35]

Once the withdrawal into Bataan was complete, MacArthur informed Quezon that he intended to set up a command post there, move to the peninsula and direct the battle in person. Quezon was horrified. He pleaded with MacArthur to think again. Occasional exposure to danger was inevitable and possibly necessary. But to share the daily risks of troops in the front line was so reckless it was irresponsible. Quezon begged him not to do it.[36]

Although the retreat had been a remarkable success, the situation on the peninsula was grim. Some 60,000 Philippine Army troops, 10,000 Philippine Scouts and 10,000 Americans were digging in across terrain that gave every advantage to the defender. But when MacArthur had ordered, "Put WPO-3 into effect," that was merely shorthand for pulling back into Bataan. The withdrawal had not exactly followed WPO-3. That plan had only envisaged pulling the Philippine Division and some smaller Regular Army units back from Lingayen Gulf and into the peninsula. It never encompassed tens of thousands of troops from the Philippine Army, a force whose existence it did not even acknowledge. WPO-3 also called for evacuating the peninsula of civilians before the troops moved in. Instead the situation now was that 25,000 refugees had moved into Bataan. In all, there were 105,000 mouths—military and civilian—to feed on Bataan, instead of the 40,000 that the Orange plans had anticipated.[37]

Drake and Beebe had come close to meeting the WPO-3 goal of stockpiling enough food to feed 40,000 troops for six months, but with 105,000 people to provide for, there was a severe food crisis. MacArthur reduced the daily ration by 50 percent. Bataan might hold out until April.

On January 10 he rode a PT boat over to Bataan to see conditions for himself. He met with Wainwright and congratulated him. "Jonathan, the execution of your withdrawal and of your mission in covering the withdrawal of the South Luzon Force were as fine as anything in history," said MacArthur. "And for that I'm going to see that you are made a permanent major general."

After talking briefly with Wainwright's generals, he turned and asked him, "Where are your 155 millimeter guns?"

Wainwright explained that two of his six 155s were nearby and suggested they go take a look at them. MacArthur shook his head. "I don't want to *see* them, Jonathan. I want to *hear* them."[38]

MacArthur had encouraging news for Wainwright and his staff. Planes were arriving at a steady rate in Australia, and Casey was preparing airfields on Mindanao to receive them. As the Japanese moved into the Philippines from the north, American reinforcements were coming in through the south. At some point he expected to launch a counteroffensive.[39]

MacArthur grilled Wainwright and his staff on everything: supply, morale, tactics, terrain, strong points, weak points, Japanese strengths,

Japanese weaknesses. Then he walked among the troops. Enemy planes circled overhead, looking for targets, and snipers shot from distant trees, but MacArthur walked from one position to another, offering encouragement: "Nice work, soldier! . . . Keep it up, men! . . ."

Back on Corregidor he settled back into what had become his new routine. After the house on Topside was obliterated, he was assigned two rooms in one of the laterals angled back at forty-five degrees from the central shaft of Malinta Tunnel. The rooms were only nine feet by seven feet, with rough concrete walls and a curved ceiling, painted white with a bucket of paint scrounged from the hospital. MacArthur refused to sleep in the tunnel, however. Its fetid air had made Quezon, who suffered from tuberculosis, so weak he could barely walk. He was confined to a wheelchair most of the time. MacArthur too was susceptible to lung infections.

He chose to take his chances out of doors and lived in a small gray house nearly a mile away. Jean, Arthur and Ah Cheu, the Chinese amah, occupied the two small rooms during air raids. Otherwise they stayed at the house with him. During air raids he went to the tunnel entrance to get a look, and as the bombing progressed, he was likely to walk out into the open to get an even better look. In this war, as in the last, he did not believe there was an enemy bomb or bullet with his name on it.

MacArthur and Sutherland set up their office at the entrance to Lateral Three, with his desk directly behind Sutherland's. Behind the desks were two tiers of metal bunk beds. MacArthur spent much of his time pacing the aisle between the bunks, looking at the floor, his mind racing.

He arrived for work about eight each morning, his mother's old walking stick jauntily tucked under his arm, looking cheerful, sounding optimistic. His former impeccable appearance had suffered a setback. Like everyone else on Corregidor, he shaved with saltwater. The result was designer stubble long before it became fashionable. His uniforms, once famously immaculate, were wrinkled and grubby. Only the highly polished shoes retained their traditional gloss.[40]

When not pacing, he sat at his desk, one foot propped on a half-open drawer, reading reports, writing messages or poring over a map of Bataan, on which he painstakingly drew the present position in pencil. Each line was farther south than the one before.

He usually took lunch with Jean, sitting at a picnic table near the mouth of the tunnel, under camouflage netting. She bore her present ordeal without complaint, and Arthur, who had gotten himself promoted from "Junior" to "Sergeant," seemed to love the excitement and novelty of the new arrangement. "He is thriving on Corregidor!" MacArthur remarked to Romulo one day.[41]

MacArthur, formerly a world-class inhaler of Lucky Strikes, was rationed to three smokes a day, plus an after-dinner cigar. He usually lit up one of the three Luckies after lunch, when he held an informal press conference for the half dozen reporters holed up on the Rock with him.

His mind was never far from the fighting on Bataan. Whenever people came back from the peninsula, he invariably asked, "How are the boys?"[42]

Several days after his visit to Bataan he received a message from Marshall. "Our heavy bombers have been arriving in theater at rate of three a day. . . . Seven thousand troops left Frisco yesterday. . . . Twenty one thousand leave east coast January 21st. . . . Another convoy of fourteen thousand leaves west coast January 30th."[43]

MacArthur assumed that these forces were heading for the Philippines. He was convinced the Japanese were mounting little more than a "paper blockade." The War Plans Division, on the other hand, had studied the question of what it would take to go to MacArthur's assistance and arrived at the opposite conclusion. The Allies lacked the shipping and airpower to push sufficient reinforcements into the Philippines to save them from conquest.[44] No one, however, told MacArthur that. Nor was it made clear to him that the forces shipping out for the Pacific were destined not for the defense of the Philippines but for the defense of Australia.

After reading this latest communication from Marshall, MacArthur penned an upbeat message that he ordered read to all troops on Bataan: "Help is on the way. . . . Thousands of troops and hundreds of planes are being dispatched . . . they will have to fight their way through. . . . It is imperative that our troops hold until these reinforcements arrive. . . . I call upon every soldier on Bataan to fight in his assigned position, resisting every attack. . . . If we fight, we will win; if we retreat, we will be destroyed."[45]

He sent a separate message to officers in the field. He reminded them that they had a special duty, in addition to their responsibility as soldiers defending their country, to preserve "that demeanor of confidence, self-reliance, and assurance which is the birthright of all cultured gentlemen and the special trademark of the Army officer."[46]

He explained to his staff why he thought it so important to send a morale-boosting message to the troops and a stern "do-your-duty" reminder to the officers at the front. "The line on Bataan is liable to go at any moment," he told them. "Morale is dangerously low." An officer from the General Staff who had been in Washington until shortly before the war began, Colonel Warren Clear, suggested that perhaps he was reading too much into Marshall's message. From his conversations with Harry Hopkins, the most influential adviser in the Roosevelt White House, said Clear, it was pretty obvious that aid to the Philippines came a long way below aid to Britain. Clear did not believe any reinforcements were heading toward the Philippines.

MacArthur thought about this, then responded, "If you are correct, then never in history was so large and gallant an army written off so callously!"[47]

Although morale was a constant concern, the fighting spirit of the Philippine Army was remarkable. Most of the fainthearted had fled in the early days. Those who remained showed that with a little practical experience of soldiering, a rifle and some ammunition, they could be tenacious in defense. They were cheerfully obedient, uncomplaining and brave, but they were constantly hungry and tired.

The troops on the peninsula were divided between the I Corps, on the western side, under Wainwright, and the II Corps, to the east, under Major General George M. Parker, Jr. Ideally there would have been a continuous front line across Bataan. Instead there was a seven-mile gap between the I Corps and the II Corps dominated by a mountain. Wainwright considered the slopes so steep and the jungle so dense that the gap was impenetrable.

For all his courage, Wainwright was probably not the right man to hold Bataan. As a cavalryman he thought in terms of shallow fronts. He knew little about the proper handling of artillery, the creation of interlocking fields of fire to defend frontline positions or the need for defensive positions in depth. He was also monumentally wrong about the impenetrability of that seven-mile gap. On January 21 some five hundred Japanese soldiers appeared a mile behind I Corps's right flank and set up a roadblock across the only decent north-south road on Bataan.

MacArthur sent Sutherland over next morning to appraise the situation. Sutherland, who had not one day of combat experience, was alarmed. Instead of organizing a strong counterattack to eliminate the penetration, he told Wainwright to fall back and improvise a new line of defense. It was a debatable decision, and Sutherland may not have been the best person to make it. The present line was well worth fighting for. Wainwright had no choice but to do as he was told by Sutherland, who spoke in MacArthur's name. The I Corps withdrew, forcing the II Corps to pull back too. Wainwright was forced to abandon most of his artillery.[48]

The Japanese meanwhile launched yet another threat, landing troops on both sides of the peninsula, behind the line of defenses Wainwright was withdrawing into. MacArthur ordered him to take charge personally of wiping out these two beachheads.[49]

With the Japanese advancing deep into Bataan and driving the defenders back to their last line, MacArthur sent a stream of urgent pleas for help to the War Department. He grew so alarmed he even sent a melodramatic cable to Marshall recommending Sutherland as his successor "in case of my death."

The officer who was handling War Department communications with MacArthur was Eisenhower. Marshall had brought Eisenhower into the War Plans Division a week after Pearl Harbor and given him the task of trying to get help to the Philippines. Marshall recognized the inevitable outcome of the campaign but told Eisenhower, "Do what you can to save them."[50]

MacArthur's old boss Patrick J. Hurley was commissioned a brigadier general and sent to Australia. His mission was to find ships and crews willing to run the Japanese blockade and take arms, food and medical supplies to MacArthur. Eisenhower put ten million dollars in gold and cash at Hurley's disposal. Despite the promise of riches, however, Hurley found only six crews willing to try, and of these, only three succeeded. None offered to make a second trip.[51]

The strain on Eisenhower as he tried to push aid through to MacArthur was intense, and he vented his frustrations in his diary, which became a ripe source of anti-MacArthur quotes. He derided MacArthur on a number of occasions: "MacArthur is as big a baby as ever . . . he still likes his boot lickers . . . a refusal on his part to look facts in the face. . . . MacArthur is losing his nerve." Damning stuff.[52]

Ike, however, was in poor health these days yet had been thrust into the biggest assignment of his life. It was a job he found irksome, depressing and ultimately futile. Not only was his health poor, but he was working an exhausting sixteen-hour day, seven days a week. His father fell gravely ill at this time, and when he died, Ike was too busy to attend the funeral, too busy even to grieve.

These early months of 1942 found him lashing out not only at MacArthur but at almost everyone. He condemned the people he worked with as talkers, not "doers." He damned the AAF for incompetence and the British for cowardice. He had nothing but contempt for the Navy, and "One thing that would help us win this war is to get someone to shoot [Admiral] King." Some days he claimed, "The Far East is critical"; at other times he accorded it no importance at all. There is a slightly hysterical tone to many of Ike's diary entries in early 1942, when he was trying, and failing, to get aid to MacArthur.

Despite the scornful comments on MacArthur, he was also moved to acknowledge at one point, "MacArthur is doing a good job." On January 25 he cabled a message to MacArthur for his sixty-second birthday saying that T. J. Davis joined him in "warmest anniversary greetings . . . we are proud to salute you [and] the inspiring record that you are establishing . . . our earnest hopes for the safety and health of Jean, Arthur and yourself are with you constantly."[53]

The anti-MacArthur entries were written by a stressed-out, tired man unable to help people he knew personally at a time when they faced death or captivity. Stimson, who took a more dispassionate view of the endgame in the Philippines, was writing coldly in *his* diary, "There are times when men must die."[54]

The heavy losses the Pacific Fleet had suffered at Pearl Harbor ruled out any rescue mission to the Philippines. So too did the grand strategy for the war agreed on in early January between Roosevelt and Churchill: Germany First. The Allies would go on the strategic offensive against Germany but assume the strategic defensive in the Pacific. MacArthur bitterly resented this decision. Not only did it place him in the secondary theater of war, but he believed as strongly as ever that America's long-term future was more closely bound up with events on the Pacific Rim than with the trials and tribulations of a declining Europe.

Once the strategy of Germany First was accepted in the War Department, it became possible to accept the inevitable loss of the Philippines. Minds started turning to salvaging something from the wreckage. The message that had gone to MacArthur on January 13 had, in its original form, stated, "We are considering ordering you out of the Philippines to exercise active command and direction of American forces now gathering in Australia. . . ." This had been dropped before the message was transmitted, but it was only a matter of time before this issue came around again.[55]

At the end of January Wainwright managed to wipe out the Japanese beachheads on Bataan, inflicting the first defeat the Japanese suffered in World War II, but Quezon was becoming more unpredictable than ever. The Japanese had established a puppet government under his former secretary, Jorge Vargas, and promised the Philippines their immediate independence if its troops would only stop fighting. Quezon proposed turning himself over to the Japanese so he could put their offer to the test. MacArthur told him bluntly, "Instead of putting you in the palace, Manuel, the Japs will more likely slit your throat. What you are proposing is ridiculous." The Japanese would not create a truly independent Philippines. If he surrendered to them, MacArthur told him, they would keep him prisoner and issue directives in his name, which would make it easier for them to control the archipelago. "We'll go back," he promised Quezon. "I will bring you in triumph on the points of my bayonets to Manila."[56]

Quezon, however, no longer believed Roosevelt's promises of help. He sent a message asking bluntly, "Has it already been decided in Washington that the Philippine front is of no importance . . . and, that, therefore, no amount of help can be expected here in the immediate future, or at least before the power of resistance is exhausted?"

Roosevelt's reply was bleak: "I cannot state the day that help will arrive in the Philippines. . . ." In other words, the islands were going to fall to

Japan. But the United States, Roosevelt pledged, would "eventually" liberate them.[57]

MacArthur sent a message to Marshall, telling him the time had come to plan on moving Quezon to safety. In the War Department, however, there was more concern about getting MacArthur out. Eisenhower had no doubt that he intended to die on Corregidor rather than surrender, but Marshall was afraid he might be captured rather than killed. To have MacArthur fall into enemy hands was simply unthinkable. It would make the loss of the Philippines doubly harmful to American morale and bring lasting shame on the Army. On February 4 Marshall suggested to MacArthur that he should go to Australia and establish a new command there. It was an idea MacArthur refused to consider. Instead he pleaded once more for the Navy to make a thrust westward and break the Japanese blockade.[58]

Quezon had meanwhile been stewing over Roosevelt's discouraging message. He came up with a plan of his own to end the fighting. He would ask the United States to grant the Philippines their independence and negotiate for the islands to be neutralized. Both American and Japanese forces would pull out, removing the Philippines from the war. Sayre more or less endorsed this idea. "If there is no hope of early arrival of American aid," cabled Sayre, "I think President Quezon's proposal . . . is a logical course of action."

MacArthur was reluctant to transmit Quezon's plan to Washington, but he had no authority to censor or veto communications between the president of the commonwealth and the President of the United States. He transmitted it, remarking to Marshall his lack of naval power and airpower made Corregidor untenable. "You must contemplate, at any date, the complete extinction of this command." As for Quezon's proposal, "The temper of Filipinos almost approaches extreme resentment against the United States" for involving them in this war and then, instead of coming promptly to their assistance, devoting most of its efforts to aiding other countries. In that context the Japanese offer of immediate independence if the Filipinos stopped fighting had made a profound impression.

MacArthur refrained from endorsing Quezon's idea explicitly, yet he remarked that from a purely military point of view there was nothing to lose by putting Quezon's proposal to the test. If the Japanese accepted it, there would be no need for a long and costly campaign to liberate the Philippines. If the Japanese turned it down, the present struggle would continue to its inevitable conclusion.[59]

Roosevelt's reply to Quezon's plan was swift and emphatic. If the Philippine Army wished to pull out of the fight, he informed MacArthur, it was free to do so, but "American forces will continue to keep our flag flying in the Philippines so long as there remains any possibility of resistance." The President suggested that before the end came, MacArthur should evacuate his wife and child.[60] MacArthur put Roosevelt's suggestion to Jean. She refused to consider it. "We drink of the same cup," she said. "We three are one." MacArthur accordingly informed the White House that his family intended "to share the fate of the garrison" with him and that he was going to fight "to the destruction of this command."[61]

Hours after Roosevelt's reply came a message from Marshall instructing MacArthur to evacuate Quezon. After Quezon had talked it over with MacArthur and his Cabinet, he decided the time had come to pay MacArthur the bonus promised back in 1935. On February 13 Sutherland composed Executive Order No. 1 of the Commonwealth of the Philippines. It awarded MacArthur $500,000. Sutherland would get $75,000, Richard Marshall $40,000 and Sid Huff $20,000. Rogers typed it up, thinking, "God, I would like to be a general!"[62]

MacArthur read through the order but remarked to Sutherland that it barely covered what he had forgone as a result of being military adviser. This may seem fanciful, until one considers the large advances he had rejected for his memoirs, the sizable amount of money Jean had been offered for a book on her life with MacArthur, the corporate directorships and other profitable ventures that he had passed up since 1935. And his commercial value was rising sharply. Shortly after this transaction in Malinta Tunnel, Viking Press offered him a million dollars for the rights to his memoirs, an offer he studiously ignored.[63]

As he accepted the $500,000 from Quezon, MacArthur may have thought if only for an instant of the irony of becoming rich at the very moment when he, his wife and his child all faced the likelihood of violent death or prolonged, humiliating imprisonment. He accepted this money with poor prospects of ever getting to spend it.

Executive Order No. 1 is one of the most controversial episodes in MacArthur's long and action-packed life. Quezon had chosen to compensate MacArthur as if the entire Philippine defense program had been carried to completion. He received what amounted to 46/100 of the $8 million-a-year defense budget for ten years ($368,000) plus loss of salary and expenses of $33,000 a year for 1942–45 ($132,000), producing a total of $500,000.

Most scholars have treated it as a corrupt transaction. Not even MacArthur's defenders have been able to explain why Roosevelt allowed it to proceed.[64] The answer is to be found in the letter from the Adjutant General to MacArthur back in September 1935. This gave him complete freedom to accept any amount of money from the Philippine government. The letter, which specifically said the secretary of war had agreed in advance to future, augmented payments, had never been revoked. Marshall's predecessor as Chief of Staff, Malin Craig, had suggested back in 1937 when MacArthur was retired that the President should consider declaring this letter null and void, but Roosevelt had chosen to allow it to stand, leaving its authority undiminished. Having declined to act then, he was not in a good position to act now.[65]

The payments to Sutherland, Marshall and Huff, however, were more than a little dubious. On the face of it they violated Army Regulations. The blanket permission MacArthur had arranged for himself said nothing about payments to his staff. However, Roosevelt allowed the entire transaction to go ahead, and MacArthur raised no question about these additional payments. They were arrived at by multiplying the recipients' annual salaries from the commonwealth by a factor of ten.

Quezon left Corregidor on February 20, aboard the submarine *Swordfish*. He bade a brief, emotional farewell to MacArthur, removing his signet ring and handing it to the general as a token of undying esteem. Quezon still hoped to reestablish his government, possibly in the Visayans, the islands in the center of the archipelago. That proved impossible, and MacArthur had him evacuated to Australia, as we shall see. From there Quezon would eventually be flown to the United States. Generous to a fault, when he reached Washington, he tried to give Eisenhower $60,000 in recognition of his services to the commonwealth in the late 1930s. Ike politely but firmly declined.[66]

Shortly after Quezon left, so did Sayre. MacArthur handed him a gift to present to Roosevelt once he reached Washington: a Japanese sword, taken from a Japanese officer killed on Bataan. It eventually came to rest at Hyde Park.[67]

While Quezon was being evacuated, Marshall was trying to convince the President that MacArthur should be ordered out too. Roosevelt was unconvinced. From a political point of view, it looked like a major mistake. "It would mean that the whites would absolutely lose all face in the Far East. White men can go down fighting, but they can't run away." McNutt agreed with him, as did Stimson.[68]

Marshall nonetheless persisted, but what eventually changed Roosevelt's mind was a sudden crisis in British-Australian relations that threatened to undermine Allied defense policy in the Southwest Pacific. The White House was itself partly to blame for the rift. On February 22 Roosevelt decided to make amends by ordering MacArthur to Australia. The Australian prime minister, John Curtin, had recently said that Australia was looking to America for help. Sending MacArthur was an implied promise that Australia would not find itself looking in vain.[69]

Next day Marshall informed MacArthur that "the President directs you to proceed to Mindanao . . . as quickly as possible. . . . From Mindanao you will proceed to Australia where you will assume command of all United States troops." This message was taken to him at his little gray house and as he read it the color drained from his face. He walked around like a man numbed or crazed. He seemed to age years in the space of a few minutes. The order to leave hit him like news of the death of a loved one.[70]

His mind in turmoil, he sat on the porch with Jean for a long time, agonizing aloud. "I am American-Army born and bred and accustomed by a lifetime of discipline to the obedience of superior orders. But this order I must disobey," he told her, and wept.[71]

That evening he composed a reply to the President, explaining why he could not leave the Philippines. He showed it to his staff, expecting them to agree with him, but to a man they vehemently disagreed. He had to obey a direct order. More to the point, he had to save himself and continue to fight against Japan. The argument ran on far into the night. If you don't obey, some of his staff argued, you will probably be court-martialed. If court-martialed, you will almost certainly be convicted. And if you are convicted, your entire career will end in disgrace, achieving . . . what? In the end he was persuaded. But that made the pill no less bitter to swallow. Next morning he cabled Marshall asking permission to make his own decisions as to when and how he departed. Permission granted.

The line on Bataan continued to hold. The Japanese campaign on the peninsula was poorly conducted, and in early March rumors floated from Manila to Corregidor that Homma, rather than face the humiliation of being relieved, had committed hara-kiri. MacArthur commented, "I suppose he messed up my bathroom."[72]

Although Bataan was holding out, the shortage of food meant it would surely fall sometime in April. MacArthur had to be out of the Philippines in good time before then, but he had no intention of leaving Corregidor on a submarine. He had a lifelong aversion to enclosed spaces. He would rather risk his life on the open sea than be cooped up in the claustrophobic environs of a submarine for a week or more. The decision was made to leave by PT boat the night of March 11, when there was just a little moonlight.

The only question was whether Jean thought that she and Arthur could stand a long, uncomfortable and perilous trip on a PT boat. MacArthur had Lieutenant John Bulkeley take her for a short ride around Corregidor one afternoon. Jean returned to Malinta to tell MacArthur that she had no objections to making a run for it by PT boat. That night MacArthur took Bulkeley for a short stroll, and when he was satisfied that no one could overhear them, he told Bulkeley to plan for an evacuation run soon, but in the strictest secrecy. "I have been peremptorily ordered to leave by the President," MacArthur told the naval lieutenant, not hiding his dismay. His own preference, he said, was to go to Bataan and die there, fighting the Japanese, but that was being denied him.[73]

As the time to leave drew near, he was plunged into turmoil all over again. He paced the floor of his house for hours each night. Jean would get up sometimes and try to comfort him, but the moment she went back to bed he started pacing again.[74]

The evening of March 9 he sent for Wainwright, who arrived next morning. They sat on the porch, and he explained to Wainwright that he was leaving "pursuant to repeated orders from the President," which was an exaggeration. "Things have gotten to such a point that I must comply or get out of the Army. I want you to make it known to all elements of your command that I am leaving over my repeated protests."

"Of course I will, Douglas," said Wainwright.

MacArthur explained that he would continue to command the Philippines but would do so from Australia. The archipelago would be split into four regions, and Wainwright would have command of the most important of the four, Luzon; in effect, he was now responsible for Bataan and Corregidor.

"If I get through, you know I'll come back as soon as I can with as much as I can," said MacArthur.

"You'll get through," Wainwright replied.

"And back."

They talked for a while about defense in depth and the employment of artillery. Then MacArthur went into the house and returned with a box of Tabacalera cigars and two jars of shaving cream, as a parting gift.[75]

There was a risk that news of MacArthur's departure would bring a collapse on Bataan. Hunger was already undermining morale. So too was MacArthur's failure to return to the front, to visit the sick and wounded as Wainwright did, to share, however briefly, the dangers and horrors of the battle.

MacArthur was, for all his awesome physical courage, frightened of hospitals. He avoided them in peace as in war. Why, though, did he not at least visit the troops who were still fighting on Bataan after January 10? Because of his proclamation of January 15 that boldly began, "Help is on the way. . . ." Having promised help, he could not face these men who had counted on it, had believed in him and were now bleeding, suffering, facing captivity, possibly torture and death.

And while he had repeatedly and bitterly criticized the Navy, had laughed heartily when Tokyo Rose accused Hart of running away and hiding in the jungles of Java, the Navy had taken its revenge with a piece of doggerel called "Dugout Doug" that became an instant classic among war poetry. There was probably hardly an American on Bataan who could not recite several verses of "Dugout Doug." The fact that "Dugout Doug" ridiculed MacArthur's physical courage and was therefore absurd did not make it any less painful. It cut like a knife. And suppose he visited the troops on Bataan now, what would he tell them: that help was *not* on the way?

His punishment for not returning to Bataan was that the gibes about "Dugout Doug" stuck for the rest of his life. He was never able to shake them off.

The evening of March 11 Bulkeley's PT boat drew up at Corregidor's north dock. MacArthur, Jean, Arthur, Ah Cheu, Sutherland, Marshall, Huff, Casey, Hal George, Willoughby, half a dozen other staff officers and the clerk, Sergeant Rogers, would depart on four PT boats for Mindanao. From there B-17s would fly them on to Australia.

As night fell, MacArthur's battered Chrysler pulled up outside the small gray house, and MacArthur, who was waiting on the porch, called to his wife, "Well, Jeannie, it's time to mount up."[76]

I Shall Return

The senior headquarters officers who were being left behind gathered at the dock to bid MacArthur goodbye. By implication, the men he did not take with him were people he judged to have performed unimpressively since December 8. They included the two officers with principal responsibility for stocking Bataan with supplies, Brigadier Generals Charles Drake and Lewis Beebe. They also included MacArthur's G-3, or chief of operations, Colonel Constant Irwin. After a brief but emotion-charged farewell, MacArthur walked across the dock to board Bulkeley's boat, PT-41. As he did so, he passed two soldiers in the darkness and overheard one say to the other, "What's his chance, Sarge, of getting through?"

"Dunno," grunted the sergeant. "He's lucky. Maybe one in five."[1]

MacArthur, Jean, Arthur and Ah Cheu boarded the boat, followed by Sutherland, Huff and an Army doctor, Major Charles H. Morhouse. The four PT boats undertaking the evacuation would set out in single file, but traveling without lights and in radio silence, they were bound to become dispersed. They were to rendezvous at Cuyo Island, an uninhabited rocky outcropping nearly two hundred miles south of Manila, around midday on March 12. A submarine was also heading for Cuyo Island to provide an alternative means of evacuation in case of problems with the PT boats or simply in case the general changed his mind.

As PT-41 pulled away from the dock, MacArthur stood on the deck and, looking toward Bataan, felt a surge of emotion—pride, sorrow, regret, remorse. He lifted his cap in a final salute to the men fighting there, men who did not yet know he was leaving, men who, he could be certain, would blame him for abandoning them, damn him for promising help that never came, curse him as they were marched into captivity and despise him even as they died. The blood drained from his head, and a convulsive twitch of agony tore at his face.[2]

He joined Jean on a mattress placed on the floor of the lower cockpit. He slumped in the darkness, a gaunt footnote to his former self: His uniform was grimy and wrinkled; he had lost twenty-five pounds; his clothes hung from his slender frame; his eyes were bloodshot from lack of sleep. MacArthur looked and felt like a grizzled, worn-out old man. Only his gold-braided field marshal's cap shone with a bold air of martial confidence amid the ashes of defeat.

The four PT boats carefully negotiated the minefields around Corregidor. Sailors leaned over the sides with long poles to push away Japanese floating mines that came within reach. Once free of the minefields, the boats moved into a diamond formation, then surged forward, straining for maximum speed. Racing southward at better than thirty knots, they were soon enveloped in huge clouds of salt spray.

During the night the four boats became separated, and shortly before dawn PT-32, carrying Brigadier General Hugh Casey and other members of the staff, spotted what the PT boat skipper thought was a Japanese destroyer coming toward them. The skipper cut loose the dozen fifty-gallon fuel drums stacked on deck and prepared to make a torpedo attack. At the last moment he recognized the "destroyer" as Bulkeley's boat. When the two boats drew alongside, MacArthur told Casey to come aboard PT-41 and share the rest of the journey with him.

Three boats made the rendezvous at Cuyo Island that afternoon. The fourth, PT-34, was assumed to have been lost, a victim of the sea or the Japanese. While the occupants of the three surviving boats tried to rest, MacArthur agonized over what to do next. The exhausting night and the loss of a PT boat carrying several members of his staff seemed to have robbed him of his decisiveness. Should he remain where he was and wait to be rescued by the submarine that had been ordered to Cuyo Island? he wondered. Or should he press on? Admiral Francis W. Rockwell, the commander of the Manila naval district, pointed out that there was no assurance that the submarine would run the blockade. "We'd better get the hell out of here fast," said Rockwell. Besides, Rockwell reassured him, the weather was going to improve and the sea would be calmer from here on. Bulkeley flatly disagreed: The weather would deteriorate and the seas would become rougher. MacArthur decided to take Rockwell's advice.[3]

The admiral assumed direct command of the remainder of the operation. Since PT-32 had jettisoned its spare fuel prior to the attack it had nearly made on PT-41 and now lacked sufficient gasoline to reach Mindanao, it was abandoned. The journey would continue with just two overcrowded boats, PT-35, carrying Rockwell, and PT-41, carrying MacArthur.

Bulkeley's forecast of worse weather and rougher seas proved only too accurate. As the little craft battled fifteen-foot waves, both MacArthur and Jean became violently seasick, but there was no turning back now.[4]

At sunset the silhouette of a Japanese cruiser appeared on the horizon, six miles distant and heading north. The torpedo boats turned hard right, putting themselves west of the cruiser and becoming virtually invisible with the brilliant disk of the setting sun behind them. MacArthur, stretched out on the mattress, said nothing during the thirty minutes the crisis lasted. Jean bent over him, rubbing his hands, trying to improve his circulation. Eventually the cruiser vanished in the fast-gathering darkness. The boats picked up speed once more.[5]

As the hours passed, many of the occupants of PT-41 fell into an uneasy sleep. Sid Huff, sitting on the steps above the lower cockpit, was dozing despite his cramped, uncomfortable position when MacArthur woke him.

"I can't sleep."

"Sorry, sir," replied Huff dutifully as if the general's slumber were part of his responsibilities.

"I want to talk."

"Yes, sir. What about?"

"Oh, anything. I just want to talk."

What followed was a strange, rambling, disjointed reminiscence as MacArthur struggled to assuage the guilt that tormented him about leaving Corregidor and abandoning Bataan. For nearly twenty years, ever since Leonard Wood had first persuaded him the islands could be held, he had fought the Navy, the General Staff, Quezon, two presidents and the empire of Japan to prove his point. And this was the result. He reflected bitterly on his long and futile struggle. Never enough money, never enough support, no understanding, nothing but obstacles put in his way, nothing but efforts to undermine him. As he told the tale, it had all the high drama of Wagnerian opera, the heart-wrenching pathos of Greek tragedy. He nearly broke down when he talked about being ordered to leave Corregidor. As he drew to a close, MacArthur became defiant. He would return to the Philippines, he told Huff. Jaw set like rock and a determined look on his face, he shouted into Huff's ear, over the noise of the engines, that he would liberate the islands one day.[6]

A few hours later dawn broke, and with the sunrise the mountainous northern shore of Mindanao loomed into view. The two torpedo boats chugged up to the dock at the small port of Cagayan de Oro at 7:00 A.M. PT-34, the boat that had missed the rendezvous at Cuyo Island, arrived an hour later. Everyone who had set off from Corregidor had made the perilous five-hundred-mile journey to Mindanao safely.

MacArthur donned his sodden field marshal's cap before stepping ashore. The Army commander on Mindanao, Brigadier General William F. Sharp, was waiting at the dock with an honor guard. Before leaving PT-41, MacArthur thanked Bulkeley profusely. "Commander, you've taken me out of the jaws of death and I won't forget it." He then told Bulkeley, "You'll take your orders from General Sharp here and conduct a defensive warfare against the empire of Japan in all the waters north of Mindanao."[7]

Stepping onto the dock, MacArthur inspected the honor guard. Before leaving Cagayan, he said farewell to the sailors. He congratulated them on the evacuation and awarded everyone, from Rockwell down to the most junior seaman, a coxswain, the Silver Star.[8]

MacArthur and the rest of his party boarded half a dozen automobiles for the five-mile drive to the Del Monte plantation and its crude airfield. Sharp had lined the route with thousands of Filipino soldiers. MacArthur was welcomed to Mindanao not like a refugee but like a conqueror.

He had nothing in his possession but the clothes he stood up in and his pipe. His suitcase been lost overboard. Not only was MacArthur reduced to the clothes he wore, but his favorite fashion statement was in jeopardy. The gold-braided field marshal's hat was shrinking as it dried out, steaming in the bright sunshine and hundred-degree heat. He continued to wear it nearly every day for the next decade, even though following its dunking it was at least half a size too small and rose an inch above his ears no matter how fiercely he jammed it onto his head.

MacArthur was informed that Quezon was in hiding on the nearby island of Negros, where he still hoped to establish a seat of government. MacArthur was appalled. It was only a matter of time before the Japanese tracked him down. He sent a message to Quezon, urging him to come to Mindanao. Quezon declined to budge. MacArthur sent a second message, telling him, "The United States is moving its forces into the southern Pacific area in what is destined to be a great offensive against Japan. The troops are being concentrated in Australia. . . . I understand the forces are rapidly being accumulated and hope that the drive can be undertaken before the Bataan-Corregidor situation reaches a climax . . . by the time you receive this note, I will have flown to Australia. I want you and your family to join me there." He entrusted this message to Bulkeley and told him not to take "No" for an answer. "I don't care how you do it," said MacArthur, "just do it!" Bulkeley did as ordered and more or less kidnapped Quezon several days later.[9]

MacArthur expected a flight of four B-17s to be waiting for him at Del Monte. When he drove up to the airfield and got out of his car, he looked up and down the runway. Puffing on a cigarette in an amber holder, MacArthur took the walnut cane he was carrying under his left arm and pushed the field marshal's cap up another inch in bewilderment. Where were the four Flying Fortresses?[10] The only bomber he could see was a beat-up, oil-spattered, war-weary machine flown in a few hours earlier by Captain Harl Pease, Jr.

Four planes *had* set out from Melbourne, but two had aborted shortly after takeoff. Another had crashed into the waters off Mindanao while on the approach to Del Monte. Pease's plane had malfunctioning brakes, and the turbo superchargers that it needed for maximum speed at high altitude had stopped working.

MacArthur was outraged, yet the four planes dispatched were, in fact, the best that Lieutenant General George Brett, the senior American officer in Australia, had to offer. Dozens of B-17s had been sent down under in the past three months, but virtually no spare parts had been shipped, there were few skilled aviation mechanics available and there was not a single repair depot in the whole of Australia able to change bomber engines. Most of the B-17s sent to the antipodes were soon unflyable. Pease's plane would have been considered unflyable in anything but an emergency.[11]

That did nothing to moderate MacArthur's indignation. He was appalled not only by the state of the plane but by Pease's evident youthfulness. He seemed not to realize that at this time only the most experienced and talented pilots in the AAF got to fly a B-17. Pease was a brilliant and courageous flier who would win the Medal of Honor just six months after MacArthur scorned him as "an inexperienced boy."

MacArthur sent a furious cable to Brett, complaining that "only one of the four planes despatched here had arrived; and that with an inexperienced pilot. . . ." He demanded, "Properly functioning B-17s must be obtained from Hawaii or the United States if they are not otherwise available." He sent a similar message to Marshall, and his anxiety for the fate of his wife and child was obvious. He insisted on the "three best planes in the United States or Hawaii. . . . To attempt such a desperate and important trip with inadequate equipment would amount to consigning the whole party to death and I could not accept such a responsibility." Soldiers and airmen routinely made perilous trips in wartime with an abundance of inadequate equipment and without a murmur of complaint. This was an embarrassing, almost hysterical communication to transmit through official channels.[12]

While awaiting a reply, MacArthur talked with Sharp and his staff and gave them instructions on what they should do if Bataan and Corregidor fell to the Japanese. They were to organize a guerrilla war on Mindanao and fight on until relief arrived.

The waiting period was enlivened by the sudden appearance of Captain Henry C. Godman, the pilot of the B-17 that had crashed off Mindanao. Godman and most of his crew had managed to swim ashore. Ushered into MacArthur's presence, the bedraggled Godman pleaded with him for a return trip to Australia. "I would like to go out with you," said Godman. "I would like to work for you."

MacArthur drew on the pipe he was smoking, thought for a moment and made a decision. "Godman, anybody as lucky as you—who can crash at night into the sea at 170 miles an hour and live to tell about it—can work for me."[13]

MacArthur's plea for more planes brought results. Four B-17s had been assigned to the admiral commanding American naval forces in Australia. Brett had requested these planes earlier, but the admiral had refused to release them. Following MacArthur's desperate plea, the admiral relented. Three were dispatched to Mindanao to collect MacArthur.

The night of March 16 he and Jean sat on her suitcase in the darkness not far from the Del Monte runway, listening for the sound of bomber engines. Suddenly MacArthur said, "I hear them!" Moments later two flares fizzed alive and spit vermilion at each end of the strip. There were only two B-17s coming in to land; the third had turned back shortly after takeoff.[14]

Landing a B-17 at Del Monte in daylight was a white-knuckle flying experience even for the best pilots. Mountains and hills surrounded it on three sides, and the sea was at the end of the runway. Putting a heavy bomber down at night, guided only by a couple of flares, took superb flying ability. MacArthur, however, was indignantly unimpressed. The planes, he complained later, were "tied together with chewing gum and baling wire."[15] Probably nothing short of a pristine civilian airliner would have satisfied him where his wife and child were concerned, but he evidently realized that he was not going to get anything else, let alone anything better. At midnight MacArthur, his wife, his son and his staff crammed themselves into the two Fortresses. Space was at such a premium Jean had to leave her suitcase behind. She was reduced to what she could push into her handbag—a lipstick, a comb, a handkerchief, a small purse and a fistful of medals.

A mattress was placed on the fuselage floor beneath the waist guns of MacArthur's plane for the benefit of Jean, Ah Cheu and Arthur. A small chair was wedged into the radio operator's compartment for the general. MacArthur sat next to the radio operator, chatting to Godman, who crouched on the floor at his feet. As the planes took wing, so did a rumor that MacArthur had left the Philippines carrying a mattress stuffed with gold coins.[16]

The flight to Australia took ten hours. Shortly after sunrise, just as the B-17s prepared to land at Darwin, Japanese fighters flying out of East Timor arrived to attack shipping in the harbor. The Fortresses flew on, to land at Batchelor Field, forty miles south of the port. As his plane settled onto the runway, MacArthur remarked to Sutherland, "It was close, but that's the way it is in war. You win or lose, live or die—and the difference is just an eyelash."[17]

MacArthur had the crews of both B-17s line up under the wing of his plane. Then he went from man to man, shook hands with each and awarded every one the Silver Star. Jean followed behind him, warmly expressing her profound gratitude for what they had done. The young pilot who had flown her to safety seemed to her to have aged a decade overnight.[18]

MacArthur arrived in Australia with his mind on the powerful army that Marshall's cables had suggested was assembling there. In a single message back in January Marshall had referred to deployments that added up to more than forty thousand troops. Encouraging messages had spoken of "every available vessel" heading for the Southwest Pacific. He had confidently assured Sharp's staff back on Mindanao, "I'm going to get help for you."[19]

He inspected a small, somewhat ragged honor guard composed of a platoon of American soldiers from the 102d Anti-Aircraft Artillery Battalion. However unprepossessing they appeared, they were a tangible sign of America's commitment to the defense of Australia. The inspection concluded, he asked an American officer where the American Army in Australia was based. "So far as I know, sir, there are very few troops here," the officer replied.

MacArthur could not believe it. He turned to Sutherland. "Surely he is wrong."[20]

There was a small knot of reporters demanding a statement from MacArthur, so he gave them one. "The President of the United States ordered me to break through the Japanese lines and proceed from Corregidor to Australia for the purpose, as I understand it, of organizing the American offensive against Japan, a primary objective of which is the relief of the Philippines. I came through and I shall return."[21]

Batchelor Field was about as basic as could be—a crude strip, a small stock of gas that had to be hand-pumped into the planes, a sorry-looking collection of tents for shelter, in the middle of what Australians called "mile after fucking mile of fuck all." The refreshments offered the MacArthurs were strong tea and canned prunes. While they were sampling this repast, Jean said she would not fly any farther, and MacArthur, who had never liked flying, demanded a train.

He was told there was no train. Besides, the radio intercept station at Darwin had just picked up a formation of Japanese fighters heading for

Batchelor Field. MacArthur, Jean, Arthur, Sid Huff and Ah Cheu scrambled aboard a fueled-up B-17 that was on the runway and ready to go. Ten minutes after MacArthur had departed, the Japanese arrived and strafed the airfield. The rest of the MacArthur party left next day aboard a C-47 that had survived unscathed.[22]

MacArthur flew on to Alice Springs, a small town in the middle of nowhere. Patrick J. Hurley had just flown in to greet them. Hurley tried to turn their reunion into a celebration. "Mac, the American people have always had a hero," he said. "In our lifetime there have been Dewey, Pershing—whether you like it or not—and then Lindbergh. Now they have taken you to their hearts. You are the hero." MacArthur, however, was not interested for once in his status as a hero. What he wanted to know was where was the army being concentrated for the relief of Bataan? Hurley hadn't a clue.[23]

The only thing he had to offer was the use of his plane, but Arthur had been airsick on the flight from Mindanao and again on the flight from Batchelor Field. Jean refused to fly another mile. Most of the staff boarded Hurley's plane, but a narrow-gauge train was dispatched from Adelaide for MacArthur. He, Jean, Arthur, Sutherland, Huff, Diller and Major Morhouse wearily boarded it on March 18. It consisted of an engine, a passenger car and two freight cars. The passenger car had nothing but a half dozen hard wooden benches to sit on. One of the freight wagons provided a Spartan simulacrum of a dining car.[24]

As the little train slowly clanked and rocked its way toward Adelaide, on the south coast, MacArthur fell asleep, his head resting on Jean's shoulder, and did not move for four hours. Jean contentedly whispered to Sid Huff, who was sitting across from her, "This is the first time he's really slept since Pearl Harbor."[25]

In Adelaide a bigger, more comfortable train was waiting to take them on to Melbourne, with a private car for the MacArthurs. Richard Marshall, who had traveled on Hurley's plane, was also waiting, bearing bad tidings. The officer at Batchelor Field had been right, after all: There were only twenty-five thousand American troops in Australia. Most were airmen or engineers. Not one was an rifleman. There were no tanks, no artillery and only a handful of poorly maintained combat aircraft. Bataan and Corregidor were doomed. Nothing could save them now. MacArthur was dumbfounded. The color drained from his face. His knees shook. His lips twitched. For a long time he was unable to speak. When he finally regained control of his body and his emotions, all he could do was whisper hoarsely, "God have mercy on us!" He spent several tormented hours pacing the corridor of the train, in utter distress, while Jean tried to calm him down and get him to rest.

Later, looking back on Marshall's news at Adelaide, he remarked, "It was the greatest shock and surprise of the whole damn war."[26]

In mid-March 1942 Australia was a nation rife with alarms and suffused with dread. To many Australians it was obvious that unless something was done soon, their country would be invaded by the onrushing—and seemingly unstoppable—Japanese. Yet there seemed little Australia could do to save itself. There were four excellent Australian divisions in North Africa, but it would take time to bring them home. The best Royal Australian Air Force units were also in the Middle East and most of the combat strength of the Royal Australian Navy was in the Mediterranean. What Australians needed at this hour was a sign that the Allies, despite the strategy of Germany First, would not allow their country to be conquered. MacArthur's arrival in Melbourne on March 21, 1942, flared like a promise written in flame across the azure antipodean sky.

When his train pulled into Spencer Street Station, some 5,000 people had gathered to cheer him. An honor guard of 360 Army engineers was drawn up on the platform. The Australian Army minister, Francis M. Forde, greeted him warmly, and 60 reporters pressed forward, scribbling.

MacArthur looked relaxed and confident. He had recovered from the arduous journey by PT boat and airplane. He was freshly shaven, immaculate once more in a faded bush jacket and well-pressed pants (incongruously shod, though, in black-and-white-checked socks and tan wing tips).[27]

He read out a brief message he had written on the train, in which he praised Australian soldiers and recalled the impression they had made on him in World War I. Then MacArthur made a plea clearly intended to echo all the way back to Washington: "I have every confidence in the ultimate success of our joint cause, but success in modern war requires something more than courage and a willingness to die: it requires careful preparation. That means the furnishing of sufficient troops and sufficient material to meet the known strength of the enemy. No general can make something out of nothing. My success or failure will depend primarily on the resources which the respective governments place at my disposal. . . ."[28]

The presence of MacArthur in Australia transformed the mood of the country. The American minister to Australia, Nelson Trusler Johnson, was astonished at the rapidity and depth of the change. "It was a stroke of genius [sending] MacArthur here . . . just the thing that was needed to boost a flagging morale. . . ."[29]

While Jean shopped for clothing, MacArthur plunged into consultations with Australian politicians and generals, but he too found time to make a purchase. He ordered a new watch for Jean, as a tribute to her uncomplaining courage on the perilous ten-day, three-thousand-mile journey from Corregidor to Melbourne. On the back he had it inscribed, "To my Bravest. Bataan—Corregidor, March 1942. MacArthur."[30]

On March 26 Godman flew him on a former KLM airliner, a DC-3, to Canberra to meet Prime Minister John Curtin and the Advisory War Council. MacArthur and Curtin had a short session alone, at which they evidently came to some kind of understanding and the basis of an enduring friendship was laid. When they emerged, MacArthur put an arm around Curtin's shoulder and told him, "You take care of the rear and I will handle the front."[31]

MacArthur told the Advisory War Council he doubted that the Japanese had the strength to mount an invasion of northern Australia. "The spoils are not sufficient to warrant the risk." The most he expected was a Japanese attempt to seize air bases in New Guinea within range of Australia. He told them frankly that he disagreed with the strategy of Germany First. The most important Allied objective now, he said, "is to make Australia secure."[32]

That evening Curtin hosted a glittering official banquet in MacArthur's honor. Ambassador Johnson electrified the gathering by reading out a message from President Roosevelt: MacArthur had been awarded the Medal of Honor.

The move to give MacArthur the medal had been started back in January by George Marshall. His intention originally was to provide a morale booster for the American people, to whom MacArthur had become one of the greatest heroes in the nation's history. Streets, babies, schools, were being named for him. Congress acclaimed him. MacArthur clubs sprang up across the United States to promote the prosecution of the war and demand support for MacArthur. At a time when Americans were still reeling from the devastating attack on Pearl Harbor there was a magic to MacArthur's name too potent to ignore. When the award was eventually made nearly two months later, however, it was done mainly to counter Axis propaganda, which derided him as a coward who had deserted his men under fire.

The citation, which was written by Marshall on the basis of information provided by Sutherland, commended MacArthur "for gallantry and intrepidity above and beyond the call of duty in action against invading Japanese forces," praised his creation of the Philippine Army, lauded his inspiring leadership and noted his "utter disregard of personal danger under heavy fire and aerial bombardment. . . ."[33]

Profoundly moved, MacArthur rose and thanked the Australians warmly for the way they had welcomed him—"I already feel at home." He went on to tell them, in a voice thick with emotion, "There can be no compromise. We shall win or we shall die, and to this end I pledge the full resources of all the power of my mighty country and all the blood of my countrymen." It was not a pledge he had any authority to make, but Australians fell on it like manna from heaven. Here was the explicit, unequivocal reassurance they desperately craved.[34]

This triumphal day ended on a strangely anticlimactic note. Godman flew MacArthur back to Melbourne and decided to test the general's nerve. On the approach to Melbourne Airport he pushed the stick over, and the DC-3 screamed toward the runway like a fighter swooping down from eight thousand feet on a strafing run. MacArthur's nerve held up, but he got off the plane with a nosebleed, while Godman, still in the cockpit, was being upbraided by Colonel Morhouse, MacArthur's doctor, for being so stupid and was warned to fly the general gently in the future.[35]

Despite fierce resistance from the British government, two Australian divisions were already preparing to leave the Middle East. Churchill pleaded with Roosevelt to send American divisions to Australia so that the British Army would not lose the services of all its fine, battle-hardened Australian units. Roosevelt responded to Churchill's plea, and two American divisions—the 32d and the 41st—were ordered to deploy to Australia. The need to defend that island continent was so pressing, in fact, that by May 1942 there were nearly a hundred thousand American troops in or on their way to the Southwest Pacific, more than twice the number deploying to Western Europe that spring.

The commander of the Australian ground forces in the Middle East, General Thomas Blamey, was recalled and arrived home on March 23. He was appointed commander in chief of the Australian Army three days later, the day MacArthur met the War Council. Blamey had run up a distinguished record on the Western Front in World War I. Between wars he had served as police commissioner of Melbourne. Short, fat, jovial and perennially rumpled, Blamey had a reputation for getting drunk at parties and knocking people's hats off when inebriated. He was not a soldier MacArthur was likely to respect. Moreover, Blamey's long spell away from active duty made him an amateur in the eyes of many American generals. It would not be surprising if MacArthur shared that sentiment.[36]

Once MacArthur had reached Australia, Roosevelt urged Curtin to appoint him supreme commander of all Allied forces in the Southwest Pacific. Curtin readily agreed in principle. It took several weeks, though, for Marshall, King and the Australian government to agree on how MacArthur's theater would fit in the Navy's Pacific.[37] The Navy saw the entire Pacific as its natural domain and only grudgingly agreed to the creation of a theater for MacArthur. The Navy got a huge area stretching from Alaska to the Antarctic known as Pacific Ocean Areas, divided into three theaters—North Pacific, Central Pacific and South Pacific—all of which came under command of Admiral Chester Nimitz. MacArthur was left with the Southwest Pacific Area, or SWPA. He became supreme commander of SWPA on April 17.

Within MacArthur's theater Blamey would serve as commander of Allied Land Forces. Brett, a former commander of GHQ Air Force, became commander of Allied Air Forces. And Vice Admiral Herbert F. Leary of the U.S. Navy assumed command of Allied Naval Forces.

Marshall suggested to MacArthur that he should create a truly Allied headquarters, incorporating Australian and Dutch officers in senior positions. MacArthur ignored Marshall's advice. When he activated General Headquarters, SWPA on April 18, all eleven senior assignments went to American officers, eight of them people he had brought with him from Corregidor.

The strategy he proposed to pursue was, for the time being, entirely defensive. He lacked the forces to do anything else. MacArthur later claimed, however, that he had arrived in Australia only to find the country in the grip of defeatism so strong that its government was preparing to abandon everything north and west of Brisbane, which would be like the U.S. government's deciding not to fight for anything north or west of the Deep South because of a threatened invasion from Canada. Rejecting this cowering posture, he had insisted on taking the war to the enemy, thrown out the Brisbane Line plan and begun making moves to defend Australia by fighting in New Guinea.[38]

There is not a word of truth in MacArthur's claim. He had completely misunderstood what the Australians had told him, but that is not surprising. At this point there was a world of incomprehension between American and Australian officers. There was no plan to abandon northeastern Australia without a fight. There *was* a plan to assume the defensive if the Japanese attacked and to yield some territory if necessary while the inflow of American and Australian manpower built up resources to a point where offensive operations became possible. MacArthur accepted these arrangements without demur but forgot to mention that in his memoirs.[39]

Besides, the truly pressing military concern his first six weeks in Australia was not the Brisbane Line. It was the grim and bloody endgame being played out on Bataan and Corregidor.

Skinny Wainwright was one of the best-loved men in the Army. He was brave, colorful, beloved by his troops and fun to be with. The cavalry that he adorned was the most high-spirited branch of the military, although much of that spirit was provided by Jim Beam and Four Roses. Drunkenness was one of the occupational hazards of cavalry life, like falling off a horse or being kicked in the head. Not surprisingly, therefore, MacArthur had his doubts about leaving Wainwright in command in the Philippines. There was a question mark over Skinny's judgment in a crisis, as there is over any alcoholic's. Before leaving Corregidor, MacArthur had promoted Lewis Beebe to brigadier general and left him behind as a deputy chief of staff through whom he could keep a tight rein on operations, and Wainwright was ordered to report directly to MacArthur, not to the War Department.

The other step MacArthur took was to divide the Philippines into four subcommands, with Wainwright responsible only for Luzon. When the inevitable end came on Corregidor, Wainwright would be able to surrender only his own troops, not those elsewhere.

For some reason, MacArthur did not explain these arrangements to the War Department before leaving Corregidor. It was the kind of oversight that casts doubt not only on his administrative efficiency but on the endless claims that even if Sutherland was an unpleasant son of a bitch, he was at the very least one hell of a chief of staff.

Shortly after MacArthur left, Wainwright started receiving communications from the War Department addressed to him as "Commanding General, USAFFE," and as seemed natural under the circumstances, he began reporting back directly to Marshall. The War Department decided to create a new headquarters for Wainwright, called U.S. Forces in the Philippines (USFIP), and Roosevelt made him a lieutenant general, in keeping with his new status. Wainwright would report directly to the War Department. He thereupon wasted no time making Beebe his own chief of staff, removing him, in effect, from MacArthur's control.[40]

When MacArthur discovered what was happening, he finally explained to Marshall the structure he had left behind, making clear his displeasure with the new arrangements. At that point Marshall got the President involved. Roosevelt told MacArthur in so many words that he considered it impossible to run a war on Luzon by radio from Australia. Wainwright could remain under MacArthur's command, but with a major headquarters of his own he would now have a large degree of autonomy on how he fought the campaign he had inherited.

However strongly MacArthur disagreed with this arrangement, he was not about to start squabbling with the President, not at a time when the question of what kind of assignment he would get, whether he would even have a theater of his own to command, was still being debated. He promptly caved in and replied that he was "heartily in accord with Wainwright's promotion" and accepted the extinction of USAFFE with good grace. Privately, however, he considered giving Wainwright command of all American troops in the Philippines a major blunder.[41]

After MacArthur returned to Melbourne from meeting Curtin and the War Council, he sent Wainwright a plan to resolve the supply crisis on Bataan. "You should attack straight north with the I Corps and reach Olongapo," he told Wainwright. "The II Corps should advance rapidly to Dinaluphihan and thence move quickly west on Olongapo, where you will join forces and be able to seize Japanese supplies." Resupplied, these troops might then head into the mountains of Luzon and begin to wage a guerrilla campaign against the invaders.[42]

As plans went, this one should have gone straight into the wastebasket. The troops on Bataan, down to less than a thousand calories a day, shivering from malaria and hardly able to stand from dysentery, could not have advanced a mile. Wainwright ignored this absurdity and sent a message to Marshall bluntly informing him that food supplies on Bataan would run out on April 15.

When MacArthur got a copy of this message, he was annoyed. He sent a cable to Marshall that was a slap in the face for Wainwright—"It is of course possible that with my departure the vigor of application of conservation may have been relaxed"—and insisted there was enough food to last until May 1.[43]

Wainwright came up with his own plan to get more food into Bataan. There were sizable stocks on the island of Cebu and ships were available in Mindanao. If the blockade could be broken even for a few days he might be able to bring supplies up from Cebu. He asked for a B-17 squadron to be sent from Australia to attack Japanese warships in the waters of the central and northern Philippines and punch a hole in the blockade. Alternatively, the bombers might fly food up to Bataan.[44]

On April 3 General Homma launched a new offensive, with fifty thousand well-rested and resupplied troops. MacArthur sent Wainwright a message telling him, "Under no conditions should this command be surrendered . . . you will prepare and execute an attack upon the enemy along the following general lines: an ostentatious artillery preparation upon the left of the I Corps as a feint and a sudden surprise attack on the right by the II Corps." The objective once again was a breakout leading to the capture of Japanese supplies, and even "If the movement is not successful and our forces defeated many increments thereof could escape through the Zambales mountains and continue guerrilla warfare. . . ."[45]

Homma expected to have to fight his way through three lines of defenses when there was really only one. Once that line was pierced on April 7, there was not much the defenders could do but die or surrender. Wainwright informed his commander on Bataan, Major General Edward P. King, Jr., of MacArthur's order to attack, but King had no intention of allowing his men to be annihilated in a pointless replay of Custer's Last

Stand. On April 9 he sent two officers toward the Japanese. One carried a white flag.

When the news that Bataan had fallen reached Melbourne, MacArthur canceled his appointments for the rest of the day. He paced his office for hours. Eventually the pacing stopped. Grim-faced and weeping, he sat at his desk and penned a last tribute. Then he summoned Diller and handed the statement to him. It read, "The Bataan force went out as it would have wished, fighting to the end in its flickering, forlorn hope. No army has ever done so much with so little, and nothing became it more than its last hour of trial and agony. To the weeping mothers of its dead, I can only say that the sacrifice and halo of Jesus of Nazareth has descended upon their sons and that God will take them unto Himself."[46]

Hardly had this statement been released before MacArthur received a message from Roosevelt modifying the no-surrender policy formulated in response to Quezon's neutralization proposal two months earlier. It was left for MacArthur to decide whether to forward Roosevelt's latest communication to Wainwright.

Wainwright's radio operators had picked up the signal as it coursed through the ether toward Australia. Next day MacArthur heard from Wainwright, who expressed puzzlement at MacArthur's failure to forward the President's message to Corregidor. MacArthur explained that Roosevelt's message "was not received here until after the fall of Bataan and was not forwarded as it referred entirely to the possibility of surrender on Bataan." He revealed his concern and frustration to Wainwright: "I cannot tell you how anxious I have been to bring you relief. My resources however are practically negligible. . . . I have not as yet been placed in command of the contemplated new area. . . . If I had any real forces at my disposal I think you know without my saying that no matter how desperate the chance of success I would move in an endeavor to reach you."[47]

Once Japanese heavy artillery was placed on the high ground of southern Bataan it would be able to pound the Rock into submission. It was a scene MacArthur could play like a mind movie. The only bright spot was the prospect that Malinta Tunnel, which was begun and nearly completed under MacArthur during his five years as Chief of Staff, might save thousands of lives.

With Corregidor likely to fall soon, MacArthur sent his two Navy PBYs up to the Rock to bring out key personnel, such Colonel Stewart Wood, a highly trained staff officer who was also fluent in Japanese, and the highly skilled cryptographers who handled secret communications. Wainwright put fifty people aboard the PBYs, more than half of them Army nurses.

Homma's artillery bombarded Corregidor for twenty-seven days and nights until, at midnight on May 5, he mounted his assault. The 4th Marine

Regiment virtually wiped out the first wave of Japanese, but the second wave got ashore with three light tanks. These puny vehicles had a shock value that made even well-disciplined troops fall back, and when Wainwright heard there were enemy tanks moving toward Malinta Tunnel, he was horrified. The prospect of high-explosive shells penetrating the tunnel, ricocheting off the walls and striking the thousand wounded men crammed into the laterals was more than he could bear. On May 6 he ordered the Stars and Stripes be pulled down and a white flag raised over Corregidor. Next day he surrendered the Rock and its eleven thousand defenders.

When the news reached Melbourne, MacArthur wrote out a statement for the press and sent for Carlos Romulo. "Corregidor has fallen!" said MacArthur in obvious anguish, handing the statement to Romulo. The press release read: "Corregidor needs no comment from me. It has sounded its own story at the mouth of its guns. It has scrolled its own epitaph in enemy tablets. But through the bloody haze of its last reverberating shot I shall always seem to see a vision of grim, gaunt, ghastly men, still unafraid."[48]

17

These Days of Stress

MacArthur on display was a reassuring sight. Hundreds of Australians gathered outside Melbourne's Menzies Hotel each day to catch a glimpse of him on his way to or from his headquarters. He strode purposefully, looking relaxed and confident as he flourished his cane. The general seemed every inch the larger-than-life figure they wanted him to be. Yet behind the stride and the cane was a man who was depressed and overwrought. He was sick at heart, and letters to old friends were filled with pessimistic observations: "If I survive the war . . ." and "If I live to return to the United States . . ."[1]

Bataan preyed on his mind and tore at his tautly stretched nerves. MacArthur spoke of it constantly to members of his staff, to Curtin, to Hurley, to almost everyone he met.[2] The telephone operators at GHQ answered the phone with a single word: "Bataan." He referred to his staff as the Bataan Gang, although most had never set foot there after the Japanese landed on Philippine soil. Bataan was both symbol of defeat and promise of return.

In the midst of these anxieties, MacArthur was shocked by the sudden, violent death of Brigadier General Hal George, the feisty fighter pilot he had come to admire in the Philippines. George was watching planes taking off from Darwin when an Australian pilot in a P-40 lost control, swerved off the runway and plowed into him. MacArthur was so upset he did something truly unusual for him: He attended a funeral. Every senior air commander in the Philippines but one—Hal George—had failed him. George's abilities, compared to the incompetence of Brereton, Brady and Clagett, made him seem truly outstanding. MacArthur had personally added George's name to the list of people to be brought out from Corregidor by PT boat.

He was so grief-stricken by Hal George's death he even wrote and delivered a funeral oration. "There is a favorite song among our veterans," he began, "that 'old soldiers never die, they just fade away.' But fate dealt otherwise with Harold George. . . . His was an irreparable loss. . . . A model for his young officers, the idol of his men, he had my unlimited professional confidence, my warmest personal admiration. He was indeed the greatest airman I ever knew."[3]

Besides grieving over Hal George, MacArthur was frustrated and angry. His own escape by sea stood, in his mind, as overwhelming proof of what he had argued for months: that the Japanese were so thinly stretched they could mount nothing but a "paper blockade" around the Philippines. Had the Navy been more resolute, it could have broken through.

Nor was his temper helped by the greatest American morale booster that spring, the attack on Tokyo on April 18, when a small force of B-25s launched from the carrier *Hornet* and led by Colonel Jimmy Doolittle, bombed the Japanese capital. MacArthur had urged two months earlier that aircraft carriers be sent within flying range of the Philippines and planes be flown off them to rebuild his air force. He had been told that was impossible. Yet here was proof to the contrary. So far as MacArthur was concerned, if it was possible to put B-25s over Tokyo, it was equally possible to fly reinforcements into the Philippines and for the Navy to break the Japanese blockade.[4]

When Theodore White came to interview him at GHQ that spring, MacArthur was in a bitter mood. He lashed out at Roosevelt, at Marshall, at the Navy and at White's employer, Henry Luce. All had in some way let him down and gotten him into his present dismal position, a general without troops, a theater commander starved of everything he needed, a man being drowned by a tsunami of history.[5]

Shortly after this Pat Casey brought a couple of his engineer officers to meet MacArthur, who sat the three men on the beat-up old chairs in his office and launched into a tirade, directed mainly at Roosevelt, pacing and ranting for an hour or more. He had appealed countless times . . . great opportunities were being lost . . . great dangers were being run . . . great mistakes were being made. He stopped abruptly, bade his visitors a courteous farewell and returned to his work. Outbursts like this were a form of therapy, but news of them was certain to find its way to Washington.[6]

While MacArthur contemplated the downside of destiny, the Japanese were still sweeping south. Imperial Headquarters in Tokyo was torn, though, on whether to invade Australia. The Japanese Navy wanted an invasion, but the Japanese Army did not. It was eventually decided to secure the whole of the Solomon Islands instead and to seize control of Papua New Guinea. By controlling the Solomons, they would pose a serious threat to the American sea lines of communications between Hawaii and Australia.

New Guinea, thirteen hundred miles long, thinly populated and poor in resources, underdeveloped and consisting almost entirely of mountains and jungle, was not worth taking. The problem was Papua, the eastern tail of this huge island. Allied bases in New Guinea would pose a threat to Japan's hold on the Philippines. Imperial Headquarters decided that if its forces could seize Papua's only sizable town, Port Moresby, and establish a handful of air bases in Papua, that would suffice to deny it to the Allies. In March the Japanese landed at Lae, on the northern coast of Papua, where they built an air base, and they captured the nearby port of Salamaua. Once the Lae airfield was in operation, they planned to capture Port Moresby, on the southern coast of Papua, in an amphibious assault around May 10.[7]

Toward the end of April 1942 U.S. Navy cryptographers informed GHQ they were monitoring a major buildup of Japanese naval forces. They assumed the likely target was northeastern Australia or Papua. The Navy hurriedly assembled a task force to intercept the oncoming Japanese.[8]

The Port Moresby invasion force steamed southeastward from the huge harbor at Rabaul, in the northern Solomons, heading for the Coral Sea, the body of water between Papua and northern Australia. On May 8 the Japanese fleet was intercepted by U.S. Naval Task Force 17. The aircraft carrier *Lexington* was sunk by Japanese planes, in a huge setback for the Navy. The Japanese lost one small aircraft carrier—and their nerve. With nothing to stop them now from sailing on to Port Moresby, the Japanese fleet turned around and headed back to Rabaul.[9]

MacArthur had no doubts, though, that the Japanese would try again. He told Blamey to expect another air and sea attack on Port Moresby "any time after June 10." He sent additional troops and air units to Port Moresby to improve its weak defenses. He also started planning to establish an air base at Milne Bay, which stands close to the most easterly point of Papua. From Milne Bay it might be possible to dominate the Coral Sea with land-based aircraft.[10]

During the days preceding the Battle of the Coral Sea, Marshall had expressed to MacArthur his displeasure that American newspapers seemed to have figured out a major battle was brewing in the Southwest Pacific and hinted strongly that he suspected a leak at GHQ. If the Japanese realized that the Allies had more information than could have been gained from reconnaissance, Marshall observed, "they would be justified in believing their codes had been broken."[11]

MacArthur vehemently denied that his headquarters had been responsible for the leak. The real problem, he insisted, was a porous Australian government undermined by an uncontrolled press. "It is utterly impossible for me under the authority I possess to impose total censorship in this foreign country," he responded waspishly. He wasted no time, though, in demanding such authority, and the Advisory War Council promptly granted it. From mid-May 1942 the principal source of frontline news in SWPA was MacArthur's General Headquarters. But while he was able to exert direct pressure on the Australian press, the news media in the United States remained, to his evident irritation, beyond his control.[12]

Equipped with sweeping powers over the media in his own theater of war, MacArthur chose to exercise them personally. Like his hero Napoleon, he not only issued a steady stream of communiqués (Napoleon had called his emanations bulletins) on the course of the fighting but wrote all of them himself. They presented one man's view of the war—and no one else's. The communiqué he penned announcing the outcome of the Battle of the Coral Sea established a worrying example. Japanese losses were heavily exaggerated, MacArthur virtually boasted that he was reading the Japanese Navy's mail—"we had ample warning"—and he could not resist publicly rebuking the U.S. Navy: "[A]n opportunity to inflict heavy losses was lost."[13]

Hardly had the smoke cleared from the Battle of the Coral Sea before Navy cryptanalysts in Hawaii scored one of the most stunning intelligence coups of the war. The Japanese attack on Pearl Harbor had been a strategic failure. The damage and destruction inflicted on eight battleships of the Pacific Fleet were poor compensation for the failure to sink a single carrier. That was an error that Admiral Yamamoto intended to put right by striking at Midway and the Aleutians in June. He would lure the Pacific Fleet into a trap and, using the large superiority he enjoyed in naval air striking power, destroy its carriers.

Forewarned, the Navy pushed three carriers into the coming battle and set a trap for the unwary and overly confident Japanese. To MacArthur's consternation, however, naval and air forces scheduled to go to SWPA were suddenly redirected to take part in the Battle of Midway.

In the huge naval engagement near Midway in early June the Japanese lost four carriers and hundreds of combat experienced pilots. The U.S. Navy lost the carrier *Yorktown* but regained the strategic initiative in the Pacific.[14]

MacArthur met with Curtin's Advisory War Council on June 17 and told its members that the threat of invasion had been lifted. "Australia was in grave danger up to the time of the Coral Sea . . . that action and the successes gained at Midway Island [have] assured the defensive position of

Australia," he said. "From the strategical point of view, we should take the initiative and not wait for results in other theaters. Our aim should be to strike at Japanese bases in islands to the north and throw the enemy bomber line back 700 miles." What he wanted now was an offensive to secure Papua and capture the large Japanese air and naval base at Rabaul before the Japanese could recover from these defeats.[15]

He already had his staff drawing up plans to take Rabaul and was begging Marshall for amphibious troops and assault shipping. Driven by a belief that he could achieve a victory on land to rival the Navy's triumph at Midway, he envisaged taking Rabaul in fourteen to eighteen days. Yet he had no idea how many troops the Japanese had there or how strong the defenses were. And seeing that he could not even keep the handful of Americans and Australians at Port Moresby adequately supplied, he clearly hadn't a clue as to the size and complexity of the logistical challenge of mounting a major amphibious assault against a vital stronghold five hundred miles away.[16]

King and Nimitz, however, had no intention of allowing MacArthur to mount an invasion of Rabaul, which was outside his theater. If there were to be an offensive in the Solomons, King informed Marshall, the Navy would undertake it. Naval cryptographers had recently intercepted a Japanese message that pinpointed where the next Japanese attack would come: against Guadalcanal, in the southern Solomons, roughly seven hundred miles east of Papua. They intended to build an air base there that would threaten America's sea lines of communication to Australia. King proposed to stop them by mounting his own assault on Guadalcanal. He made it clear to Marshall that if necessary, the Navy was prepared to conduct this operation on its own. If the Army had to be involved, it would be in a secondary role.

When MacArthur was informed of the Navy's plans, he was incandescent with rage. He sent a blistering cable to Marshall. "It is quite evident," he protested, "that the Navy contemplates assuming general command control of all operations in the Pacific theater, the role of the Army being subsidiary and consisting largely of placing its forces at the disposal and under command of Navy and Marine officers."[17]

Marshall managed to work out a compromise with King. MacArthur was informed on July 2 that operations against Rabaul would be broken into three phases, or tasks:

1. Task One. Seizure and occupation of the Santa Cruz Islands, Tulagi, and adjacent positions
2. Task Two. Seizure and occupation of the Solomon Islands, of Lae, Salamaua, and northeast coast of New Guinea

3. Task Three. Seizure and occupation of Rabaul and adjacent positions in the New Guinea-New Ireland area.[18]

The significance of the reference to Tulagi was that this was a tiny island several miles from Guadalcanal where the Japanese were establishing a seaplane base. The reference to "adjacent positions" meant Guadalcanal.

Four days after receiving this message, MacArthur attended a commander's conference at Blamey's headquarters. He told the group: "The task of all formations now is training for mobile offensive operations. Defensive preparations are of secondary importance. Valuable time is not to be wasted in digging and wiring. Physical fitness and intensive preparation for offensive action are our immediate objectives."[19]

MacArthur proposed to begin by seizing control of the northeast coast of New Guinea. There was an Australian government mission at a place called Buna. Near Buna Mission was a small airstrip that had been carved out for light planes. Could it be expanded to handle combat aircraft? If so, he intended to put ground and air units into Buna.

A recon team was sent to make a survey. It soon reported back that the Buna airstrip was not worth developing, but at Dobodura, ten miles to the south, there was an excellent airfield site. MacArthur planned accordingly to move into Buna around the middle of August and build an airfield at Dobodura, but he had another move to make first.

On July 20 GHQ was transferred from Melbourne to Brisbane, five hundred miles to the north. MacArthur installed himself in the city's finest hostelry, Lennon's Hotel. GHQ moved into an eight-story building that had formerly housed a large insurance company. In the midst of this move came news that a Japanese convoy was moving toward northern Papua. On the night of July 21 nearly two thousand Japanese troops landed at Buna. If MacArthur wanted it now, he would have to fight for it.[20]

MacArthur's greatest fear once the threat of an invasion of Australia was lifted was that SWPA would become the "forgotten front" of World War II. It was a dread he never managed to shake off. The Japanese would be satisfied with a prolonged stalemate in the Southwest Pacific, and given the strategy of Germany First they just might get it.

His demands for men, planes, ships, guns were melodramatic and emotional. When forces deploying to SWPA in May were abruptly redirected toward the Central Pacific to take part in the Battle of Midway, MacArthur sent a furious protest to Marshall. Australia, he insisted, was in imminent danger of invasion. Allied fleets in the Atlantic and Indian oceans should be "stripped," and their combat elements sent to SWPA without delay. "If this is not done, much more than the fate of Australia will be jeopardized.

The United States itself will face . . . a crisis of such proportions as she never faced in the long years of her existence."[21]

Marshall knew as well as he that there was no imminent invasion threat. In fact, he had recently justified the modest level of American forces in SWPA to the British on the ground that "there is no tangible evidence of a Japanese expedition being prepared against Australia . . . both the ground and air forces projected for Australia are sufficient for the operations now visualized for that area. . . ."[22]

The hyperbole of MacArthur's message verged on the hysterical. Even if there were an invasion of Australia, that could hardly be a greater crisis for the United States than, say, the Civil War or the Great Depression. Moreover, the Battle of the Atlantic was currently being won by the U-boats. To "strip" the Atlantic of warships at this time would be tantamount to conceding victory to Hitler.

Summer 1942 came and went without any attempt to invade Australia, but that did not stem the torrent of purple prose being transmitted from GHQ to the War Department. "I wish to invite attention to the acute danger which is rapidly developing in the Pacific theater. The situation has drastically changed," MacArthur informed Marshall on August 30. "The enemy . . . is moving the center of gravity of his forces in this general direction. . . ." Unless the strategy of Germany First was modified and forces in SWPA greatly augmented, MacArthur claimed, a military disaster was likely. He concluded, "I beg of you most earnestly to have this momentous question reviewed by the President and the chiefs of staff lest it become too late."[23]

Many an angry American general under intense pressure has been tempted to make a fool of himself by telegram but been saved by a level-headed chief of staff who talked him out of polluting the signal traffic with heat-of-the-moment nonsense. Ultimately such cables were bound to have only one result: They would undermine MacArthur's credibility with Marshall, Stimson and Roosevelt. Yet there is nothing to show that Sutherland ever tried to talk him out of sending such cables. On the contrary, Sutherland encouraged MacArthur's already deep suspicions of the War Department. Whenever Marshall turned down a request from GHQ, Sutherland responded by telling him it was the result of a two-man conspiracy to thwart him. "You see," Sutherland would say to MacArthur, "that goddamned Marshall and his boy, Eisenhower, they're just cutting your throat."[24]

MacArthur sought to press his pleas home by entrusting them to people leaving SWPA for Washington, such as John Bulkeley. The PT boat skipper had succeeded in the mission MacArthur gave him to get Quezon out of the Philippines. Once that mission had been accomplished, MacArthur ordered Bulkeley to head for Del Monte Field and catch a B-17 to Australia. He did not tell Bulkeley so, but he was recommending him for the Medal of Honor. When Admiral King learned of this, he was incensed. "No way is MacArthur going to dictate a Medal of Honor for one of my officers. *I* will make the recommendation for the Navy." And thus it was that Bulkeley was ordered home to receive the Medal of Honor from Roosevelt.[25]

MacArthur sent for Bulkeley before he left. He told the lieutenant commander not to write down anything of what he was about to say but to commit it all to memory. "When you get to Washington," MacArthur told him, "I want to you to stress to the President and the Secretary of War the crucial need to retake the Philippines at the earliest possible time." Then he told him exactly how to phrase the argument, the gist of which was that writing off Bataan on the altar of global strategy had been a body blow to the morale of the men fighting in the Pacific. He also wanted Bulkeley to tell the President that SWPA needed up to two hundred PT boats within the next eight months. Given enough PT boats, he could stop the Japanese from invading Australia. MacArthur wound up his peroration, "And Johnny, don't add or subtract anything!"[26]

When Bulkeley reached the White House, Roosevelt awarded him the Medal of Honor and whispered, "Come back tonight for a chat." Bulkeley did so and got the chance to make the pitch that MacArthur had primed him for.

On May 25 MacArthur had three unexpected visitors who had arrived the previous day from Washington. Two were colonels assigned to the Operations Division at the War Department: Samuel Anderson, an AAF officer with a brilliant four-star future ahead of him, and Francis Stevens, an able staff officer. The third was Congressman Lyndon B. Johnson. Anderson and Stevens had been sent out to SWPA as fact finders on behalf of George Marshall. Johnson was there as a Roosevelt protégé, on a mission to protect his political career. Commissioned a lieutenant commander in the naval reserve, Johnson needed at least one wartime "mission" if he was going to secure his political base back in Texas against ambitious returning war heroes a few years down the line.

MacArthur had the three visitors sit on chairs at one end of his spacious office. Then he paced for an hour behind his desk, pausing now and then to go and jab at a large map of the theater hung against one wall. He talked in his spellbinding way about the strategic challenges he faced, about the enemy's strengths and weaknesses, of the need for offensive action, the need to build up forces in SWPA and his theater's crucial role in the war. Although he did not say so explicitly, he was hoping that they, like Bulkeley, would take his message back to the War Department and the President.[27]

When Anderson and Stevens headed for Port Moresby to see conditions at the front, Johnson insisted he had to go along too. To his two traveling

companions, who were both professional soldiers, Johnson was an ignorant, vain and arrogant amateur and something of an embarrassment. After
several days traveling around the airfields near Port Moresby, Anderson
and Stevens, in keeping with their assigned tasks, were slated to accompany a mission flown by the 22d Bomb Group to attack Japanese shipping
at Lae. When Johnson learned of this, he clamored that he had to go along
and used Roosevelt's name to get his way.

The bombers were jumped by Japanese fighters as they came off the target. The B-26 carrying Stevens was shot down. Fortunately eight pilots of
the 35th Fighter Group had volunteered to fly up to Lae and provide escort
withdrawal. They intercepted the pursuing Japanese, and the surviving
B-26s returned to Port Moresby.

Returning to Australia, Anderson and Johnson reported back to
MacArthur on June 18. He told them he was awarding a posthumous DSC
to Stevens and each of them would receive the Silver Star. Almost apologetically he said, "We don't have any Silver Stars out here and the citations
haven't been written yet. But you can pick up the ribbons and start wearing them. The citations will catch up with you later." One thing puzzled
him, though. He said to Johnson, "I still don't understand why you went on
that mission."[28]

Back in Washington, Johnson gave a detailed account of his trip to
Harold Ickes, who was always fascinated to hear what MacArthur was up
to. He made some accurate comments on the inferiority of the P-39 against
the Zero, but he went on to disparage both the bomber pilots and the
fighter pilots as being unskilled. He even cast doubt on the courage of the
aircrew in New Guinea. This might seem simply churlish, considering that
he was still alive thanks to both their skills and their courage. On the other
hand, since he had survived the rigors of war despite flying with incompetents and cowards, his own feat was magnified into a heroic one in which
Lyndon's cool courage and determination had triumphed over appalling
odds. Deeply impressed, Ickes informed his diary, "MacArthur offered to
give Johnson a decoration but Johnson declined." The truth, as many will
remember, is that Johnson wore a miniature Silver Star ribbon in his lapel
for the rest of his life and boasted about his wartime "mission" in a way
that suggested he had been a participant, not merely a passenger, in aerial
combat over New Guinea.[29]

Johnson was incapable of writing a report on any serious subject. His
talents were entirely oral. The future President had no literary gifts whatever, and was hard pressed to write even a one-page letter. He persuaded
Robert Sherrod, a noted war correspondent who detested MacArthur, to
write the report for him. Sherrod produced a blistering attack on
MacArthur, his staff and his conduct of the war. It could only have rein-

forced Roosevelt's conviction to stick with Germany First and keep SWPA's role in the war to a minimum.[30]

The summer of 1942 was a miserable time for MacArthur, and it seems likely he was so depressed that low spirits affected his judgment. At times he took refuge in nostalgia. As he confessed in a telegram to one of his closest friends at the War Department, his West Point classmate George Cocheu, "In these days of stress my thoughts turn back more and more often to the boys I grew up with and so dearly loved. . . ."[31]

He felt his air commanders had failed him miserably in the Philippines, and now the one airman he trusted, Hal George, was dead. MacArthur had no confidence in the senior Army Air Forces officer in SWPA, George Brett, and was determined to get rid of him, provided he could find a suitable replacement. It was no secret around GHQ that MacArthur despised Brett. The fact that Brett had been unable to find brand-new B-17s in perfect condition with pilots who looked about thirty and with at least five thousand hours apiece in heavy bombers to bring MacArthur and his family out of Mindanao rankled.

MacArthur was in Melbourne for eight days before he deigned to summon Brett for their first meeting. Brett, moreover, seemed altogether too friendly with Australian politicians for MacArthur's liking. He told Marshall that Brett was "an unusually hard worker but his very industry leads him at times to concentrate on unimportant details . . . he is naturally inclined to more or less harmless intrigue and has a bent, due perhaps to his delightful personality, for social entertainment and the easy way of life. . . . I would rate his service during the last three months under my command as only average." In military reports, "average" is a term of condemnation.[32]

Brett was meanwhile making his own appraisal of MacArthur: "General MacArthur has not a full appreciation of air operations . . . he detests the Air Corps through his own inability to thoroughly understand it. . . . There are rumours that he refuses to fly. . . . General MacArthur has a wonderful personality when he desires to turn it on. He is, however, entirely bound up in himself. I do not believe he has a single thought for anybody who is not useful to him. . . ."[33]

The animosity between MacArthur and Brett was no secret in the War Department. When Sam Anderson returned to the Pentagon and reported to Marshall, the Chief of Staff asked him just one question: "Should I relieve General Brett?"

Anderson's answer to Marshall was "Yes, sir. As long as General MacArthur and General Brett are the commanders in the Southwest Pacific, there is going to be no cooperation between the ground and the air, and I don't think you are going to relieve General MacArthur."[34]

Shortly after this MacArthur received a message from Arnold offering him a replacement for Brett—namely, Lieutenant General Frank Andrews, presently commanding the Sixth Air Force, in Panama. MacArthur promptly turned him down, citing Andrews's lack of combat experience.[35]

Arnold then offered to send Doolittle to SWPA. MacArthur immediately replied that he would not accept Doolittle. He did not say why, but the reason was that he was still mad about the Doolittle raid. The air and naval effort that had gone into that attack should, he was convinced, have gone into the defense of the Philippines instead of being squandered on a propaganda stunt.

Arnold made a third suggestion: George C. Kenney, who was currently en route to the Middle East to activate what was destined to become the Ninth Air Force. Kenney was outspoken, opinionated, tactless. He had spent much of his career in dispute with the General Staff, and during MacArthur's tenure as Chief of Staff he had been forced to repress the ebullient Kenney's constant agitation for an independent air force. On the other hand, Kenney was smart and capable and had combat experience. As a young fighter pilot on the Western Front in 1918 he had shot down two German aircraft. MacArthur promptly replied that he would be delighted to take Kenney.[36]

Kenney spent several days in Washington being briefed on SWPA and getting pledges from Arnold for more planes and pilots. The most striking thing he learned at the Pentagon, though, was "No one is really interested in the Pacific, particularly the SWPA." This fact, however, did nothing to diminish Kenney's enthusiasm for his assignment. He had been an admirer of MacArthur's since World War I.[37]

When Kenney reached Melbourne on July 28, MacArthur had him checked into Lennon's Hotel. He sent for him late the next morning. While Kenney sat silent for an hour, MacArthur gave him a lecture on the failings of the Army Air Forces worldwide, with an emphasis on its ineptitude in the Southwest Pacific. "I believe the Air Force can do something," he conceded. "But so far I cannot see where it has done anything at all." He denounced Brett as disloyal and excoriated the way four AAF officers in SWPA had been promoted to brigadier general without Arnold's seeking his approval first. What they had done to deserve their stars was a mystery to him. So far as he was concerned, they had been promoted not for competence but for knowing the right people back at the Pentagon.

When MacArthur finally stopped pacing, Kenney told him that if he ever found he did not want to work for him or had any trouble being loyal, "I will tell you so and I will do everything in my power to get myself relieved."

MacArthur grinned and, stooping—Kenney was all of five feet five—put an arm around Kenney's shoulder. "George, I think we are going to get along all right." The two men sat down, and Kenney gave him all the latest news from Washington. The biggest piece of information was that American and British forces would land in North Africa in the fall. MacArthur said that would be a big mistake. There was nothing to be won in the Mediterranean that was worth the effort. The right strategy would be to build up the forces needed for a landing in France once air superiority had been secured over the Germans. They discussed the war on the Eastern Front, and MacArthur conceded the merits of the German Army but felt certain it was too small to defeat a country the size of the Soviet Union.[38]

Kenney was curious to know why MacArthur had been willing to take him as Brett's replacement. After all, they had clashed often when MacArthur was Chief of Staff. "In time of peace you need an officer and a gentleman," said MacArthur. "In time of war you kind of need a rebel and a son of a bitch."

"Jesus Christ," blurted Kenney, "I don't mind being called a rebel."[39]

Kenney flew up to New Guinea the next day. When he returned, he went to MacArthur's office, and the two men talked for two hours. Unlike Johnson, Kenney figured instantly what the main problems were. There was no lack of skill or want of courage. Brett had created an Allied air organization that put a handful of RAAF officers in command of a force whose combat units were almost entirely American. Brett had also mixed up flying crews so that the men aboard a bomber came from different countries, an arrangement that created a lot of friction and mutual incomprehension.

Kenney asked MacArthur for permission to send dozens of AAF officers home. Nothing could have pleased MacArthur more than to see the air officers who had failed him in the Philippines relieved and, in most cases, reduced in rank. That was what usually happened to officers who were fired and sent home in time of war. "Go ahead," said MacArthur eagerly. "You have my enthusiastic approval." He and Kenney then turned their minds to the upcoming operation in the southern Solomons. What could Kenney do to aid the Navy and marines in their assault, set for August 7, against Guadalcanal?

Although Kenney had roughly five hundred planes on the books, he could not get even a hundred into combat, for want of spare parts and regular maintenance. He intended to husband his bombers and use them only in large formations. On August 6, he said, he would send the maximum number of B-17s to strike the large Japanese airdrome near Rabaul. His B-25s and B-26s, meanwhile, would attack the Japanese airfields at Lae, Salamaua and Buna. When Kenney said he hoped to put as many as eighteen B-17s into the mission against Rabaul, MacArthur was thrilled and delighted. Up to now heavy bomber missions had consisted of five or six planes taking off, two or three aborting, and the remaining two or three carrying out the attack. Eighteen heavies sounded like a lot.

Kenney conceded that some of the criticism MacArthur's staff had made about AAF personnel's being sloppily dressed and oblivious to normal military discipline was accurate, but he would take care of that. On the other hand, MacArthur would have to help him get the GHQ staff off his back and let him run air operations his way. He did not say so outright, but up to now Sutherland and Godman had been interfering with air missions, down to specifying bombloads, altitudes and aiming points.

MacArthur was enthused by the prospect of having an effective air force. He told Kenney, "You have carte blanche to do anything you want to. As for your combat crews, you handle them. I don't care what they do, how they dress, or whether or not they salute, as long as they shoot down Jap planes and sink Jap ships. As for decorations, I'll give you authority to award any medal except the Distinguished Service Cross. That is the highest decoration I'm allowed to award and I'd like to keep one for myself. However, if one of your youngsters does something outstanding and you want to reward him on the spot with a DSC, go ahead and I'll approve it as soon as you tell me about it."

Kenney returned to his own apartment and dictated his diary entry for the day. When he recalled the expression on MacArthur's face at the possibility of mounting an attack with up to eighteen B-17s, Kenney said, "He looked as though he was about to kiss me." Shortly after this MacArthur recommended Kenney for a third star.[40]

When the Japanese had landed at Buna, Willoughby informed MacArthur that all they wanted to achieve there was what he had planned to do himself: establish an air base. When the Australians suggested that maybe the real objective was Port Moresby, Willoughby and Sutherland flatly told them they were wrong. As a result, MacArthur chose not to send more troops to New Guinea. That was a mistake.[41]

Following their setback in the Battle of the Coral Sea, the Japanese decided to take Port Moresby the way they had taken other ports, such as Manila and Singapore: from behind. That was why they had moved into Buna. Once they had secured a beachhead, they brought in more troops and soon had five thousand men and several hundred mules heading south, scaling the towering Owen Stanley mountain range, which dominates the landscape of Papua. Their first objective was Kokoda, seventy miles south of Buna, and the airfield there. Blamey, MacArthur's Allied Land Forces commander, rushed a brigade up the Kokoda Trail, to stop the Japanese from reaching the town. The Japanese infiltrated around the defenders, struck them from the flank and rear and cut the brigade to ribbons. On July 29 they reached Kokoda and several days later overran the airfield.[42]

MacArthur finally realized the seriousness of the Japanese threat in Papua. He ordered the Australian 7th Division to New Guinea. The 7th was a veteran outfit fresh from the Middle East, where it had established a fine record. It was not really ready, however, for war in the jungle. Blamey considered camouflage uniforms a waste of time, and the 7th Division plunged into New Guinea in khaki shorts and short-sleeved shirts. Its men thus provided a movable feast for just about any insect that crawled, flew, bit, scratched or stung. And their light-colored clothing made them excellent targets for the Japanese.[43]

MacArthur pushed one brigade of the 7th up toward Kokoda. The other brigade was dispatched to Milne Bay, where he now had an airfield under construction. The U.S. 32d Division, which had been in Australia since May, was alerted to move to New Guinea. MacArthur's plan was to use the Australians to stop the Japanese, after which he would use the 32d to make a counterattack. He remained confident all the same that the Japanese lacked the strength to get as far as Port Moresby. He also expected the impending assault on Guadalcanal to force the Japanese to reduce their ground operations in New Guinea.

Instead the Allies lost four cruisers the night of August 8 in the Battle of Savo Island, a volcanic feature in the waters off Guadalcanal. This defeat, and the withdrawal of the U.S. Navy only forty-eight hours after putting the marines ashore, placed the entire Guadalcanal operation in jeopardy. There was the obvious danger that if the Japanese could win at Guadalcanal, they could win in New Guinea too. MacArthur sent a message to Marshall: "If we are defeated in the Solomons, as we may be unless the Navy accepts successfully the challenge of the enemy surface fleet, the entire Southwest Pacific will be in the gravest danger."[44]

MacArthur grew increasingly anxious, as he confessed in a letter to an old friend, the eminent naval historian Captain Dudley Knox. "The way is long and hard here and I don't quite see the end of the road," he wrote. "To make something out of nothing seems to be my military fate in the twilight of my service. I have led one lost cause and am trying desperately not to have it two."[45]

Shortly after MacArthur wrote this letter, the Japanese mounted yet another assault on Papua, but this time he was ready for them. Naval intelligence detected the Japanese preparations for the descent on Milne Bay. In mid-August MacArthur rushed the Australian 18th Infantry Brigade to the area. What had begun as a construction project to carve out an airfield was shaping up into a killing ground. MacArthur had nearly ten thousand men in the area, two thirds of whom were combat troops.[46]

On the night of August 25 the Japanese landed twelve hundred troops at Milne Bay, ninety miles east of Port Moresby. This operation posed a potential second threat to the town, which would have found itself under pressure from converging Japanese columns, one coming south from Kokoda and one coming west from Milne Bay, had it not been for the fact that the enemy had just made a huge blunder. The Japanese had no idea that MacArthur was building an airfield fifteen miles inland from where they landed.

Even with a reinforcement of six hundred more men and the aid of two light tanks the Japanese found themselves heavily outnumbered and outgunned. For ten days they made futile frontal assaults against the dug-in defenders of the Milne Bay airfield. They were attacked from dawn to dusk by American and Australian fighter planes that "strafed until their gun barrels were lopsided."[47] Up to a thousand Japanese were killed or wounded in this doomed assault before the survivors abruptly withdrew. Milne Bay provided the first major Allied ground victory in the Pacific.

MacArthur issued a communiqué that proclaimed "the move was anticipated and prepared for with great care. . . . The enemy fell into the trap. . . ."[48]

Meanwhile five thousand Japanese were still moving south from Kokoda, tramping inexorably toward Port Moresby. On September 3 MacArthur had a long and depressing conversation with Kenney, who had just returned from his second visit to New Guinea. Kenney told him the dense jungle south of Kokoda would allow the Japanese to infiltrate around the Australians wherever they tried to make a stand.[49] That is exactly how it turned out: The Japanese continued to infiltrate; the defenders continued to fall back.

Although the Japanese in Papua were outnumbered more than two to one, by September 16 they had advanced to within twenty miles of Port Moresby. At night Japanese patrols could see the crisscrossing searchlights of the harbor's antiaircraft defenses. The Australians were setting up fresh defensive positions across the trail but with little promise of holding them for long.

MacArthur had a clear idea of how to stop them: make an attack against their rear. He started moving two regiments of the 32d Infantry Division toward New Guinea to launch a counterattack, but time was running out. Kenney, who had made yet another trip to New Guinea, had recently returned and told him flatly, "I believe we will lose Port Moresby if something drastic does not happen soon." He said the Australian commander in Papua, Lieutenant General Sydney F. Rowell, was "panicky and this panic is being communicated to all echelons, down to the troops themselves, who are worn out, anyhow." Kenney felt the Australians were retreating so fast they would not be able to defend his airfields.

"You've got to get some Americans up there," said Kenney. "They don't know anything about jungle fighting, but the Australians don't know that, and the Americans don't know it either. So we'll go up there all full of vinegar and the Australians will be afraid that the Americans will take the play away from them. So both will start fighting, and we'll get the damned Japs out of there." There was also a looming morale problem. "We've got to stop stories that the Yanks are taking it easy in Australia and letting the Aussies do all the fighting."[50]

It was a point MacArthur agreed with. As he informed Marshall, "The effect on the Australian soldier of aggressive action even by a small American unit would be of enormous value."[51]

The night of September 16 MacArthur called Curtin on his scrambler telephone. He admitted to the prime minister that he was seriously worried. "The retrogressive nature of the tactics of the Australian ground forces defending Port Moresby seriously threatens the outlying airfields," he said. And if the Japanese advance was not stopped, "The Allies in New Guinea will be forced into such a defensive concentration as would duplicate the conditions of Malaya."

As every Australian was painfully aware, an entire Australian division had been surrounded and captured by a smaller Japanese force in Malaya earlier that year. MacArthur said the situation was so serious he wanted Blamey to go to Papua immediately and take control of the situation personally. What he did not say, but implied, was that he wanted Blamey to make the Australians fight.[52]

This was one of the critical moments of MacArthur's life. If Port Moresby fell, his career would crash with it. He had managed to survive one defeat. He knew he would not be allowed to survive a second. It is easy to imagine him, tired, anxious, his hands trembling furiously, pacing his office on the eighth floor of the AMP Insurance Building in downtown Brisbane that night, wondering if this was the end.

18

You Must Go Forward

The MacArthurs had no trouble adjusting to life at Lennon's Hotel. As in Melbourne, and as in Manila before that, they lived at the top of the building, on the fourth floor. The hotel provided them with four adjoining suites, each of which had a bedroom, a small living room, a kitchenette and a bathroom. He and Jean lived in one, Arthur and Ah Cheu in another, MacArthur's personal doctor, Lieutenant Colonel Charles Morhouse, had the third, while the fourth was turned into a small library and office for the general.

As he did throughout their life together, MacArthur shunned socializing, to Jean's chagrin. He attended only the handful of official functions that his position absolutely required. Company for Jean consisted mainly of their Chinese servant, Ah Cheu. For Arthur, though, there was a playmate close to his own age in Neil Wall, the son of J. A. Wall, one of the assistant managers at Lennon's. The two boys soon became friends.[1]

MacArthur rose at 7:00 each morning and had breakfast at 7:30. Then he read the latest American and Australian newspapers and magazines with intense concentration. He left Lennon's for his office in the AMP Insurance Building around 10:00 A.M. "I always give my staff time to clear their desks before I go to my headquarters," he explained to Philip La Follette, a former Wisconsin governor who had been commissioned a lieutenant colonel and assigned to GHQ.[2]

He returned to Lennon's for lunch around one, but that was never certain. He could be back at the hotel as early as noon or not show up until three. Jean decided to give herself something to do by preparing all his meals, but it was a challenge to feed a man who did not come home at a set time either for lunch or for dinner. After lunch MacArthur undressed and went to bed for an hour. He returned to the AMP Building around the middle of the afternoon and might be gone for two hours, or five, or anywhere in between. After dinner he worked until midnight.[3]

MacArthur seemed, if such a thing was possible, more aloof from his soldiers than ever. Apart from his staff, few people got a good look at him. Each morning, though, there was a knot of Americans and Australians hanging around outside Lennon's, waiting for his black Cadillac to pull up, to carry him the five blocks from the hotel to the AMP Building. They were able to glimpse the brisk, confident stride, the cane and the gold-braided cap as it passed by and were treated to a view of one of the first automobile vanity plates. MacArthur's Cadillac bore his four-star plate on the front bumper, but the one at the back announced "USA-1." Jean had an ordinary Ford sedan to ride around in, with a plate that read "USA-2."[4]

During these early months in Brisbane, MacArthur was frustrated almost to the point of despair over the strategy of Germany First. It meant inevitably that SWPA's role would be a defensive one until Germany was defeated. At least whatever threat there had once been to Australia had been lifted. He had four hundred thousand troops in SWPA, the vast majority of them Australians. Only sixty thousand were combat troops, severely limiting his ability to fight, but that was still nearly three times the number of combat troops the Japanese had in Papua.

What had really secured Australia, however, was not the buildup of MacArthur's forces. It was the U.S. Navy's victories, first in the Battle of the Coral Sea, then at Midway. With the sea-lanes to Australia secure, this huge, almost empty continent could be safely left to become a backwater of the war. Despite this, MacArthur objected vehemently and repeatedly to Germany First. His mind was fixed on a single goal: returning to the Philippines.

It was not MacArthur, however, but Admiral King who won a major change to Allied strategy in the Pacific. King simply refused to allow the Navy to assume the strategic defensive against Japan. His position was supported by Congress, by public opinion and by the President. The Guadalcanal campaign was a major modification to the strategy of Germany First, and one of its most important consequences was that it gave MacArthur the chance he sought to fight a war in Papua.

He would have to do most of his fighting with Australians, but he also had two American divisions to call upon, the 32d and the 41st. Both were National Guard units, and both had been deployed to Australia before they completed the one-year cycle of division training that most wartime divisions experienced before leaving the United States.

As the Louisiana maneuvers in the fall of 1941 had shown, Guard divisions tended to have a large number of political appointees filling senior posts. The hometown character of many companies and battalions was also a source of weakness. Officers tended to go easy on discipline because Guard companies reflected political, social and business relationships back home. It was too much to expect a man to antagonize his friends, customers and voters over Army Regulations.

Following the Louisiana maneuvers, Marshall purged most Guard divisions of their colonels and generals, installing Regular Army officers in their place, but the other weakness made embarrassingly clear by the maneuvers was the low standard of training in nearly all Guard divisions. It is always possible, over time, to improve standards, but given MacArthur's determination to fight an offensive war in Papua, time was one thing his American soldiers could count on not getting.

The withdrawal of the defeated Japanese from Milne Bay at the end of August removed one threat to Port Moresby and encouraged MacArthur to believe he could wrest the initiative from the Japanese once he had stopped the Japanese column that was still advancing down the Kokoda Trail. He intended to strike at two Japanese positions on the northern coast of Papua—namely, Buna and another coastal village ten miles away called Gona. He sent a cable to Marshall telling him that if the Navy could win control of the sea-lanes between northern Australia and Papua, he would be able to go on the offensive. "Such action will secure a situation which otherwise is doubtful. If New Guinea goes the result will be disastrous. This is urgent."[5]

The presence of two American divisions in Australia in the summer of 1942 called for a corps headquarters to oversee them and coordinate their activities. A division commander spends most of his time on routine administrative and supply problems. The larger tactical battle is directed by the corps commander, who uses divisions the way a surgeon uses a scalpel or a mining engineer uses dynamite.

Marshall sent MacArthur one of the most promising generals in the Army, Robert L. Eichelberger, to serve as his corps commander. The Army was currently planning to make a landing in North Africa sometime in the fall, and Eichelberger, commanding the I Corps, was slated to command the largest American task force in the operation. Then came the urgent call from MacArthur.

Much had been expected of Eichelberger since his graduation from West Point in 1909. He had first met MacArthur in 1911, when both of them were assigned to the maneuver division at San Antonio. What had struck him then, as it struck many people, was MacArthur's almost unbelievable good looks, but his strongest memory was of seeing MacArthur outside a drugstore, "standing a bit aloof from the rest of us and looking off in the distance [in] a Napoleonic stance."[6]

Eichelberger had missed going to France in World War I, but he served in the American force dispatched by Woodrow Wilson to Siberia in 1920 and made an excellent record for himself. He returned home with a DSC. He was later graduated near the top of the Leavenworth class of 1926 (the class in which Eisenhower was graduated number one), and he met up with MacArthur again in 1935, when he served as secretary to the General Staff. He found MacArthur's unusual hours as Chief of Staff annoying but was slightly awestruck all the same. For his part, MacArthur had commended Eichelberger highly and told him, "I shall watch your future career with keen interest."[7]

In 1940 Marshall had appointed Eichelberger superintendent of West Point, where he was as much of an innovator as MacArthur had been two decades earlier. When the first draftee divisions were activated early in 1942, Eichelberger was given command of the 77th Infantry Division and proved himself a splendid trainer of troops. His career was progressing brilliantly when the call came from SWPA for a corps commander.

It was a bitter disappointment to Eichelberger to be dispatched to what was going to be, at best, a secondary theater of war, but he accepted the assignment without complaint. In late August he left Washington for Australia, taking his I Corps staff with him. The operation he had been preparing to command in North Africa would go instead to his West Point classmate George S. Patton, Jr.

MacArthur greeted him warmly when Eichelberger reported to him at Lennon's Hotel on August 26. Whatever his other achievements, one important point in Eichelberger's favor was that he had hired Earl Blaik to coach the Army football team. Blaik had been a cadet under MacArthur and remained close to him ever after.

After telling Eichelberger how delighted he was to see him again, MacArthur launched into an account of SWPA, its trials and tribulations. He explained that although Eichelberger's corps would nominally come under Blamey, acting as Allied Land Forces commander, he was to have as little contact as possible with the Australians.[8]

He concluded his monologue with a hopeless attempt to convince Eichelberger that he wasn't missing out on anything important. MacArthur ridiculed the North African landings as a pointless diversion, while in SWPA, he claimed, there were great strategic opportunities to be seized, as if New Guinea were the place that mattered most in the global struggle.[9]

The night of September 14 he summoned Eichelberger, who also had an apartment at Lennon's, to come upstairs. MacArthur paced the living room in his dressing gown while he explained that with American troops going into action, he wanted Eichelberger to move his corps headquarters to Milne Bay or somewhere nearby around October 1. Being on the spot, Eichelberger could direct the operations of American troops without interference from Blamey. The 32d Division would cross the Owen Stanley Mountains, then advance along the coast while a Marine regiment that Admiral King had promised MacArthur (a promise that was never fulfilled) would make its way toward Buna and Gona by night in small coastal vessels called luggers. The marines would hide during the day. Once both forces were in position, the 32d would make an attack from the land side of Buna and Gona, while the marines struck from the sea. Capturing these crucial positions deep in the enemy's rear would bring the inevitable collapse of the Japanese advance toward Moresby.

Eichelberger felt distinctly unenthusiastic about MacArthur's plan and asked him if Sutherland knew about it. "No. But I'll tell him tomorrow." Ever since Bataan, MacArthur explained, his staff had been afraid to take risks. Then, to encourage Eichelberger, he said, "Take Buna and Gona and I will recommend you to be a lieutenant general."[10]

Two weeks later Eichelberger brought MacArthur a plan that his I Corps staff had worked up for taking Buna and Gona. MacArthur expected Eichelberger to say the I Corps staff would move up to Papua and direct the battle. To his amazement and disgust, the plan called for Eichelberger to remain in Australia and direct the fighting from eight hundred miles in the rear! MacArthur angrily rejected this proposal and called it "defeatist."

Eichelberger protested that the problem was not fear for his own safety but the machinations of Richard Sutherland; the "Iron Duke" had vehemently argued that under no circumstances should Eichelberger go to New Guinea. "Had I been a mere brigadier general," he remarked wryly, "I don't think Sutherland would have objected." He was convinced, he told MacArthur, that Sutherland was clearly hoping to undermine him, then get him fired and be given command of the I Corps. The only sure way to block Sutherland's plan would be for Eichelberger to get a third star and outrank him. "Bob," replied MacArthur, "I am going to recommend you at once!"[11]

This recommendation surprised Marshall, who could not figure out what Eichelberger had done to deserve such a rapid promotion. MacArthur replied that he was putting Eichelberger in for a third star not on grounds of merit but simply because the corps table of organization allowed for a general of three-star rank as commander. When he put Eichelberger in for his third star, MacArthur recommended that Kenney be promoted too. But he drew an important distinction between the two generals: "General Kenney has demonstrated superior qualities of leadership and professional ability." Eichelberger, on the other hand, got his third star without doing anything for it first. It was now up to him to prove he deserved it.[12]

MacArthur visited the 32d Division to deliver a pep talk before it set off for New Guinea. He arrived at Camp Cable unannounced and told the division commander, Major General Edwin Forrest Harding, that he wanted to address the men. Harding's Signal Corps personnel hurriedly set up a microphone, but MacArthur ostentatiously stood about four feet in front of it, the better to impress his personality and his message on the fifteen thousand men who sat in a giant semicircle at his feet. This arrangement also ensured that roughly two thirds of the troops did not hear a word he said.[13]

MacArthur considered himself an expert on the Japanese Army. He had studied it at first hand in 1905, when he served as his father's aide on the trip to Japan and Manchuria. More recently he had seen the modern Japanese Army in action in the Philippines. "The Japanese soldier is no easy enemy," MacArthur told the men of the 32d Division. "He is a hard fighter, and one who fights courageously and intelligently. He gives no quarter. He asks for no quarter. . . . Never let the Jap attack you. Make it a fundamental rule, whatever your position might be, to be prepared for an attack. When the Japanese soldier has a coordinated plan of attack, he works smoothly. When he is attacked—when he doesn't know what is coming—it isn't the same.

"The Japanese soldier has an extraordinary capacity to fight to the end. He never stops. . . . All I ask of you men is that when you go into action each of you shall kill one Japanese. If you do that, you will win. . . ."[14]

The short, crew-cut, energetic and extroverted George Kenney was a cool-headed, systematic thinker with an aggressive streak as wide as MacArthur's own. Anticipating a major campaign in Papua, he had contemplated the daunting Owen Stanleys and come up with an obvious solution. Obvious, that is, to an airman. The way to cross mountains, Kenney believed, was to fly over them.

In late August he had made a command reconnaissance along the northern coast of Papua—at an altitude of one hundred feet—looking for airfield sites. Forty miles east of Buna, at a hamlet called Wanigela, he noticed the knife-sharp kunai grass was only about four feet high. Elsewhere in New Guinea it was likely to grow to a height of ten feet. The ground there, Kenney decided, was probably dry and hard. It was also flat. Airfield material. The best way to take Buna, Kenney decided, would be to fly troops over the Owen Stanleys to Wanigela and have them advance on it from there.

When he reported back to MacArthur, though, he got bawled out. MacArthur flared up angrily at the thought of losing Kenney either in an accident or to a Japanese fighter and firmly told him not to fly north of a line between Buna and Milne Bay. The Japanese owned the skies over northern Papua. He was going to get himself killed. Kenney pretended to be contrite, but Wanigela remained clear in his mind, a bright idea that would not go away.[15]

Three weeks later, when Kenney returned from yet another trip to Papua, MacArthur had him come up to his apartment one evening. Kenney told MacArthur that Port Moresby was in danger of falling. With his airfields in danger, Kenney proposed flying a regiment of American troops over to Papua to defend them. He told MacArthur that he had already discussed the idea with Sutherland and the GHQ staff, but they had shown no interest. "That is the goddamnedest way to fight a war," said Sutherland, rejecting the very idea of airlifting troops. The way Leavenworth taught officers how to mount an attack was to make sure first of all that they held a secure line of retreat in case it all went wrong. Where was the secure line of retreat in an airlift? Suppose the airfields were overrun?[16]

MacArthur, however, grasped the possibilities at once. In this crisis all that mattered was speed. The one question that troubled him was "How many will you lose flying them in?"

Kenney replied, "We haven't lost any air freight so far and the airplane doesn't know the difference between freight and doughboys."

MacArthur told him to fly one company of infantry over and see how it went. On September 15 Kenney reported back that he had delivered an entire company from the 126th Infantry Regiment of the 32d Division safely to Port Moresby. The rest of the regiment was already heading for the docks to make the crossing by boat, but "Give me the 128th Infantry Regiment," urged Kenney, "and I'll have them in Port Moresby ahead of this gang that goes by boat." MacArthur's staff objected, but he brushed their objections aside.[17]

On September 19 MacArthur flew up to Port Moresby to see for himself how well the airlift was going and was thrilled when the B-17 he was riding turned over Japanese positions on the Kokoda Trail as it came in to land. The airlift was working smoothly. Not a man had been lost, and Kenney was indeed flying in troops faster than they were arriving by boat. The Japanese, however, seemed poised to make one last push to take Port Moresby.

At this critical juncture, on September 25, MacArthur had an important visitor, Hap Arnold, who had flown out to see the situation on Guadalcanal for himself. Opposed from the first to the Guadalcanal operation, he was disgruntled at the situation he found there, which he considered a waste of good airplanes. From the Solomons, Arnold traveled on to Brisbane.[18]

MacArthur sat him on the leather sofa against one wall of his office and for two hours paced up and down, giving him an overview of conditions in his theater and venting his frustration at Allied strategy. The Japanese, he said, are better soldiers than the Germans, and the pick of the Japanese have been deployed to SWPA. If they made a concerted effort to take New Guinea, he would not be able to stop them. All he had was two partially trained American divisions and a large force of Australians, most of whom were not even good militia. The Navy was too afraid of losing ships to help him hold New Guinea, and "If New Guinea falls the Japanese will rule the Pacific for the next 100 years."

MacArthur predictably ridiculed Germany First as a hopeless strategy. He assured Arnold that England was too small to provide all the bomber and fighter bases needed to win air superiority over the beaches of northern France. A second front in Western Europe was impossible. And sending Americans to North Africa was ridiculous. The right thing to do was to give everything that could be spared to the Red Army and help the Soviets attack Germany from the east. The other thing to do was build up forces in Australia to launch an offensive against Japan.

This was MacArthur's first chance of the war to make his case face-to-face with any member of the Joint Chiefs. He protested strongly that the present situation in the Pacific was absurd. There was no unity of command—the Army had one theater, the Navy had three—and instead of having one commander over all of them, there was a huge void where someone—and he undoubtedly meant himself—should be. The problem was Admiral King, who was adamantly opposed to a unified Pacific command regardless of the handicap that placed on the war effort.

Arnold did not argue with anything MacArthur said. He was not a strategic thinker and was deeply impressed by people who were. He sat silent on the sofa, savored the performance and noted how agitated MacArthur seemed. He and MacArthur had known each other for thirty years. "Much more nervous than when I formerly knew him," Arnold recorded in his diary. "Hands twitch and tremble—shell shocked."[19]

By the time Arnold left two days later, it was becoming clear that the Japanese drive toward Port Moresby had stalled. For one thing, the column on the Kokoda Trail had run out of supplies. For another, Imperial Headquarters had decided to concentrate on the fight for Guadalcanal and to retrench in New Guinea. Just as the Australians on the Kokoda Trail were preparing for a do-or-die battle to save Port Moresby, the Japanese started pulling out, heading back over the Owen Stanleys to consolidate their hold on Buna and Gona. The Australians chased after them. In the space of a few days the initiative in New Guinea abruptly changed hands.

And as MacArthur prepared to push the 32d Division into combat, the air situation was improving dramatically. Kenney had expected to have to fight a hard and probably expensive campaign to win air superiority over Papua. Instead, because Japanese air units were shifted to Guadalcanal, he could start overflying the Owen Stanleys almost at once. There was still some danger from Japanese fighters loitering near the mountain passes, waiting for slow-flying, low-flying C-47s to come through, but apart from that, the sky over Papua pretty much belonged to Kenney's airmen.

With this stunning reversal of fortune in the air and on the ground, MacArthur gave Kenney the go-ahead to drop men and equipment at Wanigela and start building an airfield on the north coast of Papua. One regiment of the 32d Division would cross the Owen Stanleys on foot; the other would fly. Kenney was also confident that he could keep the troops supplied by air until a sea line of supply could be created from Milne Bay and along the coast toward Buna.

The GHQ staff protested all over again that operating out of Wanigela was impractical. Aerial logistics were horrendous, complicated, positively unthinkable. MacArthur sent for his chief engineer, the highly capable Hugh Casey, and told him, "Pat, I want you to build a road with the greatest speed possible from Port Moresby to the Buna area."

Casey told him flatly he was making a mistake; he was one of the few people on MacArthur's staff who had the confidence and the knowledge to contradict MacArthur to his face. MacArthur respected Casey as a thoroughly professional engineer officer and invariably paid close attention to his advice. The Owen Stanleys were the best defensive rampart Port Moresby could hope to have, Casey explained. A road going north was also a road going south. Besides, it would take all the engineering troops in SWPA to build a road to Buna. MacArthur promptly dropped the idea. "Pat, your logic is sound," he told Casey. "We won't build the road."[20]

Casey's principal assistant, a millionaire civil engineer named Leif "Jack" Sverdrup, the future mastermind behind the Chesapeake Bay bridge-tunnel, had a different idea: Why not hire gangs of Papuans to cut the kunai grass and make airstrips so C-47s could fly in supplies? This, whether Sverdrup knew it or not, was exactly what Kenney had proposed. "We will do it, and you are in charge," MacArthur said. Then, putting one arm around Sutherland and the other around Sverdrup, he told them, "Remember, my boys—food and ammunition. Time is of the essence—of the essence!"[21]

The commander of the 32d Division, Edwin Harding, protested vigorously when he realized that MacArthur was sending his division into combat without its artillery, but Kenney had an answer for Harding. "In this theater," he said airily, "the artillery flies." All the ground troops had to do was let him know when there was something they wanted bombed, and his pilots would do it.[22]

Throughout October men and supplies were ferried from Australia up to New Guinea and across the Owen Stanleys. In the midst of these preparations MacArthur received an urgent message from Marshall telling him that much of Kenney's bomber force would have to be diverted to aiding American troops on Guadalcanal.

MacArthur was willing to share what he had, he told Marshall, but unless the Navy managed to win control of the sea-lanes, Guadalcanal would be lost; the struggle was not going to be decided by airpower. Then he made an astonishing assertion: "Information has already been derived from enemy sources that an attack on Milne Bay and possibly elsewhere in New Guinea is contemplated for mid-November. I urge that the entire resources of the United States be diverted temporarily to meet the critical situation; that shipping be made available from any source; that one corps be dispatched immediately; that all available heavy bombers be ferried here. . . ." Marshall's long, homely face probably got even longer and homelier as he digested this farrago of empty threats and surrealistic demands. The threat that MacArthur described was based not on reliable intelligence but on his own fears and fantasies. It was the product of a highly strung, profoundly depressed commander at the limits of his endurance. MacArthur under intense stress was always as likely to react emotionally and melodramatically as he was to apply his formidable intellect and think the problem through calmly.[23]

He set November 15 as the date for his offensive to capture Buna and Gona, and on November 3 he and Kenney boarded a B-17 and set off for Port Moresby. He was moving up to New Guinea to be closer to the impending battle. The plane had hardly left Brisbane airspace, however, before oil pressure in one engine fell abruptly. The pilot immediately feathered the propeller. Kenney, aware of MacArthur's reputation as a man afraid of flying, went back to reassure him everything was all right and to his surprise found the general fast asleep. Kenney touched him on the knee. MacArthur blinked. "This B-17 is a good airplane," said Kenney.

MacArthur, still half asleep, was bewildered. "What about it?"

"It's so good," said Kenney, developing his sales pitch like the natural-born promoter he was, "that it flies on three engines almost as well as it does on four. In fact, you can't even notice the difference back here."

MacArthur smiled indulgently and stepped right where Kenney wanted him. "I like to see your enthusiasm, George," he said. "But that statement is a little optimistic, isn't it?"

"No. We have been on three engines for the past ten minutes and you didn't even notice it. Look out that window and you will see that the propeller on the left inboard engine has stopped."

MacArthur stared at the engine for a while, then turned back to Kenney, grinning. "Nice comfortable feeling, isn't it?" All the same, the B-17 was now heading back to Brisbane.[24]

MacArthur reached Port Moresby three days later and moved into Government House, a large, rambling affair, standing on a knoll overlooking the harbor, surrounded by palm trees and shrubbery and enjoying a magnificent panoramic view of the Coral Sea. The roof was so battered by tropical storms it seemed likely to fall off in the next breeze, but it was the most imposing structure in Papua, if not the whole of New Guinea. There were four bedrooms on each side of the building and a large book-lined living room in the middle.

Kenney had managed to make some improvements. He had a C-47 fly up the screens intended for two large mess halls and used it to screen the wide veranda that ran along all four sides of Government House. He had also installed the first flush toilet ever seen in New Guinea, for MacArthur's exclusive benefit. It was a great success. Not so the bomb shelter he had provided. He took MacArthur to look at it and suggested they try it on for size. "No, no," said MacArthur. "Those things are damp. Give you pneumonia."[25]

Once MacArthur moved his advanced headquarters into it, Government House assumed a martial air. At reveille and retreat the American and Australian flags were raised and lowered to the sound of bugles playing a strange tune that no American recognized. The color guard consisted of an impressive line of bare-chested, barefoot Papuan troops with huge mops of frizzy hair, dazzling white skirts, red silk sashes and well-filled cartridge belts slung over their shoulders. They could not have looked more picturesque.

MacArthur and his staff found life at Government House hectic but agreeable, maybe too agreeable. Neither MacArthur nor any of his senior staff officers ever went to the front lines during the battle for Buna. MacArthur rose each morning at six. Apart from his one-hour nap after lunch, he worked until midnight. His staff rose when he did and put in the same hours but had to manage without the nap. Their only relaxation was a leisurely two-hour dinner with MacArthur each evening. After dinner, however, he was likely to hold a conference to discuss future operations. Then he would sit at his desk for an hour or so writing the next day's communiqué.[26]

On the eve of battle MacArthur went to visit Harding and gave him a kind of locker room pep talk, like a football coach just before the first game of the season. "Harding," he told him, "you will be on your way in a matter of hours. You will make history. You will lead the first offensive against the Japanese. Here and now I begin a campaign of movement—where speed, and tactical surprise, and superior strategy will demonstrate again how generalship can win with lightning strategic strokes against potentially overwhelming forces. . . . With less than one infantry division and a handful of airplanes we are starting on the road to Tokyo. We shall redeem the disgrace of Pearl Harbor. We shall drive the Japanese to their knees and we shall do it by master strategy. . . ."[27]

The assault was launched on November 16, with the Australian 7th Division at Gona and the 32d Division at Buna. The 32d Division, however, was represented by only 60 percent of its manpower and 10 percent of its firepower, even though 100 percent of its reputation was at stake.

MacArthur's intelligence chief, Brigadier General Charles Willoughby, estimated there were a few thousand starving Japanese clinging to makeshift defenses at the water's edge in northern Papua. Instead there were more than four thousand well-rested, well-fed men firmly entrenched at Gona, and about twenty-five hundred at Buna. They were also hunkering down in some of the toughest defenses of the Pacific war. The system of expertly camouflaged bunkers and trenches in northern Papua was described by the official Army history of the campaign as "a masterpiece." It was an artifact that MacArthur's troops got to study at point-blank range.

If Gona was bad, Buna was worse. The Japanese position there could be approached only by four narrow footpaths through what were virtually mangrove swamps surrounded by kunai grass that was eight feet high. There were dozens of machine guns buried in the few patches of solid ground, and they covered all four trails with devastating fire. Farther back, near the water, the Japanese had scores of deep bunkers, with layers of coconut logs on top. The right weapon to open up the bunkers was a 105 mm gun-howitzer, or better still, a 155. The design concept behind the triangular division (based on three infantry regiments) was lightly equipped, highly mobile rifle units backed up strongly by the division's own artillery brigade. That was how a modern infantry division was organized, equipped and trained. Harding had been one of those Infantry School instructors under George Marshall who designed the triangular division and, unlike MacArthur and most of the GHQ staff, knew just how it was supposed to work.[28] Yet the 32d Division was about to be pitched into combat without its division artillery—forty-eight howitzers—because Sutherland had decreed that shipping artillery ammunition to New Guinea was too difficult even to attempt.

Kenney had boasted that his planes would substitute for the missing 105s and 155s, but all of them combined could not approach the amount of high explosive that a division's artillery expended when able to shoot its authorized daily unit of fire. It was a rare day, in fact, when the 32d Division got any close air support. The Fifth Air Force lacked the numbers, the technology, the technique and the experience to provide effective direct support. And on those occasions when Kenney's light bombers and mediums did show up, his pilots were shocked to discover that Harding's troops were so close to the Japanese that it was fifty-fifty as to which of them took the casualties from an American air strike.[29]

The 32d Division was forced to make brutal but ineffective frontal assaults that exacted a large price in blood for virtually no gain in ground. Harding's problems were further compounded by the fact that one of his two regiments in northern Papua was sent to join in the attack on Gona. He found himself trying to take Buna with a single regiment. He soon realized this was impossible. Buna would fall, he informed GHQ, only when he had more troops plus the support of tanks and artillery.

MacArthur's response was to order him to keep attacking, and a new attack was organized for November 30. Meanwhile the only staff officer from GHQ to get anywhere near the front, Lieutenant Colonel David Larr, sent back a censuring report on the 32d Division to GHQ. Larr had not seen the actual conditions of combat at point-blank range. He had not seen the bunkers or gone along with soldiers who were futilely trying to attack them with hand grenades in place of artillery. All he saw was the wounded, demoralized, frustrated survivors who crawled or stumbled back from the fighting in shock and disbelief.

Larr wrote scathingly of their lack of fighting spirit. Similarly Sutherland made a quick trip to see Harding and got no closer to the actual fighting than ten miles away. On the basis of this visit he informed MacArthur that what the troops were facing consisted of "hasty fortifications"—i.e., slit trenches. Not that he had actually seen them or come under fire himself. Sutherland was ignorant of the fact that what really confronted the riflemen was a system of strongly fortified positions with interlocking fields of fire, excellent concealment and secure flanks, with the sea on one side, an unfordable river on the other and a large swamp across most of the front.[30]

This was a dangerous and terrifying place, exactly the kind of scene that Sutherland was never going to explore in person. As MacArthur would one day discover, his chief of staff was, like many a bully, a grade A, triple-plated coward at heart.[31]

The troops were given a short breather, new plans were drawn up and on November 30 the 32d Division attacked again . . . and got stopped cold again. Nor was the situation at Gona much better. The Australians too had been stopped, despite being reinforced by the 32d. The entire Papuan campaign was on the brink of failure.

In the summer of 1942 Stimson asked Eddie Rickenbacker to go to England and report to him personally on how the Eighth Air Force was doing. Rickenbacker compiled a hard-hitting analysis that portrayed a different picture from the one being disseminated by the AAF. Shortly after this, Stimson, appalled at MacArthur's whining telegrams, fantastical prophecies, egotistical utterances and hysterical attacks on the Navy, decided to dispatch an emissary to SWPA. He had a severe reprimand to be delivered to the commanding general.

He sent for Rickenbacker, closed the door between his office and Marshall's, so the Chief of Staff would not hear what he had to say, swore Rickenbacker to secrecy, then more or less whispered to him the message he was to deliver to MacArthur in person. He was not to write it down, discuss it with anyone else or ever reveal it so long as he lived.

The Seventh Air Force plane carrying Rickenbacker to Australia ran out of fuel, thanks to abysmal navigation, and was forced to ditch in the Coral Sea. Rickenbacker and the other survivors spent twenty-four days bobbing around in rubber boats before being rescued. When the news came that Rickenbacker had been saved and was on his way to Australia, MacArthur sent a B-17 to collect him.[32]

Relations between them were not particularly good. Rickenbacker had been the star defense witness at Billy Mitchell's court-martial. He considered MacArthur partly to blame for Mitchell's conviction, resignation and early death. He arrived in Port Moresby in a wary frame of mind, an attitude that was underscored by the rebuke he was bringing from Stimson.

MacArthur was waiting to greet Rickenbacker's plane when it landed at Seven Mile Airdrome outside Port Moresby on November 26. He threw his arms around Rickenbacker's hollow-cheeked, skeletal form. "God, Eddie, I'm so glad to see you!" said MacArthur, deeply moved. Rickenbacker was so taken by surprise that he too was overcome by emotion. His determination to keep MacArthur at arm's length collapsed.[33]

MacArthur insisted he stay with him at Government House, which he called "my shack." When they were finally alone, Rickenbacker delivered the message from Stimson. MacArthur biographers have offered guesses as to what the message was, but none managed to guess right. Here, then, is what Rickenbacker told MacArthur: The secretary of war demanded that he stop trying to generate personal publicity for himself, stop complaining about the limited resources deployed to his theater and stop criticizing Marshall. He must also try to get on better with the Navy.[34]

Showing no emotion at this rebuke, MacArthur asked Rickenbacker to stay at Government House for several days and celebrate Thanksgiving with him. At dinner each evening they talked about people they both knew, including Mitchell, and discussed MacArthur's changing appreciation of airpower. He conceded that when he was Chief of Staff he had not had as much faith in the airplane's contribution to modern war as he should have. "But I am doing everything I can to make amends," he said, delighting Rickenbacker.

As for the fighting at Buna and Gona, MacArthur assured him that everything there was under control, which was almost certainly the message he intended Rickenbacker to carry back to Stimson. "I could take them within 48 hours," he boasted, "but in so doing I would lose a minimum of five American boys for every Jap casualty." Given enough time and firepower, however, he would blast and starve the Japanese into surrender and would suffer fewer casualties than the enemy. That was his plan.

Kenney took Rickenbacker on an inspection of the airdromes that ringed Port Moresby and the old fighter pilot talked tactics with Kenney's slightly awestruck airmen. One asked, "Colonel Rickenbacker, how many victories did you have in the last war?" Rickenbacker said he'd scored twenty-seven kills. Kenney impulsively announced that he would give a case of scotch to the first man who beat Rickenbacker's record. Rickenbacker said, "Put me down for another case." When MacArthur heard about it, he topped them both. "Whoever gets those two cases of scotch should have something to taper off on. I'll donate a case of champagne."[35]

Rickenbacker left New Guinea on November 29. If he had stayed one more day he would have had some sobering news to take back to Stimson. A few hours after Rickenbacker departed, Sutherland arrived back from his visit to Harding's command post. He predicted that the Buna attack set for November 30 would fail. The 32d was badly led, poorly organized and lacked fighting spirit, Sutherland told MacArthur. Given Sutherland's obvious ambitions, it seems certain that these damning criticisms of Harding were intended to push MacArthur into giving him command of the 32d Division. Instead, though, MacArthur had already sent for the commander of the I Corps, Lieutenant General Robert L. Eichelberger, to come up from Australia and take command at Buna.

Eichelberger reached Government House at midday on November 30 with his chief of staff, Brigadier General Clovis Byers. They found MacArthur and Sutherland on the veranda, where they had set up their desks side by side. Kenney sat in a chair, saying nothing. Sutherland looked stressed. Already accounts were arriving that indicated the new attack was in deep trouble. Moreover, MacArthur was desperate to win at Buna and Gona before Halsey could declare victory on Guadalcanal and the battle there had at last turned Halsey's way. The Navy had won control of the sea-lanes. The end was in sight on Guadalcanal.[36]

MacArthur paced the veranda, orating melodramatically. He had to have victory at Buna, and he had to have it *now.* "Bob, the number of troops employed up there is no indication of the importance I attach to this job. . . . The fact that I've sent for you, with your rank, indicates how much importance I attach to the taking of Buna. . . . Never did I think I'd see American troops quit. I can't believe that those troops represent the American fighting man of this war. I would be discouraged if I thought so. I believe they need leadership to galvanize them. . . . They are sick, but Bob, a leader can take those same men and capture Buna. . . . If you don't relieve the commanders, I shall. . . . Harding has failed miserably. Send him back to America or I will do it for you. . . . All the battalion commanders must go! . . . Time is of the essence! The Japanese may land reinforcements any night. If you don't take Buna I want to hear that you and Byers are buried there. . . . My staff tell me that you should have three or four days to get into the problem, but I can't give them to you. You must go forward in the morning!" He told Eichelberger that this was the great opportunity of his career and if he took Buna, he would give him a DSC and release his name to the newspapers.[37]

MacArthur concluded by reminiscing gloomily about the setbacks in the Philippines, the loss of Bataan, the surrender of Corregidor, the failure of Roosevelt and the War Department to provide him with the means to fight and win. Self-pity got the upper hand, and he burst out, "Why must I always lead a forlorn hope!"[38]

Overnight MacArthur began to regret his Spartan injunction to Eichelberger. At breakfast next day he put an arm around his shoulder. "Don't get killed, Bob. You're no use to me dead." He repeated what he had told Eichelberger the previous day: If he succeeded, he would receive a DSC and his name would be given to the press. America and Australia, MacArthur suggested, would hail him as the conqueror of Buna. His fame would spread around the world.[39]

With dreams of military glory fogging up his vision, Eichelberger flew to Dobodura that afternoon. He was in no hurry to relieve Harding, who was his West Point classmate. But after a brief inspection of the frontline position, he returned to Harding's CP and started to tell him his men were cowards and his officers incompetents—the Larr/Sutherland/MacArthur line.

Harding's chief of staff vehemently contradicted him, and Harding backed his chief of staff. Angered at their refusal to acknowledge that he had figured out in a few hours a tough tactical problem that they had wrestled with for weeks, Eichelberger summarily fired both of them. He installed the division artillery commander—who without his guns did not have a great deal to do—in Harding's place. Goaded by MacArthur and Sutherland, Eichelberger proceeded to relieve a score of officers, then pushed the 32d into a frontal assault that accomplished nothing except to fill up the division cemetery and the field hospital.[40]

Leadership had not been great in the 32d, but it was not the heart of the matter either. For MacArthur, though, the only thing that counted was results, whatever they cost. He needed a victory, and he needed it right now. On December 13 he wrote to Eichelberger, telling him, "Time is fleeting and our dangers increase with its passage."[41]

A dramatic improvement in the logistical situation in Papua in mid-December was meanwhile bringing dozens of artillery pieces, a handful of tanks and something resembling an adequate level of supplies into the battle. Several thousand fresh troops were deployed to the front. With this infusion of manpower and firepower, the situation was transformed. On December 9 the Australians captured Gona. Shortly after this the 32d made a breakthrough into the Japanese position at Buna. Eichelberger sent MacArthur a Christmas present from the front—an ornate sword taken from a dead Japanese officer.

MacArthur thanked him for it and added some advice. He was attacking "with gallantry, but with much too little concentration of force. . . . Where you have a company on your firing line, you should have a battalion; and where you have a battalion, you should have a regiment. And your attacks, instead of being made with two or three hundred rifles, should be made with two or three thousand. . . ."[42]

It was advice that made as much sense as telling him to send out for pizza. MacArthur seemed to be thinking of the Western Front, rather than the jungles and swamps of northern Papua. There was no elbowroom for troops fighting their way into Buna. It was like crossing a bridge or advancing into a cave. That MacArthur could even write such a letter is a comment on how badly misinformed he was by Sutherland and the rest of the GHQ staff.

It was not rifles that mattered; it was artillery and tanks. As the amount of firepower available to Eichelberger increased dramatically almost from day to day and fresh troops were brought into the fight, the Japanese defense system crumbled quickly. The battle for Buna ended on January 2, 1943, three weeks before the end of the struggle for Guadalcanal.

Harding had returned to Port Moresby feeling understandably aggrieved. MacArthur treated him sympathetically. With the battle won and his troops on the offensive, MacArthur was in a generous mood and willing to accept that Harding's relief may have been unjustified after all. He told Harding to take a long rest wherever he wished in Australia. "Forget about the war," he said. In the meantime he would explain the situation to Marshall, who was demanding the details behind Harding's relief.

MacArthur sent a cable to the Chief of Staff saying the problems of the 32d "were to some extent inherent in this National Guard division and not directly traceable to the Division commander. I believe Harding might well be given another chance with a new division. . . ."[43]

Marshall refused to be mollified. "Harding had ample opportunity to weed out incompetents prior to entering combat," he observed tartly, "and therefore cannot be absolved from responsibility for failure of his division." Harding was sent to Panama, benched, in effect, for the rest of the war.[44] Afterward, however, he got a golden opportunity to reply to his critics. He became the Army's chief of military history. Harding made sure that the official account of the fight for Buna reflected the campaign as he saw it.[45]

Eichelberger, walking over the now-silent battlefield, finally discovered the truth about the nature of the fortifications in front of him. He was shocked at their complexity, depth and ruggedness. As Byers, who accompanied him on a tour of the captured Japanese positions put it in his diary, the defenses at Buna were so strong "Description is futile!"[46]

Nearly half the troops sent up to Buna and Gona had been killed, wounded or evacuated for illness. MacArthur had been right about one thing at least. By pushing the campaign hard, his troops had suffered greater losses than the Japanese. Dislodging 2,500 enemy troops at Buna had cost him 2,343 combat casualties and 2,044 troops evacuated because of sickness, usually malaria. The butcher's bill at Gona was much the same: 7,500 men killed, wounded or evacuated to overcome 4,000 Japanese.

Overall, that is, MacArthur had incurred nearly two casualties for every Japanese who was killed, wounded or taken prisoner. Losses in the rifle companies, which bore the brunt of the fighting, virtually destroyed most of them. The 32d Division would have to be rebuilt, a task that would take at least a year. Most of what experience it had gained had been buried or crippled for life.[47]

MacArthur's victory communiqué summing up the results at Buna did not so much as hint at the true cost. "Our losses in the Buna campaign are low," he declared. "As compared to the enemy they are less than half that of his ground force losses, including not only our battle casualties but our sick from natural causes. . . . These figures reverse the usual results of a ground offensive campaign . . . losses to the attacker are usually several times that of a defender. Two factors contributed to this result: First, there was no necessity to hurry the attack because the time element in this case was of very little importance; and second, for this reason no attempt was made to rush the positions by mass and unprepared assault. The utmost care was taken for the conservation of our forces. . . ."[48]

As travesties of the truth go, this one would be hard to beat. MacArthur's communiqués, not so much the products of cynicism as the denial of painful realities, had never been reliable. But this production marked the low point. After Buna they became increasingly more accurate, without ever casting much light on anything beyond the mind of the man who wrote them. By 1943, however, no one trusted them or ever would. Instead the unreliability of MacArthur's carefully crafted missives gave rise to a pointedly mocking example of Australian wartime doggerel that was almost as enduring, and a great deal more accurate, than the scornful couplets of "Dugout Doug," viz:

> Here, too, is told the saga bold
> Of virile, deathless youth,
> In stories seldom tarnished with
> The plain unvarnished truth.
> It's quite a rag, it waves the flag,
> Its motif is the fray,
> And modesty is plain to see
> In Doug's Communiqué.
>
> "My battleships bombard the Nips
> From Maine to Singapore.
> My subs have sunk a million tons;
> They'll sink a billion more.
> My aircraft bombed Berlin last night."
> In Italy they say
> "Our turn's tonight, because it's right
> In Doug's Communiqué."
>
> And while possibly a rumor now,
> Someday 'twill be a fact,
> That the Lord will hear a deep voice say,
> "Move over, God—it's Mac."
> So bet your shoes that all the news
> That last great Judgment Day
> Will go to press in nothing less
> Than Doug's Communiqué!

When Buna fell, champagne corks popped at the Port Moresby headquarters. It was one of the few occasions in MacArthur's career when he drank with members of his staff. He raised his glass as if to propose a toast. "I am reminded," he said solemnly, "of the words of General Robert E. Lee—'It is a good thing that war is so terrible or we might learn to love it.' "[49]

Sweet though the taste of victory was, something still bothered MacArthur about Buna. Had he made an enemy of Eichelberger? If so, he might have to replace him. He sounded out Eichelberger by reminiscing that more than twenty years earlier Charles P. Summerall had ordered him to take the Côte de Châtillon or die in the attempt. "I have hated him ever since," said MacArthur.

"Well," replied Eichelberger, "I don't hate you, General."[50]

He might have given a different answer had he known that although Byers had recommended him for the Medal of Honor, MacArthur had killed this recommendation with a blistering message to the War Department. His cable faulted Eichelberger's handling of the battle, claimed he had considered relieving him of command during the fighting and criticized him sharply for abusing his rank and authority in getting a member of his staff to recommend him for the Army's highest honor.[51]

Even had he known of this message, Eichelberger, for all his physical courage, would probably have avoided any personal confrontation with "the Big Chief," as he called him. He preferred, instead, to bide his time, but time would only make things worse between them. The day *would* come when Eichelberger hated MacArthur. Hated him almost beyond reason or sanity; hated him with an obsessive, all-consuming bitterness that few even among MacArthur's large and voluble army of detractors could ever hope to match, for MacArthur broke into brave, genial Bob Eichelberger's soul and found the cracks.

19

The Continuous
Application of Airpower

On January 8, six days after the capture of Buna, MacArthur was informed that the Joint Chiefs would soon be leaving for Casablanca, where they would meet with the British and discuss Allied strategy for the coming year. While they were away, Marshall and King wanted him to formulate a plan for the capture of Rabaul, the primary objective the JCS had set for him back in July 1942.[1] He promptly issued a communiqué declaring the Papuan campaign was "in its final phase." Organized resistance had ceased. The survivors were being pursued along the northern New Guinea coast. MacArthur's communiqué struck the appropriate victorious note for his return next day to Brisbane. It also had the advantage of beating Halsey's announcement that the fight for Guadalcanal had been won by two weeks.[2]

MacArthur flew back to Brisbane with Kenney aboard Kenney's personal B-17, *Sally.* When he landed, a group of correspondents was assembled to greet him. Here was a different man. The man who descended from *Sally* in an A-2 leather flight jacket was the MacArthur who would fight the rest of the war. The apprehensive, often dejected figure of 1942 had vanished in the steamy jungles of Papua. Neither American troops nor the Australian public had ever seen the melancholy MacArthur. What they had glimpsed was a man who felt low but was masterly at pretending, briefly, that he was on top of everything. Some reporters, though, like MacArthur's staff, had seen the real man, the general staring defeat and disgrace in the eye. That man had gone missing in action. His highly polished Army low-cuts were filled after Buna by a commander who was confident, optimistic, positive and alert.

He joked with the correspondents and answered their questions frankly. The only solemn moment came when one asked him a question about Bataan. "The dead of Bataan will rest easier tonight," he replied.[3]

He celebrated victory by issuing an order of the day that awarded the DSC to ten American and Australian generals and an RAAF group captain. His order of the day contained a frank acknowledgment that the troops had succeeded "In spite of inadequate means . . ." and achieved victory largely through their courage, tenacity and adaptability. This official document concluded fervently: "To Almighty God I give thanks for that guidance which has brought us to this success in our great Crusade. His is the honor, the power and the glory forever."[4]

The eleven recipients of the DSC included Eichelberger and other combat leaders. Eichelberger was dismayed that his decoration had not singled him out individually but been part of a wide-ranging handout of medals. Four of those given this award—Blamey, Kenney, Sutherland and Willoughby—had never even come under fire. Kenney was the only one who had the grace to protest, but MacArthur refused to listen. He simply ordered Kenney to accept it.[5]

For all his present ebullience, MacArthur was not in a good position to take the war to the enemy. On paper he commanded 480,000 soldiers. On the basis of the division slice, which consisted of the 15,000 men in a division and the 15,000 men needed to support it, he had the equivalent of sixteen divisions under his command.

Most of his troops, however, were Australians, and there were two kinds of Australian soldier: the draftee, who was assigned to the Australian Military Forces, and the volunteer, who served in the Australian Imperial Forces. The AMF was a half-trained, poorly led, badly equipped militia that, under Australian law, could not serve beyond the boundaries of Australia. One Australian politician ridiculed it as really being "koala bears— you can't shoot them and you can't export them!" Under pressure from MacArthur, Curtin got this rule amended so AMF troops could serve in New Guinea, but MacArthur never believed they were much good.

The Australian Imperial Forces consisted entirely of volunteers. The AIF included five first-class infantry divisions, two of which were serving in the Middle East. The three under MacArthur's command had just been exhausted in the fight for Papua and needed an extended rest. MacArthur's American divisions with combat experience were the 32d and 41st. The 32d was so broken by the struggle for Buna it would take a year to rebuild it. The one regiment of the 41st that had served in New Guinea had suffered tremendous losses. The only fully trained and equipped American troops ready for combat in January 1943 consisted of two regiments of the 41st Division. MacArthur bluntly informed Marshall on January 10 that the bulk of the troops presently available were Australian militia, and they were "not of sufficient quality for employment in the offensive."[6]

During the next week MacArthur had several lengthy discussions with the Australian minister of war, Frederick Shedden. When Shedden expressed surprise that the fight for Buna and Gona had taken so long, MacArthur replied that the commanders there had made serious mistakes and pointedly remarked that this criticism included General Blamey. He conceded Blamey's merits. "He is a good, courageous commander in the field, but not a very sound tactician."

As he talked about Papua, however, MacArthur finally acknowledged what the troops he had so freely disparaged to Eichelberger had been up against. He told Shedden, "Of the nine campaigns I have fought I have not seen one where the conditions were more punishing on the soldier than this one."[7]

He asked Shedden to get Curtin to send Roosevelt a cable supporting his pleas for more ships, more planes and more troops. The most important lesson he had learned from the Papuan campaign, he said, was the crucial importance of airpower. Curtin responded swiftly, sending a telegram to the Casablanca Conference saying that SWPA needed another two thousand aircraft before MacArthur could go on the offensive.

The conferees, however, were not greatly impressed. Operations in the Pacific were placed well down the Combined Chiefs' list of priorities: First came the Battle of the Atlantic, then came aid to the USSR, followed by operations in the Mediterranean, followed by the buildup of forces in the UK, with the Pacific in a distant fifth place. It was manifestly a reaffirmation of Germany First.[8]

MacArthur, however, was still expected to capture Rabaul. He kept his staff hard at work, and by late February the outline was clear. Called Elkton, his plan envisaged an advance by SWPA forces along the north coast of New Guinea to Lae, while Halsey's forces advanced northward through the Solomons. Eventually these two thrusts would converge on Rabaul. Simple only in outline, Elkton involved a wide variety of ground, airborne and amphibious assaults. MacArthur did not offer target dates for any of them. Everything in Elkton depended on the forces placed at his disposal.[9]

MacArthur informed Marshall that he would have Sutherland and Kenney fly to Washington to present Elkton to the JCS. But before they could do so, naval intelligence alerted him that the Japanese were about to make a major reinforcement of their troops in New Guinea. While MacArthur hadn't been looking for a major battle anytime soon, he was about to have one thrust on him.

When USAFFE was created in July 1941, MacArthur had seized the opportunity while Marshall was in a giving mood to request the services of Colonel Spencer B. Akin, a Mississippian who was clearly one of the rising stars in the interwar Army. A highly decorated infantry officer in World War I, Akin had transferred to the Signal Corps in the 1920s. He was a graduate of Benning, Leavenworth and, unusually, the Air Corps Tactical School. Akin had also become something of an expert on the Far East and had served with the Signal Intelligence Service in the late 1930s when it broke the Japanese diplomatic code Purple.

MacArthur made Akin his signal officer, and when MacArthur left Corregidor, so did Akin. Shortly after reaching Australia, MacArthur created an American-Australian signals intelligence headquarters, called the Central Bureau, and placed Akin, by now a brigadier general, in command. Wherever MacArthur's GHQ moved in World War II the Central Bureau could always be found housed nearby. The role of the Central Bureau was to intercept and decode Japanese military signals. It had the benefit of state-of-the-art IBM equipment, and some of its cryptanalysts were highly skilled Australians fresh from operations against the Germans in the Middle East. MacArthur had also secured something close to complete autonomy for the Central Bureau. It maintained close links with the Signal Intelligence Service outside Washington, but it remained firmly under MacArthur's control—not Marshall's, not SIS's, not the Australians', but his.[10]

Akin had unrestricted, direct access to MacArthur at any time. He was inclined to take the most important material directly to MacArthur but showed it to Sutherland too. During the Central Bureau's first year of operations, however, Akin did not have much high-grade material to offer. The Central Bureau had little success breaking Japanese Army codes before April 1943. Its most successful operation until then was probably monitoring radio traffic from the Japanese air bases on East Timor. This provided the 49th Fighter Group with an hour's warning when the Japanese launched air attacks on Darwin. The 49th was able to get into position on most occasions, ambush the enemy and disrupt his attacks.[11]

Until the spring of 1943 most of the important signals intelligence provided to MacArthur came from the Navy, which had broken into the main Japanese fleet code, JN 25, shortly after Pearl Harbor. It was this success that had enabled MacArthur to turn Milne Bay into a killing ground in August 1942. And in early January 1943 it alerted him to an impending Japanese attempt, following the loss of Buna, to send a regiment from the 51st Infantry Division to Lae. Some four hundred Australians were hanging on to an airstrip thirty miles from Lae, at a hamlet called Wau. The Japanese had originally bypassed Wau, assuming it would fall into their hands once the Americans were defeated at Buna. Now, however, they were determined to take Wau. The Japanese planned to use the regiment's three thousand troops to capture the airstrip.[12]

Sutherland told MacArthur that Wau was not worth defending. Kenney, on the other hand, said just as emphatically that it was. MacArthur ordered Kenney to give the Australians whatever help they needed by flying in men and supplies.[13] Meanwhile he had Kenney's Fifth Air Force launch heavy bombing strikes against the convoy even before it left Rabaul. The convoy was attacked as it steamed toward Lae and while the troops debarked. Only a thousand Japanese reached Lae safely. Kenney's airlift increased the size of the garrison at Wau until it eventually numbered thirty-two hundred men.

On the morning of February 6 the Fifth Air Force hit the Japanese airfield at Lae with fifty-eight bombers and fighters. On the return to base, they ran into a Japanese force of fifty planes that had just finished attacking Wau. A huge dogfight ensued. Kenney's pilots landed jubilant, claiming to have shot down twenty-five enemy planes, yet not a single Allied plane had been lost.

To Kenney's astonishment, MacArthur's communiqué reporting these events concluded, "Our losses were light."

Kenney objected vigorously. "We didn't lose a single airplane!"

MacArthur proceeded to tell Kenney a story his father had told him from his experience out on the frontier with General Sherman. The general had to negotiate with the Sioux and told his interpreter, Wild Bill Hickok, to impress on the Sioux chiefs that the Indians stood no chance if they persisted in fighting the white man. The white people were inventive and resourceful. Why, they had invented the railroad, a mighty machine that could haul all the buffalo meat the Sioux could shoot in a month and carry it three times faster than the fastest horse the Indians possessed. "Tell 'em about the railroad, Bill."

Hickok did so, but the chiefs were unimpressed. They grunted a brief reply. "What did they say?" asked Sherman.

"They don't believe you," Hickok said.

"All right. Tell 'em about the steamboat. Tell them how the white man made a big boat driven by steam that would carry all the Sioux up and down all the rivers."

Hickok did as Sherman ordered, but the Sioux were still mightily unimpressed. "General, they don't believe you," said Hickok.

"Bill," said Sherman, playing his trump. "Tell them about the telegraph. Tell them how I have a little black box out here and the Great White Father in Washington has a little black box. When I talk into my box, the Great White Father in Washington hears me, and when he talks into his little black box, I hear him." Hickok stared at Sherman. "What's the matter now?"

"General," said Hickok, "now *I* don't believe you."

"So," MacArthur concluded, "I think we'd better say, 'Our losses were light.' "[14]

Determined still to take Wau, the Japanese decided to ship the rest of the 51st Division to Lae. In late February, as MacArthur's energies were devoted increasingly to selling Elkton to the JCS, naval intelligence warned that up to twelve large transports, well protected by destroyers, would carry the 51st Division from Rabaul across the Bismarck Sea.

MacArthur sent for Kenney on February 25 and spent several hours discussing the Navy's report. Kenney guessed the convoy would sail during the first week in March, if the weather was bad. MacArthur asked Kenney if he was going to call off all other operations, to concentrate on stopping the convoy. Kenney replied that apart from keeping supplies going to Wau and Dobodura, that was exactly what he intended to do. In fact he was planning to hold a rehearsal of the low-level attacks he planned to unleash against the Japanese ships.

Kenney's airmen had been practicing various techniques for attacking ships after discovering that bombing from high or even medium altitude was almost worthless against a moving vessel. They had modified their planes and their tactics. The upcoming operation was going to provide them with the chance to show what they had learned. Kenney went up to the fourth floor of Lennon's on February 28 to describe the final plan. His intention, he said, was to strike the Japanese ships as far out as he could, in deep water, making rescue difficult, maybe even impossible. MacArthur listened carefully, then told him, "I think the Japs are in for a lot of trouble."[15]

But even as they spoke, the convoy—consisting of eight transports and six destroyers—had set sail. It was carrying roughly half the 51st Division. Next day it was discovered. Reconnaissance pilots caught fleeting glimpses of it through holes in the squally low clouds that blanketed the Bismarck Sea. On March 3 the weather improved, to the serious disadvantage of the Japanese. American and Australian aircrews bombed and strafed the convoy to destruction. In the confusion of combat the number of vessels reported as being sunk rose to twenty-two. Given a choice between naval intelligence figures, which suggested a total of twelve to fourteen ships sunk, and the reports of his airmen, Kenney did not hesitate. He believed, adamantly, then and later, that his men had destroyed twenty-two enemy ships and up to fifteen thousand Japanese troops in the Battle of the Bismarck Sea.[16]

This figure was phoned through to Kenney in the early hours of March 4. Too excited to sleep, he went upstairs and woke MacArthur at 3:00 A.M.

to tell him that the convoy had been destroyed and an entire enemy division more or less eliminated. MacArthur was jubilant. Kenney returned to his apartment on the second floor to pack before leaving for Washington with Sutherland to present the Elkton plan to the JCS. While Kenney was packing, MacArthur wrote out a message for him to transmit to the Fifth Air Force before he departed. It read, "Please extend to all ranks my gratitude and felicitations in the magnificent victory which has been achieved. It cannot fail to go down in history as one of the most complete and annihilating combats of all times. My pride and satisfaction in you all is boundless. MacArthur."[17]

MacArthur accepted Kenney's figure of twenty-two enemy vessels sunk and fifteen thousand Japanese soldiers drowned. Diller suggested that maybe it was too high. There was a tendency in air operations by all World War II air forces for excessive claims to be made, often for the most innocent reasons. MacArthur, however, simply said, "I trust George Kenney," and so far as he was concerned, that was the end of the matter.[18]

The fact that signal intelligence decrypts showed there were only fourteen ships in the convoy prompted an intelligence officer on the Air Staff ("that high school bunch," as Marshall derisively termed them) to query MacArthur's account of this engagement. What was more the intelligence officer had routed the memo he had compiled on the subject over to the Operations Divisions, and it soon came to Marshall's attention. Six months after the Battle of the Bismarck Sea MacArthur found himself under intense pressure to justify the claims made in his communiqué.[19]

He was outraged and had good reason to feel aggrieved. Theater commanders were not expected to make their own investigations into official reports from their senior commanders. To do so was to suggest there was something wrong with the commander, in which case the best thing to do was relieve him and find someone more reliable. The Eighth Air Force, for example, repeatedly made claims for German planes shot down that were simply impossible, and Ultra intelligence showed how grossly inflated they were. Even so, Eisenhower was never criticized by the War Department for the publication of these figures or expected to fire the commander of the Eighth Air Force. Kenney's reaction to the War Department's inquiry into the Bismarck Sea operation was to hint that if it were pursued any further, he would demand a court-martial to clear his name. In effect, he said, he was being accused of knowingly submitting a false report.

Arnold found the whole business excruciatingly embarrassing. Questions about the Bismarck Sea engagement had been raised when he was on a trip to Europe, he apologetically informed Kenney. Had he known what was happening, he would have stopped it at once. By the time he got back to the Pentagon, the Operations Division was involved, and it was beyond

MacArthur's grandfather Arthur McArthur arrived in the United States from Scotland as a child. He was a promising politician and lawyer in Milwaukee in his early years; by the time Douglas was born, in 1880, he had become a distinguished judge and legal scholar in Washington, D.C.

Arthur MacArthur, Jr., Douglas MacArthur's father, as a teenaged lieu-tenant in the Civil War. He commanded regiment before he was old enough to vote, and won the Medal of Honor in he Union victory at Missionary Ridge.

Douglas's mother, Mary Pinkney Hardy Norfolk, Virginia, shortly after her marriage to Captain Arthur MacArthur, Jr. Four of her brothers had fought for the Confederacy; the two who survived boy cotted her wedding.

Douglas (left) at the age of four, photographed with his eldest brother, Arthur III, who would go on to Annapolis, a promising naval career and a tragically early death.

At West Point, the football-mad MacArthur (at right, in light-colored uniform) was too thin and too slight to play football—so he became manager of the team instead.

During his first two years at West Point, MacArthur's mother was in residence at a nearby hotel. MacArthur claimed that his mother had made his father a three-star general, but that her having an earlier start with him had got him up to four stars, the maximum available at the time of her death in 1935.

While MacArthur was at West Point his father was in the Philippines, suppressing the insurrection the and antagonizing William Howard Taft, creating a rift that ultimately prevented Arthur MacArthur from concluding his career as Chief of Staff of the Army.

Veracruz, 1914: MacArthur's individualistic interpretation of U.S. Army uniforms is already apparent.

In 1916, MacArthur, now a captain on the General Staff, became the War Department's first censor. His real job, though, was cultivating journalists in order to prepare the way for public acceptance of the draft should the United States be drawn into World War I.

MacArthur was the most highly decorated American soldier of the war, with two DSCs, a DSM, seven Silver Crosses, two Purple Hearts and three French decorations for bravery. General Pershing is shown awarding him his second DSC. To MacArthur's left are George Leach and William "Wild Bill" Donovan.

Back home, MacArthur's mother kept a huge scrapbook of clippings on her son's battlefield exploits. Here, she gazes adoringly at the first photograph taken after his promotion to brigadier general.

On St. Valentine's Day, 1921, MacArthur married the fabulously wealthy Louise Cromwell Brooks, a divorced mother of two. At their wedding in Palm Beach, the groom wore white and the bride wore apricot.

Louise tried to get MacArthur to leave the Army and become a businessman. This
photograph was taken on Louise's Rainbow Hill estate, outside Baltimore, in 1925.
MacArthur may be dressed up like a banker, but his heart was still with the Army.
Two years later he and Louise divorced.

In 1925, MacArthur (fourth from the left) served on the court-martial of the outspoken Army aviator Brigadier General "Billy" Mitchell. Claims that MacArthur voted against Mitchell's conviction are probably unfounded, but he almost certainly prevented Mitchell's being dismissed from the service.

The most controversial episode in MacArthur's long career was the rout of the Bonus Army from Washington in 1932. MacArthur (right) took charge—in person. The figure in the foreground is one of his aides, Captain Thomas Jefferson Davis. Just behind Davis is MacArthur's senior aide, Major Dwight D. Eisenhower.

MacArthur rarely socialized. Here, however, he is seen at an official dinner at the Army and Navy Club in Manila in 1938, accompanied by T. J. Davis (left) and Dwight Eisenhower.

August 24, 1937. President Manuel Quezon makes MacArthur a Field Marshal. Shortly after this, their relationship began to deteriorate as Quezon began to question the viability of MacArthur's defense plans for the Philippines.

Early 1942 found Manila in Japanese hands and MacArthur conducting the fight for the Philippines from Malinta Tunnel, on Corregidor. By this time he had come to rely heavily on his chief of staff, the abrasive Richard K. Sutherland (right).

MacArthur's young son, Arthur MacArthur IV, brought an irrepressible note of cheerfulness to the grim days on Corregidor, helping to sustain his father's spirit at the worst time in the general's eighty-four years.

MacArthur visited the troops fighting on Bataan only once, for which he has been heavily criti-
ized. He is shown here with Jonathan Wainwright, who would eventually be forced to surren-
er to the Japanese in April 1942 and spend the rest of the war as a prisoner.

Under orders from Franklin Roosevelt to move to Australia, MacArthur escaped through the Japanese blockade, despite numerous hazards. He took his second wife, Jean Faircloth MacArthur, his son and fifteen members of his staff with him. Here, he and Jean are seen eating breakfast aboard the train to Melbourne, two days after their arrival in Australia.

rom his Australian base, MacArthur organized and led the campaign to return to the Philippines.
ere he is seen visiting troops in training and talking to the commander of the 41st Division,
orace Fuller (left), and the commander of the I Corps, Robert Eichelberger (right).

In July 1944, MacArthur was summoned to Hawaii to discuss strategy with President Roosevel
and Admiral Chester Nimitz (extreme right). Seated between FDR and Nimitz is Admiral
William D. Leahy.

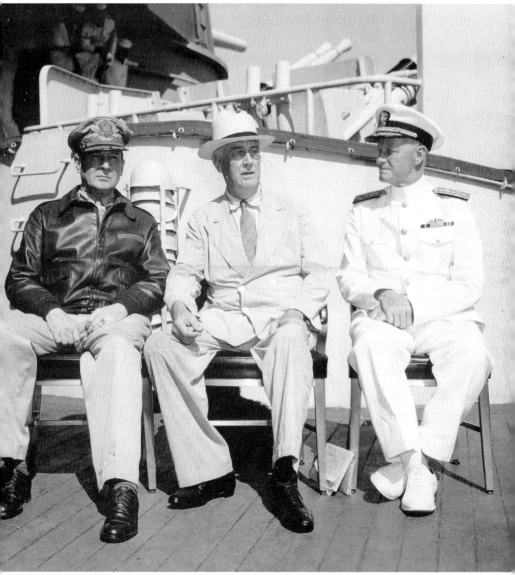

imitz argued that there was no need for a landing in the Philippines. MacArthur insisted that
ere were good military, political and moral reasons for liberating the islands. He convinced
oosevelt, but the President left the final decision to the Joint Chiefs. In the end, logistics dic-
ted that the Philippines would be freed, not bypassed.

MacArthur took great pains to control press coverage of his campaigns and attempted—not always successfully—to win journalists over to his side. He is shown here with four reporters he had chosen to accompany him when he made good his pledge "I shall return."

When MacArthur went ashore at Red Beach on Leyte the afternoon of October 20, 1944, two cameramen who had ridden with him in the landing craft had already rushed down the ramp to film and photograph the event. Later claims that MacArthur had rehearsed his arrival or staged it several times for publicity purposes are untrue.

Once ashore, MacArthur called on the people of the Philippines to "rally to me . . . rise and strike!" as a tropical rainstorm burst over the landing beaches. Behind MacArthur, the president of the Philippine Commonwealth, Sergio Osmeña, drinks from a canteen.

Stung by a mocking Navy song called "Dugout Doug," MacArthur exposed himself to enemy fire throughout the war. He is seen here (center, rear), dressed conspicuously in a faded khaki uniform, in the midst of a firefight on Luzon. At the left and right, an infantry squad is ducking low; in the foreground, a rifleman in the "infantry crouch" moves forward while a casualty is carried away by medics. Meanwhile, MacArthur calmly studies a map and discusses the situation with other officers.

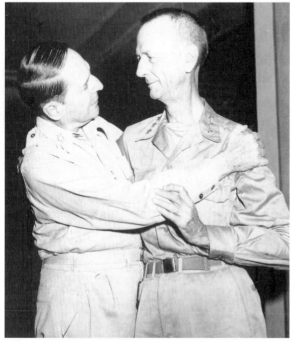

One of MacArthur's first actions on reaching Japan was to order that Jonathan Wainwright be set free and brought to him. They shared an emotional reunion in a hotel dining room the night before the formal surrender of Japan.

MacArthur organized the elaborate but brief ceremony aboard the U.S.S. *Missouri* in Tokyo Bay on September 2, 1945, to make it memorable as both an end to the war and the start of the occupation of Japan. Standing at left are Jonathan Wainwright and Lt. Gen. Sir Arthur Percival, former commander of the British garrison at Singapore, who had been imprisoned by the Japanese for most of the war.

Urged by his staff to call on Emperor Hirohito, MacArthur declined. "He will come to me," said MacArthur, and that was how it turned out. A good relationship was quickly established, in no small part because MacArthur rejected every attempt to indict Hirohito as a war criminal.

The North Korean invasion of South Korea in June 1950 nearly drove U.N. forces off the peninsula. MacArthur reversed the North Korean victories with a single stroke—landing in Inchon, deep in the enemy's rear. Shown here during the landing of the 1st Marine Division are Courtney Whitney (left front), who had become MacArthur's right-hand man in Japan, Brigadier General Edmund K. Wright, MacArthur, and MacArthur's chief of staff, Edward Almond.

As he had done numerous times in World War II, MacArthur visited the beachhead and viewed some of the enemy's dead.

cArthur was one of the foremost public speakers of his generation. Some found his style
lodramatic, but most people were spellbound. Here he is caught in full flow, addressing the
vly reinstalled government of South Korea in recently liberated Seoul.

In October 1950 MacArthur and President Harry S. Truman met, for the first and last time, on Wake Island. Truman was there hoping to get some political benefit from the Inchon landing. An overconfident MacArthur assured the President that the Chinese would not enter the war; was a mistake he soon lived to regret.

glas and Jean MacArthur congratulate Arthur IV on his graduation from the Browning ool, New York, 1956. Arthur, a highly talented pianist, went on to study music at Columbia.

Following his dismissal from command in April 1951, MacArthur returned to the United Stat His efforts to wrest the Republican presidential nomination from Dwight Eisenhower failed, despite the outpouring of public emotion on his return. Close to death, he entered Walter Ree Hospital in March 1964 (Jean MacArthur is shown at left; at the extreme right of the photo is Lt. Gen. Leonard D. Heaton, Surgeon General of the Army). On April 5, MacArthur died as I was born, in the embrace of the United States Army.

his control. He promised Kenney there would be no repetition and urged him to believe that he, Hap Arnold, had never doubted the accuracy of his reports.[20]

Marshall meanwhile was demanding that MacArthur issue an amended communiqué, with a significant reduction in the number of Japanese ships claimed to have been sunk. MacArthur replied that he was standing by the figures in his original communiqué, and Marshall backed down.[21]

MacArthur was not simply being stubborn or stiff-necked. He did not believe that anyone on the American side knew the exact losses inflicted on the Japanese in the Battle of the Bismarck Sea. "Expect only five per cent of an intelligence report to be accurate," he once remarked. "The trick of a good commander is to isolate the five per cent."[22]

After the war research into Japanese records showed actual losses were eight transports, four destroyers and three thousand men. What mattered, though, was not the number of ships sunk or soldiers drowned. The fact was that in destroying the convoy the Fifth Air Force had in the space of twenty-four hours changed the military balance in New Guinea.[23]

The strategic initiative had shifted firmly to MacArthur, as his Bismarck Sea communiqué exultantly proclaimed: "Our decisive success cannot fail to have most important results on the enemy's strategic and tactical plans. His campaign, for the time being at least, is completely dislocated."[24] The Japanese abandoned their campaign to take Wau. They mounted no more offensives in or against New Guinea. Instead they dug in and waited for MacArthur's forces to come to them.

The Buna campaign had left MacArthur deeply disappointed in Blamey. He could not fault his land commander's loyalty to him, but that hardly compensated for his mediocrity as a tactician in the heat of combat. Besides, MacArthur was convinced, rightly or wrongly, that Blamey had political ambitions for the postwar and was trying to curry favor with powerful Australian politicians. He was irritated too by the way the Australian Army had tried to control command arrangements in New Guinea by promoting nearly everyone who had to deal with the Americans one grade higher than his American counterpart.[25]

Two days after returning to Brisbane from New Guinea MacArthur sent a message to Marshall: "Experience in this area indicates the imperative necessity for the tactical organization of an American army. The Australian forces are organized into armies and it becomes increasingly advisable for many reasons to provide a corresponding American organization. . . . I recommend that the Third Army under General Krueger be transferred to Australia. . . . I am especially anxious to have Krueger because of the long and intimate association with him. Eichelberger appears to be a competent corps commander but he will not now fulfill the instant requirement of an army commander."[26]

Marshall was surprised to receive this request. He did not himself think of Walter Krueger as a combat commander. Indeed, Krueger had no combat experience at all. A dour, slow-moving and bookish soldier, Krueger also lacked social skills and seemed to travel through life with a boulder-size chip on his shoulder. When Marshall promoted Krueger to lieutenant general in 1941, he'd done so with considerable misgiving, but there was no question about Krueger's ability as a trainer of troops, which was the principal mission of the Third Army. Although he had his doubts about Krueger as a combat commander, Marshall would not deny MacArthur's request. If anything, the fact that he had no major role in mind for Krueger made it easy for him to accede to it. Three weeks later Krueger found himself flying to Australia with sixteen members of the Third Army headquarters staff.[27]

Like Willoughby, he was German-born. Like him too, he had joined the Army to become an American. Enlisting at the age of seventeen, he had risen to sergeant and eventually won a commission. He had first encountered MacArthur in 1904, when they were both lieutenants in the Philippines. At the Army Staff College at Fort Leavenworth in 1907, they had met up once again.

In 1911 Krueger made the first translation into English of Balck's manual on infantry tactics, for which he was highly commended by the Chief of Staff, General Leonard Wood.[28] As a staff officer at various higher headquarters in France during World War I he created an impressive record for himself, received the DSM and at the end of the war was promoted to colonel. In the 1920s the Air Corps tried to recruit him, but eager as he was to learn to fly, it proved too great a challenge for a forty-five-year-old body to meet the exacting demands of Army aviation. He nonetheless graduated from both the Army War College and the Naval War College. The Navy liked him so much that from 1927 until 1931 Krueger served as an instructor at the Naval War College.

After his five years teaching naval officers Krueger had assumed command of the 6th Infantry Regiment at Jefferson Barracks, Missouri. When the CCC was launched in 1933, he established one of the most successful CCC programs in the country.[29] A year later MacArthur had Krueger assigned to the General Staff as head of the War Plans Division. Six years later Marshall had given Krueger command of the Third Army, and in the Louisiana maneuvers in the fall of 1941 Krueger's troops had won an unexpected victory over the Second Army by stopping an armored attack with infantry. The mastermind behind this victory, however, was not Krueger but Dwight Eisenhower, the Third Army chief of staff.

Whatever Marshall's reservations about Krueger, there were factors working in his favor as a commander under MacArthur. For one thing, there was a long acquaintanceship. For another, Krueger was one of the best-read officers in the Army and widely considered an expert on tactics. Krueger was also on unusually close terms with the secretary of war, Henry L. Stimson, whom he had taught at the AEF staff college in World War I.[30] Finally there was Krueger's familiarity with naval operations. MacArthur was going to launch dozens of amphibious assaults. When Krueger reached Brisbane on February 8, 1943, MacArthur greeted him warmly, not just as an old acquaintance but as the solution to various problems.[31]

As Krueger soon discovered, the command structure in Australia was complex. MacArthur commanded GHQ, Southwest Pacific Area. This was an Allied headquarters, with personnel not only from the United States and Australia but from Britain and the Netherlands as well. GHQ was concerned entirely with military operations. Under GHQ, MacArthur had an Allied land commander (Blamey), an Allied air commander (Kenney) and an Allied naval commander (Vice Admiral Arthur S. Carpender, USN), all of whom reported directly to him.

He also commanded U.S. Army Forces in the Far East (USAFFE), which consisted solely of the U.S. Army troops in his theater. Then there was the U.S. Army Service of Supply (USASOS), which was MacArthur's administrative and supply organization. And now there would be yet another headquarters, the Sixth Army, under Lieutenant General Walter Krueger.

MacArthur had the right, under the agreement that established GHQ SWPA, to create and direct the employment of task forces. The original thought behind this proviso was that there might be occasions when a specially structured ad hoc force might be formed to pull off a crucial but fairly small-scale mission. Once the mission had been accomplished, the task force components would revert to their permanent organizations. MacArthur, however, was going to call the Sixth Army a task force and in this guise direct the operations of American combat troops free from Blamey's control. It was a subterfuge that fooled no one.

The arrival of Krueger was a blow to Eichelberger, who believed he had performed well at Buna under nearly impossible conditions. It was bad enough to be denied the Medal of Honor, but to be denied an army command and see it given to someone who had never commanded troops in combat only rubbed salt into the wound. Shortly after Krueger arrived, Eichelberger went to see MacArthur and asked him what he intended to do now with the I Corps.

MacArthur told him that the I Corps would come under Krueger's Sixth Army headquarters. "Krueger is the one who will determine how and when you will fight."[32]

Chafing at being denied command of the Sixth Army and harboring an intense dislike of Krueger, Eichelberger sought a transfer back to the United States. His old friend and mentor former Chief of Staff General Malin Craig suggested Eichelberger for command of the First Army. MacArthur accordingly was asked if he would allow Eichelberger to leave SWPA. He tried to talk Eichelberger out of it but said he would approve this request if it was what Eichelberger wanted. Later, however, he sent a very different message to Marshall: "His services are of more value here than they could be in any assignment to which he could aspire in the United States."[33]

This was MacArthur the manipulator and user. He had been disappointed by Eichelberger's frontal assaults at Buna and probably held him partly to blame for the appalling casualty toll. A war correspondent, E. Z. Dimitman, remarked to MacArthur on the striking physical resemblance between Eichelberger and Marine Corps legend and double Medal of Honor winner Smedley D. Butler. Dimitman suggested he might prove to be another Butler. MacArthur was incredulous. "Never in a million years. Butler was a really great general."[34]

Even so, he had good reasons to hang on to Eichelberger, who had shown himself to be an excellent trainer of troops. Besides, Eichelberger could step in and take over the Sixth Army if Krueger failed or fell ill. And suppose he did let Eichelberger go, whom would he get in his place? Probably someone like Alexander Patch, who had commanded Army troops on Guadalcanal but turned in such a lackluster performance that Marshall had brought him back to the United States, pointedly refrained from promoting him to a third star and given him a training command instead.

It was not MacArthur's job to keep Eichelberger happy, much as he liked him personally. MacArthur was there to use him to win the war, whatever Eichelberger's feelings may have been. That is exactly what he did, to Eichelberger's immense bitterness and frustration. Nor was MacArthur completely underhanded about it. He showed Eichelberger the telegram he had sent to Marshall and tried to placate him. If you go home now, he told him, the War Department "would feel I had gotten rid of you," much as he had gotten rid of Brett. That would probably kill his prospects of getting another combat command. But by staying with MacArthur, he would see combat again. In the meantime MacArthur tried to mollify him by giving Eichelberger two weeks' leave to return to the United States to see his wife. For a brief while at least, Eichelberger was overjoyed.[35]

Krueger's arrival was a disappointment not only to Eichelberger but also to Sutherland. As chief of staff of both GHQ and USAFFE Sutherland wielded great power, and his relationship with MacArthur appeared close.

Even so, he continued to yearn for a combat command. And there were subterranean strains in his relationship with MacArthur, who was beginning to have doubts about Sutherland. The GHQ chief of staff was exceptionally efficient at routine tasks and phenomenally hardworking, but there was no imagination and hardly a spark of daring.

Moreover, the competence and grinding effort he offered were at times outweighed by the resentments Sutherland created. Whether having him as a chief of staff represented a net gain or a net loss was far from clear. There were occasions when Sutherland blocked the flow of ideas and information to MacArthur simply because he happened to disagree with them or disliked the person who wanted to present them.[36]

Shortly before Sutherland and Kenney set off for Washington to present the Elkton plan for the capture of Rabaul to the Joint Chiefs of Staff, MacArthur told Kenney to get more airplanes from Arnold and to try to keep Sutherland in line. "Sutherland is unpopular and sarcastic and might get us in Dutch."

Kenney replied that if he did not get more airplanes, Elkton would be dead no matter what Sutherland did. MacArthur laughed. "That's right, George. Get the planes *and* take care of Dick, too."[37]

True to form, Sutherland managed to antagonize most of the people he encountered in the War Department. With his abrasive manner and exaggerated idea of his own abilities, that was probably inevitable. MacArthur, however, had only himself to blame. Shortly before Pearl Harbor, Sutherland had grown so worried about his health that he wanted to retire from the Army. MacArthur had talked him out of it. Sutherland drank too much but seemed alert and highly competent. With war likely to erupt at any time, MacArthur did not want to break in another chief of staff.

It wasn't until the fall of 1942 that MacArthur began to regret his decision. Sutherland suddenly started to show signs of failing memory and poor concentration. When MacArthur tried to point to errors in Sutherland's memory, his chief of staff flared up angrily and vehemently denied he had been mistaken when he clearly had been. A chief of staff who could not hold his thoughts together and was suffering memory loss was a liability, not an asset.[38]

MacArthur became increasingly dissatisfied with Sutherland, and one evening, while talking to Kenney, he suddenly blurted out, "I wish I could get a chief of staff."

"What's the matter with Sutherland?"

"You know what's the matter with him. He is a brilliant officer whose own ego is ruining him. He bottlenecks all action over his own desk. The staff is scared to death of him and they all hate him. I've tried to get someone else but anyone I want is either in Europe or indispensable in Washington."

Kenney suggested Eichelberger as a possibility, but MacArthur said, "No. I like Bob and I don't want not to like him. Bob talks too much when I don't want conversation and I would probably get irritated and I don't want to get irritated with Bob because I like him too much."

Kenney came to Sutherland's defense, praising him as the most competent staff officer in SWPA. MacArthur did not say anything for a minute or two, then abruptly changed the subject.[39]

The officers at GHQ MacArthur admired most were Pat Casey, his chief engineer, and Kenney. He told them as much. On one occasion he threw his arms around the two of them and said, "How are my two aces today?"[40]

He felt an affinity with Casey, partly because he had spent more than a decade as an engineer. Up to a point the two of them talked the same language. MacArthur probably understood engineering problems better than almost any infantry officer in the Army, and in his opinion Casey was the best engineer in the wartime U.S. Army. Fighting in SWPA involved overcoming some of the most difficult terrain on earth in some of the remotest parts of the globe at the end of a long and anemic logistical line. MacArthur could not have moved far without a truly outstanding chief engineer.

When a fresh operation was being discussed, he was likely to send for Casey at the outset, take him over to the huge maps pinned on his office wall, explain the size and nature of the operation, then tell him, "Pat, I've got to have an airstrip so it can take our fighters by D-plus-five. Do you think you can do it?"

Casey would talk over the engineering problems—drainage, grading, vegetation, subsoil—and ponder solutions. Finally he would look MacArthur in the eye and say, "I'll do my best, sir." Casey never failed to deliver.[41]

As for Kenney, he was probably closer to MacArthur than anyone but Jean. Several evenings each week when he was in Brisbane, he went upstairs to chat with MacArthur. There was a bond of professional admiration between them that would be hard to exaggerate.[42] Kenney considered MacArthur the greatest general in American history. MacArthur considered Kenney the greatest airman of the war and made him his most trusted confidant on the GHQ staff.[43]

Kenney was combative, piercingly intelligent, imaginative and bold. He could think on a large scale yet kept a sharp eye out for the details that could ruin even the best plan if they were neglected, such as making sure that men were rested, decorated, their morale and their weapons properly maintained. He could fight any kind of air war, as the occasion arose. The flexibility of airpower made it a mystery to all but a handful of ground commanders. As a rule, soldiers recognized only one kind of airpower, and that was when they saw combat aircraft directly overhead. They wanted bombs put down right in front of them, on top of the enemy.

To the airmen, however, the first requirement was to secure air superiority. That meant shooting down the enemy's fighters and attacking his air bases—activities few ground soldiers ever saw. Without air superiority, other kinds of air operations were almost impossible. With it, the full range of airpower could be deployed, from strategic bombing to air evacuation of the wounded and flying in C rations for troops in the front line. And to Kenney, the best way to stop the Japanese from advancing was to sink their ships, not to fight them in the jungle man to man or to try blasting them out of deep bunkers.

The way a commander used his bombers, fighters and transports could change radically almost from day to day, depending on what the enemy was doing, what the commander was planning or what the weather allowed. When MacArthur took command of SWPA, he had virtually no understanding of how airpower worked or what it could do. He saw airplanes as weapons of opportunity, little more, to supplement the operations of soldiers on the ground.

A year later, under Kenney's tutelage, he had come to recognize that air was the key to everything he hoped to accomplish. And Kenney, articulate, clearheaded, someone who, like MacArthur, scorned the spit-and-polish ideas of the traditional military man, was just the person to provide it. His disdain for military conventions was part of his charm. Above all, though, Kenney was the first airman MacArthur had ever known who actually did what he said he would do. He was lucky, to be sure. He did not have to fight to win air superiority over Papua, for example, but luck is as much a part of war as new cemeteries.

MacArthur publicly offered Kenney one of the finest compliments he received in his entire career. MacArthur held a press conference on January 20, 1943, and when a journalist asked, "What is the Air Force doing today?" MacArthur replied, "Oh. I don't know. Go ask General Kenney."

The journalist was taken aback. "General, do you mean to say you don't know where the bombs are falling?"

MacArthur smiled broadly. "Of course I know where they are falling. They are falling in the right place. Go ask George Kenney where it is."[44]

Several days later MacArthur, making a bid for more airplanes, issued a press statement that declared, "The outstanding military lesson of this campaign was the continuous, calculated application of airpower. . . . The offensive and defensive power of the air . . . will permit the application of offensive power in swift, massive strokes, rather than the dilatory and costly island-to-island advance that some have assumed to be necessary in [this] theater. . . ."[45]

In Kenney's view, MacArthur acquired the best grasp of airpower of any ground commander of the war. It was a development that brought praise from Arnold, who wrote to MacArthur in the summer of 1943: "I have followed your operations in the use of aviation, naturally with a great deal of interest, and want to congratulate you on the excellent way in which you have made use of the air arm both tactically and strategically. The results have been most effective."[46]

At the beginning of the war MacArthur had been an airpower skeptic. He still saw it as he had during his time as Chief of Staff, as a weapon of opportunity. He compared it to Civil War cavalry—capable of quick, deep strikes against an enemy's flank or rear but lacking weight and stamina. When there was fog or rain, snow or darkness, airplanes were grounded. Yet the infantry had to fight around the clock, in all weather, day after day. The most that airplanes could do was supplement the infantry's efforts.[47]

He had undergone a total conversion and acquired a faith that was almost religious in its intensity. Airpower, he now realized, was the key to offensive operations in SWPA and probably everywhere else in the world. A senior RAF officer passed through Brisbane in the fall of 1943 on his way to join the staff of Admiral Sir Louis Mountbatten, recently appointed to command the Southeast Asia theater. MacArthur gave him some advice for Mountbatten. "Tell him he will need more Air," said MacArthur firmly. "And when you have told him that, tell him again from me that he will need *more Air!*" As the RAF officer digested this information, in what is likely to have been sheer delight, MacArthur brought his fist down on his desk. "And when you have told him that for the second time, tell him from me for the third time that he will still need MORE AIR!"[48]

And Mountbatten did indeed discover it *was* air that alone made possible an eventual Allied offensive in the jungles of Burma, taking in troops, bringing out the wounded and dropping huge quantities of supplies. Throughout the Pacific, far from being a sometime thing, the air weapon was in operation virtually every day. Infantry units, on the other hand, could spend an entire year in MacArthur's theater without being in contact with the enemy.

MacArthur took an avuncular interest in Kenney's pilots. Shortly after the fall of Burma, MacArthur arrived at GHQ one morning and found Sutherland and Major General Richard Marshall, the commander of USASOS, berating Kenney for the rambunctious behavior of pilots on leave in Sydney. "I think it's time these brats grew up and behaved themselves," said Marshall.

Kenney responded vehemently. "I don't want them to grow up, get respectable and fat and bald headed because I know if they do they won't any longer be shooting down Nip planes and sinking Nip boats."

While the three men argued, they suddenly sensed MacArthur was standing in the doorway. He grinned. "Dick," said MacArthur, "leave George's kids alone. I don't want them to grow up either. I'd like to see Jap planes shot down and Jap ships destroyed."[49]

MacArthur flagrantly identified himself with Kenney and his airmen. After Buna, his favorite garment, excluding the glittering field marshal's cap, became a leather flight jacket. He made a couple of minor modifications to turn his own jacket into a unique garment, but it is in all essentials the wartime A-2, whose original specifications stated it was "suitable for high speed, low level flight." Despite the heat of the tropics, he wore it regularly. He flaunts it still. In front of the MacArthur Memorial in Norfolk he stands on a five-foot marble shaft, the flight jacket draped over his left arm. At West Point there stands a copy of this same statue. MacArthur gazes loftily across the Plain, toward "the million-dollar view." Dressed in an open-neck shirt, sharply creased pants and the field marshal's cap, he seems to be looking for somewhere to hang up his A-2 in eternity.

20

Boom! Boom!

MacArthur's first nine months in Australia were so stressful he might well have cracked up had it not been for the presence of his wife and son. Love is as addictive as any drug ever manufactured, and MacArthur had been hooked all his life. His mother had sustained him from childhood to middle age with her complete adoration. Louise had been a great disappointment—too much concerned with herself to make him the center of her universe. Jean, however, was absolutely devoted to him, and so was young Arthur. The presence of his wife and son made it possible for MacArthur to bear up under the strain of defeats, setbacks and frustrations that a man as proud and as highly strung as he might have found otherwise impossible to bear.

Except for the fact that he saw less of Jean and Arthur than he had done in Manila, the pattern of MacArthur's home life was much the same as before. In this, he was uniquely privileged, although chances are he simply accepted it as his due. Among all American theater commanders during the war he alone had the emotional sustenance and stability of keeping his family with him. Others, such as Eisenhower, tried to create an imitation of a family atmosphere, with all that implies of mutual understanding and unquestioned devotion, from among members of their staffs. In allowing MacArthur to keep Jean and Arthur with him, Roosevelt and Marshall conferred an extraordinary favor. MacArthur complained vehemently to nearly everyone he encountered or corresponded with that he got little material support, yet other commanders could as easily have protested against the favoritism MacArthur enjoyed in unlimited emotional reinforcements.

After rising each morning, MacArthur went to his son's bedroom at seven-fifteen for a solemn exchange of salutes. Then the two of them marched around the bedroom shouting "Boom! Boom! Boomity . . . boom!" for a minute or two, until MacArthur felt the moment had come to give his son that day's gift. Arthur would hide his face in a large chair while the general brought the present from a pocket. *"Boom!"* The offering was dropped onto the chair, to be gleefully snatched up by Arthur, who ran to Jean's bedroom, crying, "Look at the boom-boom present papa gave me!" It wasn't particularly fancy or expensive—a red pencil, some colored ribbon, a small toy, a comic book, a few crayons. Expensive gifts were saved for Arthur's birthday, when there was a present from his father for every year of his age.[1]

When retired General Robert E. Wood, the president of Sears, Roebuck, an old West Point friend, fellow Rainbow warrior and Republican moneybags, visited Australia in October 1943 to sound out MacArthur's political ambitions, he promised that on his return to the United States he would send Arthur a Sears, Roebuck catalog. "He can pick out anything in it he wants," said Wood. "I'll see that he gets it."

"Better be careful," said MacArthur. "He might want a tractor!"

Wood was as good as his word. The catalog showed up, and what Arthur finally decided to have was a packet of colored straws. He'd heard about straws but never actually seen them.[2]

Whenever MacArthur was in New Guinea, he wrote regularly to his wife and son. On one occasion he delayed an important conference at Port Moresby for half an hour because he had just heard that Arthur had lost a baby tooth. He spent the time writing a long message of commiseration to Arthur on his loss. The letter was entrusted instantly to a colonel who was about to return to Brisbane, and it was delivered to Arthur next day.[3]

One of the few happy moments for him during his first few months in Australia came when he was named Father of the Year in June 1942. He responded:

Nothing has touched me more deeply than the action of the National Fathers' Day Committee. By profession, I am a soldier and take pride in that fact, but I am prouder, infinitely prouder, to be a father.

A soldier destroys in order to build; the father only builds, never destroys. The one has the potentialities of death; the other embodies creation and life. And while the hordes of death are mighty, the battalions of life are mightier still.

It is my hope my son, when I am gone, will remember me not from the battle but in the home, repeating with him our simple daily prayer—"Our Father who art in Heaven."[4]

Around the time he was five, in February 1943, Arthur was deemed old enough to have breakfast with his parents. To MacArthur's discomfort, however, he tended to dawdle, dragging a meal his parents could get through in twenty minutes into something that took more than an hour. The reason seems fairly obvious: This was the only time he was allowed to spend each day with them both. Otherwise he passed nearly every waking hour in the company of women—with Ah Cheu, with his tutor, an Englishwoman named Phyllis Gibson, or with his mother. While MacArthur doted on his son, fretted over him and seemed unable to deny him anything, virtually the only time they had together was an hour or so each morning. MacArthur's relationship with Arthur was more like that of a grandparent than a father—fitful, indulgent, gift-wrapped.

His relationship with Jean, on the other hand, remained exceptionally close despite the limited time they could spend together. The Puritan in him chose to give up alcohol for the war, so there were no more predinner cocktails. And the war gave him the perfect excuse to cut out nearly all social engagements, official or otherwise. Jean tried for a time to carry the social burden alone but soon found herself snared in the undercurrents of Australian high society, which was riddled with petty jealousies and vague resentments. Australians were notorious for their feuding, and Jean, who was invited to everything in sight, became a pawn in other people's struggles.

As the strain took hold, she started getting terrible headaches. MacArthur came home for lunch one day to find his wife agonizing over which invitations to accept and which to turn down. "What will I do?" she moaned. "What *will* I do?"

MacArthur sent for Lieutenant Colonel Morhouse, his personal doctor. Morhouse examined Jean and found nothing physically wrong, beyond the need for some rest. "If you don't stop fussing like this," MacArthur told her, "we'll just write 'What will I do?' on your tombstone!" Jean accepted no more invitations.[5]

On the few occasions the MacArthurs entertained, it was nearly always for old friends, like Robert Wood, who had traveled all the way from the United States. MacArthur was also starstruck, not surprisingly, given his love of movies. Visiting entertainers found him ready to welcome them, and one, the comedian Joe E. Brown, became a family friend. Brown admired MacArthur's A-2 so much he got the general to promise to give it to him as the ultimate war souvenir once Japan surrendered.[6]

Mostly, though, what MacArthur did in Brisbane was work. He put in twelve to fourteen hours a day, every day of the week. Compared to the magnificent office he had created for himself at 1 Calle Victoria, the one he occupied in the AMP Insurance Building was austere; another expression of the purging spirit of wartime puritanism. There was no dazzling display of flags, no expensive furniture. He had a large desk—clear of papers when he was not working at it—facing the door. There was no telephone in his office. It was an instrument he seemed to distrust as well as dislike. Apart from his desk, there was little furniture. A black leather couch was placed against one wall, with a table against the wall opposite. There were several chairs near his desk for visitors to sit on. And that was it. While there were maps pinned to the wall of his advanced headquarters up in New Guinea, his Brisbane office walls were adorned only with two portraits, one of Washington, behind him, the other of Lincoln, in front of him.[7]

His relationships with Australians were cordial, and with some, such as John Curtin, there was a genuine closeness. He took a liking too to the governor-general, Lord Gowrie, and when Gowrie's son was killed in action in North Africa in February 1943, MacArthur composed a heartfelt message of condolence:

My dear Friend:
At such a time as this I realize the complete uselessness of words. You have had a mortal blow and not even time can do more than temper the hurt. That the people of two nations stand in reverential salute for your hero son can well fill your heart with pride but not the void in your heart. Take comfort in the thought that through all the skein of man's sorrowful existence there runs a holy pattern handed down to us by the Man of Galilee and that each great sacrifice brings us a little closer to God. We shall pray for you both that your grievous wound may gradually seem an accolade of celestial honor to perpetuate the glorious memory of a man who died that his country might live.[8]

In February 1943 Brigadier General Albert C. Wedemeyer arrived in Brisbane. One of the brightest young officers in the Army, Wedemeyer was something of a Marshall protégé and the author of the Victory Program, the pre–Pearl Harbor document that provided the framework for the mobilization of the economy and the expansion of the Army if the United States entered the war. Wedemeyer had accompanied Marshall to Casablanca, and his mission to MacArthur was to explain what had transpired at the Casablanca Conference.

Churchill and the British chiefs had argued that the momentum of the North African landings had to be maintained, that operations during the coming year should be focused on the Mediterranean. Once the Germans had been defeated in North Africa, the Allies would make a landing in Sicily, and beyond that an invasion of Italy was likely. MacArthur's response was to urge Wedemeyer to stress to Marshall on his return that there was even more momentum to be exploited in SWPA than there was in North Africa. While victory in Tunisia was still months away, he had already defeated the Japanese at Milne Bay, Buna and Gona and forced them to retreat.[9]

MacArthur dispatched Kenney and Sutherland to Washington to present his plan for taking Rabaul and to beg for major reinforcements to implement it. Sutherland's baggage included a huge chip on his shoulder. A morose, prickly individual, he viewed the Pentagon as enemy territory. To him, the War Department was the vipers' nest where plots were hatched to bring MacArthur down. Kenney considered that ridiculous and concentrated on one thing: getting more airplanes. The current replacement rate barely covered his losses. A couple of bad days and the Fifth could be flat on its back and its airfields wide open to attack.

Despite this, he had no success persuading Marshall and Arnold to let SWPA have 10 percent of total American aircraft production. One third of American production was already going to the British and the Soviets under lend-lease. Arnold was trying to build up the Eighth and Ninth air forces so they could win air superiority in time for an invasion of France in 1944. Every theater commander in the world was clamoring for more airplanes. SWPA was going to have to take its chances like all the others.

Just when things looked grim, Kenney got a break. Roosevelt was always curious to know what MacArthur was up to, so he sent for Kenney. He asked about MacArthur's health, which Kenney said was excellent. He also wanted to know if MacArthur had any political ambitions. Kenney said MacArthur had none. When they got around to talking about SWPA, Roosevelt surprised Kenney with his knowledge of airpower. That gave Kenney a perfect opportunity to make his pitch, way over the heads of Marshall and Arnold. Roosevelt listened with interest as Kenney described the Battle of the Bismarck Sea, the tactics his men had devised for attacks on Japanese shipping, the way the two sides played a cat-and-mouse game to strike at each other's airfields, how the skies over New Guinea turned from sunny and clear to stormy and dark within minutes, how good pilots and crews set out on long flights over water and were never heard from again. There were more ways to lose planes and crews in that part of the world than just about anywhere else. Roosevelt got the point. "Write down on this pad what you need. Be reasonable about it and I'll see what I can do, even if I have to argue with the whole British Empire about it." By the time Kenney returned to Brisbane he had a promise from Arnold of enough planes virtually to double the size of the Fifth Air Force.[10]

The JCS studied MacArthur's plan and put Rabaul in abeyance as his strategic objective. Instead MacArthur and Admiral Halsey, the commander of the South Pacific theater, were ordered to undertake operations in 1943 that would eventually enable Allied forces to seize the Bismarck Archipelago, as a probable prelude to an assault on Rabaul. To enable MacArthur to fulfill his part of this plan, he was promised two more divisions, both of them first class: the 1st Cavalry Division and the 1st Marine Division. And to ensure that SWPA's operations would be harmonized with those of the South Pacific theater, MacArthur would exercise broad strategic direction over Admiral Halsey's drive north.[11]

While the quality of the reinforcements MacArthur was getting was excellent, he remained profoundly dissatisfied. He wanted more, especially in the air. There was no bigger convert to airpower than MacArthur. Thanks to Kenney's chat with Roosevelt, he was getting another 860 airplanes, which would increase the effectiveness of the Fifth Air Force by 100 percent, but not even this was enough. He put out a press release that seemed to disparage the Navy but was really a blatant plea for more airpower: "The Japanese . . . have complete control of the sea lanes in the Western Pacific and of the outer approaches toward Australia. Control of such sea lanes no longer depends solely, or even perhaps primarily, upon naval power, but upon air power. . . . The first line of Australian defense is our bomber line. . . . If we lose the air, naval forces cannot save us. . . . The vital factors in the Southwest Pacific are the air forces to strike and the ground forces to conquer and hold . . . the battle of the Western Pacific will be won or lost by the proper application of the air-ground team."[12]

This statement was released only twenty-four hours before Halsey arrived in Brisbane to confer with MacArthur, but while some admirals were indignant at what they saw as another MacArthur attack on the Navy, Halsey took it in his stride. During the course of the three days he spent conferring with MacArthur, they formed a mutual admiration society that lasted the rest of their lives. The restless, combative element in each responded to the same fire burning in the other. In peacetime the surest way for a naval officer to sink his career was to lose a ship. When war came, the dread of risking ships made many admirals excessively cautious. Halsey was the buoyant exception, and MacArthur admired him for it and praised him at every opportunity. During their conference there were no serious disagreements between them, no personality clashes, no hidden agendas. "The 'Bull' is a real fighting admiral," MacArthur told Kenney. "He has some faults, likes a headline, thinks a lot of himself, but he's not dumb. Neither is he brilliant and sometimes he might be erratic. He has color and he's a showman. However, he *is* a fighter and as a general rule, people like him. Lots of them will follow him blindly." Apart from the comment on Halsey's intellect, it was a description that could just as easily have been applied to MacArthur. In effect, he was saying, we're like brothers—only I'm brighter.[13]

MacArthur's staff and Halsey's put together an interlinked series of operations, consisting of more than a dozen amphibious assaults, which they gave a collective code name, Cartwheel. These operations would conclude near the end of 1943 with a landing on Bougainville. Beyond that, nothing was settled, but it seemed likely that they would lead to further operations to secure bases in the Bismarck Archipelago from which an assault could be mounted against Rabaul.

Amid a picture postcard setting of shimmering coral reefs and six smoking volcanoes, Rabaul currently provided a comfortable base for nearly a hundred thousand Japanese troops. The Imperial Japanese Navy enjoyed a great natural harbor, large enough to shelter every vessel in the emperor's fleet. A mile or so back from the water were excellent level, well-drained sites for airfields. Rabaul was primo military real estate, well worth fighting for. It was essential to attack it so hard and so often it would lose its value to the Japanese. Ultimately it might be necessary to invade it.

MacArthur had committed himself to undertaking a variety of amphibious assaults, but his means of putting troops ashore in the face of opposition were meager. The U.S. Navy's Seventh Fleet, commanded by Vice Admiral Arthur S. Carpender, was assigned to SWPA, but its major combat elements consisted of three obsolescent cruisers, one American, the other two Australian.

Besides the Seventh Fleet, MacArthur had the Seventh Amphibious Force, an organization he had created days after the fall of Buna. The commander of Seventh Amphib would be Rear Admiral Daniel E. Barbey. When Barbey reported for duty, MacArthur gave him the same kind of lecture on the crucial importance of loyalty that Kenney had received six months earlier. And if MacArthur had been mad at the Army Air Forces then, he was livid about the Navy now. At Buna, he told Barbey, the obvious and logical thing to do was send in some warships and shell the Japanese from the sea, but the Navy was too afraid of losing ships to play its proper part in the campaign. It was so afraid of losing ships it had refused to open up a supply line along the northern coast of Papua to keep his troops in combat.[14]

Barbey vowed to do his best, but when the Seventh Amphib made its first assault, it was not going to boast anything more than four obsolescent destroyers converted to troop transports, six LSTs and roughly thirty landing craft.

King had been indifferent to the need for amphibious forces beyond the small-scale needs of the Marine Corps. After Pearl Harbor he sought to concentrate on building warships, preferably aircraft carriers and submarines. It was the Army that foresaw the need to build a wide variety of vessels, from four-thousand-ton LSTs down to modest landing craft holding thirty infantrymen.

In the summer of 1942, with plans being drawn up for the North African landings, Army engineers created and trained the 1st Engineer Amphibious Brigade at Martha's Vineyard. Only at the last moment did Admiral King realize that the Army was prepared to man thousands of LSTs and landing craft if necessary and put hundreds of thousands, maybe even millions of soldiers ashore against hostile fire, an enterprise that might raise questions about the long-term need for a large navy. By turning to the openly and fervently pro-Navy Roosevelt, King was able to force the Army to shelve its plans to use the brigade in North Africa. The Navy would put the troops ashore after all.[15]

Dismayed but determined to keep a good idea afloat, one of the creators of the Engineer Amphibian Command, Colonel Arthur Trudeau, flew to Brisbane in November 1942 and talked to Casey and MacArthur about the specialized skills and equipment developed at Martha's Vineyard. MacArthur promptly wired Marshall, requesting that all three engineer amphibian brigades be allowed to complete their training and be assigned to his command. By the time this message arrived, the 1st Brigade had already been broken up, under Navy pressure, but he would get the 2d Brigade as soon as shipping could be found for it and the 3d sometime in the future.[16]

During the April 1943 conference in Brisbane, Halsey had proposed having South Pacific (SOPAC) theater forces land on New Georgia on May 15. MacArthur got him to delay this assault until June 30, when SWPA forces would land on two small islands between Papua and Guadalcanal, called Woodlark and Kiriwina. Intelligence showed that both were unoccupied by the Japanese, but MacArthur intended to use their capture to round out the training program of Eichelberger's I Corps and Barbey's Seventh Amphibious Force. If the troops did not know they would not have to fight their way ashore, they would train harder and would conduct the operation as if their lives depended on it.

MacArthur visited Rockhampton in late May to see for himself how the training was coming along. He seemed pleased with what he saw and gave a pep talk to Eichelberger's staff. "You have made an enviable record as the result of your activities at Buna," he told them. "A hard task now confronts you, but when it is finished I'm sure you will realize that it isn't by accident that you are known as *the I Corps!*"[17]

On June 30 Barbey put fifteen thousand soldiers and one thousand marines ashore on Woodlark and Kiriwina. Casey's engineers were at work within hours creating airstrips for Kenney's fighters. Halsey's forces meanwhile mounted an amphibious assault against the Japanese defenders of New Georgia. Cartwheel was finally rolling.[18]

MacArthur's campaign in New Guinea in the summer and fall of 1943 was built around two kinds of operations: an air war conducted mainly by Americans and ground thrusts conducted mainly by Australians. It was for him to weave the two together into a coherent whole. Nowhere in World War II were military operations as complicated as they were in SWPA, because nowhere was the geography more problematical or the enemy more difficult to reach.

Following the Battle of the Bismarck Sea the Japanese still clung to Lae, even though they had major problems reinforcing it now that the direct sea route from Rabaul had been cut by Kenney's B-25s. And Lae itself was so vulnerable to air attack that the Japanese began to concentrate their air strength at Wewak, three hundred miles northwest of Lae on the northern coast of New Guinea.

Kenney monitored the buildup of Japanese aircraft at Wewak all spring, itching to get at them, but he could reach Wewak only with B-17s, which had to fly at night for lack of long-range daylight escorts. Bombing Wewak in the darkness, the Fortresses were merely rearranging the jungle and depriving the Japanese of some sleep, nothing more.

Kenney's proposed solution was to build an airfield quickly and secretly deep in the jungle, near Marilinan, only sixty miles inland from Lae. In effect, he wanted to build an airfield behind enemy lines and right under the Japanese nose. When he suggested this to MacArthur, there was only one question: "How are you going to protect it against Jap ground forces?"

Kenney said he was going to get some troops from the Australians and fly them into Marilinan at night. MacArthur was delighted. "Good, good," he said, grinning. Then a thought occurred to him. "Say, George, have you told my staff about all this?"

"Hell, no."

"Don't tell them yet," said MacArthur. "I don't want them scared to death."[19]

Once he had Marilinan in operation, Kenney hit Japanese air bases hard, inflicting heavy losses and paving the way for major advances at sea and on the ground. On August 24 MacArthur returned to his advanced headquarters at Port Moresby to oversee the the final push to capture Lae. It also gave him the perfect excuse to avoid an important visitor, Eleanor Roosevelt.

Shortly before leaving, MacArthur had sent for Eichelberger and informed him that Mrs. Roosevelt was planning to visit SWPA. She wanted to visit American troops and tour the military hospitals. Eichelberger would fly to Nouméa, meet Mrs. Roosevelt there, bring her to Australia and accompany her throughout her trip.[20] MacArthur feared, however, that she would insist on visiting the troops in New Guinea. He told Eichelberger that on no account was Mrs. Roosevelt to be allowed anywhere near it. His fears were misplaced. She never made such a request, to his, and Eichelberger's, intense relief.[21] And although Eleanor Roosevelt did not get to meet MacArthur, Jean hosted an official dinner in her honor at Lennon's, just as events at the front came to a dramatic climax.

Lae was isolated from reinforcement by land, sea or air, enabling MacArthur to play his ace: He would have the 503d Parachute Infantry Regiment dropped onto an abandoned Japanese airstrip, at Nadzab, twenty miles northwest of Lae. When he and Kenney discussed SWPA's first airborne assault at Government House in Port Moresby, Kenney mentioned casually that he was planning to go along and see how the drop of the 503d went. MacArthur told him, "George, I don't think you should go." Kenney protested that he had a right to see how his airmen handled an operation like this. It was their first airborne drop. Besides, they were his "kids."

"You're right, George," MacArthur decided. "We'll both go. They're my kids too."

Kenney objected vehemently. "That doesn't make sense. Why is it necessary for you to risk having some five-dollar-a-month Jap aviator shoot a hole in you?" MacArthur stared for a moment at Kenney. His short, crewcut air commander seemed to have forgotten something: MacArthur never feared shot or shell. The idea that he even thought of such things was more wounding than bullets. "I'm not worried about getting shot," MacArthur told him evenly. "Honestly, the only thing that worries me is the possibility that when we hit the rough air over the mountains my stomach might get upset. I'd hate to get sick and disgrace myself in front of the kids," he said, hinting obliquely at his seasickness during the escape from the Philippines.[22]

Kenney could see the uselessness of argument. MacArthur was going along, and that was it, but it would be foolish to have both of them fly in the same plane. He would fly in one B-17, with MacArthur in another. They would fly above and to one side of the ninety-six C-47s that dropped the seventeen hundred paratroopers onto the heavily overgrown airstrip.

Came the day, the C-47s, escorted by more than two hundred bombers and fighters, carried the 503d into the first successful Allied combat jump of World War II. The drop took only three minutes and the paratroopers landed exactly where they were supposed to. It looked flawless to MacArthur, who was enthralled by both the spectacle of this new form of warfare and the skill of its implementation. And adding to his delight, Kenney awarded him the Air Medal for being part of the operation. The airstrip was seized, the tall grass swiftly cut, troops pushed down the trail toward Lae and at daybreak next morning the C-47s came back, ferrying in the Australian 7th Division.[23]

Lae was now under strong attack from three sides. The town fell on September 16. Thousands of Japanese escaped into the jungle-clad mountainous terrain north of the town. But cold, hunger and tropical diseases would kill many of them. With the Japanese no longer posing a threat to Papua, MacArthur was poised to seize control of the western side of the Vitiaz Strait. Cartwheel was unfolding almost exactly as planned, but to MacArthur's dismay and frustration, instead of exploiting these victories, the JCS had abandoned its declared goal of capturing Rabaul. Worse, it seemed set to throw out his own declared goal of returning to the Philippines too.

Admiral King was a hard-drinking sailor who had vowed to remain abstinent for the duration. At Casablanca, however, he came crashing off the wagon, got noisily drunk, to Marshall's embarrassment, but sobered up sufficiently to convince the rest of the Combined Chiefs to sanction, in principle, a powerful Navy drive across the Central Pacific. Nimitz thought it a bad idea. Halsey, when he learned of it, was also opposed. Marshall had grave doubts that it would achieve anything beyond the capture of a lot of useless islands.[24]

If that was what King wanted, though, he was almost certain to get it. The admiral held four aces: a Navy President, public opinion (which was thirsting to avenge Pearl Harbor), King's unshakable confidence in his own strategic ideas and the immense fleet that would be commissioned in 1943. The vessels laid down before Pearl Harbor were pouring out of the shipyards in 1943: fast carriers, light carriers, escort carriers, all in abundance; fast battleships, powerful modern cruisers, dozens of submarines, scores of destroyers. And there would be even more to come in 1944.

This awesome host in steel gray was built around the ninety-six-plane *Essex*-class fast carrier. It was designed from keel to bridge to conduct an offensive naval war, and the United States had too much invested in these warships not to employ them. To bring forth the full measure of deadly advantage latent within it, the fleet of 1943 needed the broad waters of the Central Pacific. When the Combined Chiefs met in Quebec in August 1943, King won the authority needed to unleash his Central Pacific drive.

What, though, should be done about Rabaul? King's answer, supported by the Joint Staff planners, was to isolate it, neutralize it and leave it to rot. The Navy no longer needed its huge harbor. The focus of operations would now be much farther north and west.

Marshall reluctantly went along with the new offensive and the new axis of advance it implied, but MacArthur found it intolerable. For one thing, if the drive across the Central Pacific succeeded, SWPA would become a backwater in the Pacific war. And if it did not succeed, Rabaul would have to be taken after all. He continued to believe that Rabaul would have to be captured eventually, if only for its wonderful harbor. Besides, the operations to isolate and neutralize Rabaul that fall would go ahead as planned. There was no instruction to cancel them.[25]

MacArthur and his staff met with Halsey's staff on September 10 in Brisbane. MacArthur proposed to have the air forces of both SWPA and SoPac launch an aerial blitz against Rabaul in late October that would neutralize Japanese airpower sufficiently for Halsey to grab a large piece of Bougainville around November 1. If these operations succeeded, his and Halsey's airmen would then launch another aerial campaign in December to allow SWPA to mount an amphibious assault against Cape Gloucester, on the southwestern coast of New Britain, in the last week of the year. Halsey raised some objections about timing, but by and large this became the plan for SWPA and SoPac operations.[26]

No matter how well MacArthur planned these assaults he still faced a desperate shortage of shipping. Any merchant ship that arrived in SWPA was likely to find itself more or less commandeered. This brought protests from the War Shipping Administration, but MacArthur circumvented the WSA and put the problem squarely in the lap of the commander of the Army Service Forces, Lieutenant General Brehon Somervell. The pace of operations was being held back by the shipping crisis, MacArthur informed him, and "sustained effort may be impossible in this theater because of a lack of mobility." Even when he had been able to scrape up enough men and matériel to attack the Japanese, he was never able to exploit his victories. "This results from lack of shipping."[27]

These frustrations found melodramatic expression in letters to old friends. In a self-pitying mood, he wrote to George Van Horn Moseley that fall, "Out here I have had a hard time from the very beginning. . . . I often recall Stonewall Jackson's remark—'If necessary I will fight them with sticks and stones.' "[28]

To John Callan O'Laughlin, he complained even more bitterly, "Probably no commander in American history has been so poorly supported. If I had not had the Australians I would have been lost indeed. At times it has looked as though it was intended that I should be defeated."[29]

MacArthur often kept his deepest feelings and real intentions from his subordinates, but there were times when his frustration grew so great his self-control broke down. He concluded one planning session that fall, at which the lack of shipping forced him to postpone an amphibious assault by a couple of weeks, by complaining bitterly, "There are some people in Washington who would rather see MacArthur lose a battle than America win a war."[30]

Correspondents such as Moseley and O'Laughlin could have been forgiven for imagining that MacArthur had been told to win the war in the Pacific more or less on his own, then expected to do it with a rowboat and a platoon of musketeers.

In 1942–43 ground commanders around the world were operating on threadbare shoestrings. So were air commanders. In the CBI Stilwell was trying to stop the advancing Japanese but could not get his hands on a single American division despite being a favorite of both Marshall and Stimson. At Casablanca Eisenhower nearly burst into tears as he described his logistical problems to Marshall. In England the Eighth Air Force was getting its clock wiped in the summer and fall of 1943 by the Luftwaffe's day fighter arm. Short of planes, experience and range, it seemed set to lose the struggle for air superiority, and its commander, Ira Eaker, was fired. The assault by Mark Clark's Fifth Army at Salerno in September 1943 was so short of shipping, men and firepower it nearly ended in disaster. MacArthur's problems were compelling but not remotely unique.[31]

Yet unlike Kenney, who got the most he could out of whatever was handed him and never complained, MacArthur felt victimized. It may have been due in part to the fact that his was not and would never be the principal theater of war. This was a constant irritant, raising a barrier to objectivity too high for him to overcome. Bad enough to be given a secondary theater. Totally galling to have the salt of penury rubbed into the wound.

One thing he did get that fall, though, was his own airplane. When news got out early in 1943 that the AAF was developing the four-engine C-54 transport, MacArthur, like a lot of generals, asked for one. Arnold had to turn him down but started action to provide him with his own B-17. It would never be as comfortable as a C-54, but some improvements were made and armor plate was added.[32] One day toward the end of October MacArthur sent for Henry Godman, his personal pilot.

He told Godman to go to Wright-Patterson Air Force Base in Dayton, Ohio, and collect the B-17. "Godman, I want the plane named *Bataan,* and the artist is to paint a map of the Philippines on the side of the nose and then to have the word *Bataan* painted across it. That's an order."[33]

While Godman was collecting the plane, Kenney was conducting the aerial offensive MacArthur had proposed at the September 10 conference with Halsey's staff. With airfields on Kiriwina putting his P-38s in range of Rabaul, Kenney had stopped bombing Rabaul (ineffectively) at night. The Fifth Air Force was blasting Rabaul in broad daylight. Halsey's Third

Fleet pilots joined in this offensive. Between October 12 and November 11 the Japanese lost more than two hundred planes at Rabaul, mainly on the ground, and more than a dozen ships.[34]

Even so, this bastion of enemy strength had not been made untenable to shipping. Nor had it been isolated from air reinforcement. In fact, its air strength had been maintained. But this had been achieved by flying planes down from the Central Pacific—just as King's Central Pacific offensive was unleashed. This drive opened with the Marine Corps' famously bloody assault against Tarawa on November 20. The Imperial Japanese fleet pulled back from Rabaul, to fight the U.S. Navy farther north, abruptly reducing Rabaul's military value to close to zero, more or less neutralizing it overnight.

By this time the Australians had secured the Huon Peninsula in an arduous campaign against formidable terrain and tenacious defenders. With the peninsula firmly in his hands, MacArthur now had control of the New Guinea side of the Vitiaz Strait. What remained was to secure the New Britain side. On that side of the water all he needed, he decided, was a large level site for an airfield and a small harbor suitable for a PT boat base.

His G-3, Brigadier General Stephen Chamberlin, argued for Cape Gloucester as the airfield site and persisted even after Kenney told him the ground there might be too swampy to take bombers. Kenney, on the other hand, knew next to nothing about naval operations but was arguing that the place to go for was Arawe. MacArthur accepted Chamberlin's argument about the airfield and Kenney's about the PT boat base![35]

He was worried up to the last minute about the possible strength of enemy resistance at Arawe. MacArthur did not want on his conscience a bloodbath like Tarawa, where three thousand marines were killed or wounded taking an area half the size of Central Park. He insisted on extensive and detailed photo reconnaissance before okaying the attack.[36]

The assault would be mounted from Goodenough Island, just off the Huon Peninsula. MacArthur flew up to Goodenough on December 13 to watch the loading of the troops. Arawe would provide Krueger's Alamo Task Force, i.e., Sixth Army, with its combat debut. The unit selected to make the assault was the 112th Cavalry Regiment.

The morning of December 14, as the 2d Engineer Special Brigade prepared to put the 112th Cavalry ashore at Arawe, Kenney's Fifth Air Force hit the defenders with the heaviest bombing so far seen in the Pacific. The invaders took Arawe slowly, but at a cost of fewer than five hundred casualties.[37]

The morning of the Arawe attack Kenney flew George Marshall to Goodenough from Port Moresby. The Combined Chiefs had met in Cairo earlier that month. MacArthur had sent Sutherland to the meeting, but

Marshall evidently felt there were some things he ought to tell MacArthur personally. It was something he had hoped to do months earlier, but more urgent business had always intervened.[38]

For two years now Marshall had been on the receiving end of messages from MacArthur decrying the lack of support for SWPA and blaming, by implication, the War Department for letting him down. At this, their only personal meeting in the course of the war, Marshall wanted to tell MacArthur that his problems did not stem from the War Department. They came, he said, from Admiral King, who did not believe there was any need for the Army to control even one theater in the Pacific. The Pacific belonged to the Navy. The admiral, Marshall remarked, "resents the prominent part you have in the Pacific war," and King's criticisms of MacArthur were personal and vehement. The Navy also encouraged the production of publicity that disparaged MacArthur. King's hostility was supported, in a general way, by the secretary of the navy, Frank Knox, by the chairman of the JCS, Admiral William D. Leahy, and by Roosevelt. Against that kind of opposition, there was little that he, Marshall, could do to get a higher priority for SWPA.[39]

MacArthur ruminated aloud about the Navy's failures and defeats in the Pacific war to date and pointedly remarked that there had been no naval debacles in *his* theater. He was appalled that interservice rivalry should be allowed to undermine the prosecution of the war and repeated what he had said before: that there should be unity of command in the Pacific. If that meant his becoming a subordinate commander, he would accept the assignment.

Marshall was sympathetic to MacArthur's concerns about being bottled up in New Guinea as the Navy thrust across the Central Pacific but was not encouraging about being able to change it.[40] So long as there was a president whose favorite garment was a blue Navy cape Marshall would always be at a disadvantage in the struggle over Pacific strategy, and MacArthur knew that as well as he.

SWPA's last major operation went ahead as planned. Shortly after Marshall's departure for the United States, MacArthur returned to Goodenough Island. Despite suffering from a sore throat and a heavy cold, he wanted personally to wish the marines well in their scheduled assault on Cape Gloucester. "I know what the marines think of me," he told the division commander, Major General William H. Rupertus, "but I also know that when they go into a fight, they can be counted on to do an outstanding job. Good luck."[41]

On Christmas Day, the 2d Engineer Special Brigade put the 1st Marine Division ashore. There was only slight opposition to the assault, but the terrain was as swampy and treacherous as Kenney had feared. The marines found the risk of drowning almost as great as the risk of being shot. It took three weeks to secure Cape Gloucester.

It would soon become clear that neither Arawe nor Cape Gloucester had any real military value. No PT boat base was ever created at Arawe. No bombers ever flew from Cape Gloucester. In early 1944 MacArthur's war made a sudden change of direction, leaving these hollow victories on New Britain far behind.

My Ku Klux Klan

The atmosphere at MacArthur's Government House headquarters in Port Moresby reflected the commander himself—so casual it could be taken for a mockery of traditional military ideas of good order and discipline. The relaxed ethos at Government House was more like that of a military base of the 1990s than one of the 1930s. Guards were permitted to lounge at their posts, lean against the walls, gossip among themselves, stirring languidly from time to time to toss off a sketch of a salute when an officer appeared, before resuming their conversation where they'd been forced to leave off. MacArthur sometimes wandered the grounds in white silk pajamas and a Japanese silk dressing gown with a large black dragon embroidered on the back, deep in thought as reality and fantasy merged among the frangipani trees. At other times he sprawled in an overstuffed chair out on the veranda, smoking a pipe, reading reports, chatting with an aide and paying little heed to the awestruck passersby gawping at him from the street that bordered the lawn.[1]

For all the insouciance of his demeanor, MacArthur remained as attentive to his image as ever. Like his hero, Napoleon, once he had established a totemic picture of himself as the most resplendent figure in uniform, he suddenly enfolded himself in a simplicity equally extreme, equally noticeable now that there were generals parading across the pages of every American newspaper, nearly all of whom proudly sported growing medal collections. Much as he had done when he took up the superintendency at West Point, MacArthur chose to have legend ornament his chest. From the summer of 1943 he wore not a single ribbon, badge or stripe, nothing but the insignia of his rank. Above all, though, he retained the field marshal's cap. After its ordeals by tropical sun and a seawater dunking, its glitter had faded. In the summer of 1943 he got the cap overhauled in New York.[2]

Sid Huff returned from the United States bearing the rebraided cap and told MacArthur that while there was a lot of interest in him back home, "One of the things people asked me was this: 'Why does MacArthur carry that cane around all the time? Is he feeble?' " Pinky's walnut cane went into retirement overnight.[3]

The military victories of 1943—the Battle of the Bismarck Sea, the defense of Wau, the drop at Nadzab (the first strategic airborne success of the U.S. Army and the crucial jump that probably saved the 82d Airborne Division from being broken up after its bad experiences in Sicily), the capture of Lae, the clearing of the Huon Peninsula, the assaults on Arawe and Cape Gloucester—had restored MacArthur's reputation as a brilliant combat commander. His stock rose sharply in the War Department. New Year's Day 1944 brought a surprisingly warm message from Stimson, who was not normally a MacArthur admirer. Stimson, a restrained, buttoned-up ornament of the Wall Street Republican establishment, effusively signed himself "Very sincerely, your friend. . . ." On his sixty-fourth birthday, January 26, MacArthur was awarded his third Distinguished Service Medal, by Marshall.[4]

However gratifying such gestures were, he continued to keep the Pentagon at arm's length. The bright young lieutenant colonels who provided the bulk of the brains in the Operations Division regularly came up with ideas intended to help the various theater commanders achieve the objectives set for them by the Combined and Joint Chiefs. They were trying too to ensure that what was being done in one theater was coordinated with operations elsewhere in the world.

When they sent their planning outlines to GHQ, though, MacArthur was nearly always dismissive. He was likely to make a cutting remark such as "Well, the boys are getting pretty good at making these plans," crumple up the document and throw it into his wastebasket.[5]

He made his own plans, often down to the last detail. MacArthur's knowledge of the finer points of operations was remarkable. It was often misunderstood, by admirers and detractors alike, if for different reasons. The admirers saw it as brilliance at work; the detractors as high-level meddling in nuts-and-bolts issues that in a well-run command were left to majors and lieutenant colonels. MacArthur immersed himself in the details of operations not because he was an egomaniac but because he had little choice.

Almost everyone who dealt with MacArthur's staff, from Marshall down, remarked on its general mediocrity. There was, for example, an exceptionally able young officer in the Fifth Air Force named Colonel Frederic Smith,

Jr. He had brought the 8th Fighter Group to New Guinea in 1942, led it superbly and been rapidly promoted to run the V Fighter Command. One piquant detail about Smith was that he also happened to be Admiral King's son-in-law. He was nonetheless a fervent MacArthur man, convinced he was the greatest commander of the war. At the conclusion of a long and successful military career that brought him four stars, Smith looked back at the GHQ staff with nothing but contempt. He called it "as inept a staff as I have ever operated with." On the other hand, Smith observed, "MacArthur had a grasp of the situation which was magnificent."[6]

Visitors such as Eddie Rickenbacker were often struck by how hard MacArthur made his staff work. A typical day for an officer assigned to GHQ ran from 7:00 A.M. until 9:00 P.M., seven days a week. Sundays were like Mondays. A visitor from the War Department in 1944 suggested to him that he was working his staff to death. MacArthur seemed almost amused at the prospect. "Well, could they die a nobler death?"[7]

All the same, he kept a watch on their well-being. In February 1944 MacArthur's doctor, Lieutenant Colonel Charles Morhouse, returned to the United States. His replacement was Lieutenant Colonel Roger O. Egeberg. At their first meeting MacArthur told Egeberg, "I also want you to be the doctor for the officers at GHQ. These officers need a bit of special help. As you know by now, officers in the field, in combat, relieve their emotions, their energy, in action. . . . In the intermediate headquarters the officers can kick up their heels on Saturday nights and at parties. But the officers at GHQ have neither of these outlets. They are working hard, long hours. . . . I can see that some are already pretty tense. . . . I want you to get to know those officers. . . . If you think that one of them is near the end of his rope and needs to get away for a week or two, tell me about it and I'll do my best to see that it's made possible."[8]

One reason he worked the GHQ staff so hard was that grinding effort, a steady, flat-footed plod toward eventual victory, was really all that most of them had to offer. There was no inspiration there, no daring, no imagination or cleverness. MacArthur had to provide that for himself or seek it elsewhere, from people such as Kenney.

He had learned not to expect it from Sutherland, that supreme workaholic and master of the book solution. Such traits were why he had excelled in the schools and as a peacetime chief of staff. These were, even now, reasons why many of those who dealt with him thought Sutherland was outstanding: They could see the effort, they could applaud the mastery of doctrine, but being limited people themselves they remained oblivious to what was missing.

While MacArthur worked as hard as his staff, he covered his tracks in various ways. He was so successful that a respected writer like Eric

Larrabee could conclude that MacArthur was not the inspired commander his admirers believed but merely a pompous mediocrity who did nothing but okay what a hardworking staff brought to him.[9]

There are few documents bearing MacArthur's signature that prove he ever thought of this or ordered that. Ever since his time as superintendent he had shown his preferred way of getting things down was by conversation, not correspondence. He destroyed letters once he had answered them. He abhorred paperwork, meetings and routine—everything a trained staff officer lives by. His myth of himself was MacArthur the commander, not MacArthur the wizard of staff work. He had responsibilities like Eisenhower's but a self-image like Patton's. "What the hell is the use of a staff?" he once remarked to Kenney. "All they do is write the histories after the war is over. The decisions ought to be made by the commander and his fighting subordinates. What the hell is the staff man? What's he doing in this conference making a decision? My three fighting commanders and I will decide what to do."[10]

MacArthur's management style seemed almost calculated to frustrate historians. He gave firm orders to his staff that all drafts of letters, plans, reports and communiqués that flowed from those decisions had to be destroyed. A document could go through half a dozen permutations, yet in most cases not a trace of the effort involved or of any individual's contribution can be discerned. By and large, however, MacArthur provided the original ideas, demanded changes as Sutherland or the staff worked to turn his ideas into a plan or a communication and gave his approval only when he was satisfied they had done what he wanted. The fact that a document was signed by Sutherland or someone else means little. The communiqués, for example, were signed by Diller, but MacArthur wrote all of them.[11]

Sutherland continued to intimidate the GHQ staff and tried to justify his bullying ways as being the most effective method of waging war. At breakfast one morning he held forth on the shortcomings of democracy in times of conflict. A strong, authoritarian government under one man, he argued, was more effective in a crisis than any democratic government with its cumbersome procedures and endless debates. What could be more absurd than wasting a nation's political energies in a national crisis than fighting elections or having debates in Congress? In wartime a dictatorship came into its own.

MacArthur listened attentively, then told him, "Dick, you are wrong," and proceeded to extol the flexibility of democratic government and its way of drawing on all the talents of a nation. "Democracy costs money and lives and at times it does look inefficient," he conceded, "but it wins in the end. No matter how you look at it, in the final analysis, democracy as we have it in the United States is the best form of government that man has ever evolved. The trouble with you, Dick, is that you are just a natural born Fascist."[12]

MacArthur's dissatisfaction with Sutherland's bullying methods continued to grow. As the reader may recall, in May 1943 MacArthur had talked with Kenney about his desire to get rid of Sutherland, but Marshall had declined to give him any of the people he wanted as a replacement. There were by now many reasons for him to want to be rid of Sutherland.

For one thing, Sutherland was suffering from high blood pressure and a frighteningly erratic pulse. His medical problems and the medication for them probably aggravated an already cantankerous temperament.[13] More important than any of that, though, was the fact that Sutherland, despite being married and with a family back in the United States, had fallen head over brass hat for an upper-class Australian woman, Elaine Bessemer-Clarke. This affair has inspired a novel by the Australian writer Thomas Keneally, the renowned author of *Schindler's List*. What most Americans know of it, however, is based on the account in *American Caesar*. Unfortunately William Manchester, in his enthusiasm to tell this story, managed to get nearly every detail wrong. According to him, for example, Elaine Bessemer-Clarke "fucked her way to the top." She began by seducing junior officers and worked her way up the chain of command until she reached Sutherland.[14]

The fact is, she started at the top. Her father, Sir Norman Brooks, was the outstanding Australian tennis player of the 1920s. Her mother, Dame Mabel Brooks, was Australia's leading socialite. Elaine grew up surrounded by people with titles and millions. The idea that she would bother with obscure U.S. Army lieutenants and captains is ludicrous.

Like Sutherland, Elaine was married. But while he had married an ordinary middle-class woman of no particular distinction, she had married an English millionaire, Reginald Bessemer-Clarke, one of the heirs to the Bessemer steel fortune. Her husband was no impediment: He had been taken prisoner when the Australian 8th Division surrendered in Malaya and would spend most of the war in Singapore's Changi Jail, one of the most nefarious prisoner of war camps of the twentieth century. Only one man in fifteen survived imprisonment in Changi.

Manchester calls Elaine "a beautiful Australian girl," which is stretching the truth more than somewhat. At the time she met Sutherland she was thirty-two and had a three-year-old son. She was also, as her photographs show, remarkably plain, with heavy features, a nondescript figure and mousy hair. Certainly there had been no rush of young men eager to marry her. She was approaching thirty when she married. Women of her class usually married in their early twenties. Those few who did not often had careers to pursue instead. Elaine, however, had never had a job, had no skills or training to do anything.

Shortly after MacArthur and his staff reached Melbourne, some of the city's leading lights held a party to welcome them. Elaine met Sutherland at this party and within a few weeks, possibly only a few days, the two of them were lovers. When GHQ moved to Brisbane, Elaine soon followed.[15]

Sutherland could not get enough of her. Sex was obviously part of it. But by all accounts Elaine was a domineering, unpleasant person—much like Sutherland himself. It is a guess, no more than that, but it may well be that Sutherland, like other bullies who are really cowards at heart, had fallen in love with her because she dominated *him*.

In early 1943 he managed to get her commissioned in the Women's Army Corps by exploiting a loophole in the law that created the WAC. Two other Australian women, the secretaries of George Kenney and Richard J. Marshall, were commissioned at the same time. No one at GHQ minded the two secretaries being commissioned. They both were highly trained, well experienced and an asset to GHQ's efficiency. Elaine, on the other hand, wasn't qualified to do anything. Yet Sutherland was totally blind to her shortcomings and made her assistant to the headquarters commandant. Captain Clarke supervised the guards and the receptionists and issued passes to the GHQ staff. She liked to perch herself in a white summer uniform on a high stool near the entrance to the AMP Building, where she could get a good look at everyone as he or she entered. MacArthur had to pass under her gaze several times a day.[16]

While we can be sure she always had a pleasant greeting for him, she showed a different face to everyone else. Elaine Clarke was a sharp-tongued upper-class rich bitch who regarded most people she encountered as trash in human form. MacArthur's pilot, Major Henry Godman, for example, had managed to obtain a jeep. He was so thrilled to have his own vehicle he paid to get the seats upholstered in red leather. Captain Clarke admired Godman's jeep, and one day, when Godman was away on a trip, she called the motor pool and commandeered it. On his return, he soon tracked it down and, using his spare keys, reclaimed it. Two days later Godman was called in by Sutherland, who told him bluntly, "You have been transferred from MacArthur's headquarters. I'm sending you back to combat."

Godman was astounded. He had already flown his full quota of thirty-five combat missions, but back to the war he went. MacArthur later learned what had happened and was reported to be furious. Even so, Godman flew another thirteen missions. It speaks volumes about Sutherland and his mistress that they were prepared to put a man's life at risk over possession of a jeep, and had Godman been killed or crippled, it's unlikely that either one of them would have been troubled for an instant. Little wonder, then, that both were detested by nearly everyone at GHQ.[17]

Despite his growing disenchantment with Sutherland, MacArthur put him in for promotion. MacArthur demanded loyalty of an almost feudal nature from his subordinates. One way of cementing it was to reward them even when he was unimpressed by their performance. He promoted people partly on the basis of hard work because he believed strongly in loyalty down as well as up and partly because he was not prepared to see his own command slighted. When Eisenhower's chief of staff, Walter Bedell Smith, was promoted to lieutenant general in January 1944, MacArthur promptly recommended Sutherland for a third star. The award came through two months later, and it was taken by the GHQ staff, including Sutherland, as approbation for outstanding work during the past year, although it was, in fact, nothing of the kind.

MacArthur had few illusions about his chief of staff, who regularly blocked access to him, spoke in MacArthur's name on matters over which he had no authority whatever, lied to MacArthur whenever it suited him and continued to defy him over the privileges and perquisites showered on Elaine Clarke.[18]

When specific idiocies were drawn to his attention, MacArthur acted swiftly and firmly to correct them. Casey, for example, had secured the offer of the services of Leif Sverdrup, one of the most successful civil engineers in the United States and a master of large-scale construction projects. Delighted at his coup, he swiftly drafted a cable to the Pentagon recommending that Sverdrup be commissioned a colonel and assigned to GHQ. As a matter of routine, he handed the cable to Sutherland, expecting him to pass it on to MacArthur. Instead Sutherland, fortified by a boundless ignorance of engineering in modern war and asserting an authority he did not possess, brusquely swept it aside. "I can't approve that."

Outraged, Casey grabbed at the cable and, before Sutherland could move, headed for MacArthur's office, told him that Sverdrup was a brilliant engineer capable of supervising construction of the big engineering projects that would be needed, such as airfields and harbors, and showed him the wire. MacArthur immediately initialed it "OK—MacA." On this occasion Sutherland was thwarted. There were many others when he wasn't.[19]

In January 1944, as MacArthur planned the battles ahead, Australian troops were driving the Japanese from the northern coast of the Huon Peninsula. On January 15 the Australians overran the small coastal town of Sio, which the Japanese 20th Division had successfully defended for two months. The Australians probed the beach for booby traps and unearthed something much more interesting—a hurriedly buried trunk filled with Japanese Army codebooks. The covers had been ripped off and probably sent to Tokyo as proof that the codebooks had been destroyed. When the contents of the trunk were flown back to MacArthur's code breakers at the Central Bureau, they could hardly believe their luck. For more than a year they had struggled to crack two hundred to three hundred Japanese Army messages each month. Now, with the entire cryptographic library of the 20th Division to draw upon, they could read more than five hundred messages every day almost as easily as if they had been transmitted in pig Latin.[20]

The Central Bureau's product went to MacArthur's assistant chief of staff, G-2, Brigadier General Charles Willoughby, who handled everything that might be termed combat intelligence. Willoughby analyzed all the intelligence material that came in, whether from the code breakers at the Central Bureau, spies behind enemy lines, aerial reconnaissance, interrogations of Japanese prisoners or translations of enemy documents.

His evaluations could vary almost from day to day. Willoughby had a habit of submitting what amounted to back-to-back contradictory assessments, like a man trying to cover both sides of the coin or at least his posterior.[21] Some of his assessments had been almost tragically wrong. He had regularly dismissed Australian intelligence summaries, including those that forecast the Japanese attempt to capture Port Moresby. Sutherland openly detested him, probably because Willoughby had unrestricted access to MacArthur. Other officers simply despised Willoughby as a pompous and fundamentally mediocre man elevated to an important position mainly on the basis of doglike devotion to MacArthur. As another GHQ staffer remarked, "Willoughby has the best hindsight of any intelligence officer in the Army." And Kenney said flatly, "Willoughby was a better historian than an intelligence man."[22]

Throughout the operations of 1943 it was noticeable that MacArthur seemed to pay almost no attention to what Willoughby told him. No operation was called off because of Willoughby's analyses; no operation was mounted on the basis of them. MacArthur did what he wanted to do regardless of the combat intelligence picture. In 1944, however, as both the quality and quantity of the intelligence available improved, that would change. MacArthur came to rely increasingly on intelligence—particularly signals intelligence, otherwise known as Ultra—to guide him.

One thing that did not change was his determination to exercise total control of intelligence activities in SWPA. The War Department, concerned with both efficiency and security, repeatedly sought to coordinate MacArthur's intelligence operations with those at Arlington Hall, the principal Signal Corps code-breaking center, near Washington. Marshall wanted strict and uniform controls on the handling of Ultra throughout the world, and a small number of highly intelligent Ultra liaison officers (usually lawyers with Wall Street backgrounds) had been trained for that purpose. They would decide who saw Ultra decrypts and ensure the safe handling of them. It was an arrangement other theater commanders accepted, but MacArthur managed to resist. He insisted that anyone sent to SWPA to conduct intelligence activities had to be assigned to his command. The Central Bureau maintained a close relationship with Arlington Hall when it came to exchanging technical knowledge. Apart from that, it remained under MacArthur's control, and so, for all practical purposes, did the Ultra liaison officers who were allowed, grudgingly, into his theater.[23]

The Office of Strategic Services meanwhile sought to establish a foothold in SWPA. The OSS, run by MacArthur's former Rainbow comrade and fellow Medal of Honor winner "Wild Bill" Donovan, was by 1944 conducting clandestine operations in half a dozen countries, with even more ambitious plans for the year ahead. Donovan had tried repeatedly to get MacArthur to permit the OSS to operate in SWPA and failed every time. "I am completely opposed to the establishment in this theatre of a subordinate military operative agency directly connected with my headquarters and the local war effort, yet not subject to the command and control of the commander in chief," MacArthur informed Marshall in August 1943, and he never budged from that line.[24]

Every Donovan biographer has tried to explain it by inventing a feud between MacArthur and Donovan, supposedly dating back to their days in the Rainbow Division and claiming it was because MacArthur was jealous of Wild Bill's Medal of Honor. There is no evidence of envy, however, and even had someone other than Donovan been running OSS MacArthur would have still been determined to exercise tight control over his theater. What's more, his attitude was shared by Nimitz, who adamantly refused to allow the OSS to operate in any of the three theaters he commanded. So far as is known, Nimitz had no feud with Donovan. He had never even met him.

While MacArthur was always vigilant to maintain complete control over intelligence operations in his theater, the only covert ventures in which he showed anything that could be considered a strong personal interest were those involving conditions in the Philippines. In the spring of 1943 he managed to get an old Manila acquaintance, Courtney Whitney, assigned to SWPA. Whitney, a former Army Air Corps pilot, had for thirteen years practiced law in Manila, where he had belonged to the same Masonic lodge as MacArthur and been on excellent terms with Quezon. Recalled to active duty in 1940, he had spent nearly three years in air intelligence when he was assigned to GHQ. On his arrival in Brisbane,

MacArthur greeted him like an old friend and told him to take control of guerrilla operations in the Philippines. He was to improve the guerrillas' organization, get supplies to them and get information out. He was to conduct a propaganda campaign to undermine the Japanese occupation and pave the way for the eventual liberation of the archipelago by stirring up resistance among the people. Whitney was to report not to Willoughby but directly to MacArthur.

At first astonished, but soon inspired, Whitney waited for MacArthur to finish, rose to leave and said, "General, I will deliver you periodic reports from my own operatives in the city of Manila within three months." MacArthur was surprised, thought for a moment, then laughed, delighted at Whitney's enthusiasm. "And what will be the penalty if you fail?" he asked. The question, although lightly put, was left hanging in the air.[25]

Almost nothing had been learned of conditions in the Philippines since the fall of Corregidor, and the prospects of Whitney's succeeding in his promise did not seem bright. Several weeks after this meeting Quezon's personal physician, Dr. Emidgio C. Cruz, arrived in Brisbane from the United States one night and insisted on seeing MacArthur. Quezon wanted Cruz to go to Manila, discuss the situation in the Philippines with General Manuel Roxas and report back to him. MacArthur considered it a fantastic and hopeless project. He told Cruz that his chances of getting into Manila were, at best, one in ten. As for getting out again, he said frankly, "Your chances are none at all." Nevertheless he had Cruz flown to Perth and put aboard a submarine, the USS *Thresher,* about to sail for a rendezvous with guerrillas in the southern Philippines.[26]

Whitney soon provided dramatic news of what had happened after the surrender of Corregidor. Three officers—AAF Captain William E. Dyess, Major Steven Mellnick and Commander Melvin H. McCoy—had escaped from the penal colony on the island of Davao with the aid of the guerrillas. They were brought out by the *Thresher* in early July. Dyess had survived the Bataan Death March, one of the most infamous episodes of the war.

MacArthur met with the three escapers, listening with evident emotion to their stories of how the Japanese were treating their prisoners of war. His jaw tightened. "The Japanese will pay for that humiliation and suffering," he said, before decorating all three men with the Distinguished Service Cross.[27]

He sought permission from the War Department to release the information they had given him to the press. Roosevelt instructed Marshall to turn down MacArthur's request, for fear that the inevitable public outcry would jeopardize the delicate talks already under way to get the Japanese to give the International Red Cross greater access to the prison camps. The story did not break until January 1944.[28]

MacArthur directed Whitney to limit guerrilla activities to gathering information and communicating it to Australia. There was no point in launching gesture pinprick attacks against the Japanese and bringing reprisals on helpless Filipinos. Nor did he want the Japanese to realize how extensive the guerrilla network was. That might only provoke them into mounting a major campaign to root it out.

Carlos Romulo suggested that one way to keep hopes of liberation high in the Philippines would be a personal pledge from MacArthur, the one man nearly every Filipino admired. Why not flood the archipelago with small items that were easy to carry, cheap to produce but in desperately short supply, such as pencils, candy bars, sewing kits and cigarettes? They could be packaged in wrappers that sported the U.S. and Philippine Commonwealth flags on one side, with "I Shall Return," superimposed over MacArthur's signature, on the other side. Whitney submitted a memorandum supporting Romulo's idea. MacArthur scrawled at the bottom of the memo, "No objection—I *shall* return. MacA."[29]

New Year's Day 1944 found the Australians closing rapidly on the north shore of the Huon Peninsula. MacArthur mounted an operation to trap the retreating Japanese by landing three thousand men at Saidor, roughly a hundred miles west of the Huon Peninsula, on January 2. The American commander, Brigadier General Clarence Martin, remained close to the water. Even after his men had been reinforced until they numbered more than seven thousand, he still chose not to drive inland. This allowed the Japanese to swerve around Saidor without difficulty and thwarted MacArthur's intentions. Even so, this operation moved Allied forces a hundred miles farther along the New Guinea coast from where they had been a month earlier.[30]

Meanwhile MacArthur had the GHQ staff draw up plans for an assault on Hansa Bay, some 150 miles northwest of Saidor. Hansa Bay, with its superb natural harbor and promising airfield sites nearby, was an obvious target. MacArthur did not intend to drive as far as Hansa Bay, however, without taking Rabaul first. For one thing, he needed a large advanced harbor for his Seventh Fleet. For another, he intended to make sure that his right flank was secure as he moved toward the Philippines.

As he pondered the huge maps pinned up on the walls at Government House, MacArthur was looking for a way to avoid storming Rabaul, where the Japanese were known to have seventy to eighty thousand troops, well dug in, with plenty of firepower. Even though the Imperial Japanese Navy had pulled out and its air defenses had been weakened, Rabaul remained a formidable target. During the August 1943 meeting with Halsey they had agreed on a strategy of "avoiding and by-passing strength wherever practicable instead of direct attack to obtain occupied areas."[31]

On January 26, MacArthur's sixty-fourth birthday, he visited Eichelberger's I Corps headquarters at Rockhampton. He said he wanted to be photographed with "the victorious troops of Buna in the field" and made an inspection of the 32d Division.[32] Eichelberger was surprised and embarrassed when MacArthur showed up without warning in the middle of a command post exercise. The general found Eichelberger in the jungle, dressed as if ready for war and slightly chagrined that he had forgotten this was the boss's birthday. MacArthur got into a jeep, with Eichelberger driving, as photographers crowded around. To Eichelberger's astonishment and disgust, GHQ later released some of the photographs taken that day with the caption "General MacArthur at the Front."[33]

Lunching with Eichelberger, MacArthur was in an expansive mood. Major strategic decisions were about to be made and, MacArthur said, he was taking a strong line with the War Department. "I told them they had to use me or I'd go home. I've accomplished my defensive mission. Our supply line to Australia is now safe. Two days ago, I won out. Halsey is now under me. I have 36 LSTs. I need 12 more, but if necessary I'll use Liberty ships.

"Nimitz wanted to take the islands north of Rabaul, but Tarawa scared the admirals so much they now plan to take some unoccupied coral atolls instead. I'll take Rabaul through starvation in four months. . . . The I Corps will go to Hansa Bay in April. . . . Nimitz must guard my right flank. I'll starve out Rabaul. . . . I'll have an army group out here, with at least four corps. . . . Arnold has fallen for my plan to group all the air forces into the largest fleet yet, so he is backing my plan."[34]

MacArthur remained obsessed with Rabaul even though the JCS had indicated months earlier that it was no longer his objective. Following the Quebec Conference in August 1943 he had been given clear, explicit instructions on the strategy he was to follow: "An advance along the north coast of New Guinea as far west as Vogelkop, by step-by-step airborne-waterborne advances."[35]

MacArthur deeply resented strategic directives such as this. As Kenney had discovered, "MacArthur believed that the commander out there, 10,000 miles away from Washington, should be entitled to run the war, that the duty of Washington was to pick out a good general and then give him the means and the money and the backing to win the war and get it over with as soon as possible to save money and lives. That was his whole theory."[36]

MacArthur's approach to strategy was also shaped by the near disaster at Buna. He sought, wherever possible, to move between and around Japanese strongpoints. His statements on the virtues of bypassing enemy strength encouraged journalists at the time to write about MacArthur as if he were the first commander in history to operate in this way. He himself never made any such claims. The kind of strategy he pursued was, MacArthur rightly said, "as old as war itself."

It had already been implemented to free the Aleutians. In May 1943 Rear Admiral Thomas C. Kinkaid had persuaded the Joint Chiefs to abandon their plan to seize the island of Kiska, which was the strongest Japanese position in the Aleutian chain, by direct assault. Kinkaid argued instead that Kiska should be isolated and bypassed and the more lightly defended island of Attu be seized instead. Once Attu had fallen, the Japanese abandoned Kiska without a fight.[37]

Toward the end of 1943 MacArthur managed to get rid of Vice Admiral Arthur Carpender, whose caution he had despised and railed against throughout the Buna campaign. Admiral King offered MacArthur the services of Kinkaid, partly because he did not think Kinkaid was very bright. The Navy was not going to lose much by having him assigned to MacArthur's command.[38]

The relationship between Kinkaid and MacArthur was never close. It nearly ended before it really began. During a discussion of proposed operations to isolate Rabaul, Kinkaid remarked, "Well, I will have to check with Admiral King."

MacArthur was incensed. "You have the right to send communications to Admiral King any time you want to," he said pointedly, "but the day you do I will request a new commander for the Seventh Fleet."[39]

MacArthur was equally wary at first with the commander of the VII Amphibious Force, Rear Admiral Daniel Barbey, who got much the same lecture on loyalty during his first meeting with MacArthur that Kenney had received. He told Barbey bluntly, "Since you were on Admiral King's staff, I assume you will write to him from time to time. But it is well to remember that echoes of what you say will come back to me." Barbey was stung by this remark. He seemed to have been judged guilty of disloyalty before he had actually done anything.

MacArthur didn't leave it there. He launched into a furious denunciation of the Navy and how it had failed him at Buna. The only sailors for whom he had a good word were the PT boat crews.

He told Barbey that GHQ was "a smoothly functioning team," which was almost funny, considering the hatreds and rivalries between Sutherland and Willoughby, Sutherland and Krueger and so on. Strategy in SWPA was directed toward a single goal, said MacArthur: the reconquest of the Philippines. Not only did the United States have a moral obligation to free the Filipinos from Japanese occupation, but an Allied drive toward the islands would embolden people throughout Southeast Asia to defy the Japanese invaders of their countries. "Your job is to develop an amphibious force that can carry my troops in those campaigns," said MacArthur.

With that off his chest, he then turned to Barbey and asked a question that left the admiral bewildered: "Are you a lucky officer?" Like Napoleon, MacArthur seems to have felt that the most important attribute a commander could possess was good luck.

Barbey was not sure how to answer the question or what to make of his new boss. It was a worrying beginning for the admiral, but his ultimate judgment was this: "MacArthur proved to be the finest commander I ever worked for."[40]

One of the most important reasons he inspired such loyalty was his way of giving a subordinate a mission, then leaving him alone while he sought to fulfill it. Unlike many senior commanders, MacArthur was not a back-seat driver. He assumed that other people could be trusted to do their jobs, and once he had them pointed in the right direction, he got out of their way. It was a method so different from their previous experiences that Krueger, Kenney and Kinkaid all found it liberating.

The way he initiated plans also bolstered their confidence. He would tell Sutherland to send for "my Ku Klux Klan." Closeted in his office with Krueger, Kenney and Kinkaid, MacArthur discussed the idea for the new plan with them alone. Sutherland was not there, or anyone else. This was a commanders' meeting, and staff officers were kept where they belonged—busy with staff work. MacArthur would present his idea for some future operation. The KKK considered whether it was feasible from an air, ground or naval point of view, offering whatever suggestions or objections they wished. Once the four fighting men had reached an agreement, their respective staffs were told what decision had been made. It was then up to them to draw up plans to implement it.[41]

MacArthur had to work, all the same, within the strategic limits set by the Joint Chiefs. Marshall had managed at the Cairo Conference to keep open the possibility of a return to the Philippines but had been obliged to accept that if a choice had to be made between one offensive or the other, the Central Pacific would get priority. The Navy intended to aim for a summer assault on the Marianas. An axis of advance so far north amounted to a threat that MacArthur's drive toward the Philippines would be bypassed. He could find himself concluding the war only as the conqueror of New Guinea, not the liberator of Manila.

From the Marianas the Navy's strategy pointed straight toward Formosa. King hoped to ignore the Philippines, except possibly for grabbing just enough real estate on northern Luzon to carve out an airfield to aid in the attack on Formosa. That was something the Marine Corps could probably handle without any help from the Army. King did not share MacArthur's belief in the importance of liberating the Philippines. If anything, he despised MacArthur's pledge to return as putting sentiment ahead of strategy.[42] King already seemed to be trying to force MacArthur onto the sidelines. In early February he got Marshall and Arnold to agree that the operations MacArthur had scheduled for April should be postponed if doing so would accelerate Nimitz's advance.[43]

On February 17 the Navy captured Eniwetok two months ahead of schedule. This news sent a shock wave through GHQ. While MacArthur was still trying to isolate Rabaul, Nimitz was making gigantic leaps westward. MacArthur had to do something dramatic to keep pace with Nimitz and prevent SWPA from becoming a backwater of the war. He decided to make a grab for the largest island in the Admiralties, Manus.

Almost unpopulated, Manus had a magnificent natural anchorage, Seeadler Harbor, and the nearby island of Los Negros boasted a large airfield, at Momote. Starting in mid-February the Fifth Air Force had begun flying regular reconnaissance missions over the Admiralties. On February 24 Kenney received a message that Los Negros and Manus appeared to be deserted. Three B-25s had flown over the islands as low as twenty feet and seen no signs of Japanese occupation. No one had shot at them. There was no washing on the laundry lines. Grass was growing in the bomb craters at Momote Airfield. Dirt had piled up in front of the field hospital doors. Gun positions that had recently held artillery pieces were empty.

Excited at this news, Kenney went to see MacArthur that evening and made a daring proposal: Invade the Admiralties immediately. Kenney did not believe there were more than three hundred Japanese troops left on the island. Eight hundred men of the 1st Cavalry Division taken in by destroyers could grab Momote Airfield. A small party of engineers should be able to get it operating pretty quickly. Kenney would then fly in reinforcements if they were needed. MacArthur was intrigued, but he did not think his staff could organize an assault on such short notice. Besides, the Central Bureau's information was that there were twenty-five hundred Japanese on Manus and fifteen hundred on Los Negros, and the two islands were so close together that troops on Manus could easily be moved to Los Negros to join in the battle.[44]

MacArthur sent for Kinkaid and for his G-3, Brigadier General Steve Chamberlin, to meet with Kenney next day. If Kenney could convince them, he said, he would okay the idea. Kenney argued for an hour and a half, at the end of which they agreed the risk was worth taking. Without any warning, Krueger was told to "prepare plans for an immediate reconnaissance in force on Los Negros island in the vicinity of Momote airstrip, with the object of remaining in occupancy in case the area is found to be inadequately defended by the enemy; or, in case of heavy resistance, to withdraw after all possible reconnaissance has been accomplished." The assault would be made on February 29, just four days away.[45]

The prospect loomed of MacArthur's reliving one of his father's most famous feats, the reconnaissance in force on the outskirts of Atlanta as Sherman prepared to capture the city. And like his father, he knew how easily a reconnaissance in force can turn into a military defeat.

Both Barbey and Krueger seethed at this decision. They had planned to assault Los Negros with the entire 1st Cavalry Division, on the assumption that the intelligence reports of four thousand Japanese troops on Manus and Los Negros were accurate. The defenses were to be heavily bombarded for weeks before the assault. And almost the whole of the VII Amphib would take part. Instead of that, Barbey was being pushed into a hasty operation, on a small scale, against a defender whose position had barely been weakened. He would not be able to employ his slow-moving LSTs and landing craft but would be forced to rely on destroyers, thrusting them into a narrow, shallow channel dotted with coral outcroppings that could rip open their thin-skinned hulls. As for Krueger, he was being asked to strike with a force of only nine hundred men at a target he'd planned to hit with nine thousand. MacArthur was risking a disaster that could end both their careers.[46]

He not only insisted on mounting the assault but intended to go along with the troops. He would make the decision himself whether the resistance encountered warranted pulling out or pressing on. Kenney was appalled. He told MacArthur that he was only going to get seasick if he went on a destroyer. "I'll fly you over on a B-24. You can even pull the bomb release yourself." Normally this might have appealed to the small boy in MacArthur, but he turned down Kenney's bribe. Frustrated, Kenney said that MacArthur would stand out clearly among the troops and some Japanese sniper was likely to try to shoot him.

MacArthur replied, "I have been taking the chance of being shot at all the years I have been in the Army. I am going to continue taking that chance when it is advisable." The one compromise he would make was to travel on a cruiser, the *Phoenix,* instead of a destroyer.[47]

He had given strict orders to Krueger that he was not to accompany the troops in any assault. When Krueger learned that MacArthur intended to go to Los Negros, he was shocked. It would be a calamity, he told MacArthur, if anything happened to him. MacArthur, however, told him simply, "I have to go." End of discussion.[48]

On February 27 he flew to Milne Bay to board the cruiser. Krueger was waiting for him there. When MacArthur went aboard, he shook hands with Krueger, told him how glad he was to see him, but Krueger said nothing. "What's the matter, Walter?" asked MacArthur, knowing full well that Krueger was angry, but still Krueger kept mum. The impromptu deed was not Krueger's idea of how to make war. Stolid and methodical, he was a man who soldiered by the book, not the inspiration. All the same, he was not going to argue with MacArthur. He was a taciturn, almost diffident figure, a man who wisely avoided arguments, because in debate with someone as articulate as MacArthur, he was certain to lose.[49]

That night Krueger had a party of six Alamo scouts go ashore on Los Negros. They reported back, "The place is lousy with Japs." MacArthur, however, would not even consider calling off the operation. The best way he could hold on to the Admiralties and prevent them from being transferred out of his theater was to take them. And if he went ashore and risked his life to help capture them, it was almost inconceivable that the JCS would respond by ordering him to give over to the Navy something he had seized, almost with his own hands and under enemy fire. Besides, if he failed to keep the Admiralties, there would be no return to the Philippines. His war would be as good as over. This was a high-stakes game, well worth gambling his soldier's life to win.[50]

As the invasion fleet sped toward the Admiralties in the early-morning hours of February 29, MacArthur was restless. He was too excited to sleep. Around one-thirty he sent for his doctor, Colonel Egeberg. MacArthur paced around his small cabin for half an hour, emotionally recalling his years as a cadet and his exploits on the West Point baseball team. As he spoke, he gradually calmed down. Egeberg took his pulse, which was slow and regular. MacArthur decided he was at last ready to go to sleep.[51]

At first light the invasion force closed on the beaches. MacArthur watched with keen interest as the *Phoenix* and its sister ship, the *Nashville,* bombarded Los Negros with their six-inch guns. When the bombardment lifted, three of Barbey's destroyer-transports rushed toward the beach and decanted nine hundred men of the 1st Cavalry Division under Brigadier General William C. Chase. The cavalrymen took less than two hours to reach Momote Airfield. By noon they were driving the defenders into the jungle. Enemy resistance was slight; losses were negligible. At 4:00 P.M. MacArthur went ashore.[52]

Accompanied by his aide Colonel Lloyd "Larry" Lehrbas and by Colonel Egeberg, he walked the thousand-yard length of the Momote airstrip, under fire from Japanese mortars and snipers. Disdaining a helmet, he wore his glittering field marshal's cap and bore no weapon but his corncob pipe. An alarmed cavalry officer pointed toward a stretch of jungle only fifty yards away. "Excuse me, sir, but we killed a Jap sniper in there just a few minutes ago."

"Good," replied MacArthur. "That's the best thing to do with them." A few minutes later he came across the bodies of two recently killed Japanese. "That's the way I like to see them."[53]

Out on the airstrip, he measured craters, comparing the damage of Kinkaid's shells with that of Kenney's bombs. At one point he knelt down.

"Let's dig into this coral surfacing and see how deep it is," he said to Lehrbas. "I promised General Kenney I'd give him a report on the field. He said he hoped the Japs had put enough coral on it to take our heavy planes and I've got to get that information for him." The coral proved to be only a couple of inches deep. "I'm afraid General Kenney isn't going to like this," MacArthur said, standing up.[54]

After ninety minutes ashore he had not only inspected the airfield but read the battle erupting around him. He knew that so far his troops had engaged only a small part of the estimated fifteen hundred enemy troops on Los Negros. He turned to Egeberg and said he had a feeling the Japanese were preparing to launch a banzai charge.[55]

Back at the beach, he decorated the first man ashore, First Lieutenant Marvin J. Henshaw, with the DSC. Before returning to the *Phoenix,* he shook hands with Chase. "You have all performed magnificently," MacArthur told him. "Hold what you have taken no matter against whatever odds. You have your teeth in him now. Don't let go."[56]

Aboard the *Phoenix* once more, he gently chided Egeberg for going ashore wearing only a cap. "You probably took a look at me and put it on," said MacArthur. "Well, I wear this cap with all the braid. I feel in a way I have to. It's my trademark . . . a trademark that many of our soldiers know by now, so I'll keep on wearing it. But with the risks we take in a landing, I would suggest you wear a helmet from now on."[57]

That night the Japanese launched their banzai charge and nearly drove Chase's men into the sea. They hung on over the next five days despite repeated, ferocious attacks. MacArthur meanwhile returned to Brisbane elated at his exposure to fire once again. Elated too by the near certainty that he had just saved SWPA's drive toward the Philippines from being sacrificed on the altar of Nimitz's barnstorming offensive in the Central Pacific.[58]

A New Kind of Warfare

On March 3, the day after MacArthur returned to Brisbane, Halsey arrived to discuss strategy. MacArthur, however, seemed obsessed with Manus. Admiral King wanted the splendid harbor and airfield at Manus transferred to Nimitz's theater. Manus, MacArthur sternly informed Halsey, was his, and he intended to keep it. Halsey listened with some impatience as MacArthur ranted about a conspiracy being operated by King, Nimitz and the rest of the Navy—which presumably included Halsey—to reduce his authority. He was not going to be pushed around. He had given orders, MacArthur said, that the only ships that would be allowed to use Seeadler Harbor were vessels of Kinkaid's Seventh Fleet and some Royal Navy ships due to arrive in SWPA in the next few weeks. Halsey was amazed. "If you stick to this order of yours," he protested, "you'll be hampering the war effort!" MacArthur's staff gasped. Nobody talked to the general that way.[1]

The other subject they argued about was Kavieng. This was a strong Japanese base at the northern neck of the island of New Ireland. MacArthur had been pressing Halsey for several months to seize Kavieng. Halsey had persistently declined and continued to do so. He preferred to seize the lightly held island of Emirau, north of Kavieng, instead. MacArthur nonetheless told him that once Emirau had been captured, he had to seize Kavieng. Taking Kavieng would complete the isolation of Rabaul.[2]

MacArthur's interest in making an assault on Rabaul had more or less vanished in the space of a week. With the capture of Manus and Los Negros he now had the advanced naval base he needed to continue driving westward along the northern coast of New Guinea.[3]

Even without his conquest of the Admiralties, though, Rabaul was no longer a threat. Nimitz's carrier pilots had struck heavy blows at Rabaul and at Truk, the huge Japanese naval anchorage in the Central Pacific, in late February. Both places, so recently the focus of much concern, were found to be occupied almost entirely by ground units. Their air and navy elements had been destroyed by American attacks or withdrawn westward. Without ships and planes, the troops on Truk and Rabaul were effectively neutralized. MacArthur's feeling now was "Let 'em die on the vine."[4]

With Rabaul and Kavieng settled, the conferees turned their attention to Hansa Bay. This was a superb natural harbor nearly two hundred miles northwest of the most advanced Allied position on the northern coast of New Guinea, at Saidor. Just inland of Hansa Bay was level, well-drained open ground that to a military planner almost demanded airfields. The GHQ staff had been poring over maps and photographs of Hansa Bay for the past four months. It was taken for granted that MacArthur would have to seize it at some point, and planning was fairly well advanced by the time the Los Negros operation was mounted.[5]

The Japanese, however, guessed that MacArthur would try to assault Hansa Bay and moved in two more divisions to defend it. By March 1944 it was held by forty thousand men, well dug in and well armed. The Japanese turned it into a huge killing ground.[6]

Fortunately the Central Bureau monitored the massive reinforcement of Hansa Bay. MacArthur would have to look for another place to put Krueger's Sixth Army ashore. One of his operations officers, Brigadier General Bonner Fellers, produced a report that urged him to make an assault on Hollandia, which had a natural harbor and three airfields.[7]

At first glance, an assault on Hollandia looked impossible. MacArthur's troops had advanced as far along the New Guinea coast as Saidor. The distance from Saidor to Hollandia was 550 miles. Yet Ultra intercepts indicated that while Japanese positions between Saidor and Hollandia were strongly defended, Hollandia itself was vulnerable. The Japanese were counting on distance to spare the force at Hollandia from the attentions of MacArthur's troops.

To make a 550-mile leap on the basis of intelligence that might be right, but might also be wrong, was a huge gamble. Besides, MacArthur had never made an attack without advancing toward his objective under the cover of land-based airpower. If he chose to make a landing at Hollandia, he would have to rely on Nimitz to provide carrier air cover. He realized that Nimitz—and King—would be reluctant, even on a good day, to do it. Naval doctrine held that bombers operating from secure airfields might overwhelm a carrier force and wipe it out within hours, possibly minutes. Whatever carrier air cover he got, it would be pulled out after a few days.

MacArthur had a feeling, though, that despite the risks, he could pull off a successful assault on Hollandia. He cabled the JCS for permission to land two divisions at Hollandia in the period April 15–24, when the tides would favor a daylight assault.[8]

MacArthur's decision to invade Hollandia came at a critical moment in the debate over Pacific strategy. King and Nimitz were trying to get SWPA's boundaries redrawn so that MacArthur's advanced bases in the Admiralties would be turned over to the Navy. MacArthur was outraged. He sent a blistering cable to the Pentagon saying this proposal reflected so adversely on his reputation that unless it was dropped, he wanted to return to the United States and see the President. He hinted strongly that if the President decided in the Navy's favor, he would resign his command. Marshall got King's proposal withdrawn but was annoyed and puzzled that MacArthur had made it a resignation matter. "I cannot see that a change in boundary in your area, in itself, could be regarded as a serious reflection on your capacity to command," Marshall told him.[9]

The Chief of Staff revealed here how little he understood the way MacArthur's mind worked. To MacArthur, it was not simply a question of his professional reputation—although he viewed it as being exactly that—but, more important still, a matter of his personal honor. He had stated repeatedly, publicly and vehemently that he would return to the Philippines. Rightly or wrongly, he was convinced that transferring his bases in the Admiralties to Navy control would prevent that. In that case he might as well go home. But if he did return to the United States, his mission aborted, that would be an ignominious end to what he saw as an almost holy crusade. Marshall did not invest strategy with religious sentiments or understand those who did.

Although the Navy had dropped its proposal, Admiral King was pressing harder than ever for everything in the Pacific to be put behind the awesome force of Nimitz's offensive. He wanted the Central Pacific drive to move into top gear and promised the Navy would take the Marianas in June if the JCS gave its approval. Hap Arnold suddenly found himself the key player in an argument over strategy. It was one of the little ironies of Pentagon politics that he of all people should be thrust into this role. Arnold by his own admission knew next to nothing about questions of grand strategy. But he had no doubt of how to vote on this one.[10]

The biggest project of the war, in terms of money, was not the atomic bomb, which cost $2 billion, but the B-29, which cost nearly $2.3 billion. Arnold, indeed the entire AAF, as well as the American taxpayer, was betting heavily on the success of the Superfortress. Arnold thought it might be possible to bomb Japan into submission, an achievement that should bring air independence when the war ended. All he needed was airfields within range of Japan for his B-29s, and that was exactly what the Marianas offered. The Superfortress had enough range to bomb Tokyo from Saipan. The Navy should be able to ship enough fuel and bombs out to the Marianas. The B-29 might be saved after all.

As a rule, Arnold was Marshall's loyal subordinate on the JCS. In the March 1944 debate over strategy, however, he went his own way and would not be deflected. With Arnold strongly supporting King, Marshall was completely outgunned. Nimitz personally put the case for his Central Pacific drive to the Joint Chiefs. The next day Sutherland presented MacArthur's alternative, making a strong argument that the principal axis of advance should be along the northern coast of New Guinea and up to the Philippines. Sutherland might as well have saved his breath. Even had he been blessed with MacArthur's eloquence, it would have made no difference.

On March 12 the JCS drew up its directive on strategy for the rest of 1944. MacArthur's proposed landing at Hollandia was approved. Nimitz would occupy the Marianas in June. MacArthur was expected to go ashore on Mindanao in the southern Philippines sometime in November, but everything was really geared to a naval assault on Formosa in February 1945.

The directive held out a slight possibility of a landing on Luzon, but even then it was presented as a secondary effort—"should such operations prove necessary prior to the move to Formosa." That was the only concession Marshall could wring from King on MacArthur's behalf. The best MacArthur might hope if King got his way was a symbolic return to the Philippines, in some remote area far from Manila—nothing that could be viewed as either a triumph of arms or the liberation of an occupied nation groaning under the heel of a rapacious conqueror.[11]

In an almost defiant mood, he responded by publicly repeating the most famous mission statement in modern military history. On March 17 the Australian prime minister, John Curtin, hosted a state dinner to celebrate MacArthur's arrival two years earlier and to acknowledge his deeds since then. MacArthur responded with a short speech of thanks to the Australian government and observed, "The last two years have been momentous ones for Australia. You have faced the greatest peril in your history. With your very life at stake, you have met and overcome the challenge. It was here the tide of war turned in the Pacific and the mighty wave of invasion rolled back. Two years ago when I landed on your soil I said to the people of the Philippines whence I came—'I shall return.' Tonight I repeat those words. I *shall* return. Nothing is more certain than our ultimate reconquest and liberation from the enemy of these and adjacent lands."[12]

After the dinner MacArthur had a long talk with Curtin and his defense minister, Sir Frederick Shedden. He told them that he was going to mount an assault on Hollandia in the near future. As for Rabaul, which the RAAF had attacked repeatedly, it was now completely neutralized. It would not be invaded.

Curtin was about to leave for Washington and his first meeting with Roosevelt. There was a wide variety of questions his government wanted to put to the United States. What would happen to the islands taken from the Japanese after the war ended? Would Australia have a role in the peace negotiations with Japan? What kind of organization would the United Nations be: a peacekeeper, a peacemaker, or both? Australia was already worrying about its security in the postwar world.[13]

MacArthur advised Curtin on how to present Australia's concerns but told him not to take Roosevelt's promises too seriously. "He is quite unscrupulous . . . in getting away from his own expression of agreement and repudiating his word if it suits him." And yet, MacArthur said, he should devote as much of his time as he could to discussions with the President. There was not much point in meeting with the Joint Chiefs. They had little power to decide on issues concerning the making of the peace or on possible security pacts in the postwar world. But just in case Curtin was introduced to the JCS, MacArthur offered some thumbnail sketches: "Marshall is a very well informed and pleasant person, but he really does not have a strategic mind. King has a hard and unattractive personality." As for Arnold, he was a lightweight figure whose main interest was the strategic bombing of Germany. Australia and SWPA were of no great concern to him.

Curtin asked if there was anything he could do to further MacArthur's views on Pacific strategy in Washington. MacArthur responded that any such effort, coming from the prime minister, might be taken as political interference in military matters. That was one battle, he suggested, that it was better for him to fight alone.[14]

Shortly after Curtin departed for the United States, Nimitz arrived in Brisbane to confer with MacArthur on implementing the new directive from the JCS. As they discussed the problems of naval air cover for Hollandia, it was evident the admiral was still apprehensive. The Navy feared there might be two to three hundred enemy planes defending Hollandia by the time the operation was launched, posing a major threat to his carriers. Kenney confidently (and typically) reassured him: "I will have the Jap planes rubbed out by April 5." Everyone present seemed astonished at what sounded like a rash promise—everyone, that is, except MacArthur.[15]

The two staffs talked about coordinating other operations after Hollandia. The Navy intended to seize the Palau Islands around September 15, and naval planners wanted to know, What will SWPA do then? The GHQ staff hadn't a clue. Palau was a long way from New Guinea, and one reason for seizing it was to clear the way for MacArthur to land on Mindanao in November. But from Hollandia to Mindanao was another five-hundred-mile leap. And if Nimitz was tied up in the Palaus, MacArthur could not count on getting enough assault shipping and carrier air cover to make an assault on Mindanao at the same time. So if Nimitz really did seize the Palaus as early as mid-September, MacArthur might well find himself looking on desperately from afar.

It was a sobering prospect for MacArthur and his staff. As they gloomily turned it over in their minds, Nimitz let slip confirmation of something MacArthur already feared and suspected. He had recently written to John Callan O'Laughlin, "There is apparently a concerted plan to by-pass the Philippines," but no one in the War Department had confirmed it, nor had any senior naval officer done so—until now.[16] Although he personally felt it would be necessary to land on Luzon, said Nimitz, Admiral King was intending to use the Marianas and the Palaus as a springboard to make a direct attack on Formosa.

MacArthur was roused to indignation. He denounced King's plan as being strategically and tactically unsound. Important as the military considerations might be, MacArthur said, "It is also immoral. It would abandon all the American prisoners that the Japs hold in the Philippines and 17 million Filipinos to the mercies of the enemy."[17]

Behind MacArthur's outburst there was a bottomless well of passionate commitment. There was something else too. He was sending a message to King, through Nimitz, that whatever the JCS directive said about strategy in 1944 the debate was far from over. If anything, it had barely begun.

When George Kenney was in Washington in March 1943 to beg for more airplanes, he was invited to the White House and had a long talk with Roosevelt. The President demonstrated a remarkably detailed grasp of the military problems and possibilities in SWPA. But he also expressed interest in something else. He asked about MacArthur's health. How was it?

There were rumors among MacArthur's friends in the United States that he was a physical wreck from the strain of trying to get men and supplies. Other accounts said he was on the verge of a nervous breakdown.[18] Evidently some of these rumors had reached the Oval Office. Kenney assured Roosevelt that MacArthur's health, both mental and physical, was excellent.

The President then asked if MacArthur was thinking of entering the 1944 presidential campaign. Kenney gave him a categorical answer: "General MacArthur has one ambition, and that is to ride down the Ginza at the head of the parade when we enter Tokyo, and I have an ambition to sit in the car alongside him."[19]

Despite this reassurance, doubts about MacArthur's political ambitions persisted, and shortly after Kenney returned to Australia, Henry Stimson reminded journalists that Army regulations prevented any career officer from becoming a political candidate for any office he had not held before being called to active duty. Stimson's statement was taken by press and Congress alike to be aimed at discouraging one officer and only one from getting into the 1944 presidential primaries—namely, MacArthur.

Various Republican politicians protested that the Roosevelt administration was trying to deny the American people a free choice in their political candidates. Among those who spoke up for MacArthur's right to run was Senator Arthur Vandenberg of Michigan.

MacArthur had never met Vandenberg or corresponded with him. He was sufficiently impressed now, however, to write to the senator. "I am most grateful to you for your complete attitude of friendship. I only hope that I can some day reciprocate. . . . In the meanwhile I want you to know the absolute confidence I would feel in your experienced and wise mentorship."[20] Surprised and flattered by this invitation to be MacArthur's fugleman on the tortuous roads of Republican politics, Vandenberg began organizing a semisecret pro-MacArthur movement within the Republican party to secure the presidential nomination for him in 1944.

MacArthur's old friend and World War I comrade Robert Wood offered to provide whatever money was needed to get MacArthur nominated. Wood had been the president of both Montgomery Ward and Sears, Roebuck. When World War II broke out in Europe in September 1939, Wood had thrown his energies into keeping the United States out of the conflict. A bred-in-the-bone midwestern isolationist, he swiftly became chairman of the ultra-isolationist America First Committee. Only the Japanese attack on Pearl Harbor brought him around to a more internationalist outlook.[21]

There was strong behind-the-scenes support for a MacArthur candidacy from Herbert Hoover. When it was suggested that MacArthur would never live down the routing of the Bonus Army and was therefore unelectable, Hoover let it be known that he was prepared to swear out an affidavit that he had issued the orders under which MacArthur had acted and given him full authority to do what he had done. Hoover would publicly exonerate him from all blame or responsibility for driving the bonus marchers out of the District.[22]

MacArthur did not provide any overt encouragement to his political backers. He acted by indirection. Letters to his supporters were invariably opaque. At no point did he commit himself in writing to wanting the Republican nomination. All the same, he did nothing to discourage the efforts being made to secure it. And there was no mistaking the interest he took in what was going on. Willoughby made a brief visit to the United States in the summer of 1943 and at MacArthur's behest went to see Vandenberg. Sid Huff, who also returned to the United States that summer, was told by MacArthur to keep his ears open for political news.

His conversation betrayed what was on his mind. At lunch at I Corps headquarters in late May he held forth for the best part of an hour on the executive duties of the president. Two weeks later he virtually boasted to Eichelberger that he could win the Republican nomination in 1944, although whether he was serious or not is open to doubt. He may simply have been trying to impress Eichelberger. It would not have been the first time.[23]

Certainly he had not been told to expect the nomination. On the contrary. Neither Vandenberg nor Wood nor anyone else who was closely involved told him he had anything but a remote chance of becoming the Republican candidate. He was, they assured him, a very long shot. If Governor Thomas E. Dewey of New York chose to run, he was almost certain to get the nomination. And the least hint in the press that MacArthur had any political ambition, they informed him frankly, would kill what slight chance he currently possessed stone dead. In time of war Americans expected their generals to devote their energies to fighting military, not political, campaigns.

The strategy of the sub rosa MacArthur for president movement was as banal as could be. It consisted almost entirely of dreaming about that fabled political beast much loved by the low-hopers and the no-hopers of every generation, the totally deadlocked convention. Vandenberg and his helpers were trying to win friends and influence people behind the scenes just in case a stalemate developed between Dewey and Wendell Willkie. MacArthur's name might then be submitted as a compromise candidate on whom everyone could agree. There was no denying his enormous popularity with the people. In 1944 voters of all parties and none regarded him as the greatest American soldier of the war.[24]

During Willoughby's trip to the United States in the summer of 1943 he met up once more with Clare Boothe Luce. Their pillow talk seems to have included earnest discussions of MacArthur's political prospects. They contemplated the paradoxical political situation in which MacArthur was the potential candidate with the most popularity, but that would remain so only so long as he was not a candidate. Willoughby took Mrs. Luce's thoughts on the subject back to Brisbane. She followed this up with a long letter to MacArthur.

In it she urged him not to do anything publicly to encourage the movement, but not to do anything to discourage it either. Not yet, anyway. There was a good reason, she advised, to let it develop. "I believe you should allow the MacArthur sentiment here to grow unchecked . . . let people talk of MacArthur-for-President when such talk is of material help to your theater by helping to focus the public's attention on its problems and needs . . . this political talk, painful as it may be to you, is of military value to the SWPA . . . for these reasons you should not discourage it *now.*"[25]

Using the prospect of a presidential bid as leverage probably struck MacArthur as shrewd advice. Anything that would bring him more men, planes and ships was welcome; anything that would help him win out in the debate of strategy was doubly so. Mrs. Luce was offering what seemed at first blush to be an excellent reason not to make any explicit public declaration that he was not a candidate and would not become one. That was exactly what he did. He enfolded himself in impenetrable layers of insubstantiality, an armory of hints, coy looks, ambiguous murmurs and empty compliments. It probably seemed pretty clever to him. But, then, what did MacArthur know about politics?

While making no public disclaimer MacArthur sought to cover his back by conveying a message to Stimson. Brigadier General Frederick H. Osborn, one of the Army's experts on troop welfare and morale, visited SWPA in January 1944. MacArthur sent for him and told him, "Tell Mr. Stimson I have no political ambitions. I have but one ambition—to return to the Philippines, to save the Philippine people, who are a great people, from their present agony, and to restore the prestige of the United States. That is all that is moving me."[26]

The Vandenbergers were dismayed meanwhile to find they were not toiling alone. Dozens of MacArthur-for-President clubs sprang up, mainly on the West Coast and across the Midwest. No one controlled them. They represented in nearly every instance the popular support that MacArthur enjoyed among ordinary people. In early 1944 these clubs managed to get MacArthur's name onto the ballot in two states that did not require a candidate's consent in the primaries. One of them happened to be Wisconsin (the other was Illinois). Although his links with the Badger State had grown pretty tenuous since his father's death in 1912, he could still hope to benefit from the native son effect in the Republican primary.

It was possible to block his name from appearing on the Illinois ballot by signing a certificate of withdrawal. Wood promptly dispatched a certificate to Brisbane, but MacArthur did not send it back. Nor did he ever speak out publicly against the efforts to get his name onto primary ballots without his consent.[27]

When the Wisconsin primary was held, on April 4, it provided all the evidence needed as to how MacArthur stacked up against Dewey. The election was held to select twenty-four delegates for the Republican convention in July. MacArthur won three delegates. Dewey got seventeen. Willkie got none and promptly quit the race.

However much the people admired MacArthur as a general, few really saw him as a potential president. There is a huge gap between popularity, which MacArthur had in abundance, and political support, which he lacked. Public opinion polls clearly showed the lack of political support across the entire United States. People wanted MacArthur as a general, not as a candidate. Vandenberg and Wood alike drew the obvious conclusion: Dewey was going to win the nomination. There would be no hopelessly deadlocked convention. The MacArthur bubble had just been pricked.[28]

Yet some admirers still refused to give up. One was a freshman congressman from Nebraska, Arthur L. Miller. He had written to MacArthur in the fall of 1943, damning the New Deal, telling him he expected the GOP to offer him its presidential nomination and urging him to accept: "You owe it to civilization and to children yet unborn." MacArthur replied, saying he did not expect to be a candidate but lauded the "complete wisdom and statesmanship" of Congressman Miller's observations.[29]

Six months later the congressman wrote MacArthur again, to let him know "there is a tremendous revolution on in this country. It is more than a political revolution. It is a mass movement by the citizens who are displeased with the many domestic mistakes now being made by the administration. They are also convinced that the events leading up to Pearl Harbor and since Pearl Harbor in the allocation of war supplies [are] not above critical examination. . . . If this system of left wingers and New Dealism is continued another four years I am certain that this monarch [*sic*] which is being established in America will destroy the rights of the common people. . . ." The best hope in this crisis was MacArthur as "Commander in Chief and President of a free America."[30]

MacArthur took this nonsense seriously enough to write back to Miller: "I appreciate very much your scholarly letter. . . . Your description of conditions in the United States is a sobering one indeed and is calculated to arouse the thoughtful consideration of every true patriot. . . ."[31]

Miller then demonstrated that he was as naïve as MacArthur: He published their brief correspondence. These four letters created a furor in the liberal press, which accused MacArthur of being disloyal to his commander in chief, of being a candidate for the presidency and, by implication, of devoting time and talent to party politics and personal advancement that any good soldier and true would expend on winning the war.[32]

MacArthur had a penetrating intelligence and was one of the most highly educated men of his generation. He had imagination and a mind that was broad and powerful. His thirst for knowledge combined with a capacity for abstract thought made him an intellectual as much as a soldier. Few, if any, American generals could match him for the ability to examine a problem in all its important aspects, relate each to the rest and come up with a novel yet workable solution. He was remarkably articulate and a gifted writer. He had spent much of his life mastering the small world of military politics. Yet in the larger world of ordinary American life and party politics, he was almost completely ignorant of those treacherous hidden currents that either sweep a man into the White House or produce a public drowning. MacArthur's 1944 noncandidacy for the Republican nomination was a fine example of what brains are worth when parted from common sense.

The best and only chance MacArthur had of getting the Republican nomination would come after the war, in 1948. For a general to do anything in wartime other than to declare loudly, publicly and convincingly that he had no—that is, NO—political ambitions, would not run if chosen, would not serve if elected, would not even discuss the matter with anyone, in public or in private, would not correspond on the subject or express an opinion, was foolish. Stimson's reminder about what Army regulations said had provided an ideal opportunity to squash all speculation early on. MacArthur did not simply ignore that opportunity; he failed even to see it for what it was. Worse, he had reacted to it by encouraging Vandenberg, Wood, Clare Luce, Hoover and others to promote him as a potential candidate.

Perversely, this was so even though what he really wanted to do was what Kenney had told Roosevelt: to return to the Philippines in triumph, liberate them and take Japan's surrender in Tokyo. That did not prevent him from taking his eye off the ball.

Why would an intelligent man act so dumbly? MacArthur had a lifelong fascination with the White House that was disconnected from even the slightest interest in being a politician. He believed the ultimate accolade the people could grant a victorious American general was the presidency.[33] In his mental universe, military success on a grand scale meant the grubby world of real-life politics was tossed aside and the hero was anointed president by a grateful nation.

MacArthur never shook off his unworldly, apolitical attitude to the presidency. His view of the White House, with himself in residence, was as romantic as his view of just about everything else. Had he left it at that, as a kind of intellectual eccentricity, he would have escaped serious damage to his reputation. Unhappily for his good name as a soldier, he could not resist a little political flirtation when the chance arose. Since at least the mid-1930s admirers such as John O'Laughlin had been telling him he was a potential president.[34] Like many an aging gent who can't help being curious about whether that look in the eyes is a come-on or merely a trick of the light, MacArthur in 1944 stumbled onto the rutted path that leads even great men to the fool's destination—the table heaped with humble pie.

When Miller published their correspondence, MacArthur was appalled and possibly scared of being dismissed from his command. The story broke on April 17, when he was in Port Moresby. Late that evening he dashed off a blanket denial of political ambition or disloyalty to Roosevelt. His letters to Miller, he protested, "were neither politically inspired nor intended to convey blanket approval of the Congressman's views. I entirely repudiate the sinister interpretation that they were intended as criticism of any political philosophy or any personage in high office." As for his supposed presidential hopes, "I can only say as I have said before, I am not a candidate for the office nor do I seek it. I have devoted myself exclusively to the conduct of the war." Just when he had "said before" that he was not a candidate was not indicated. Whatever denials he had made had been expressed in private, to people like Kenney, not in public and definitely not to the press.[35]

A clutch of war correspondents was hastily summoned to Government House at midnight from beds and bars. As a tropical downpour shook the night, they assembled on the veranda and MacArthur's statement was read out to them. The bedraggled journalists hurriedly scribbled it down in dim light to a furious arpeggio of massive raindrops bouncing off the overhanging palm-covered roof. Some of them distrusted MacArthur so much they thought his statement was a way of saying he *was* a candidate. In the United States, however, it was taken for what it was: the first public declaration that he was not a candidate, a genuine disclaimer and an action roughly a year overdue.[36]

His misguided political flirtation ended in this bathetic denouement on the eve of the biggest operation SWPA had attempted in its two years of existence. That afternoon the invasion convoys had put to sea, heading for a rendezvous that would take them to Hollandia.

The greatest strength of the U.S. Army in World War II was its unprecedented and unrivaled development of combined arms, pulling together air, infantry, armor, artillery and, if necessary, naval operations into well-coordinated thrusts that multiplied the strength of each element, raising the intensity of combat to new heights and posing more challenges than any enemy—German, Japanese or Italian—could cope with.

MacArthur delighted in his mastery of combined arms, and the way he had employed it from Buna to Los Negros, by striking deep into the Japanese flanks and rear, was masterly. His success was so complete that some of his admirers seemed to think he had invented modern war, especially bypassing. This was a boast he never made, but writing to an old friend, Brigadier General Perry L. Miles, he observed that what he was conducting now was "a new kind of warfare."[37]

For all the victories since Buna, however, MacArthur had not traveled far. Saidor was just 240 miles from Buna, and Manila was still more than

2,000 miles from Saidor. At this rate he was on course to liberate the Philippines in 1953 or 1954. But MacArthur knew, as Marshall once put it, "A democracy cannot fight a seven-years' war."[38] Nor could he risk letting Nimitz get too far ahead of him. The pressure beating on MacArthur every day in the spring of 1944 was to speed up the tempo of operations. He needed Hollandia badly.

Kenney set about "rubbing out" the Japanese Air Force in New Guinea with a series of raids on the huge air base at Wewak. The Fifth Air Force struck Wewak every day for two weeks in the second half of March. By April more than a hundred planes had been destroyed. The rest had been pulled back to Hollandia. Kenney then turned his attention to destroying Japanese airpower at Hollandia, which was soon wiped out.[39]

There were eleven thousand Japanese at Hollandia, yet if Ultra was right, nearly all were rear-echelon support troops. MacArthur nonetheless was not going to take any chances. He planned to strike with two divisions of Eichelberger's I Corps, operating as a task force under Krueger's Sixth Army headquarters. The Hollandia area was dominated by two huge indentations in the New Guinea coastline—Tanahmerah Bay and Humboldt Bay—nearly twenty-five miles apart. The 24th Division would go ashore at Tanahmerah Bay; the 41st Division would land at Humboldt Bay. On April 8, with the assault only two weeks away, Kenney's reconnaissance pilots returned with photographs showing that the landing beach at Tanahmerah Bay was a virtual swamp and probably impassable. Eichelberger insisted all the same that this part of the assault had to go ahead.[40]

The basic plan, once both divisions were ashore, was that they would drive inland to Lake Sentani and seize the three airfields there. Nearly fifty-five thousand men would make the assault, two thirds of them combat troops.[41]

Nimitz was prepared to provide cover from his fast carriers for only three days. After that he would pull them out. MacArthur's solution to this problem was to make a supplementary landing at Aitape, roughly halfway between Wewak and Hollandia, where there were two small Japanese fighter strips, one of which was in operation and the other of which was nearing completion. If Aitape could be seized quickly and its airstrips secured, it might be able to provide air cover from one of them, maybe both, for the troops at Hollandia when Nimitz's fast carriers departed.

On April 19 MacArthur flew to Finschhafen and boarded the cruiser *Nashville*. Before heading for Hollandia, he had the *Nashville* take him across the Vitiaz Strait to Cape Gloucester, where the 1st Marine Division was still exchanging potshots with a handful of Japanese. The marines were fed up with being left to flounder around in the mangrove swamps, instead of being given a worthwhile objective. MacArthur went ashore to thank the division for its efforts in his theater.[42]

The invasion convoys rendezvoused north of the Admiralties on April 20, having followed courses that would make the Japanese think they were heading for the Palaus. Once assembled, the fleet turned about under cover of darkness, heading for Hollandia. MacArthur spent much of the next day sitting on a chair outside his cabin, thinking, napping, chatting with his aides, signing short snorters for naval officers who approached tentatively, eager to collect his signature and shake his hand.[43]

He also had an important guest, William Donovan, the head of the OSS. Donovan wanted to make a personal appeal to MacArthur to allow the OSS to operate in his theater. MacArthur was glad to see his old Rainbow Division comrade again, but he still refused to have the OSS in SWPA if he could not have complete control of its operations there. That was more than Donovan was able to concede. The only thing MacArthur was prepared to accept was Donovan's offer of OSS frogmen in future landings.[44]

As dusk fell on the evening of April 21, the invasion fleet neared the latitude of Aitape. A small group of ships turned to port, taking the three thousand men of the 163d Regimental Combat Team with them.

Next morning dawned hot and humid. The cruisers of the convoy closed to within two miles of Hollandia and began bombarding shore targets with their six-inch guns while carrier-borne attack aircraft struck Japanese positions inland. MacArthur watched, fascinated, from the bridge of the *Nashville* as the cruiser approached the beaches of Humboldt Bay, where the 41st Division would land.

The first wave of assault troops hit the beach at 7:00 A.M. There was nothing but sporadic opposition at either Tanahmerah Bay or Humboldt Bay. But while the 41st Division was soon in control of the beaches at Humboldt Bay, three battalions of the 24th Division found themselves standing on two narrow strips of sand at Tanahmerah Bay that were hemmed in by coral and the impassable swamps that Kenney's recon pilots had photographed at low level two weeks before.[45]

At 11:00 A.M. MacArthur went ashore at Humboldt Bay to take a look at the 41st Division's rapidly expanding beachhead. He strode through the soft sand at a pace that left his aides panting, and while they were soon soaked with sweat, he seemed hardly to perspire at all. After walking roughly a mile, he turned around and retraced his steps. He spoke for a few minutes with the division commander, Major General Horace Fuller, then returned to the *Nashville*.[46]

While MacArthur had lunch, the cruiser steamed the twenty-five miles to Tanahmerah Bay, where Eichelberger had set up his command post. Eichelberger came out to the cruiser to report on the situation ashore. He complained that Krueger was breathing down his neck to push inland, but it was simply impossible.[47] MacArthur decided to go take a look for himself.

Going ashore at three o'clock with Krueger and Eichelberger, he found several thousand men milling about, wondering how in the hell they were going to get across the swamp. MacArthur and Krueger agreed the troops should be reembarked and the 24th Division moved by sea over to Humboldt Bay. During the hour MacArthur spent on the beach there was almost no enemy fire.[48]

Back aboard the *Nashville* he called a meeting with Krueger, Barbey, Eichelberger and their chiefs of staff. He pronounced the Hollandia operation a complete success. Then, to Eichelberger's consternation, he urged him to make another landing, a hundred miles farther west, within seventy-two hours, to seize Wakde Island, which was defended by only eight hundred Japanese. There was a Japanese airfield on Wakde—in fact, virtually the whole of that small island consisted of runways—which I Corps troops were already scheduled to seize on May 18. Barbey said the VII Amphib could get the troops there. Krueger was opposed to the idea but would not say so outright. It was left to Eichelberger to juggle this proposition unaided.[49]

He objected furiously to MacArthur's proposal. His men had not yet taken their primary objective, the three airfields at Lake Sentani, so the fight could not yet be said to be won. Nor were the ships he would need to make another assault combat-loaded. At present they were loaded with follow-on supplies for the troops at Hollandia. It would take more than seventy-two hours just to rearrange the cargoes. Besides, the intelligence picture farther up the coast was unclear.

MacArthur had tried to mollify Eichelberger in recent months over his disappointment at having to remain in the Pacific, and on the eve of the Hollandia assault MacArthur told him that if this operation went well, he would make him an army commander. They solemnly shook hands on it.[50]

It was obvious to MacArthur by the afternoon of April 22 that the I Corps had enough manpower and firepower at Hollandia to spare part of its strength to grab another airfield a hundred miles away. And to tell MacArthur that rearranging cargoes ruled out a chance to speed up the timetable by four weeks was the kind of quibble he might excuse when it came from the GHQ staff, but what kind of talk was that from an experienced combat commander and would-be Medal of Honor hero?

This, I believe, is how MacArthur's mind worked: Two of the 24th Division's regimental combat teams were still aboard the assault ships that had carried them to Hollandia. The third RCT, stranded on the beaches at Tanahmerah Bay, was about to be extracted by landing craft and moved over to Humboldt Bay. Why not send the two RCTs that were still on the assault ships straight to Wakde? They could be there in twelve hours and make a dawn assault. It would be possible for Nimitz to reposition a couple of his fast carriers during the night to provide air cover for a Wakde attack. There was a fleeting chance to catch the enemy totally unprepared and speed up the timetable. If the Wakde assault were held back another four weeks, the Japanese would be able to regain their balance, guess that Wakde was next and reinforce it.

Whichever way an improvised Wakde landing turned out, it could not possibly jeopardize the conquest of Hollandia. Eichelberger currently had a manpower advantage at Hollandia of five to one. He could also count on continuing air supremacy and nearly complete control of the sea-lanes. The Japanese were not going to reinforce the defenders of Hollandia. Sending two RCTs and their support troops to Wakde would reduce Eichelberger's manpower advantage to around three to one, but the outcome at Hollandia would not be altered by their absence. Such is likely to be the way MacArthur analyzed the situation that afternoon.

Eichelberger simply did not think like that. He was a good tactician and an excellent trainer of troops, but not for one day was he ever a strategist (nor, for that matter, was Krueger). He also seemed oblivious to the need for speed. Buna had left a mark on his soul. MacArthur did not express his disappointment, but put to the test, Eichelberger proved to be no more adventurous than Krueger. A good opportunity was missed, and MacArthur almost certainly revised the mental scorecard he carried in his head on Eichelberger the fighter.[51]

During the night the *Nashville* headed east, traveling back along the New Guinea coast. By daybreak it was off Aitape. MacArthur went ashore to see how the 163d RCT was doing. The troops had overrun both airstrips. Fighters would be able to operate from Aitape to cover the troops at Hollandia even before Nimitz's fast carriers pulled out. On this triumphant note, MacArthur returned to the cruiser and as it headed back toward Finschhafen, he began writing the communiqué: "We have seized the Humboldt Bay area on the northern coast of Dutch New Guinea, approximately 500 miles west of Saidor. . . ."[52]

23

I Will Push on That Plan

The biggest weakness of the wartime Army was the homesickness of American soldiers.[1] The morale situation in SWPA was increasingly bleak as it became obvious to MacArthur's men that the only ticket home was a coffin, blindness or loss of a limb. Only the dead and the permanently disabled ever seemed to be allowed out of the theater, except for generals, such as Eichelberger, who went home for a rest.

During Eleanor Roosevelt's tour of SWPA's military hospitals in the fall of 1943 she had assumed that here, as in other theaters, the seriously wounded were routinely sent home. Eichelberger, who accompanied her on these hospital visits, found it too painful to tell her the truth. So in her kindly, motherly way she blithely tried to revive the spirits of grim-faced men recovering from grievous wounds by talking about how they would soon be on their way back to their families while Eichelberger, standing just behind her, stared at the floor or looked out of the window. Almost none of the wounded men she met would be returned to the United States, no matter how long it took for them to recover.[2]

MacArthur's manpower problems grew even more acute at the end of 1943, when the War Department suddenly woke up to the unwelcome fact that the pool of healthy eighteen- to twenty-six-year-old males was nearing exhaustion. Only a few weeks earlier Washington had boosted morale by introducing a rotation policy under which a theater commander could send 1 percent of his combat troops home each month. This news briefly sent morale in SWPA soaring. Then, on January 6, 1944, Marshall bluntly informed MacArthur: "The present manpower situation is critical. There is a shortage of planned strength by several hundred thousand men. The situation has been aggravated by a tendency to discharge men who could render further useful service . . . the Army must be maintained with the personnel at hand . . . it is desired that this matter be given your prompt, personal and continuing attention."[3]

MacArthur's response was to draft a personal message to the troops. Several hundred copies were run off on a mimeograph machine at GHQ, and MacArthur signed every copy. The forms were then sent to units in the field, with instructions that these messages were to be pinned on company, battery and detachment bulletin boards at 11:00 A.M. on a particular day. As soldiers returned for lunch that day, they clustered around the bulletin boards.

"Soldiers of the Southwest Pacific—through your superb fighting qualities we have won impressive victories over our enemies. As military men, I know you will understand that it is imperative that we exploit our successes by driving on in relentless attack before the enemy can regroup. Therefore, in order to have enough men to follow-up our hard won successes and thus avoid unnecessary casualties and suffering later, I have ordered that the rotation policy be discontinued until further notice." They stared in astonishment at MacArthur's distinctive signature. This really was a personal communication from him to them.[4]

That helped take some of the edge off their disappointment, but it was still profound. For all his enormous popularity at home, MacArthur was not greatly liked by his troops. They respected his generalship, which, after Buna, saved many lives that might otherwise have been lost. Yet admiration for the skill was never translated into affection for the man. In cultivating aloofness, he had surrendered his gift for winning the hearts of ordinary soldiers. When MacArthur's face appeared on movie screens in Australia, American soldiers were reported to boo him.[5]

He tried to sustain troop morale by setting up an Army radio station in Port Moresby in February 1944, and he used it to address them directly the day the station began broadcasting. He told them that the limited recreational facilities in New Guinea caused him great anxiety. "No campaigns in history have entailed greater hardships than here," he said, "and no one appreciates more than I the need of relaxation and recreation. . . . To know what is transpiring in the world, to hear occasionally the tinkle of music and laughter, to feel something of the little familiar things that link us with home—that is what I hope this station can do for you."[6]

He sought to look after them in other ways too. The huge disparity in pay between a GI and his Australian counterpart was an endless source of inter-Allied friction, and the Australian government hinted that the solution was to let American servicemen receive only part of their pay while they were overseas. MacArthur's response was that the only solution, he insisted, was for the Australian government to pay its troops better.[7]

The most effective and valuable way of raising troop morale and sustaining it was a soldiers' newspaper. The World War II *Stars and Stripes* was the proof of that. Its success was such that many officers in the European theater disliked it intensely, and Patton would gladly have seen it put out of business. Written by soldiers for soldiers, especially for the men who fought the battles, *Stars and Stripes* provided an invaluable safety valve for men whose emotional lives were in a pressure cooker. Enlightened commanders, such as Eisenhower and Mark Clark, recognized that and protected the paper from its high-ranking critics. In the CBI, General Stilwell allowed a similar paper, the *CBI Roundup,* to operate without interference from himself or his staff. He told the *Roundup*'s editors, "If you can prove it, you can print it," and was as good as his word.[8]

MacArthur was too sensitive to slights ever to allow his troops to run a newspaper that had anything resembling freedom of expression. What might be good for the men's morale could be devastating for his. A small group of enterprising Americans and Aussies got hold of a printing press in Port Moresby and put out a paper called *Guinea Gold* that was widely distributed among soldiers in SWPA, but it was a harmless rag, consisting almost entirely of wire service stories and MacArthur's communiqués.

Even without a soldiers' paper, he knew what his men thought of him. His principal counterintelligence officer, Brigadier General Elliott Thorpe, took him a résumé each month of what the troops were thinking and saying. These were drawn from various sources: opinion surveys; the routine censorship of letters; even pillow talk. One of Thorpe's officers was convinced American officers were blabbing secrets to impress Australian women they were sleeping with. He hired a couple of sexy teenage girls to compile reports on what their American boyfriends talked about when not otherwise engaged.[9]

Thorpe's résumés covered gripes about Army food, what the troops thought about the Australians, what officers thought about the way the theater was run, what the troops thought about the abilities of their officers and what officers and men thought about MacArthur. No punches were pulled. A typical résumé might offer such prime quotes as "He's a brass-hatted old bastard . . . the flannel-mouth fool . . . that egotistical ass. . . ."

MacArthur usually read these remarks without saying anything, but on one occasion he was provoked into telling Thorpe, "I don't care what people say, if I know in my heart I am doing the right thing."[10]

The truth, of course, was that he cared deeply. He was an excessively thin-skinned man. The least slight left bruises. He lamented his unpopularity among his soldiers. "I know the troops don't like me," he wistfully told

Sutherland one day. "It wasn't always that way. Back in France, I was a combat officer out in front of my men. Now I'm an old man. My legs are like toothpicks. I can't operate any more. But it wasn't always that way."[11]

Following the landing at Hollandia, it took Eichelberger less than a week to secure the three airfields at Lake Sentani. The 11,000 Japanese defenders, who consisted mainly of service troops, melted into the surrounding jungles and mountains. Tracking them down produced some intense firefights, and up to 3,000 Japanese were killed. Most of the remaining 8,000 died of starvation or disease. Eichelberger's combat losses came to 150 men killed, 1,100 wounded.[12]

Although the captured airfields at Hollandia could take Kenney's mediums, they lacked the drainage to handle heavy bombers during the rainy season, which would start around September 1. Kenney needed more airfields. He demanded the capture of the small island of Biak, 225 miles northwest of Hollandia. Biak had three operational airfields, including one, Mokmer, that Kenney was certain would handle his B-24s. Biak also had another attraction. It was within range of the Marianas. Bombers flying from Biak could assist Nimitz's assault on Saipan, which was set for June 15.

To provide air cover for the Biak assault, MacArthur made a landing at Wakde on May 17. The airfield there was used to support the invasion of Biak on May 27.[13] The highly experienced 163d Regimental Combat Team made the Wakde assault. Nearly 150 soldiers were killed or wounded taking Wakde from its 800 Japanese defenders, but the island was completely in American hands within less than forty-eight hours. Aviation engineers were repairing the runways even before the shooting stopped. This swift conquest of Wakde by a single regimental combat team was all the proof needed that MacArthur's proposal five weeks earlier to Eichelberger to grab Wakde and speed up the advance had been the right strategic move.[14]

The challenge now, though, was Biak. Mokmer Airfield, on the southern coast, was the real prize on that rugged, virtually uninhabited island. Krueger created a task force numbering twenty-eight thousand men around the 41st Infantry Division. The division commander, Major General Horace Fuller, would also serve as task force commander. There were nearly twelve thousand Japanese defending Biak, of whom roughly five thousand were combat troops. Coral reefs fringing the southern coast of Biak made a direct attack on Mokmer impossible, so the landings would take place five miles to the east of it.

When the assault was made on the morning of May 27, the Japanese commander chose not to fight at the water's edge. He had prepared a defensive position based on caves and tunnels, supplemented by a well-arranged network of pillboxes, bunkers and rifle pits. Although taken by surprise at the landing, the Japanese quickly deployed themselves within these positions and improved on them. Imperial Headquarters meanwhile prepared to send reinforcements.[15]

MacArthur was starting to take success for granted in the wake of the great gamble that had paid off at Hollandia. The day after the Biak assault was made he proclaimed in a communiqué, "This marks the practical end of the New Guinea campaign." On June 3 he announced that "mopping up is proceeding," as if the battle had been won. In fact, it was only now that Fuller was getting into position to make his main assault.[16]

He was an able, experienced combat soldier. Once ashore, he systematically probed the enemy positions and tested their strength. He had no intention of making a beeline for Mokmer Airfield by simply driving along the coast road toward it. That was exactly what the Japanese defenses had been organized to prevent.

The Infantry School under George Marshall simplified infantry tactics between the wars until the Army really only had one tactic, the holding attack. This consisted of putting pressure on the enemy from the front, to pin him down, then hitting him hard from a flank or the rear. Once he had worked out the placement of the Japanese defenses, Fuller prepared to mount a holding attack.

MacArthur meanwhile was fretting over Fuller's advance. With each passing day he grew alarmed at the looming certainty of being embarrassed in front of the Navy. Even if Fuller succeeded, it looked unlikely that the runways at Mokmer could be patched up in time to contribute anything to Nimitz's June 15 assault on Saipan. He put pressure on Krueger to speed up the capture of Mokmer. "I am becoming concerned about the failure to secure the Biak airfields," he informed Krueger on June 5, only two days after announcing that the mop-up was under way. "Is the advance being pushed with sufficient determination? Our negligible ground losses would seem to indicate a failure to do so."[17]

Krueger sent his chief of staff, Brigadier General George Decker, to Biak to see what was happening there. Decker, a 1937 Infantry School graduate (and a future Army Chief of Staff), saw the situation much as Fuller did. On June 8 he reported back that the defenses were formidable, the terrain daunting and the heat overwhelming. The temperature was above a hundred degrees, yet a severe shortage of water restricted men to less than one canteen a day. Despite these obstacles, Fuller was making progress. His troops had just captured one of Mokmer's five airstrips.[18] The strip could not be used until Japanese guns in caves overlooking it had been seized, but Fuller now had a regiment well established on the high ground.

Instead of complimenting Fuller on taking one of Mokmer's runways and encouraging him to press the current operation to complete success,

Krueger bombarded him with insulting messages, casting doubt on his competence and his courage and demanding to know why he had not yet taken the entire airfield.[19] Just as his holding attack started yielding results, Fuller was forced to change tactics. Krueger demanded that the regiment he had managed to get onto the high ground was to abandon its position and join in a frontal assault along the coast road.

The way combat command worked in much of the Army was to apply the lash to whoever was below you, whether he was a three-star general or a second lieutenant. That wasn't MacArthur's normal style, though, and the fact that he resorted to it now showed how much pressure he felt he was under. Krueger was so alarmed by this development he did something that was equally unusual for him: He interfered with a perfectly good plan and ignored the advice of his trusted chief of staff, who had actually seen the situation for himself. This idiotic decision was bitterly protested by Fuller and by his assistant division commander, Brigadier General Jens Doe, the officer who had conducted the successful assaults on Aitape and Wakde. Doe had incomparably more combat experience than Krueger, who had been a staff officer in the last war and still did not wear a single combat decoration. Doe vehemently told Fuller he was throwing victory away. Fuller agreed with him, but what could he do?

Krueger did not seem to know or care that even if the frontal attack he was demanding brought the capture of the entire airfield, it would be pointless. Mokmer's runways were useless without control of the caves overlooking them. Bringing the troops down from the high ground surrendered the chance to grab the caves as well as the airfield. As the Army's official history records, "The attacker now placed himself where the defender most wanted him to be"—on the low ground, making frontal assaults against tunnels and bunkers.[20]

MacArthur was monitoring the battle closely by radio, and the impending loss of face was simply too humiliating to contemplate. On June 14, with the Navy's attack on Saipan less than twenty-four hours away, he sent an angry cable to Krueger: "The situation at Biak is unsatisfactory. The strategic purpose of the operation is being jeopardized by the failure to establish without delay an operating field for aircraft."[21] His credibility as a professional soldier was on the line.

Krueger sent for Eichelberger, told him to go up to Biak, fire Fuller as task force commander and take control of the operation himself. When Eichelberger arrived next day, he was met by a tearful Horace Fuller, who demanded to be relieved not only of his task force command but from command of the 41st Division too. He had tolerated Krueger's stupid and hostile messages until now, he said, but enough was enough. Eichelberger gave command of the division to Doe.[22]

Not too amazingly, Doe prepared to make a holding attack. And Eichelberger, who had been a classmate of Doe's at Leavenworth in 1926, did the best thing he could: He got out of Doe's way. Apart from making some minor changes to Doe's troop dispositions, he let the new commander of the 41st Division fight the battle much as Fuller had planned to fight it. A regiment of troops was directed to get up onto the high ground again.

The holding attack worked. Mokmer Airfield was taken in three days, the caves overlooking it two days later. Had Fuller been allowed to proceed without Krueger's interference, Kenney might just have had planes operating from Mokmer on June 15 and flying up to Saipan. Instead some of Kenney's heavies flying from Momote Airfield on Los Negros had to bomb targets in the Marianas that day. That allowed MacArthur to claim he had aided the Navy's assault on Saipan, but from Biak? Not a single sortie. It was June 22 before American fighters began operating from Mokmer. It took another three weeks to secure the two airfields farther west, and it was the end of July before all resistance ceased on Biak.[23]

After the battle MacArthur regained his poise and freely acknowledged the injustice Krueger had done to Fuller. He awarded Fuller the DSM, citing "his exceptional ability and sound judgment" both before and during the battle. He even remarked to Eichelberger that Fuller was "a grand soldier." Nonetheless, for MacArthur as for Horace Fuller, victory on Biak proved to have a stale, flat taste not much more palatable than the lees of defeat.[24]

In June 1944, shortly after D Day, Marshall, King and Arnold visited the Normandy beaches. Fighting raged a few miles inland. They were close enough to hear the thunder of artillery fire churning the marlaceous soil of northern France and see bomber formations wheeling overhead to drop their loads on German positions. The beachhead was secure, even if expanding it was proving frustratingly slow. Strategy from Normandy to Berlin could safely be left to Eisenhower.

Having savored the success of the greatest combined arms operation in history, the Joint Chiefs returned to Washington with minds increasingly focused on strategy in the Pacific. The more the Joint Chiefs discussed it, the more Marshall was impressed by King's demands for picking up the tempo.

MacArthur was informed during the battle for Biak that the JCS was thinking of speeding up the advance by making a direct attack on Formosa or maybe even southern Japan.[25] There was no need to reconquer the Philippines.

Appalled, he fired back an angry reply. Either operation would have to be made without land-based air cover and was fraught with enormous risk.

"The hazards of failure would be unjustifiable when a conservative and certain line of action is open. . . . [Recent] successes must not lead us into a suicidal direct assault without air support and with inadequate shipping and bases against heavily defended bastions. . . ." He argued the political side of the case: If the American people knew the military did not intend to liberate the Philippines, there would be "an extremely adverse reaction." And raising the specter of a resignation threat once more, he concluded, "If serious consideration is being given to the line of action indicated . . . I request that I be accorded the opportunity of personally proceeding to Washington to present fully my views."[26]

Words. Words. Marshall had heard them all before and was becoming less convinced by them than ever. What MacArthur stood in need of at this point was some kind of minor miracle. It was Marshall alone who had thus far stymied King's demand for bypassing the Philippines, but now, after reading MacArthur's impassioned reply to his cable, Marshall told Stimson the Philippines were not essential to defeating Japan. "We would be going the slow way. . . . We would have to fight our way through them and that would take a very much longer time than to make the cut across."[27]

In his response to MacArthur's protest, Marshall told him bluntly, "It seems to me that you are allowing personal feelings and Philippine political considerations to override our great objective which is the early conclusion of the war with Japan. Also that you confuse the word 'by-pass' with 'abandonment.' The two are in no way synonymous in my view." As for MacArthur's returning to Washington, Marshall was sure he could arrange a meeting with the President.[28]

Despite this discouraging message, MacArthur had the GHQ staff draw up a plan for liberating the Philippines. Called Musketeer, it projected an assault on Mindanao on November 15, an advance to the island of Leyte, in the central Philippines, on December 20, and a landing at Lingayen Gulf, roughly 120 miles north of Manila, around the middle of February 1945.

While the JCS was wrestling with Musketeer, MacArthur received a message from Marshall: "Arrange your plans so as to arrive in Honolulu July 26. It is of the utmost importance that the fewest possible number of individuals know of your expected departure or of your destination." MacArthur waited more than a week, expecting further details, and, when none was forthcoming, sent a message back: "Will I receive further instructions? I know nothing of the purpose of my orders." Marshall sent a tight-lipped reply: "Purpose general strategical discussion. . . . I will be in Washington but you will see Leahy, etcetera."[29] That was a pretty good hint of whom he would really be talking to. Admiral Leahy was the Chairman of the Joint Chiefs and, as such, Roosevelt's chief military adviser. The "etcetera" was a veiled reference to the President.

MacArthur set off from Brisbane on July 26 (it was still July 25 in Hawaii) aboard a C-54, a design based on the DC-4 airliner. There were only two C-54s in the whole of SWPA, and every air force commander in the world was clamoring for them. The *Bataan,* MacArthur's personal B-17, was just about adequate for flying between Australia and New Guinea but was too cramped and uncomfortable to be truly suitable for carrying passengers. Kenney got the head of the Air Transport Command to release one of the two C-54s in SWPA for the flight to Hawaii, and for MacArthur, who had never flown in a C-54 before, it was love at first sight. Even though this was a military cargo plane, it was a huge improvement on the *Bataan.*

He was accompanied by Brigadier General Bonner Fellers, who would act as his military secretary, one of his senior aides, Colonel Larry Lehrbas (who had spent most of his professional life as a journalist), and an Army doctor. Sutherland was left in Port Moresby to mind the store.

On the first leg of the flight, to New Caledonia, MacArthur spent most of the four and a half hours the plane was in the air pacing the aisle. What did the President want to talk to him about? Was he being relieved of his command because he would not accept King's plans? Was he going to get the green light to follow his own strategy? Was he simply being summoned so Roosevelt could pretend to confer with him before the November election? He decided the political motive was the most likely explanation. Roosevelt was not going to let Dewey use MacArthur's military difficulties as ammunition against him. Well, if so, he was going to turn this political stunt to his own advantage and put his case for liberating the Philippines to Roosevelt personally.[30]

He continued his pacing on the second leg of the flight, to Canton Island, shunning the army cot that his pilot, Major Weldon "Dusty" Rhoades, had fixed up for him in the rear of the plane. When the C-54 touched down at Canton just before dawn, there was a courier waiting with a telegram from Nimitz. MacArthur read it with obvious irritation. His plane was scheduled to arrive in Honolulu at 2:30 P.M., but Nimitz suggested he should hold off until 5:00 P.M. The message did not offer any explanation for this request.

MacArthur resented being told what to do by an officer junior to him. Besides, he had no desire to spend an extra two and a half hours in the air, flying in circles. "Not only are they telling me what to do," he fumed, "but they're telling me how to do it." He dictated a brief and pointed reply: He did not care if Nimitz could not meet him personally and had to send an ensign to the airfield instead, but he was going to arrive as scheduled. Period.[31]

As MacArthur's plane approached Hawaii in midafternoon, Rhoades had to avoid hundreds of fighters and bombers maneuvering into a huge formation over the deep green mountains of the Big Island. Here was all the confirmation anyone could ask for; only the President got an air show like this. Roosevelt was indeed approaching, aboard the heavy cruiser *Baltimore,* presently coming around Diamond Head.

Nimitz was on hand to greet MacArthur's plane when he landed at Hickam Field and took a brief ride with him over to Fort Shafter, where the general would be staying. Nimitz looked immaculate while MacArthur, who had not slept or changed for about thirty hours, looked like a crumpled brown paper bag. He had no intention of meeting the President unwashed and unshaven.

When the *Baltimore* docked, Roosevelt was met by an array of admirals in dazzling whites and glittering gold braid. He was greeted too by the Hawaiian department commander, Lieutenant General Robert C. Richardson. But where, the President wanted to know, was MacArthur? Nimitz chose not to say anything. After making small talk for nearly an hour, Roosevelt decided to go ashore. At that point an automobile siren was heard wailing in the distance.

Minutes later, escorted by MPs on motorcycles, a long red convertible pulled up at the dock. There were only two red convertibles in Honolulu, the fancier of which was owned by the madam who operated Hawaii's most expensive whorehouse. The other belonged to the chief of the Honolulu fire brigade. Nimitz had wisely decided to commandeer the fire chief's car to provide transportation for MacArthur, even if it was not quite as long or as showy as the alternative.[32]

MacArthur sat alone in the back making a fashion statement. He wore a fresh uniform, his field marshal's cap, A-2 flying jacket, and Ray-Bans, and carried an enormous corncob pipe, a puffer virtually impossible to smoke, and the effect of this eclectic ensemble of objects, some tacky, some classy, was one of the most memorable personal images of the century, recognized in all lands where photography was known or cartooning practiced.

The crowd gathered at the dock burst into a loud, spontaneous ovation. MacArthur descended from the car and strode briskly to the *Baltimore*'s gangplank. Halfway up, he turned to the crowd to acknowledge another ovation before stepping onto the deck and being piped aboard. Roosevelt was waiting, in his wheelchair, to greet him.[33]

"Mr. President, it is so nice to see you again after all these years," said MacArthur, reaching down to shake hands. "When last I saw you, I was your Chief of Staff."

"Hello, Douglas," Roosevelt responded. "What are you doing with that leather jacket on?" He was evidently annoyed at being kept waiting and probably irritated, too, by MacArthur's dramatic appearance. "It's darned hot today."

"Well, Mr. President, I've just landed from Australia." He pointed at the sky. "It's pretty cold up there."

"I guess you know what this conference is for?" said Roosevelt.

"No, Mr. President. I am completely unprepared."

Admiral William Leahy, the chairman of the JCS, intervened. "We thought we would have photographs taken now."[34]

Once the snapping and filming stopped, the assemblage of pomp and power dissolved rapidly. The general was driven back to Fort Shafter, the President to an estate on Waikiki Beach. MacArthur spent that evening dining with Richardson. Their friendship, formed at West Point when they were cadets and renewed in the Philippines in the 1920s, had suffered a crippling blow in the summer of 1942. MacArthur had needed a commander for the I Corps that summer, someone who would mount an offensive in New Guinea. Marshall had offered the assignment to Richardson, who claimed to be delighted but invented various flimsy excuses to avoid taking it. It soon became evident that he had no intention of exposing his precious person to danger. The I Corps had then gone to Robert Eichelberger. Richardson had seriously disappointed both Marshall and MacArthur, but what of it? His long friendship with Stimson soon brought what he really wanted: command in Hawaii and a third star.[35]

And now, as he took in Richardson's millionaire lifestyle—a large, beautiful house with a magnificent view, a host of servants and a fleet of large cars on call—as he studied with a critical eye this life of privilege far removed from the discomforts and dangers of the front lines of Biak, where the I Corps had just suffered twenty-five hundred combat casualties, MacArthur was pleased to make a discovery: Richardson was a deeply unhappy man. The Navy really ran Hawaii. His authority as a department commander counted for nothing, and he was reminded of it nearly every day. Fluttering aimlessly within a sunlit gilded cage, Richardson survived on a steady diet of coprophagy served up by snotty admirals.[36]

Next day MacArthur spent six hours with Roosevelt, Nimitz and Leahy, inspecting Army and Navy installations. MacArthur was shocked at the President's deathly gray pallor, the way his jaw sagged, the obvious fading of the spark of life. Roosevelt would almost certainly win in November, he decided, but he would never survive another term of office. It was doubtful he would even live long enough to see the end of the war. Throughout these six hours MacArthur and Roosevelt talked at length. There was something of a reunion here between old sparring partners. Nimitz and Leahy said almost nothing. The two sailors were really outsiders.

After dinner that night at the Waikiki estate, Roosevelt, MacArthur and Nimitz got down to business. The Navy had covered one wall with a huge map of the western Pacific. Studies and reports were piled on tables. The purpose of this meeting, Roosevelt said, was to discuss strategy. He picked up a long bamboo pointer and tapped Mindanao on the map. "Well, Douglas, where do we go from here?"[37]

This was the moment MacArthur had been preparing for since that jolting, sickening ride by PT boat, scurrying away in the darkness past brave men left to die or become prisoners of war, an act that would always look shameful however it was dressed. There was not an argument he could offer that he had not rehearsed many times, not an angle that he had not examined, not a shade of meaning that he had not learned how to convey. He argued strategy: From the Philippines he would be able to cut off the flow of oil and metals the Japanese military needed to sustain its war machine. He argued tactics: The Japanese were so widely spread throughout the Philippines they were as vulnerable to attack there as they had been in New Guinea. He argued logistics: There was enough sealift available to mount the campaign he proposed and keep it going until it proved victorious. "I can do no more than tell you I can land in the Philippines in three months and have the task completed six months thereafter," MacArthur concluded. "The blockade that I will put across the line of supply between Japan and the Dutch East Indies will so strangle the Japanese Empire that it will have to surrender." There would be no need to mount an invasion of Japan.[38]

Nimitz had been extensively briefed by King on what he should say. Over the next two hours he made the argument that King wanted him to make. Luzon could and should be bypassed. It had little military value. The Navy could now operate freely at great distances from friendly ports and airfields. The fast carrier force would be able to bring more than a thousand combat aircraft to bear on any target the Navy was allowed to strike, and Nimitz currently had enough sealift available to put up to twelve divisions ashore. There had never been a seaborne force like this in the history of war. Here was a crushing weapon that demanded continuous employment. The Navy's strategy was designed to do just that. The way to defeat Japan was to isolate the home islands and choke the empire into submission. The next big attack should be launched at Formosa, not Luzon, and be followed rapidly by assaults against Iwo Jima and Okinawa. Once the home islands were isolated, a campaign of air and naval attacks would bring victory without an invasion of Japan.

MacArthur responded coolly, "I don't think we could ever justify liberating the Chinese on Formosa and abandoning millions of Filipinos on Luzon." As for attacking Iwo Jima and Okinawa, what the Navy proposed was nothing more than bloody frontal assaults against two strongly held positions. The heavy loss of life involved would never justify the slight military benefits taking either would bring.[39]

The meeting broke up at midnight, and discussion resumed in the morning. There was no rancor, no impatience or point scoring. MacArthur even claimed to hold Admiral King in high esteem.[40] Nimitz reiterated what he had said the previous evening about isolating Japan. MacArthur continued to demand the reconquest of the Philippines.

Roosevelt interrupted him this time. "But, Douglas, to take Luzon would demand heavier losses than we can stand." There were nearly half a million Japanese troops in the Philippines.

"Mr. President, my losses would *not* be heavy, any more than they have been in the past. The days of the frontal attack should be over. Modern infantry weapons are too deadly, and frontal assault is only for mediocre commanders." He did not say so outright, but everyone there knew Saipan, seized by frontal assault, had cost fifteen thousand American casualties.[41]

The discussion ground to a halt at noon, and the conferees moved into the dining room for lunch. The serious talking seemed to be over, everything that could be said seemed to have been said, and repeated more than once, but when lunch concluded, MacArthur asked if he could have ten minutes alone with Roosevelt. The President's advisers, Samuel Rosenman and Elmer Davis, shook their heads. He had a schedule to keep. After a brief pause, however, Roosevelt said, "All right, Douglas." The room was cleared, leaving them alone.

When everything else was stripped away, Roosevelt was a politician. MacArthur had come to Hawaii to make not one argument but two. The first, the strictly military one, was presented in front of Nimitz and Leahy. The second one, the political pitch, had to be made in private. He was not going to give King the chance to say he was dragging in nonmilitary considerations, even though that was exactly what he intended to do. Roosevelt was more likely to be swayed by a political argument than one that was purely military, and MacArthur was ready. He kept it brief and to the point.

"Mr. President, the country has forgiven you for what took place on Bataan. You hope to be reelected President of the United States, but the nation will never forgive you if you approve a plan which leaves 17 million Christian American subjects to wither in the Philippines under the conqueror's heel until the peace treaty frees them. You might do it for reasons of strategy or tactics, but politically, it would ruin you. And now, Mr. President, duties at my headquarters are calling me, and I shall withdraw." He shook Roosevelt's hand, turned and had reached the door before the President called him back. He seemed reluctant to say goodbye and asked MacArthur to join him on a last tour of inspection.[42]

As they rode along to visit yet another military base, MacArthur said, "What chance do you think Dewey has?" Roosevelt replied that he had been too busy to think about politics. MacArthur threw back his head and laughed heartily. Roosevelt stared at him for a moment, then broke out laughing too. When they had calmed down, he remarked that Dewey was a nice man but a little inexperienced in politics. Even so, he concluded, "If the war with Germany ends before the election, I will not be reelected."[43]

When the inspection concluded, MacArthur returned to Fort Shafter, said farewell to Richardson and took off on the return flight to Brisbane in an excited, confident mood, convinced that he had finally won, that Roosevelt would back his plan to liberate the Philippines. Earlier in the war the President had stepped in and dictated strategy to the JCS. Since the Quebec Conference in August 1943, however, he had increasingly left the Joint and Combined Chiefs to make the big decisions. His opinion nonetheless counted for something, and if there was a deadlock over Luzon versus Formosa, it could be decisive.

When MacArthur got back to Australia he electrified the GHQ staff by telling them that the President was backing his strategy.[44] Shortly afterward Roosevelt confirmed it. "I will push on that plan," he wrote MacArthur, "for I am convinced that as a whole it is logical and can be done. . . . Some day there will be a flag raising in Manila—and without question I want you to do it."[45]

To complete his advance along the coast of New Guinea, MacArthur would have to control the dominant terrain features at the western end of that huge island, Geelvink Bay and the Vogelkop Peninsula. There were three Japanese airfields on Noemfoor Island, fifty miles west of Biak. If he had planes operating from Noemfoor, Kenney advised him, it would be possible to make a major assault against the Vogelkop Peninsula and secure control of Geelvink Bay.

MacArthur decided to seize Noemfoor with a combined airborne and amphibious assault as soon as the fight for Biak had been won. On July 2 the 158th Infantry Regiment landed at Noemfoor, coming ashore only a hundred yards from one of the three airfields. Next morning a battalion of paratroopers from the 503d Parachute Infantry Regiment was dropped onto the airfield to reinforce the assault. A second battalion was dropped on Independence Day.[46]

The two thousand Japanese defending Noemfoor pulled back to the high ground in the center of the island. They fought desperately but were eventually overrun. American losses came to four hundred killed or wounded. Only a handful of Japanese survived.[47]

With Noemfoor in his hands, MacArthur mounted an assault against the fishing village of Sansapor, on the Vogelkop Peninsula, on July 30. The 6th Infantry Division landed in force, along with several thousand Army engineers, ready to carve out an airfield. There were few Japanese anywhere near Sansapor. It was two weeks before the invading troops were attacked, and they beat off the halfhearted thrusts that were made against them with little difficulty.

MacArthur now controlled the entire thirteen-hundred-mile length of New Guinea. There were no worlds left for him to conquer in its mist-shrouded mountains and stinking swamps. It abruptly ceased to be a stage where great dramas were played out. The scene of action had moved on. From Sansapor MacArthur planned to seize the island of Halmahera, roughly halfway between Geelvink Bay and Mindanao, but while he was in Hawaii, Ultra revealed the Japanese were constructing a defensive triangle to block his advance from New Guinea to the Philippines.

The triangle was based on Halmahera, on the Palau Islands to the east of Mindanao and on Mindanao itself. Eighty thousand Japanese ground troops and three air armies, operating five hundred planes, held the triangle. Nearly half the Japanese troops were on Halmahera. The enemy seemed to have been reading MacArthur's mind.[48]

MacArthur came back from Honolulu, looked at the maps, listened to Willoughby and Kenney, then put his finger on the island of Morotai, ten miles from Halmahera. Virtually undefended Morotai had promising sites for the airstrips and radar stations he would need to mount an assault against the island of Talaud, standing halfway between Morotai and Mindanao, on October 15. From Talaud, he would make the jump to the southern coast of Mindanao, on November 15. Five weeks after landing at Mindanao, he intended to land in Leyte Gulf, on December 20. The JCS approved this plan, but what happened beyond Leyte still had not been settled when Barbey's assault shipping began heading for Morotai.

MacArthur decided to get away from GHQ for a few days and accompany the 31st Division in its assault. On September 10 Dusty Rhoades flew him from Port Moresby to Hollandia. Two days later MacArthur boarded the *Nashville,* and the cruiser sailed out to join the invasion convoys streaming northwest along the New Guinea coast. When dawn broke on September 15, the *Nashville* sailed into Halmahera Bay with other warships and bombarded the coastline. The Japanese kept their heads down, but nature responded. The volcano Gam Konora erupted in flame and smoke, sending up huge clouds of dust that blackened the sky over the invasion fleet as it turned northeast for Morotai.

The 31st Division put its first wave of troops ashore at 8:00 A.M. The landing craft ground to a halt on a long sandbar a couple of hundred yards from shore. The soldiers calmly got out and waded the rest of the way, holding their M-1 semiautomatic rifles over their heads, while Kenney's

C-47s flew over them and lavishly sprayed the beach and the jungle nearby with DDT. Typhus was going to be more of a threat than the Japanese.[49]

At 10:15 MacArthur went ashore with Egeberg and Lehrbas. There was no immediate sign that the island was even occupied, although there were in fact three fishing villages not far away and a leper colony a few miles inland. After three hours ashore MacArthur headed back to the *Nashville.*

The cruiser steamed back to Hollandia, still keeping radio silence. The ship could receive messages but not transmit anything until the operation was over, for fear of giving its presence and position away to the enemy. Although MacArthur has always been presented by historians who have dealt with this subject as being out of touch and thus ignorant of one of the most dramatic developments in the brief history of the JCS, Navy records show he was well aware of what was going on.

The Joint and Combined Chiefs of Staff were meeting in Quebec when, late on the evening of September 15, Nimitz forwarded a message to them that he had received a few hours earlier from Halsey. One of Halsey's fast carrier task forces was currently attacking targets on Leyte and had encountered virtually no opposition from Japanese planes. A downed pilot had also been rescued, after spending a day in hiding on Leyte. The pilot reported the Filipinos who had helped him said the island was "wide open to attack." Halsey wanted permission from Nimitz to scrape together a landing force and make an immediate assault to seize Leyte.

Nimitz had turned him down. After all, this was really MacArthur's territory. He should be given a chance to grab it if he could. Nimitz was willing, he informed GHQ, to release various Marine and Army units presently under his command and earmarked for operations in the Central Pacific if MacArthur would use them to make a Leyte assault on short notice. Nimitz would also provide the necessary shipping.[50] Copies of his cable and Halsey's report were transmitted to Quebec.

They were also transmitted to the *Nashville.* As MacArthur read them, his filmic imagination put before him a vision of one of the most audacious attacks in military history, a great battle to rank with Cannae or Waterloo, a strategic masterstroke that even the Corsican genius would have savored. With the sealift available to Kinkaid's Seventh Fleet plus the extra assault shipping that Nimitz was offering, he might just be able to put six divisions ashore. But why put all of them onto the beaches of Leyte? That was the safe and obvious thing to do. A great captain would bet everything on one roll of the dice and strike Leyte and Luzon simultaneously. Hammer and anvil: He could land four divisions in Lingayen Gulf, put two ashore at Leyte and crush the 425,000 Japanese troops in the Philippines between them like a nut!

He wrote out a message for Sutherland: "Magnificent opportunity presents itself now that air resistance over Philippines will be neutralized to combine projected initial and final operations in one comprehensive pincer movement. Six divisional lift divided four and two with rapid buildup would be sufficient. Have staff study tonight with idea of presenting plan to Washington tomorrow. I am completely confident that it can be done and will practically end the Pacific war. It is our greatest opportunity. The double stroke would be a complete surprise to the enemy and would not fail." If the JCS accepted this brilliant and daring plan, the great debate over Luzon would be settled once and for all.[51]

The *Nashville* would not break radio silence, however. MacArthur's message was marked by the cruiser's coding clerk, "Deliver by safehand." It was not going to reach Hollandia any faster than a humble Navy messenger courier could carry it. At a guess, it seems likely that it did reach Sutherland, but only after MacArthur had already returned to his headquarters. In his *Reminiscences,* however, MacArthur asserted that he had telegraphed his agreement to the Halsey proposal, which made it seem that he had made the decision.[52] Yet with MacArthur still incommunicado, Sutherland had to reply for him.

On receiving Nimitz's message, Marshall had fired a cable straight to Hollandia: Could SWPA follow through on Nimitz's recommended hurry-up assault on Leyte?

"The Joint Chiefs of Staff are of the opinion that this operation is highly to be desired and would advance the progress of the war in your theater by many months. . . ."[53]

Sutherland sent for Kenney and MacArthur's G-3, Brigadier General Steve Chamberlin. Was it possible to mount a Leyte assault on such short notice? What about air cover? What would happen if they said No?

They decided that if they took the shipping and ground units Nimitz had offered, scrapped the October 15 landing on Talaud and the November 15 assault on southern Mindanao, they would be able to mount a four-division assault on Leyte. That would still leave them short by up to a hundred landing ships, two infantry divisions and hundreds of thousands of tons of supplies that they had counted on being available for a Leyte assault in December.

The biggest problem was air. Chamberlin argued the Navy would provide all the air cover that was needed. Kenney told him flatly he was about as wrong as he could be. Besides, Halsey was also wrong about the Japanese defenses on Leyte. There were reliable reports from Whitney's guerrillas of nearly twenty thousand Japanese on Leyte, well dug in and supported by tanks.

Leyte Gulf was out of range even for Kenney's P-38Js, and any carriers Nimitz provided would pull out in a few days. Nor were there good airfield sites in the vicinity of Leyte Gulf for Kenney's aviation engineers to build on. The assaulting units could easily find themselves fighting a battle for survival without air cover.

An hour and a half after receiving Marshall's cable, Sutherland sent a reply. He disagreed with Halsey's estimate of the strength of the defenses on Leyte, he said, but conceded there would be just enough troops, airplane and assault shipping to make a landing feasible. As commitments went, it was a pretty tepid response. It was, that is, a perfect reflection of his doubts and hesitations.

While it was being coded and transmitted, Sutherland and Kenney talked some more, worried some more, turned the implications of Halsey's recommendations over in their minds, and a terrifying prospect seized hold of them: If the Joint Chiefs got anything less than an unequivocally positive commitment, King might say it demonstrated SWPA's lack of confidence in its ability to mount a major campaign in the Philippines and proof that MacArthur was unable to act as quickly and flexibly as the Navy. They were horrified. King might even use that cable to get authority for Nimitz to put together a landing force and make the assault!

If the Navy got its hands on Leyte, King would control whatever happened in the Philippines. No triumphant return. No liberation. No vindication. Sutherland wrote out a second cable, one with a resoundingly confident tone: "Subject to completion of arrangements with Nimitz, we shall execute the Leyte operation on 20 October. MacArthur." Marshall received it on his way to dinner with the Combined Chiefs and passed it among them over the hors d'oeuvres.[54]

When the *Nashville* docked at Hollandia at 9:00 A.M. on September 17, MacArthur left the cruiser in an ebullient mood. So far as he knew, the GHQ staff was now working on his plan to strike Leyte and Luzon simultaneously. The trip had lifted his spirits and made destiny seem almost palpable. During his walk along the beaches of Morotai, MacArthur had chatted with a group of officers for a while, then turned his gaze to the northwest. He seemed to see something beyond the horizon, something they could only imagine: the mile-high purple outline of the Mariveles Mountains looming over Bataan? Or the sinuous, low silhouette of Corregidor? "They are waiting for me there," he murmured. "It has been a long time."[55]

24

Rally to Me

There were a lot of rumors about how MacArthur lived during the war. One of the most famous was that he had built himself a palace on the scale of San Simeon or Versailles in the unlikely environs of Hollandia. There was no denying that Army engineers built a large new structure there for GHQ in the summer of 1944, but as palaces go, this one was not in the Taj Mahal bracket. It was built out of the prosaic, flat-packed materials that were normally used for the erection of three standard Army-style prefabricated houses. The most impressive thing about MacArthur's new residence-cum-headquarters was the magnificent setting.

The site was atop a hill that looked out over the deep blue waters of Lake Sentani. The six-thousand-foot peak of Mount Cyclops rose majestically behind the headquarters building, and as in a Hollywood epic, a spectacular waterfall erupted from the center of the mountain, sending a long plume of water cascading in an exuberant white arc far into the jungle below. Nearly one thousand feet up, MacArthur's combination of office and home stood high enough to catch the ocean breezes circulating above the stifling heat and stinking swamps of the shoreline below.

Kenney flew some rugs, furniture and a bathtub from MacArthur's office in Brisbane to make the place seem comfortable and familiar. There was a conference room, eight or nine offices and half a dozen bedrooms for Sutherland and other key members of the GHQ staff.[1]

Before the war the hillside and the narrow strip of flatland at its base had seen no structures more ambitious than a few grass huts. After three months of American occupation there was a canvas city housing nearly a hundred thousand people. The engineers bulldozed dusty roads out of the jungle, a large field hospital sprang up, the Navy erected a complex of Quonset huts for the Seventh Fleet headquarters, supply officers put up crude warehouses made of sheet metal, canvas and odds and ends of lumber salvaged from packing crates, while snaking around the base of the hill was row upon row of brown Army tents. The unstated design principle of this instant city was to center it on MacArthur's new Advance GHQ.[2]

The relative comfort of this structure in the midst of one of the most forbidding places on Earth drew cynical remarks from some soldiers. There was a legend that MacArthur had built himself a "million-dollar mansion" so he could wallow in luxury while his men lived in the dirt. The actual construction cost was about two zeros less than a million, and even if we allow for the occasional eccentric plutocrat who becomes a Buddhist or volunteers to clean out the sewers of Calcutta, it isn't easy to imagine the average American millionaire would have felt pampered to live and work in a dull rectangular structure a hundred feet long by forty feet wide consisting mainly of waist-high wallboard, screen doors and whitewashed canvas.[3]

The biggest advantage the Lake Sentani headquarters possessed over Government House in Port Moresby was that MacArthur was finally able to get Kenney's Far Eastern Air Forces, Krueger's Sixth Army and Kinkaid's Seventh Fleet to put their headquarters in the same place where GHQ did most of its work. The result was a lot less commuting among the various headquarters, and decisions were made more quickly, no slight consideration given the speed with which the details of the Leyte landing had to be worked out.[4]

When MacArthur returned to this new headquarters at Hollandia on September 17 following the successful landing on Morotai, Sutherland was waiting to greet him and obviously nervous. He asked Kenney to be present, a request Kenney rightly interpreted as a bid for moral support. Like a teenager confessing to dad, Sutherland told MacArthur about Halsey's proposal to make an immediate landing, about Nimitz's offer of troops and shipping and, with evident obvious trepidation, that he had agreed to this proposal in MacArthur's name.

This was the first MacArthur knew that Sutherland had not yet received his message from the *Nashville*. Without bothering to mention that, he chose to take his chief of staff completely by surprise by putting the suggestion directly to him: Why not make two landings instead of just one? Really catch the Japanese between the rock and a hard place, hit Leyte and Luzon simultaneously!

Sutherland was staggered, the GHQ staff incredulous. A quick rundown of what was available ruled it out, Sutherland reported shortly afterward. According to Chamberlin's figures, if they allowed for some sardine-style packing and left a lot of useful stuff back in the warehouses and depots, there was just enough sealift, maybe, in what Kinkaid already had and Nimitz was offering to lend them to put five divisions maximum ashore, and not one soldier more. If they stuck their necks out and hit Leyte with only two divisions, that would leave three for Luzon, where the Japanese had at least two hundred thousand troops—the equivalent of six divisions. MacArthur didn't hide his disappointment, but he was a realist, even when he took big chances. He was hoping they could come up with a way to put at least four divisions on the beaches of Lingayen Gulf, but when he realized that was impossible, he dropped the idea.[5]

MacArthur spent a couple of days talking to Kenney, Krueger and Kinkaid about the hurry-up assault on Leyte. In the evenings he relaxed by reminiscing and talking politics with his old friend Robert Wood, who had somehow managed to get military transportation all the way to Hollandia. They agreed that Roosevelt was almost certain to be reelected in the upcoming presidential election.[6]

Two days after returning to Hollandia, MacArthur flew back to Brisbane. Over the next three weeks he spent more time with Jean and Arthur than had been possible since the war began. The one sad note to his prolonged visit to Australia was his farewell to John Curtin. Something close to friendship had developed between these two very dissimilar men. Curtin was an outspoken, patchily educated working-class politician who had risen to power through the Australian labor unions. He had none of MacArthur's patrician air or polished manners. Yet there was a lot of integrity in Curtin, a quick intelligence and a wealth of common sense. He had seen earlier than most politicians that if Australia were to be saved, America, not Britain, would have to do it. He put his political career and his country's security firmly in MacArthur's hands and did what MacArthur would have done had their positions been reversed: He backed him completely against any critic, took his side against every foe.[7]

MacArthur owed a lot to Curtin, and if he could not resist manipulating him at times and was not always candid with him, there was nevertheless a genuine affection in his feelings toward the prime minister and a willingness to acknowledge that he owed him a great deal. And now Curtin had such serious heart disease he was not expected to live much longer.

On September 30 MacArthur flew to Canberra for a final conversation with the prime minister, discussing the closing campaigns of a war that Curtin had lived to see won but would probably never live to see finished. It was a deeply emotional farewell for both of them. MacArthur boarded the *Bataan* for the return flight to Brisbane clearly moved.[8]

During his first three weeks back in Brisbane MacArthur was on tenterhooks. The JCS still had not decided whether to attack Formosa or Luzon.

MacArthur had been intensely irritated that Marshall had not been at Honolulu to back him up in what had amounted to a head-to-head slugging contest with the Navy. Although King had not been there either, he had discussed strategy with Nimitz extensively only a few days before MacArthur's arrival. Moreover, Nimitz had benefited from the presence of Admiral Leahy, the Chairman of the JCS. MacArthur had been maneuvered into fighting his corner alone, and with no advance preparation, unlike the admirals, who had shown up loaded for bear.

Whether Marshall was trying to make amends or not isn't clear, but days after MacArthur returned to New Guinea, Marshall sent Major General John Hull, the head of the Operations Division, out to Australia. Hull wanted to know more about MacArthur's plan for liberating the Philippines. MacArthur told Hull that it was Formosa, not Luzon, that ought to be bypassed. Air and naval units based on Luzon could easily isolate Formosa. There would be no need to take it. On the other hand, he scorned King's proposal to cripple the Japanese forces in the Philippines with a naval blockade. If such a blockade hurt anyone, said MacArthur, it would be the Filipinos, not the Japanese. His own objective was feasible: He would liberate Manila thirty days after landing on Luzon. That was a clear, unequivocal pledge.[9]

When there was still no decision on Luzon versus Formosa even after the capture of Morotai, MacArthur sent Major General Richard J. Marshall to the Pentagon to press the case for a landing in Lingayen Gulf in January 1945.[10] In Washington Marshall found King's staff was still resisting MacArthur's strategy as vigorously as ever. But the minor miracle MacArthur needed was finally in the pipeline. It was not a gift from George C. Marshall. Nor was it a presidential favor granted by Franklin D. Roosevelt. Nor yet was it the fruit of MacArthur's strategic insights and eloquence. It came from a handful of obscure Army lieutenant colonels and Navy commanders working eighteen-hour days on the Joint Logistics Committee of the Joint Planning Staff of the JCS. The more they looked at the figures on sealift, troop deployments, assault shipping, airplane availability rates, projected manpower loss rates, units of fire, the number of replacements in the pipeline, plus factors of time and distances, one simple fact kept looming up before them: Formosa could not be invaded before February 1945, and then only if it got priority over everything else, such as the defeat of Germany. King may or may not have been a great strategist, but one thing was beyond doubt: The Navy's numbers did not add up.

MacArthur's numbers came out the way he said they did. He could make a six-division assault on Luzon with the resources that would be available to him in January. And the JCS would not have to halt the war in the rest of the world for him to do it. Once this became clear in late September 1944, the Chairman of the JCS, Admiral Leahy, threw his weight behind MacArthur's plan. Marshall and Arnold backed it too. There was no Army-Navy deadlock for Roosevelt to resolve, as had seemed likely a few months earlier. Instead King found himself outvoted three to one. He had finally lost his long and bitter campaign to block MacArthur's plan for a triumphant return to Luzon with enough troops, enough firepower and more than enough authority to liberate Manila.

On October 5 MacArthur finally got the word he had been begging for since the spring of 1942: He would make the Luzon assault. But he was in no hurry to return to Hollandia and leave his wife and son behind. During the past year he had seen little of them. He delayed his departure as long as he could. Then, on October 14, he flew back to Port Moresby. Next morning he set off for Hollandia . . . and Leyte.[11]

By the summer of 1944 every important move MacArthur made was a vote for airpower. He had learned to get as much out of it as any ground commander of the war. He understood both its flexibility and its fragility. He knew what the airmen could do, and what they couldn't, appreciated how the air war changed from day to day, depending on the weather, the mix and number of planes able to fly, the immediate needs of the ground troops, the overall needs of the air campaign and the enemy's actions. The story of the war in the air was like the Gospels, largely figurative, a tale reconstructed from fragmentary evidence and conflicting reports presented in a manner designed to encourage faith. It called on the powers of imagination rather than the physiology of sight. Few people ever saw what actually happened in the air war. It was not like a ground battle, something a four-star general could go and get the feel of as his nostrils contracted spasmodically, twitched by the sharp odor of cordite, while his mind, teeming with all he had ever seen of combat, absorbed a new chapter in the protean panorama of war.

One hundred and fifteen miles long, forty miles wide in the north and south but only fifteen miles wide in the middle, Leyte was an obvious place for MacArthur to land. Airfields there could put Kenney's fighters within range of the beaches of Lingayen Gulf and cover an amphibious assault on Luzon. But when Kenney contemplated the four airfields known to be in operation on Leyte in the summer of 1944, one thing was obvious: They were on the wrong side of the island. All four were on or near Leyte Gulf, on the eastern side—the side, that is, which got the worst of the island's weather, and the assault would be made during the rainy season. The land they stood on was poorly drained. They had been placed there originally for commercial reasons and were adequate for handling lightplanes heading to and from the regional capital, Tacloban. They were also more or less capable of handling Japanese fighters, undernourished and flimsy craft compared with Kenney's P-38s and P-47s. And there was no way they could take his bombers without being rebuilt.

Kenney insisted that the plan for Leyte had to include an assault against the west coast of the island, to provide him with flat, well-drained land for airfields. Sutherland agreed, and in the original plans for Leyte the island was going to be struck from both sides. There would be an amphibious assault on the eastern side, in Leyte Gulf, and the 11th Airborne Division would be dropped on the western side to seize land for an airfield.[12]

That plan was thrown out, though, when the date of the assault was brought forward to October 20. MacArthur's engineers told him that the Tacloban area was a poor place to build airfields in the rainy season, but he already knew that, had known it, in fact, since before some of them were even born. He had surveyed the coast near Tacloban back in 1903, when he too was an Army engineer. Nevertheless he put their protests to one side and demanded they have a five-thousand-foot strip in operation at Tacloban five days after the landing that would be capable of handling a fighter group (roughly seventy-five planes) and other airfields shortly thereafter to handle bombers, photorecon and more fighter groups.[13] He was counting on Halsey to provide him with fighter cover from his fast carriers during those first five days ashore, while Casey's engineers tried to wrestle airstrips out of the mud.

After lunch on October 16 MacArthur, Sutherland and Kenney boarded the captain's barge that would take them out to the *Nashville* for the voyage to Leyte. As he prepared to step onto the landing platform at the base of the cruiser's side ladder, a powerful wave abruptly pitched the barge above the platform. MacArthur, off-balance and in midstep, crashed face-down across the barge's deck. While sailors lining the rail above gasped and waited expectantly for him to react, he picked himself up, calmly stepped onto the platform, mounted the ladder and saluted the *Nashville*'s quarterdeck without any change of expression, as if being ambushed by the treacherous sea were all part of the game.[14]

Shortly after he had settled in aboard the cruiser, he received a message from Halsey: The number of fast carrier groups assigned to provide air cover was being cut from four to two. Halsey was evidently still convinced there was no real air threat on Leyte, that the Japanese Army Air Force and the air arm of the Imperial Japanese Navy in the Philippines had been virtually destroyed. MacArthur had his doubts. "I wish I had my own air in direct support," he told Kenney. "If it hadn't been for the pressure of the Navy in the JCS to grab control of this show and sidetrack me, I would never have gone to Leyte their way, prior to establishing our own air on

Mindanao." All the same, he added, he believed in his own luck; this assault would succeed.[15]

In midafternoon on October 18 the eastern horizon seemed to turn into a solid black line; the main invasion convoy was in sight. By evening the seas around the cruiser had filled with ships. The ocean seemed studded with metal, as if the center of the Earth were throwing up gobbets of steel. More than seven hundred vessels took a north by northwesterly course for the central Philippines.

The cross-Channel attack of June 6, 1944, was a ferrying operation compared to this one. Here really was an armada, whole fleets of assault ships protected by more than twenty aircraft carriers, a dozen battleships, nearly a hundred cruisers and destroyers, and close to a thousand planes, all to protect and move an entire army of 175,000 soldiers across a vast expanse of open sea and put them on a distant shore deep in the enemy's rear with all their supplies and artillery and ready to fight. For nearly every man on every ship it was a nerve-jangling, am-I-really-part-of-*this*? arsenal-of-democracy, managerial-revolutionary, remembering-Pearl-Harbor-in-spades spectacle, on a steady twelve-knot zigzag sub-dodging course to the biggest assault of the entire Pacific war. This was Iwo Jima, Okinawa and Saipan all rolled into one—only bigger.

MacArthur read and wrote telegrams in the mornings, napped after lunch, relaxed on deck in the late afternoon by reading reports and chatting with George Kenney or Courtney Whitney or with his aides Roger Egeberg and Larry Lehrbas. The astonishing sight of the invasion fleet drew him, like just about everyone else, to the rail from time to time. He stood there seeming to feast on this living painting of gray steel and blue water with flying fish. Whitney, standing alongside him the afternoon of October 19, was moved to remark, "General, it must give you a sense of great power having such a mighty armada at your command."

"No, Court, it doesn't," said MacArthur. "I cannot escape the thought of those fine American boys who are going to die on the beaches tomorrow morning."[16]

In the evenings he worked on that day's communiqué and on the two speeches he was planning to give—one on the beach and one when he restored the government of the Philippines. He tried the final draft of the beach speech on Egeberg and Lehrbas the evening of October 19. When he reached a passage that declared, "The tinkle of the laughter of little children will again be heard on the streets," Egeberg was appalled.

"That's a time worn sentimental cliché," he said, interrupting the general in full flow. "It stinks."

A stricken expression flashed across MacArthur's still-handsome features. His feelings were plainly hurt. Defensively he said he thought what he had written was okay, but Egeberg would not back down. MacArthur picked up his pen and crossed it out, then returned to his dress rehearsal. When he finished the speech, Egeberg told him it was excellent . . . now.[17]

Before retiring, MacArthur wrote out a letter to Roosevelt that he would send from the beach once he got ashore. He dated it "October 20." Then he wrote a letter to "Dearest Jeannie," telling her that he was "in good fettle and hope to do my part tomorrow and in the days that follow." He signed it "Sir Boss."[18]

At 11:00 P.M., wrapped in the depths of a black Pacific night with thick, low clouds that smelled of rains to come, the *Nashville* was off the entrance to Leyte Gulf. MacArthur prepared to go to bed still wishing he had Kenney's planes to support his troops come morning.[19]

Before falling asleep, he read a few pages from his mother's Bible. Then he prayed and asked God for the impossible, but what else is faith for? Would the Lord, could the Lord, find a way that not a single American soldier died in the assault tomorrow? He then drifted off to sleep, under the eternally unblinking black and white gaze of his father, his mother, his dead brothers, his wife and his son, their silver-framed faces lined up on a small table beside him.[20]

At dawn, battleships and cruisers closed on the invasion beaches and opened fire with their big guns. The thunder of their bombardment rolled across the waters of Leyte Gulf and flowed over the *Nashville,* bringing MacArthur awake. Dressing quickly, he slipped his father's old two-shot derringer into his right pants pocket. It was a simple precaution, something he did not expect to need, but whatever happened ashore, he would never be taken alive.[21]

The assault was going to be made by four divisions: The 1st Cavalry and the 24th Infantry would go ashore near Tacloban Airfield, the most important tactical objective of the day; two other divisions, the 7th Infantry and the 96th Infantry, would land ten miles farther south, near Dulag, where there were three airstrips that Kenney wanted to seize and develop.

The first wave of assault troops hit the beach at 10:00 A.M. They found little resistance in most places. The Japanese had about twenty thousand troops on Leyte but realized they could not build bunkers strong enough to withstand the kind of naval bombardment the Pacific fleet brought to bear against beach defenses. Where there were caves, as at Biak, there was a possibility of strengthening and deepening them so that not even sixteen-inch one-ton naval shells would destroy them except with a very lucky hit. But Leyte's beaches had few caves. Most Japanese defenders had been pulled back to the hills overlooking the beaches, where they could rake the landing force with mortar and machine-gun fire.

From the deck of the *Nashville* ten miles out it was hard to see anything of what was happening on the beaches. The stunning concussions from the barrage, the kaleidoscopic patterns of rockets flashing overhead, the roar of Navy fighters somewhere in the low clouds, the smudged streak along the shoreline where thick black pillars of smoke with tongues of fire for roots rose to touch the clouds were context for the battle being fought but not the thing itself, the drama that MacArthur was straining to see from his vantage point on the cruiser's bridge.

At 11:00 A.M. he sent for the four war correspondents who were aboard the *Nashville* to join him. He chewed on the corncob pipe and told them everything was going according to plan. And here he was, he went on, exactly forty-one years to the day when he had first seen this place, on October 20, 1903, a still-wet-behind-the-ears second lieutenant of engineers, crossing these waters on a little interisland steamer. His mission then had been to do a survey and build some piers at Tacloban.[22]

After lunch MacArthur was preparing to go ashore when his deputy chief engineer, Brigadier General Jack Sverdrup, brought him some bad news. Pat Casey, who had stepped into a hole back at Hollandia, had wrenched his back. Despite still suffering from intense pain, Casey was demanding that he be taken ashore today. Egeberg went and examined him, then reported back to MacArthur that he did not think Casey should leave the ship. It looked like a slipped disk.

It was inconceivable to MacArthur that the challenge of building airfields in the gumbo that passed for rainy season terrain around Tacloban could be overcome without Casey's brain and will. "Doc," he said firmly, "I don't think I have ever called anyone indispensable, but at this time Pat Casey is indispensable to me. So you get him ashore and find some way in which he can work." Casey was taken to the beach at Tacloban strapped to a stretcher and shot full of painkillers.[23]

At 1:00 P.M. MacArthur boarded an LCM (landing craft, medium) accompanied by Kenney, Kinkaid, Sutherland, Whitney, Egeberg, Lehrbas, four journalists and his orderly, Sergeant Francisco Salveron. On the ten-mile run to shore the landing craft made a slight diversion to the Liberty ship *John Land* to collect the new president of the Philippines, Sergio Osmeña. Quezon had died in the United States in July 1944, killed mainly by a lifelong commitment to heavy smoking. Osmeña was one of Quezon's oldest friends. They had been law students together at the turn of the century. Shy, reserved, honest, not overly ambitious, no threat to the maestro of Philippine politics, he was, that is, the ideal vice-president for the glamorous Don Manuel.

MacArthur had known Osmeña as long as he had known Quezon, had met both of them at the same time, at the Army and Navy Club in Manila one evening in 1903. Yet they had never been close. Even during the two months Osmeña spent at Hollandia waiting to join this expedition MacArthur more or less ignored him. He treated Osmeña with all the courtesy he was due, but nothing more. There was never any sign that he liked him or thought highly of his abilities.[24]

During the ninety-minute journey toward the shore MacArthur sat on the LCM's engine housing, with Osmeña on his left, Sutherland on his right. As the LCM approached the beaches, it ran into scores of landing craft returning to the LSTs after putting the first three waves ashore. Among them was a barge from one of the big warships. MacArthur told the LCM's coxswain, "Hail that barge." The cox did so, and the barge came about.

MacArthur shouted to its helmsman, who was staring in complete disbelief. Was that MacArthur? "Son," he called out, "where is the hardest fighting going on?" The helmsman wordlessly pointed almost directly ahead of them, to Red Beach, where the 24th Division had landed. MacArthur shouted his thanks and turned to the LCM coxswain. "Head for that beach."[25]

As the landing craft neared the shore, he was thrilled to see souvenirs of his youth jutting like a dark line into the water farther north, near Tacloban. Some of the piers he had built as a shavetail were still intact, still in use. He turned to Sutherland and said simply, "Believe it or not, Dick, we're back!"[26]

At 2:30 the LCM nudged a sandbar and came to a halt near four other beached landing craft, one of them on fire. Just inland from where the LCM halted, three Navy dive-bombers were making an attack on Japanese positions. The ramp went down, and the four journalists rushed down the ramp. Two of them carried cameras to record the moment when the general set foot on Philippine soil once more. MacArthur disembarked, closely followed by his staff, Osmeña, Kenney and Kinkaid. At the bottom of the ramp he was in water up to his knees.

There were stories that MacArthur had staged his arrival for maximum dramatic impact. Such tales were still circulating during the celebrations to mark the fiftieth anniversary of the return to the Philippines. The coxswain of the LCM and his friend the coxswain of the barge that MacArthur had hailed both denied these assertions. So did William Dunn, one of the four journalists traveling with MacArthur. It was also claimed by some writers that MacArthur was tight-lipped and angry at having to get his feet wet. Their only evidence is what they have tried to read from the expression on his face. In fact, he had made the same kind of arrival during the landing at Morotai five weeks earlier, when he had waded through water that was even deeper to reach the shore. Getting his feet wet was neither new nor unexpected.

Chin thrust vigorously forward, MacArthur strode on about fifty yards until he reached the soft sand of the beach. Then, once his party of Americans and Filipinos had gathered around him, he said simply, "I have returned." A simple, incontrovertible statement of fact, delivered in a normal tone of voice, as if dropped into a conversation. The time for speeches would come later. Osmeña reached out, shook MacArthur's hand and officially welcomed him back to the Philippines.[27]

He asked a soldier where the nearest command post was and set off to reach it. Striding briskly along the coastal road, he saw a dozen or more dead Japanese but only one American casualty. When he passed a rifle squad prone behind some palm trees, trying to locate enemy snipers, one of the soldiers looked up and nudged the rifleman next to him. "Hey, there's General MacArthur."

The other soldier was not going to fall for a dumb gag like that. "Oh, yeah? And I suppose he's got Eleanor Roosevelt with him." He didn't even bother to look.[28]

Reaching the CP, MacArthur found the commander of the 24th Division, Major General Frederick Irving, directing the battle for Red Beach. Irving said he had about fifteen dead and thirty wounded. His men had advanced inland only three hundred yards, where they had run into some concrete pillboxes. MacArthur could hear the firing even as he talked to Irving, and to Kenney some of the rifle fire sounded no more than a hundred yards away.[29]

MacArthur continued striding along the beach, talking to small groups of soldiers, while the Signal Corps brought a weapons carrier to Red Beach with a portable transmitter that would create a radio link between the beach and the *Nashville*. The cruiser would then transmit his speech to the rest of the Philippines.

About an hour after the party had come ashore, everything was ready, except for the weather: A fierce tropical downpour drenched the beachhead. William Dunn, a CBS radio correspondent who had known MacArthur since his days as military adviser, spoke into a handheld portable mike for fifteen minutes while voice levels were checked and radio circuits tested. When everything was ready, he handed the mike, which resembled a large black Bakelite soupspoon, to MacArthur.[30]

Holding the mike in his left hand as water dripped from the brim of his cap and rain pitter-pattered off the helmets of curious soldiers clustering around, MacArthur delivered the speech he had worked on during the voyage to Leyte. His hands shook wildly as he intoned in his deep, mellow voice: "People of the Philippines, I have returned. By the grace of Almighty God, our forces stand again on Philippine soil. . . . Rally to me. Let the indomitable spirit of Bataan and Corregidor lead on . . . rise and strike. . . . Strike at every favorable opportunity. For your homes and hearths, strike! For future generations of your sons and daughters, strike! In the name of your sacred dead, strike! Let no heart be faint. Let every arm be steeled. The guidance of divine God points the way. Follow in His name to the Holy Grail of righteous victory!"[31]

He gave the mike to Osmeña, who made a short, low-key speech announcing the restoration of the commonwealth government. At the conclusion of this address MacArthur took Osmeña by the arm and led him to a fallen tree trunk in a nearby clearing, where they sat in the rain and talked for an hour about the relationship of the newly restored civilian government and how it would function while American troops were liberating the Philippines. During their discussion two enemy planes flashed low over the beach and dropped their bombs. MacArthur and Osmeña simply ignored them. By the time they finished their conversation, the rain had stopped and the sun had come out.

MacArthur and his party returned to Irving's CP. He paid no attention to the sniping and machine-gun fire erupting all around, but he suddenly noticed his pilot, Major Dusty Rhoades, edging toward a tree as the shrill whistle of incoming mortar rounds announced a fresh delivery of Japanese ordnance. MacArthur walked over to Rhoades. "What's the trouble, Dusty, are you worried?" Rhoades readily confessed that he felt a lot more comfortable at times like this if he could establish a close relationship with a large tree. "Well," said MacArthur, "the Almighty has given me a job to do and he will see that I am able to finish it."

Rhoades said that was a wonderful thing, no doubt about it. "I'm just not convinced that God is equally interested in *my* survival." MacArthur strode on, a broad smile on his face.[32]

Back at Irving's CP, there was one more task he wanted to tackle before returning to the *Nashville*. He entrusted the letter he had written to Roosevelt the previous night to a Signal Corps officer. It read:

Dear Mr. President:

This note is written from the beach, near Tacloban, where we have just landed. It will be the first letter from the freed Philippines and I thought you might like to add it to your philetic [*sic*] collection. I hope it gets through.

The operation is going smoothly. . . . Strategically it pierces the center of his [the enemy's] defensive line. . . . Tactically it divides his forces in the Philippines in two and by bypassing the southern half of the islands will result in the saving of possibly 50,000 American casualties . . . a successful campaign of liberation if promptly followed by a dramatic granting of independence will place American prestige in the Far East at the highest pinnacle of all time. . . .

He urged Roosevelt to come to the Philippines for the independence ceremony and, well aware of Roosevelt's aversion to airplanes, assured him a fast cruiser would be able to get him out and back in a reasonable period of time. He closed, "Please excuse this scribble but at the moment I am on the combat line with no facilities except for this field message pad."[33]

Boarding the LCM once more, MacArthur headed back to the *Nashville.* A low-flying Japanese torpedo bomber flew past, but its pilot was not interested in a humble landing craft. He was heading for the cruiser *Honolulu,* made his attack and got away unscathed. The ship immediately began to list. Its crew managed to back it onto a sandbar and saved it from sinking.[34]

That evening MacArthur went to the *Nashville*'s communications room, where Dunn was waiting for him. He was going to deliver his "Rally to me!" speech again, this time for transmission to the United States, and Dunn would provide the introduction once more. Dunn could not help commenting on how MacArthur's hands had shaken when he gave the speech the first time. Did having to talk into a microphone make the general feel nervous? he tactlessly inquired. MacArthur looked at him for a moment in astonishment, then shook his head. "Bill, I am *never* nervous."[35]

That evening four Japanese planes tried to attack the *Nashville,* but antiaircraft fire drove them away. Shortly after this came a message from Halsey: Three of his fast carriers were pulling out. They had to go refuel and rearm. The rest were moving north but would be "strategically located" so they could still provide air cover over the beachhead.

MacArthur had staged the landing with eight hundred combat aircraft at his disposal. Roughly half were on Halsey's fast carriers and light carriers; the remainder were aboard sixteen escort carriers, or baby flattops. An escort carrier's role in life was antisubmarine warfare, close air support and antiaircraft defensive fire. MacArthur was relying on the fast carriers to provide fighter cover over Leyte Gulf. And now Halsey was trying to get into position so he could ditch this operation and go pursue one of his own. There were intelligence reports of a Japanese carrier force somewhere to the north, off Luzon.

MacArthur was disgusted. He sent for Kenney. "Get the Fifth Air Force up here as fast as you can," he ordered. "I'm never going to pull another show without land based air, and if I even suggest such a thing, I want you to kick me where it will do some good."[36]

Reports from the beachhead indicated this was going to be one of the least costly major landings in military history. (The final figures were 49 dead, 192 wounded.) It was not remotely like the bloodbath recently concluded in the Palaus, where Nimitz had incurred more than 10,000 casualties to seize Peleliu, an island no longer of any strategic importance. More than 50,000 men were put ashore on Leyte that day, along with 4,500 vehicles and 107,000 tons of supplies. Although it was not the bloodless victory he had asked for the previous night, MacArthur almost certainly felt his prayer had been answered anyway.

There was one last chore to take care of that would round out this momentous day, the communiqué. "In a major amphibious operation," he wrote, "we have seized the eastern coast of Leyte Island in the Philippines, 600 miles north of Morotai and 2,500 miles from Milne Bay whence our offensive started nearly sixteen months ago. . . . The Commander-in-Chief is in personal command of the operation. . . ."[37]

Between the wars the Imperial Japanese Navy had a dream: One day it would destroy the Pacific Fleet in a huge battle somewhere in the triangle formed by Formosa, the Marianas and the Philippines. It built its ships, established its bases and trained its crews for that decisive operation. The attack on Pearl Harbor was meant to be a prelude to this cataclysmic fight, not a substitute for it. MacArthur's landing on Leyte looked like the opportunity the IJN had sought for twenty years.

The Japanese objective was to smash Kinkaid's Seventh Fleet and defeat MacArthur's landing. A carrier force would be trailed as bait to lure the modern battleships and fast carriers of Halsey's Third Fleet north toward Formosa. If Halsey pulled out, MacArthur's air cover would be cut to almost nothing. Two Japanese fleets would then sail into Leyte Gulf, one from the north, the other from the south, and trap Kinkaid's motley fleet of transports, ancient battleships and escort carriers between them and crush it in a gunnery duel in which the Japanese would have a firepower advantage of nearly ten to one.

MacArthur followed the Japanese moves fascinated but worried too. The first three planes to fly over Leyte Gulf at dawn on October 21 were Japanese. There was no combat air patrol up and ready to intercept. Two were shot down by antiaircraft artillery, but the third scored a direct hit on the bridge of the cruiser *Australia,* killing or wounding half a dozen senior Australian naval officers. The first U.S. Navy fighters did not show up until an hour later.

An exasperated George Kenney remarked, "If Halsey decides to go on a wild goose chase of the Jap fleet he will pull out of this show in a minute," exactly what MacArthur feared.[38]

At 9:30 A.M. MacArthur, Kenney and Sutherland boarded a landing craft. They wanted to look at the Tacloban airfield. Landing at White Beach, MacArthur was gratified to find the 1st Cavalry Division, under

Major General Verne D. Mudge, had conducted its assault almost flawlessly. MacArthur, Kenney and Sutherland got into a jeep and headed for the airfield, passing several dead Japanese lying alongside the road.

The airfield was small and soggy, but Casey's engineers were already patching it up. Kenney was disappointed. The field might take one group of P-38s, but no more, even after the runway had been extended and covered with pierced-steel plank. Sutherland meanwhile was losing his nerve and becoming agitated. He kept worrying out loud that the Japanese might have buried mines under the strip and insisted they ought to get off it. MacArthur was puzzled. He had always assumed that his thick-skinned chief of staff Sutherland was a brave man. This indication that he lacked physical courage was worrying.

After riding around on the airstrip, MacArthur headed toward Tacloban, two miles away, but had not gone far when his jeep driver stopped. A column of Sherman tanks was blocking the road ahead of them and fighting its way into the town. MacArthur had the driver turn around and returned to the *Nashville*.[39] Once back aboard, he asked Egeberg about Sutherland's loss of nerve. "What's the matter with him, Doc? Why do you suppose Dick was so concerned about mines?"[40]

Next day he and Kenney went ashore again and visited Dulag, ten miles south of Tacloban, to inspect the airfield there. This time he left Sutherland behind. The Japanese were holding a hill overlooking the western end of the runway. As the two generals walked across the eastern end of the strip, a fierce firefight was raging at the opposite end of the runway, with mortars and artillery joining in. MacArthur asked Kenney what he thought. Kenney said he'd like to be able to inspect the whole thing—"preferably from an airplane."

MacArthur laughed. "George, it's good for you to find how the other half of the world lives."[41]

Before leaving Dulag, MacArthur talked to the commander of the XXIV Corps, Major General John R. Hodge, and told him the 96th Division, attacking the hill west of the airfield, was trying to make a frontal assault across ground that consisted mainly of swamps. This was the division's first battle, and the lack of experience was all too obvious. He ordered Hodge to get the division out of the swamps and bypass the hill.[42]

The next morning, October 23, MacArthur left the *Nashville* with his staff to install Osmeña as president of the Philippine Commonwealth. The setting was the front steps of the provincial capitol building in Tacloban, at noon. The building, like the town, had escaped serious damage during the fighting. After the ceremony MacArthur awarded the DSC to the Leyte guerrilla leader Colonel Ruperto Kangleon, and Osmeña appointed Kangleon governor of the island.[43]

MacArthur went to take a look at the large, handsome cream-colored house of an American plantation owner, Walter Price, killed by the Japanese early in the war. The house was a solid brick-and-concrete structure built around a courtyard. It had been used as a Japanese officers' club until a few days earlier. Kenney and Sutherland thought MacArthur and the advanced GHQ staff ought to move in, but there was one thing MacArthur did not like about the Price house. A large dugout, with electric lights, furniture, rugs, ventilating fans and other refinements, raised its humped back between the main gate and the front door—a dugout fit for a general. But this general had two good reasons for avoiding dugouts: a belief since his days on the Western Front that they bred pneumonia and the taunting echoes since Bataan of "Dugout Doug."

"Level it off and fill the thing," said MacArthur. "It spoils the look of the lawn."[44]

Before returning to the *Nashville* for the night, he had a brief talk with Krueger and told him he wasn't satisfied with the pace of movement off the beach. Only the 1st Cavalry Division was seizing its objectives on time. The other divisions—the 7th, the 24th and the 96th—were lagging behind, and their commanders weren't pushing them hard enough. It was obvious by now that the Japanese were dug in up on the hills west of Leyte Gulf. The time to hit them was when they were still trying to consolidate their position, not later. He wanted Krueger to step up the pace.[45]

Back aboard the *Nashville* that evening, he learned that Halsey had unceremoniously pulled out. A major naval battle was beginning to roil the waters of Leyte Gulf. The Japanese looked as if they had the edge in firepower, Kinkaid told him, and the *Nashville* ought to be there to add its guns to the battle.

"Of course, Tom, send her in," MacArthur replied.

"But I can't, General, if you are on board."

"There is every reason why I should be present during such a crucial engagement," said MacArthur. "Besides, I have never been in a major naval action and I am anxious to see one." Kinkaid abandoned the argument and returned to his own flagship.[46]

The next night Leyte Gulf rocked to the sound of gunfire. The blackness of the night was ripped by orange flames and dazzling white flashes. The waters shook with the concussion of exploding magazines. Halsey's Third Fleet meanwhile was racing north at flank speed, in pursuit of four carriers that had all of twenty-nine airplanes among them. His thirty-knot withdrawal uncovered the principal approaches to Leyte Gulf from the waters of the central Philippines. On the morning of October 25, as the battle came to its climax, Kinkaid insisted that MacArthur leave the *Nashville* so it could go into action. He reluctantly transferred to another ship, the *Wasatch,* where Krueger had his Sixth Army command post.

The Japanese fleet entering Leyte Gulf from the north was deployed in a column and ran smack into six elderly battleships, five of which had been salvaged off the mud of Pearl Harbor. The American commander was able to pull off the classic naval maneuver of crossing the T—bringing the massed fire of his six veteran battlewagons against one oncoming ship at a time. After seeing several cruisers blown up, the rest of the Japanese fleet turned about and fled, into the path of stalking American submarines. Halsey too made a contribution. After receiving a stinging rebuke from Nimitz, he sent some of his planes back toward Leyte Gulf.[47] After attacking the Japanese ships, they lacked the fuel to return to their carriers. They had to make emergency landings at Tacloban and Dulag. MacArthur, deeply saddened at the sight, watched them from the rail of the *Wasatch* as they crashed and cartwheeled all over the slick, potholed strips.[48]

The Japanese fleet approaching Leyte Gulf from the south had five fast battleships, nine cruisers and fourteen destroyers. It had lost two warships to American submarines during the night, but it now bore down menacingly on the sixteen baby flattops in Leyte Gulf. Their pilots were not trained for attacking warships, nor were their planes usually armed for combat at sea. Nonetheless they swarmed over the oncoming Japanese, forcing them to take evasive action, while Kinkaid's American destroyers hurled themselves at the battleships and cruisers to make torpedo attacks. After several hours of wild maneuvering, the Japanese admiral's nerve broke, and he pulled out his fleet, stalked by submarines.[49]

The combined fleet's losses in the Battle of Leyte Gulf came to three battleships, four carriers, six cruisers and fourteen destroyers. As the light faded on October 25, however, the Japanese Navy unveiled something for which there really was no answer—the kamikaze. Nine Japanese planes flew over Leyte Gulf, and instead of trying to bomb Kinkaid's ships, they crashed into the escort carriers, sinking one and seriously damaging three.

MacArthur returned to Tacloban that evening for dinner in the Price house. When the small GHQ advance staff sat down to eat, the subject on everyone's mind was the naval battle. They roundly damned Halsey for chasing the Japanese carriers, calling him a "stupid son of a bitch" and "that bastard Halsey." MacArthur brought his clenched fist down on the table. "That's enough," he barked. "Leave the Bull alone. He's still a fighting admiral in my book."[50]

After this epic battle Halsey's fast carriers headed east, so they could refuel and give their pilots a rest. Meanwhile the kamikazes had reduced the number of operational escort carriers still in the gulf from sixteen to twelve. Progress at Tacloban had been delayed by the Navy's decision to have twenty-four LSTs dump their contents right where Army engineers were attempting to build the new airstrip. Just hauling the stuff away not only took valuable time but created huge ruts and potholes.

MacArthur needed some land-based planes whatever the condition of the Tacloban airfield. When Kenney went to see him the evening after they moved into the Price house, he found MacArthur reading Douglas Southall Freeman's life of Robert E. Lee. "You know," he said, putting the book down, "both Lee's and Stonewall Jackson's last words were 'Bring up A. P. Hill's light infantry.' " He thought for a moment, then added, "If I should die today, tomorrow, next year, anytime, my last words will be, 'George, bring up the Fifth Air Force.' "[51]

Two days later MacArthur was having lunch when he heard a familiar sound, the engines of P-38s being throttled back. Kenney had ordered half the 49th Fighter Group to fly up from Morotai but had not told him. MacArthur called for his car and headed for the airfield to greet the thirty-four fighter pilots. He shook hands with the first three as they descended from their planes onto the half-finished strip. One of them was the AAF's top scoring ace, Major Richard Bong, with twenty-eight victories to his credit. "You don't know how glad I am to see you," he told them, beaming. He turned to the journalists who were clustering around. "The Fifth Air Force has never failed me."[52]

The Japanese destroyed nearly half the P-38s over the next twenty-four hours. Kenney flew up the rest of the group, but his fighters continued to take a beating. The town and the airfield were being bombed up to a dozen times a day. The heaviest raids were at night, and for some officers on MacArthur's staff, such as Willoughby, it was a terrifying experience, but MacArthur as always ignored air attacks.

The Japanese did not know MacArthur was living in the Price house, but as one of the few modern structures in Tacloban it was an obvious target of opportunity for Japanese pilots. They tried to flatten it at least a dozen times, yet only one bomb scored a direct hit. It landed in the bedroom adjoining MacArthur's but failed to explode. On another occasion a three-inch antiaircraft round fired at a low-flying intruder landed on the couch in MacArthur's bedroom, but it too was a dud. When his antiaircraft artillery commander, Major General William Marquat, returned to the house for dinner that evening, MacArthur plunked it on the dining table in front of him. "Bill," he said, "ask your gunners to raise their sights a bit higher."[53]

During air attacks nobody at headquarters could seek cover, however much he felt like ducking, because MacArthur simply sat where he was and went on talking even when it sounded as if a dive-bomber had just flipped over directly above the Price house and were heading straight for it.[54]

Bombs fell all around the house, and some exploded in the garden, but he seemed as bulletproof now as he ever was during his service on the Western Front. Age had not wrinkled his armor. One evening in early November a Japanese light bomber flew overhead and strafed the street outside. MacArthur was sitting at his desk when two .30-caliber bullets flew through the open window and thudded into a beam eighteen inches above his head. Larry Lehrbas rushed in and found MacArthur still seated, working as if nothing untoward had occurred. "Well," said MacArthur, looking up, "what is it?"

"Thank God, General! I thought you'd been killed," said Lehrbas.

"Not yet. Thank you for coming in." He returned to his work but later had his orderly dig the two bullets out of the beam. Then he wrapped them up and wrote a few lines to his son: "Dear Arthur—Papa is sending you two big bullets that were fired at him and missed. He misses you and Mama and sends you both his love. Poppie."[55]

The key to securing Leyte was not Tacloban but Ormoc, the island's largest port, on the western shore, thirty miles from where the Sixth Army had made its assault. To reach Ormoc, Krueger's soldiers would have to fight their way over the line of hills in front of them and descend into the Leyte Valley. Crossing the rice paddies of Leyte Valley, they would have to scale a mountain range to get into the Ormoc Valley. Once there, they would have to surmount even more mountains to reach the coastal plain on the western shore to seize the town of Ormoc itself. The more closely the staff at Imperial Headquarters in Tokyo studied the maps, the more convinced they became that it was worth fighting a major battle for Leyte. The topography was all on the defender's side.

The Japanese commander in the Philippines, General Tomoyuki Yamashita, argued that Leyte was not a good place to fight despite the favorable terrain. Yamashita was renowned as the man who had seized Singapore from the British. He was short, bald, muscular and highly intelligent; no one could doubt either his ability or his pugnacity. It seemed obvious to Yamashita that it was simply pointless to try holding on to Leyte after the combined fleet's defeat in the Battle of Leyte Gulf. Although the Japanese could make the Americans pay a high price for Leyte, the Americans would inevitably capture it. He thought it made more sense to put everything into a battle for Luzon and let Leyte go.

Yamashita's thinking was sound, but he still lost the argument. Imperial Headquarters pushed reinforcement convoys toward Ormoc, determined to make the Sixth Army fight a bruising, bloody campaign among those remote hills and valleys.[56]

Krueger's advance was steady rather than spectacular, despite the Sixth Army's huge advantage in manpower and firepower. Just as engineer officers had forecast, the monsoons turned the valley into a shallow lake. The worst monsoon season in a generation lashed the central Philippines that fall. Landing craft had to be brought in to move supplies and equipment across the Leyte Valley, and at Tacloban and Dulag the efforts of aviation engineers to create adequate airfields were almost completely frustrated. On the days when the weather was flyable the Japanese had parity in the air. The Sixth Army was fighting its way forward, in effect, without the air superiority American soldiers had come to take for granted. The Leyte Valley was not secured until mid-November.

Krueger's two corps commanders, John Hodge and Franklin Sibert, were ordered to move through the mountains at the northern and southern ends of this position and break into the Ormoc Valley. Their attacks were launched in torrential rains and awesome storms that turned day into night. Even before they mounted these attacks, captured intelligence documents indicated that the Japanese were planning a major counterattack against Krueger's right flank and rear. Despite the loss of dozens of ships and tens of thousands of troops to Kenney's planes and the Navy's ships, the Japanese had managed to land forty thousand reinforcements at Ormoc. Krueger seemed afraid to advance far for fear of exposing himself to a powerful counterattack. The Sixth Army moved slowly toward the Ormoc Valley despite repeated pleas from MacArthur that he display some urgency and get this show rolling.[57]

It was obvious by now that the engineers were not going to pull off a miracle and create the airfields he needed. Tacloban and Dulag were simply too muddy. The only well-drained land near Leyte Gulf was halfway between Tacloban and Dulag, near a hamlet called Tanuan, and Krueger's Sixth Army headquarters was sitting on it. Krueger himself had moved into a house on the beach two miles away, at a place called Tolosa. While MacArthur's GHQ staff was floundering in the mud at Tacloban, Krueger and his staff were living in relative comfort. Kenney meanwhile was clamoring to get his hands on Tanuan. It took MacArthur more than a month to persuade Krueger to evacuate Tanuan and turn it over to Kenney. MacArthur sent him a message of thanks, concluding, "Knowing the privations that this entails from you and your headquarters, I hereby nominate you as the Hero of Tolosa, and a mighty wet hero, too."[58]

When it came to prodding Krueger into action in the advance across Leyte, MacArthur had a card up his sleeve that he had been getting ready to play for months. Back in August, after the conquest of Biak, MacArthur had, to Krueger's dismay, created another army, the Eighth, and given it to Eichelberger. With Krueger bogged down, MacArthur started hinting that if the Sixth Army could not finish the job, maybe he would have to hand the task over to Eichelberger and the Eighth.

It rankled Krueger and his staff that the Sixth Army's unbroken run of victories had gone unrecognized. Throughout the arduous New Guinea campaign it had been known only as Alamo Force, to prevent the Australians from getting control of it. So long as it was disguised as a task force, MacArthur could keep the Sixth Army directly under GHQ. Leyte was the Sixth Army's chance to emerge into the full light of day and garner the glory its successes deserved. Bringing the untried Eighth Army into Leyte now would be a wounding blow to Krueger, his staff and the entire Sixth Army, which was thirsting for recognition.

MacArthur had just gotten command of the 77th Infantry Division, which had taken part in the conquest of Guam back in June. He told Krueger that if the Sixth felt unable to take Ormoc, Eichelberger would assume command of the Leyte campaign, and the Eighth Army would mount the Ormoc assault, using the 77th Division as its spearhead. At this point Krueger caved in, begged for three more weeks to secure Leyte and said the Sixth Army would be glad to take the 77th Division and would use it to make the landing at Ormoc.

On Pearl Harbor Day the 77th Infantry Division landed on the beaches a few miles south of Ormoc, catching the Japanese completely by surprise. The town fell three days later.[59] It had been a completely successful operation, except for one thing: There were more than forty thousand Japanese still fighting on Leyte, and they would not quit. The Japanese still held most of the Ormoc Valley. Krueger's logistical situation was precarious. Kenney was still short of the runways he needed to establish air superiority. And the damned rain was still falling in cataracts.

The slow-motion advance across central Leyte and the failure to develop the airfields had forced the postponement of the scheduled landing on Luzon, to MacArthur's embarrassment and chagrin. He told Eichelberger he was considering relieving Krueger. "I've kept him on over-age because I expected him to be a driver," said MacArthur one day. It was not Leyte that worried him so much, though, as what would happen when they got to Luzon. Suppose Krueger performed as poorly there as he had here? But whatever he may have said about firing Krueger, it was unlikely to happen. MacArthur hardly ever fired anybody. So long as people showed loyalty to him, he returned it, no matter what.[60]

His relationship with Sutherland, however, was becoming increasingly strained. In July 1944, to MacArthur's amazement, Sutherland had moved

Elaine Clarke to Hollandia, where she acted like an aristocratic hostess welcoming generals and admirals to her country home with lemonade and small talk. When MacArthur discovered she was there and not back in Brisbane, he flew into a rage and told Sutherland to send her back to Australia at once. Sutherland demanded to be relieved or transferred, but MacArthur would not give him that satisfaction. Instead, and making it clear that he was not going to let Sutherland use his faltering memory as an excuse for not doing as he was told, MacArthur gave Sutherland a written, direct order: Captain Clarke would return to Australia and remain there. When MacArthur returned to Hollandia after the Morotai landing, she was gone. So far as he was aware, the Elaine problem had finally been settled.[61]

He was underestimating Sutherland's lust and Captain Clarke's determination to be close to the scene of action. Brisbane was a dull, provincial place compared to an advanced headquarters where powerful men made important decisions and the air was electric with historic events. Shortly after American troops landed on Leyte, so did Elaine.

Sutherland ordered Sverdrup to build her a house, using materials that had been shipped thousands of miles to help provide airfields. Sverdrup was appalled, but he wasn't going to be the one who blew the whistle on Sutherland. He thought that was a job for MacArthur's aides Roger Egeberg and Larry Lehrbas. Neither of them, however, was in any hurry to tell MacArthur that the Elaine problem was just a few miles down the road from Tacloban in a brand-new house, courtesy of Army engineers, where she entertained her three-star lover.

Egeberg and Lehrbas knew it was only a matter of time before MacArthur either found out for himself or became curious as to what had happened to Sutherland's mistress. MacArthur had told Blamey that Australian women would not move beyond New Guinea, but that seemed to apply only to Australian women serving in the Australian armed forces. It did not apply to Australian citizens in the U.S. Army. George Kenney and Richard Marshall both had brought their WAC assistants with them to Leyte, and there was neither a murmur of protest from the Australian government nor a word of complaint at GHQ.

One evening in mid-December MacArthur was having a postprandial chat with Egeberg on the porch of the Price house when he suddenly asked, "Say, Doc, whatever happened to that woman?"

"Woman?" said Egeberg. "What woman, General?"

"Oh, you know, *that woman.*"

"You mean Captain Clarke?

"Yes, Captain Clarke . . . where is she now?"

She was, Egeberg informed him, living only five miles away.

MacArthur reacted like a man who had just been plugged into an electric socket. *"What!"*[62]

For a minute or two he could hardly believe his ears as Egeberg filled him in on Elaine's present arrangements. MacArthur went into Sutherland's office quivering with rage. He bellowed at his chief of staff, who was seated at his desk, "Dick Sutherland, I gave you an order. You disobeyed it. You are under arrest!"[63]

For fifteen minutes MacArthur raged at Sutherland, screaming every profanity acquired in a lifetime of military service. The sentry at the entrance to the house put his fingers in his ears. Sutherland was bewildered. He tried to argue back. He could not understand why MacArthur was so mad at him.

William Manchester put it down to MacArthur's prim sense of morality, but it had nothing to do with that. MacArthur turned a blind eye to the fact that at least half the generals at GHQ were conducting adulterous affairs. There were always WACs, American Red Cross workers and Army nurses around. MacArthur was incensed to discover that Sutherland had disobeyed a written, direct order. He was also angered not by Elaine's contempt for bourgeois morality but by the damage she was doing to morale. She was a disruptive force that a combat headquarters could well do without. Only the day before MacArthur's latest confrontation with Sutherland, Elaine had gotten Sutherland to fire a captain in the GHQ commandant's office for getting in her way.

"That woman will be flown out of Tacloban immediately!" MacArthur raged. "And if she is not out of here within 24 hours I will court martial you for disobedience of a direct order!"[64]

MacArthur had the unlucky captain recalled to GHQ and promoted him to major for standing up to Elaine. He did not fire Sutherland, but their relationship was never close again. They dragged it out to the end of the war, like a deeply estranged married couple sticking together for the sake of the children until they left home. Many of Sutherland's more important responsibilities were transferred to Richard Marshall, and there were long periods when Sutherland went back to Australia, on one excuse or another, to be with Elaine.

As 1944 drew to a close, MacArthur was alienated from Sutherland, disappointed with Krueger, questioning Kinkaid's loyalty (for reasons to be explained in the next chapter) and frustrated by having to postpone the assault on Luzon. Yet his relationship with Kenney remained as strong as ever. One day in early December, Kenney came to him holding a piece of paper. "General," he said, "I want a Medal of Honor for Dick Bong." He had written a citation, which stressed that Bong had just shot down his eighth plane since arriving at Tacloban, bringing his total score to thirty-six. MacArthur warmly endorsed Kenney's recommendation, and the War Department approved it almost immediately. Medal of Honor cases usually took weeks, if not months or years, to come through.

Kenney asked MacArthur to decorate Bong publicly, but MacArthur refused. He usually decorated men at headquarters, with the exception of a few battlefield awards for morale purposes. "I'm not running for any office," he said, "and I don't want the publicity." That should go to the man who got the award, not the man who presented it. For all his love of seeing his name in the newspapers, MacArthur genuinely felt that when a medal was awarded, attention should be focused firmly to the recipient. Besides, he had been on the receiving end of more medal ceremonies than almost any officer in history. It was easy for him to identify with the man who was being honored and to see himself when he too had been young and savoring the taste of military glory. There were some experiences on which he did not want to encroach. But Kenney persisted, and MacArthur relented.

On December 12 on the muddy strip at Tacloban Bong stepped forward, MacArthur saluted him; Bong returned the salute; then MacArthur reached out, put his hands on Bong's shoulders and delivered one of the best short speeches of the war: "Major Richard Ira Bong, who has ruled the air from New Guinea to the Philippines, I now induct you into the society of the bravest of the brave, the wearers of the Congressional Medal of Honor of the United States." He then pinned the medal on Bong's chest.[65]

Shortly after this MacArthur was himself honored. On December 18 he was promoted to the newly created rank of General of the Army, with date of rank two days behind Marshall and two days before Eisenhower.

On Christmas Day he wrote out a telegram to Jean, with instructions that it was to be delivered on her birthday, December 27. It read, "Many happy returns of the day. The entire command joins me in saluting our staunchest soldier."[66]

That same day he also issued a special communiqué declaring Leyte secure, bar some mopping up. He handed responsibility for that to Eichelberger and the Eighth Army. Krueger and the Sixth Army were pulled out. They had a date to keep on Luzon.

Go to Manila

When Krueger handed Leyte over to Eichelberger in December 1944, he told him all that remained was mopping up; there were only about five thousand Japanese left for the Eighth Army to deal with. "Mopping up, hell," said Eichelberger at a staff conference a month later. "We have already killed 27,000."[1] The fighting dragged on, keeping four divisions tied down until the spring of 1945. The eventual cost of the Leyte campaign came to thirty-five hundred Americans killed and twelve thousand wounded. The Japanese lost around fifty thousand troops defending Leyte and up to forty thousand more aboard ships carrying them there but sunk en route by American submarines and aircraft.[2]

Although the Leyte landing had been a strategic victory, the subsequent campaign had been a mixed blessing. MacArthur had defeated the Japanese but not won himself the all-weather airfields needed to keep his advance moving. Despite the efforts of Sixth Army's engineers, it simply proved impossible to create adequate airfields out of the sludge around Tacloban and Dulag.[3]

MacArthur was nonetheless as determined as ever to make a landing on Luzon. To his intense frustration, Krueger's two-and-one-half-mile-per-week advance across Leyte forced him to postpone it from December 20 to December 30. His plan for Luzon was to put four divisions ashore in Lingayen Gulf, roughly a hundred miles north of Manila. He absolutely needed to put fighter cover over the invasion fleet as it sailed up the west coast of Luzon, and to do that, he would have to take another island first.

He opted to seize Mindoro, some twenty miles south of Luzon but within fighter range of Lingayen Gulf. Kenney said he could develop three airstrips on Mindoro in time to support the assault.

MacArthur was confident it would work, and so was Kenney, but Admiral Kinkaid balked. He was willing to risk the Seventh Fleet, and especially its six escort carriers, on one mission only—the dash to Lingayen Gulf. He was not going to risk them twice by going to Mindoro too. To make a landing on Mindoro and then make a second assault, on Luzon, several weeks later, was like asking him to play Russian roulette and pull the trigger twice.

What Kinkaid feared was the loss of his escort carriers. The baby flattops, with their thin decks and even thinner hulls, were frighteningly vulnerable. A single kamikaze hit could sink one. That had happened in the Battle of Leyte Gulf. Kinkaid told MacArthur he would commit most of the Seventh Fleet to the Mindoro landing, but not the escort carriers. The risk from the kamikazes was simply too great.

MacArthur, on the other hand, would not even think about mounting a landing without air cover. In his office-cum-bedroom at the Price house, MacArthur argued with Kinkaid for hours, until a weary Kinkaid finally blurted out that he intended to tell Admiral King that the general was rejecting his professional advice. That did it. MacArthur was roused to fury and tore into the Seventh Fleet commander. He paced more furiously than ever, waved his arms and made melodramatic gestures, shouted and whispered like the innate actor he was, forcing Kinkaid to lean against MacArthur's bedstead like a man in need of physical support. What kind of loyalty was this, threatening to go running like some whining child to Admiral King? Kinkaid feebly protested that he *was* loyal, but seeing that he did not sound as if he had convinced himself, there was no chance he was going to convince MacArthur.

While MacArthur was berating the hapless Kinkaid, Sutherland came into the room with a message that had just arrived from Halsey. Halsey's fast carriers had been assigned to neutralize the Japanese airfields on Formosa prior to MacArthur's landing on Luzon. He needed more time than he'd anticipated, however. Halsey wanted to know if MacArthur would agree to postpone the Luzon landing for ten days. MacArthur reluctantly agreed to the postponement, and Kinkaid left to consult his staff.[4]

They told the admiral he'd made a serious mistake in rejecting MacArthur's plan to land on Mindoro with air cover from the escort carriers. Kinkaid returned to the Price house that evening for dinner. MacArthur began to berate him all over again, but Kinkaid told him this time that he would make the Mindoro assault after all—and commit his escort carriers—provided this operation too was postponed for ten days. MacArthur reached out, put his hands on Kinkaid's shoulders and told him, "Tommy, I love you still. Let's go to dinner!"[5]

On December 15 the 19th Regimental Combat Team and the 503d Parachute Infantry Regiment mounted an amphibious assault on the southwest coast of Mindoro. This attack caught the Japanese completely by surprise. By Christmas Day one fighter strip was in operation and two more were under construction. The sole untoward note was the kamikaze onslaught against the invasion convoys. It was not half as bad as Kinkaid had feared, but it was bad enough. There were fewer than two hundred combat casualties in the fight to secure Mindoro, but more than a thousand men were killed or wounded by kamikaze attacks on the invasion fleet.[6]

Kenney soon had some of his best fighter groups flying out of Mindoro. They were escorting his heavy bombers flying up from Leyte in daylight to pound Japanese air units at Clark Field. With Mindoro's three strips in full operation by January 4, everything was in place for the campaign that meant more to MacArthur than all the others put together: the return to Luzon, home to half the population of the Philippines, site of the country's capital city and the stage on which he had endured those defeats that tormented him still. Physically he was already back in the Philippines. Emotionally and spiritually he had yet to return. He had to liberate this country to be a free man himself, the exorcist at last over his failures, his ghosts and his guilt.

Despite the fact that Leyte had cost him nearly 100,000 troops, General Yamashita still had 275,000 men available for the defense of Luzon. He had no intention of squandering them in a fight to the death on the beaches of Lingayen Gulf, where they would be blasted into oblivion by American naval gunfire. He had no intention of trying to hold on to Manila either. To do that, he would have to fight and win a battle on the central plain of Luzon, and he lacked the firepower and mobility for any head-to-head contest with MacArthur on terrain where the Americans had maneuver room. About the only thing he could do was get onto the high ground—a commodity with which Luzon is exceptionally well endowed—dig in and wait for the Americans to come to him. He deployed roughly 150,000 men in the mountains of northern Luzon; a further 75,000 were posted in the high hills to the east of Manila; another 30,000 were dug in along the hills overlooking Clark Field, leaving only 20,000 soldiers to occupy Manila and 16,000 naval infantry defending the port and the harbor.[7]

MacArthur had intended to participate in the Mindoro assault but was talked out of it by his staff. Nothing, though, was going to keep him from the landing in Lingayen Gulf. The night of January 3–4 he paced the porch of the Price house for the last time, alone, bareheaded, hands clasped behind his back, lost in the intense concentration of silent prayer. In the morning his jeep pulled up, with a brand-new screaming red plate bearing five bright white stars, to take him down to the Tacloban dock.[8]

The voyage to Luzon aboard the cruiser *Boise* was like the famous medieval military punishment running the gauntlet. The closer the invasion convoy drew to Lingayen Gulf, the greater the number of kamikazes. Kenney and the Navy had devised an air plan to have sixty fighters on combat air patrol over the fleet from dawn to dusk, but some suicide pilots were certain to pierce even this strong umbrella.

MacArthur watched the action from the ship's rail sometimes. At other times, he stood next to a gun turret fascinated at the sight of Japanese pilots plunging into black walls of exploding antiaircraft fire like carrion trying to batten on field mice. On the four-day voyage north one of Kinkaid's six baby flattops went down and two more were seriously damaged. Kamikazes exploded into the bridges of two battleships, and five cruisers were struck. Torpedoes were fired at the *Boise* by a midget submarine, but they missed, as did a bomb dropped by a Japanese dive-bomber pilot who'd taken aim at it.

"Thank God," MacArthur said to Egeberg in the middle of one furious kamikaze attack, "they're after our men-of-war. Most of them can take a hit or a number of hits, but if they attack our troop ships so ferociously I think we will have to turn back."[9]

After visiting the bridge, he then returned to his cabin for his afternoon nap, ignoring the ferocious roar of antiaircraft fire, exploding bombs and shouting men. Egeberg later found him there, fast asleep, and took his pulse; it was a steady 68. Absolutely normal. MacArthur woke up. "What's the matter, Doc?"

Egeberg was amazed. "I just wanted to be sure you were all right. How could you sleep with all those guns going off above and around you?"

"Doc, I watched the battle for several hours. I got the feel of it and then decided I'd seen enough. There was nothing I could do that was my business, so I thought I'd catch a little sleep. Why did you say you were taking my pulse?"[10]

As the *Boise* passed Corregidor and Bataan, he was like a man transfixed. "I could not leave the rail," he recalled in his memoirs. "One by one, the staff drifted away, and I was alone with my memories. . . . I felt an indescribable sense of loss, of sorrow, of loneliness, and of solemn consecration."[11]

The invasion armada gathered in Lingayen Gulf under the cloak of darkness the night of January 8. When dawn broke next morning, the gulf swarmed with shipping; eight hundred gray vessels crowded it from horizon to horizon.

The Joint Staff planners had proposed making a landing on the shores of southern Luzon, but MacArthur rejected this as being too timid and too obvious. He would land along Lingayen Gulf, but he would try to make it appear that he was using Mindoro to mount an attack against southern Luzon. He later claimed this deception had been an overwhelming success, but in truth the Japanese never doubted he would make his main assault where they had made theirs in December 1941—on the beaches of Lingayen Gulf.

They had chosen to invade its eastern shore, because this littoral had the best beaches for a landing. Yamashita assumed MacArthur's troops would do the same and had many of his best units dig in on the hills overlooking them. Krueger meanwhile was planning to land at the southern end of Lingayen Gulf, on beaches that were partially blocked by sandbars and subject to heavy surf. By doing the unexpected, he hoped to reap the benefit of surprise and keep his casualties down, something he was as keen to achieve as MacArthur.[12]

Krueger was nevertheless not going to take any chances. He believed there were strong Japanese forces ready to defend the beaches, and he had no intention of pushing forward rapidly in the direction of Manila. During the intelligence briefing at which MacArthur had been given the details of the invasion plan, he had openly scoffed at the huge numbers of Japanese the briefing officer said were defending the beaches of Luzon. "There aren't that many Japanese there," MacArthur said firmly.

"Well," said the briefing officer, "most of this information came from your headquarters."

Willoughby jumped up from his chair like a man who had been jabbed in the posterior with a large needle. "Didn't come from me!" he spluttered. "Didn't come from me!"

When the meeting ended, MacArthur took the briefing officer to one side. "Sit down," he said. "I want to give you my ideas of intelligence officers. There are only three great ones in the history of warfare—and mine is not one of them."[13]

The Sixth Army put four divisions—the 6th, 37th, 40th and 43d—ashore in midmorning on January 9 after the naval bombardment lifted. They ran into little resistance, and in some areas the troops almost raced inland. After lunch MacArthur, Sutherland, Egeberg, Lehrbas and several other members of the staff boarded a landing craft and headed for the beach near San Fabian.

Navy Seabees had anticipated his arrival and with their bulldozers created a small jetty of sand so MacArthur could come ashore this time without getting his feet wet. Whether or not MacArthur had found wading ashore at Leyte on October 20 unpleasant, fate had dealt him a saltwater ace that day. It lives on as a kind of perfection, beyond all contriving, beyond even MacArthur's extravagant hopes. It is all there in a single, compelling shot: the last full general to exercise command at the front and under fire, the hero as man of action advancing through water up to his knees, the vigorous stride trampling down every obstacle, the resounding promise redeemed and honor—his honor, his country's honor, the Army's honor—saved by one man's will.

Step onto dry Seabee sand? Not a chance. MacArthur had the cox ignore their handiwork. The landing craft's ramp was dropped in two feet of water, and he strode down it to reenact on Luzon that Leyte moment of triumph. Hundreds of Filipinos had gathered on the beach to greet him. They cheered lustily and shouted, "*Mabuhay!*" (Welcome!) as he splashed toward them, but there was no imperishable image a second time. Perfection defies imitation.[14]

After a couple of hours ashore talking to the people and the troops he returned to the *Boise.* The most pressing task right now was beyond his control. The engineers absolutely had to get a fighter strip in operation before Halsey's fast carriers pulled out one week from now. Brigadier General Jack Sverdrup had bet Kenney a bottle of scotch he would have a five-thousand-foot strip operational seven days after the landing, but no sooner were the troops ashore than it seemed he was going to lose his bet.

One of the worst obstacles to progress at Tacloban had been the Navy's decision to dump the contents of twenty-four LSTs right where Kenney planned to put new airstrips. And now, as Sverdrup pulled up in a jeep to examine the crude Lingayen airstrip, a tank battalion started to roll across it, threatening to turn it into a mudhole. Sverdrup jumped out of his jeep, brandishing a big black Colt .45 in his right hand and screaming at the tank crews to back off. MacArthur heard about it that evening. "I'll promote Sverdrup," he said, amused and delighted, "and I'll give him the Distinguished Service Cross."

Even before the strip was finished, MacArthur went out to look at it and pin a DSC on Sverdrup's sweaty shirt. A few weeks later Sverdrup became the only reserve engineer officer to become a major general in World War II.[15] He also collected his bottle of scotch. The day the carriers pulled out, Kenney was able to fly a fighter group into Lingayen, and the day after that he had the B-24s of the 308th Bomb Wing flying missions from it.[16]

MacArthur moved his advance headquarters ashore on January 13 and placed it in the buildings of a secondary school in Dagupan, four miles inland from the gulf. He took a bungalow in the school grounds for his own residence and office. The first couple of days he was there his mood was optimistic and expansive, but then he started clashing with Krueger. He wanted Krueger to launch a drive south to capture Manila by January 26,

MacArthur's sixty-fifth birthday (which was, by a remarkable coincidence, Krueger's birthday too). Krueger was worried about what the Japanese might do to him if he attempted any major advance. He intended to do little more than consolidate the beachhead seized the first day of the landing until reinforcements arrived later in the month. Yet not only was MacArthur urging him to mount a drive toward Manila, but Kenney was clamoring for the army to take Clark Field, standing roughly halfway between Lingayen Gulf and the city.

At this point MacArthur received a message from Marshall, telling him that the War Department was about to submit a promotion list to the President. Was there anyone MacArthur would like to recommend? On January 18, in an attempt to woo Krueger into a more cooperative frame of mind, MacArthur put Krueger's name forward for promotion to four-star rank.[17]

Whether moved by the prospect of a fourth star or because the Sixth Army needed all the air support it could get, Krueger relented and allowed the 37th and 40th divisions to advance on Clark Field. It was like pushing at an open door. They advanced down Highway 3 at a rate of ten miles a day against light opposition. MacArthur could not resist following them, at times even going ahead of them in his jeep. Like dozens of World War II generals, he loved to sit in the front passenger seat, barreling down the road, clinging to the windshield post with his right hand, while an aide rocked around in the back.

On January 20, approaching Tarlac, nearly fifty miles south of the landing beaches, MacArthur was scouting the front line and artillery was peppering the road ahead, when he yelled, "Stop!" The jeep crunched to a screaming halt. He got out and led Egeberg over to an old-fashioned black-painted cannon embedded by the roadside in a large block of concrete. He knew this place well. MacArthur turned to Egeberg, forefinger extended, and, strangely proud and excited about something, poked his chest.

"On that spot, Doc, about forty five years ago," he announced, "my father's aide-de-camp was killed standing at his side!"

Egeberg thought about this for a moment, wondered if MacArthur, a firm believer in history as repetition, was hoping for a second performance and decided not to push his luck. He abruptly barked at MacArthur's driver, "Let's get the hell out of here," and scrambled back into the jeep.[18]

Seizing Clark proved to be easy. The tricky part was making it useful. The tens of thousands of Japanese dug in on the mountains overlooking it had its six airfields under artillery fire. The 40th Division would have to go up into the mountains, drive them beyond artillery range and eventually dig them out.[19]

Even before the 40th overran Clark, Krueger made it clear that he had no intention of advancing any farther in the direction of Manila. He was convinced that the tens of thousands of Japanese holed up in the mountains to the north and east of the central plain of Luzon would suddenly thrust down toward Highway 3, the principal route linking Lingayen and Manila, and destroy his right flank, or else they might counterattack the beachhead and destroy his left flank. He was not going to take any more chances until his follow-up forces, mainly the 1st Cavalry Division and the 32d Division, had been brought up to Lingayen from Leyte.[20]

MacArthur considered Krueger's reading of the situation about as wrong as it could be. He blamed Willoughby for encouraging Krueger's fears by exaggerating Japanese strength. If Yamashita pushed his men onto the plain, they would be setting themselves up to be wiped out by American tanks, planes and self-propelled artillery. Indeed, when an armored regiment from the Japanese 2d Tank Division did move down from the high ground in an attempt to cut Highway 3 during the fighting for Clark, that is exactly what happened to it.[21]

On January 21 MacArthur had another heated hourlong discussion with Krueger and told him he had to have troops in Manila by February 5. He had promised the JCS he would reach the city within four weeks of landing in Lingayen Gulf. Time was fast running out. Krueger adamantly refused to sanction a drive on Manila. MacArthur returned to Dagupan in his jeep, shaking his head in dismay, murmuring, "Walter's pretty stubborn. Maybe I'll have to try something else."[22]

The solution he came up with was to set up a race or, rather, two races. He would pit the Sixth Army against the Eighth. And within the Sixth Army he would set two divisions in competition against each other.

By giving an Eighth Army division the chance to come up from Leyte and seize Manila, he could be certain of provoking a (belated) response from Krueger, who still resented the fact that the Sixth Army's achievements in New Guinea had gone almost unrecognized. To have Eichelberger's Eighth Army troops burst onto the scene at this late stage of the war and snatch the glory of liberating Manila from the Sixth Army was intolerable. Krueger finally agreed to MacArthur's demands that the Sixth mount a drive to capture the city.[23]

The Eighth Army's contribution would be made by its most prestigious division, the 11th Airborne. Even before MacArthur landed on Luzon, GHQ was planning to have the division mount an amphibious assault forty-five miles southwest of Manila, at Nasugbu Bay, and make a reconnaissance in force of the defenses of southern Luzon. Now, though, MacArthur had a different idea about how it should be employed. Sutherland told Eichelberger bluntly, "General MacArthur would like you to capture Manila if possible." Kenney confirmed it. He told Eichelberger MacArthur had said that if Eichelberger used the 11th Airborne boldly and got into the city first, he would make Eichelberger "King of Manila," with all that implied: a fourth star and an offensive role as big as—possibly even bigger than—Krueger's in the liberation of Luzon.[24]

Kenney advised Eichelberger to cancel the 11th Airborne's landing at Nasugbu Bay. Instead he should have the entire division dropped onto Nichols Field, on the southern edge of the city and barely three miles from downtown.[25] Eichelberger had been urged once before to make a similarly daring move, back during the first day of the landing at Hollandia, when MacArthur had urged him to reach out another hundred miles and grab Wakde while the Japanese were still reeling from the Hollandia assault. Eichelberger had balked and thereby lost MacArthur the chance to speed up his advance by four weeks.

Since then MacArthur had worked to bolster Eichelberger's confidence. Before the Eighth Army took over on Leyte, he had told Eichelberger he expected him to be a modern Jeb Stuart or Stonewall Jackson, a master of the daring, surprise attack that threw the enemy into confusion. Eichelberger had lapped it up.[26]

Here, then, was Eichelberger's second chance. Seizing Nichols Field in a stunning coup de main that would put American troops into Manila on or about February 1 was exactly what a modern Jeb Stuart or Stonewall Jackson would have done. Alas, poor Eichelberger! He was a personable, charming, intelligent and physically courageous man, but he lacked vision and the boldness that springs from vision. Nichols Field? Too risky. Too dangerous. He was going to stick to the tame, safe landing on the shores of Nasugbu Bay, even though that was going to leave him a long way short of Manila.[27]

Kenney warned him that if he didn't seize this opportunity, Eichelberger could expect to spend the rest of the war in secondary operations elsewhere in the Philippines, mopping up bypassed Japanese garrisons. Eichelberger was astounded. He refused to believe what Kenney told him and said it had to be a joke. He had seriously misjudged his man. MacArthur could not have been more serious.[28]

Eichelberger failed to see that the only strategic objective in sight right now was Manila and the only correct use of the 11th Airborne was to put it into that fight by landing the entire division on Nichols Field. If there was one lesson that World War II taught about airborne operations, it was that you dropped as close to the target as you could go. Parachutists and glider men were too lightly armed to make a long, fighting advance. It was better to take the losses on the drop than bleed to death in a slugging match. Both combat drops in MacArthur's theater to date—at Nadzab and Noemfoor—had put the 503d Parachute Infantry Regiment right on the target, not miles away from it, and both operations had succeeded.

The 11th Airborne Division numbered only eight thousand men, but it was superbly trained, well led, battle-hardened, confident and eager to make its first combat jump. Kenney offered to give Eichelberger all the air support he would need to secure Nichols if he would only agree to make the drop, but Eichelberger refused. He was going to stick to the planned landing at Nasugbu Bay and proceed toward Nichols Field from there.

The 11th Airborne Division's role in the race for Manila got under way on January 31, when the division's two glider regiments were loaded aboard landing craft for the amphibious assault on Nasugbu Bay. Its sole parachute regiment was dropped three days later to seize the high ground ten miles inland from the landing beaches. The closer the division got to the southern outskirts of Manila, the stronger the resistance it encountered. The only approach into the city that the Japanese had well covered was the one the 11th Division was trying to advance on. It ground to a halt, stopped by enemy defenses two miles south of Nichols Field.[29]

This failure meant Eichelberger had lost his fourth star, yet in his own mind he *was* a bold, risk-taking Army commander, unlike Krueger, whom he considered an expert in risk avoidance. He managed to convince himself that the 11th Airborne's landing at Nasugbu Bay and its tortuous advance toward Nichols Field were among the most outstanding feats of the war. It was a judgment that was not shared by MacArthur, the Japanese or the Army's official history of the Luzon campaign.[30]

Eichelberger never figured out where his career had gone wrong, never understood why Krueger got a fourth star, never comprehended why he didn't. Yet so far as MacArthur was concerned, justice *had* been done. He'd given Eichelberger two golden chances—and he'd blown both of them. Eichelberger concluded he had been cheated out of the promotion that he, as an army commander, deserved. He became a self-pitying and embittered man, his formerly open and generous character curdled by an undying hatred of MacArthur, whom he came to look upon as a great fraud and his worst enemy.

After Eichelberger refused to have the 11th grab Nichols in a coup de main, MacArthur turned all his energies to the race from the north. He was going to encourage it, monitor it and, to some degree, take part in it. On January 29 he shifted his advanced headquarters fifty miles south of Dagupan and moved into Hacienda Luisita, a large whitewashed sugar mill outside Tarlac.

Two of the Sixth Army's best divisions were chosen to race each other to Manila: the 1st Cavalry, due to arrive at Lingayen Gulf on January 27, which would advance down Highway 5, and the 37th Division, which would start the race from its position near Clark Field, and approach the city along Highway 3. In effect, the 37th was already halfway from Lingayen to Manila, but the 1st Cav had more mobility and tremendous esprit de corps. It considered itself the best division in the Army. Some commentators have said it was not really a race because the 1st Cavalry had a huge mobility advantage.[31] In fact, an American infantry division in World War II had nearly four thousand vehicles, mainly jeeps and trucks. None of its soldiers absolutely had to walk. It also had a tank battalion attached to it. The 37th had as good a chance of winning as the 1st Cavalry.

At times MacArthur's eagerness to get to Manila pushed his jeep ahead of his most advanced troops. On January 30 near Clark Field he managed to drive into the middle of a firefight, with three Japanese machine-gun crews less than a hundred yards to his left firing at an American artillery battery less than a hundred yards to his right that was shooting over open sights at the entrenched enemy.[32]

Meanwhile the 1st Cavalry was racing south from the beaches of Lingayen Gulf. That evening MacArthur visited the division commander, Verne D. Mudge, and told him, "Go to Manila. I don't care how you do it, but get in there and get in fast. And save your men. Go around the Nips, bounce off the Nips, but go to Manila. Free the internees at Santo Tomás. Take Malacañang Palace and the Legislative Building."[33]

Mudge organized a flying column of eight hundred enthusiastic volunteers in jeeps, trucks and light tanks who would make a dash for the city. Two days later the column reached Cabanatuan, seventy-five miles northeast of Manila. The cavalrymen forded a river, forced the Japanese out of Cabanatuan and got onto Highway 5. The column covered those seventy-five miles in sixty hours and crossed the Manila city limits at dusk on February 4. The 37th Division, hotfooting it down Highway 3, was twelve hours behind and reached the city at dawn the next day.[34]

MacArthur had made good on his pledge to be in Manila within four weeks of the landing. He was hoping too that a rapid penetration of Manila by a small, fast-moving force would so confuse the Japanese that his troops would be able to free thousands of Allied prisoners in and around the city. If he got troops into the city quickly, he might capture the camps without a fight. But if he was drawn into a grinding, bloody siege, the Japanese could easily be prompted, in the closing days of a hopeless struggle, to massacre their prisoners. The fate of Allied prisoners weighed heavily on MacArthur's conscience these days.[35]

On the morning of February 5 the 1st Cavalry's flying column thrust deeper into the northern suburbs and headed for Santo Tomas University, where the Japanese were holding thirty-five hundred people, mainly American civilians. The 37th Division meanwhile was making for Bilibid Prison. The infantrymen grabbed a bridge over a ravine before the Japanese could blow it, seized the prison and freed its eight hundred inmates without a fight.

Mudge sent a message to MacArthur that night, asking him if he would like to join the 1st Cavalry Division's main force on its entry into Manila in the morning. MacArthur's reply was a prompt and enthusiastic affirmative, but his departure from Tarlac was delayed by several important cables from Washington that required immediate replies. It was midmorning on February 6 before he reached the head of the 1st Cavalry's column, which was halted ten miles north of the city. Minutes before MacArthur's jeep pulled up, the Japanese blew the bridge spanning a deep ravine a mile or so ahead of the cavalry division. Mudge's engineers had to give him the bad news: It would be at least twelve hours before they could put a Bailey bridge across the ravine. MacArthur returned to Hacienda Luisita crestfallen and silent throughout the long drive back.[36]

The 1st Cavalry and the 37th Infantry moved into Manila in force before nightfall. Next day MacArthur was too busy reading and drafting telegrams to get away from the sugar mill, but that evening he issued a triumphant communiqué: "Our forces are rapidly clearing the enemy from Manila. . . ." The complete destruction of the city's defenders was "imminent." It was a typically optimistic—and in the event overly optimistic—announcement. Confidence is essential in a successful commander, but MacArthur's volatility often meant that he took bad news too hard and gilded good news until it bore only a passing resemblance to mundane reality.[37]

On February 7 he was at last able to go to Manila. MacArthur, Egeberg, Lehrbas and half a dozen other members of the GHQ advance echelon staff drove from Tarlac down to the city in several jeeps. MacArthur headed straight for Bilibid Prison. The first prisoner to greet him looked like a skeleton rattling itself to attention and trying to salute. "Welcome to Bilibid, sir," said this dried-up husk of a man who seemed barely strong enough to stand. He identified himself as Major Warren Wilson, an army doctor and the senior officer in charge of the prison hospital.

MacArthur shook hands with this almost spectral apparition. "I'm glad to be back," he said simply.

Advancing into the prison, he found himself in a Dantesque scene painful to see, agonizing to become part of. Hundreds of men gazed up at him too weak to do anything but attempt to smile from where they lay, stretched out like corpses on filthy cots, closer to death than life, almost ready for burial. He shook their hands gently or patted their shoulders, fighting to keep his emotions under control. "You made it," one of them whispered.

"I'm a little late," he said, almost apologetically, "but we finally came."[38]

He returned to his jeep and drove over to Santo Tomas, where conditions were better than at Bilibid. It was a harrowing scene all the same. The prisoners here had just enough strength to pull on his jacket and weep on his chest, to fall on their knees and kiss his hand, to throw their sticklike arms around him in rapture. "To be a life-saver," he thought, "and not a life-taker!"[39]

After an hour at Santo Tomas, MacArthur drove on, moving toward the bay and the Manila Hotel. One of the members of his staff, Colonel Andres Soriano, owned the San Miguel brewery. The jeeps carrying MacArthur's party slowed to a halt outside the famous brewery, which had been captured only an hour or so before their arrival. Within minutes jubilant troops, Filipino brewery workers and Soriano had brought out bottles and glasses to toast Manila's liberation.

MacArthur joined them, but his lips barely touched the glass of beer he raised to them. What moved MacArthur as he held the foaming glass of San Miguel in his shaking right hand and stared through his Ray-Bans at the filtered, familiar sights of downtown Manila crowding around him was more like a sense of mourning than anything resembling elation.

He drove on, to Malacañang Palace, which had been captured intact. His old Cadillac was restored to him. It had been used by the Japanese commander of the Manila occupation troops and was still in good condition.[40]

He wanted to move on, to step once again into the Manila Hotel penthouse, to see for himself if the rumors were true that the Japanese, awed by the huge vase given to his father by the emperor of Japan and standing, with a partner, at the apartment entrance, had been awestruck into treating MacArthur's home like a sacred site. He continued his progress, following the line of the Pasig River, until he reached the frontline troops and dismounted from his jeep.

Shrugging off warnings that the whole neighborhood was crawling with Japanese troops, he started walking toward Manila Bay. He had not advanced more than a block or two before sniper bullets began ricocheting off the sidewalks or flew past his head like vengeful hornets. Yet he continued on foot until a machine gun burst into life not far ahead.[41]

MacArthur stepped into a doorway. What was going on? Yamashita was not going to make a fight for Manila. If that was his intention, he would not have pulled out nearly all his troops and pushed them into the mountains. Yet the closer American patrols drew to the old walled city, the Intramuros, and the Luneta, the park overlooking Manila Bay, the more shooting there was. Huge fires were already burning in the northern suburbs. And the 11th Airborne Division had spent the past three days battling against strong defenses south of Nichols Field. Someone wanted to fight. In that case this city was doomed.[42]

On January 29 MacArthur set in motion the operation to retake the Bataan Peninsula, a battle that would pave the way for an attempt to recover the island of Corregidor. He had Eichelberger land the 38th Division, reinforced with the 34th Regimental Combat Team, on the west coast of Luzon a few miles north of Bataan. Over the next three weeks, these units cut the peninsula at its base, then drove south. To aid their advance, yet another RCT was landed on the southwest coast of Bataan to strike at the Japanese, who held the line across the center of the peninsula.[43]

MacArthur could not wait for Bataan to be recaptured. On February 16 he made a command reconnaissance, taking a party of six jeeps, two generals, several aides and a dozen gun-toting infantrymen deep into the peninsula. "It's been a long time since I led a patrol into No-Man's Land," he remarked to Egeberg. "Makes you tingle a bit, doesn't it?"[44]

They reached a pair of scouts probing the Japanese lines and asked where the enemy was. The scouts said the Japanese were in the jungle just ahead. MacArthur told his aide to keep their carbines ready. Then, reduced to just two jeeps, he drove on for another four or five miles. The jeeps came to a sudden halt in a clearing. Rice was still warm in the cooking pots, and a hastily abandoned Japanese machine gun sent a shiver down Egeberg's spine. Even now MacArthur would not turn back. He drove on, hoping to get far enough south to see the parachute drop scheduled to take place over Corregidor that day. The jeeps drove on another mile or so, until they were halted by a blown bridge blocking a wide, deep stream.

MacArthur got out of his jeep and paced in frustration, trying to decide what to do, when a formation of P-38s providing air cover for the incoming C-47s swooped low over the jeeps and radioed for permission to attack this "enemy convoy." Fortunately the ground general the air request was routed to vetoed it. He knew that MacArthur was somewhere on Bataan that morning.

MacArthur reluctantly concluded there was no chance of going any farther and had the jeeps turn around. He was disappointed but relieved all the same. "You don't know what a leaden load this lifts from my heart," he said to his aides. "This day has done me good."[45]

When GHQ started planning the recapture of Corregidor, Willoughby estimated there were only eight to nine hundred Japanese holding the Rock. This low figure gave Sutherland an idea. Why not try to hit it with the ultimate in combined arms operations—a simultaneous airborne and amphibious assault? Even Kenney, that lover of the daring stroke, had his doubts about this one and told MacArthur he could not recommend it. He did not think much of Willoughby's abilities, and what if this guess proved to be as dumb as some of his others? MacArthur nevertheless okayed Sutherland's proposal.[46]

There wasn't a suitable drop zone anywhere on Corregidor. Either the 503d Parachute Infantry Regiment could drop onto the relatively flat land at the eastern end of the island and fight its way toward Malinta Tunnel, or it could be dropped onto the parade ground and the adjoining two-hole golf course at Topside. Both the parade ground and the golf course were bordered by cliffs. Krueger opted to make the drop at Topside, where the Japanese would never expect to see parachutists descending on them.[47]

On February 16 some two thousand men of the 503d made the drop while a thousand infantry landed on the tiny strip of beach at the bottom of the cliffs. This attack took the Japanese completely by surprise—all five thousand of them. A reinforcement drop by another thousand parachutists was made the next day. Getting the Rock back produced a ferocious battle in which the Fifth Air Force's heavy bombers almost drowned much of Corregidor in napalm while Navy destroyers offshore fired at point-blank range into the island's caves and tunnel entrances.[48]

The fight for the Rock was a vicious close-quarters struggle against a well-entrenched, well-armed foe. Up to two thousand Japanese blew themselves up in Malinta Tunnel the night of February 21 in a suicidal detonation of hundreds of tons of high explosive, yet still the battle went on. It took another week before organized resistance ended. The cost of recovering Corregidor was a thousand dead or wounded.[49]

While this fight was still raging, MacArthur mounted yet another prison raid. There is a huge lake south of Manila called Laguna de Bay. On its southern shore stood the internment camp of Los Baños, holding more than two thousand Americans and Filipinos, many of them missionaries and nuns. On February 24 several hundred glider men of the 11th Airborne Division made an amphibious assault across the lake. The Japanese guards at the camp were too surprised to offer resistance, too bewildered to slaughter their prisoners. All the internees were freed unharmed.[50]

This dramatic raid was the one bright spot in an otherwise tragic picture. The Japanese admiral in command of Manila, Sanji Iwabuchi, had thirty-five thousand troops under his orders. Rejecting Yamashita's policy of sparing the city, Iwabuchi imposed his own nihilistic vision on its helpless inhabitants, its historic buildings and his hapless troops. There was no strategic or tactical advantage to be won by turning Manila into a battle-ground, no honor in its destruction, no glory for Japan. Killing Manila would not delay the empire's defeat by a single day. No matter. There were plenty of automatic weapons available to the defenders, and ammo bunkers overflowed with ordnance. Barricades were built across every major intersection; the streets were lavishly mined; thousands of buildings were booby-trapped; naval vessels in Manila Bay were stripped and their guns hauled ashore. And much as they had done elsewhere in the course of conquest, the Japanese rounded up large numbers of civilians and simply murdered them. These atrocities were beyond reason or excuse.[51]

MacArthur found himself forced to fight a battle for the city, a battle he knew would raze it. He tried where he could to spare its people. When Kenney proposed bombing the old walled city, the Intramuros, and blasting it into dust, thereby saving the infantry from having to try digging out its defenders, he refused to consider it. "No, I can't let you do that," he told Kenney. "You would probably kill off the Japs, all right, but there are several thousand Filipinos in there who would be killed, too." As it turned out, MacArthur refused to let Kenney drop bombs on anything in Manila. Bombing simply wasn't accurate enough to avoid killing large numbers of innocent civilians in a densely populated city.[52]

At first MacArthur tried to prevent heavy artillery from being used in this battle, but when his troops came under fire from Japanese guns, he was forced to drop these restrictions. American artillery was by this time the best in the world. It was superbly coordinated and controlled. As MacArthur realized, once it was unleashed, it could destroy just about anything human beings could build. In the Battle of Manila American guns destroyed most of the structures, while the Japanese killed most of the hundred thousand Filipinos who perished.

Downtown Manila was taken apart building by building, almost room by room. It produced one of the most spectacular funeral pyres of history's bloodiest century. "Flames billowed 1,000 feet and then belched huge clouds of black smoke to 20,000 feet," recorded an awestruck general viewing the early stages of the battle from an airplane.[53]

Manila's destruction could not have been more complete if all the general staffs in the world had gotten together to plan it. War correspondents who had seen other devastated cities, from London to Warsaw, Rotterdam to Stalingrad, could hardly believe the scenes erupting around them as artillery fire blasted whole neighborhoods out of existence within hours and Japanese booby traps blew entire buildings apart in seconds. "Manila is dying," some of them wrote in their accounts of the battle. MacArthur angrily censored their copy and ordered them not to use such phrases. The trouble was not that what they had written was false but that it was all too obviously, only too painfully true.[54]

On February 22 MacArthur could not resist joining the cavalrymen fighting their way up Dewey Boulevard toward the Manila Hotel. "Suddenly, the penthouse burst into flame. They had fired it. I watched, with indescribable feelings, the destruction of my fine military library, my souvenirs, my personal belongings of a lifetime." The troops fought their way into the hotel and captured it before nightfall. The fires in the penthouse were extinguished, and MacArthur climbed the stairs to his former home. Sprawled in the entrance was the bloodstained corpse of a Japanese colonel. Scattered around him like stone petals were the shards of the two huge ceremonial vases, their protective magic, like all magic, a myth after all. A young officer carrying a carbine saw MacArthur standing there and called out cheerily, "Nice going, chief!," thinking that for the general as for the troops who had captured the hotel this was a moment of triumph. But for MacArthur it was another tragedy, another dead dream. Nothing turns out the way we expect. It is always a lot better . . . or far worse.[55]

Shortly after American troops had entered the city, the GHQ staff had drawn up plans for a victory parade, but the fighting forced it to be post-poned, and postponed, and finally abandoned. By the time Manila was secured there were only four intact public and commercial buildings left in the entire city. Most of "the Pearl of the Orient" consisted of nothing but low heaps of rubble stretching to the horizon in every direction. Virtually all thirty-five thousand Japanese had been killed. MacArthur's combat casualties came to sixty-five hundred men dead or wounded.[56]

As the fighting died down, MacArthur fulfilled the promise he had made to Quezon in Malinta Tunnel in February 1942: "I will put you back in the Malacañang on the point of my bayonets." On February 27, 1945, at a ceremony in the Malacañang he reinstalled the government of the Philip-pines. Quezon's close friend and successor, Sergio Osmeña, made a brief address. MacArthur responded with a long, emotional speech.

"More than three years have elapsed—years of bitterness, struggle and sacrifice—since I withdrew our forces and installations from this beautiful city that, open and undefended, its churches, monuments and cultural cen-ters might, in accordance with the rules of warfare, be spared. . . . The enemy would not have it so and much that I sought to preserve has been unnecessarily destroyed by his desperate action. . . ."

MacArthur spoke slowly, pausing often, fighting a losing battle to keep his emotions in check. "Then we were but a small force struggling to stem the advance of overwhelming hordes. . . . That struggle was not in vain! God has indeed blessed our arms! The girded and unleashed power of America, supported by our Allies, turned the tide of battle. . . . My country kept the faith!" As he drew to the close of his speech, MacArthur's mellow voice quavered, then broke. He stared hard at the floor for a minute, unable to trust himself to speak. He tried to go on, stopped in mid-sentence, gulped hard, then concluded by asking those assembled to join him in reciting the Lord's Prayer.[57]

On March 2 he returned at last to Corregidor, where he was greeted by the commander of the 503d Parachute Infantry Regiment, Colonel George M. Jones. The colonel saluted and declared, "Sir, I present to you—Fortress Corregidor!"

MacArthur congratulated the colonel on the brilliant operation that had recovered the Rock and awarded him the Distinguished Service Cross. "I see the old flagpole still stands," said MacArthur in a loud parade ground voice. "Have your troops hoist the colors to its peak, and let no enemy ever haul them down."[58] In what was possibly the only truly happy moment for him in the liberation of Manila, he stood with his trembling right hand raised in salute as Old Glory made a halting ceremonial ride up the bent and battle-scarred fifty-foot flagpole.

26

It Will Terminate
This Year

During the closing stages of the Battle of Manila, MacArthur sent for Jean and Arthur. They boarded a Norwegian ship on a two-week voyage from Brisbane to Manila with a cargo of frozen food. MacArthur had his staff look for a suitable place for his family to live. They reported back that he ought to move into the former German Embassy, down by the Pasig River. The best thing about the place was that it was intact; the worst was the smell from the nearby sewers gushing into the river.[1]

During the occupation the Japanese had created a puppet government and conferred on the Philippines a quasi independence, a charade that called for having a Japanese ambassador. News of the American landing on Leyte prompted the ambassador, ensconced at first in the Manila Hotel, to seek somewhere less likely than the hotel to become a target when the Americans reached Manila. He had moved into a house called Casa Blanca, the home of a rich German family named Bachrach, the biggest importers of automobiles into the Philippines before the war. As Germans they were citizens of a power allied to Japan and assumed their property and their lives were safe but the Japanese not only seized his house, they had shot Herr Bachrach dead before he could inform them of his German nationality. Thereafter, however, the beautiful fourteen-room Spanish colonial villa was spared the usual plundering and wrecking practices perfected by Japanese soldiers from Nanjing to Singapore.

When the ambassador moved in, his baggage included a large wooden chest of souvenirs collected from the Manila Hotel. These consisted of more than the usual tourist trove of towels and swizzle sticks. The ambassador had scooped up a load of MacArthur family heirlooms—the sterling silver tea service the Japanese government had commissioned from Cartier back in 1905 as a gift for General Arthur MacArthur, a pair of silver candlesticks passed down through several generations of Jean's family and other possessions of considerable sentimental value. The chest was stamped "Medical Supplies," a deliberately dull way to describe the balm of conqueror's loot and clearly intended as a curiosity killer. With American troops advancing on Manila, the ambassador fled, leaving his "Medical Supplies" behind. Frau Bachrach informed an American Army officer that she had something belonging to General MacArthur, and would he please arrange to collect it?[2]

Meanwhile George Kenney was also looking for a place to live. He had spent most of the past two years living in grass shacks, metal huts and canvas tents. He ordered his staff to scour the more attractive districts of Manila and find him a nice place to plant his flying boots. It did not take long before American spotter planes came across the charming, spacious and untouched Bachrach mansion. Kenney went to inspect it. He liked the look of the swimming pool, the wine cellar, the steam bath, the massage room, the exquisite furniture, the lovingly tended garden, the cool, high-ceilinged rooms. Perfect. A true *repos du guerrier.*

That evening over dinner at the spacious, whitewashed but Spartan Hacienda Luisita, he told MacArthur about the great house he'd found. He realized next morning when MacArthur did not show up for breakfast that he had made a mistake. While Kenney was working his way through the cornflakes, MacArthur was touring Casa Blanca and thinking how much better this place was than the dump his staff had recommended down by the Pasig River. There was an old Army expression: RHIP, "Rank has its privileges." The Bachrach house was an RHIP dwelling, or he did not deserve the five stars made from the silver coins of five Allied nations (the United States, Britain, Australia, New Zealand and Holland) shining brightly on his shirt collar.

Shortly after MacArthur left for Manila, Kenney put a call through to Frau Bachrach, told her he was new to the area and asked if she could give him any advice on house hunting. A rich lady in a nice house can usually be trusted to know where the other nice houses inhabited by rich people are to be found. As it happened, said Frau Bachrach, her sister lived in a *really* wonderful place. She had given the architect some simple, competitive instructions: "Build me a better house than my sister's." Kenney jumped into a plane, flew down to Manila, went to take a look at it and agreed with Frau Bachrach. The architect had done a wonderful job on her sister's house.

When MacArthur came back that evening for dinner, he told Kenney, "I stole your house. What are you going to do now?"

"I've got a house," said Kenney. "I was in Manila today getting me another one."

"Is it any good?"

"It's better than yours."

"Where is it?"

"I'm not telling you a thing about that house, but it's a better house than yours."

"Son of a bitch," said MacArthur. "Why didn't I wait a little longer and get that one!"[3]

Jean and Arthur arrived in Manila on March 6, and MacArthur took a small boat out to meet them. When the boat returned to the dock, Kenney was there. Hundreds of fighters and bombers flew over the bay just then, heading north, to attack Japanese troops still dug in on the hills overlooking Clark Field. When the roar of their engines faded into the distance, Jean smiled at Kenney. "Isn't it wonderful to hear *our* airplanes? The last time I was here, they were all Japs and instead of watching them we were running for cover."[4]

A couple of days later MacArthur took his wife and son to the Manila Hotel. The roof was gone, and the upper floors were burned out, but life on the ground floor was much as it had always been. The bar was crowded with servicemen buying one another drinks. The MacArthurs climbed the rubble-strewn stairwell to the penthouse. They stood in disconsolate remembrance of the many happy days they had spent here together. The apartment had been completely gutted by the fire. It was nothing now but a blackened shell, open to the sky, carpeted with ash five inches deep, from which chunks of Jean's baby grand stuck out like polished black granite tombstones.[5]

A gregarious and sociable person with a strong feeling for the welfare of others, Jean had barely unpacked before she decided to go visit the prisoners at Bilibid. When she arrived, though, the weak and sickly inmates, many of them still bundled in vermin-ridden rags, stared in disbelief at her perky hat and dazzling white gloves. Embarrassed, she whipped off the hat, pulled off her gloves and dumped them in the back of the general's old black Cadillac sedan.[6]

She won the affection of soldiers throughout the Philippines by her visits to the four military hospitals operating in Manila. Conditions in some of them were not much better than in the prisons, but just as nothing would make MacArthur go to the hospitals, nothing would keep Jean away.[7]

On one occasion Egeberg took her to visit a field hospital up near Baguio, in the mountains of northern Luzon, where fighting was still going on. She talked to men who had, in some cases, been wounded only an hour or so earlier. When Jean and Egeberg returned to Manila, Egeberg was summoned to MacArthur's office. "You took her to a field hospital under intermittent enemy fire. I don't like it!" MacArthur said angrily, and banged his desk with his fist. "You cannot—you must not—expose her like that. If anything should happen to her while you were taking her forward . . ." For a moment he didn't know what to say. The prospect was so terrible no words could express it. "I don't know just what I would do to you," he said, exasperated. He took out his rage on the desk instead of the doc and thumped it for the second time. "Don't ever do that again!"[8]

Jean's devotion to him was as great as his devotion to her. And on January 26, his sixty-fifth birthday, she had written him a message on Lennon's Hotel stationery:

Dearest Sir Boss—
I love you more than you will ever know.[9]

Arthur was as adored, indulged and overprotected as before. Back in Manila, he had no playmates of his own age, but one day MacArthur came home with a starving, emaciated mongrel picked up from the streets, in the Manila vernacular, a barrio hound. The dog was brought back to good health and named Spottie. It proved to be a lively, affectionate creature, and Arthur loved it. One day the dog was struck and killed by a visiting officer's car, breaking young Arthur's heart. MacArthur ordered the gates to the driveway locked thereafter and made another dog-hunting trip through the barrio. He came back with yet another scrawny but affectionate mutt. This one was called Blackie, but after a few months he developed distemper and was in such constant pain he had to be destroyed. Arthur had had his heart broken all over again. MacArthur too.[10]

The boy, now seven, had reached an age where Jean felt she ought to hand him over to a teacher, and MacArthur hired an Englishwoman, Mrs. Phyllis Gibbons. Over the next six years "Gibby" not only proved a good teacher for Arthur but was also a charming, agreeable companion for Jean. The boy, his teacher decided, was "quite intelligent, but a poor speller, like any other American boy."[11]

Gibby was a proficient pianist and was delighted to find that Arthur possessed considerable musical ability. He would happily sit at the piano for hours, learning to sight-read and practicing diligently. Arthur had been gifted with the ability to produce a passable rendition of just about any tune that he heard played or sung only once.[12]

To add to MacArthur's delight, he not only had his family with him once more but finally got a C-54, with *Bataan II* painted on both sides of its prominent nose. The Douglas Aircraft Company made so many modifications to it the plant had lost the production of another four or five planes.

Hap Arnold's reaction was "Jeezus Christ! @#&%ÿπ£!" but the result was a plane that even Jean, with her unhappy memories of air travel, thought was terrific.[13]

MacArthur would have been thrilled to return to his old headquarters, at 1 Calle Victoria, but the building was almost completely wrecked. He had Manila's bullet-scarred city hall patched up and moved GHQ into it in early May. He took over the mayor's office as his own. With a comfortable home and a spacious headquarters once more, MacArthur was able to resume his well-practiced routine of going to work in midmorning, returning for a late lunch and a nap, putting in a few more hours at the office before coming home for dinner and a movie, then an hour or two of reading before going to bed. Much of his reading in the Casa Blanca library now consisted of histories of Japan and accounts of how its government functioned.[14]

Roosevelt's policy toward Filipinos who collaborated with the Japanese could not have been clearer: They were traitors to the commonwealth and to the United States. They should be arrested, tried for treason and punished severely. MacArthur felt this was a matter for the commonwealth government, not the Army, to deal with, but Osmeña lacked the resources to launch a major roundup of collaborators. It was left to MacArthur to do it. By the spring of 1945 the head of MacArthur's counterintelligence section, Brigadier General Elliott Thorpe, had brought in more than five thousand Filipinos suspected of collaboration.[15]

The leading figures were nearly all members of the commonwealth's political and financial elite. Ordinary Filipinos had remained faithful to the United States. Ironically, it was the class of people closest to Quezon who had shown the greatest willingness to work for the Japanese. Don Manuel himself cultivated contacts with the Japanese as early as 1940, fearing that the United States was planning to leave the islands to their fate. He intended to cooperate with whoever came out on top in the struggle for mastery over the western Pacific. Besides, it was almost inevitable that the Philippines' ruling class would fall into bed with the Japanese without much wooing beyond a little heavy breathing over the sake cups for the sake of appearances. Survivalism had always been the elite's lodestar.[16]

It reflected a creed rooted in four centuries of Spanish occupation. Filipino officials had a long history of attempting, with good conscience, to do something that Anglo-Saxons are inclined to consider a moral impossibility: They truly believed they could satisfy the demands of the conqueror and protect their own people at the same time. As General Arthur MacArthur had reported to Congress in 1902, during the insurrection, "The presidentes and other officials act openly in behalf of the Americans and secretly in behalf of the insurgents and, paradoxical as it may seem, with considerable apparent solicitude for the interests of both."[17]

As his life ebbed away during his two-year exile in the United States, Quezon tried to exonerate virtually all the leading collaborators, many of whom were close to him, such as Jorge Vargas, his former executive secretary, and José Laurel, his minister of justice. They were not truly collaborators, he swore. There was no treason in what they did. It was only through appearing to cooperate with the Japanese that they were able to protect ordinary Filipinos from an even harsher occupation regime. Quezon's assertions might have been more convincing had he not tried to support them by claiming he was in regular radio contact with Laurel and Vargas, something that was patently untrue.[18]

Laurel, whom the Japanese installed as president of the Philippines in October 1943, claimed that even before leaving Corregidor MacArthur had explicitly approved his collaborationist actions. MacArthur strongly denied it. "I gave no instructions to [any] Filipino leaders on leaving the Philippines. . . . Every Filipino, except those in the armed services, acted according to his own conscience so far as I know."[19]

Even so, he had no intention of implementing Roosevelt's stern anticollaborationist policy if he could avoid it. Nor had Osmeña, who traveled to Hot Springs, Georgia, in March 1945 to persuade the President to modify it. Virtually the entire Philippine ruling class was tainted by collaboration. Many of Osmeña's relatives—including his two sons—had worked for the Japanese. Roosevelt indicated he was willing to soften his hard-line policy by trying only those who had sworn allegiance to Japan on charges of treason, but he died on April 12. His successor, Vice President Harry S. Truman, was content to leave it to MacArthur to decide how the collaborators ought to be treated.

During his three-year struggle to return to the Philippines, MacArthur had been infuriated at times by stories coming out of the Philippines of Japanese atrocities inflicted on prisoners and ordinary Filipinos. That anger stayed with him during the Leyte campaign. He had wanted retribution not only on the Japanese but on those Filipinos who had been only too willing to help them, such as Laurel and Vargas. By the time he reached Luzon, however, his attitude had softened. For one thing, the Philippines were scheduled to become independent on July 4, 1946. Investigating and trying big-time collaborators could take years. With the United States about to pull out, this was really a matter for the Filipinos to deal with. For another thing, the more he learned of what conditions had been like during the occupation, the less ready he was to be judgmental toward people who had not been masters of their own fate.

He remarked to his pilot, Lieutenant Colonel Dusty Rhoades, one day, "It's hardly fair for us from our safe and unthreatened vantage point to judge or criticize people for employing almost any means to save their own lives and the lives of their families, particularly when relief from their oppression was nowhere in sight." Besides, there was no legal definition of what "collaboration" was, but "The French," he observed wryly, "have a definition of a collaborationist—'Somebody who collaborates more than you do.' "[20]

MacArthur was well acquainted with nearly all the principal figures in the puppet government created by the Japanese. In his years as military adviser and, even before that, as commander of the Philippine Department, he had hailed them as "brothers" at Manila's Masonic Lodge No. 1, dined with them at official banquets in the Malacañang, partied with them at the Army and Navy Club, watched the fights with them at Rizal Stadium and flattered their wives at government receptions. He had not pursued much of a social life, but what there was of it had been spent almost entirely with them.

Throughout the Japanese occupation he had relied on his guerrilla contacts to provide him with information on what the collaborators were up to. Were they really trying to protect the people? Or were they only trying to protect their own families, their own businesses and their own fortunes?

Unfortunately the information he received came to him through the twisted conduit of Courtney Whitney. This portly lawyer was a clever and persuasive man, but one so in love with intrigue, so determined to feather his own nest and so addicted to manipulation that little he said or wrote about the Philippines could be taken at face value.[21]

It was only when MacArthur reached the Philippines and was able to talk to the guerrilla leaders that he finally received unbiased reports. When it came to the collaborators, the one who concerned him most was not Laurel but Manuel Roxas, the former speaker of the commonwealth Assembly and scion of the family that owned the biggest paper in the archipelago, the *Manila Daily News*. MacArthur had known the workaholic, chain-smoking Roxas for twenty years and had appointed him to his staff during the siege of Corregidor.

In his judgment, Roxas was an able, energetic and popular politician, the absolute antithesis of the colorless, elderly Osmeña. Roxas would make a better president for an independent Philippines—if, of course, the collaborationist taint was not too strong. Although Roxas had served as Laurel's minister of food, MacArthur was convinced he had offered the Japanese no more than a minimum of cooperation.

The reader may recall that in May 1943 Quezon had asked his personal physician, an elderly medico named Emidgio Cruz, to slip into Manila and try to talk to Roxas about conditions under the occupation. MacArthur had sent Cruz to the Philippines aboard a submarine but never expected him to succeed. Cruz was, as he made clear to the good doctor's face, almost certainly a dead man. Well, Cruz had got through, and Roxas had helped prevent the Japanese from finding him. The doctor had gone underground in Manila, and eventually been smuggled out of the Philippines.[22]

The Cruz case in itself was not enough to exonerate Roxas. On February 6 MacArthur summoned to the Hacienda Luisita Major Edwin Ramsey, a cavalry officer who had spent the past three years leading thousands of guerrillas on Luzon. This once-dashing young officer who had rivaled Errol Flynn for looks and made an impact on the belles of Manila society before the war showed up that evening as a man transformed by war into a scrawny, exhausted-looking figure clad in threadbare fatigues and worn-out boots. MacArthur talked to him for an hour, but virtually the first thing he wanted to know was, What did Ramsey make of Roxas? Ramsey told him Roxas had never really collaborated with the Japanese. He had tried to help the guerrillas when he could and had done no more than pay lip service to the puppet government run by Laurel.

"I am very glad to hear you say that," said MacArthur, plainly relieved. "I know Roxas well and I cannot believe that he is a traitor."[23] There was nothing he could do right now, though. The Japanese had removed the puppet government to Baguio, in the mountains of northern Luzon, when MacArthur landed at Lingayen Gulf.

It was mid-April before Roxas fell into American hands. Until then he was a prisoner of the Japanese, in Baguio. MacArthur had him flown to Manila immediately for an emotional reunion. Shortly thereafter he promoted him to brigadier general, a step that amounted to a public declaration that he believed Roxas had remained loyal to the United States. Then, to Osmeña's intense discomfort, Roxas resumed his political career, a career that would see him become the first president of an independent Philippines—exactly the result that MacArthur wanted.

On April 1 Nimitz landed two Army and two Marine divisions on Okinawa. The troops walked ashore, facing virtually no opposition. Within days, however, they found themselves drawn into one of the biggest and costliest battles of World War II. The Navy came under a storm of kamikaze attacks.

Military operations south of Okinawa ceased to have any strategic importance to the Japanese. All air and surface movement between Japan and the Philippines stopped. No more oil came up from the Dutch East Indies; no more Japanese planes operated from Formosa; no more Japanese ships dared sail across the seas of Southeast Asia.

For the past two years American forces had been advancing toward Japan along two axes: The Navy, under Nimitz, was moving west across the Central Pacific, while MacArthur was moving northward from the Southwest Pacific. As they advanced, Nimitz's forces and MacArthur's steadily converged. The question was, What would happen when they did finally link up? It was obvious that MacArthur would refuse to come under Nimitz's command, and there was no chance that King would allow Nimitz to come under MacArthur.

Three days after the assault on Okinawa, MacArthur was informed by Marshall that an agreement had been reached with the Navy: Once the battle for Okinawa ended, MacArthur would have command of all the Army forces in the Pacific, including those currently under Nimitz's control. Nimitz would have control over all naval forces, including Kinkaid's Seventh Fleet. Strategic planning from now on would have one objective: the invasion of Japan.

MacArthur put his GHQ staff to work on plans for two operations: Olympic, an invasion of the southernmost of the home islands, Kyushu, on October 1, 1945, and Coronet, a landing thirty miles from Tokyo two months later. Personally, though, he did not believe that either one would be mounted. Japan would quit first.[24]

In February 1945 Navy Secretary James Forrestal had visited MacArthur at the Hacienda Luisita. MacArthur had told Forrestal that there should be no hasty attempt to invade Japan. "We should secure the commitment of the Russians to vigorous and active prosecution of a campaign in Manchuria to pin down a large part of the Japanese army. Once this campaign is engaged we should then launch an attack on the home islands." MacArthur calculated the Soviets would need at least sixty divisions to defeat the one-million-plus troops that the Japanese had deployed in Manchuria.[25]

When MacArthur and Forrestal were having dinner, the navy secretary asked, "Do you wish to hazard a guess upon the end of the war in the Pacific?"

MacArthur replied, "I predict that it will terminate this year."

A look of incredulity appeared on Forrestal's broken-nosed black Irish features. The current betting in the Navy Department was that it would end sometime in 1946. Nor did MacArthur's intelligence chief, Charles Willoughby, anticipate a Japanese surrender any time in the next eighteen months. "May I quote that to Washington?" Forrestal asked. It was as much a dare as a question. MacArthur told him to do so by all means.[26]

Krueger was meanwhile grinding down the 150,000 enemy troops bottled up in the remote mountains of northern Luzon, as grueling and unglamorous a task as the war provided. The terrain was the greatest enemy, with tropical diseases a close second. Since the Japanese had lost all ability to maneuver against the Sixth Army's flanks and were too weak to make frontal assaults, MacArthur stripped divisions from Krueger and transferred them to Eichelberger.

Even so, Krueger kept pounding away at the well-entrenched Japanese for no good reason. MacArthur ought to have wound down this campaign sooner than he did. The continuing effort to dig the Japanese out of the mountains of northern Luzon inflicted a steady loss on the American units involved. Taking Luzon would eventually cost nearly nine thousand American dead and more than thirty thousand wounded, making it one of the bloodiest campaigns of the Pacific war. As one of Krueger's division commanders remarked later, "MacArthur violated the principles of shopping"—i.e., he paid too much for what he got.[27]

By reassigning half of Krueger's divisions to Eichelberger's command, MacArthur enabled the Eighth Army to mount a liberation campaign against Japanese-held islands in the central and southern Philippines. The return was not enough in itself. When he restored the government of the Philippines at Tacloban on October 23, 1944, MacArthur had called the landing "a prelude to the liberation of the entire Philippines . . ." and referred to himself as "the Commander in Chief of the military forces committed to the liberation of the Philippines. . . ."[28]

He had no explicit authority from the JCS to make such a pledge, which led his most respected biographer, Professor D. Clayton James, to accuse him of exceeding his orders. William Manchester, taking his cue from James, enthusiastically weighed in with a charge that MacArthur had been guilty of flagrant insubordination, appalling arrogance, unbridled egotism et cetera.[29]

As both MacArthur and the JCS were well aware, the liberation of the Philippines was American policy. The JCS did not establish war policy; that came from Roosevelt, acting as commander in chief. The role of the JCS was to implement the policy, and so was MacArthur's. Even before Corregidor fell, Roosevelt had explicitly pledged to Quezon that the United States would free the Philippines.[30] Not some of it, but all of it. That commitment had not been withdrawn or amended.

Moreover, Roosevelt's statements to MacArthur in Honolulu and his correspondence with MacArthur about a return to the Philippines clearly anticipated that the President's promise would be made good. When MacArthur landed at Lingayen Gulf, he was intending to reconquer all of Luzon, including Bataan and Corregidor, and then go on to launch a liberation campaign in the rest of the Philippines. Once the Eighth Army started liberating islands south of Luzon, the JCS finally bestirred itself and sanctioned what he was doing, a development that to James made it seem that MacArthur had moved too quickly when in fact, what it really indicated was that the Joint Chiefs had moved too slowly, probably because Admiral King was as convinced as ever that a campaign in the Philippines was a monumental mistake.[31]

Liberating the islands south of Luzon consisted mainly of low-risk operations against an enemy so weakened it could rarely manage to launch even local counterattacks. From a military point of view, it was merely large-scale mopping up. But MacArthur slaked Eichelberger's almost pathetic desire for praise by flattering him to a point where even Eichelberger felt uncomfortable at times.[32] Giddy on C in C soothing syrup, the Eighth Army tackled its liberation assignment with an enthusiasm rarely seen in mopping-up operations.

Only on Cebu was there strong opposition. There some fifteen thousand Japanese held three layers of strong defensive positions. Cebu was tackled, however, by the aggressive, well-led American Division. The American eventually won this battle despite eight thousand cases of hepatitis and two thousand combat casualties.[33]

Liberating the central and southern Philippines cost 850 American lives. The limited nature of these operations did not mean they were easy or free, but to MacArthur they had a moral importance that completely justified the losses. Retaking these islands was the only way the United States could redeem the national humiliation of earlier defeats.

The Australian premier, John Curtin, was also seeking a liberating role for his troops. Australian forces had attacked the large garrisons that MacArthur had bypassed on New Guinea, such as Wewak, instead of merely containing them. They were also attacking Japanese garrisons on Bougainvillea and New Britain. In February 1945 Curtin, who was still (barely) alive, informed MacArthur that Australian forces should be either used or demobilized. He and Blamey feared that unless the Australians continued to fight to the end of the war, they would be shut out from the political settlements that were reached in the final stages and their interests ignored.[34]

MacArthur obliged by assigning them targets in the Dutch East Indies, but without consulting them closely. The JCS did not see the point of invading places like Borneo, which would soon fall into Allied hands anyway, but MacArthur felt he had a moral obligation to the Australians, without whose wholehearted support he could never have taken the offensive in New Guinea in September 1942. If they wanted to fight, he would not stand in their way. Besides, the Dutch East Indies were within the boundaries of SWPA. He felt he could not hand these islands back to the Dutch without taking at least one important town from the Japanese first.[35]

The Borneo campaign would be mounted in three stages: a landing to seize the small nearby island of Tarakan and build airstrips; an assault on

Brunei, the oil-rich British possession that comprised the northern half of the island; and a landing at Balikpapan, site of the oil refineries, in the southern Dutch-owned half. Blamey had no objection to taking Brunei but was strongly opposed to Balikpapan. MacArthur ignored Blamey's protests.

On June 2 MacArthur called Kenney and asked him if he would like to go with him to watch the Brunei assault. Kenney tried to beg off, saying he had too much work to do. "Come along with me, George," MacArthur urged. "We'll have a good holiday." Then the killer blow: "Besides, there will be chocolate ice cream sodas three times a day."[36]

MacArthur and Eichelberger boarded the cruiser *Boise* next day for a leisurely tour of the central and southern Philippines, visiting the islands that the Eighth Army had recently liberated. Along the way MacArthur had the cruiser pull in at Palawan so he could visit the prison at Puerto Princesa. This was where Thorpe was holding most of the top-ranking collaborators. "These were men I used to see frequently, socially or on business," he explained to Roger Egeberg. "They were friends in a way."[37]

When the cruiser reached Mindanao and docked at Del Monte, MacArthur was eager to find the place where he and Jean had spent three anxious days and nights waiting for planes to come and take them to Australia. The building had vanished.[38]

Kenney flew down and boarded the *Boise* on June 8. The Brunei assault would be made by the Australian 9th Division. The landing was made the morning of June 10 and met only sporadic opposition. The troops showed no lack of courage, and their officers seemed eager. But both men and officers were undertrained and inexperienced. Too many of the veterans of the 9th Division had been killed or crippled and been replaced by green recruits. Instead of exploiting their success and pushing rapidly inland, they were still clinging to the sand.[39]

MacArthur went ashore in midafternoon. Using himself as an example of what was needed, he briskly crossed the beach and started walking along a road five hundred yards inland that ran parallel to the shore. Sniper fire and the chatter of a Nambu light machine gun sounded from the jungle up ahead. He strode on, leading a party of increasingly apprehensive brass hats straight toward the firefight. As he drew near, a tank rumbled toward them, heading back from tackling the machine-gun nest. A jubilant Australian soldier poked his head out of the turret to announce, "We got the fucking bastards!"

MacArthur walked on, curious to see the dead Japanese. An Australian photographer rushed up and started taking photographs, trying to get MacArthur and two enemy corpses into the same frame. Standing a few feet from MacArthur, he abruptly fell to the ground, shot by a sniper hidden somewhere in the jungle nearby.

Kenney walked up to MacArthur and said it seemed pretty clear to him that this "holiday" would be ruined if MacArthur got what the photographer had just got. And now that MacArthur had conducted a successful command reconnaissance, it seemed to him, Kenney said, that this was where the infantry was supposed to come in. Besides, the Navy was expecting them back in good time for dinner. It would be impolite to keep their hosts on the *Boise* waiting. And what about the chocolate ice cream sodas he had been promised? "All right, George, we'll go back," said MacArthur. "I wouldn't want you to miss that ice cream for anything."[40]

He returned to the beach next day and wanted to take a look around Brunei town, but the Australians hadn't finished securing it. Back aboard the cruiser, MacArthur headed for the Sulu archipelago, to meet with the sultan. This small group of islands was home to the Moros, a fierce warrior breed practicing Islam. Pershing had made much of his early reputation as the conqueror of the Sulu archipelago during the insurrection. To an Army officer of MacArthur's generation, this was an almost legendary place.

The small, bald, aged and seminaked sultan greeted MacArthur warmly. They exchanged a few words in English, but most of the conversation that followed was translated by the sultan's vizier. The sultan presented MacArthur with a ceremonial creese, a wavy blade with inscriptions from the Koran. MacArthur turned to Eichelberger, who in turn looked around, gazed briefly at the fine binoculars hanging from a colonel's neck, transmitted his orders wordlessly, and the colonel handed his binoculars to MacArthur with a gloomily resigned expression. RHIP. MacArthur in turn graciously handed this splendid example of modern optics to the sultan. The exchange of gifts completed, they stood and chatted for a while as the sultan's young grandson relieved himself freely over MacArthur's gleaming low-cuts, Eichelberger's highly polished boots and the slippered feet of both Gramps and his vizier. All four notables ignored this steaming intervention and continued conversing calmly, as men of the world do whenever they meet. "That little pisser *was* the apple of the Sultan's eye," MacArthur remarked philosophically once back aboard ship and able to change his socks.[41]

With Tarakan and Brunei town taken, the third stage of the Borneo operation was launched on July 1 with the landing of the Australian 7th Division at Balikpapan. This oil-refining center had long been one of the most important strategic targets in the whole of SWPA.

Kenney mounted some B-24 raids against Balikpapan, but they were not particularly effective. In any case, by July 1945 Balikpapan was no longer a strategic objective. The Japanese had not been able to ship oil from it for nearly six months, but MacArthur wanted to see this place that he and

Kenney had talked about many times. He expected the Japanese to defend it strongly even though its strategic value had gone.

The naval bombardment of Balikpapan produced some of the most spectacular fireworks of the war. Naval shells ignited huge fireballs in the refineries. Storage tanks erupted in sheets of flame. Rivers of fire girdled the low hills as ruptured pipelines gushed oil onto the landscape.

MacArthur gave orders that he wanted a barge alongside the *Baltimore* at 9:30 A.M. to take him ashore. Admiral Daniel Barbey, the commander of the VII Amphibious Force, sent a message back: "[T]he beach is under enemy mortar fire and it is not safe for the commander-in-chief to proceed." MacArthur's reply was "Send barge at once." It was there in less than two minutes.[42]

The Australians were still fighting to secure the beach when MacArthur arrived. He strode across the sand, passing a company of Australian infantrymen in firing positions, shooting at the enemy somewhere ahead. He headed for a nearby ridge to get a better look. When he reached the summit, an Australian major ran up to him and said there was a Japanese machine gun on a nearby hilltop. MacArthur paid no heed. Instead he stood atop the ridge, ostentatiously studying the landscape, hands on hips. Most of the officers around him assumed crouching positions. One terrified colonel simply sat down, while Barbey and a war correspondent ardently kissed the dirt.[43]

MacArthur and the major pored over a map and discussed the tactical situation, studiously ignoring the machine-gun bullets flying past and making their usual ripping-cloth noises. "By the way," he told the Australian officer as he turned to go back down the ridge, "I think it would be a good idea to take out that machine gun before someone gets hurt."[44]

MacArthur returned to Manila two days later. On July 5 he received two important messages. One was that Curtin had died. The other was an "Eyes Only" cable from Marshall. Kenney was already deploying his heavy bombers to Okinawa and would soon start striking targets in Japan. The cable from Marshall informed MacArthur that Kenney's bombers were not under any circumstances to make attacks on four Japanese cities: Kyoto, Kokura, Niigata and Hiroshima. Marshall did not explain why.[45]

In July 1945 the Army was moving hundreds of thousands of men from the European theater to the Pacific and the War Department was monitoring the massive Japanese buildup on Kyushu. Ultra provided a daunting picture of a vast killing ground in preparation. Nearly 5,000 kamikazes were being stockpiled, with enough fuel to provide all of them with a one-way flight. It had cost 50,000 American casualties to take Okinawa from 80,000 Japanese troops. If that was the yardstick, as Marshall feared it was, then seizing Kyushu would bring a casualty toll of 275,000 dead and wounded Americans.[46]

MacArthur, however, did not believe Olympic would ever be launched. While Krueger's Sixth Army staff was studying aerial photographs of southern Kyushu and deciding which divisions to put on which beaches, MacArthur was telling Sutherland, "Dick, don't spend too much time planning for OLYMPIC and CORONET. If you can find a way to drag your feet, do so, because we are never going to have to invade Japan."[47]

That was his conviction even though he still did not know about the development of the atomic bomb. Neither did Kenney. The first successful explosion, in the New Mexico desert, occurred on July 16. Ten days later Brigadier General Thomas F. Farrell arrived in Manila to brief MacArthur on the Manhattan Project and explain why the JCS was sparing the four Japanese cities. Farrell told him the estimated power of the bomb was twenty thousand tons of TNT, that two bombs were ready to be dropped and the missions would be flown from Tinian, the main B-29 base in the Marianas.[48]

General Carl Spaatz, recently appointed to command the strategic air forces in the Pacific, arrived in Manila on July 31 and showed MacArthur the order to drop the bomb. Stimson had managed to get Kyoto, the cultural heart of Japan, taken off the list of cities to be spared. Its place had been taken by Nagasaki. Everything was now in place, said Spaatz.[49]

MacArthur was certain the bomb would knock Japan out of the war. On August 1 he told Kenney the war would be over within two weeks. Five days later the skies were clear over southern Japan. That afternoon MacArthur summoned twenty-five war correspondents to Manila City Hall for a rare off-the-record press conference. He talked about the war, but what was really on his mind was wars to come. He seated himself in a comfortable leather armchair and spoke for an hour. "Atomic disintegration bombs," he said, would magnify the horrors of war ten thousandfold. Technology was in the saddle now. He remembered vividly how, only ten years earlier, the first Pan Am Clipper had arrived in Manila and the flight had been hailed throughout the world as a stupendous achievement. In 1945 hundreds of planes flew across the Pacific every day and no one thought anything of it.

As for Japan, it had been defeated and its rulers knew it. The Soviet Union was poised to enter the war against Japan and add its strength to the fight, a development he welcomed. "Every Russian soldier killed is one less American death." The Soviets would neutralize the two Japanese field armies presently deployed in Manchuria. He did not expect the conflict to last much longer. The correspondents returned to their offices and arrived just as the news clattered over the teletype from Washington that Hiroshima had been destroyed by a single atomic bomb.[50]

Even now, however, the six military officers who were, for all intents and purposes, the government of Japan refused to surrender. They believed that an American invasion would prove so bloody, so ghastly that the United States was sure to offer them better surrender terms. They voted unanimously to continue fighting.

Two days later, on August 8, the Soviets declared war on Japan. Stalin had no intention of being left out when it came to distributing the spoils of victory in the Pacific. On August 9 the second bomb was dropped, obliterating Nagasaki. The Japanese War Cabinet split three to three, and for the first time since 1941 the emperor's opinion was sought. He advised his government to find a way to surrender.[51]

Theodore White, who had interviewed MacArthur in the fall of 1941 and again in Melbourne shortly after MacArthur's arrival in Australia, hastened to Manila to see him once more. He found a different man. This MacArthur was not the roaring, angry, frustrated general he had seen in 1942. Nor was he in a triumphant mood, puffed up with victory. All he wanted to talk about now was the atomic bomb. "White, do you know what this means?"

"What, sir?"

"Men like me are obsolete," he said, pacing with his hands behind his back. "There will be no more wars, White, no more wars."[52]

War was now in the hands of scientists and thinkers, not soldiers. Individual courage: what was that against an atomic bomb? Tactics were irrelevant, infantrymen doomed, artillery was outclassed, armor old hat. MacArthur jokingly remarked to Kenney one day, "The winner of the next war is going to be some 2nd Lieutenant who pulls the string on the A-bomb—and he should be made a full general immediately. The winner of a war deserves four stars."[53]

On August 15 MacArthur was named Supreme Commander for the Allied Powers (SCAP)—the officer, that is, who would take the Japanese surrender. He had no intention of keeping this event private, unlike Eisenhower, who had allowed the Germans to surrender in a dull provincial schoolroom in the early hours of the morning. MacArthur wanted a ceremony, something grand and memorable that all the world could see. The Navy was less than happy about having him take the surrender, but holding the ceremony on the battleship *Missouri* helped salve its wounded pride and was sure to please Harry Truman. The President's daughter, Margaret, had launched this forty-five-thousand-ton behemoth.

It took nearly two weeks for MacArthur, Washington and the Japanese government to work out the details of a ceremonial end to the war. While they were doing so, Thorpe came to see him. He wanted to turn the six thousand collaborators he was currently holding over to the Philippine government. "They'll whitewash them, or they'll just let them out for political reasons. I know that," said Thorpe. "But we will have done our duty." MacArthur agreed with him.[54]

On August 23 all the suspected collaborators were handed over to Osmeña. With that action MacArthur's interest in the Philippines came to an abrupt, anticlimactic end. He was never again involved in the life of that nation, never took much interest in it. If anything, he seemed relieved it was finally over. The Philippines as he had known and loved them no longer existed. This was a new country, setting out on a new course. So was he.

Six days later he boarded his C-54, and Rhoades flew him up to Japan.

Big Number One

MacArthur's dramatic and adventurous life seemed to have reached its apogee. He had worked on it, shaped it, but mainly willed it into existence out of the bric-a-brac provided by fortune. His good looks and high intelligence were pure gifts. On the other hand, the expectation that he would enter his father's profession and exceed his father's achievements was a cruel burden to impose on anyone. Shy and aloof by nature, he had taught himself how to win the devotion of others. Intellectual by inclination, he had nevertheless risen to the top of the most pragmatic of vocations. Imaginative and highly strung, he was not a soldier by temperament but had steeled himself to live with the deafening noise of gunfire, with appalling scenes of human violence, with the groans of men dying around him and the brutal extinction of people in his charge. The cost to his psyche can scarcely be imagined. By the age of sixty-five he had realized to the full the imagined life of action that had filled his childhood dreams at dusty Army posts along the western frontier. And now, at a time of life when nearly all other soldiers eased themselves gently into retirement, MacArthur stood on the threshold of his greatest achievement.

It was a turn of events that he had not planned for and could not have foreseen. Although there was no fixed retirement age for a General of the Army, there was no doubt that the other five-star officers of his generation—Leahy, Marshall, King and Arnold—would retire once the shooting stopped. Besides, for the first time in his long career MacArthur had an implacable enemy in the White House. He could expect no favors from Harry Truman.

Despite the complex tensions that underlay their relationship, MacArthur and Roosevelt had nurtured a wary respect for each other's gifts and larger-than-life personalities. Great actors both, they understood and could savor the art behind the artifice. Their political and personal differences obscured how much they held in common, in large matters as well as small. Their class backgrounds were much the same; both were profoundly influenced by overpowering mothers; from childhood both had been trained for leadership. They were, by blood, distant cousins. They were so much alike the handwriting of the one could be mistaken for the penmanship of the other.

Apart from their American citizenship and their commitment to public service, there was almost nothing in common between MacArthur and Harry S. Truman. Far from it. Truman hated MacArthur more than any man alive. At least, if he loathed anyone more than MacArthur, no evidence of it has ever come to light. There was something slightly strange about Truman's hatred. He was himself a man strongly attracted to military life and immensely proud of his service as an artillery officer in World War I, yet he had nothing but disdain for the most obvious of MacArthur's military attributes—his physical courage. Truman scornfully called MacArthur Dugout Doug. To his commander in chief, the most highly decorated soldier in American history was a contemptible coward. The fact that he held more than a dozen decorations for gallantry and two Purple Hearts counted for nothing. To Truman, everything about MacArthur was fake, including his bravery.[1]

As the President turned his mind to what he should do with Japan once the emperor had surrendered, he raged at the thought of having to deal with "Mr. Prima Donna, Brass Hat, Five Star McArthur [*sic*]. He's worse than the Cabots and the Lodges. They at least talked to one another before they told God what to do. Mc tells God what to do right off. It is a very great pity we have to have stuffed shirts like that in key positions. I don't see why in Hell Roosevelt didn't order Wainwright home and let McArthur be a martyr. . . . We'd have had a real general and a fighting man if we had Wainwright and not a play actor and a bunco man such as we have now."[2]

Truman's anger and contempt had no basis in personal knowledge or experience, although there was no shortage of reasons for Truman to dislike a man he had never met and who had never done him harm. There was the all-too-evident vanity, the tacky props, the repellent adulation of the right-wing Republican press; there was the routing of the Bonus Army; there was Harold Ickes's bottomless fund of stories that MacArthur was a bungler, a fraud and a crook. Even so, the depth of Truman's bitterness toward MacArthur at this point is not easy to explain.

Given the President's implacable hostility, the sensible thing to do was to have MacArthur take the surrender, bring him home, wish him a happy retirement and appoint someone else to run the occupation of Japan, which is what MacArthur half expected. Belying his reputation as a decisive executive and plain-speaking man, Truman shrank from ordering MacArthur home. The general had too many admirers on Capitol Hill and was too popular with the nation at large for the President to contemplate doing so. The political cost was too high. Truman took out his frustration by disparaging MacArthur in private. It did not take long for his views to spread beyond the White House and be absorbed by senior officials, especially in the State Department.

If one thing was certain, it was that the President's scorn would be reciprocated in full measure, for MacArthur was every bit as touchy and excitable as Truman. Already, then, an epic clash was in the making, and when it came, there could be only one result.

On August 14 a deeply reluctant Truman informed MacArthur, "You are hereby designated as the Supreme Commander for the Allied Powers. . . . You will take the necessary steps to require and receive from the duly authorized representatives of the Japanese Emperor, the Japanese Government, and the Japanese Imperial General Headquarters the signed instrument of surrender."[3]

MacArthur was both overjoyed and slightly surprised. He had more or less braced himself for disappointment. Paranoid about the Navy, he half expected King to get his way and for Nimitz to take the surrender. "They haven't gotten my scalp yet!" he exulted to Eichelberger when Truman's message naming him SCAP arrived. He hugged this appointment like a personal triumph within the greater victory.[4]

Japanese representatives flew to Manila to work out the choreography of the formal surrender ceremony with MacArthur's staff and to arrange for the peaceful entry into Japan of American troops. MacArthur recalled Sutherland, who was in the United States on leave and dividing his time between seeing his wife and Captain Elaine Bessemer-Clarke, whom he had managed to get assigned to the San Francisco port of embarkation. Her sudden appearance there aroused curiosity that reached all the way to the White House. Truman demanded to know what was going on, and when he found out, she was ordered back to Australia and discharged from the Army.[5]

Eisenhower had taken the German surrender on French soil, not German, in the middle of the night, and without any press being present, sparing the feelings of the Nazi generals who signed the document. MacArthur thought that was all wrong. He intended to have a ceremony in broad daylight, in Tokyo and covered by the world's media. He did not intend to humiliate the Japanese by demanding they hand over their swords or by holding a victory parade. Unlike Mountbatten, who felt the emperor should be forced to come to Manila and surrender personally to MacArthur, the general felt that kind of thing was passé and would do nothing to reconcile the Japanese to their defeat. What he wanted was something that would provide a dignified end to the war and serve at the same time as the beginning to the occupation.[6]

On August 29 MacArthur flew to Okinawa aboard the *Bataan*. Next day he received further instructions: He would not only take the surrender but supervise the demilitarization and demobilization of Japan. What would happen after that was uncertain. Eisenhower had taken the German surrender, but once Germany had been disarmed, he returned to Washington. The same might happen to MacArthur, although he spoke and acted as though he intended to remain in Japan for a long time.

From Okinawa he flew on to Atsugi Airfield, forty miles southwest of Tokyo, escorted by two B-17s. One contained Kenney, the other Spaatz. Kenney had chosen Atsugi for its concrete runways and had already flown in an advance party of aviation engineers, weathermen and soldiers from the 11th Airborne Division.[7]

MacArthur spent much of the flight in an excited state. He paced the aisle of his C-54 and kept ducking into the cockpit to talk to Dusty Rhoades, but he was napping when volcanic Mount Fujiyama came into view. Whitney nudged him awake. "Fuji—how beautiful!" MacArthur murmured, even though the mountaintop was seasonally denuded of its usual crown of glistening ice and snow. Bereft of its glory, to some of those with him it seemed a drab, anticlimactic sight that was faintly menacing, like a sign of greater disappointments to come.[8]

Kenney and other officers had armed themselves with shoulder holsters and Colt .45 pistols. They were apprehensive at the thought of setting foot on enemy territory, of entering a land containing three million fully armed Japanese troops and only four thousand American paratroopers. MacArthur, however, was unconcerned. He knew just what the Japanese troops would do: nothing.

Back in 1905, when he was serving in Japan as his father's aide, the Japanese Army had been stricken with cholera. Military doctors had concocted some pills for the troops to fight off the disease and a Japanese general soberly informed Lieutenant MacArthur that every soldier would take three pills a day. The lieutenant couldn't help laughing. The general was irritated. "Why are you laughing?"

"If American troops were given pills and told to take them three times a day," explained MacArthur, "they would throw them away at the first opportunity."

That was just what the Japanese soldiers did. The medics tried again, but this time the pills were distributed in boxes which read, "The emperor requests that these pills be taken three times a day." The pills were duly consumed as directed. The emperor had spoken.

So now, forty years later, he knew what would happen: nothing. The Tennō's command—the "Voice of the Crane"—had been heard by Japan's soldiers once again.[9]

When his plane touched down at Atsugi, Eichelberger was waiting to welcome him to Japan. "Bob," said MacArthur, "this is the payoff!" He was probably the best American orator—not public speaker but orator in the old-fashioned bloviating style—of his time, yet MacArthur was not much of an extempore speaker. This flat, uninspired utterance, the limply understated counterpoint to a moment of heightened emotion, was typical. Oratory apart, MacArthur was as banal as the rest of us when we find ourselves slightly unprepared and acting almost like unexpected guests at the defining moments of our lives. "This is the payoff" plodded its flatfooted way into books about MacArthur along with his dull remark to Sutherland when he returned to the Philippines: "Believe it or not, Dick, we're here!"[10]

MacArthur and his staff were driven the twenty miles to the New Grand Hotel in Yokohama without a military escort. A large, square structure, the hotel had somehow survived B-29 raids almost intact, while the city around it was burned and blasted into ruins. MacArthur gazed somberly at the devastation. It was a stirring, melancholy sight. He saw in his mind's eye the fleets of B-29s that had wrought this destruction but reflected that without their attacks, Japan would not have surrendered. Still, there was something shocking about seeing the results at street level. Here was the true horror of war, of total war. The people who lived on these streets were not soldiers but civilians, many of them women, like Jean, and children, like Arthur. It was a thought that made him uncomfortable and slightly depressed.[11]

Over the next two days MacArthur wrote the two speeches he intended to deliver, drew up three proclamations that he would issue once the surrender had taken place and informed field commanders throughout the Far East not to accept any local surrenders by the Japanese until after the ceremony on the *Missouri*. Camps holding Allied prisoners of war would remain under Japanese control, but food and medicine were dropped into many of them by parachute. While release was postponed for nearly all the Allied POWs, MacArthur ordered that two people—Jonathan Wainwright and the British officer who had surrendered Singapore to the Japanese, Lieutenant General Arthur E. Percival—be brought to him.[12]

They arrived the evening of September 1. MacArthur and nearly a score of Allied officers were seated at a large table in the private dining room in the hotel basement, about to tuck into steaks that the Japanese had astonishingly produced, when Wainwright entered the room, leaning heavily on a stout walnut cane with a large curved handle—a cane that MacArthur had given him in Manila. Percival was only a few steps behind. There were gasps of astonishment, and everyone in the room stood up. It was a gesture of surprise and respect, but one propelled by raw emotion too.

MacArthur turned around, rose from his place and threw his arms around this lopsided skeleton dressed as a man. Wainwright's hair, what wisps remained of it, was white. His head, little more than a skull tautly covered in yellowing rice paper, seemed too large for the pathetically sticklike body. His hollow-cheeked face and deeply sunk eyes were lambent with suffering and dulled by a numbing fear. For nearly four years he had stared at prison walls and wondered how he would defend himself at his court-martial, asked himself whether he could survive more imprisonment, this time at Leavenworth, for defying MacArthur's orders and surrendering all of the Philippines to the Japanese.

MacArthur hugged Wainwright tenderly, stepped back and held him by the shoulders while he looked closely at the revenant's otherworldly visage—"The emotion registered on that gaunt face still haunts me," he wrote nearly twenty years later—then enfolded him in his arms once more. "Jim, Jim," MacArthur whispered hoarsely, using Wainwright's cadet nickname. "I'm glad to see you." The eyes of both men filled with tears. The other officers at the table applauded, breaking the tension, then sat down fumbling for their khaki, government-issue handkerchiefs.[13]

Once the high tide of emotion had passed, MacArthur, Wainwright and Percival sat and chatted for more than an hour. MacArthur offered Wainwright command of a corps, an offer that gave Wainwright his first realization that there would be no court-martial. In fact, although neither of them knew at the time, Stimson had already revived the question of giving Wainwright the Medal of Honor.

Marshall had first proposed this back in 1942, after the fall of Corregidor, but MacArthur had vehemently opposed it, claiming that Wainwright had not fought effectively and had exceeded his authority when he ordered men throughout the Philippines to surrender to the Japanese. He had already given Wainwright the DSC, but to go all the way to the Medal of Honor, he asserted, would strike at the morale of those brave men who had gone on fighting rather than quit.

MacArthur also dropped heavy hints that Wainwright was unsuitable for such an award but did not say why. That added an element of mystery to his message but also made it seem cheap and pretentious. What he was trying—ineptly—to hint at, but was unwilling to state explicitly, was that Wainwright was an alcoholic (and keeping this out of the newspapers was to prove a headache for the Army until Wainwright died). Now, however, such issues were irrelevant. Wainwright would get the Medal of Honor he richly deserved, not only for the stoical way he had conducted the tragic and inevitable endgame on Bataan but for the manly way he had resisted Japanese efforts to break his spirit during nearly four years of captivity.[14]

The morning of September 2 MacArthur rode a Navy destroyer to the *Missouri,* anchored eighteen miles out in Tokyo Bay. The ceremony would be held near the number two main turret, on the starboard side of the ship, at a large table covered with a green rug. The American flag flown above the Capitol on December 7, 1941, flew now from the main yard of the battleship. The thirty-one-star flag under which Commodore Matthew Perry had brought his fleet of seven black warships into Edo Bay in 1853 and forcibly opened Japan to the West was draped over a bulkhead near the table.

At 8:50 A.M., MacArthur arrived and was piped aboard. He walked past the serried ranks of nearly 150 generals and admirals formed into lines and squares on the battleship's deck and went into the captain's cabin. Minutes later the Japanese delegation arrived: four diplomats, led by Japan's one-legged Foreign Minister Mamoru Shigemitsu, and seven soldiers, led by Army Chief of Staff General Yoshijiro Umezu. Three of the diplomats wore frock coats, striped pants and silk top hats, but one incongruously had chosen to wear a crumpled white linen suit. The soldiers were in unpressed uniforms and scuffed, unpolished boots, like adolescents trying to defy and annoy their stern, boringly conventional parents.

As they came aboard, the Japanese had to be disarmed. They handed over a formidable armory of samurai swords and ceremonial daggers for safekeeping before stoically shuffling into position.[15] Shigemitsu lurched forward in obvious pain from his badly fitting artificial leg. A Korean had tried to assassinate him in Shanghai in the early 1930s with a bomb. His life had been saved by a Canadian doctor (no Chinese doctor could have treated him without being murdered) named Llewellyn Cosgrave. To his amazement, he saw Cosgrave facing him barely fifty feet away, as the representative of Canada. Shigemitsu broke into a delighted smile.

Alas, poor Cosgrave! He was as unsteady on his feet as Shigemitsu. Either the prospect of seeing his former patient again was too much for him or he was unnerved by the grandeur of the occasion, but at all events Cosgrave was drunk.[16]

MacArthur's most important performance was finally at hand, and his emotions were stronger than he was. When feelings run too deep for words, the body finds a way, in blood or tears, excrement or vomit, to express the true intensity beneath the civilized shell. MacArthur was bent over in the captain's head noisily throwing up his half-digested breakfast.[17]

While he washed his face and shook himself into his normal ramrod-straight posture, the ship's loudspeaker system tinnily carried a brief invocation by the *Missouri*'s chaplain to the deepest recesses of the battleship. When the chaplain finished speaking, a phonograph began cranking out "The Star-Spangled Banner." The music faded away. MacArthur put on his stained and tattered field marshal's cap, its gold braid now so dulled it looked like lead, and stepped out onto the quarterdeck. It was 8:58.[18]

Two minutes later he launched into his brief opening address. He held a single sheet of paper in his right hand, which trembled visibly. His knees shook so violently a small gale seemed to be troubling his well-worn khaki pants. Yet the timbre of his voice when he spoke was as firm and resonantly confident as ever. Willpower again.[19] "We are gathered here, the representatives of the major warring powers, to conclude a solemn agreement whereby peace may be restored. The issues [of the war] are not for our discussion or debate. Nor is it for us . . . to meet in a spirit of malice, distrust or hatred. But rather is it for us, both victors and vanquished, to rise to that higher dignity which alone befits the sacred purposes we are about to serve. . . ."

Then, giving notice that this ceremony marked not so much the ending of the war as the beginning of the occupation of Japan, he declared, "As Supreme Commander for the Allied Powers, I announce it is my firm purpose . . . to proceed to the discharge of my responsibilities with justice and tolerance, while taking all necessary dispositions to insure that the terms of surrender are fully, promptly and faithfully complied with." He looked directly at Shigemitsu and Umezu. "I now invite the representatives of the Emperor of Japan and the Japanese government and the Japanese Imperial General Headquarters to sign the instrument of surrender at the places indicated."[20]

Two copies of the instrument of surrender lay open on the table. One, bound in dark green leather, was America's copy, certain to be displayed. The other, cheaply bound in black canvas, was Japan's, just as certain to be hidden in a vault somewhere. Shigemitsu approached in a state of bewilderment, evidently overcome by emotion. He removed his silk top hat and his white gloves, put them on the table, picked up his hat, looked despairingly around and swayed as if he might fall over at any moment. "Sutherland," barked MacArthur, "show him where to sign!"[21]

After Umezu had signed on behalf of the Japanese military, MacArthur called on Wainwright and Percival to step forward, sat at the table and signed the English-language copy, writing "Douglas" with one pen, "Mac" with another and "Arthur" with a third. He then performed the same orthographic ballet on the Japanese copy. Six pens in all—one for Wainwright, one for Percival, one for West Point, one for the Naval Academy, one for the National Archives and a small red one with "Jean" inscribed in gold letters along the barrel.[22]

MacArthur signed on behalf of all the Allied nations united against Japan. Nimitz then came forward and signed on behalf of the United States, followed by representatives from China, the United Kingdom, the Soviet Union, Australia, Canada, France, the Netherlands and New Zealand. Cosgrave was up to the challenge of signing the English-language copy on behalf of Canada, but when he turned to the Japanese version, he missed a line and signed on behalf of France.[23]

Once the ritual of signing was finished, MacArthur stepped to the microphone near the table for the last time. "Let us pray that peace be now restored to the world and that God will preserve it always. These proceedings are closed."

The Japanese bowed stiffly, took up their swords and daggers and departed. As they transferred to the destroyer waiting to carry them back to shore, the sun, unseen since MacArthur's arrival in Japan, broke through the clouds over Tokyo Bay, burnishing the gray ships and murky waters. From the east came a tremendous roar, a sound capable of bringing terror to the heart of any Japanese—the awesome throbbing noise of four hundred silver B-29s. They had flown up from the Marianas to pass over the *Missouri* at the appointed hour. And behind, above and around the formations of huge bombers rose fifteen hundred dark blue Navy fighters, swift, deadly and beautiful. The shadows of their passing wings danced triumphantly black on black across the charred carcass of Tokyo.[24]

Through the long roll of conquered nations forced to endure the presence of an occupying army ran a common thread: bitter resentment. About all that MacArthur had to guide him as he embarked on the occupation of Japan was his own overly idealistic conception of what the occupation's aims ought to be. Just how he was going to realize them, he could not say. The instructions he had so far received on how to rule Japan were ambiguous on all the big questions and fuzzy on most of the little ones.

Japan's right to govern itself was left a mystery. Was the country a sovereign power any longer? What role, if any, would the emperor play? The Japanese had been assured that the position of the emperor would be retained. That concession had been a powerful inducement to get them to surrender, but the emperor's place in governing Japan was vague. "The authority of the Emperor and the Japanese Government will be subject to the Supreme Commander," MacArthur was informed. That made it seem that he would tell the Japanese leaders what to do, and they had to do it. Yet "The Supreme Commander will exercise his authority through the

Japanese governmental machinery and agencies, including the Emperor";
that suggested that he had to secure their cooperation.[25]

Interpretations and clarifications could, and no doubt would, be worked
out, but in the meantime MacArthur had to get the machinery of the occupation into gear. One of the first things he did after reaching Japan was to
draw up three proclamations. The first announced the installation of what
amounted to military government and made English the official language
of that government. The second introduced military courts and punishments up to and including the death penalty for Japanese who resisted the
occupation. The third declared that military currency—or scrip—would be
legal tender in Japan. MacArthur signed all three and ordered they be
issued at 10:00 A.M. on September 3.

When the Japanese Cabinet learned of the three proclamations, its
members were shocked and horrified. Shigemitsu went to see MacArthur
before the proclamations were published and begged him not to issue
them. If military government was introduced, he warned MacArthur, "it
may well be that utter confusion will result." This was a diplomat's way of
saying that if the emperor was brutally elbowed aside like this, public
order was going to break down. In that case the Americans could find
themselves having to take Japan street by street from three million
Japanese soldiers, surrender ceremony or no surrender ceremony.

Anyway, Shigemitsu assured him, there was no need for military government. All MacArthur had to do was tell the Japanese Cabinet what his
policies were. If the government then somehow failed to carry out his
wishes as he desired, he had the power to direct it to do so. This was
MacArthur's first indication that the Japanese were more than willing to
follow where he chose to lead, so long as he treated the emperor with
respect.

The way to make the occupation succeed had just been handed to him.
He was not going to have to force the occupation on the Japanese; they
were already prepared to accept it, provided he worked through the government they already had. It was a bargain no one had foreseen and no sensible person would refuse. For ultimately it was not he or the Allies, the
State Department or the Pentagon that would make the occupation work. It
was the Japanese. Either that, or they would make sure it proved a disaster,
a continuation of the war by other means. Here, then, in Shigemitsu's
demand that he kill these three proclamations were both a threat and a
promise.

MacArthur chose to ignore the threat and pocket the promise. "While
the government must fulfill its duties," he told Shigemitsu sternly, "the
Supreme Commander has no intention of making slaves of the Japanese
people." He turned to Sutherland and ordered him to scrap the three

proclamations. Shortly after this the Joint Chiefs sent him a clarification of his authority that amounted to approval for his decision to allow the Japanese to implement occupation policy, provided "that such an arrangement produces satisfactory results."[26]

The Joint Chiefs soon followed up with a long, two-part directive that created the basis of occupation policy for the rest of MacArthur's time in Japan, JCS 1380/15. This document runs to nearly eight thousand words and covers everything of importance in reforming Japan. MacArthur's earlier instructions, which were drafted by the State Department, were overtaken by the new directive, which, crucially, was worded as an order.[27] Within GHQ SCAP it was treated like Scripture. Nearly everything MacArthur did was explicitly supported by reference to the relevant section, subsection or paragraph in this directive, from trust-busting Japanese business to giving women the vote.[28]

The military way is to give a commander an objective, provide the means for achieving it and leave it up to him to figure out how he is going to do it. That is what the JCS did with Japan. The MacArthur publicity machine in Tokyo and the adoring right-wing press in the United States, however, made it appear that no sparrow could fall dead from a Japanese tree, its claws forever curled, without MacArthur's knowing about it and probably authorizing its demise in advance. The reverential attitude of the bulk of the Japanese, who elevated him to the status of a minor god, only seemed to confirm the legend of MacArthur the omnipotent.

Two weeks after his meeting with Shigemitsu, MacArthur moved his headquarters into the six-story Dai Ichi (Big Number One) Insurance Building in downtown Tokyo, one of the few large structures still intact. The building faced the outer moat of the imperial palace. Symbolically, at least, MacArthur was looking down on the emperor, even if the palace was hidden behind a thick screen of trees.

The same day he moved SCAP headquarters into the Dai Ichi Building, the Japanese prime minister, Baron Naruhiko Higashikuni, accepted Shigemitsu's resignation. Deeply humiliated by his prominent role in the establishment of the occupation of his country, Shigemitsu had had enough. He was replaced as foreign minister by an elderly career diplomat who was fluent in English, Shigeru Yoshida.

On September 20 Yoshida went to meet MacArthur for the first time and to sound him out on the position of the emperor. MacArthur's sixth-floor office was not particularly large, and it had no view of anything much. His aides had splendid offices at the front of the building, with magnificent views over the grounds of the imperial palace. He had only one window, and that faced the blank gray walls of an inner courtyard that echoed the clatter and din from a mess hall on the floor below.

His choice of this unprepossessing room seemed perverse to some visitors and staff members, but in its self-conscious austerity it was intended to say that here, beneath the panoply of great power, is a simple man at heart. It was like the iron cot that he had kept in the basement of the supe's house at West Point and may actually have slept on a few times as a reminder of the hardships being endured by soldiers in the field. His Dai Ichi office was like his earlier offices. There was the usual large desk, free of papers and telephone, a portrait of Lincoln, a portrait of Washington, a few family photographs, several chairs, two leather couches for visitors. It could have been Melbourne or Brisbane or Manila.

Yoshida was politically conservative, quick-witted and morally courageous. He had vigorously opposed the rise of the military clique that had plunged Japan into war. He spent the war years in a kind of internal exile, shut out from government and untainted by the crimes his country committed. Short, chubby and dynamic, he was sometimes called a pocket Churchill, a compliment he gladly accepted. "Yes," he cheerfully agreed, "but one made in Japan!"[29]

Speaking a quaint, Dickensian brand of English, Yoshida welcomed MacArthur to Tokyo. He had also come, he added, to convey the emperor's cordial regards and to ask if there was any prospect of their meeting anytime soon.

MacArthur's staff had raised this question a short while before. They advised him to summon the emperor to a meeting. That would show the Japanese who was the boss. MacArthur flatly disagreed. "To do so would make a martyr of the Emperor in their eyes. No, I shall wait and in time the Emperor will voluntarily come to see me."[30] To Yoshida, however, he blandly remarked that his position did not allow him to pay a call on the emperor. Did that mean, Yoshida inquired, that the supreme commander was expecting the emperor to call on him?

"It would give me the greatest pleasure to see the Emperor," MacArthur replied, but added that he did not want to embarrass him in any way. Once this matter had been settled, MacArthur got up and started to pace. He could not resist giving Yoshida the benefits of his reflections on Japan's strategy in the war, which he described as being suicidal. He then turned his mind to the challenge of disarming and demobilizing millions of troops and militia, rebuilding Japan's devastated cities and introducing democracy to the people.

Yoshida watched him stride back and forth behind the desk with intense curiosity. He did not mind MacArthur's theatrical manner. A diplomat sees all kinds of idiosyncratic behavior in the course of a long career. But all this pacing reminded him of visiting the zoo, and he started to laugh. MacArthur was puzzled. What did the foreign minister find so amusing? "I feel," he said, "as if I'm listening to a lecture inside a lion's cage!" MacArthur glared at him for a moment, then diplomatically laughed too.[31]

A week later a cortege of black limousines pulled up at the American Embassy, which MacArthur had taken over as his residence. The emperor alighted, followed by a dozen courtiers. No emperor had made a call on a commoner in twenty-five hundred years of imperial history. Hirohito was dressed in a morning coat and striped pants. MacArthur greeted him in his work clothes—faded suntans, no jacket, no tie—and led him into the embassy's large and gloomy drawing room.

A fire was burning in the huge fireplace, in an attempt to provide a welcoming atmosphere, even though it was a warm day. The two men sat on a davenport near the fireplace surrounded by overstuffed silk-covered furniture, and MacArthur attempted to put Hirohito at ease. He recalled meeting the emperor's father forty years earlier, at the end of the Russo-Japanese War. He offered his guest a cigarette, and while Hirohito—a lifelong nonsmoker but ready to make a sacrifice—held it in a shaking hand, MacArthur carefully lit it for him.

They were alone, save for the emperor's interpreter. This was another courteous gesture; MacArthur chose not to have his own interpreter present and to rely on Hirohito's.[32] And alone so long as we don't count Jean and Colonel Roger Egeberg, who had secreted themselves behind the heavy draperies that framed a balcony overlooking the room and were peeking down on this historic meeting, hardly daring to breathe.[33]

MacArthur assumed that Hirohito had come to make a personal plea that he not be tried as a war criminal. The institution of emperor had been guaranteed, but this did not exempt Hirohito personally from standing trial for signing the imperial rescript that declared war on the United States.

Once the initial pleasantries were concluded, Hirohito wasted no time in telling MacArthur why he had been so eager to meet him. He was prepared, he declared, to accept complete responsibility for Japan's actions— from Pearl Harbor to the most unspeakable atrocities. The Allied Powers were free to put it all on his shoulders and impose whatever punishment they thought fit.

MacArthur was astonished. It was the last thing he had expected to hear. Hirohito's full acceptance of responsibility for his nation's misdeeds disarmed him as nothing else could.[34] He responded by speaking for twenty minutes on the devastating power of airpower and atomic bombs. It might have been thought that no one appreciated these additions to the armory of mass destruction more than the Japanese, but the emperor tactfully avoided the subject. Perhaps it was simply too painful.

Humanity, MacArthur reflected portentously, could now destroy itself. The next big war would be the last. The responsibility of political and military leaders in this terrifying new age was not to think of how to win wars but of how to guide their countries toward peace. He congratulated the emperor on taking the steps that had ended the war, thereby sparing his country from total destruction.[35]

Hirohito assured MacArthur that he had not wanted the war. He had grieved when his country attacked the United States, but he had had to accept the advice of his ministers. "Well, why didn't you, at a certain point, just tell your ministers that this couldn't be done?" asked MacArthur, puzzled.

"But I'm a constitutional monarch," replied Hirohito. "If I am advised by my prime minister and the other ministers that this must be done, I must do it, even if I don't like it." MacArthur was staggered. In all his vast reading on Japan nothing had prepared him for this revelation of total imperial impotence. Respected scholars still argue that the emperor had some, if severely limited, room for maneuver.[36]

Whatever the truth of the matter, MacArthur was convinced of his sincerity. Hirohito concluded by saying he and his people alike accepted the war had been lost. All his efforts would henceforth be dedicated to the creation of a peaceful Japan.

MacArthur replied that he would be grateful to receive the emperor's advice at any time, then turned to some immediate political problems. Maybe a different Cabinet was needed to oversee the demobilization of the Japanese military. And abolishing the existing army staff could be complicated. Hirohito agreed with him on both points.[37]

They concluded their first meeting like ordinary people, with some trite observations about the weather. MacArthur then summoned his official photographer, Major Gaetano Faillace, to take a photograph of the two of them together. Faillace had them stand in front of a table near a window. MacArthur put his hands on his hips, and Faillace took three photographs. After that MacArthur escorted the emperor to the embassy's front door.[38]

After the cortege pulled away for the short drive back to the palace, MacArthur turned to Jean, who had reappeared from her hiding place in the drawing room. "I was born a democrat, and I was reared as a liberal." He sighed. "But I tell you I find it painful to see a man once so high and mighty brought down so low."[39]

Only one of the three photographs proved to be any good, and MacArthur ordered it published in the Japanese newspapers two days later. It showed him towering over Hirohito, who looked like his valet. To millions of Japanese that black-and-white image came as a shock. It immortalized for them, as the surrender aboard the *Missouri* ceremony immortalized for Americans, the face of the victor and the face of the vanquished, showed beyond all argument just who had the power and who did not.

Whatever personal sympathy MacArthur felt for Hirohito, this one photograph did more than anything else to make the Japanese cease to regard their emperor as a god and to look on him as MacArthur wanted and needed them to do, as a man, fully as mortal and as fallible as themselves.[40]

There could be no question, though, of treating him like a Japanese war leader. Dozens of Japanese were indicted for war crimes, and the Australian government was eager to see Hirohito join them. Willoughby agreed with the Australians. He called Hirohito "This modern Genghis Khan."[41] MacArthur refused to consider it. First, he was personally convinced that Hirohito did not have the power to prevent atrocities, even if he had known about them. Second, it was too risky. According to a memo submitted to MacArthur by Brigadier General Bonner Fellers, his expert on Japanese psychology, "If the emperor was tried for war crimes the governmental structure would collapse and a general uprising would be inevitable. . . . The period of occupation would be prolonged and we would have alienated the Japanese."[42]

The question arose again, however, toward the end of the first Tokyo trial of Japanese war criminals. There were rumors that Hirohito was going to abdicate, as a way of expiating his own sense of guilt for the war. MacArthur's attitude was firm. "I will not allow him to abdicate," he told a Canadian diplomat. "I will require him to stay as a matter of duty." And when the emperor raised the matter directly with him, that was exactly what MacArthur did. His refusal to have the emperor put on trial did more to ensure the success of the occupation, said Yoshida, than anything else could ever have done.[43]

On September 8 MacArthur was driven from the New Grand Hotel into Tokyo, to reclaim the American Embassy and make it his home. That called for a ceremony, a symbolic reconquest combined with reconsecration of this one spot of American territory landlocked on Japanese soil.

When his car drew up at 11:00 A.M., an honor guard ringed the charming lily pond in front of the chancellery. The soldiers proudly held aloft the guidons and regimental battle flags of the 11th Airborne Division. An Army Air Forces bomb had blown away much of the chancellery's roof, but a wobbly flagpole had been erected by Army engineers in readiness for today's ceremony.

MacArthur and the division commander, Major General William C. Chase, led Halsey, Eichelberger, Sutherland and various generals and admirals in a brisk short walk up the slight incline to the front of the chancellery. "General Eichelberger," MacArthur commanded in a loud, clear voice, "have our country's flag unfurled and in Tokyo's sun let it wave in its full glory as a symbol of hope for the oppressed and as a harbinger of victory for the right."

An Army chaplain pronounced an invocation. The guard of honor was ordered, "Present arms!" and as the same American flag that had been flown over the *Missouri* during the surrender ceremony rode slowly up the flag-pole, the 11th Airborne band threw itself into "The Star-Spangled Banner."[44]

The emotional significance of the moment gripped the assembled generals and admirals by the throats as powerful memories flashed unbidden through their minds: the early defeats, the deaths of friends, the gut-wrenching fear, the haunting sense of loss, the crushing sense of relief when the war finally ended. Now this. Right hands raised stiffly in salute, many tried to fight off the tears welling in their eyes. It is never seemly for officers to cry in front of the men—bad for morale, looks like weakness, got to set a good example, I'm not a kid anymore—but goddammit, sometimes it happens.[45]

After the flag-raising ceremony MacArthur walked into the chancellery with Halsey and Lieutenant General Barney Giles, the deputy commanding general of the AAF. The walls were pockmarked with shrapnel scars, and there was rubble piled in corners. There were shattered pipes and pools of standing water, cracked windows and damaged furniture. "Now, Bill, aren't you ashamed?" said MacArthur, pretending to admonish Halsey.

"Don't blame the Navy for this," replied Halsey. "Blame the 20th Air Force." He pointed at Giles. "Blame Barney there."[46]

The chancellery was the embassy's principal office building. At the top of the hill was the main building within the embassy compound, the ambassador's residence, which was known as the Big House, a name usually applied to state penitentiaries. It remained much as the last U.S. ambassador, the aristocratic and erudite Joseph C. Grew, had left it in 1941. He, like his predecessors, had made the residence comfortable in the overstuffed but understated manner of the Anglo-American upper class and furnished it with many of his own antiques.

Days after MacArthur moved into the Big House, he sent for Jean and Arthur to fly up from Manila. MacArthur greeted his family at the airport accompanied only by a single unarmed aide. As they drove into the city without a guard of any kind, Jean grew apprehensive. The place seemed spooky. There was hardly anyone on the streets, and an air of menace seemed to scream from the shattered buildings. "Is this safe?" she asked. He smiled down at her. "Of course it's safe." She remained on tenterhooks despite this reassurance until the car drove up to the gates of the embassy. At the sight of American MPs, tall and immaculate in white helmets and gloves, she let out a sigh of relief and finally relaxed.[47]

Reunited with Jean and Arthur, MacArthur resumed his daily routine much as before, but with some Big Number One refinements. Up at 7:00 he got into his dressing gown and breakfasted with Arthur and Jean. After breakfast he did some calisthenics in his bedroom, watched with rapt attention by Arthur's three dogs, Blackie, Brownie and Yuki, who seemed to take this morning ritual as seriously as he did. After an hour or so of reading the newspapers, he headed for the Dai Ichi around 10:30 A.M.[48]

He rode in his prewar Cadillac V-12 sedan, which had been brought from the Philippines. There were two fender flags, one Old Glory, the other a red flag with five silver stars, and a license plate reading "1." The ride to the Dai Ichi covered less than two miles through the heart of Tokyo. Traffic along the route was stopped, and all traffic lights between the embassy and the headquarters turned green in his favor. With the car traveling at the legal speed limit, the journey would not have taken more than ten minutes. MacArthur took a magisterial twenty. And the general seemed to love every moment, comfortably seated on the faded gray upholstery at the back, contentedly humming to himself, looking out on a city that he could see slowly but inexorably coming back to life. His aides worried that his "dead-march" progress through the streets was making it easier for somebody to try bumping him off. Assassination was as much an element in Japan's politics as in America's, but MacArthur never gave it a thought. For a while he was escorted to work by a jeep carrying a couple of MPs, but he never liked being escorted, and after a few months he ordered the practice stopped.

The next day his car broke down on the way to work. The aide riding with him flagged down a passing jeep driven by a young corporal and ordered him to take MacArthur to the Dai Ichi. The corporal looked terrified. "You worried, son?" MacArthur asked.

"Yes, sir. You don't know my major."

"Do you think it would help if I gave you an excuse?"

"Yes, sir, if you'll write it. Otherwise, nobody—and especially the major—is going to believe my excuse for being late." MacArthur wrote out a message to the major and thereafter submitted to being escorted again.[49]

There was a street sweeper who was normally to be seen sweeping part of the route the general followed each morning. Whenever he noticed the Cadillac approaching, he turned his back. That was what a commoner did when an emperor passed by. MacArthur's democratic instincts were increasingly irritated by this ritual, and one morning he told his driver to stop the car and got out, followed by an aide who spoke Japanese. He had the aide tell the furiously bowing street sweeper that in America the custom when two people met was for them to face each other and say hello.

Thereafter, when the Cadillac approached him, the Japanese stopped sweeping, shouldered his broom on his left shoulder and threw a snappy salute with his right hand. MacArthur returned the salute with a smile and a friendly wave. One small step for democracy.[50]

Once he reached the Dai Ichi, he could count on there being a couple of hundred Japanese on hand, intensely curious and almost blushingly respectful. He loved that too. He repeated the journey in reverse at 1:30 for lunch with Jean. He napped for an hour in midafternoon, then between 4:00 and 5:00 made a stately return to the Dai Ichi, where he would remain until he had cleared the paperwork on his desk, which often kept him in his office until 9:00 P.M. Dinner usually concluded with coffee, chocolate candy and a Philippine cigar.

Occasionally he had a dinner guest, usually someone on his staff, like his counterintelligence chief, Brigadier General Elliott Thorpe. Army counter-intelligence was monitoring Japanese politicians and other people. Phones were being tapped, mail was being opened and informers were being hired. Thorpe had the dirt on countless figures in Japanese public life and, it seems a fair bet, on many of the Allied soldiers and diplomats assigned to Tokyo. Over dinner Thorpe passed on interesting tidbits of what was really going in behind the façade of propriety. MacArthur was fascinated, but one night some particularly interesting item made him burst into laughter. "Thorpe, I'd hate to have your conscience!"[51]

After dinner he and Jean watched a movie. MacArthur would don a monogrammed silk smoking jacket given to him by his thirty-man honor guard and seat himself in the middle of the front row in a wicker rocking chair, light up a Tabacalera corona from the Philippines and watch yet another film about cowboys, Indians and the Army on the frontier. The Old West of the movies bears no resemblance to the reality. It is a sanitized, glorified, impossibly heroic fake, a confection drenched in poignant trea-cle—and he, an Army brat reared on those dusty posts, could have given a lecture series on how contrived and phony it all was. But no. What was real to him *was* the romance, the adventure, the numinous beneath and beyond dull realities. It was the meaning that mattered, of America as an epic.[52]

His other relaxation was following the progress of the West Point foot-ball team, which had been at its absolute peak during the war, for obvious reasons. MacArthur desperately hoped that this was the turning point, that Army would become a perennial powerhouse, like Notre Dame or Ohio State. Every Monday during the football season he spent hours studying newspaper accounts of Saturday's game. Once he had analyzed them, he wrote out a long telegram, or an even longer special delivery letter, to Red Blaik, telling him where the team had gone wrong and needed improve-ment. "Let's get these things straightened out!" he wrote.[53]

Before 1948 every player was expected to play both offense and defense. A more liberal substitution rule changed that, to MacArthur's immense delight. Players could now specialize. He wrote to Blaik in some excitement, "It makes the game more and more in accord with the development of the tactics of actual combat." The following year he sent an inspirational message to the football team at the start of the new season: "From the Far East I send you one single thought, one sole idea—written in red on every beachhead from Australia to Tokyo—there is *no* substitute for victory!"[54]

He did not go to parties, official banquets or almost any other social occasion if he could avoid it, and he nearly always could. Visiting dignitaries were invited to a large lunch at the embassy, seated next to or near him, regaled with his courtesy, his charm, his large fund of amusing stories, for an hour, and that was as far as he would go in dining with them. He made no secret of the fact that he considered this side of his duties a great bore, and he was probably right.

Arthur was nearly eight when he reached Tokyo. MacArthur informed his staff that his son was not going to attend school but would continue to be educated by the redoubtable Mrs. Gibbons. He insisted that the boy would live a "normal" life, that he was not going to be force-fed and turned into a genius. MacArthur's idea of a normal life for a growing boy was so bizarre it was weird.

Breakfast was the only time of the day Arthur spent with his father, who was too old and too busy to do many of the things a boy needs a father for: to teach him how to hit a curveball, take him fishing, play catch, put up a basketball hoop over the garage door, help him with his homework, pick him up when he falls down and give him a man he can relate to rather than a god he can worship from afar. Arthur rarely saw him at lunch and was in bed by the time the general came home for dinner.

Arthur was deprived not only of his father's time but of friends his own age. For the first year or so he was in Tokyo there were hardly any American children for him to play with. Later, as officers assigned to SCAP brought their families to Japan, children were taken to the embassy to keep him company at weekends. But while they went to school, he was privately tutored. His father was their fathers' boss, and they were taken to him as if they existed for his amusement. It's obvious they would be told to be careful about what they said about life at home, not to repeat *anything* they had heard Daddy say, to keep themselves clean, be polite at all times and never, under any circumstances, to lay a hand on the little prince. Careers were at stake here. A real boy would have gone once, then refused to go back.[55]

Most of Arthur's playmates were not children but colonels. He was spared the struggle for acceptance and the challenge of making new friends. This was not remotely like MacArthur's own childhood. When he was a boy, he got into fights and went weeping home to Pinky. His mother studied his cuts and bruises, decided nothing was broken and told him to go out and fight some more until he'd won.[56]

Had he been a father at an earlier age, MacArthur might have done the same with his own son. Instead, if Arthur was bruised or scratched, his father got frantic. And when the boy broke his arm ice-skating shortly after moving to Tokyo, MacArthur was hysterical. During Arthur's stay in the hospital he visited the lad five times a day, armed guards were posted, the hospital was ordered to take dozens of X rays—which MacArthur studied intently—and SCAP duties were put on hold. "The General simply would not keep his appointments and could not do his work," said his military secretary. Or, as another staff member put it, "The general went crazy." After Arthur recovered, he was never permitted to go ice-skating again.[57]

With no close friends his own age, he was surrounded by adults, accompanied everywhere by adults and had to act like a miniature adult. Nearly all children have secret lives their parents know not of. It is an essential part of growing up. MacArthur, however, allowed his son no breathing room. He smothered Arthur yet neglected him at the same time. He was far from being unique in this, but in American life in the first half of this century, MacArthur may have been the only person who considered it "normal."

By the end of 1945 MacArthur was comfortably settled at both the embassy and the Dai Ichi. With his family occupying one pole of this axis and the most devoted members of the GHQ staff clustered at the other, he was cocooned once more in a small world of hermetic oddities, a small world that he completely controlled.

Let History Decide

During the first year of the occupation MacArthur relied heavily on the staff that had fought the war. There was still an inner circle, the old "Bataan Gang," and a prickly, jealous outer circle that competed with them for the old man's attention. But many of the men who had been close to MacArthur during the war lost their stars in 1946 as the Army dwindled to a shadow of what it had been. Officers who had been generals abruptly reverted to their permanent rank—usually colonel—and found it too painful to remain on active duty denuded of a general's prestige.[1]

As the old campaigners departed, they were replaced by officers who were strangers to MacArthur, and destined to remain that way. He continued to regard the old staff as an extended family and virtually ignored the newcomers. "The staff weren't arguing with him," observed Willoughby's deputy, Colonel James H. Polk. "They weren't disagreeing with him, and they weren't giving him different options. . . . The old guard that had been around him so long were just like his sons, and the new guard he never saw."[2]

There were two American armies in Japan in the fall of 1945: Krueger's Sixth and Eichelberger's Eighth. The worldwide demobilization of the wartime U.S. Army meant that one of them would have to be inactivated, and as Krueger would reach the Army's mandatory retirement age in January 1946, the Sixth was the logical choice.

MacArthur had made sure that Eichelberger did not get a lot of publicity during the war. Now, though, the wraps were off, and that fall Eichelberger's open gaze stared out from the covers of *Time* and *Life*. This blaze of publicity and the flattering letters it brought his way were bad for the judgment. Eichelberger, a nice man but no sophisticate, was so bedazzled by fame he concluded it meant he had "joined the fraternity of the great or near-great." MacArthur felt the occasion warranted a tribute of his own and gave him an autographed photograph, inscribed: "No Army of this war has achieved greater glory and distinction than the Eighth." Eichelberger was such a sucker for praise he read and reread the inscription in a state of rapture. This was, he told his wife, "one of the greatest moments of my life."[3] Yet the inscription was no more than typical MacArthur hyperbole. Don't tell someone he's done a good job; tell him he's a genius and get him to eat out of your hand.

Eichelberger's sudden emergence from the shadows brought an unexpected offer from the new Army Chief of Staff, Dwight Eisenhower, his 1926 Leavenworth classmate. Ike offered him the post of deputy chief of staff. Acceptance was almost certain to bring the longed-for fourth star. It was no secret that Eisenhower had spent much of the war dreaming about retirement. He had to have his arm twisted halfway up his back to become Chief of Staff. He acceded to Truman's demands only on the understanding that the President would find a replacement within two years. Eichelberger could conceivably have become Chief of Staff of the Army.[4]

MacArthur was reluctant to release him, probably fearing that an Eichelberger sitting in a big office on the E Ring of the Pentagon could prove a powerful enemy. Eichelberger was, after all, a man with a number of grievances, which had accumulated steadily from the day MacArthur had told him to capture Buna or die there. All the same, it might be unwise to send a flat no to Eisenhower. His relationship with Ike had not been entirely harmonious, and Ike might all too easily sympathize with someone who felt he had been treated badly by MacArthur. No point in stirring up unhappy memories over something like this. MacArthur dutifully informed Ike that he was prepared to let Eichelberger go. He added that if Eichelberger left Japan, Krueger would have to stay. The Eighth Army, instead of the Sixth, would be inactivated.[5]

While Eisenhower was digesting this message, MacArthur was telling Eichelberger about it and pointing out some of the implications. If the Eighth was inactivated, said MacArthur, Krueger was certain to claim the services of whichever Eighth Army officers he wanted for his own staff. He knew exactly which buttons to press. Eichelberger was vain, ambitious but, above all, sentimental. He simply could not bear the thought of men who had loyally served him for more than three years having to take orders from Krueger, whom he completely despised. He rejected Ike's offer. It was a romantic gesture that cast a rosy glow on his character . . . and doubt on his brains.[6]

Had he been half as astute as MacArthur, Eichelberger would have said, "General, I must accept this assignment." Once installed as deputy chief of staff, he would have had more than enough clout to get his former staff officers sent wherever they wanted to go and to steer them into slots that were likely to bring promotion. He would be able to do more for them by going than he could ever do by staying.

Whatever discomfort they would have had to endure under Krueger would be brief and be amply rewarded thereafter. In peace as in war, however, Eichelberger could always be counted on to kiss off opportunities that most soldiers can only dream about. Twice he had pulled strings to get a transfer from SWPA to the European theater, twice the offer came through, and he balked both times. He had also been given the chance to liberate Manila, only to chicken out.

Far from being grateful that Eichelberger had chosen to remain in Japan, MacArthur had only an icy contempt for the sentimental gesture he had himself prompted. Beyond the windy cave where he composed compliments and inscribed photographs there was a walk-in refrigerator, where whatever warmth he felt for other men vanished. It was here that MacArthur made ruthless judgments on the abilities of other men. For the next two years he treated Eichelberger like dirt.[7]

Uncle Bob became embittered. He decided that MacArthur had cheated him not only of a well-deserved star but of his portion of glory too. To correct that imbalance, he got one of his corps commanders to bypass MacArthur and recommend him directly to the War Department for various decorations, including the Bronze Star and the Air Medal. Once the awards were authorized, he pinned the medals on himself in a secret ceremony in his office.[8]

The only comfort Eichelberger could take from his decision to remain in Japan was that Krueger had to depart. By coincidence, Krueger and MacArthur had the same birthday—January 26—and on that day in 1946 Krueger went to the Dai Ichi to bid MacArthur goodbye.

MacArthur had the staff lined up against one wall of the reception room adjoining his office. Placing his right hand on the back of a large armchair, he stared pensively at Krueger. It was a Pinteresque pause—packed with emotion, its significance uncertain, the dramatic tension almost unbearable. He finally spoke, declaring slowly, "When the final pages of the history of World War II are written no army commander will emerge greater than Walter Krueger. I feel greatly honored to be in the position to present to him the Distinguished Service Cross, for valor which I myself observed on several occasions." He also awarded him his third Distinguished Service Medal.

MacArthur advanced to pin the DSC, Krueger's first and only combat decoration, on the general's chest, above the four rows of ribbons he already wore. He then reached out and grasped Krueger by the shoulders, intoning theatrically, "You have been a peerless commander." He released his grip momentarily, only to grasp Krueger again. "You have been a great soldier." Release, grasp for the third time, stare deep into the eyes. "And you have been a loyal and devoted friend."

Krueger, standing stiffly at attention, tried to speak, choked up and began to weep. The tears flowed swiftly into the ravines and crevices of his deeply lined, craggy face as if seeking a place to hide. It was all too much. He bowed his head, reached out and patted MacArthur on the arm. MacArthur then took him to the embassy for a birthday luncheon that Jean had prepared for them both.[9]

Lieutenant General Richard K. Sutherland, MacArthur's longtime chief of staff, had been brought back from the United States, where he was on leave, ostensibly to plan the surrender ceremony. It is hard to believe the GHQ staff could not have worked out the mechanics of that event, while MacArthur composed the mood music. The real reason, I believe, was that MacArthur felt it only fitting for Sutherland to be on the *Missouri*. For all his faults he had played an important role in MacArthur's war against Japan. Besides, his absence would have been noticed and was likely to excite unwelcome curiosity about their relationship—a relationship that MacArthur had always tried to portray to Marshall and Stimson as something remarkably close and harmonious.

Once the occupation began, however, MacArthur virtually ignored Sutherland, who had become obsessed with his high blood pressure, as if hypertension were a death sentence. It was evident that MacArthur intended to continue working his staff as he had during the war. He still expected them to be on duty from 7:00 A.M. to 9:00 P.M. seven days a week. They had no lives of their own. Their existence was merely an extension of his.

That kind of regime was less attractive than ever to a hypochondriac. Shortly before Christmas 1945 Sutherland told MacArthur he was thinking of going home and seeking medical advice. If his health was up to it, he would remain in the Army but not return to Japan; otherwise he would apply to retire. MacArthur eagerly told him that was a good idea. Sutherland, who had cherished a myth of himself as the man who had made MacArthur great, was crushed. And when he departed a few weeks later, MacArthur, normally effusive at times of farewell, pointedly refrained from thanking him for anything. He bid Sutherland goodbye like a man scraping something unpleasant off his shoe.[10]

Although MacArthur was Supreme Commander for the Allied Powers and devoted nearly all his energies to reforming Japan on their behalf, he remained responsible for large numbers of ground troops. His U.S. military command, known as Army Forces in the Pacific (AFPAC), controlled

Army personnel between Hawaii and the Asian mainland, excluding Korea. Running AFPAC was the last thing MacArthur was interested in. He let his chief of staff run it.[11]

Disarming Japan was AFPAC's first priority. A month after the surrender MacArthur told Karl Compton, the president of MIT, that he was hoping to disarm the entire Japanese Army within the next thirty days. Otherwise, he said, recalcitrant elements in the military might head into the mountains, taking their weapons with them and launching a guerrilla war.[12]

As it turned out, there were no guerrillas to be hunted down. Some Japanese did bury their weapons, and half-forgotten arms caches were still being unearthed twenty years later, but in the four and a half months between the surrender and Krueger's departure Japan was almost completely demilitarized. Its seven-million-man army was demobilized, its navy was abolished and 420 naval vessels were scrapped. American troops seized and destroyed millions of firearms, nearly 1.5 million tons of ammunition, 8,000 combat aircraft, 2,500 tanks, nearly 200,000 artillery pieces and coastal guns. The swiftness and efficiency with which Japan was demilitarized would have been impossible without the cooperation of the Japanese government and was really the first test of how willing it was to implement MacArthur's directives. The success of this operation got the occupation off to an auspicious start.[13]

By the time Japan was defanged most of the combat veterans of the Eighth Army had departed or were about to do so. The occupation force increasingly consisted of downy-cheeked youths who had come to Japan to enjoy themselves. AFPAC (later renamed the Far Eastern Command) became little more than a constabulary. Its combat ability was low, its training schedules were undemanding and its relationship with the young women of Japan was exhausting. If it ever had to fight, it was likely to find it had left its best performance in bed.

As SCAP MacArthur was explicitly authorized to do anything he considered "advisable and proper" to implement the policy directives he received from Washington. He thus possessed more freedom to interpret his instructions than he had ever enjoyed during the war. The American military tradition since Grant's time had been to allow a field commander a lot of leeway when it came to interpreting his instructions and not to try micromanaging his every move. The JCS approach after 1945 was more in the American tradition—a tradition MacArthur believed was absolutely right—than it had been during the war. He had the kind of freedom to interpret his instructions that Pershing had been granted back in 1917.

The amount of leeway he enjoyed was wildly exaggerated by his critics at the time, who chose to portray MacArthur as a headstrong figure who turned the occupation into a one-man show. Interestingly, that was much as Courtney Whitney portrayed it too: "No proconsul, no conqueror, no generalissimo ever had more power over his subjects than MacArthur had over the people of Japan. His authority was supreme."[14]

While not going as far as Whitney, MacArthur himself seemed to support Whitney's claim: "From the moment of my appointment as supreme commander, I had formulated the policies I intended to follow."[15] This was a considerable exaggeration. It was the details that came from MacArthur. The policies came from Washington. As Professor James observes, "The constraints on him were many."[16]

Even so, MacArthur brought a comprehensive philosophy to this new challenge. Six months before the surrender he had told Robert Sherwood, one of Roosevelt's closest advisers, that a harsh occupation policy would bring nothing but problems, but if the United States treated the Japanese with fairness and liberality, "we shall have the friendship and cooperation of the Asian people far into the future."[17]

Every major initiative MacArthur undertook in Japan was to be found in the instructions he received from the JCS. Japan in defeat was viewed like Japan in war—as a military problem. Occupation policy came from the Pentagon. It suited MacArthur's vanity to have it appear that he was in complete control, but he never had a totally free hand, and most of the time he was only carrying out instructions like any other Army officer.[18]

He was limited further by the fact that commanders from the ETO—such as Eisenhower, Bradley and Spaatz—now dominated the Pentagon. There had been a glimmer of hope toward the end of the war when Jack Sverdrup went home on leave and was summoned to Washington for a meeting with Truman. Stimson was itching to step down as secretary of war the moment the shooting stopped. Truman had known, liked and trusted Sverdrup for nearly twenty years. It was even claimed that when Truman's haberdashery business failed, it was Sverdrup who had paid off his creditors. Be that as it may, as the founding partner of one of the biggest construction companies in the Midwest and a man who had risen to two-star rank in the war Sverdrup was, in Truman's view, the right man to be the next secretary of war.

Sverdrup listened to what Truman had to say but wanted to talk it over with MacArthur. When he returned to the Pacific, MacArthur tried for more than an hour to talk him into accepting the appointment. He desperately needed "a friend at court," he told Sverdrup, who by this time had more or less made up his mind to turn down Truman's offer. There was a huge backlog of engineering projects that had been shelved because of the war. American businesses and governments had huge piles of cash they had not been able to spend. Sverdrup & Parcel, based in St. Louis, had a choice—to become a truly big, rich company or see its competitors move in and steal fat contracts from under its nose. The more he thought about it, the more Sverdrup wanted to return to his company and steer it through the exciting times ahead. Eloquent as MacArthur was, even he had his limits. And loyal as Sverdrup was, he had limits too. By the time he reached Japan MacArthur knew he would have no friend at court, not in the Pentagon, not in the White House.[19]

Unlike his relations with Hoover and Roosevelt, MacArthur had virtually no direct dealings with the new President, and the two men, one already hostile, the other extremely wary, got off to a spectacularly bad start. The surrender ceremony on the *Missouri* had been broadcast live to the United States. After the formal proceedings on the top deck ended, MacArthur went below, sat at a microphone and broadcast a twenty-minute, sometimes perfervid oration to the American people. "Today the guns are silent," he intoned slowly. "A great tragedy has ended, a great victory has been won. . . ." He talked of the way nations had historically resorted to war to resolve their differences. But the destructive power of modern weapons meant those days were over. "We have had our last chance. If we do not now devise some greater and more equitable system, Armageddon will be at our door." The only hope of salvation was a higher stage of human development. "It must be of the spirit if we are to save the flesh."[20]

MacArthur had given much thought to this speech and anticipated an audience of many millions. What he had not anticipated was that Truman would steal his thunder. The moment the surrender ceremony ended, the President went on the air to give a fireside chat. By the time he finished, so had MacArthur, whose fervent speech evaporated into the ether, unheard, unapplauded, undone.

The administration meanwhile was trying to demobilize the huge wartime Army, which consisted mainly of draftees. At the same time it did not intend to see the United States disarmed, and it was trying to persuade Congress to continue Selective Service even though victory had been won. The justification that government spokesmen were making was the need to station large numbers of troops in Germany and Japan for the indefinite future.

No one in the War Department or the White House bothered to advise MacArthur on what was happening or tried to get him on board before using Japan as an example. Even so, he was well aware of what was going on. He did not believe Congress would continue the draft (and it didn't). Not having been consulted, he saw no reason to stick his neck out on behalf of something he foresaw was doomed to failure. On the contrary, he was eager to distance himself from it. MacArthur announced that in another six months he would need only two hundred thousand men, instead of the half million currently under his command.[21]

Truman was infuriated at what he saw as an inexcusable attempt to sabotage his efforts to secure a peacetime draft. He angrily informed his staff, "I intend to do something about that fellow." Several days later Acting Secretary of State Dean Acheson publicly criticized MacArthur. He conceded that the draft was a military question and not really within the purview of the State Department's concerns. But instead of letting the matter drop right there, he went on to declare that "the occupation forces are the instruments of policy and not the determinants of policy . . . and whatever it takes to carry this [policy] out will be used to carry it out."[22]

There was no doubt among journalists or politicians that Acheson had gone out of his way to deliver a public rebuke to the general. MacArthur's admirers in Congress were outraged, and the general was both hurt and astonished. Nothing like this had happened to any American officer since 1901, when Secretary of War Elihu Root had criticized the commanding general of the Army, Nelson Miles. In that instance, though, Miles had begun matters by making an outspoken attack on Root to a congressional committee. MacArthur's statement may have been impolitic, but he had been careful not to criticize any individual, directly or indirectly.

He was stung by Acheson's rebuke. It was made all the more wounding by his conviction that someone as cool and cerebral as Acheson would never make such an attack on him except under orders to do so from the President. MacArthur sent a message to the War Department saying that so far as he had been aware, he was "acting in complete conformity with the War Department's announced policy of demobilizing as rapidly as possible." What he said was true, as far as it went, and the administration had been remiss in not securing his support before using Japan as an argument for continuing the draft.[23]

Truman decided the time had come for MacArthur to pay a visit to his native land. The general seemed to be losing touch with the mood and outlook of his own country. Like other victorious commanders, MacArthur was due in any case to receive the gratitude of the nation for his services in the war. Marshall duly sent MacArthur a cable suggesting a visit to the United States and added that the Army needed him to testify before Congress on the nation's military needs now that the war was over. MacArthur had no doubt that this cable came not from Marshall but from Truman.

The President's request was not presented as an order. It read, "I suggest that you make a visit home," but as everyone who has ever served in the armed forces knows, be it ever so politely expressed, a suggestion from your commanding officer is really an order. MacArthur himself preferred not to give direct orders. He usually thought something was a good idea or asked if such and such an action was possible or made a recommendation, whether it was to an orderly or an army commander. His response to this cable was inexcusable. He sent Marshall (and, by implication, the President) an unequivocal No. He said the present situation in Japan was "extraordinarily dangerous" but offered no evidence for this assertion.[24]

During World War II Marshall and Roosevelt had left Washington from time to time. The war continued in their absence. Eisenhower had returned home for ten days during the buildup to D Day, and the invasion still succeeded. The idea that the occupation of Japan might fall into chaos if MacArthur was absent for two weeks was not simply lame but ludicrous.

True, MacArthur *did* believe he held the fate of Japan in his hands. He may also have feared that if he did leave Japan for two or three weeks and nothing untoward happened in his absence, that might plant the idea in Truman's head that the occupation could be run without MacArthur. A visit could be but a prelude to retirement.

There were other reasons. For one thing, he still disliked flying, and a trip to Washington would take three days, most of it in the air. He jokingly claimed he would be happy to fly to Washington—when there was a plane able to get him there in twelve hours.[25]

The most compelling reason for him to reject Truman's invitation, however, was not fear of flying but fear of a direct confrontation. "He probably hates me," MacArthur glumly told Eichelberger.[26] Like most people, as he grew older, MacArthur loathed fuss, atmosphere, open disagreement. He still had all the old appetite for fame and power, but there was a deepening appreciation too of the delights of a quiet life. Besides, these days he hobnobbed with royalty and highly cultured men like Yoshida, people who made Quezon and his cronies look like vulgarians. As he moved into old age, MacArthur increasingly cultivated a sense of himself as a gentleman of the Old South, a man of fine breeding, impeccable manners, an aristocrat without a patent of nobility. The routines he had established were intended to produce—and for the most part did produce—a calm, unruffled aura that blended military efficiency with high-minded tranquillity. He had no intention of going to a meeting with Truman where there was any risk of a frank exchange of views. No telling where that might lead.

Truman had to settle for sending Assistant Secretary of War John J. McCloy to give MacArthur a private briefing on the administration's thinking about Japan and the postwar Army. McCloy, who had been Stimson's wartime troubleshooter, was no fan of MacArthur's either, but if Truman expected McCloy to put MacArthur firmly in his place, he was in for a disappointment. McCloy was a hard-bitten, tough-minded Wall Street lawyer and not easy to impress. He despised MacArthur's staff and had spent five years listening to Marshall and Stimson talk about MacArthur's shortcomings. He had personally objected to MacArthur's receiving the Medal of Honor back in 1942.[27] Still, eleven hours of discussion seemed to turn his opinion inside out. They argued heatedly over MacArthur's refusal to allow the Soviets a role in making occupation policy, and McCloy left MacArthur's office in a state of shock. "My God!" muttered McCloy as he wrestled himself into his overcoat. "How does he do it? He's in better health than when I saw him before the war. More fascinating than when he was Chief of Staff. What a man! What a man!"[28]

Truman tried again a year later to get MacArthur to come home for a visit. This time he got his military aide, Major General Harry H. Vaughan, to write to MacArthur and ask him to return home for a brief visit. Vaughan had served under MacArthur in Australia, as the provost marshal of Brisbane, and Truman probably thought that the personal connection would help. Besides, the occupation was by this time more than a year old and conditions in Japan were more settled. "The President directs me to advise you that he thinks [a visit] would be very appropriate and timely," wrote Vaughan. MacArthur once more claimed the situation did not allow him to leave. This was when Truman should have issued a direct order to return, but he did not. In backing down for a second time, he only reinforced MacArthur's contempt for him.[29]

MacArthur meanwhile had to run the occupation knowing that he could expect no public support from the President. The only chance he had of holding on to his position as SCAP was to run the occupation so well that Truman could not justify firing him without risking a public relations disaster.

While MacArthur's relations with the President were getting worse, his relations with the War Department improved once Eisenhower succeeded Marshall as Chief of Staff. Ike's elevation brought a renewal of their relationship in a way that neither could have expected when they parted at the Manila docks in 1939.

Although MacArthur could not resist putting Ike down from time to time and Eisenhower made cutting remarks about MacArthur, the fact remained that there was still an emotional tie between them, one that endured despite the friction. As Chief of Staff Eisenhower wrote regularly to MacArthur or sent him telegrams asking his advice—on decorations policy, on whether it was worth keeping permanent bases in the Philippines, on recruitment problems, on which combat commanders should get high-level Pentagon slots, on making War Department personnel justify their visits to overseas theaters, on the size of the Army and the struggle to maintain its effectiveness.[30]

However critical he had been of MacArthur's conduct of the Bataan campaign, Ike had nothing but admiration for the campaigns in New Guinea and the Philippines. These, he told Major General Lucius R. Holbrook, "have no equal in History." And on the first anniversary of the Japanese surrender Eisenhower sent MacArthur a personal message: "During the dark days of the war your military leadership, repeatedly proved against staggering odds, inspired free men the world over. . . . The entire Army joins me in saluting you on this memorable day."[31] There were also personal messages, such as this one, dated February 8, 1946: "A man just came into my office to suggest an engagement for February 21st. It instantly flashed across my mind that that date is young Arthur's anniversary, so I am dashing off this note in the hope that it will reach him in time to say 'Happy Birthday.' "[32]

MacArthur responded in kind. He sympathized with Eisenhower's efforts to protect the Army from the zeal of a peacetime, budget-cutting Congress. "The deflation of the Army with which you are now faced," he observed, "recalls so vividly many of the incidents of our struggle in the early 1930s to save the remnants and nucleus of the service. The individuals involved have changed [but] [d]on't let it get you down and don't worry at losing many of the skirmishes." He sent Eisenhower a birthday message in 1946: "Many happy returns, dear Ike. May each succeeding year merely add to your success and content."[33]

In May 1946 Eisenhower decided to pay a brief visit to Japan during a journey through the Far East. When MacArthur's Japanese-language interpreter, Major Faubion Bowers, placed the cable announcing Ike's trip on MacArthur's desk, the general's immediate response was defensive. "Up to no good," said MacArthur. "He'll look for trouble and I hope he doesn't find it. Got the roar of the crowd in his ears, that boy. Can't sit still and do his job. Got to junket around." To Ike, however, he sent a cable saying, "Look forward with greatest pleasure and anticipation to your visit."[34]

Eisenhower was one of the few visitors who rated more than a lunch. Jean and the general hosted an official dinner for him. Once the meal ended, MacArthur dismissed the other guests and took Eisenhower into the embassy library. They reminisced about the old times and then got down to what was really on their minds. For more than an hour they argued amicably about which one of them ought to run for the White House. Eisenhower told MacArthur that he absolutely had to make a bid for the 1948 Republican nomination. "I'm too old," MacArthur insisted, and urged Ike to run instead. They waltzed around the subject until 1:00 A.M. Both men were fascinated by the idea of running for the presidency, but neither was prepared to admit it to the other.[35]

Two years later, when Eisenhower's time as Chief of Staff drew to a close, his thoughts turned to MacArthur again. The last thing he did before stepping down as head of the Army and going into retirement was to write his onetime mentor a letter: "In 20 minutes I shall be relieved as Chief of Staff. I am taking occasion to write you because it suddenly occurs to me that in all my years in the Army I served directly under your supervision longer than any other. Another reason for writing is because of the efforts that some [journalists] have been making to prove that you and I are deadly enemies. . . ." He went on to assure MacArthur that he had tried to disabuse them. "I told them I hoped you treasure our old friendship as much as I do."[36]

MacArthur almost certainly treasured it, but whether he did so quite as much as Ike is doubtful. MacArthur's respect for other soldiers was never complete unless spiced with the odor of cordite and the prospect of violent death. Eisenhower had never served in the front line, had never shot anyone, had never been shot at. This was always a sore point with Ike himself, who looked enviously on combat veterans. So while MacArthur liked Eisenhower personally and acknowledged his excellence as a staff officer, he was constitutionally incapable of according him the full measure of a soldier's admiration. Eisenhower knew it. He would never have worked as closely as he did with MacArthur for as long as he did without being able to read his mind. Theirs was never a truly equal relationship not because Ike had once served under MacArthur but because Ike did not wear a single decoration for gallantry. "He never fought in Europe," MacArthur said to Bowers. "He let his generals in the field fight the war for him. . . . Lucky he had Patton."[37]

The officer closest to MacArthur in Japan was Courtney Whitney, who had more access than the rest of the staff combined. Whitney held a reserve commission, and as was true of most reservists, his active duty ended with the fighting. MacArthur soon got him back, with a regular commission and a star. Short, pudgy and moon-faced, he was once described as looking "like a pig with a mustache."[38] No one was more devoted to MacArthur than Whitney. There was something either touching or slightly creepy about the depth and breadth of his adoration. No matter how close he got, he wanted to be closer. He even invented a shared past for them both.

Whitney claimed, for example, that when MacArthur went ashore at Leyte, he had carried Whitney's watch in his shirt pocket. Close examination of the photographs of MacArthur wading ashore shows that there *was* something in his left breast pocket—his tobacco tin. Whitney had not taken part in the landing in Lingayen Gulf, a fact that pained him. His solution to it was to have a copy of the photograph of MacArthur wading

ashore in Lingayen Gulf doctored. He had his head put on the slender body
of Colonel Larry Lehrbas, one of MacArthur's aides. He liked to show his
fake photograph to visitors and reminisce about wading ashore at
MacArthur's side when the general had returned to Luzon. Knowing how
highly MacArthur regarded combat soldiers, he even claimed he had been
recommended for the Medal of Honor. It was a fantasy and, like most fantasies of·desire, slightly sad.[39]

When Lehrbas returned to the United States at the end of 1945 to
resume his career in journalism, he was replaced by Colonel Laurence E.
Bunker, a tall, strikingly handsome man with polished manners, a Harvard
law degree and extreme right-wing views that would one day make him
vice-president of the John Birch Society. Bunker chose to assert himself
shortly after arriving at GHQ SCAP by clamping his own control over
MacArthur's appointment schedule. No one, he informed the GHQ staff,
would see "the General" without clearing the meeting with him. The ink
was hardly dry on Bunker's memorandum before Whitney was knocking
on MacArthur's door, holding a sheet of paper in his hand. It read, "I
hereby resign my position in this headquarters. Courtney Whitney."
MacArthur reached for a match, as if intending to light his pipe while he
pondered this development. Instead he held up the paper, applied the
match to the bottom edge and, once it was blazing vigorously, dropped it
in the steel wastebasket next to his desk. "Court, the side door is open any
time you want to come in." Whitney alone had direct access to MacArthur
whenever he wished, a privilege keenly resented by the rest of the staff.[40]

MacArthur gave Whitney control of the most important single compo-
nent in the machinery of the occupation, the Government Section. Whitney was a shrewd and hardworking officer. His greatest gift, however, was
his ability to understand how MacArthur's mind worked, to fathom from
the sometimes gnomic observations of his master just what it was that he
wanted. MacArthur was surrounded by people who were passionately
loyal to him. What made Whitney different was not his doglike devotion
but his intellectual penetration of the general's thoughts. He could tell the
real belief from the mere thinking out loud, the appearance of uncertainty
that contained, within it, a decision that was already fixed.

A lawyer by training and an advocate by inclination, Whitney enjoyed a
good argument. He told one surprised civil affairs officer, "I look forward
to the time when a lieutenant will barge into my office, bang my desk, and
say, 'Goddammit, general, such-and-such a proposed directive is prepos-
terous and you would be out of your mind to ask General MacArthur to
approve it!' "[41]

Essentially he got what he wanted when Lieutenant Colonel Charles E.
Kades arrived in January 1946. In the later stages of the war the Army

trained thousands of people at some of the best universities to manage the affairs of the vast areas that American troops were liberating. Hundreds of these civil affairs officers were sent to MacArthur, but his decision to rely almost entirely on the Japanese to implement occupation policy reduced their significance dramatically.[42] They had been trained to act as key players in managing the occupation, only to discover that compared with the military personnel at the Dai Ichi, they carried as much weight as the janitors. Only a few civil affairs officers were ever allowed to handle anything important, and among those happy few Kades was a mile ahead of the rest.

Kades was another Harvard Law graduate, had spent five years as assistant general counsel for the Treasury Department before the war, had graduated from the Infantry School and Leavenworth, then served in the invasion of southern France before becoming a civil affairs officer. He had expected, and wanted, an assignment in Europe. Everything he had heard about MacArthur's staff made it sound disgusting—a collection of mediocrities fawning on their greatly overrated chief and cutting one another's throats to get into better groveling positions around the legs of the throne. Kades had a clear idea of what GHQ SCAP was like: "a Byzantine court."[43]

Despite his objections, he was sent to Japan anyway. A lifelong Democrat, Kades proved to be the grit that Whitney was looking for to make an oyster. While MacArthur had much in common with the conservatives, such as Yoshida, who presently ruled Japan and ran Japanese business, Kades looked on them all with a liberal's jaundiced eye. The ruling class was a creature he recognized, a combination of plutocrats and reactionaries whose principal interest was to preserve their power and privileges at the expense of the ordinary Japanese.

Far from being irritated by Kades's New Deal philosophy, MacArthur and Whitney were delighted. They had found, they believed, the essential counterbalance needed to craft an occupation that was neither too hard nor too soft, neither too liberal nor too conservative.

There was no precedent for turning a non-Western, militaristic, ultraconservative and xenophobic country like Japan into an antimilitaristic parliamentary democracy. In the first drive to modernize, the Japanese had taken many of the worst elements of Western civilization—the tools of war, the imperialistic imperative, the political propaganda machine—while ignoring the best. It fell to MacArthur to force or persuade them to accept that Japan did not have to loot its neighbors to become rich, did not have to be armed to the teeth in order to be secure.

Having disarmed Japan, MacArthur set about democratizing it. Japanese politicians like Yoshida tried to tell him that Japan had been a democratic country after World War I, but the Great Depression had brought the military to power. Why, Yoshida, informed him, Japan was by its very nature an inherently democratic country.[44]

The result, however, was not democracy as it was known in America or Britain. Early in the twentieth century, Japan had copied some of the outward trappings of Western democracy, but there was no free press, no wide range of voluntary associations to lobby for social change, no guarantee of human rights or civil liberties. Women had the vote on paper, but political and social pressures barred them from exercising it.

Had there been a real democracy in Japan, it would have been impossible for the military to seize control of the government under any circumstances. MacArthur intended to introduce the missing political and economic elements to Japan. Women would not only get the vote but be able use it. Nearly 70 percent of the adult male population consisted of tenant farmers who were utterly dependent on an unscrupulous and overweening landlord class. He intended to impose land reform. Organized labor had been under government control. He planned to change that. There would be a free press too.

MacArthur's path toward these objectives was blocked by the Meiji Constitution. Adopted in 1889, it had been the work of reformers and Westernizers, but its inherent weaknesses had been exploited by three generations of Japanese politicians and soldiers. When MacArthur decided to rely on the existing government, he more or less accepted its legitimacy under the Meiji Constitution, but within weeks he realized it would have to be revised in at least two ways: Its authority had to be based on popular sovereignty, instead of divine will, and the emperor must be transformed from a deity into a constitutional monarch.

When the Allied leaders met in Potsdam in July 1945, they had issued a declaration that spelled out the various demands on the Japanese as part of any surrender. These demands amounted to a requirement that Japan create a modern, democratically accountable system of government. The Japanese government had already accepted the need for constitutional reform, and in October 1945 it created a committee to make recommendations. After three months of deliberations it became clear that the committee chairman intended to produce a report that left the status of the emperor intact and did little to acknowledge the sovereignty of the people. MacArthur was already under pressure from most of the Allied governments that he represented to take a tougher line with the Japanese. He was being pressured too by the State Department to make far-reaching changes. He sent for Whitney. "Well, do I have the power to change a written constitution?"[45]

Kades produced a study that concluded that MacArthur could not only revise the Meiji Constitution but throw it out and introduce a new one. For ten days in February 1946 Whitney's Government Section turned itself into an unelected constitutional convention.[46] The resulting document was radically different from the Meiji Constitution. MacArthur left Whitney and Kades to write most of it but told them they had to include three essential provisions: The emperor would be subject to the will of the people, war would be renounced as a means of settling disputes and all manifestations of feudalism, such as the peerage, would be abolished.[47]

MacArthur later claimed that the idea of having a clause that explicitly rejected war originated not with him but with the Japanese prime minister, Baron Kijuno Shidehara. It is inconceivable, however, that MacArthur would have permitted any constitution that allowed for the remilitarization of Japan. Yoshida was convinced that MacArthur had hinted at the possibility of such a clause to Shidehara, who, being an astute man, later presented it back to him as something the Japanese wanted. What better way to get the Japanese not only to accept it but to abide by it for generations to come?[48]

The resulting document met MacArthur's three basic demands. Whitney and Kades stitched together the executive powers of the American system and the parliamentary institutions of the British. Japan was to become a representative democracy, the emperor was reduced to a figurehead, civil liberties were guaranteed and the executive branch became answerable to the legislature. Writing a text that both Americans and Japanese could agree on tested the linguistic and philosophical abilities of the Government Section almost to breaking point. Western concepts such as sovereignty had no exact Japanese equivalents. Agreement was possible only because of the ambiguity inherent in many of the basic terms, which permitted MacArthur to believe key phrases meant one thing and the Japanese to believe they meant another.[49]

Yoshida and most of the Cabinet resented the draft of the new constitution. It went far beyond anything they had been prepared to accept. MacArthur, however, knew just how to persuade them: He proposed to put the draft directly to the people in a referendum. The prospect of allowing ordinary Japanese in their millions a direct say in something as important as this was more than the old guard could stomach. They caved in at once, and the new constitution was passed by the Diet with only minor changes.[50]

MacArthur later remarked, "The new Japanese constitution is merely an amendment to the older Meiji one."[51] He was trying to make the document as palatable as he could to the Japanese, but the fact remains that the MacArthur constitution represented a complete break with the past. It was the most important single achievement of the occupation. The new constitution put Japan on the path to becoming a truly free and democratic country in a part of the world where freedom and democracy had never existed before. It helped make Japan a country that was the envy, not the scourge, of East Asia.

There were only a few occupation issues in which Truman took a direct interest. The prosecution of war criminals was one of them. Just four days after the surrender the President informed the JCS that MacArthur was to "proceed, without delay" in bringing war criminals to trial. When McCloy visited Japan six weeks later, he reminded MacArthur that the President wanted action.[52]

Most prosecutions were for crimes against humanity or crimes against peace, which were new offenses in the history of war. These crimes were prosecuted before Allied tribunals in Nuremberg and Tokyo. While these tribunals were being established, MacArthur responded to Truman's demands by using the powers he possessed as commander of AFPAC to bring General Tomoyuki Yamashita to trial in Manila for war crimes. Yamashita was charged with failing to prevent the massacre of Filipino civilians and the wanton destruction of Manila.

MacArthur's prosecution of Yamashita was seen at the time and later as nothing but revenge. Typical is the comment in one recently published work that his handling of the trials of his former enemies reflects "extraordinary discredit on him." The biography of MacArthur by Professor D. Clayton James takes a similar view.[53]

Yamashita was not in Manila at the time it was destroyed, nor did he order the city be turned into a battleground. He was 150 miles away, in the mountains of northern Luzon, when these terrible events unfolded. He was charged nevertheless on the ground that as he was the commander of all Japanese forces in the Philippines, he had a duty to know what was happening and to prevent the commission of atrocities.

In creating the military commission that tried Yamashita, MacArthur did not act in an arbitrary way to stack the deck against the defendant. He was guided by the recommendations of the War Crimes Office, Harry Truman, John McCloy and the proceedings of the London Conference, at which the Allies had discussed how war trials should be handled. When it came to the rules of evidence, he adopted those contained in the leading authority available, the British government's "Regulations for the Trial of War Criminals," and added a provision against self-incrimination. In some respects, the procedures under which Yamashita was tried were more liberal than those that were being employed at Nuremberg.

On the other hand, Yamashita would be tried by a panel of American officers. What he faced was a lot closer to a court-martial than a civilian trial, and courts-martial are notorious for dispensing rough justice.

Yamashita was hampered too by his chief defense counsel, A. Frank Reel, whose conduct of the case was bizarre. Reel, for example, protested that his client was denied a fair trial because he was not given enough time to prepare the defense case. Yet it was Reel who asked for only two weeks to prepare, startling the military commission trying the case. The commission offered to give him more time, but he refused to take advantage of the offer. The commission also prodded Reel several times to bring in more lawyers to aid the obviously overworked defense team, a suggestion that he resisted.[54]

One of the most troubling aspects of the Yamashita case was the fact that there was no precedent for charging a combat commander with failing to control his troops and therefore being responsible for crimes they had committed. And when a Japanese-speaking naval lieutenant on Yamashita's defense team, Samuel S. Stratton, traveled to Tokyo to assure MacArthur personally that Yamashita *had* tried to prevent his troops from committing atrocities, MacArthur was unimpressed. "Let history decide."[55]

The law is still making up its mind as to just how far a commander is expected to control his subordinates, but there was no doubt in MacArthur's mind. His father had taught him a number of important lessons about being an officer. One was "Always look after your men." Another was "Never give an order unless you are sure it will be obeyed." If Yamashita really did try to prevent atrocities, that meant he knew they were being committed and failed to prevent them. Being ineffectual does not remove a commander's responsibility.

Yamashita was convicted and sentenced to death, but the defense promptly appealed the case to the Supreme Court. The judges decided, by a 6–2 margin, that the court had no jurisdiction, and the majority included three of the most esteemed judges in American history—Felix Frankfurter, William O. Douglas and Hugo L. Black. Two strong dissents were entered, by Justices Frank Murphy and Wiley Rutledge. They damned the trial as "a legal lynching."[56]

MacArthur had the right to review the conviction and reduce the sentence. "It is not easy for me to pass penal judgment upon a defeated adversary in a military campaign," he acknowledged in a statement to the press. "I have reviewed the proceedings in vain, searching for some mitigating circumstances on his behalf. I can find none. . . ."[57] Yamashita was hanged on February 23, 1946.

The establishment of the Yamashita precedent doomed the man who had conquered the Philippines in 1942, sent MacArthur fleeing by PT boat and forced Wainwright to surrender, Masaharu Homma. The main charge against him was responsibility for not preventing the horrors inflicted on Americans and Filipinos during the infamous Bataan Death March.

Homma was convicted but received a sentence more acceptable to a soldier than hanging: "to be shot to death by musketry." His wife went to see MacArthur. She spoke movingly of her feelings for her husband and pleaded with MacArthur to spare his life. It was, MacArthur reflected, "one of the most trying hours of my life."[58]

Whatever his personal sympathy for Mrs. Homma, he could not get out of his mind the way Homma had forced Wainwright to surrender all the troops in the Philippines. He had threatened to murder the Americans he had captured on Corregidor unless Wainwright got commanders elsewhere in the Philippines to surrender their men. As MacArthur described these events to Averell Harriman, the ambassador to the Soviet Union, tears slid down his cheeks. Homma was executed in April 1946.[59]

The International Military Tribunal for the Far East had meanwhile indicted twenty-eight Japanese, including the former head of the military cabal that had plunged Japan into war, General Hideki Tojo. MacArthur had left it to his counterintelligence chief, Brigadier General Elliott Thorpe, to collect evidence and decide who should be put on trial. MacArthur personally put Tojo's name at the head of the list, but Thorpe provided the rest of the names. The whole business made Thorpe uneasy. In his knowledge of military history, the victors did not put their defeated enemies on trial, and they certainly did not execute them, for obvious reasons. Who would ever believe this was justice?[60]

He recommended to MacArthur that he do what his father had done when he pacified the Philippines. Instead of trying the insurgent leaders, Major General Arthur MacArthur had banished them to Guam, and there they remained until long after the insurrection was defeated. Thorpe advised him to round up the Japanese war leaders but refuse to allow any death sentences. Instead those convicted of the most serious offenses should be imprisoned indefinitely on the bleak, remote Bonin Islands. "That's a good idea, but I can't do it," said MacArthur. "Our allies want blood, and our people want blood, and they're going to have blood, and I can't stop it." He wanted the accused to be charged with the kinds of offenses of violence commonly dealt with under the criminal law, unlike the defendants at Nuremberg, most of whom were charged with "crimes against peace" or "crimes against humanity." All the same, he found the whole business sordid and sought to keep his involvement to the minimum that his orders required.[61]

MacArthur appointed the tribunal's members and had the right to reduce or alter (but not increase) the sentences. The trial dragged on for two years. By the time it ended, in November 1948, two defendants had died and a third been declared insane. All twenty-five surviving defendants were found guilty. Tojo and six other defendants were sentenced to death;

the others received long prison sentences. MacArthur allowed the death sentences to stand but claimed reviewing them was the most "utterly repugnant" duty he had ever performed.[62]

The Tokyo trial, like the trials of Yamashita and Homma, was severely criticized at the time and ever after as being "victor's justice"—the law as a harlot in black robes servicing an unbridled lust for revenge. Most of those charged with war crimes, whether in the Far East or in Europe, were indicted for offenses that did not even exist when the war began. That in itself made many who had grown up with the tradition of the common law uneasy.[63] Moreover, international law was—and half a century later, still is—a half-formed creature compared with the domestic law of nation-states. With the best will in the world, it is doubtful that anyone could have come up with a way of trying war criminals that would have matched the rules of evidence, jury selection and criminal procedure found in a federal district court in New York or San Francisco. The choice, though, was not between fair trials or flawed trials but between show trials or no trials.

The system MacArthur employed was imperfect, not because he set out to create a blunt instrument that would murder old enemies but because neither he nor anyone else could come up with anything much better. The trials in Manila and Tokyo were seriously flawed, but no worse than happened elsewhere. Chief Justice Harlan Fiske Stone privately condemned what he called "the high-grade lynching party in Nuremberg." Victor's justice? Yes. But unavoidable too.[64]

MacArthur was the son of a man who was both a general and a lawyer. His grandfather had been one of the most successful jurists of his generation. He had acquired a legalistic view of the world without a day spent in law school. Almost from the moment Japanese troops landed on Luzon he had seen this was how it would end. He had threatened Japanese commanders with retribution for their misdeeds. To them that was unimaginable. To him, only too real. He seemed from the first to hear the clatter of the hangman's drop, glimpse the rope, foresee that the last shots would not be fired on the field of battle. They would come from the leveled rifles of a grim-faced firing squad taking aim at pathetic, shrunken figures slouched in grubby, discarded work clothes against a prison wall.

29

Ten Thousand Angels

MacArthur's remoteness from Japan and the Japanese became legendary. It was a constant source of puzzlement, not so much to the Japanese—who had hardly ever seen or heard the emperor before 1945—as to Americans. He did not travel around Japan. Instead he encouraged Jean to take trips to various parts of the country and act as his eyes and ears. He also had a Signal Corps cameraman travel around making movies about everyday Japanese life. These became a staple of the nightly movie show, along with American newsreels, film of Army football games and the latest westerns flown in from Hollywood.

He met with comparatively few Japanese, and the only ones he saw on a regular basis were Yoshida, whom he saw about once a month, and the emperor, who visited him twice a year. MacArthur met some Japanese Cabinet members, but they were the favored few. Occasionally he greeted groups of Japanese, such as thirty-five women elected to the Diet in 1946, and the Japanese swimming team, in 1949.

MacArthur made only one trip outside Japan during the first three years of the occupation, when he attended the ceremonies that launched the Philippines as an independent country in July 1946. But he had become disenchanted with his "second home." Thorpe's agents unearthed documents in Japanese archives that showed Quezon had been planning even before December 1941 to sell out to the Japanese. He was a collaborator-in-waiting, positioning himself to cut a deal before the first Japanese soldier ever set foot on Philippine soil. MacArthur had never really trusted Quezon; that was why he had him more or less kidnapped and taken to

Australia in April 1942. So when Thorpe showed him the documents, MacArthur wasn't in the least surprised, but he was disappointed all the same. Thorpe wondered if he wanted to release the material for publication. "No," said MacArthur. "He's dead. Let's just leave it that way."[1]

MacArthur had done all he could to help Manuel Roxas become the first president of an independent Philippines, and when Roxas won the election in April 1946, MacArthur publicly hailed the result as "the repudiation by the Filipino people of irresponsible charges of collaboration" that had been leveled at Roxas.[2]

The date set for Philippine independence was July 4, 1946, and elaborate ceremonies were planned, but MacArthur—the greatest living hero of the Filipino people—expressed no interest in attending. It was only at the last moment that the White House was alerted and MacArthur was ordered to go to Manila.[3]

The city was still a scene of appalling devastation, and on the drive from the airport into the city, he stared balefully at the shattered buildings, the heaps of debris that covered block after block. He thought about Tokyo and Yokohama. A year ago they too had looked like this. But now most of the rubble had been cleared away and the Japanese were industriously building on the ruins, burying their dead cities under freshly poured concrete. Why weren't the Filipinos doing the same? Their indifference to healing the scars of war did not bode well, he gloomily concluded, for their future as an independent nation.[4]

Instead of traveling widely to see things for himself, MacArthur much preferred that people come to him. If nothing else, it put him in a superior position, and he used it to pick their brains clean. He could get more information out of a visitor than the visitor sometimes realized he possessed. There was a steady procession of distinguished visitors through Tokyo. American politicians, generals, admirals, foreign diplomats, famous journalists, movie stars, old MacArthur friends, book writers, professors, cardinals, sporting heroes, newspaper publishers, all came to call.

Jean organized an official lunch for visiting notables two or three times a week. MacArthur timed his arrival home from the Dai Ichi so that everyone would be in the embassy drawing room, chatting to Jean and one another, when he returned. As he appeared in the doorway, Jean was likely to turn around and trill, "Why, there is the general!" as if he had taken her by surprise.

MacArthur walked straight to her, ignoring everyone else in the room, grasped her firmly, kissed her warmly and said, "Hello, Jeannie!" or "Darling!" like a man who has not seen his wife for a month. It was a performance, but sincere at the same time. They were like Scott and Zelda Fitzgerald, who always had to be *seen* to be Scott and Zelda. These existential niceties out of the way, MacArthur turned to his guests and greeted them as if their coming had answered his deepest wish. He was likely to say, "I'm hungry," and ask his wife playfully, "Have we got anything to eat?" Then he and Jean led the way into the dining room.[5]

The table would be set for about twenty people, most of them senior officials (both military and civilian) at GHQ SCAP. MacArthur sat at the head of the table, with the guest of honor on his right and probably another guest on his left. Jean sat at the foot, with a visitor on either side. Other than that, people sat where they wished, sometimes producing unseemly jostling for positions near the general. MacArthur's political adviser, a career diplomat from the State Department, pointed out that "protocol requires that diplomatic representatives be seated in a prescribed order." MacArthur replied, "Not at my table. If any question is raised as to my informality, you merely say that it is the MacArthur protocol."[6]

Over a leisurely lunch MacArthur gently grilled the guest of honor, tapping the veins of knowledge, sampling the quality of the opinions, weighing up what the man was worth and planting seeds that might bear fruit one day. He loved to talk, but he did not love wasting his time. Even talk with these transient luminaries had to have some meaning, some purpose, no matter how light and conversational it seemed. Usually he did most of the talking, but that too had its purpose. Few could resist it. Time and again visitors arrived vowing not to be taken in by the man's charm or wit, nor to be ensnared by his huge personality, only to fail. The range of his interests was vast, and he had a story—sometimes moving, sometimes tragic, deeply personal or hilariously funny—for just about every visitor and any occasion.

This did not mean he had a real sense of humor. He could not laugh at himself. The sense of destiny, of God's hand gripping his shoulder got in the way. He could never see himself as being ridiculous, never openly acknowledge the absurdities in his own attitudes and behavior. But he laughed easily and knew how to turn a joke to his own purposes. Visitors who came to see him in his office at the Dai Ichi had a tendency to fall under his spell and refuse to budge at the end of their allotted fifteen or thirty minutes. So MacArthur would bring the conversation around to a story about a young British subaltern who was drilling a platoon of soldiers at Dover Castle. The subaltern (the equivalent of a second lieutenant) called out the wrong command by mistake and sent the men heading toward the edge of the cliffs. Panicking, he tried to remember which command would turn them around, but his mind went blank and his vocal cords tied themselves into knots as images of men tumbling over the cliffs flashed through his mind. All he could do was emit strangulated, squawking noises of terror. As the troops marched briskly toward disaster, a sergeant rushed up to the subaltern. "For God's sake, sir," he pleaded, "say something—even if it's only goodbye!" The visitor got the point, laughed heartily and said he simply had to go now.[7]

At an age when most men are inclined to give up the unequal struggle, MacArthur was as vain as ever about his appearance. He had put on about twenty pounds during the war, and his waist had vanished. Like that of many an aging gent, his once-splendid form now resembled a tree trunk. His eyesight was failing, making it impossible for him to read without glasses. It was clear by this time that the tremor in his right hand was a symptom of Parkinson's disease, which was slowly but steadily growing worse.[8]

MacArthur did what he could to hide the signs of deterioration. He dyed his hair black and sought to disguise his increasing baldness by growing it long on the right side and trailing the resulting strands over the top of his head. He also tried to ensure that whenever his photograph was taken his spectacles were out of sight and he was wearing his cap.[9] Some things could not be hidden. Russell Brines, a journalist who had more access to MacArthur than most, noticed "the thinness of his hands, his increased nervousness and irritability, his growing sensitivity."[10]

Despite the remorseless advance of old age, his health remained robust, and visitors were likely to remark that he looked more like a man in his fifties than someone approaching seventy. He was sick only twice in Japan. On one occasion he had an abscessed tooth, which had to be removed. On the other, he had a strep infection in his throat. His doctor, Colonel Douglas Kendrick, wanted to give him a shot of penicillin. MacArthur had a dread of doctors, hospitals and shots. No doctor had been allowed to give him a complete physical examination since World War I. "Doc," he said firmly, "I don't believe I'll take the needle." Kendrick gave him six sulfanilamide tablets instead, but MacArthur swallowed only one of them.

At two o'clock the next morning Kendrick got a call from Jean. She had just taken the gin'ral's temperature and discovered it was 104° Fahrenheit. After hurrying to the embassy, Kendrick found MacArthur stretched out on his bed, dressed in a West Point bathrobe and looking contrite. "I didn't mean to pull rank on you, Doc," he croaked sheepishly. "I'll take anything you suggest." Kendrick gave him a penicillin jab, and within a few days he had recovered completely.[11]

As his body dragged him inexorably into old age, his spirit resisted. He refused to surrender the central vision that had inspired his youthful imagination: the dashing young colonel of infantry, physically fearless, handsome and good, leading brave, patriotic men into battle, where they would win or they would die. MacArthur did not have much depth to his hinterland. There were no interests there that did not touch on his work, except for West Point football and cowboy movies: no interest in art, literature or music; no physical activity, such as tennis or golf; a vast range of interesting acquaintances, but not one real friend with whom he could talk freely and openly, whose joys were his joys, whose griefs were his griefs and whose destiny was part of his own. One way or another, it was a fairly chilly place, empty and echoing. Dominating that hinterland was a soldier's lean, erect silhouette, casting an ever-lengthening shadow down the years, from his childhood, through virile manhood and now penetrating into old age. Everything that embellished or enhanced the mental portrait of himself as a soldier mattered. It mattered as much in the waning days of his career as it had ever done.

When Congress created the rank of General of the Army, it had done so in a hurry, and there were some important ambiguities. MacArthur seized on them to demand that he be restored to the active list. Being on the retired list, but temporarily restored to active duty, affronted his sense of self. Congress changed the law, and in 1948 MacArthur was restored to the active list.[12]

This, though, was not enough. In 1944 Congress had created the Combat Infantryman's Badge. The law specifically barred senior officers from receiving it. But by the time the war ended, the prestige of the CIB was so great that generals from Burma to Berlin were slavering for the silver Kentucky rifle on an enamel rectangle of infantry blue surrounded by a truly handsome laurel wreath. Most awards for gallantry involve an element of favoritism or dumb luck. The Purple Heart and the CIB alone were awarded solely because a man had earned them. Stilwell was typical of the yearning generals. He, like MacArthur, saw himself as a real soldier, a fighting man. He pestered the War Department for a CIB, and screw Congress. He finally got his way. As Stilwell lay dying, the secretary of war, Robert Patterson, awarded him "an honorary CIB," and he was buried with it, but the Army did not publicize what it had done. That, of course, did not prevent his family from having a posthumous portrait painted showing the CIB on Stilwell's left breast, above four rows of ribbons.

MacArthur too wanted a CIB, but not some second-rate honorary version and certainly not on his deathbed. He asked the War Department to change the regulations. The CIB was, he pointed out, "the most coveted of Army awards." He urged "that provisions be made for the awarding of the Combat Infantryman Badge to former assistant division commanders and commanders of divisions . . . who meet the requirement of having commanded such units in combat." To his keen disappointment—and that of a lot of other generals—the Army said no.[13]

And always, always there was West Point. He thought of it constantly. He sent his alma mater a message in March 1947 on the occasion of its

145th anniversary: "Nearly 48 years have gone since I joined the long grey line. As an Army 'brat' it was the fulfillment of all my boyish dreams. The world has turned over many times since that day and the dreams have long vanished with the passing years, but through the grim murk of it all, the pride and thrill of being a West Pointer has never dimmed."[14]

Each morning and afternoon hundreds of Japanese stood patiently at the entrance to the Dai Ichi Building to watch MacArthur coming and going. Their attitude was almost reverential and seemed all the justification in the world for MacArthur's trust in them. But it would take only one person, with a knife or a gun, to turn the occupation inside out. Important figures in the State Department, the War Department and among the Allies scoffed at his faith in the former enemy, but he never wavered. The Japanese, he insisted, could be trusted. They were no threat, not to him, not to anyone. Then, one day in 1946, a man emerged from the crowd as MacArthur stepped out of the shiny black Cadillac, and in his hand was a knife. He got to within a couple of feet of MacArthur before the MPs grabbed him.

MacArthur proceeded to his fifth-floor office as though nothing had happened, but when he got there, he ordered the man brought up. Over tea and coffee they discussed the man's grievances for a while; then MacArthur told him to go home. The would-be assassin turned into a fervent admirer from that moment.[15]

The incident was never reported in the press. No one in Washington was informed about it. Few people at GHQ SCAP even knew what had happened. The story did not come to light for forty years. But there, in microcosm, was his entire approach to the occupation: Disarm them, try to resolve their grievances and after that leave them alone.

Japan was struggling with three revolutions at once: from empire to nation-state, from military power to military impotence and from a command economy to a free market. To the surprise of many of MacArthur's critics, and to the surprise at times of members of his staff, the political and economic philosophy that guided him through this challenge was not the reactionary vision of people like Robert McCormick and William Randolph Hearst, who fondly imagined he was one of them. MacArthur's political and economic views were those of a radical Republican, a Bull Moose Progressive, much like his mentor Leonard Wood. There was a strong populist element in his approach to Japan's three revolutions.

He had little knowledge of or interest in modern political or economic theory. He sought inspiration, instead, in abstract principles and heroic figures. "My major advisers now," he told a journalist, "have boiled down almost to two men—George Washington and Abraham Lincoln. One founded the United States, the other saved it. If you go back into their lives, you can find almost all the answers."[16] It sounded pretty cornball, but it was backed up by some concrete evidence. When MacArthur looked up from his desk, there was, on the wall facing him, a portrait of Lincoln with this quotation framed underneath: "If I were to try to read, much less answer, all the attacks made on me, this shop might as well be closed for any other business. I do the very best I know how, the very best I can, and I mean to keep on doing so until the end. If the end brings me out all right, what is said against me won't amount to anything. If the end brings me out wrong, ten thousand angels swearing I was right would make no difference." And on the wall behind MacArthur, looking over his shoulder, was a portrait of Washington.[17]

One of the first actions MacArthur took on reaching Tokyo was to release nearly five hundred political prisoners and have the five thousand members of the government's "thought police" fired.[18] He introduced habeas corpus, feeling immensely proud. His father, who had been both a lawyer and a general, had counted it one of his greatest achievements to have brought habeas corpus to the Philippines in 1900. The son was thrilled to think that he was following once more in his father's footsteps.[19]

MacArthur waited until he had disarmed Japan before he tried to rearrange it politically. He had been ordered to purge from Japanese public life those suspected of war crimes, all the senior officials in the military and anyone who had been actively involved in promoting "militant nationalism and aggression" since 1931. The first purge was launched in January 1946, to the horror of Yoshida and other conservatives. They could easily imagine many of their old friends and colleagues being thrown out of public life, leaving the way open for the Communists to move in. The purges were a tremendous shock to the Japanese and the most unpopular action of the occupation. Yoshida reportedly asked MacArthur, "Are you trying to turn Japan Red?"[20]

Nearly 720,000 Japanese were ultimately screened. Of these, some 200,000 were barred from politics, business, the armed forces and the civil service. The first purge was the most wide-reaching, and it removed 400 members of the Diet that was sitting when the purges began, as well as half the members of the Cabinet. Its impact was enormous.

This was not enough for Whitney and Kades, however. They convinced MacArthur that the first purge had not gone far enough. At the end of 1946 a second purge was launched, this time aimed at ultranationalists in the media, industry and local government. The Japanese were forced to swallow a second dose of the same bitter medicine, while the aftertaste of the first still soured their palates. Even so, MacArthur had not gone as far as the JCS probably had in mind. In the American occupation zone in Germany 2.5 percent of the entire population was barred from public life or positions of influence. In Japan the figure was less than half of 1 percent. In Germany thousands went to prison, tens of thousands more received heavy fines or had their properties confiscated. In Japan no one went to jail, was fined or lost his property.[21]

Despite this, there were strong protests in the United States that MacArthur was trampling on civil liberties. Kades proposed to counter this by getting some American experts to come to Japan. He convinced Whitney to ask the War Department to request the services of three famous figures in the American Civil Liberties Union: Roger Baldwin, Morris Ernst and Arthur Garfield Hayes. When MacArthur learned of it, he sent a cable to Washington canceling the request. Kades did not realize it, but Ernst was Drew Pearson's lawyer and, in MacArthur's eyes, the man who had blackmailed him out of fifteen thousand dollars back in 1934 by threatening to publish his love letters to Isabel Rosario Cooper and put her on the witness stand. Hayes and Ernst dropped whatever plans they had to go to Japan, but Baldwin, having been invited, refused to be uninvited. He was going, he said, and if necessary would pay his own way. MacArthur's only option now was to charm him into submission.[22]

Did it work? Did it work! Baldwin spent nearly three months in Japan. GHQ was ordered to give him all the cooperation he needed. He was to be taken wherever he wanted to go, shown whatever he wanted to see, and his questions were to be answered frankly and fully. Half forgotten now, Baldwin was as much a hero to liberals as MacArthur was to conservatives. He had devoted his entire adult life to upholding the rights of individuals against the growing power of the state. He had founded the ACLU at the height of the Red Scare back in the early 1920s. In the course of his career Baldwin opposed fascism, racism and nativism with intelligence, wit and courage. During the late 1920s he had briefly been misled into praising the Soviet Union, but unlike many of his liberal contemporaries, he soon came to recognize communism for the monstrous tyranny that it was.

He arrived in Japan in a skeptical frame of mind, though it did him little good. "I had seen enough of so-called big men to discount the virtues attributed to them," he recalled several years later. "But I observed in General MacArthur the qualities which would make of him, if wholly unknown, a character so arresting and unusual that people would be drawn to him by the force of his convictions and the eloquence of his expression. . . . Doubtless he struts in company, though in personal interviews he is relaxed, charming, witty, and an attentive listener. All testimony by those close to MacArthur attributes the strutting, posing and posturing to what few would accept—a persistent shyness, an acute self-consciousness which finds its compensation and defense in the grand manner."[23]

Baldwin was disturbed by what he saw of GHQ's press censorship machinery. MacArthur had emulated the British system, in which reporters and editors were briefed on the stories GHQ wanted to see covered and advised on which facts should be left out of stories the authorities did not want to see published but knew they would just have to live with. Baldwin told MacArthur that however subtly it was done, precensorship undermined free expression. MacArthur responded, "Under the Occupation there are some of our policies that we can't let them criticize, because that would make it too difficult for us to carry them out." It would be some time before there was any noticeable relaxation of press censorship.[24]

At another meeting Baldwin complained that mail was being opened. MacArthur blandly assured him that mail tampering had ceased, although he probably knew better. Baldwin assured him he had actually seen the mail censors at work in the Osaka post office. The next time he saw MacArthur the general told him, "You're right, Mr. Baldwin. Even my own mail was opened. I found a letter that had been opened and resealed and I put a stop to the whole system." By the time he left Tokyo, Baldwin had established the Japanese Civil Liberties Union, convinced MacArthur to make it easier for American soldiers to marry Japanese women, helped end mail tampering and, with MacArthur's help, met the emperor.[25]

While he was changing his mind about the general, the general was also becoming a fan of his. In 1949 MacArthur sent a letter to be included in a *Festschrift* honoring Roger Baldwin on the occasion of his retirement. He hailed him as "one of the architects of our cherished American way of life." Baldwin scrawled across the bottom of this letter a wry comment that although written "in the general's best hyperbole, it has not hurt me, even among liberals."[26]

MacArthur counted heavily during his first couple of years in Japan on reforming the country politically by weakening Shinto, which as the state religion was inevitably associated with Japanese militarism and aggression. He realized the futility of removing one faith without putting another in its place. He was, as he had been since childhood, a devout Episcopalian. He still read the Bible daily even if, a few funerals excepted, he did not attend church. Jean went regularly and carried that burden for both of them. MacArthur worked on a Sunday as if it were just another day, which, in Japan, it was. One of his fondest dreams was that by the time he left the country Japan would be a Christian nation.

MacArthur ordered government subsidies to Shinto temples stopped. He got the emperor to distance himself from Shintoism by publicly renouncing his own divinity. And he actively tried to spread Christianity from the few hundred thousand Japanese adherents it already claimed into the principal religion of Japan. He encouraged Christian missionaries to come to Japan and forced the Japanese government to finance them.[27] He convinced himself that Japan was primed for conversion and informed the American Bible Society, "The demand for Bibles, testaments and gospels is insatiable. . . . There is great demand by millions of Japanese who have become interested in Christian principles."[28] More than ten million Japanese translations of the Bible were distributed during the occupation.

For a time he thought the program was working. "The Japanese have got the Spirit of the Sermon on the Mount," he told a journalist. "Nothing will take it away from them."[29] His hopes of spreading Christianity to the masses were nonetheless doomed. They might have been realized if the missionaries' efforts had produced one convert, the emperor. It could have been the story of Rome all over again: fierce resistance to Christianity until the conversion of Constantine.

In early 1946 rumors started circulating that Hirohito was thinking of becoming a Christian. The papal nuncio went straight to Thorpe, who was in effect the Allied custodian of the emperor, and demanded to see him. Thorpe himself had a strong feeling Hirohito was toying with the idea of a conversion and was prepared to go through with it if he could be convinced it would benefit his people. The papal nuncio seemed to have come to exactly the same conclusion and was panting to woo Hirohito into the Vatican's embrace. Thorpe, however, refused to let the papal nuncio anywhere near the emperor.

After a brief but heated discussion, the Pope's representative departed, to be followed soon thereafter by the arrival of three Protestant heavyweights. They too demanded to see Hirohito, and Thorpe gave them the same dusty answer. Then he went to tell MacArthur what had happened. "Sir," he concluded, "we're in trouble if he becomes a Christian." If Hirohito converted to Catholicism, tens of millions of American Protestants would be outraged. And if he became a Protestant, tens of millions of American Catholics would be equally incensed. "I don't think we can afford to let him change religions."

MacArthur saw a dream die before his eyes. "You're right." He sighed. "I can't let him become a Christian." And that was how the convert of the century slipped right through his trembling fingers.[30]

Japan's economic plight in the winter of 1945–46 was wretched almost beyond description. The rice harvest was two thirds its normal level. Food consumption in the cities had fallen from an average of eighteen hundred calories per day per adult to one thousand calories a day. At his first meeting with MacArthur Yoshida asked for four million tons of American food to prevent mass starvation. Herbert Hoover, who had become famous as "the Great Humanitarian" by feeding starving Belgians in World War I and had saved the Bolsheviks by feeding starving Russians in the early 1920s, was also alarmed. He wrote to MacArthur, advising him to "borrow" up to a million tons of Liberty ships and move surplus rice from Indochina and wheat from North America to nip this crisis in the bud.[31]

MacArthur had no means of getting hold of large amounts of shipping nor the money to buy up large amounts of food. He used the limited amount of shipping that he had available to bring in 350,000 tons of food from Army stocks in the western Pacific. The Japanese government emptied the warehouses that contained its emergency food supplies.[32]

MacArthur was criticized in Congress for feeding the hated enemy. He later claimed that his response was to tell the War Department that unless he fed the Japanese, there would be "mass unrest, disorder and violence. Give me bread or give me bullets." In fact, what he really cabled was a warning that starvation "can only precipitate calamitous reactions. . . . Either food or soldiers must be brought to Japan."[33]

The food crisis gave added urgency to SCAP's plans for land reform. Nearly half of Japan's limited supply of arable land was farmed by tenants who tried to scratch a living from plots the size of some American lawns and turned over much of their yield to the landlord. MacArthur's solution was the fulfilled hope of generations of populists: Absentee landlords were required to sell all their land to their tenants at prices the tenants could afford. Those who worked the land would own the land; at least, they owned 90 percent of it by the end of the occupation. For those who still rented, there was a ban on payment in kind. What a farmer grew was for him to sell or eat, as he chose.[34]

The Diet passed the two bills that imposed land reform on Japan on a day in mid-October 1946. MacArthur was in his office when Kades brought him the news. His father had tried, and failed, more than forty years earlier, to convince Taft of the need for land reform in the Philippines, where the oppression of tenant farmers was as great as anything to be found in Japan. He looked hard at the framed photograph of his father that he kept on his desk. "Dad would have liked this," he said.[35]

Another key economic reform was the creation of an organized labor movement free of government control. There had been unions in Japan for half a century, but over the years they had lost their independence. MacArthur was under orders to give it back to them. His prolonged absence from the United States and his reading of right-wing newspapers had, inevitably, given him a weird perspective on American labor history. He was convinced, for instance, that under U.S. law every worker was required to be a member of either the AFL or the CIO.[36]

He persuaded the Japanese government to enact three major labor laws. No Japanese was required to join a union, but those who wished to do so found it easy. It was easy too to create a union. MacArthur encouraged American labor leaders to come to Japan and help their Japanese counterparts seize the opportunities the new legislation provided.[37]

Organized labor grew at a phenomenal rate. Before the war Japan had fewer than a dozen unions and about 100,000 members. Between 1945 and 1948 the number of unions rose from 5 to more than 34,000, and the number of union members topped 6.6 million.[38]

This tremendous growth was accompanied by numerous strikes. Living conditions in Japan were appalling for the urban masses. The principal objective of most of the new unions was to demand higher wages for their members. Moreover, Communists managed to seize control of some of the new unions and intended to use them as instruments for prosecuting class war. In January 1947 they threatened a general strike that would bring the entire country to a standstill. MacArthur hoped desperately that the government would find a way to prevent the strike, but even the offer of a 40 percent pay increase failed. When, at the last minute, it became clear that the strike would go ahead unless he intervened, MacArthur crossed his fingers, held his breath and banned it. If the Communists challenged the ban, he knew, there was likely to be bloodshed. To his immense relief, there was no trouble. The workers pocketed the 40 percent pay raise, and something like peace broke out across organized labor now that the Communist labor leaders had been publicly humiliated.[39]

MacArthur did not share the almost pathological fear of Communist influence that afflicted people like Willoughby. When George Kennan visited Tokyo in 1948 and asked him about rumors of there being Communist party members working in GHQ SCAP, MacArthur responded, "We have probably got some of them. The War Department has some. So does the State Department. It doesn't mean very much."[40] He was troubled nonetheless by the prevalence of Communists in the leadership of unions that represented government workers, such as schoolteachers. Before he left Japan, he launched yet another purge, to root them out of the labor movement, an action that brought renewed cries that he was trampling on civil liberties.[41]

MacArthur's orders required him to break up the huge holding companies, known as zaibatsu, that dominated Japanese industry. The fifteen biggest zaibatsu—such as Mitsubishi, Mitsui and Sumitomo—were owned by a handful of families whose members were widely held to be active partners in Japanese militarism and aggression. They dominated entire industries, such as steel, chemicals and machinery production. They controlled the biggest banks and insurance companies too. The zaibatsu families had profited from the rule of the military, had helped finance the military's domination of Japanese political life and had put no obstacles in the way of

Japan's career of conquest. Such, at least, was the view in Washington. When MacArthur reached Japan and met this supposedly fearsome and ruthless business elite, he was underwhelmed. They reminded him, he remarked dismissively, "of the most effete New York clubmen."[42]

One object of the purges was to break up the zaibatsu. It seemed essential to rid Japan of this feudal element before a free market could develop. The purges removed more than a thousand executives and managers from zaibatsu-run companies, and other members of the families that owned them were barred from taking their places. Most of the zaibatsu were broken up, despite cries of alarm from Yoshida and many conservative Japanese politicians.

Some Allies, strongly supported by the State Department, demanded heavy reparations, but MacArthur resisted every attempt to strip Japan of its industrial base to pay for the ravages of war. He had to give way eventually, and Japanese industry was stripped of many of its machine tools. These were parceled out to the Russians, the British, the Dutch, the Filipinos and various Southeast Asian countries. How much these tools contributed to Allied economies is debatable, but the effect on the war-shattered industries of Japan seems pretty obvious.

The United States took nothing in reparations. Instead it provided about two billion dollars in economic assistance, mostly to relieve the privations suffered by millions of Japanese. MacArthur meanwhile managed to persuade the Japanese government to accept legal responsibility for repaying the costs of the occupation. The Japanese eventually paid the United States nearly five billion dollars in occupation costs, more than twice the amount expended on relief.[43]

Strange as it may seem, MacArthur was not instructed to revive the Japanese economy. He was told to democratize it, by broadening ownership and increasing the participation of formerly powerless groups, such as workers and farmers. There is, in modern philosophy, a category known as "a necessary but not sufficient condition." Democratizing the Japanese economy amounted to exactly that—a condition that was necessary for its revival but not sufficient to bring about a revival. In 1946 industrial output was less than one third its wartime peak. Inflation was running at 50 percent a month. Incomes were rising, but not as fast as inflation. Japan's foreign trade was virtually zero. Investment was stagnant. Unemployment was around 20 percent. Land reform, political reform, breaking up the zaibatsu, the growth of organized labor, emergency relief and the like were not enough to pull Japan out of its malaise.

MacArthur was fiercely criticized by *Fortune* and *Newsweek* for failing to revive the Japanese economy.[44] These attacks infuriated him, and he responded vigorously, but he knew as well as anyone else just how parlous the economic situation had become. "The only remaining problem of magnitude lies in the rehabilitation of the Japanese economy," he told Herbert Hoover in October 1947. And in a New Year's Day 1948 message to the people of Japan, he told them frankly, "Individual hardship is inevitable. Your economy . . . is now impoverished," and held out no hope of any significant improvement in the near future.[45]

The solution to Japan's economic dilemmas, MacArthur believed, was a peace treaty. So long as Japan remained formally in a state of war, it was not an attractive place for investment. It would have to continue paying for the occupation, and it was under constant pressure for reparations. Once it rejoined the international community, on the other hand, its economic prospects would be transformed. Without a treaty, any recovery was going to be slow and fitful, because there was no Marshall Plan for Japan and no chance of there being one.

In March 1947 MacArthur had made his one and only visit to the Tokyo Press Club. The journalists there were simply flabbergasted to see him drop in like this. It seemed too good to be true. There was a scramble for paper and pencils, and he acted so relaxed they knew it was too good to be true. Was the meeting on the record or off? they asked warily. On, he said. So they could quote him? Absolutely. Were there any subjects he was not prepared to discuss? No. They blinked in amazement. He'd not only come to them but was actually going to hold an on-the-record press conference, something none of them had ever imagined would happen. They were right to be astonished because it never happened again. He was obviously up to something, but what?

The very first question was the pitch he was looking for. He had planted the seed a few days earlier by telling several reporters that the UN might want to take over responsibility for Japan. Was it true, a reporter asked, that Japan was going to be placed under the control of the UN? "The time is now approaching when we must talk peace with Japan," said MacArthur. "The military purpose [of the occupation] has been, I think, accomplished. The political phase is approaching such completion as is possible under the Occupation. . . . The third phase is economic. . . . But this is not a phase the Occupation can settle. We can only enforce economic strangulation." What was needed now was a peace treaty—"as soon as possible."[46]

In Washington the head of the State Department's Policy Planning Staff, George Kennan, was arguing the opposite case. Back in 1945 the State Department had lost out in the turf war over Japan to the War Department. Washington's turf wars are partly about ideas, but mainly about power, money and prestige. The department was filled with people every bit as idealistic as MacArthur, but because they had comparatively little say about how the occupation was run, State's senior officials liked to imagine that MacArthur was a loose cannon on the deck of the good ship *America,* likely to shoot off in any and all directions. They seized on his demands for a peace treaty as proof they were right.

Kennan was the father of the containment doctrine against Soviet expansionism and possessed one of the keenest minds in Washington. He was, to a large degree, the mastermind behind Truman's policy of resisting the threats and encroachments of the Soviet Union until communism evolved beyond the evil system of lies and mass murder that currently kept it afloat into something half civilized, or until it collapsed from the weight of its stupidity, whichever came first. Fearing Communist designs to exploit whatever weaknesses were to be found in Japan, Kennan told the new secretary of defense, James Forrestal, that MacArthur had allowed socialism to reach such a point that if there was a peace treaty now, something close to anarchy would break out. Effective government would be impossible, and the economy would collapse—"precisely what the Communists want."[47]

Kennan traveled to Japan to see things for himself. He had dinner with Willoughby, who was agitated by what he saw as the growing influence of Communists within GHQ SCAP. Kennan concluded that MacArthur had "brought Japanese life to a point of great turmoil and confusion [and] a serious degree of instability." The purges, far from democratizing Japanese politics and business, seemed almost ideal "for the specific purpose of rendering Japanese society vulnerable to Communist pressures and paving the way for a Communist takeover."[48] Kennan spoke with MacArthur at length but never expressed what he really thought. As a result, their meetings were as harmonious as they were meaningless.

Far from there being a meeting of minds, they were as far apart in their views of a peace treaty as it was possible for two people to get. MacArthur thought the economy would not recover without one. Kennan was just as convinced that without an economic recovery, there could be no peace treaty. Paradoxically, both were right. The solution was as plain as Washington's face on the one-dollar bill. Japan needed a large infusion of capital, for new plants and equipment, for infrastructure projects and for retraining its work force. It was already being done . . . in Europe. By 1949 the United States was pumping a billion dollars a month into nearly a dozen European countries, via the Marshall Plan. This money had even been offered to countries like Czechoslovakia in an attempt to keep them out of Soviet hands.

The Marshall Plan was a brilliant example of enlightened self-interest, but the Truman administration refused to countenance a Marshall Plan for Japan. American public opinion remained fiercely hostile to the Japanese. The Pearl Harbor legacy died hard, and sadly, racial antagonism probably played a part too. If the Japanese were going to get up off their knees, they would have to find a way of doing it themselves. For the present the Japanese economy would continue to scrape along, desperate for investment, stripped of machine tools and unable to modernize.

Kennan's visit marked a turning point. MacArthur had just passed the high-water mark of his time as supreme commander. From mid-1948 on his powers were increasingly circumscribed and the scrutiny of his actions was more tightly focused. The creation of the Department of Defense and the National Security Council had changed the machinery for international security policy. There were also more players in the game, and they played by different rules.

Kennan's visit brought various changes in occupation policy. Some of them, such as persuading MacArthur to moderate the heavy-handed methods the GHQ staff employed to curb the black market, were minor but overdue. He also helped bring about a more relaxed approach to fraternization between American soldiers and the Japanese. The important changes, however, flowed from a recognition in Washington that Japan would have to be turned into the bulwark of American opposition to Soviet expansionism in the Far East. The crooked and ineffective government of Chiang Kai-shek had failed to stem the advance of the Chinese Communists under Mao Tse-tung. Nothing could now stop China from falling under Communist rule.

In October 1948 a new directive, known as NSC 13/2, was drafted following Kennan's recommendations. MacArthur reacted to it fiercely: "NSC 13/2 has not been conveyed as an order to SCAP by appropriate directive . . . therefore SCAP is not responsible in any way for its implementation."[49] Messages like this were seized on by MacArthur's critics as proof that he was insubordinate. Yet he was on solid ground. The only agreed method was for the NSC to submit documents like this to the JCS, which would turn them into military orders that MacArthur would have to obey. There was a clear chain of command, but it was being ignored.

MacArthur's resistance to NSC 13/2 proved to be more a matter of irritation at the NSC's high-handed approach than anything else. Having made his point, he gradually began acting as if NSC 13/2 were an order. Nearly all its provisions were ultimately implemented by GHQ SCAP. MacArthur reduced the size of the SCAP bureaucracy, handed more and more powers over to the Japanese and cracked down on the Communists. The democratizing, reforming phase of the occupation came to an end in 1949. Japan was increasingly treated as an ally, less and less like a defeated and occupied nation.

In May 1946 MacArthur had the pleasure of welcoming Herbert Hoover to Japan. The former President, the man who had made him Chief of Staff, had come to examine the food situation. The two men nevertheless talked about many things, including politics. Hoover told MacArthur that he was still immensely popular and urged him to run for the White House in 1948. At the very least a MacArthur candidacy would allow him to awaken America to the dangers it faced and raise the level of political debate. Hoover said he was certain MacArthur could be elected. MacArthur's response was "I want none of it." Disappointed, Hoover concluded he meant exactly what he said.[50]

Even so, after waiting six months, Hoover tried again. "The whole nation will listen to you as to no other man," he informed MacArthur. He got, if anything, an even more emphatic rejection. First, said MacArthur, he would probably have to retire from the Army to become a candidate. Second, he did not want to leave before a peace treaty was signed. And "Third is the very definite feeling on my part that no one would seriously listen to me. . . . On military or Occupation matters, yes, but on other questions I am doubtful."[51]

While Hoover and others tried to convince him he was still enormously popular, there was no sign that his popularity was not only broad but deep, and he probably suspected as much. MacArthur personally opened every letter that was addressed to him and delighted in opening them. They tended to be jejune effusions of admiration or requests for photographs, but a few were genuinely touching or informative. The envelopes were slit half open by an aide to speed the operation, then placed on his desk, awaiting his own surgical stroke. "My fan letters," he called them, but there were only about half a dozen each day.[52]

If he looked to the press for signs of popularity, there was as much against him as for him, as he well knew. MacArthur could count on right-wing Republican newspapers in the Midwest, such as the self-styled "world's greatest newspaper," the *Chicago Tribune*. This meretricious rag was the personal organ of the pompous and blinkered Robert McCormick, one of MacArthur's most devoted admirers. But the East Coast newspapers of the center-right, such as the highly respected *New York Herald Tribune*, did not do MacArthur any favors. Periodicals that had been ardently pro-MacArthur during the war, such as the *Saturday Evening Post*, were losing interest, and even the Luces seemed to have gone cold on him, as the attack in *Fortune* showed. MacArthur hoped passionately to see his face on the cover of *Time* as the Man of the Year for 1946, in recognition of his handling of the occupation, and was crushed when the magazine chose Secretary of State James F. Byrnes.[53]

Convinced, of course, that he was merely defending the occupation from its enemies, he manipulated press censorship in Japan to his own ends. His way of dealing with a journalist was usually to flatter and seduce him. Just about every journalist granted access to MacArthur ended up writing favorably about him, more or less. But there were more than a hundred accredited American and British journalists in Japan, and the vast majority never got to interview MacArthur. Anyway, the people he was likely to talk to were publishers, not reporters; the generals, not the lieutenants. And he could charm even their defenses away. A distinguished correspondent of *The New York Times,* Cyrus L. Sulzberger, visited Tokyo determined not to be taken in by this general who seemed to have snake-charmed so many others before him. And failed. When he was asked some months later, "How long did it take MacArthur to get you in his pocket?" Sulzberger replied wryly, "About thirty seconds."[54]

While he was charming the publishers, MacArthur was inclined to be ruthless with reporters who disagreed with him or looked as if they were going to disagree with him. There were more than a dozen respected journalists whom he tried to keep out of Japan on the ground that they were too far to the left. He was told to let them in by the Pentagon in nearly every case.

One of the few journalists granted an interview was a British writer, Malcolm Muggeridge, who was both a staunch liberal and vehement anti-Communist. MacArthur regaled him for nearly an hour with a stream of clichés ("Freedom is a heady wine," "the Japanese have gotten the spirit of the Sermon on the Mount") and allowed Muggeridge to interpose hardly a word, let alone a thought. Democracy and Christianity had completely revolutionized Japan, MacArthur intoned. Muggeridge was bored much of the time, and slightly embarrassed too. "He seemed to me," Muggeridge informed his diary, "like a broken-down actor of the type one meets in railway trains or boarding houses in England." The next day Muggeridge had dinner with a State Department official and mockingly described his interview with the general. Their conversation was overheard by a SCAP official seated at a nearby table and was swiftly reported to MacArthur. Muggeridge would soon be leaving for Hong Kong, so there was not much point in expelling him for lèse-majesté. MacArthur got what revenge he could by personally ordering the expulsion of his dinner companion.[55]

With this kind of example to guide them, it was not surprising that SCAP's public relations officers tried to bully correspondents into writing favorably or at least not writing unfavorably about the way the occupation was going and how the general was doing. For the first three or four years the correspondents depended on GHQ SCAP for housing, travel and rations. MacArthur's staff used this leverage with such a heavy hand that the main result of their efforts was to generate more bad publicity than would have been likely had they treated the scribblers as minor partners in a historic enterprise and not as carping, left-wing scum trying to stir up trouble.

MacArthur had once advised his wartime aide Colonel Larry Lehrbas, "Never get in an argument with the press. . . . If you argue, they keep the controversy going [and] [t]hey always have the last word. On the other hand, if you ignore their statements there is little they can do but let the issue die and label you as being uncooperative."[56] Lehrbas had returned to civilian life, his place taken by Brigadier General Frayne Baker, a man who believed in the frontal assault, the most suicidal of tactics. When, for example, a CBS reporter named William Costello wrote a piece for *The New Republic* claiming the occupation was failing in its major objectives, Baker sent Edward R. Murrow a three-page, single-spaced, almost word-by-word rebuttal of Costello's article. Murrow, the legendary head of CBS News, replied, "Your letter has greatly increased our confidence in Mr. Costello's work."[57]

MacArthur usually followed the advice he had given Lehrbas, but occasionally his combative nature got in the way. As William Sebald, MacArthur's political adviser, noticed, "his reaction to press attacks was painful to watch."[58] He sent furious personal rejoinders to critical articles in various magazines, denouncing some of them as stemming from "a Communist-inspired smear campaign." Several times he tried to get the Pentagon to stop the publication in the United States of articles attacking the way he ran the occupation but never succeeded.[59] The first thing any serious contender for his party's presidential nomination needs to do is get the media on his side. Far from doing that, from 1945 to 1950 MacArthur increasingly alienated journalists, editors and publishers.

Although he had discouraged Hoover in 1946, by the fall of 1947 MacArthur was having second thoughts about running for the White House. For one thing, Truman was deeply unpopular, and nearly every poll indicated how vulnerable he was to a strong Republican challenge. For another, as supreme commander MacArthur had shown he could run a country. He was more than a general now. In October 1947 he wrote his old friend and West Point classmate Robert Wood, "I certainly do not covet nor actively seek any other office, but should the movement become more expressive of the desire of good and loyal friends and well wishers, and take on the character of popular will, I should be left no alternative but to consider it a mandate which I could not in good conscience ignore."[60] In other words, I don't intend to campaign, but I wouldn't mind a coronation.

Eisenhower was meanwhile being urged to run too, but Ike's response was completely different. In January 1948 he wrote to a New Hampshire newspaper to take himself out of the race just as the primary season really got rolling. "I am not available for and could not accept nomination for high political office," he declared. But instead of leaving it there, he went on to say, "It is my conviction that the necessary and wise subordination of the military to civic power will be best sustained . . . when lifelong professional soldiers, in the absence of some obvious and overriding reason, abstain from seeking high political office." That looked suspiciously like a twenty-four-inch torpedo aimed at sinking MacArthur's hopes.[61]

MacArthur was incensed. If Ike wanted to rule himself out, that was one thing, but dog-in-the-mangerism was a provocation that could not go unanswered. Ike's statement, he told the British ambassador, was both "a slur upon the U.S. Army" and "the reason I felt obliged to offer my own candidacy."[62] He now made public what he had so far told only a few people, like Wood, in private. He released a statement to the press, saying that while he was not actively seeking elective office, "I would be recreant to all my concepts of good citizenship were I to shrink . . . from accepting any public duty to which I might be called by the American people."[63]

The first Republican primary would be held in Wisconsin in April, and news that one hundred thousand signatures had been collected on a MacArthur-for-President petition in that state sent his hopes soaring. Dewey privately concluded that Wisconsin was as good as lost to MacArthur and gave it little of his time or money. Meanwhile Louise was asked what she thought of MacArthur's chances as "a dark horse candidate." Showing she had lost none of her tartness since divorcing him twenty years earlier, she replied, "If he's a dark horse, he's in the last roundup."[64]

On election day Harold Stassen from next-door Minnesota took nineteen of Wisconsin's twenty-seven delegates to the Republican convention. MacArthur got the other eight, and Dewey got shut out. Coming in a distant second was no consolation to MacArthur. When Sebald went to the Dai Ichi Building for a routine conference with MacArthur the morning the Wisconsin results were announced, the chief of staff, Major General Paul J. Mueller, held up a hand, like a traffic cop. No entry. "The general is as low as a rug," said Mueller. "He's very disappointed."[65]

The Nebraska primary was held a week later, and MacArthur's showing was even more humiliating than it had been in Wisconsin. He asked his supporters to withdraw his name from further primaries. Old friends like Robert Wood tried to convince him to come home and salvage his tattered candidacy, but he refused to consider it. He stuck by what he had said on March 9, and that was it.[66]

Dewey was duly nominated at the Republican convention in late June. MacArthur got eleven delegate votes, out of nearly eleven hundred cast. After Dewey's nomination MacArthur was sounded out on becoming Dewey's secretary of defense should Dewey win the presidency, but MacArthur was no more interested in taking orders from Dewey than he was in taking them from Truman.[67]

MacArthur was reported to have said when he arrived in Japan, "If the Occupation lasts two years, it will be a great success. If it last three years, it still has a chance of being a success. If it lasts beyond that, its success is doubtful."[68] By his own measure, his time in Japan was up. Whatever good he might do had been done.

Shortly before the November 1948 election Truman arrived at a similar conclusion. He expected to win, despite what the polls said, and when he became President in his own right, he was finally going to force Mr. Brass Hat, Five-Star MacArthur, to do what he, the President, wanted. He was going to make MacArthur come home and retire.

Just about the time that ballots were being printed and distributed, the military governor of West Germany, General Lucius D. Clay, was asked by the Pentagon to go to Tokyo and take over from MacArthur. Clay had been a cadet at West Point under MacArthur and had worked for him in the Philippines in the late 1930s. One of the ablest young officers in the Army, he had made as great a success of his German assignment as MacArthur had achieved in Japan.

It had not been easy. Clay had been under enormous pressure from the Soviets, who were determined to push the Western Allies out of Berlin. When Stalin tried to starve and freeze the city into submission, Clay organized and ran the Berlin airlift. At the age of fifty-one he was in the prime of life and more than a decade away from the Army's mandatory retirement age, but the strain of his assignment had burned him out. All Clay wanted to do now was leave the Army. He refused the assignment and put in for retirement. With that, Truman's hopes of getting rid of MacArthur collapsed. They were stuck with each other for as far ahead as either one of them could see.[69]

30

With One Arm
Tied Behind My Back

MacArthur had been eager to get the Soviets into the war, but he had no intention of allowing them into Japan. The division of Germany into zones of occupation turned millions of Germans over to Communist indoctrination, terror and coercion and did nothing toward achieving a peaceful, prosperous Germany. The advance of the Red Army deep into Western Europe, however, had made that inevitable. When Stalin demanded that Japan too be carved into zones of occupation and proposed taking a large chunk of the most northerly of Japan's main islands, Hokkaido, Truman was willing to accommodate the Soviets on the understanding that their presence in Japan would be temporary. MacArthur did not believe that if they were allowed in they would ever leave willingly, and was adamantly opposed to this idea, but he did not have the power to reject it.

It was up to him as Supreme Commander for the Allied Powers, however, to decide where Allied occupation troops would be deployed. He pretended to welcome Stalin's offer of "help" and said he had just the place for his troops, a desolate spot in the middle of Honshu, the main island, and that spot just happened to be ringed by American military bases.[1] Stalin hinted that he might simply send troops to Hokkaido anyway and assert the Soviet Union's rights at the point of a bayonet. MacArthur's off-the-record response, according to his counterintelligence chief, Brigadier General Elliott Thorpe, was, "If you land one Russian soldier, I'll have an American division up there to run them right back into the water." The version he gives in his memoirs is slightly different. He claims he told Stalin's representative in Japan, Lieutenant General Kuzma Derevyanko, "If a single Soviet soldier enters Japan without my authority, I will at once throw the entire Russian mission, including you, into jail."[2]

Stalin's response to MacArthur's tough line was to stop hinting that he would use force if necessary, but he continued to insist that the Soviet Union had the right to put troops into Hokkaido. In that case, said MacArthur, they would have to come under the Eighth Army's control. Rather than place Soviet troops under American command, Stalin abruptly dropped all demands for a piece of Japan.[3]

The British and Australians were meanwhile making similar claims for a zone of their own and equal status with the Americans. To their chagrin, MacArthur gave them Hiroshima, one of the most depressing places in the whole of Japan. Nor did they have any real say in occupation policy. The commander of the British Commonwealth Occupation Force reported, through clenched teeth, to Eighth Army headquarters. He had no direct access to MacArthur.[4]

The Soviets bitterly resented the way MacArthur froze them out and when their opportunity came, they grabbed it with both hands. The day that Dean Acheson publicly rebuked MacArthur for saying he needed no more than two hundred thousand troops to occupy Japan, Stalin seized the moment and demanded an Allied control commission similar to the one already in operation in Germany. Having itself held MacArthur up to public scorn, the Truman administration found itself instantly backed into a corner by Soviet diplomats arguing that anyone so wayward obviously had to be brought under control. The United States was forced to give ground.[5]

The result was a conference in Moscow that brought the creation of two bodies, the Allied Council for Japan and the Far Eastern Commission.[6] The four-member ACJ comprised representatives from the United States, the Soviet Union, China and the British Commonwealth. Its role was limited to giving the supreme commander advice on occupation policy.

The role of the FEC, on the other hand, was to ensure that the Japanese carried out the surrender terms. The FEC was authorized to issue directives to SCAP, *but* these directives had to go first to the U.S. government, which would in turn "transmit them to the Supreme Commander through the appropriate authority. . . ." In other words, through the JCS. It was obvious that neither the President nor the Joint Chiefs would transmit any directive to MacArthur that conflicted with American policy, and that policy, Truman told Secretary of State James Byrnes in December 1945, was simple: "We should maintain complete control of Japan and the Pacific. . . ." Nor was Truman prepared to make any more concessions to Stalin. "I'm tired of babying the Soviets," he fumed.[7]

Given its limited, advisory role, it was easy for MacArthur to ignore the ACJ whenever he chose, which turned out to be most of the time. SCAP rarely put anything on the agenda for it to discuss, so most of its meetings were short if nothing else. John Gunther attended a typical session. "The official report notes soberly that the meeting opened at 10:03 A.M. and closed at 10:04 A.M."[8]

MacArthur eventually found a use for the ACJ—as a forum to raise the question of what had happened to nearly two million Japanese soldiers who had surrendered to the Red Army in Manchuria. Most were kept as POWs until 1949, and enormous efforts were made to convert them to communism before they were returned to Japan. Even after repatriation more than three hundred thousand Japanese remained unaccounted for; they have not been accounted for to this day. It has to be assumed they were victims of Soviet revenge or were murdered for resisting the indoctrination program. This was an issue that touched a raw nerve in Japan, and the Soviets were outraged whenever MacArthur raised it, whether in public or private. When he put it before the ACJ, the Soviets made a great show of flouncing out and did not return for six months.

While MacArthur found it easy to ignore the ACJ, he had to pay more attention to the Far Eastern Commission, given its right to issue directives on how to run the occupation. Established early in 1946, it sputtered into life about the time the Government Section was drafting the new Japanese constitution. The FEC insisted on having its say, but beyond being allowed to recommend a few minor changes, it was treated with the deepest suspicion by GHQ SCAP. Yet not even the paranoid Charles Willoughby realized there was a Soviet agent among the delegates to the FEC—the British diplomat Donald Maclean. A committed Stalinist, Maclean was the secret guardian of Soviet interests in Japan.[9]

MacArthur resisted every Soviet attempt to win a major role in the occupation. Anticommunism was blood of his blood, bone of his bone. He took a certain delight in baiting Derevyanko. When MacArthur banned the general strike the Communists had organized in early 1947, Derevyanko hurried around to the Dai Ichi and demanded to know what authority MacArthur had for acting in this high-handed manner. Why, in that haven of liberty the USSR, workers' rights were guaranteed by law and people could go on strike whenever they wished. A ban like this was impossible there. MacArthur got up from behind his desk, stared Derevyanko in the eye and out of the side of his mouth said to the Russian-speaking interpreter, "What's the Russian word for 'nuts'?" Derevyanko knew enough English to follow what MacArthur was saying, said goodbye and left.[10]

When Derevyanko was recalled to Moscow, MacArthur gave him a message for Stalin. It was a message that took an hour to deliver, as MacArthur paced behind his desk pouring scorn on every flaw, weakness and provocation in Soviet foreign policy. MacArthur finally stopped pacing. "Now," he concluded, "you tell that to Marshal Stalin." The Russian departed and did not return to Japan for nearly a year. When he called once more at the Dai Ichi, MacArthur greeted him like an old friend. "Why, General Derevyanko! Delighted to see you back. When you failed to return sooner, I feared they had shot you!"[11]

In Washington MacArthur's critics—such as George Kennan—ridiculed the "peace" clause in Japan's constitution. One reason MacArthur disclaimed his authorship of the constitutional renunciation of war was probably the fact that he had no specific authority to demand it and had never consulted Washington about it in advance. American diplomats were convinced a permanently disarmed Japan would wreck any chance of creating a secure military presence for the United States in East Asia. MacArthur, however, had no such doubts. Not only was it right to keep Japan disarmed, but it would not even be necessary for the United States to maintain its own bases in the home islands after a peace treaty had been signed, so long as it retained control of Okinawa, four hundred miles to the south.

Okinawa was a Japanese possession, but most of the people there were not ethnic Japanese. It was not one of the home islands, and the United States saw no serious obstacles in turning virtually the entire island into a permanent military base. But the inevitable response from the Soviets was a fierce written protest to GHQ SCAP that MacArthur was exceeding his authority again. He replied with icy contempt. "I cannot accept the integrity of your letter," he informed the Soviet mission in Tokyo. "It can only be regarded as a provocative impertinence."[12]

For the conservative politicians who ran Japan one of MacArthur's greatest achievements and a crucial reason for the success of the occupation was the fact that he kept the Soviets from landing troops in their country. A divided Japan would be a different, poorer and less stable Japan. And MacArthur's skillful propaganda concerning the fate of the missing Japanese POWs helped foster a deep and lasting revulsion against the Soviet Union. Kennan was right: It *was* crucial to the strategy of containment that Japan become a strong and active partner in the resistance of the Western democracies to Soviet expansion. Few played a greater role than MacArthur in the achievement of that geostrategic objective.

Secretary of State Dean Acheson and George Kennan wanted to end what they saw as the one-man occupation of Japan and install a regime more like that operating in West Germany, where John J. McCloy had been appointed high commissioner and policy was micromanaged from Washington. What the department had in mind was to insert an American ambassador who would control the occupation, leaving GHQ SCAP with little more than responsibility for the military security of Japan. And if the plan were fully implemented, MacArthur would be brought home and replaced by Major General Maxwell D. Taylor.[13] State's plan was supported by various colonels and generals in the Defense Department. It was endorsed too by Eisenhower's successor as Chief of Staff, Omar Bradley, another Missourian who detested MacArthur. Bradley informed MacArthur in June 1949, "We should try to get the State Department to take over the Military Government in Japan."[14]

MacArthur was incensed. How could Bradley be so ignorant? There was *no* American military government in Japan and never had been. Seething, he put Bradley straight with a four-page, single-spaced letter on how the occupation actually worked. His letter was worded politely, but with a subtext that was all furious indignation. Bradley was too stunned, or intimidated, to favor MacArthur with the courtesy of a reply but was quoted posthumously as calling MacArthur's letter "a scathing diatribe the like of which I have seldom read." He claimed to have known nothing of the mutual animosity between MacArthur and Acheson. If so, he must have been just about the only person in the Pentagon who was unaware of it.[15]

Detecting State's none-too-subtle hand in what had been proposed, MacArthur sent a stiff protest to Acheson too. The secretary of state thought for three months about what kind of answer to send, then opted for implausible denial. He replied blandly that the proposals MacArthur was objecting to "do not reflect any trend of thought in official circles—certainly not in the Department of State." Here was a pluperfect example of that old definition of a diplomat: "A man paid to lie for his country." Acheson, a dedicated and able public servant, was much like MacArthur in one respect: fundamentally high-minded but without feeling any compulsion to be honest with people he despised.[16]

While Bradley's clumsy handling of the affair wrecked this effort to undercut him, MacArthur had nevertheless come to a realization that the State Department had a better grasp of the situation in Japan than the Pentagon. State had changed its mind and was now in favor of a peace treaty, unlike the JCS, which was still afraid of a Communist takeover in Japan if the occupation ended.[17]

The role of the State Department in Far Eastern affairs was growing not only in Japan but also in Korea. When the war ended, two Army colonels, named Dean Rusk and Charles Bonesteel, were entrusted with organizing surrender arrangements in Korea, which had been occupied, looted and raped by the Japanese for nearly fifty years. Purely for the sake of convenience, they decided to have all Japanese forces north of the thirty-eighth parallel surrender to the Soviets and all Japanese south of the parallel surrender to the Americans.[18]

It was optimistically assumed that all Korea would be united in a couple of years under a democratically elected government. That did not happen. Under the Japanese, there had been no free Koreans. By 1948 there were exactly two. One was the elderly, Bible-thumping Syngman Rhee, who ran a right-wing police state under American protection; the other was Kim Il Sung, a vainglorious thug who ran a Communist prison camp under Stalinist guidance.

The surrenders south of the thirty-eighth parallel were taken by the XXIV Corps, under Lieutenant General John R. Hodge, but rapid postwar demobilization soon reduced the corps's strength to less than that of a full division, and still it continued to shrink. MacArthur recommended that if the United States did not intend to maintain a force in South Korea capable of defending the country, it should pull all the troops out. "In the event of any serious threat to the security of Korea," he told the JCS, "strategic and military considerations will force abandonment of any pretense of military support. . . . We must increase the strength of the XXIV Corps decidedly or turn the U.S. interest in the Korean occupation over to the State Department for handling."[19] His suggestion was accepted without demur by Truman, the Joint Chiefs, the National Security Council and the State Department. All American combat troops were withdrawn by June 1949, leaving nothing but a force of five hundred American military advisers, whose sole task was to help train a South Korean army.

On January 12, 1950, Dean Acheson went to the National Press Club in Washington, and for the benefit of a lunchtime audience of reporters juggling pencils and coffee cups he traced the line of American defenses in the Pacific. It ran, he said, from the Aleutians to Japan, down to Okinawa and continued south to take in the Philippines. The United States had no intention to defend South Korea. What the secretary of state said was undeniable, but why he chose to say it at all is a mystery. Delivering this speech was not the brightest idea Acheson ever had.[20]

On May 18 MacArthur had Cyrus L. Sulzberger join him for lunch at the embassy. He gave Sulzberger his views on why the Russians were more Oriental than Occidental, on the reasons why the UN should try to abolish war, and on the essentially conservative character of the Japanese, which made 99 percent of them virtually immune to communism. When Sulzberger asked about the possibility of war, MacArthur told him there was little chance of that. The Chinese Communists were not a military threat. Only the Soviets could strike Japan, but the 750,000 troops they had in the Far East at present were deployed on the defensive.[21]

That was what he told Sulzberger, and he probably believed it. But he was also under orders from the Defense Department "to avoid statement or speculation on the possibility of proximity of war with Russia . . . a non-aggressive attitude should be displayed to the public." Washington had also ordered him "to have confidence in the United Nations as an instrument to assure world peace."[22]

The real reason for MacArthur's confidence, however, was less the so far untested UN than the four infantry divisions assigned to the Far Eastern Command (FECOM) and the B-29s of the Fifth Air Force. But what he did not know, or would not acknowledge, was that FECOM was a pretty weak reed.

The Joint Chiefs visited Japan in February 1950. Unlike MacArthur, they actually visited the four American divisions, watched them in training in the field and talked to their officers. Although MacArthur was the commanding general of the Far Eastern Command and had a responsibility to try to correct any major defects in its fighting ability, he never showed any interest in finding out for himself what kind of shape it was in. Instead he busied himself with the much more interesting task of being supreme commander acting on behalf of thirteen Allied nations in the occupation of Japan. Stand in the mud and the rain to watch troops in training? Find out why it had become impossible to hold maneuvers for anything bigger than a battalion? He had been elevated to a sphere far beyond such mundane concerns.

The Fifth Air Force was in a high state of combat readiness, but this only underlined the mediocre condition of the ground combat units. The difference was largely the superiority of Air Force leadership. MacArthur's failure to ensure that his ground troops maintained the same high standard as the airmen was an appalling instance of neglect. No one, however, seemed to care how low the fighting ability of MacArthur's troops fell—not the President, not the secretary of defense, not the secretary of the army, nor even the Joint Chiefs. So why, he might well have reasoned, should he?

Eighth Army officers not only knew their tactical units were at best only 40 percent combat-ready but told the Chiefs so. The troops on occupation duty had volunteered for a Far Eastern assignment so they could get laid for "50 cents short time, one dollar all night," drink beer at fifteen cents a bottle, have bowing Japanese clean their boots and rifles, see something of the world and generally have a good time for a few years. Their commanders had no illusions about their fighting ability. The Chiefs, however, claimed to be impressed! Excellent troops, they said, well trained, well led, with good morale. As experienced field commanders they knew how to inspect troops and talk to their officers. But they knew something else, too—any serious attempt to raise the combat readiness of MacArthur's command would cost money . . . and a fight.[23]

The secretary of defense, Louis Johnson, was a brash presidential crony. Roosevelt had dumped Johnson as assistant secretary of war back in 1940.

Stimson thought he was one of the most disloyal men ever appointed to high office, and Truman would wake up in September 1950 and arrive at the same conclusion. For now though Truman had raked Johnson off the dead pile and made him secretary of defense after Drew Pearson had hounded James Forrestal into jumping out his office window.[24] Because the postwar popular mood favored spending less on defense, Johnson was trying to ride the budget-cutting trail straight to the White House, and the Chiefs were too intimidated by this foulmouthed, overbearing buffoon to recommend anything that might get him mad at them. On their Far Eastern trip they did not raise a single question about the low combat readiness of FECOM's ground forces during their discussions with MacArthur.[25]

Meanwhile, Brigadier General William L. Roberts, the commander of the Korean Military Advisory Group, was training the nascent South Korean Army, under the direction of the State Department. In the spring of 1950 Roberts too reported all was well on the Eastern Front. He told a reporter from *Time,* "The South Koreans have the best damn army outside the United States."[26]

The telephone in MacArthur's bedroom rang shrilly at 5:00 A.M. on Sunday, June 25, 1950. The GHQ SCAP duty officer informed him that North Korean troops were reported to have crossed the parallel "in great strength" some hours earlier. MacArthur dressed, but he felt no sense of alarm, no profound concern. Everything was under control. For the past year the Koreans had exchanged potshots across the parallel. They had sent raiding parties into each other's territories to engage in economic sabotage and spread alarm. This was just another provocation, if on a bigger scale. The whole thing would soon blow over.[27]

The decision to pull American ground troops out of South Korea in 1949 was one of the most reckless and baffling moves of the Cold War. Japan consists of islands. The security of islands depends almost entirely on control of the sea-lanes. The American pullback in effect wrote off the Korea Strait, the narrow sea that separates Korea from Japan. Without a strong American presence on *both* sides of the strait the security of Japan was going to be put at risk if by war, coup d'état or revolution the Communist regime in the North managed to seize control of the South. The fate of Czechoslovakia, the recently concluded Greek civil war and the growing political and military strength of the Vietminh in Southeast Asia demonstrated beyond peradventure that such risks were not fanciful, not remote, not specks in the myopic eyes of knee-jerk anti-Communists. They were something any intelligent person could read about every day in *The New York Times* or *The Washington Post.* In 1949 one did not have to be a George Kennan to realize that Communist leaders in both Europe and

Asia were testing the limits of Western resolve, probing for weak spots they might exploit.

The fate of South Korea was not in itself of great importance to anyone but the Koreans. But the fate of Japan was. The Japanese military had for centuries viewed the Korean peninsula as "a dagger pointing at the heart of Japan." Control of the Korea Strait is as crucial to the military security of Japan as control of the English Channel is to the security of the British Isles. And by effecting a complete withdrawal of combat units from South Korea, the United States was removing the only guarantee against the risk of war, coup or revolution on the far side of the strait, which is barely forty miles wide. MacArthur, who could talk for hours, if not weeks, about global strategy, had taken his eyes off the ball, the Joint Chiefs had let it slip through their fingers and then it had bounced up to strike Dean Acheson in the head. What were the Chiefs thinking of when they made this blunder?

JCS meetings in 1949 were characterized by tantrums and sulking, more like scenes from a nursery than a military high command considering the nation's security. The Army and Navy were embroiled in a bitter, often personal confrontation over missions, roles and money. The Army Chief of Staff, Omar Bradley, and the Chief of Naval Operations, Louis E. Denfeld, could hardly bear to be in the same room. The Air Force Chief of Staff, Hoyt Vandenberg, was both a superb pilot and a master of military politics, but too much of an intellectual lightweight to mediate between Bradley and Denfeld.[28] The Chiefs spent so much of their time and energy squabbling among themselves they had little left over for long-term strategy. There *were* generals and admirals who realized that pulling ground forces out of Korea was a strategic mistake, but they operated far below the bickering JCS.[29]

General Roberts's estimate of the fighting ability of the South Korean Army was so far off the mark it was laughable. Some hundred thousand strong, it had no tanks, no heavy artillery, few modern field radios, no close air support. Its logistics were of the chewing gum and baling wire variety. It had no combat experience and little expectation of acquiring any. It was less an army than a paramilitary constabulary designed to keep the unpopular Syngman Rhee in power.

The North Korean Army—or Inmun Gun—was a different proposition. It numbered nearly 150,000 men, who were well trained and well equipped by the Russians. It boasted tanks, self-propelled artillery and more than a hundred combat aircraft. Many of the Inmun Gun's officers were Red Army veterans of battles against the Japanese in Manchuria. It was a tough, self-confident force capable of running the South Korean Army all the way down to the Korea Strait and driving the survivors into the sea.[30]

MacArthur, moreover, was completely unaware of that. Korea was outside the zone of his responsibilities and had been for more than a year. At a meeting in his office several hours after he had learned of the North Korean onslaught, he confidently declared that all the South Koreans faced was "a reconnaissance in force." The United States had no commitment to defend South Korea, nor did he expect Truman would do much about it. But "If Washington only will not hobble me, I can handle it with one arm tied behind my back."[31]

Some hours later, in Washington, Truman authorized MacArthur to ship mortars, artillery and extra ammunition to the South Korean Army, which was preparing to launch a counterattack against the North Korean tank units already closing on Seoul. MacArthur was also told to send a survey group to monitor the situation as it developed. The Air Force was ordered to go on alert so it would be able "to wipe out all Soviet air bases in the Far East" in case Stalin decided to enter the war.[32]

Throughout June 26 MacArthur remained confident the South Korean counterattack would succeed when, in fact, the Inmun Gun was brushing it aside with contemptuous ease. By nightfall its tanks were rolling into the suburbs of Seoul. The morning of June 27 the American ambassador to South Korea, John Muccio, informed MacArthur that the situation was desperate. Seoul was about to fall and the South Korean Army was in full flight, heading south. MacArthur was flabbergasted. He could not believe things were as bad as that. Muccio assured him they were. "All Korea is lost," MacArthur said despondently. "The only thing we can do is get our people safely out of the country."[33] There was no trace now of his normally confident, optimistic manner. This was a MacArthur most of the GHQ SCAP staff had never seen, one who was depressed and despairing.

He informed the Pentagon bleakly of the situation in South Korea: "Complete collapse is imminent."[34] Truman promptly convened a conference with his military and foreign policy advisers. MacArthur was alerted and told that a teleconference message—or telecon—would soon be on its way to Tokyo. This involved a linkup between teleprinters and movie screens. The participants at each end dictated their messages, which were encoded, transmitted by teleprinter, then decoded at the other end, and the text was flashed on a screen.

MacArthur was in the teleprinter room when the message from Washington came through. As he read the words marching down the screen, he received his second great shock that day. MacArthur's mind reeled. He could not believe it. Harry Truman, that equivocating politician whom he could face down whenever he chose, that Missouri hayseed accidentally shot into the White House by the death of a far greater man, a pusillanimous nobody so easy to intimidate that he had never done anything but hint that he wanted MacArthur to come home—unlike Roosevelt, who would have told him to come home and made it a direct order—that same Harry Truman, surrounded by a bunch of mealymouthed liberals, had somehow found the balls to fight?

Two crucial days had been lost while the President made up his mind, but there it was, scrolling soundlessly down the glowing telecon screen: The United States was going to commit its air and naval forces to defend South Korea. MacArthur gasped, "I don't believe it!" *Truman was actually going to war?* He turned to some of the officers standing near him. Maybe they could explain what was going on. But they too were staring at the screen, in open-jawed amazement. "I don't understand it!" said MacArthur. He returned to his office in a daze and ordered the commander of the Far Eastern Air Force to start striking North Korean forces south of the thirty-eighth parallel. By nightfall American planes were strafing North Korean convoys and shooting the North Korean Air Force out of the sky.[35]

Seoul fell to the Inmun Gun next day, and Syngman Rhee fled to Pusan, two hundred miles to the southeast and the biggest port on either side of the Korea Strait. Although he had a fifteen-man team of military observers in South Korea, MacArthur decided to inspect the rapidly deteriorating situation for himself. On June 29 he flew to Suwon Airfield, twenty miles south of Seoul, aboard the *Bataan*. When his plane touched down at Suwon, there were fresh craters and wreckage still burning at one end of the runway, which had been attacked five minutes earlier by North Korean planes.

This was still not close enough to the action to tell him anything, so MacArthur headed north, toward the Han River, in a convoy of three battered automobiles. As the convoy jolted along, it passed thousands of South Korean soldiers heading in the opposite direction. When MacArthur got to within a mile of the river, he left his automobile and walked to the top of a hill. Mortar rounds exploded nearby, but he ignored them. From his vantage point, it was obvious that the North Koreans were already crossing the river and there was no sign of the South Koreans digging in to stop them.[36]

Returning to the car, he was driven back to Suwon. During the entire two-hour journey to the front line and back he spoke only once. "It is a strange thing to me," he said to his chief of staff, Major General Edward Almond, "that all these men have their rifles and ammunition, they all know how to salute, they all seem to be more or less happy, but I haven't seen a wounded man yet. Nobody is fighting."[37]

Back in Tokyo that night, MacArthur called J. Lawton Collins and told him he would have to use FECOM troops if South Korea were going to be saved. Collins told him he could send a regimental combat team (roughly five thousand men) immediately to Pusan. MacArthur replied, "That is not enough." Collins's message paraded across the telecon screen: "How many troops do you recommend?"

MacArthur's answer was a regimental combat team to defend Pusan, followed by two divisions to launch a counteroffensive. If he did not get what he wanted, "The fighting will be terminated within 10 days. Please tell the President that. Time is of the essence and a clear-cut decision is imperative." Collins pointed out that it was 3:00 A.M. in Washington and the President was asleep. MacArthur concluded the conference: "Then wake him up."[38] The secretary of the army waited until 5:00 A.M. before calling Truman. Within twelve hours MacArthur had the authorization to move two of his four divisions to Korea.[39]

Truman's decision to commit large ground forces to the campaign did not mean that his confidence in MacArthur had grown during this crisis. Far from it. The President directed the Joint Chiefs to send MacArthur "an order from the President,. . . telling him that the President wants full reports every day." During World War II, Truman grumbled to the National Security Council, "I practically had to telephone General MacArthur to get information from him." It wasn't going to happen again.[40]

If Truman was suspicious, MacArthur was disgusted. The teleconference system was intended to improve communications and speed decision making. Using the telephone was too insecure, but with a teleprinter, everything could be securely coded and decoded. Truman's distrust of MacArthur meant, however, that nothing was going to be decided quickly. Everything would have to come from the President himself. Whenever MacArthur asked a question, the answer he got back was "Wait a few hours and we'll let you know." The question then went to the secretary of defense, who went over to the White House and got the answer from Truman. After being told several times that he would have to wait for an answer, MacArthur snapped, "This is an outrage. When I was Chief of Staff I could get Herbert Hoover off the can to talk to me. But here, not just the Chief of Staff of the Army delays, but the Secretary of the Army and the Secretary of Defense. They've got so much lead in there it's inexcusable."[41]

During the Inmun Gun's advance from Seoul to the Pusan perimeter, the Joint Chiefs flew to Tokyo to confer with MacArthur. He was confident, he told them, of holding Pusan. He urged the Chiefs to "grab every ship in the Pacific" and build up American strength in Korea. "To hell with business as usual." There was no point debating whether Europe mattered more than the Far East. "We win here, or we lose everywhere. But if we win here, we improve our chances of winning everywhere." And to do that, he intended to mount a counteroffensive. He could not say when he would do that. He could not say where he would do that. But they were to make no mistake: He intended to destroy the Inmun Gun and not merely drive it back across the thirty-eighth parallel. Once that had been achieved, the United Nations would be able to "compose and unite Korea." The Chiefs concluded the visit with a little ceremony on the roof of the Dai Ichi Building. Collins presented MacArthur with the flag of the United Nations, symbolizing his appointment as chief of the United Nations Command in Korea. MacArthur solemnly accepted the blue and white standard from Collins. "I accept this flag with the deepest emotion," he said. The strain of the past two weeks had etched deep lines and dark shadows across MacArthur's ashen face. He looked every one of his seventy years.[42]

Meanwhile the North Koreans continued their advance down the few good roads leading from Seoul to Pusan. The handful of American troops who were thrust into Korea to stop them were brushed aside. Even so, the Inmun Gun moved at a plodding six miles a day. It showed no ability to improvise and feared to risk exposing its tanks to American airpower. Its cautious progress enabled MacArthur to feed three divisions into South Korea and get them dug in along an arc that ran thirty miles east and fifty miles north of Pusan, well out of artillery range of the city. It was late July before the Inmun Gun came up against this defensive line and started trying to break through.

The general who had activated the Eighth Army and made it his own proud creation, Robert Eichelberger, had returned to the United States in 1948, a deeply embittered man. He would eventually get his fourth star, but it brought him no happiness. It was awarded posthumously, after both he and MacArthur were dead. Eichelberger had handed the Eighth over to Lieutenant General Walton H. Walker, a short, fat, pugnacious Texan. Walker had made his reputation as commander of an armored corps under George Patton in World War II, but whether he was the right man to command a green, undertrained, poorly equipped army in a complicated and nerve-racking defensive battle is open to doubt. MacArthur did not think he was smart enough or, at age sixty-one, vigorous enough to handle the rigors of a field command; neither did Bradley.[43]

When Walker's frontline position came under pressure from the North Koreans, his chief engineer, Brigadier General Garrison Davidson, jumped into an L-5 spotter plane, flew around at low level and traced a new defensive line much closer to Pusan. This was a much shorter line and put the city within range of enemy artillery, but Davidson was confident that it could be held by the poorly trained American and South Korean troops under Walker's command.[44] On July 26 Walker informed Tokyo that he was planning to retreat. He was moving his command post into Pusan. Next morning MacArthur and Almond flew to Korea to see the Eighth Army commander before he pulled back. "Walker," said MacArthur sternly, "you can make all the reconnaissance you want. You can put your engineer to work if you like preparing intermediate trenches. But *I* will give the order to retire from this position. There will be no Dunkirk in this command. To retire to Pusan is unacceptable."[45]

This so emboldened Walker he issued a "stand or die" order to his army: "There will be no Dunkirk, no Bataan, a retreat to Pusan would be one of the greatest butcheries in history. We must fight until the end. Capture by these people is worse than death itself. We will fight as a team. If some of us must die, we will die fighting together." MacArthur could not have expressed it better.[46]

Throughout August the North Koreans pounded and probed the perimeter remorselessly. There was a crisis nearly every day, but somehow the position held. MacArthur had, in a way, fought this battle before—on Bataan. And during those desperate days in February 1942 he had sent a message to Marshall telling him that now that the Japanese had pushed everything south the thing to do was strike deep in the enemy's rear.[47] Nothing had come of his idea then. Maybe this time, though, he could pull off a masterstroke that he had only been able to imagine in that evil-smelling tunnel in the bowels of Corregidor. A double envelopment against an oncoming enemy, the ultimate battle of annihilation, was the one military maneuver he had never accomplished and the mark of great commanders from Hannibal down to Napoleon.

Shortly after the Inmun Gun crossed the parallel, MacArthur started thinking of making a move to strike them in the rear and requested a Marine regiment, but by the time Truman approved his request it was clear that the marines would be needed to defend Pusan. On July 10 MacArthur received a visit from Lieutenant General Lemuel C. Shepherd of the Marine Corps. MacArthur paced back and forth as he explained what he really wanted. There was a map of the Far East next to the door. "I wish I had the entire 1st Marine Division under my command again," said MacArthur. "I have a job for them to do." He stopped pacing and jabbed at the map with his meerschaum. "I'd land them here . . . at Inchon." He was pointing at a port 150 miles northwest of the Pusan perimeter and only 30 miles east of Seoul. Shepherd, who had come to advise him to ask for an entire Marine division instead of requesting smaller units and feeding them piecemeal into the war, responded, "General, why don't you ask for them?"[48]

MacArthur did so, but without much hope of getting the entire division. The Joint Chiefs were lukewarm about his proposed landing, and Bradley was on record as saying that there would never again be an amphibious assault. Truman, who loathed the Marines, also had his doubts. It was at this time that he bluntly informed a pro-Marine congressman, "For your information the Marine Corps is the Navy's police force and as long as I am President that is what it will remain."[49]

Suspicious as ever of MacArthur, he sent a special envoy, Averell Harriman, to find out what was really happening at the Dai Ichi. This was one of the rare occasions when MacArthur went out to Tokyo's Haneda Airport to greet a visitor. MacArthur had known Harriman for thirty years. While superintendent at West Point, MacArthur had played polo against Harriman's "Orange County" team and gone duck hunting on Harriman's estate near Tuxedo, New York.[50] They had always gotten along well and did so now.

MacArthur asserted that a rapid military victory was crucial. The longer the war lasted, the greater the risk of Chinese or Soviet intervention. The main objective of the campaign should be to destroy the Inmun Gun "before the onset of next winter." A winter campaign in the mountains of Korea would produce enormous casualties and achieve nothing. But if he got the reinforcements he was seeking, including the entire 1st Marine Division, he would be able to destroy the North Korean Army. He concluded his peroration by intoning slowly, with an emotion-charged delivery, "I cannot believe that a great nation such as the United States cannot give me these few paltry reinforcements for which I ask. Tell the President that if he gives them to me, I will, on the rising tide of the fifteenth of September, land at Inchon and between the hammer of this landing and the anvil of the Eighth Army, I will crush and destroy the army of North Korea." It was spine-tingling and left Harriman deeply moved.[51]

Harriman reported back to the President, "In a brilliant 2½ hour presentation, made with utmost earnestness, supported by every logical military argument of his rich experience, and delivered with all of his dramatic eloquence, General MacArthur stated his compelling need for additional combat ground forces."[52]

Convincing Harriman was not enough. MacArthur still had to convince the JCS. The more the Chiefs looked at Inchon, the less they liked it. A Navy officer who studied the proposal said, "We drew up a list of nearly every natural and geographic handicap—and Inchon had 'em all."[53] Collins and the Chief of Naval Operations, Forrest P. Sherman, flew to Tokyo to discuss it with MacArthur in detail. Collins was more than ever convinced the operation would fail.

On August 23 a tense, dramatic meeting was held in the small conference room adjoining MacArthur's office. Collins, Sherman, Almond, Shepherd and various naval experts crammed themselves into the room. They were almost sitting in one another's laps. Collins was worried by the thought of MacArthur's forces being so widely split there was a 150-mile gap between them.[54] But MacArthur brushed aside Collins's efforts to have the landing made much closer to the Pusan perimeter. The result, he said scornfully, would be "ineffective and indecisive. It would be an attempted envelopment which would not envelop. The amphibious landing is the most powerful tool we have. To employ it properly, we must strike hard and deep!" As he spoke, an echo came to him, an echo of his father's voice, telling him again something he had told him once long, long ago: "Doug, councils of war breed timidity and defeatism." It was for the commander to make the decision and impose it on these dull committeemen, by the force of his personality and the strength of his case.[55]

He emphasized the strategic importance of Seoul, which was the road and rail hub for the whole of South Korea. It was to the peninsula what Paris is to France. If he captured Inchon, Seoul and its airport would fall quickly. The only alternative to an amphibious landing on the west coast of Korea was a breakout from the Pusan perimeter, but that would be a frontal attack against prepared defenses, leading to a massive loss of life. He acknowledged the problems of making a landing at Inchon, where the tidal range was thirty-two feet. What was even worse, the assault would have to be split into two phases more than eight hours apart, because it would be necessary to seize an island in the shipping channel first. Only after it had been secured could the main assault be made, on the next tide. But, MacArthur said emphatically, the U.S. Navy had never failed him before, and he knew it would not fail him now. He did not argue hydrographic details, tide tables or weather hazards. He relied instead on emotional blackmail and an appeal to the Navy's pride.

While MacArthur made his case, he was also calculating the best way to overcome resistance from Collins and Sherman, especially Collins. Their fear of failure was greater than their drive for success. So he tailored his pitch to their fears as he drew to a close: "If my estimate is inaccurate, and should I run into a defense with which I cannot cope, I will be there personally and will immediately withdraw our forces before they are committed to a bloody setback. The only loss will be to my reputation. But Inchon will not fail. Inchon will succeed. And it will save 100,000 lives.

"I realize this is a 5,000 to 1 gamble. But I am used to taking such odds." MacArthur's voice dropped to a whisper. The people in the conference room could hardly hear him as he said, "We shall land at Inchon . . . and I shall crush them!"[56] An awestruck silence filled the small conference room. Six days later the JCS authorized MacArthur to make a landing at Inchon . . . "or at a favorable beach south of Inchon if one can be located." Collins was still worried.[57]

On September 13 MacArthur and Shepherd flew down to Sasebo, to board the command ship, the USS *Mount McKinley*. On the ride from the airport to Sasebo docks, the sun was setting and a light rain began to fall. MacArthur looked up. A brilliant rainbow was stretching its shimmering embrace across the darkening sky. "That's my rainbow!" he said excitedly. He turned to Shepherd. "I commanded the Rainbow Division in the first war. That's my lucky omen. This landing is going to be a success."[58]

On the high tide of the morning of September 15 a force of marines seized the small island of Wolmi-do, guarding the narrow channel that led to Inchon, and captured its gun emplacements. A second force of marines landed at the harbor front of Inchon on the afternoon high tide. Opposition was sporadic and poorly organized. MacArthur, dressed in his A-2 jacket and field marshal's cap, watched fascinated and thrilled beyond words as the marines launched their flawless and daring assault from the *Mount McKinley*.

That, however, was not enough. MacArthur had to get closer to the action. He insisted on going to Wolmi-do. Shells fell around the boat that carried him there, but he wanted to move even closer to the beach, where mortar and machine-gun fire indicated a firefight was in progress. Shepherd was alarmed and tried to get the admiral commanding the landing force to order the boat to come back, but the admiral declined. To Shepherd, nothing could be more calamitous than to have the theater commander killed by enemy fire. Years later he was still asking people, "Don't you think I was right?" They invariably said yes, but the correct answer was no.[59]

There was one day in MacArthur's life when he was a military genius: September 15, 1950. In the life of every great commander there is one battle that stands out above all the rest, the supreme test of generalship that places him among the other military immortals. For MacArthur that battle was Inchon. The landing produced all the results he had promised. By the end of September Seoul had been recaptured, the Eighth Army had broken out from the Pusan perimeter and the Inmun Gun was destroyed. The survivors were fleeing across the thirty-eighth parallel with UN forces in hot pursuit. The most fitting conclusion to MacArthur's life would have been to die a soldier's death in the waters off Inchon at the height of his glory, with his legend not simply intact but magnified beyond even his florid imaginings. There was only way it could go from here—down.

31

We're Going Home

In the fall of 1949 Chinese Communist forces led by Mao Tse-tung took Peking and established themselves as de facto rulers of mainland China. Chiang Kai-shek's troops and hangers-on fled to Formosa. The United States had armed the Nationalists during World War II to fight the Japanese, but Truman had no intention of being dragged into the conflict between Chiang and the Communists. When the Korean War began in June 1950, the U.S. Navy was ordered to place itself between Formosa and the mainland and block any attempted invasion in either direction. American policy was to "neutralize" Formosa.[1]

MacArthur considered the President's attempts to distance himself from Chiang Kai-shek foolish. He was convinced that Formosa was "an unsinkable aircraft carrier and submarine tender" from which American power could be projected over the Chinese mainland. Instead of supporting the President's policy of neutralizing Formosa, MacArthur assumed the policy would fail and started planning to move American combat aircraft to Formosan bases and had jet fighter pilots flying there on "familiarization flights."[2]

The Pentagon meanwhile estimated there were several hundred thousand Chinese Communist troops massing at mainland ports on the Formosa Strait, and an invasion fleet of four thousand vessels—mainly wooden junks—had been assembled. On August 1, 1950, MacArthur flew to Formosa to steady the hapless and ineffectual Chiang, whose Nationalist troops were no match for the Communists but hell on the poor Formosans, many of whom openly resented the influx of two million rapacious Chinese

Nationalist carpetbaggers from the mainland. During his brief visit MacArthur tried to encourage Chiang to impose his will on the mediocrities and crooks who ran the Nationalist government, but neither he nor Chiang really expected anything to change. The corrupt Nationalist regime continued to loot American military supplies for personal gain, thereby undermining Formosa's defenses, and MacArthur knew it.[3]

Before returning to Tokyo, MacArthur was photographed kissing the dainty hand of Madame Chiang. He did so with an eagerness that made him appear ready to devour the lady. Almost to the day he died, he remained highly susceptible to feminine beauty and responded to it with all the ardor of youth rather than the mixed sentiments of advancing age. Photographs of him kissing Madame Chiang's hand created a furor in American newspapers. To all but the small number of right-wing Republicans who considered Chiang some kind of upholder of democratic values MacArthur's visit to Formosa was a nauseating demonstration of kissing more than the Dragon Lady's digits.

Yet MacArthur believed all he was doing was pursuing a hardheaded policy of realpolitik, merely following the old precept that "The enemy of my enemy is my friend." "If he has horns and a tail, so long as Chiang is anti-Communist, we should help him," MacArthur told a State Department official. "Rather than make things difficult, the State Department should assist him in his fight against the Communists—we can try to reform him later!"[4]

Truman and Acheson were outraged by MacArthur's Formosa trip. There had been no change in American policy, but MacArthur's highly publicized visit had made it appear that there were, in effect, two policies on Formosa: his own and Truman's. One of the reasons why Truman sent Averell Harriman to Tokyo in early August was to set MacArthur straight on the Formosa question.[5]

So far as that part of Harriman's mission was concerned, however, he failed. He repeatedly tried to get MacArthur to understand that the United States had no intention of getting involved in a war with China over the fate of Formosa. American policy was to hold the ring while the UN tried to work out a modus vivendi between the Communist government in Peking and the Nationalist government in Taipei.

This was not good enough for MacArthur. Instead of seeing Formosa for what it really was—a political distraction and a military liability—he continued trying to present it as a valuable asset that had to be defended. MacArthur had believed for many years that it was better to have Asians fight Asians than to have a race war between Orientals and whites. And now, Chiang was offering to send three divisions to fight in Korea. MacArthur seemed eager to accept this offer, which was bizarre. If Formosa was under such an imminent threat that it needed American fighter pilots to defend it, stripping it of tens of thousands of its best troops to go and fight elsewhere made no sense at all. Yet it was obvious to Harriman that far from having problematical Formosa figured out, MacArthur was going around in circles.[6]

One of those who traveled to Japan with Harriman was Colonel Edwin Lowe. The colonel was a courtly Maine farmer and an old Truman friend who had undertaken various sensitive missions for the President in recent years. Lowe's mission now was to act as Truman's "eyes and ears" around the Dai Ichi. Truman did not believe he was getting enough information about or from MacArthur. Lowe also had a message to give the general directly from the President's lips, a message that was so obviously untrue it is surprising Lowe could deliver it with a straight face. "I have never had anything but the utmost confidence in the general's ability to do that Far Eastern job," said Truman via Lowe.[7]

The colonel was at pains to assure MacArthur that being the President's eyes and ears did not mean he was spying on him. In an attempt to reassure him of this, Lowe provided MacArthur with a copy of every report he sent to Washington. While this gesture enabled Lowe to act in all good conscience as a decent, honorable man, it is hard to imagine that MacArthur considered this evidence of anything much. Lowe could always give his real reports orally to general officers passing through Tokyo on their way to Washington. Besides, MacArthur knew how to play the game of ostentatious cooperation with the best of them. He gave Lowe an office only a few doors away from his own and granted him complete access to everyone in the Dai Ichi. What he did not give him was entrée to the only territory that mattered—the mind of Douglas MacArthur.

Several weeks after Lowe arrived, the general sent a statement to the Veterans of Foreign Wars. His message stressed the strategic importance of Formosa. MacArthur could not resist pontificating on "the Oriental mind," something he had been doing for years. Indeed, among his admirers MacArthur was believed to have a uniquely powerful insight into the thought processes of the people of Far Eastern countries. The truth was he knew next to nothing about "the Oriental mind." The key to any culture is language. MacArthur did not speak or read any Asian language. He had not set foot on the mainland of Asia since 1905, and his visit then was fleeting. The few Asians he actually conversed with consisted of a handful of conservative Japanese politicians. He knew no more about the Chinese, the Burmese, the Koreans and others than anyone else with access to a handful of academic texts, the most important characteristic of which was their superficiality. Orientals, he claimed, only respected strength (that would have come as news to Buddhists and Confucians), and he concluded defiantly: "Nothing could be more fallacious than the threadbare argument by those who advocate appeasement in the Pacific that if we defend Formosa we alienate continental Asia."[8]

Truman was outraged when he read this sentence. It looked like a thinly veiled attack on his refusal to commit the United States to the defense of Formosa. MacArthur made matters worse by distributing copies of the statement to publications that were hostile to the administration, such as *U.S. News & World Report*. By the time Truman learned of it, the presses were already rolling and the wire services were distributing MacArthur's statement all over the planet.[9]

Truman contemplated firing MacArthur as UN commander in chief, leaving him as Supreme Commander for the Allied Powers but giving responsibility for Korea and Formosa to Omar Bradley. Once more, however, Truman shied away from the political repercussions of a confrontation with MacArthur—who would almost certainly have resigned had he been publicly humiliated in this way—and instead sent a message that was fundamentally absurd and bristling with indignation: "The President of the United States directs that you withdraw your message for the National Encampment of the Veterans of Foreign Wars because various features with regard to Formosa are in conflict with the policy of the United States and its position in the United Nations."[10] MacArthur strongly protested his innocence, and it was obvious he could no more "withdraw" his statement than he could bring back yesterday. All he could do was put out another statement disavowing what he had told the VFW, and that was what he did.[11]

In the fall of 1950 Harry Truman and the Democratic party were apprehensively contemplating a midterm election that looked like a potential disaster. Truman became incomparably more popular after he died than he ever was during his lifetime. The only time he enjoyed anything resembling strong public support during his presidency was the day he beat Dewey in November 1948.

Following Inchon, Truman decided to boost his popularity by conferring personally with MacArthur, the man of the hour. Truman's most successful biographer, David McCullough, firmly denies that Truman was prompted by politics, and he quotes Omar Bradley as dismissing such claims as "sheer nonsense." The fact remains, however, that Bradley is hardly an objective witness. Anything short of a blanket denial would amount to an admission that he, as Chairman of the Joint Chiefs, had been a willing participant in party politics. Other Truman biographers, such as Cabell Phillips, who was personally acquainted with almost the entire Truman staff, frankly acknowledge that the point of the meeting was indeed a political one, and as we shall see, there was no serious discussion of strategy when the President and the general finally met.[12]

The composition of Truman's party showed what the President's real intentions were. Omar Bradley and Secretary of the Army Frank Pace flew to Wake with Truman, but the new secretary of defense, George Marshall, was not there. A month before the trip to Wake, Truman had finally gotten fed up with the overly ambitious and truculent Louis Johnson and fired him. Marshall returned to the Pentagon, with profound reluctance but unable to resist yet another call to duty. That sense of duty had its limits, though, and being party to Truman's vote-chasing journey to Wake was beyond them. Dean Acheson too was determined not to get involved in something so obviously political, and he did not go to Wake either.[13]

The absence of Marshall and Acheson was itself a good indication that nothing of real importance was going to be discussed. There was going to be no serious discussion of essential strategic questions. Truman wasn't bothered by that. The main thing was to make sure the meeting got plenty of press coverage. An entire planeload of journalists was flown out to Wake to record this historic encounter.

MacArthur was asked to meet Truman in Honolulu, which stands roughly halfway between Tokyo and Washington. Alternatively, he was informed, a meeting might be possible on Wake Island, which is a coral speck less than two thousand miles from southern Japan. Not surprisingly MacArthur opted for Wake. This meeting was Truman's idea and, MacArthur was certain, was a political move. If Truman insisted on chasing votes in the middle of a war, MacArthur was the last man in the world to make it easy for him. Truman thus found himself making a round-trip journey of nearly fifteen thousand miles.[14]

Their brief encounter on October 15 was the first, last and only meeting between them. It has figured heavily in every post-1950 biography of MacArthur and Truman, been re-created in at least one feature film and a television documentary. It has also been portrayed on the Broadway stage. Pro-MacArthur accounts, such as *American Caesar,* draw heavily on MacArthur's unreliable *Reminiscences* and Whitney's adulatory biography of the general.[15] Not much to be trusted there. On the other hand, the pro-Truman accounts depend largely on Truman's version of events, which consists of a rich tapestry of half-truths, nonsense and contempt.

According to the account Truman gave several interviewers after he left the White House, his plane, the *Independence,* arrived over Wake at the same time as MacArthur's Lockheed Constellation, the *SCAP.* MacArthur told his pilot not to land until Truman's plane was on the ground. Truman's reaction was to order MacArthur's pilot to land immediately. With both planes finally on terra firma, MacArthur skulked by the airport administration building for forty-five minutes, refusing to approach the *Independence,* in an arrogant attempt to make the President disembark and come over to him. But by refusing to budge, Truman won this farcical Mexican standoff. Once disembarked from his airplane, he proceeded to give MacArthur the mother of all tongue-lashings, leaving the general "as red as a beet" and promising to behave himself in future. All good knockabout stuff, and not a word of it is true.[16]

What really happened was this: MacArthur *was* discourteous and provocative, but Truman, politician that he was, actually overlooked that. So long as the President got what he wanted out of this meeting he was prepared to tolerate MacArthur's annoying lapses of courtesy. It was only later, when the expected political boost failed to materialize, that Truman, recalling the general's eccentric and disrespectful attitude, grew wrathful and indignantly inflated these incidents until they bore not even a passing resemblance to what actually occurred.

MacArthur's Constellation landed at Wake twelve hours before the President's plane was due to arrive. MacArthur spent most of the flight from Japan pacing the aisle, fuming at Truman for dragging him away from the war in a disgraceful effort to round up some extra votes for deserving Democrats in November. By getting MacArthur to Wake twelve hours ahead of Truman, the general's staff was trying to ensure that MacArthur would have a chance to sleep before the conference as well as having him in place to greet the President on his arrival. By the time the *SCAP* reached Wake, however, MacArthur was so angry he could not sleep. All he managed was an uneasy nap.[17]

It was well-established custom and practice for the senior military officer present to be in place to greet the commander in chief when he alighted from a plane, an automobile, a horse, a ship or any other conveyance. But when the *Independence* rolled to a stop, there was no reception party headed by MacArthur standing on the tarmac to greet the President as he stepped onto the island. Instead MacArthur was twenty-five yards away, sitting in a jeep. The ramp was pushed up to the plane, the door opened and Truman emerged. As he started to descend the ramp, MacArthur set off to cross the intervening twenty-five yards. Lengthening his stride, the general managed to get to the bottom of the ramp at the same moment Truman did.[18]

It probably seemed to MacArthur to be a dramatic way to handle the instant of their first meeting, but symbolically it put him on an equal footing with the President. As if to confirm this, he did not bother to salute his commander in chief but shook hands instead. MacArthur had long disdained saluting. He considered this ancient ritual a military relic, along with the surrender of swords and kissing the regimental flag. Modern man preferred a handshake. And, it's true, Roosevelt had not been a stickler for salutes either. But MacArthur neither knew nor cared whether Truman wanted to be saluted. A handshake was all he was going to get.

As they shook hands, Truman said, "How are you, General? I'm glad you are here. I have been a long time meeting you." To which MacArthur responded, "I hope it won't be so long next time."[19]

The two men walked over to the only automobile on the island, a small, elderly Chevrolet sedan, which took them a hundred yards to a small building where they could have a private chat. The twenty-four members of the President's party and the handful of people who had accompanied MacArthur boarded a bus that took them to another building, where the conference would be held.

MacArthur and Truman both claimed they got on well during the forty minutes they were alone together. Truman said he found MacArthur "a most stimulating and interesting person." MacArthur lauded Truman's "engaging personality" and said flatly, "I liked him from the start." Neither man really believed any of this. In all likelihood, their friends and advisers urged them to insert these expressions into their memoirs. As both men made clear in private conversation, they never wavered in their mutual contempt.[20]

Alone at last, they did not know what to talk about. Neither felt he could be frank with the other. The closest they came to honesty was MacArthur's apology for getting involved in politics in 1948. "They made a chump out of me," he said, referring to those Republicans who had encouraged him to seek the presidential nomination. Truman told him the matter was closed and not to worry about it.

Beyond that, they spoke about safe, inconsequential matters, such as the financial problems the Philippine government faced. It would not be surprising if they were reduced to talking about their flights to Wake and wasn't this pleasant weather. One thing is certain. Neither one dared approach the edges of the huge chasm that yawned between them. Too dangerous. Either one could easily go over the edge and would probably drag the other man with him.[21]

Having pretended to confer privately, they were driven over to the conference room, where they could pretend to do the same thing in front of witnesses. Once all the conferees were seated, MacArthur got out his pipe, filled it with tobacco, pulled his matches from a pants pocket and was just about to light up when he remembered something: He was not the boss here. This wasn't the Dai Ichi. He turned to Truman and asked if the President had any objections. Truman adroitly replied, "No. I've probably had more smoke blown in my face than any man in America."

This witty rejoinder got them both over a discourteous act. MacArthur had gone so far in the preliminaries of pipe smoking that it was almost impossible for Truman to say he objected. And in a small, hot, crowded room the smell of pipe tobacco can be overwhelming. When it came to indulging his dependence on nicotine, MacArthur was, like most addicts, totally insensitive to the wishes of others.[22]

For ninety minutes Truman and his advisers questioned MacArthur. The commonest features of the thirty-four questions they posed were banality and complacency. At the time of the Wake Island Conference UN forces were deep into North Korea and closing on Pyongyang. It was assumed by everyone in the room, from Truman down, that the Korean War would soon be over. Bradley expressed the JCS's concern that the strategic reserve of American forces had been cut to the bone to provide MacArthur with troops, leaving Europe vulnerable to Soviet threats and pressure. MacArthur responded, "I will make one division available by January," and advised Bradley to take one of the best divisions in Korea, the 2d Infantry.[23]

The subject that got the most attention during these talks was planning for the rehabilitation of South Korea once the fighting ceased. Truman also raised the question of a peace treaty with Japan. MacArthur told him emphatically that Japan was ready for a treaty. "All occupations are failures," said MacArthur, and the occupation of Japan should be ended soon.

A week before this meeting the Chinese government had warned the United States, via an Indian diplomat, that if American troops approached China's border along the Yalu River, China would enter the Korean War.[24] The question of Chinese intervention was raised just once, by Truman. "What are the chances of Chinese or Soviet interference?" he asked.

"Very little," MacArthur replied. "Had they interfered in the first or second months it would have been decisive. We are no longer fearful of their intervention. . . . Only fifty to sixty thousand could be gotten across the Yalu River. They have no air force. Now that we have bases for our Air Force in Korea, if the Chinese tried to get down to Pyongyang there would be the greatest slaughter." He was equally dismissive of the threat from the Soviets.

Truman had raised the most important question of all, the one the conference should have focused on. In fact, in his memoirs he claimed the Chinese threat was one of the two reasons he traveled to Wake (the other reason was the chance to get to know MacArthur better).[25] Yet there was no indication whatever of interest in what MacArthur had said. His view was neither challenged nor supported, neither questioned nor praised.

Assistant Secretary of State Dean Rusk was alarmed at the superficiality of the questions being put to MacArthur and the speed at which the President was firing them. It worried him that the President was paying so little attention to the general's replies that his indifference would be obvious to anyone reading a transcript of the meeting. The planeload of journalists would be briefed when the meeting concluded, but they would not know any more than the President and his staff told them. There were no reporters present at the meeting. The transcript, however, was something else. It would be circulated within the highest reaches of government and eventually find its way into the archives.

Truman was rushing from one question to the next, without even pretending to digest the answers. Rusk feared this would make the whole conference seem too hurried and pointless to be taken as a genuine discussion of strategy. He scribbled a note to Truman, urging him to slow down, "to lend a note of seriousness to the meeting." Truman scribbled on the note and pushed it back to Rusk: "Hell, no! I want to get out of here before we get into trouble!"[26]

Truman, Pace or Bradley should have seized this opportunity to give MacArthur the latest thinking from the NSC, the JCS, the CIA and the National Security Agency on the risk of Chinese or Soviet intervention. Strategic intelligence was, and still is, directed from Washington, and the results disseminated to commanders in the field. Truman, Pace and Bradley, however, were just as complacent as the general, despite the recent warning from the Chinese. Yet MacArthur was the only person there who put his overoptimism on record. He had delivered up one of the fattest hostages to fortune ever seen in a century that has been filled with calamitous bad guesses. His judgment this day was so poor and his staff so inept that neither he nor they had a clue as to what he had just done. He was right in his evaluation that the purpose of this "conference" was political. A more astute person would have acted accordingly and, like a politician, qualified just about everything he said. For all his keen intelligence, MacArthur could be staggeringly naïve.

During the Wake Island Conference various people around the table were taking notes. These were fragmentary rather than complete. There was, however, a verbatim account, which was the work of someone who was not even in the room, Vernice Anderson. She was the secretary to Philip Jessup, an ambassador-at-large who had accompanied the President to Wake. Miss Anderson had traveled nearly halfway around the world aboard the *Independence* with her portable typewriter. Her task was to type out the communiqué that would be issued when these proceedings were closed.[27] While the conferees sat at five small folding tables that had been pushed together, Miss Anderson was out of sight, behind a half-closed slatted door.

Sometime later Truman tried to suggest he had planted her there to bring down MacArthur, a man whose arrogance had led him straight into a trap that wily old Harry Truman had set for him. Whitney—and, therefore, William Manchester—protested vigorously in their biographies that Miss Anderson was a stenographic time bomb hidden behind that slatted door to blow the general's reputation to smithereens. Manchester portrayed her hidden presence at Wake Island as one of the dirtiest tricks every played by a politician on a soldier.[28] In fact, Truman did not even know she was there.

Whitney, on the other hand, not only knew Vernice Anderson was on Wake but also knew she was somewhere in the building because he had been introduced to her shortly before the conference began. She had been introduced too to MacArthur's pilot, Lieutenant Colonel Anthony Story. When Truman and MacArthur arrived at the conference room, there were seats for everyone but Miss Anderson. Being a self-effacing secretary, she "simply receded into the background," she recalled later, "and that could only be the small ante-room where the refreshments were and where someone had earlier taken my typewriter." After the conference got under way, she thought of going for a walk along the beach and opened the ante-room's external door, only to find herself staring at the backs of rifle-toting marine MPs and being glared at by unsmiling Secret Service men. She closed the door. Then "I sat down and since I was there with a pad, pencil, and typewriter ready to assist with the communiqué, it was quite natural for me to write down what I heard."[29]

After the conference concluded, what did this presidential secret weapon do? Miss Anderson went into the other room, to chat with various people and, she hoped, someone might be kind enough to introduce her to her hero Douglas MacArthur. Her wish came true, and MacArthur beamed down at her, asking in his usual gallant way, "And where did this lovely lady come from?"[30]

Truman invited MacArthur to stay for lunch with him, but in yet one last demonstration of disrespect MacArthur said he had to return immediately to Tokyo—as if to say that his duties as SCAP were more important than Truman's duties as President. Besides, when the commander in chief asks any officer to lunch, there is only one appropriate response: "Thank you, sir. I'd be delighted." MacArthur knew that. So did Truman.[31]

The President awarded the general his fourth Distinguished Service Medal. MacArthur bade farewell to Truman and wished him "Happy landings." He boarded his Constellation eager to escape from Wake, glad to escape from Truman, but there was no escaping his destiny, for he carried the spores of disaster within him. The general was the quintessential twentieth-century incarnation of the tragic hero as immortalized by great playwrights down the ages. MacArthur's complex nature and dramatic life made him the living breathing brother of Coriolanus, Hamlet or Macbeth. Like the tragic heroes of the theater, he would finally be brought down not by his enemies but by an immutable fault line that ran through the bedrock of his character. When the SCAP got airborne from this remote coral island, MacArthur was set on a direct course to the ultimate destination of all tragic heroes: the spectacular, irreversible fall.

Following the historic victory at Inchon, a delirious mood of optimism swept through Washington and Tokyo. The Korean War seemed to be virtually over. The North Korean Army was in full retreat, and Seoul was swiftly recaptured. MacArthur, weeping copiously, reinstalled Syngman Rhee as president of South Korea, much as he had restored the Philippine government in 1945.

The United Nations had a standing commitment to bringing about a united Korea, under a freely elected government, but Stalin had blocked every move toward a peaceful unification of the peninsula. Now, though, there was a dazzling chance to implement the UN policy, provided UN forces under MacArthur were permitted to cross the thirty-eighth parallel, capture Pyongyang and complete the destruction of the North Korean Army.

In late September 1950, while the UN debated calling for a united and democratic Korea, MacArthur received a directive from the Joint Chiefs that authorized him to cross the thirty-eighth parallel. "Your military objective is the destruction of the North Korean Armed Forces," it began. "You are authorized to conduct military operations north of the 38th Parallel in Korea, provided that at the time of such operations there has been no entry into North Korea by major Soviet or Chinese Communist forces, no announcement of intended entry, nor a threat to counter our operations militarily in North Korea." This directive spelled out in the clearest terms that he was not to send any but South Korean troops into the provinces bordering on China and the USSR.[32]

MacArthur's plan for conquering North Korea called for splitting his ground forces into two commands. Walton Walker's Eighth Army, numbering roughly two hundred thousand men, would advance along the west coast from the Inchon-Seoul area. The X Corps, numbering nearly a hundred thousand men, would advance along the east coast, under the command of MacArthur's former chief of staff, Edward Almond. The JCS had its doubts about the wisdom of dividing his forces in this way, but after Inchon, who was going to argue with a military genius? The Joint Chiefs gave formal approval to MacArthur's plan.[33]

One reason why MacArthur was deploying his ground units under two commands was to avoid putting everything under Walton Walker, in whom he had no confidence at all. He kept Walker so much in the dark that as the Eighth Army approached the thirty-eighth parallel, Walker told journalists that he expected he would halt along the parallel and regroup his forces until the UN decided to sanction an advance into North Korea. The one thing Truman did not need at this point, however, was for the UN to be asked point-blank to sanction an advance into North Korea. It would either dither or say no. Either way, the momentum that was carrying UN forces northward would soon be lost. In the belief that Walker's remarks might indicate some uncertainty in Tokyo, Marshall sent MacArthur a message that read: "We want you to feel unhampered strategically and tactically to proceed north of the 38th Parallel." MacArthur sent back a robust response: "I regard all of Korea open for our military operations." On October South Korean troops crossed the parallel, and MacArthur broadcast a proclamation calling on the North Korean government to capitulate.[34]

The response to these events came not from Pyongyang but from Peking. The Chinese premier, Chou En-lai, informed the U.S. government, via an Indian diplomat, that while China would not respond to the entry into North Korea of South Korean forces, "an American intrusion into North Korea will encounter Chinese resistance." MacArthur was promptly informed of this message but remained resolutely unimpressed. Back in July he had considered the question of Chinese or Soviet intervention when Hoyt Vandenberg, the USAF Chief of Staff, was in Tokyo. "The only passages leading from Manchuria and Vladivostok have many tunnels and bridges," he confidently told Vandenberg. "I see here a unique use for the atomic bomb. . . . Sweeten up my B-29 force." Even without atomic weapons, he was convinced that his airpower alone would make it impossible for large numbers of Chinese troops to enter North Korea undetected and equally impossible for China to maintain tens of thousands of men in North Korea even if it did find some way to smuggle them across the Yalu River. At most, MacArthur believed, the Chinese might be able to get a few thousand "volunteers" into action.[35]

Truman too declined to take Chou's threat seriously. The Indian diplomat was regarded as a fellow traveler and a mere pawn of the Chinese government. He had delivered dire warnings in the past, and nothing had come of any of them.[36]

Walker's Eighth Army and Almond's X Corps continued to advance into North Korea. In the plan that MacArthur had submitted to the JCS he had said he would have American forces press forward roughly 125 miles and establish a strong defensive line across the narrowest section of the Korean peninsula, running from Chongju to Hungnam. Only ROK (Republic of Korea) forces would operate north of this line, in accordance with the Joint Chiefs' directive.

On October 17, however, with American forces closing on Pyongyang, MacArthur changed his mind. Without consulting the JCS, he bluntly informed the Chiefs that he intended to have American and other allied troops advance to a line close to the Chinese and Soviet borders, a line, that is, nearly forty miles north of the line he had planned to place across the narrow "waist" of the peninsula. The new line was one third longer than the old one and would be much harder to defend.

This was the kind of question MacArthur and the JCS ought to have discussed, but he did not offer discussion, nor did the JCS demand it. He would never have gotten away with anything like this in World War II, and he knew it. The Chiefs, it was clear by now, were too inert to restrain him. They were men of less stature and ability than the people they had replaced, epigones stumbling along in the footsteps of giants.

What happened next was almost predictable. MacArthur ordered Walker and Almond "to drive forward with all speed and . . . use any and all ground forces . . . to secure all of North Korea."[37] At a stroke he overturned the restrictions on not employing American troops in areas adjacent to China and the Soviet Union. The Chiefs were stung into protest this time. They informed MacArthur that this order violated the directive that authorized him to advance into North Korea and concluded, with almost risible understatement, "Your action is a matter of some concern here."[38]

MacArthur responded with a message that said he could not employ ROKs as directed because he did not have enough of them, that ROK commanders were emotionally unstable and not to be trusted and that his order was not in conflict with the JCS directive. Besides, Marshall's message that he should not feel hampered strategically and tactically when he crossed the parallel gave him all the authority he needed to modify his instructions. What MacArthur was doing was to take Marshall's message completely out of context and pretend it was a blank check, something he surely knew he did not really possess. Then, in true MacArthurian mode, he concluded his cable on a dire note, hinting darkly that "tactical hazards might even result from other action than that which I have directed."[39]

Here, then, was the crux of command relationships in the Korean War: Who would make the strategic decisions? The Chiefs, rightly, did not wish to micromanage the war from a distance of ten thousand miles. The American tradition was to allow the commander in the field considerable leeway in interpreting his orders. On the other hand, there was not a scintilla of ambiguity or doubt in the injunction against employing American forces close to the borders of China and the USSR. There was not anything that sanctioned the kind of change MacArthur had unilaterally imposed without prior agreement.

The reason for allowing only ROK troops to advance all the way to the borders of Russia and China was obvious. The United States was not going to provoke the Chinese or the Russians to intervene in Korea, nor would it give them any excuse for doing so. Truman also needed to take cognizance of the anxieties of his allies if this war was going to retain international support. The British in particular had opposed crossing the parallel for fear that the Chinese would respond by seizing Hong Kong. What made MacArthur's action unjustifiable was that he had not modified U.S. strategy—which was as much political as military—but had changed it. A strategy designed to avoid a widening of the war had been turned into one that openly courted that risk.

MacArthur had done this without discussion, without even having the courtesy to inform his superiors of what he was thinking. He had instead presented them with a fait accompli. He had no authority to alter Korean War strategy, and no amount of sophistry or casuistry could alter that fact. What was happening was that as he got older, MacArthur's judgment deteriorated along with his health. Like many people as they enter old age, he was becoming increasingly emotional in his responses to problems and less able to think clearly under pressure. Even so, Truman, Marshall and the Joint Chiefs backed down yet again and allowed MacArthur's order to stand. That made them as culpable as he for the disaster that followed.

Meanwhile the Chinese had infiltrated nearly a hundred thousand men into North Korea. Marching by night and hiding by day, they had gone undetected. With the strategic initiative in their hands, these veteran troops moved into the huge gap between the Eighth Army and the X Corps.[40] On October 25 they struck, concentrating their attacks against the most advanced ROK regiments and virtually wiping them out. Despite this debacle, MacArthur refused to acknowledge that the Chinese had entered North Korea in force. He was supported by the ever-loyal, rarely reliable Charles Willoughby, who insisted that only sixteen thousand Chinese troops had crossed the Yalu.[41]

MacArthur's response to Chinese intervention was to order the Far Eastern Air Forces to mount a two-week aerial blitz against the enemy's lines of communication in North Korea, including the bridges spanning the Yalu. The JCS swiftly responded by ordering him not to bomb any of these bridges. When this message flashed onto the telecon screen, MacArthur was roused to fury. He returned to his office enraged and wrote out a cable demanding immediate relief from his command. His acting chief of staff, Major General Doyle Hickey, pleaded with him not to send it. If you quit now, he told MacArthur, it will undermine the morale of the troops in the field at a time when they are under attack.[42]

MacArthur scrapped the resignation cable, which he would probably never have sent anyway—writing it out and talking it over with Hickey were a form of stress management—and dictated a message to the JCS that verged on hysteria. He damned the Chinese intervention as "outrageous international lawlessness," criticized the Chiefs for "the disastrous effect, both physical and psychological, that will result from the restrictions which you are imposing," demanded that Truman be consulted, "as I believe your instructions may well result in a calamity of major proportion," and urged "immediate reconsideration of your decision."[43]

Truman reluctantly permitted FEAF to bomb the bridges but insisted that air attacks must be limited to the North Korean end only; there were to be no attacks on the Chinese side. It was a wonderfully weird order. It may have made sense politically but was ludicrous militarily. It simply wasn't possible to bomb one end of a bridge with B-29s; they lacked the accuracy to do anything like that.

Suddenly, however, the Chinese Communist forces disengaged. They melted away abruptly. It seems, in all likelihood, that the Chinese Communists felt they had made their point: They would not tolerate the presence of American troops on their borders. This was hardly an unreasonable stance. The United States, after all, would never allow the Chinese to put an army on the Canadian or Mexican border. The Chinese disengagement gave American policy makers a chance to draw the obvious lesson. MacArthur, however, did not draw it. Neither did Truman, the NSC, the State Department or the JCS. After a ten-day pause to straighten out his logistics, MacArthur resumed his advance to the Yalu, and no one in Washington told him to halt.

On November 24 he flew to Korea to visit the front lines. When the commander of the 24th Division, Major General John Church, remarked that he felt confident his troops could go all the way to the Yalu, MacArthur responded in a lighthearted way, "Well, if they go fast enough, maybe some of them can be home in time for Christmas." Several journalists standing nearby caught only the phrase about troops being home for Christmas. They hurriedly filed dispatches asserting that MacArthur had solemnly said the troops now in Korea would be home by Christmas. They added to the verisimilitude of their copy by adding details that were entirely fictitious and invented some extra "quotes" from MacArthur to round out their pieces. When the "Home by Christmas" story got out, MacArthur tried to correct it, without success. It appears in nearly every history of the Korean War.[44]

Before returning to Tokyo on November 25, he had his pilot fly the *SCAP* along the Yalu River at a height of five thousand feet. MacArthur gazed down at the harsh landscape stretching bleakly along both sides of the river: treeless mountains and steep ridges, their blackness made starker by dazzling patches of snow in the valleys and necklaces of ice glittering in the crevices. It was a desolate, merciless-looking place, without any evident trace that huge numbers of Chinese troops had crossed it in recent weeks. He flew back to Japan confident he had the situation under control.[45]

That night the Chinese struck again, this time in massive numbers. They now had more than three hundred thousand troops in North Korea. The Yalu had frozen over, so whether the bridges were knocked down or not made little difference. They would be resupplied and reinforced. Once in position, the Chinese ambushed the leading elements of the Eighth Army and the X Corps. By the end of November the entire UN command was in full retreat.[46]

MacArthur cranked out a special communiqué that denied he had ever mounted an offensive to reach the Yalu. All he had done was make a reconnaissance in force to determine the enemy's strength and intentions. This patently false contention was the reaction of a man who feared his reckless drive north would place him before the bar of history as the fool who had provoked the Chinese into making the massive intervention they had threatened and brought about a national humiliation for the United States. The only truthful passage in this communiqué was a sentence that read, "We face an entirely new war."[47]

A week later J. Lawton Collins flew to Korea and visited the front, where he found Walker confident that he could hold the Seoul-Inchon area once he reached it. In Tokyo, however, Collins found despair rather than optimism. Still shaken and in a defeatist mood, MacArthur told him that unless he received up to two hundred thousand more men in the near future, "The United Nations command should pull out of Korea." MacArthur was planning to fall back all the way to Pusan.[48]

Over the next few weeks both Walker and Almond made fighting withdrawals southward. Thousands of American soldiers and marines were killed or wounded. Hundreds more died of hypothermia and pneumonia. Winter campaigns in the mountains are probably the most arduous ordeals that ground troops ever have to endure, and conditions in North Korea that winter were worse than most of the men fighting there had probably ever imagined. Yet no matter how bad the weather, no matter how rugged the terrain, the Chinese continued to attack. The UN command's superior firepower inflicted many thousands of casualties on the Chinese and Far Eastern Air Forces ruled the skies, but neither airpower nor artillery was able to achieve much against an enemy who was willing to absorb so much punishment.[49]

The Eighth Army fell back to the thirty-eighth parallel, and still the Chinese advanced. Having driven the UN forces out of North Korea, they seemed intent on "liberating" South Korea too. On December 23, as the Chinese closed on Seoul, Walker was killed when his jeep collided with a South Korean weapons carrier.[50]

Early in the war MacArthur had been tempted to fire Walker and put someone else in command of the Eighth Army. The officer he had in mind was Lieutenant General Matthew Ridgway, one of the finest combat commanders of World War II, a man of keen intelligence, awesome courage and aggressive instincts. MacArthur had known and admired Ridgway since the early 1920s, when he had placed the young Captain Ridgway in charge of the physical education department at West Point. Walker's death gave him the opportunity he needed to ask for Ridgway and be certain to get him. On Christmas night Ridgway arrived at Tokyo's Haneda Airport to assume command of the battered and reeling Eighth Army. MacArthur's instructions to him were simple and clear: "The Eighth Army is yours, Matt. Do what you think best."[51]

The Chinese entry into the Korean War coincided with humiliating Democratic losses in the midterm elections. Truman had gained nothing from traveling to Wake Island and tolerating MacArthur's rudeness. And the eruption of Chinese armies onto the field of battle made a mockery of MacArthur's confident assertions, at Wake and after Wake, that the war was virtually over. As he mulled over these disappointments, Truman confided his angry recollections of the Wake Island meeting to his diary: "Gen. MacArthur was at the airport with his shirt unbuttoned, wearing a greasy ham and eggs cap that evidently had been in use for twenty years . . . the General assured the President that the victory was won in Korea, that Japan was ready for a peace treaty and that the Chinese Communists would not attack. . . ."[52]

Not only had they attacked, but at the end of November MacArthur granted an interview to *U.S. News & World Report.* He informed two of its reporters that all his problems dealing with the Chinese were due to the restrictions placed on him by Washington. These amounted to "an enormous handicap, without precedent in military history." Truman was enraged, and the administration swiftly issued a blanket gag order on military commanders and senior civil servants. From now on, ran the order, they would have to clear with their departments all statements intended for public consumption prior to releasing them. Although it looked like a restriction imposed on thousands, it was really aimed at one man. MacArthur's response was to write out a press release criticizing the Pentagon, the State Department and the CIA for their faulty intelligence on Chinese intentions. He submitted this, with what amounted to a poker face, to the JCS. They played out their part in this minifarce by solemnly telling him his statement was not in accord with official policy concerning press coverage of intelligence matters.[53]

MacArthur continued to inform Washington that there were only two ways the Korean War was going to end if he did not get another two hundred thousand men. Either the UN command would be annihilated or it would have to be evacuated. In January 1951 the Chinese captured Seoul. UN forces were still backpedaling, and MacArthur's grim postulates seemed increasingly believable. He himself seemed unable to rally his usual optimism. The few people who saw him regularly found him uncharacteristically tired and depressed.[54]

Perhaps Colonel Lowe informed Truman about the general's low spirits because at this critical juncture Truman tried to patch up his relationship with MacArthur by sending him a long letter spelling out ten good reasons why the United States was following its present policy in Korea. The President concluded with a personal tribute. "The entire nation is grateful for your splendid leadership in the difficult struggle in Korea," he wrote, "and for the superb performance of your forces under the most difficult circumstances."[55]

While MacArthur was digesting this message, J. Lawton Collins and Hoyt Vandenberg were making yet another trip to Korea. Ridgway assured them the Chinese were virtually played out and vulnerable to a counteroffensive. In February Ridgway launched the Eighth Army in a series of attacks that brought the recapture of Seoul a month later and drove the Chinese back to the thirty-eighth parallel. MacArthur's bleak assertion that the choice in Korea was annihilation or evacuation was suddenly revealed for the defeatism that it was. The mantle of military genius draped around him since Inchon was trailing in the mud. Without major reinforcements Ridgway had inflicted a massive defeat on the Chinese Army. This showed beyond peradventure that the general who now had the best understanding of the position on the ground was not MacArthur but Ridgway.[56]

MacArthur tried to claim credit for the aggressive spirit Ridgway had put into the Eighth Army and in his memoirs baldly asserted, "I ordered Ridgway to start north again." Ridgway, reading this sentence shortly after MacArthur's death, was irritated and bemused. He wrote in the margin of his copy of MacArthur's *Reminiscences* next to the offending passage, "No such order was ever issued."[57]

With the Chinese having suffered a severe defeat, Truman and Acheson thought the time was ripe at last to bring a negotiated end to the war. MacArthur was informed accordingly that the President was planning to make an announcement calling on the parties involved to enter into discussions. MacArthur thought about this prospect for several days, before deciding to halt the President's initiative in its tracks. Victory had not been won. All that Truman seemed ready to settle for was an end to the war with the two sides more or less where they were before the North Koreans attacked. All that suffering, all that destruction, all that loss of life had been for nothing. MacArthur issued a long message, addressed to the Chinese, calling on them to admit defeat or face the risk of "a decision by the

United Nations to depart from its tolerant efforts to contain the war to the area of Korea, through an expansion of our military operations to [China's] coastal areas and interior bases, [which] would doom Red China to the risk of imminent military collapse"—i.e., quit now, before we destroy you. Needless to say, he did not clear this in advance with the Joint Chiefs.[58]

Truman was once again outraged. At a stroke MacArthur had made it impossible for him to try to get peace negotiations going. MacArthur disingenuously protested that all he had done was issue a routine press release. His action was so blatantly counter to the President's initiative, though, that it is impossible to believe for a moment that he was unaware of what he had done. It is altogether likely, in fact, that he had enough of the Korean War. If it was not going to be fought to a victory, he might as well get out now and claim the martyr's crown, a fighter to the end, sacrificed on the altar of political cowardice. The alternative was to spend the final years of his illustrious career in turgid soapbox negotiations with the Communists, begging them to agree to an armistice. Better to damn their eyes, demand a change in strategy and risk dismissal.[59]

For Truman, MacArthur's blustering message to the Chinese was brazenly insubordinate. To the public, however, MacArthur's blast at the enemy was the kind of triumphalism that was balm to the soul after a winter of defeats and retreats. This was not a good time to fire the general. The President would have to wait for MacArthur to make some other, more obviously egregious misstep.[60]

He did not have long to wait. While MacArthur was pondering how to respond to Truman's proposed offer to the North Koreans and Chinese to enter truce talks, he had written a letter to Joseph Martin, the Republican speaker of the House of Representatives. In his letter he criticized the Eurocentrism of American foreign policy, which was at the expense of the Far East: "[I]f we lose this war to Communism in Asia, the fall of Europe is inevitable; win it, and Europe most probably would avoid war and yet preserve freedom." What really galled him, though, was the prospect of how the Korean War was going to end, and he let out a scream of rage: "There is no substitute for victory."[61]

MacArthur did not ask Martin to keep his letter confidential. He knew from experience that when he wrote to a congressman, that congressman was more likely to make his letter public than to keep it to himself, so he can hardly have been surprised when, on April 5, Martin read it out on the floor of Congress. That evening an irate Truman informed his diary, "This looks like the last straw. Rank insubordination."[62]

Just to make sure, though, MacArthur had given interviews to a pro-Republican periodical, *The Freeman,* and to a conservative British newspaper, the *Daily Telegraph,* in which he outspokenly attacked the restrictions under which he had to operate. For good measure, he damned U.S. strategy in the war as "ludicrous."[63] The restrictions and the strategy were dictated, ultimately, by the President. If this was not the action of a man trying to get himself fired, it certainly was not the action of a man eager to hold on to his job.

On April 9, when Almond came to see him before returning to Korea, MacArthur said somberly, "I may not see you anymore, so goodbye, Ned."

"I don't understand what you mean," said Almond, puzzled. "You have been coming to see me frequently during the past six or eight months."

"That isn't the question," MacArthur replied. "I have become politically involved and may be relieved by the President."[64]

Less than twenty-four hours later Truman signed the order relieving MacArthur of all his commands. Word soon leaked out, and Bradley hurried to see Truman late at night on April 10. He told the President that if MacArthur heard about Truman's order before it reached him, he was likely to resign immediately. Truman flared up angrily: "The son of a bitch isn't going to resign on me. I want him fired."[65] A press conference was convened at the White House at 1:00 A.M. to announce the President's decision: MacArthur had been summarily relieved.

Sid Huff heard the news of MacArthur's dismissal over the radio and informed Jean. She in turn informed the general. Official confirmation came while the MacArthurs were having lunch on April 12, when a Signal Corps courier arrived with a pouch containing Truman's order. A weeping Huff approached the dining table carrying an brown envelope marked "Action for MacArthur." MacArthur opened the envelope and read: "I deeply regret it becomes my duty as President and Commander-in-Chief of the United States military forces to replace you as Supreme Commander, Allied Powers; commander-in-chief of the United Nations command; commander-in-chief, Far East; commanding general, U.S. Army, Far East.

"You will turn over your command, effective at once, to Lt. Gen. Matthew B. Ridgway. You are authorized to issue such orders as are necessary to complete desired travel to such place as you select. Harry S. Truman."[66]

MacArthur turned to his wife without any display of emotion on his normally expressive face. There was nothing to be read there, no clue to what he was really thinking. MacArthur's strange calmness looked remarkably like an iron will at work, when it was most probably the blank expression of someone who was emotionally and physically exhausted. "Jeannie, we're going home at last."[67]

32

I Bid You Goodbye

All three MacArthurs were prone to airsickness. They planned to return to the United States by ship and enjoy a long, leisurely voyage together while the general adjusted to a new world, one much smaller than the empire of his own that they were leaving. Herbert Hoover considered a slow return by boat a serious mistake, and he urged MacArthur to come home at once, by air. Any delay would allow the White House an opportunity to turn public opinion against the general before he ever set foot on the continental United States.[1] At present the mood was generally hostile to Truman and favorable toward MacArthur, but as every politician knows, public opinion can turn around 180 degrees from one week to the next. MacArthur accepted Hoover's point. He and his family would fly home at once.

Hoover was evidently thinking of MacArthur's political prospects, and who could say what a triumphal return might lead to? With the nation deeply involved in an unpopular war, the people could well be in the mood to put a general into the White House in 1952.

MacArthur made no complaints then or later against being relieved. He accepted Truman's absolute right to fire him. What rankled was the shabby way it was done, allowing millions, if not tens of millions, to know of it before he did. "Publicly humiliated after fifty-two years in the Army," he reflected somberly to his political adviser, William Sebald. Years later he wrote, "No office boy, no charwoman, no servant of any sort would have been dismissed with such callous disregard for the ordinary decencies," and he was right.[2]

For millions of Japanese, word of MacArthur's dismissal struck them hard, like news of a death in the family. Much of Japan was thrown into a state that resembled mourning. On April 12, when the MacArthurs left the embassy for the last time, some 250,000 Japanese lined the streets to the airport, many of them with heads bowed and faces streaked with tears. MacArthur got a nineteen-gun salute, a warm tribute from Ridgway and an army band that broke into "Auld Lang Syne." Deeply moved, he bade emotional farewells to tearful GHQ staff members and their families.[3] MacArthur's airplane, the *SCAP,* had been renamed the *Bataan,* and a freshly painted nose was the result. MacArthur would return to his country not as the recent proconsul of Japan or as the recent commander in Korea. No, he would come home as the conquering hero of World War II, the man who had lost Bataan only to redeem it and so save America's honor along with his own.[4]

MacArthur had been invited to address both houses of Congress. During the twelve-hour flight to Hawaii he worked on the address he would deliver. When the silver Constellation landed in Hawaii, young Arthur finally stepped onto American soil for the first time in his thirteen years. Next day MacArthur laid a wreath at the Punchbowl, the brooding volcanic crater that is the National Memorial of the Pacific, where thirteen thousand Americans who died fighting in World War II are buried. "I do not know the dignity of their birth," he intoned sorrowfully, "but I do know the glory of their death."[5] It was an expression he had coined back in December 1941, to honor Captain Colin Kelly, the B-17 pilot credited with sinking a Japanese battleship when the Japanese first landed on Luzon.

MacArthur flew on to San Francisco, and by the time his plane arrived he had finished writing his speech to Congress.[6] Even though the MacArthurs did not reach the city by the bay until late at night, there were still some five hundred thousand people on hand to welcome them home. The following day MacArthur delivered a short speech at the Civic Center Plaza, interrupted by cries of "MacArthur for president!" But in his speech he declared, "I have no political aspirations whatsoever. I do not intend to run for any political office and I hope my name will never be used in any political way. The only politics I have is contained in a simple phrase known to all of us—'God Bless America!' "[7]

From San Francisco he flew on to Washington, to address Congress. When his plane landed at Washington airport, Marshall, Bradley, Collins and more than a dozen three- and four-star generals were on hand to greet him. To MacArthur it seemed a cynical and hypocritical performance.[8] He was convinced that Marshall and Bradley were two of the most important players (along with Truman and Acheson) in a conspiracy to bring him down and introduce appeasement of the Communists into American security policy. He never ceased to believe that without their machinations he could have won the war in Korea. Even so, he smiled and shook hands with Marshall and Bradley and acted out his part, much as they steeled themselves to act out theirs, for the benefit of the cameras and posterity.

MacArthur's address to Congress was an epic moment in the early days of television. It brought history with a capital *H* to the flickering round screens of Stone Age TV and left a grainy, if indelible, impression on millions of Americans of what a living legend and walking myth looked like in the flesh. MacArthur spoke for nearly an hour and a half. Mainly he talked about Asia: how impoverished and war-ravaged it was now, but how important it was going to become. He dwelt in particular on China, which had risen in one generation from poverty and passivity until it threatened to dominate Asia. This was a China that was an expansionist, nationalistic and military power. It was the Chinese, not the Soviets, he asserted, who were the real force behind the Korean War. It was only by exerting America's economic and military strength against China that the war could be won.

MacArthur's speech was interrupted by wild applause and standing ovations every couple of minutes. At such moments Democrats sprang to their feet as readily, applauded just as enthusiastically and cheered just as loudly as did Republicans.

MacArthur complained about the lack of reinforcements to his command and railed at the restrictions imposed on him as a commander in the field. With that off his chest, he then concluded magnificently, with a bravura passage of farewell: "I am closing my fifty-two years of military service. When I joined the Army even before the turn of the century, it was the fulfillment of all my boyish hopes and dreams. The world has turned over many times since I took the oath on the Plain at West Point, and the hopes and dreams have long since vanished. But I still remember the refrain of one of the most popular barrack ballads of that day which proclaimed most proudly that—'Old soldiers never die, they just fade away.' And like the old soldier of that ballad, I now close my military career and just fade away—an old soldier who tried to do his duty as God gave him the light to see that duty. Goodbye."[9]

There were shouts from the floor of "No! No!" A storm of raw, naked emotion burst upon this august body made up largely of gray-haired elderly gents. The Speaker of the House, Joe Martin—the man whose release of MacArthur's letter had helped bring about this drama—had never seen such a tidal wave of passion in nearly half a century of political life. He later reported to a friend, "When MacArthur finished there wasn't a dry eye on the Democratic side of the House . . . nor a dry seat among the Republicans!"[10]

MacArthur's father had been fascinated by China for much of his adult life. China was one of those subjects on which MacArthur considered himself exceptionally well informed, having inherited his father's interest in that huge country, along with his father's books on the subject. Even so, the intellectual fascination of father and son had proved no obstacle to seriously misjudging the Chinese in November 1950. Angered and humiliated, MacArthur became obsessed with making the Chinese pay for what they had done to him and to his troops.

In war and peace alike, his every instinct was to strike back whenever he was attacked. In December 1950 he had urged the Joint Chiefs to sanction a strategic bombing campaign against China's military-industrial base, but his Far Eastern Air Forces had only 90 B-29s available. FEAF was too small to mount a sustained bombing campaign. Moreover, there were approximately 250 MiG-15 jet fighters based in Manchuria, up to 100 of which were flown by Soviet pilots. Unless FEAF were allowed to win and maintain air superiority over Manchuria, the B-29s would be wiped out within days of launching any strategic bombing campaign. The Joint Chiefs turned down his proposal.[11]

In his address to Congress, MacArthur demanded increased military and economic pressure on China and the provision of American logistical support to the forces of Chiang Kai-shek. The United States would, in effect, use its air and sea power to defend Formosa, thereby allowing Chiang to send several hundred thousand troops to Korea, where they would turn the tide of battle.

MacArthur may have been the only commander in the world who considered Chiang's troops capable of overcoming anything stronger than the Boy Scouts. They had been comprehensively defeated by a ragtag force of underarmed peasants whom Mao and his generals had turned into a tough, highly committed army. Mao's soldiers had had no outside military assistance. They had armed themselves by capturing weapons from Chiang's well-armed but demoralized and badly led forces. The Nationalists stood no more chance of defeating the Chinese in Korea than they had of defeating them in China, with or without American logistical support.

Beyond that, any attempt to escalate the war by moving hundreds of thousands of Chinese Nationalists into Korea and making the war there an extension of the Chinese civil war would have one certain consequence: UN support would collapse, leaving the United States fighting a new war whose focus was China, not Korea. Such a change in direction was politically impossible at home as well as abroad. You would have to go a long way in 1951 to find Americans who favored going to war with China. Such a struggle could be fought and won only with the use of nuclear weapons against China's population centers. The deaths of millions of innocent people was hardly a reasonable reaction to a limited setback in Korea. All in all, MacArthur hadn't a clue as to how to deal with the Chinese. He had managed to get himself lost in a Red mist.

The administration had taken advantage of his intellectual confusion by portraying MacArthur as an out-of-control commander who was pressing a course of action almost certain to ignite World War III. This legend clings to his reputation, and nothing seems likely ever to dispel it. Ironically, Truman and Acheson themselves were drawn to MacArthur's idea of launching a bombing campaign against China to force an end to the war. The President considered going even further. If the Chinese did not respond to strategic bombing, Truman mused, maybe he should issue an ultimatum to the Soviets, threatening them too with "all-out war" if the stalemate in Korea persisted. In the end, however, he chose to leave this unwinnable war for his successor to wrestle with. Truman had no more idea than MacArthur how to bring it to an end without drastic escalation.[12]

MacArthur was keen to refute this portrait of himself. "It has been said that I was in effect a warmonger," he had told Congress during his farewell address. "Nothing could be further from the truth. I know war as few other men now living know it, and nothing to me is more revolting. I have long advocated its complete abolition. . . . But once war is forced on us, there is no other alternative than to apply every available means to bring it to a swift end. War's very object is victory—not prolonged indecision. In war, indeed, there can be no substitute for victory."[13]

This observation brought one of the most ecstatic of his many standing ovations. And yet, and yet . . . war's very object is victory only in a world of pure nihilism, when killing and destruction have no higher purpose. MacArthur seemed in his anger and frustration to lose sight of the fact that among modern nations wars are fought for clear and attainable political ends. Many times those ends can be achieved only by victory; sometimes, however, they might actually be reached by prolonged indecision. Most wars in the course of Western history have probably ended in stalemate rather than in victory parades and surrenders. The United States had itself fought just such a war. Congress had declared war on Britain in 1812 without for an instant thinking the United States would be able to defeat the British and dictate peace terms. MacArthur was not a man to fight that kind of war, and in retrospect it is clear that it was a monumental mistake on Truman's part to expect him to do so. He was not and never would be a limited war commander.

On May 3, two weeks after MacArthur's speech, Congress opened hearings on the Korean War. MacArthur was the first witness and testified for the first three days. The hearings were closed, but a transcript was issued each day, and virtually nothing that was said went unreported. MacArthur claimed that all his recommendations on how to fight the war had been accepted by the Joint Chiefs but were turned down by the White House and the State Department. The claim that the JCS had agreed with him was, on the face of it, astonishing. There was a huge documentary record to the contrary, as he well knew.

What was at work here was institutional self-preservation. Many senior commanders tacitly accept that it is bad for the military to appear divided in front of politicians or the press, no matter how deeply they may disagree among themselves. Indeed, the more they disagree, the more necessary some may feel it is to give an appearance of service unity. There are times, of course, when that tacit understanding breaks down.

What MacArthur probably was not prepared for was the fact that the Joint Chiefs would come before Congress and contradict his claims. He may have read too much into the way they had greeted him on his arrival in Washington. Bradley said flatly that MacArthur's proposal to make China the focus of the struggle "would involve us in the wrong war, at the wrong place, at the wrong time, and with the wrong enemy."[14]

The chief rebuttal witness for the administration, however, was not Bradley but Marshall. It was a less than edifying spectacle to have two five-star generals politely calling each other liars. This dismal conflict between two old men who had both dedicated their lives to public service was made incomparably worse by Senator Joe McCarthy, an outspoken admirer of MacArthur's, who seized this opportunity to make a three-hour attack on the Senate floor against Marshall. McCarthy painted one of the greatest men in the history of the Republic as a Communist fellow traveler, a man whose entire career was "steeped in falsehood," and effectively accused Marshall of treason. "Support" like this did MacArthur's reputation lasting injury, but he chose not to distance himself from that feculent wretch Joe McCarthy, probably for fear of antagonizing the Republican party's ultra-right wing.[15]

To the disappointment of his many Republican admirers, MacArthur did not dominate the congressional hearings on the Korean War. Most of his testimony was clear and straightforward, but whenever his own conduct came under close scrutiny, he became defensive or uncommunicative. It seems likely that he hoped these hearings would help his political ambitions, but they had exactly the opposite effect. There was a stark contrast between the way he was greeted in late April, before the hearings, and the welcomes he received a month later.

The day after his farewell address to Congress, for example, MacArthur journeyed to New York, where an estimated seven million people turned out; it was the biggest reception the city had ever given anyone. One person who wasn't there was Governor Thomas Dewey, who chose to leave the state rather than be pressured into meeting MacArthur. Dewey despised MacArthur almost as much as Truman did, if for very different reasons. He considered MacArthur partly responsible for his defeat in 1948.[16]

On April 27, a week after receiving the accolades of New York City, MacArthur visited Milwaukee, and the glow was still strong. Nearly half the population of Milwaukee was estimated to have turned out to greet him on his first visit in nearly fifty years to what MacArthur called "my ancestral home."[17]

By late May, however, after MacArthur's appearance at the Korean War hearings, the crowds were considerably smaller than they had been back in April. He traveled to Texas, expecting to be met by huge crowds, but the largest gathering he addressed consisted of twenty-seven thousand people at the Cotton Bowl in Dallas. As one of Truman's friends in Texas gleefully informed him, "a high school football game would have drawn a bigger crowd."[18]

The most obvious lesson to draw from the falling away of popular interest was that MacArthur's political prospects were nil. Nevertheless, in the spring of 1952, when convention time drew near again, his name was canvassed once more by a handful of diehard admirers. Old friends such as Herbert Hoover and Robert E. Wood, men who had long urged him to enter politics, had not completely given up. They were intent on securing the Republican presidential nomination for Senator Robert A. Taft of Ohio, but it seemed to them that while MacArthur stood no chance of securing the top spot on the Republican ticket, he might well win the vice presidential nomination. When they put this idea to MacArthur, he was delighted to accept it.[19]

One thing seemed certain: The Democrats were going to lose in November. After twenty years of Democratic rule the United States was more than ready for a change of leadership. And if Taft, who was nearly seventy, died in office, MacArthur might still become president, if by the back door. The best way for MacArthur to push himself forward as Taft's running mate, his handlers agreed, was for the general to ignite the Republican convention with some of his brilliant oratory.

Late one July night in Chicago, with fat little Courtney Whitney sitting behind him basking in reflected glory, MacArthur delivered one of the dullest, most turgid keynote speeches ever heard at a political convention. The day before the first ballot Hoover concluded that Taft did not have enough votes to win the nomination, and unless something dramatic happened, the nomination was going to go to Eisenhower. He pleaded with Taft to stand aside and urge his delegates to vote for MacArthur. If Taft's sizable block of committed votes combined with the small hard-core pro-MacArthur vote, argued Hoover, it might just be possible to stop Eisenhower from winning and get the right general into the White House. Taft refused to stand aside. Ike won the nomination easily, and MacArthur's political ambitions guttered out like an exhausted candle.[20]

He was in a sulk all the way to election day. A handful of pro-MacArthur supporters had managed to get his name onto the ballot in Texas and California. His Republican friends urged him to get his name removed to make it easier for Eisenhower to win those two states, but he adamantly refused. It was churlish and pointless, but he was so embittered he could do no other.[21]

After his election Ike fulfilled his campaign pledge to go to Korea to examine the situation there for himself. During his absence MacArthur made a speech to the National Association of Manufacturers in which he said he knew how to end the war. The JCS urged MacArthur to reveal his "secret" plan to them, but he preferred to offer it directly to the President-elect. Shortly before Christmas, when Ike returned from Korea, he went straight to MacArthur, taking his secretary of state designate, John Foster Dulles, with him.

MacArthur at first proposed to end the war by delivering an ultimatum to the Chinese to pull out of Korea or see their cities bombed and their fragile industrial base wiped out. Ike said he doubted that America's allies would go along with expanding the war into China. The other possibility, said MacArthur, was to have the Air Force drop nuclear waste across North Korea, just south of the Yalu. This radioactive belt would make it impossible for the Chinese to resupply or reinforce their three hundred thousand men in Korea and make it equally impossible for those three hundred thousand to get out. They would be trapped. The second part of the plan was to mount amphibious assaults against the east and west coasts of North Korea, while UN forces moved north of the thirty-eighth parallel once more and wiped out the Chinese by enveloping them from three directions.[22]

This was, as Eisenhower realized, a perfectly infeasible plan. It simply demonstrated that MacArthur had absolutely no comprehension of the problems of handling nuclear waste and no concern whatever for the environmental or political consequences of what he was proposing. Radioactive material scattered over the North Korean landscape would have been at the mercy of every wind that blew and would threaten serious nuclear contamination not only to China and the USSR but to at least two of America's allies, South Korea and Japan, not to mention the threat it would pose to the health of the 350,000 American soldiers in the Far East. Ike was too sensible to take such a bizarre idea seriously, one reason why he became President and MacArthur did not.

Seeing Eisenhower preparing to be sworn in as President was not easy for MacArthur. Much as he liked Ike personally, it was impossible for him to consider his former assistant presidential material, and he never changed his mind that Eisenhower was a lightweight. He could not have been more mistaken.

MacArthur's political hopes finally ended in one of the oldest stories of all: the talented pupil who exceeds the master, the prince's servant, not the prince, who wins the kingdom. There would be a Republican in the White House at last, something he had longed for since the defeat of Herbert Hoover in 1932, but what a Republican! Far from toasting the success of an old colleague, MacArthur took Eisenhower's election as yet another bitter defeat.[23]

Back in 1919, when Brigadier General Douglas MacArthur returned from France as the most highly decorated American soldier of World War I, he had been ordered off the ballroom floor at the Waldorf because he insisted on wearing spurs. He had sworn then that he would never set foot in the Waldorf again, yet he and Jean had eaten their wedding breakfast there the day they were married in 1937, and irony of ironies, it was the Towers at the Waldorf-Astoria that became MacArthur's last home. The owner, Conrad Hilton, admired MacArthur so much he knocked three apartments into one to provide the general with a spacious and luxurious dwelling on the thirty-seventh floor. Hilton, it was reported, charged MacArthur a mere $450 a month, which was less than the price of four nights in a Waldorf suite.[24]

The focal point of MacArthur's last home was a huge salon filled with works of Oriental art, many of them gifts from the Japanese. The salon's walls were covered with large paintings in gilded frames. There were mementos from Jean's travels around the Far East. And there was a Japanese butler who greeted guests at the door and ushered them into this room to wait for MacArthur to appear. One old friend who came to call was William Ganoe, MacArthur's adjutant back during his days as superintendent at West Point. "Alone in the vast splendor, I had the feeling I had barged into a palace," wrote Ganoe.[25] MacArthur, like Franklin Roosevelt and others of their class, combined a basic indifference to money-making with a preference for sumptuous surroundings.

Another occupant of the Waldorf Towers was Herbert Hoover, but neither Hoover nor anyone else in the Waldorf—apart from Jean and Arthur—saw much of the general. He was as reclusive and uninterested in socializing as he had ever been. To Jean's embarrassment, the Hoovers regularly invited them to come and have lunch or dinner, but MacArthur rarely accepted these invitations, and on those few occasions when he did so, he never invited the Hoovers to dine with them in return.[26]

MacArthur cared only for the most familiar faces, visages lambent with adoration: Jean and Arthur, Courtney Whitney and Sid Huff. On his return to the United States he had persuaded Huff to be restored to active duty and remain with him until 1961, when Huff reached the Army's mandatory retirement age of sixty-four. The Army provided MacArthur with an office on Church Street in Brooklyn, to which Huff and Whitney were assigned. Huff collected MacArthur's mail every morning, took it to him and spent hours talking to him about whatever the general wanted to talk about: politics, Army gossip, the old days in the Far East. Above everything else, MacArthur loved to talk about the prizefights on television. In the 1950s there were at least two big fights each week. Huff loyally stayed up late at night, his eyes glued to the television screen long after his wife had gone to bed, watching the boxing so he would be able to talk about right crosses, left-hand leads, cut men and referees with the general next day.[27]

One of the things MacArthur enjoyed most about being back in the United States was the fact that he could go to boxing matches, baseball and football games once more. He distilled from the fevered, competitive atmosphere of the ring and the gridiron a kind of nectar that had always soothed the restless, aggressive spirit that had made him a brilliant battlefield commander, and in his mind he was an athlete still. Nor did his enthusiasm for the sporting heroes of his youth ever diminish, and near the close of his life MacArthur wrote the foreword to Ty Cobb's autobiography, *My Life in Baseball.*[28]

MacArthur was, as always, the biggest fan the Army football team could ever hope to have. Although he was a practicing Episcopalian—he, Jean and Arthur said grace together before every meal—he sometimes seemed to have even greater faith in the redemptive power of football to raise fallen humanity to a higher plane. The Army coach, his old friend Earl Blaik, wrote him every week during the season, to provide an inside account of the previous Saturday's game. He offered his thinking on future fixtures, training problems, possible lineups, formations, plays, players and rule changes, knowing the general would have an opinion to offer on all of these. Even this was not enough. Blaik, who revered MacArthur above all other men, also came to see him every two weeks or so, in season and out.[29]

Besides stadiums and arenas, MacArthur loved going to the theater. His favorite shows were lavishly produced Broadway musicals, such as *The King and I,* or trivial pursuits, like *Holiday on Ice.* Theater crowds invariably burst into applause as MacArthur walked down the aisle to take his seat. After the show he delighted in going backstage to mingle with the cast, especially the pulchritudinous actresses, whom he hugged and kissed with obvious delight.[30]

Apart from the fights, the baseball contests, the football games and the Broadway shows, MacArthur preferred to remain in the Waldorf Towers. A multimillionaire insurance executive, Neil Starr, offered him the use of a spacious country house, outside Brewster, New York, whenever he wanted to use it. Jean managed to get MacArthur to spend a day there from time to time, but even these short breaks from the Waldorf were rare. After MacArthur returned from Korea, he spent most of his time in what amounted to internal exile.[31]

Although he had no great interest in making money, MacArthur believed strongly in the value of work to keep a man alive. Two years before he left Japan MacArthur had agreed with the president of the Sperry Rand Corporation, James H. Rand, to join the company's board as chairman once he returned home. MacArthur's salary was reported to be a hundred thousand dollars a year.[32]

The company's biggest customer was the Pentagon, so having a five-star chairman was good for business. Sperry Rand's nondefense interests included manufacturing the Remington shaver. MacArthur had used a cutthroat razor all his life, but now he loyally began each day by running a Remington electric over his face.[33]

Sperry Rand's headquarters were a one-hour drive from New York City. After consuming a leisurely breakfast and digesting several newspapers, MacArthur set off for work at 11:00 A.M. on three or four mornings each week. He usually arrived in time for lunch, after which the board got down to discussing business for several hours. Around 4:00 P.M. MacArthur would be driven back to Manhattan. He played no role in the day-to-day running of the business. Jim Rand remained the chief executive officer and handled that. What MacArthur did was lend his prestige to the company and offer his advice on international affairs. Should the company build a plant in India? MacArthur said that was a bad idea. Then how about Taiwan? Excellent![34]

MacArthur diligently fulfilled the not very onerous demands that Sperry Rand made on him, which still left him with plenty of time to pursue other interests. During his first few years in the Towers, however, he seemed unconcerned about anything much except sports. He had been offered huge sums for his memoirs but turned down every contract that was suggested to him. He even spurned a million dollars for the rights to make a Hollywood epic based on his life, provisionally titled *I Shall Return*.[35]

His return from Japan moved American publishers to bring out nearly a dozen books about MacArthur, and he cooperated with at least one author,

Frazier Hunt, whom he had known since World War I. Apart from that, he took little interest in MacArthur biographies. It was only when he heard in 1954 that Truman was writing his memoirs that MacArthur shook off this indifference. He still had no interest in writing his memoirs, but as touchy as ever on what he considered matters of honor, he was going to defend his reputation from the fierce attacks Truman was sure to launch. MacArthur pressured Whitney into writing a biography, a task that Whitney did not feel he could handle successfully. He was a memo writer, a legal brief writer, a staff study writer, but he lacked the skills and the confidence to write a big book. No matter. Whitney was forced to yield. Henry Luce agreed to buy the serial rights for Time-Life and Alfred A. Knopf would publish the book.

Whitney proved to be just as incapable of writing MacArthur's biography as he had feared. In the end the staff at Time-Life had to write Whitney's *MacArthur: His Rendezvous with History*. Day after day MacArthur dictated extensive passages to the bewildered but obedient Whitney. These were carried over to the Time-Life building, where the staff writers assigned to write the book were horrified. Much of what MacArthur had dictated was appallingly self-serving, biased or simply untrue. Even so, it went into the book in one form or another, because MacArthur usually refused to agree to alterations.

Desperate for another view, the Time-Life staffers found themselves relying as far as the laws of plagiarism allowed on a mediocre MacArthur biography published in 1954, *MacArthur, 1941–1951,* purportedly written by Charles Willoughby. Yet "Sir Charles," like Whitney, had found it impossible to produce an acceptable manuscript. His publisher had forced him to hire a professional writer, John Chamberlain, to turn his effusive, disorganized scribblings into a publishable book.

Whitney's contribution to "Whitney's book" was marginal, but the objective was achieved: *Douglas MacArthur: His Rendezvous with History* beat Truman's memoirs into the bookstores by one month. Published in August 1955, it sold in huge quantities and got almost nothing but ecstatic reviews. Until the publication in 1978 of William Manchester's *American Caesar* this huge gray slab of modern hagiography stood unchallenged as the standard one-volume biography of MacArthur.[36] Manchester himself drew extensively on it in his own book, citing it more than a hundred times and paraphrasing large chunks of it.

Through contacts on *The New York Times,* MacArthur obtained advance copies of the page proofs of Truman's book. It was sharply critical of him, as he no doubt expected it to be, but he was nonetheless roused to fury by Truman's account of their meeting on Wake Island and by Truman's assertion that he had relieved MacArthur because "I could no longer tolerate his insubordination." MacArthur's response was a blustering rejoinder that was short on factual details but overflowing with wounded pride. Luce published Truman's version of events, and MacArthur's reply, in *Life* magazine in early 1956. While the laws on libel constrained him in print, in private MacArthur called Truman "a vulgar little clown [and] an inveterate liar."[37]

The battle of the books continued. In 1957 the chief of military history, Brigadier General Richard W. Stephens, invited MacArthur for his comments on the first volume of the Army's official history of the Korean War. MacArthur was indignant that the author, Lieutenant Colonel Roy E. Appleman, portrayed him as underestimating the abilities of the North Korean Army early in the conflict. He partially accepted criticism of the poor fighting ability of the four divisions on occupation duty in Japan but argued vehemently that he was in no way responsible for this state of affairs. Poor leadership, low morale and inadequate training characterized the entire Army in the late 1940s, said MacArthur.[38]

In 1958 the *Encyclopaedia Britannica* commissioned a five-thousand-word piece on the history of amphibious warfare from a young Marine major who was also a scholar, Edward H. Simmons. The more he thought about how to handle the topic, the more problematical Inchon seemed. Simmons eventually decided that because Inchon defied just about every rule there was on how to conduct an amphibious assault, he would leave it out. The *Britannica* editors, following their customary procedure, sent Simmons's article to an independent, expert reader for comments. The reader wrote back that the article should be rejected or extensively rewritten; it did not even mention one of the most brilliant of all amphibious assaults, Douglas MacArthur's landing at Inchon. Simmons rewrote the piece to include Inchon. After publication, he discovered the outside reader was . . . Douglas MacArthur.[39]

Sometime around 1960, when he reached his eightieth birthday, MacArthur finally decided to write his memoirs after all. A book would provide an inheritance for Jean and Arthur after his death. Henry Luce paid him nine hundred thousand dollars for all the rights to his book—in 1996 values, roughly four million dollars.[40] Like Grant, MacArthur spent the last few years of his life writing a memoir that would both provide financial security for his wife and son while offering history a strong defense of his controversial career. And like Grant, he would live just long enough to finish the writing but die on the eve of publication.

MacArthur's former deputy chief engineer in the Southwest Pacific, Jack Sverdrup, was a brilliant civil engineer from Missouri. He was a can-do, will-do millionaire businessman who was determined to do something for the man he admired most in the world, in fact, the only man he admired even more than his old friend Harry S. Truman. Sverdrup organized and paid for a party in the Waldorf every January 26, MacArthur's birthday. He invited one hundred people, nearly all of them individuals who had served the general during the war. The true devotees, such as George Kenney and Charles Willoughby, attended every year, while others, such as Sutherland and Krueger, came only a couple of times.

As MacArthur's eightieth birthday approached, his old colleagues feared this might be the last of these celebrations.[41] MacArthur's health was obviously failing rapidly. Ike could not be there but sent a warm tribute: "Normally I tend to feel that birthdays should, if possible, be overlooked—especially my own. But when such an event as your eightieth anniversary comes along, it brings to all our people a renewed feeling of gratitude for your dedicated services to our common country. And to those of us who have been privileged to work with you, the occasion has an importance all its own. . . . My affectionate greetings to Jean—and with warm personal regard for yourself."[42]

MacArthur never changed his mind that Eisenhower did not belong in the White House and was convinced the administration was somehow hostile to him, but at this late stage in his life he did not want to die on bad terms with Ike. Shortly after this birthday he traveled to Washington for a brief, emotional reunion that was also their final parting.[43]

The eightieth birthday bash was held in the Jade Room, on the third floor of the Waldorf. The assembled guests wore their Army blue dress uniforms, except for Herbert Hoover, who wore a dinner jacket. At exactly 7:00 P.M., as MacArthur slowly entered the room with Jean on his arm, all the old soldiers responded to a shout of "Tenshun!" MacArthur shook hands with all his guests and had a brief word and a smile for each. The West Point choir sang "Happy Birthday to You" before the company sat down to dinner.

There was roll call, and each man stood as his name was called, to wave a greeting to the rest. Ike's birthday message was read out. The Air Force Chief of Staff presented MacArthur with the command pilot wings that Dusty Rhoades had worn while flying MacArthur around SWPA in World War II.[44] Admiral Kinkaid presented him with the command ship flag from the *Nashville,* the cruiser that had carried him to Morotai, Hollandia and Leyte Gulf. The undersecretary of the army presented him with the chair he had used as Chief of Staff. MacArthur responded with a brief speech of thanks to his guests for their presence on this night and their services to him in years gone by.

There was a birthday cake in red, white and blue to be cut, more anecdotes to be swapped, more well wishes to be exchanged. MacArthur suddenly felt unwell, and his former aide, Dr. Roger Egeberg, took his temperature and measured his pulse. There was something seriously wrong with the general, but he refused to leave the party until 11:00 P.M. Then, as MacArthur and Jean strolled back toward the elevator, his guests started singing. The strains of "Old Soldiers Never Die" floated upward with him on his journey back to the thirty-seventh floor of the Towers.[45]

Many of those who attended MacArthur's eightieth birthday party were shocked by his appearance. He looked too frail to survive more than another year. Indeed, it seemed unlikely he would survive another week. The once hale and vigorous MacArthur had suddenly become a skeletal, ashen-faced old man. The day after the party he collapsed and was rushed to St. Luke's Hospital. His prostate gland had swollen to such a size he could no longer urinate, and death seemed near. MacArthur had always feared hospitals, scalpels, needles. He had numbered a doctor among his aides for the last twenty-six years of his military career not because he expected to need medical help but as a talisman against illness. But now doctors and scalpels were his only hope. As he was being wheeled on a gurney from his hospital room to the operating theater, MacArthur opened one eye and saw Jean looking down at him, her small, bony face a picture of anxiety. He reached up and weakly stroked her cheek. "Don't worry, Jean," he said. "I shall return."[46]

MacArthur made a rapid and complete recovery, and in April 1961 the new President, John F. Kennedy, paid a courtesy call on him during a visit to New York. As a Democrat and as a former naval officer Kennedy was well steeped in anti-MacArthur sentiment. The sole reason for his visit was curiosity. Visiting the general was like making a slight detour to get a glimpse of a famous monument, and all it would cost him was some perfunctory politesse. The general, Kennedy firmly believed, was a pompous, overrated stuffed shirt, a living legend utterly lost in the smoke and incense of an ego so vast it defied human comprehension.

What Kennedy found instead was one of the most interesting people he had ever met. MacArthur's conversation was simply enthralling. Three months later MacArthur traveled to Washington for lunch at the White House. When the meal ended, Kennedy engaged MacArthur in even more conversation, and this time they talked for nearly three hours.

The general was, the President had discovered, both intellectually sharp and politically shrewd. They talked, inevitably and at length, about the threat of Communist expansion in Asia. MacArthur urged Kennedy never to commit American forces to the defense of Vietnam and ridiculed the domino theory that influential Kennedy advisers such as Dean Rusk and Robert McNamara were promoting as justification for military intervention. The real crisis the United States faced, said MacArthur, was not overseas but at home; not in the green jungles of Southeast Asia but in the concrete jungles of American cities. Sterling advice, sadly ignored.[47]

In July 1961 MacArthur returned to the Philippines, to be present at the celebrations marking the fifteenth anniversary of Philippine independence. His real motive for going, however, was to seize this final chance of a reunion with the survivors of Bataan and Corregidor.[48]

In 1962 West Point invited him to accept the Sylvanus Thayer Award, which the academy grants each year to an American who has performed outstanding services to his country. Ike had received the award in 1961; there was a certain logic in choosing MacArthur in 1962. He was nonetheless in such poor health that all his doctors urged him not to travel. By now he looked like a sheet of yellow parchment wrapped around a bundle of sticks. He was suffering from biliary cirrhosis, the result of a large accumulation of gallstones that was pressing on the bile duct. MacArthur was in pain much of the time and tormented by ferocious itching, yet the chance to return to the Point and address the cadets was too strong to resist. To Jean's gentle pleas that he put his health first, he responded emphatically, "I will attend the Thayer Award ceremony if I have to crawl there on my hands and knees."[49]

This, MacArthur knew, would be his last trip to Highland Falls, his last chance to absorb the severe beauty of the academy's gray, granite buildings redolent of order, discipline and purpose where he had once lived, studied and dreamed, to feel the stiff ryegrass of the Plain yield beneath his feet again as he had felt it for the first time sixty-five years before with a black plumed shako on his head and a Krag-Jorgensen rifle cradled in a white glove on his right hand, to stand at Trophy Point and gaze at "the Million-Dollar View," to see himself when young again.

No one witnessed it, but MacArthur practiced his last speech. It would take nearly an hour to deliver. There were passages that referred to satellites and "space ships to the moon," but much of it consisted of passages from speeches he had given in the course of his long life. To the cadets, it was all new, all dazzling. Most young soldiers are idealists and romantics anyway, and to hear MacArthur give his last speech, to see so much of the nation's military history still alive in the form of one man, to hear it uttered with that still-thrilling voice, was beyond rationality or calculation. It was a magical, mesmerizing experience.

He ended his speech by telling them, "I listen vainly, but with thirsty ear, for the witching melody of faint bugles blowing reveille, of far drums beating the long roll. In my dreams I hear again the crash of guns, the rattle of musketry, the strange mournful mutter of the battlefield. But in the evening of my life, I always come back to West Point. Always there echoes and re-echoes in my ears—Duty, Honor, Country. Today marks my final roll call with you. But I want you to know that when I cross the river my last conscious thought will be of the Corps . . . and the Corps . . . and the Corps. I bid you farewell."[50]

MacArthur glanced over at his wife, blew her a kiss and sat down, while grown men fumbled for their handkerchiefs and blew their noses in a vain effort to hide their tears.

By early 1964 MacArthur's biliary cirrhosis had grown so severe it threatened to kill him. Yet his civilian doctors could not convince him to undergo surgery. Ever since his return from Korea he had neglected his health, tolerating two inguinal hernias that almost any other man would have had treated. The negligent attitude he adopted toward his health in old age was in stark contrast with his earlier view, which was that taking care of his body was "the first duty of a soldier."

However, he was still an Army officer. The surgeon general of the Army, Lieutenant General Leonard Heaton, came to New York and told him he had to have an operation. President Lyndon Johnson sent Air Force One to fly him to Washington. MacArthur reluctantly allowed himself to be checked into Walter Reed.

To his immense delight, he discovered that the doctor who would operate on him, Norman Scott, Jr., was the son of the Dr. Norman Scott who had treated his mother back in 1920.[51] The doctors removed his gallbladder and cut out the gallstones that were obstructing his bile duct.

For a week or so MacArthur seemed to be recovering. Then he developed severe bleeding. A second operation was performed to stanch it and was successful. But a few days later one of the inguinal hernias became strangulated, making a third operation necessary. His weakened eighty-four-year-old body wasn't up to it. On April 5, 1964, MacArthur died. Jean, Arthur and Whitney were at his bedside as he lapsed from a deep coma into everlasting sleep.

He had decided to be buried in a place that meant nothing to him—Norfolk, Virginia—rather than alongside his parents in Arlington or at his spiritual home, West Point. True, Norfolk was his mother's birthplace, but it held no fond memories for him. This was the rough, unprepossessing Navy town where as a lad he had had to fight with his fists just for a chance to sell newspapers on a street corner. So why Norfolk?

He claimed it was because of the connection with his mother, but it is more likely that he was prompted by the fact that four of his contemporaries—Hoover, Roosevelt, Eisenhower and Truman—were going to be laid to rest in splendid presidential libraries: the body of the man enshrined with the body of his papers, a monument that would keep the flame burning brightly beyond the grave's ghastly maw. A fifth, George Marshall, was not entitled to a presidential library, but VMI was planning to house a splendid Marshall research library and foundation on its beautiful campus to serve Marshall's memory for generations to come.

What MacArthur was offered by the city of Norfolk was a square city block to himself, featuring four picturesque buildings. He would be interred in a crypt beneath an imposing dome, much like his hero Napoleon, and his papers would be preserved on the same site into perpetuity. There was to be a theater, a museum, an archive and a gift shop. This ensemble was too much like a presidential library to be a coincidence.

Norfolk's bid for MacArthur's body came as a complete surprise, as if destiny was getting into gear again as he turned into the home stretch. Here was a shrine MacArthur could never have resisted. Only great men get an arrangement as fancy as this. Yet there was another side to this story.

MacArthur was unaware of it, but the memorial he was being offered was part of a complex land deal engineered by the longtime mayor of Norfolk, Fred Duckworth. A bullying, crooked figure known as the Boss Crump of the Tidewater, Duckworth saw that one way to push the land deal through was to save the block that became known as MacArthur Square. Moreover, the MacArthur Memorial would enshrine not only the general's memory but the mayor's as well.

In 1972 Duckworth was murdered. He was found on a sidewalk a few blocks from his home, his body riddled with bullets. It is said in Norfolk that "Duckworth had so many enemies the police didn't know where to begin. So they didn't." Duckworth's killer has never been found.

And there MacArthur rests, in Norfolk, Virginia, his memory diligently served by a fine, mainly young, staff, waiting for Jean, surrounded by parking lots, boarded-up storefronts and banks. In the next couple of years, though, the city council plans to build a MacArthur Mall across the street, with a Nordstrom store to tempt the middle classes back downtown.

Even if Norfolk is a strange choice of resting place, the memorial itself is somehow all of a piece with the man and his career. His memorial is not as well endowed financially as the Marshall Foundation, but it was Marshall who was his boss in World War II and again in Korea. Besides, Marshall outranked him. Although both were five-star commanders, Marshall had seniority, by two days.

The MacArthur Memorial is not as splendid as a presidential library, and never will be. But he was not a president, much as he would have liked to have been. On the other hand, no American combat commander has a memorial remotely as magnificent as MacArthur's. Insofar as such things can be measured, what MacArthur ended up with is probably just about right.

MacArthur cared profoundly about his reputation, so it is probably as well that he is dead. He has in recent years been excoriated by some scholars and journalists as a military blunderer and a grade A charlatan. Yet he also continues to be revered as a great soldier and patriot. What's more, the MacArthur Memorial continues to attract a steady flow of Japanese visitors, to whom MacArthur remains a heroic figure.

The strong contradictions in MacArthur's character make it inevitable that he will be both reviled and revered. But to paraphrase Max Beerbohm, only mediocrity is consistent. Genius contains the latitude for failures proportionate to its triumphs. And on one day of his long life—September 15, 1950, at Inchon—he proved himself a military genius.

Was he a great man then? MacArthur's life was shaped by the nineteenth-century belief that history is created by the actions of great men. He told Quezon, a man he regarded as driven by ambitions comparable to his own, "The birthdays of great men mark the milestones of the world's progress. History is merely the sum of their biographies."[52] His only goal in life was to be numbered with the great. But educated people no longer believe that a single individual can change the history of the world. Although MacArthur became, by his lights, a great man, we navigate by other beacons now.

He found the path to the top of his profession an ordeal, and only his extraordinary self-discipline made any of his achievements possible. "Powerful personalities, organized for conflict, crises, great events . . . are usually blunt and uncompromising, without social graces. Although deep down the masses may obscurely do them justice, recognizing their superiority, they are rarely loved and in consequence do not find an easy way to the top." Not MacArthur's words, but those of Charles de Gaulle, delivered at a lecture on leadership to French Army officers in 1927. The sentiment, however, is one MacArthur shared. He told his first wife shortly before their marriage, "Life for me has always been so stern, so fierce, so bitter a struggle."[53]

What is remarkable is that he felt this way when he was the second-youngest superintendent in the history of West Point, the most highly decorated American soldier of the war and a glamorous, widely envied young man. He felt much the same way in 1948, when he referred to his career as "a long public service replete with very many bitter, lonely and forlorn assignments." If we put aside the slightly self-pitying tone of this observation, MacArthur's life was in many ways such a constant test of nerve and will it is open to question how much happiness he derived from it.

He himself occasionally acknowledged the sense of isolation that went with being the boss. "When you become a general," he once noted wistfully, "you haven't any friends." That was why it was so important to create a kind of family around him from the members of his staff. A man with real friendships to sustain him would feel no compulsion to operate like that.[54]

Phil La Follette, the three-term governor of Wisconsin who served on MacArthur's staff in World War II, remarked that MacArthur was really an intellectual and was never, in his experience, put on his mettle. It was a perceptive observation. MacArthur had arranged his mental universe so that he could feel superior to every officer in the Army. He never wavered in his conviction that the real soldiers were the fighting men. That meant that no matter how brilliant a staff officer might be, including men of enormous talents such as Marshall and Eisenhower, that man was not a *real* soldier. That left MacArthur, with his fifteen awards for gallantry, far above them in the basic and brutal business of what soldiers really do for their country.

On the other hand, few combat commanders are likely to be considered intellectuals. A taste for abstract thought and a fascination with ideas are not likely to put a man in command of a regiment or a division engaged in close combat. There *were* a few such men among MacArthur's contemporaries (such as John S. Wood, Maxwell D. Taylor and Harold K. Johnston), but MacArthur could use the English language more powerfully than they, whether in conversation or in writing, which not only set him apart from but placed him slightly above all other career officers of his generation.

What made his career so emotionally burdensome to MacArthur were the very qualities that underpinned this sense of superiority. Most soldiers are comparatively ordinary people in their temperaments. MacArthur was not. He was highly strung, overly sensitive and unusually imaginative. He had, that is, the temperament and talents of a writer or a scholar.

Toward the end of his career he told a distinguished international lawyer, Joseph Choate, how much he envied him. He had pursued a military career only to please his father, said MacArthur. "When a man hangs up his shingle," he continued, "he is a free man. He is on his own and can pursue his own destiny unfettered."[55] It is easy to see him employing his gifts as a highly successful lawyer, a field in which egos and arguments abound, easy to picture that speaking style—the sudden fortissimos, the dramatic whispers, the instant access to the emotions—being used to mesmerize a courtroom or a boardroom.

MacArthur's most obvious trait was his vanity, which is often seized on as if it were the key to the man. It seems to me, however, that while MacArthur *was* infuriatingly vain, *was* egotistical, *was* fascinated by himself, he was not in the deepest sense ego-driven. The motor that powered his ascent was his amazing willpower, the same willpower that made him control his body under fire, that made him study his way to the top at West Point, that made him impose his strategy on a reluctant government in World War II.

MacArthur's parents had planted a vision of himself in the deepest, richest soil of his character. That vision never changed from childhood to old age. He had a destiny to fulfill. The thirst for medals, trophies, publicity, flattery and an adoring staff was vanity, but more than vanity. These were his compass bearings, the way he confirmed that he was on the right track to his destination. But it was his implacable, inexhaustible will that was the engine taking him toward his goal. It was that will that made him a difficult subordinate and distanced him from other men—at times even distanced him from himself—yet it finally got him where he intended to go.

> Hard is the stone, but harder still
> The delicate, preforming will
> That guided by a dream alone
> Subdues and moulds the hardest stone. . . .

The fact that Truman had to fire him brought it all to a painful and anticlimactic end. But that is nearly always how the lives of those who strive for greatness have concluded, in failure or disappointment. Few great men have gone to their graves feeling they completed the task they had set for themselves, truly realized the vision of their early years.

Even allowing for the failures, the disappointments, the scorn and rebuffs, wasn't MacArthur, as William Manchester claims, the greatest soldier in American history? Not in my view. MacArthur was too difficult a subordinate to be an entirely successful commander. He created far more problems for Marshall, Stimson, Roosevelt and Truman than any general has the right to make, especially in time of war. He also spent time and energy toying with political ambitions when everything that was in him should have gone into fighting the enemy. At his best he was probably the second-greatest soldier in American history, second only, that is, to Ulysses S. Grant. And along the way he did lead the most adventurous and dramatic life in American history, which makes him a gift to biographers and a subject of enduring interest to Americans.

As for Jean and Arthur, both are still alive at the time of writing. She lives in the Waldorf, but in a much smaller apartment than the one that she and the general occupied. In her nineties, she has to rely on a wheelchair.

Contrary to William Manchester's claim, Arthur did not change his name. Rather, he lives in an unpretentious midtown hotel under an assumed name. A handsome man even in late middle age, he bears a strong resemblance to his father, a resemblance that he sometimes hides under a bushy black beard. The musical abilities that Arthur showed in his early years were developed through study, and he graduated with a music degree from Columbia. At times he has worked as a musical arranger, using a pseudonym. He sees his mother regularly. Like his father, he is a voracious reader and a nonstop talker. Arthur reads everything he can get his hands on about his father's career. He has never married, and it seems almost certain that when he dies, so will the direct line of descent from Douglas MacArthur. Only then will this story really reach its end.

Notes

Abbreviations

CAFH	The Center for Air Force History, Bolling Air Force Base
EL	Dwight D. Eisenhower Presidential Library, Abilene, Kansas
FDRL	Franklin D. Roosevelt Presidential Library, Hyde Park, New York
GCMF	George C. Marshall Foundation, Lexington, Virginia
HHL	Herbert Hoover Presidential Library, West Branch, Iowa
HI	Hoover Institution, Stanford University
HRA	U.S. Air Force Historical Research Agency, Maxwell Air Force Base
HSTL	Harry S. Truman Presidential Library, Independence, Missouri
MD, LC	Manuscript Division, Library of Congress
MMA	The MacArthur Memorial and Archives, Norfolk, Virginia
NA	The National Archives, Washington, D.C.
USAMHI	U.S. Army Military History Institute, Carlisle Barracks, Pennsylvania
USMA	United States Military Academy, West Point, New York

1. The Sound of Bugles

1. Clark Lee and Richard Henschel, *Douglas MacArthur* (New York: 1952), 9.
2. Letter, Arthur MacArthur to Arthur MacArthur, Oct. 28, 1843, RG 20, MMA. This letter was written to a namesake, who had asked whether they were related.
3. D. Clayton James, *The Years of MacArthur* (Boston: 1970), I, 9.
4. J. A. Watrous, "How the Boy Won: General MacArthur's First Victory," *Saturday Evening Post* (Feb. 24, 1900).
5. Letter, Arthur McArthur to Abraham Lincoln, May 13, 1862, RG 94, NA.
6. Arthur MacArthur 201 File, AGO Records, RG 94, NA.
7. Muster-in Roll, 24th Wisconsin Volunteer Regiment, Aug. 22, 1864, RG 20, MMA.
8. Watrous, op. cit.
9. Letter, Arthur MacArthur to Sidney Burbank, Oct. 20, 1866, RG 94, NA.

10. Anonymous biographical sketch, n.d. but apparently early 1899, in Arthur MacArthur Papers, RG 20, MMA. This sketch was written by someone who served in the 24th throughout the Civil War.

11. Robert C. Johnson and Clarence Buel, *Battles and Leaders of the Civil War* (New York: 1887), III, 707.

12. Ibid.

13. Philip Sheridan, *Memoirs of General Philip S. Sheridan* (New York: 1888), I, 170–173.

14. War Department, *The War of the Rebellion: A Compilation of the Official Records,* Series I (Washington, D.C.: 1880), XII, Part 2, 208; letter, Carl von Baumbach to Edwin M. Stanton, n.d., Arthur MacArthur 201 File, loc. cit.; Kenneth Ray Young, *The General's General: The Life and Times of Arthur MacArthur* (Boulder, Colo.: 1994), 73. Seizing an enemy flag or saving one's own regimental colors and advancing with them in the heat of battle were the most common deeds for Medal of Honor awards in the Civil War. See Jeffrey W. Anderson, "Military Heroism," *Armed Forces and Society* (Summer 1986).

15. MacArthur to Burbank, loc. cit.

16. Arthur L. Wagner, *Service of Security and Information,* rev. ed. (Washington, D.C.: 1903), 92n.

17. Douglas MacArthur, *Reminiscences* (New York: 1964), 9.

18. Letter, Emerson U. Opdyke to Edwin M. Stanton, April 11, 1865; MacArthur to Burbank, loc. cit.

19. Letter, Edward Brown to Douglas MacArthur, Oct. 16, 1937, MMA.

20. David L. Cockrell, "Forgotten Reformer: Arthur MacArthur," M.A. thesis, University of North Carolina (Chapel Hill, N.C.: 1988), 16.

21. Letters, Halbert E. Paine to Edwin M. Stanton, Aug. 8 and 16, 1866, and Matthew Carpenter to Stanton, Aug. 6, 1866, RG 94, NA.

22. Letter, Arthur MacArthur to A. W. Randall, Sept. 24, 1866, ibid.

23. Letter, Arthur MacArthur, Jr., to John C. Kelton, Dec. 6, 1867, ibid.

24. Lucile M. Kane, ed., *Military Life in Dakota: The Journal of Philippe Régis de Trobriand* (St. Paul, Minn.: 1951), xx–xxv.

25. See the War Department's *Annual Reports* for this period. Also, Robert M. Utley, *Frontier Regulars: The United States Army and the Indian, 1866–1891* (New York: 1973).

26. *History of the 13th Infantry Regiment,* n.d., RG 98, NA.

27. MacArthur, 14.

28. Jerry M. Cooper, *The Army and Civil Disorder: Federal Military Intervention in Labor Disputes, 1877–1900* (Westport, Conn.: 1980).

29. Letter, Woodlief E. Thomas to George C. Marshall, May 12, 1942, MMA.

30. Letters, Arthur MacArthur, Jr., to the Adjutant General, Sept. 11, 1879, and Oct. 28, 1879; the Adjutant General to Arthur MacArthur, Jr., n.d. but evidently Aug.–Sept. 1879, and Nov. 6, 1879, RG 94, NA.

2. The Happiest Years

1. Fiorello La Guardia, *The Making of an Insurgent: An Autobiography 1882–1919* (Philadelphia: 1948), 19. On the lives of Army children out on the frontier, there are two fine works: Merrill Mattes, *Indians, Infants and Infantry* (Denver: 1960) and Patricia Y. Stallard, *Glittering Misery: Dependents of the Indian-Fighting Army* (San Rafael, Calif.: 1978).

2. Douglas MacArthur, *Reminiscences* (New York: 1964), 15.
3. Babcock memoir, 21, Conrad S. Babcock Papers, HI.
4. Martha Summerhayes, *Vanished Arizona* (Salem, Mass.: 1911), 224, 231.
5. Letter, Edward Brown to Douglas MacArthur, Oct. 16, 1937, MMA.
6. Letter, Ulysses S. Grant to Arthur MacArthur, June 10, 1882, RG 165, NA.
7. Letter, William T. Sherman to Arthur MacArthur, Jr., Aug. 16, 1862, MD, LC.
8. Telegrams, Arthur MacArthur, Jr., to the Adjutant General, April 9 and 18, 1883, RG 94, NA; MacArthur, 14.
9. Letter, the Adjutant General to Arthur MacArthur, Jr., Nov. 8, 1883, RG 94, NA.
10. MacArthur, 15.
11. Letter, Eleanor P. Cushman to Douglas MacArthur, May 10, 1944, MMA.
12. Letter, Douglas MacArthur to Adolphus Ragan, May 28, 1956, MMA.
13. Inspector General's Report, Sept. 22, 1885, Arthur MacArthur, Jr., 201 File, RG 94, NA.
14. Letter, Sherman to Sheridan, July 31, 1881, William T. Sherman Papers, 1881, MD, LC.
15. For a memorable, if mocking, account of Army social life in this period, see Duane M. Greene, *Ladies and Officers of the United States Army* (Chicago: 1880). The cultural attainments of officers and their wives tended to be mediocre at best, with the inevitable result that they provided tedious companionship to those few who were quick-witted and well educated.
16. MacArthur, 16.
17. Babcock, 43, loc. cit. Babcock, who was three years older than Douglas and almost the same age as Arthur, was at Leavenworth when the MacArthurs were there.
18. Clark Lee and Richard Henschel, *Douglas MacArthur* (New York: 1952), 242.
19. Edward Coffman, *The Old Army* (New York: 1988), 317.
20. MacArthur, op. cit.
21. Timothy Nenninger, *The Leavenworth Schools and the Old Army* (Westport, Conn.: 1975), 28.
22. Letter, G. H. Burton to the assistant Adjutant General, Dec. 12, 1887, RG 19, NA; undated letter, but evidently Aug. 1887, headed "To accompany Captain MacArthur's application for Inspector General," RG 94, AGO file, NA. To judge from the handwriting, the captain appears to have written the letter. It seethes with indignation at the promotion system.
23. Letter, Alexander M. McCook to the Adjutant General, July 16, 1888, RG 19, NA.
24. "Application of Captain Arthur MacArthur Jr. for the junior vacancy of Major, to occur in the Adjutant General's Department," May 28, 1889, RG 94, NA.
25. For an excellent account of how this system worked, see Allan Millett, *The General: Robert L. Bullard and Officership in the U.S. Army* (Westport, Conn.: 1975), 81–82.
26. Thaddeus M. Szetela, pamphlet, "Chicopee, Massachusetts, Birthplace of Lieutenant Arthur MacArthur," MMA.
27. Letter, the Adjutant General to Arthur MacArthur, Jr., n.d., but evidently late fall 1890, MacArthur 201 File, loc. cit.
28. Kenneth Ray Young, *The General's General: The Life and Times of Arthur MacArthur* (Boulder, Colo.: 1994), 160–162.
29. Efficiency report, May 1, 1890, Arthur MacArthur, Jr., 201 File, loc. cit.
30. John Hersey, *Men on Bataan* (New York: 1942), 56.
31. Letter, Jesse N. Bigbee to LeGrande A. Diller, Sept. 4, 1943, MMA.
32. D. Clayton James, *The Years of MacArthur* (Boston: 1970), I, 58–59.
33. Kathryn Hardy (Brower interview), July 13, 1966, MMA.
34. Letter, L. H. Jameson to MacArthur, Dec. 20, 1941, MMA.
35. MacArthur, 18.

36. Letter, Charles H. Quinn to Douglas MacArthur, March 31, 1944, MMA.
37. Letter, Edward T. Coleman to MacArthur, July 20, 1942, MMA.
38. Frazier Hunt, *The Untold Story of Douglas MacArthur* (Chicago: 1954), 18.
39. Letter, Arthur MacArthur to the Adjutant General, June 1, 1896, RG 94, NA; T. M. Paschal to Grover Cleveland, June 5, 1896, MD, LC.
40. Letter, Roscoe H. Piety to MacArthur, April 2, 1942, MMA.
41. Hunt, 21.
42. Jean MacArthur interview, Tape 30, MMA.
43. Letter, MacArthur to Edward J. Condon, Oct. 2, 1936, MMA.
44. MacArthur, 18.
45. Letter, Frank C. McCutcheon to Douglas MacArthur, May 5, 1942, MMA.
46. See Hiram Rickover et al., *How the Battleship Maine Was Destroyed* (Washington, D.C.: 1976), 93–106.
47. MacArthur, op. cit.
48. Bernard C. Korn, "MacArthur Goes to West Point," *Historical Messenger of the Milwaukee Historical Society* (Autumn 1974).
49. *Evening Wisconsin,* June 13, 1898.
50. Korn, op. cit.
51. Francis T. Miller, *General Douglas MacArthur* (New York: 1942), 38.

3. The Corps, and the Corps, and the Corps

1. Douglas MacArthur, *Reminiscences* (New York: 1964), 19.
2. Registration form No. 153, Douglas MacArthur File, USMA Archives.
3. *Report of the Board of Visitors* (West Point: 1901), 8.
4. George W. Cocheu, "The MacArthurs," *Assembly* (April 1964).
5. Pershing unpublished autobiography, Chapter 2, John J. Pershing Papers, MD, LC.
6. These examples have been taken from the *Official Register* (West Point: 1903), 33–40.
7. Allan Millett, *The General: Robert Lee Bullard and Officership in the U.S. Army* (Westport, Conn.: 1975), 39–40.
8. There were only nine Army officers' sons among the 143 cadets who entered West Point in 1899: *Circumstances of the Parents of Cadets,* No. 2 (West Point: 1899). Cf. Richard Brown, *The Social Attitudes of American Generals* (Madison, Wis.: 1950), 15. Brown found that only 14 percent of the West Point graduates in his study came from military families.
9. Francis T. Miller, *General Douglas MacArthur* (New York: 1942), 52.
10. See letters of Charles F. Crane, May 1890–June 1894 and Charles D. Rhodes, *Diary of a Cadet at the U.S. Military Academy,* both in the West Point Special Collections, for accounts of hazing in the 1890s. Cf. Hugh T. Reed, *Cadet Life at West Point* (Chicago: 1896).
11. John Hersey, *Men on Bataan* (New York: 1942), 68; Robert E. Wood, "The MacArthurs," *Assembly* (April 1964).
12. *Report of the Board of Visitors,* 5.
13. Richard Goldhurst, *Pipe Clay and Drill* (New York: 1977), 23.
14. Donald Smythe, *Guerrilla Warrior: The Early Life of John J. Pershing* (New York: 1979), 13.
15. *Report of the Board of Visitors,* 6.
16. Superintendent's statement, March 6, 1899, *Regulations of the Academy* (West Point: 1899).

17. Marti Maher, *Bringing Up the Brass* (New York: 1951), 88.
18. *New York Sun,* Aug. 20, 1899; Hugh S. Johnson, *The Blue Eagle from Egg to Earth* (New York: 1935), 23.
19. Forrest C. Pogue, *George C. Marshall: The Education of a General* (New York: 1963), 44.
20. U.S. House of Representatives, *Investigation of Hazing at the United States Military Academy,* Fifty-sixth Congress, Second Session (Washington, D.C.: 1901), IV, 1713–1716; Johnson, 24–25.
21. Arthur P. S. Hyde, "Douglas MacArthur," *Assembly* (Oct. 1942).
22. Frazier Hunt, *The Untold Story of Douglas MacArthur* (New York: 1954), 25.
23. Babcock memoir, Conrad S. Babcock Papers, HI.
24. *Regulations for the Interior Discipline and Police of the United States Corps of Cadets* (West Point: 1902), 4.
25. Letter, Arthur P. S. Hyde to Elbert E. Farnam, Feb. 21, MacArthur File, 1942, Special Collections, USMA.
26. Arthur Hyde, "MacArthur," *Hudson Views* (April 1942); letter, Julian L. Schley to Elbert E. Farnam, March 6, 1942; Johnson, 21–22; Hugh J. Casey, *Engineer Memoirs* (Fort Belvoir, Va.: 1993), 129; Earl Partridge (Reynolds interview), 59–60, HRA.
27. Smythe, 40–45; Frank Vandiver, *Black Jack* (College Station, Texas: 1977), I, 169–172.
28. D. Clayton James, *The Years of MacArthur* (Boston: 1970), I, 75; George Van Horn Moseley, "One Soldier's Story," I, 34—"French was taught by men who couldn't speak it . . ." George Van Moseley Papers, MD, LC.
29. Orders No. 181, West Point, Nov. 19, 1895, USMA.
30. Johnson, 21.
31. T. Bentley Mott, *Twenty Years a Military Attaché* (New York: 1937), 41.
32. War Department, *Report of the Superintendent of the Military Academy* (Washington, D.C.: 1902), 15.
33. Alfred Steinberg, *Douglas MacArthur* (New York: 1961), 25–26.
34. Hunt, 27.
35. *Investigation of Hazing at the Military Academy,* III, 916–932.
36. MacArthur, 25.
37. From time to time the War Department applied pressure on the board to readmit the sons of generals or powerful politicians who had been dismissed for academic or other failings. In such instances the board nearly always complied. See USMA, *Staff Records,* No. 16, Jan. 13, 1898, and Feb. 14, 1898.
38. *Investigation of Hazing at the United States Military Academy,* IV, 1713–1718.
39. Act of Congress, March 2, 1901; general order No. 10, March 29, 1901, USMA.
40. Special orders No. 70, April 16, 1901, in *Post Orders No. 15,* USMA.
41. *Proceedings of a Board of Officers,* April 17, 1901, and special orders No. 71, April 18, 1901, both in USMA Archives; cf. Johnson, 24; George Pappas, *To the Point* (Westport, Conn.: 1993), 414.
42. Hagood memoir, "Down the Big Road," 132, Johnson Hagood Papers, USAMHI.
43. Memo, Feb. 23, 1901, Stephen Abbot Papers, Special Collections, USMA.
44. Hunt, 30.
45. Jean MacArthur interview, Tape 30, MMA.
46. Edward Coffman, *The Hilt of the Sword: The Career of Peyton C. March* (New York: 1966), 16–17.
47. Frederick Funston, *Memories of Two Wars* (New York: 1911), 251; Babcock, 147, loc. cit.

48. There is extensive official correspondence on the wide range of issues he had to deal with as military governor in the sole extant volume of Arthur MacArthur's *Letterbook,* covering the period July–Nov. 1900, in the MacArthur Memorial Archives.

49. Letter, William H. Taft to Helen Taft, June 6, 1900, William H. Taft Papers, MD, LC.

50. Letters, William H. Taft to Elihu Root, Nov. 15, 1900, Elihu Root Papers, and WHT to Charles P. Taft, Aug. 31, 1900, Oct. 2, 1900, and Jan. 9, 1901, Taft Papers, loc. cit.

51. U.S. Senate, Fifty-seventh Congress, First Session, *Hearings on Affairs in the Philippines* (Washington, D.C.: 1902), II, 876.

52. Letter, WHT to Elihu Root, Feb. 24, 1901, Root Papers, loc. cit.

53. William E. Birkhimer, *Military Government and Martial Law* (Washington, D.C.: 1892); Frank Friedel, "General Orders 100 and Military Government," *Mississippi Valley Historical Review* (March 1946).

54. "Annual Report of Major General Arthur MacArthur," in War Department, *Annual Report of the Secretary of War* (Washington, D.C.: 1901). Cf. Kenneth Ray Young, *The General's General* (Boulder, Colo.: 1994), 279–281; Brian McAllister Linn, *The U.S. Army and Counterinsurgency in the Philippine War 1899–1902* (Chapel Hill, N.C.: 1992), 23–24; John R. Gates, *Schoolbooks and Krags* (Westport, Conn.: 1973), 204 passim; and Russell Roth, *Muddy Glory* (West Hanover, Mass.: 1981), 84.

55. James Parker, *The Old Army* (Philadelphia: 1929), 355, 364.

56. Frederick Funston, "How Aguinaldo Was Captured," *Army and Navy Journal* (July 20, 1901).

57. Manuel Quezon, *The Good Fight* (New York: 1944), 5–8. Quezon was Aguinaldo's principal aide at the time and, once he was assured of his capture, simply gave himself up.

58. Letter, Hyde to E. E. Farnam, Feb. 21, 1942, Special Collections, USMA; Hyde, "Douglas MacArthur," *Assembly* (Spring 1964); Francis T. Miller, *General Douglas MacArthur* (Philadelphia: 1942), 52.

59. Clark Lee and Richard Henschel, *Douglas MacArthur* (New York: 1952), 20.

60. Letter, Max Clayton Tyler to E. E. Farnam, Feb. 19, 1942, Special Collections, USMA.

61. George C. Kenney, *The MacArthur I Know* (New York: 1952), 230.

62. Letter, Everett Bowman to E. E. Farnam, March 11, 1942, Special Collections, USMA.

63. Robert Considine, *MacArthur the Magnificent* (New York: 1942), 36.

64. Marti Maher, *Bringing Up the Brass* (New York: 1954), 91.

65. See *Register of Delinquents,* No. 37, USMA Archives.

66. Letter, John C. Montgomery to E. E. Farnam, Feb. 25, 1942, USMA; Mott, 41.

67. Cocheu, loc. cit.

68. Considine, 35.

69. MacArthur, 27.

70. Bess B. Follansbee diary extract, Douglas MacArthur file, Special Collections, USMA.

71. Earl Blaik (Mattox interview), 5, MMA.

72. Letter, Frank C. McCutcheon to MacArthur, May 5, 1942, MMA.

73. William Ganoe, *MacArthur Close-Up* (New York: 1955), 134.

74. Hunt, 33; Considine, 37.

4. A Tragic Joke

1. Letter, Charles Telford to E. E. Farnam, March 22, 1942, Special Collections, USMA.

2. Douglas MacArthur, *Reminiscences* (New York: 1964), 28–29.

3. MacArthur statement issued on hundredth anniversary of Pershing's birth, Aug. 22, 1960, MMA.

4. Donald J. Smythe, *Guerrilla Warrior: The Early Life of John J. Pershing* (New York: 1973).
5. Pershing unpublished autobiography, XIV, 8, John J. Pershing Papers, MD, LC.
6. Letter, William Wallace Chapin to MacArthur, Aug. 20, 1945, MMA.
7. Hugh Johnson, *The Blue Eagle from Egg to Earth* (New York: 1935), 40.
8. Leslie Groves (Brower interview), 4, MMA.
9. MacArthur, 29.
10. Wood diary, Aug. 29, 1924, Leonard Wood Papers, MD, LC. Wood got this information from Pershing's lawyer in Manila, who handled the money Pershing transmitted for their upbringing. Neither one survived beyond adolescence.
11. Robert Considine, *General Douglas MacArthur* (New York: 1964), 13.
12. Letter, William H. Rose to MacArthur, Sept. 14, 1944, MMA.
13. Jean MacArthur interview, Tape 31, MMA.
14. MacArthur, 29.
15. John Hersey, *Men on Bataan* (New York: 1942), 76.
16. The pamphlet is referred to in a document titled "Account of Service" in MacArthur's 201 File at MMA; cf. Harold H. Elarth, *The Story of the Philippine Constabulary* (Los Angeles: 1949), 21.
17. Lewis Gleek, Jr., *The Manila Army and Navy Club* (Manila: 1946), 36–37.
18. Manuel Quezon, *The Good Fight* (New York: 1944), xi–xii.
19. Rose, op. cit.
20. *New York Herald Tribune,* Dec. 11, 1903; *Honolulu Commercial Advertiser,* Dec. 10, 1903.
21. Letters, Elihu Root to Theodore Roosevelt, Dec. 30, 1903, RG 94, NA, and Theodore Roosevelt to William Howard Taft, March 7, 1904, in Elting E. Morison, ed., *The Letters of Theodore Roosevelt* (Cambridge, Mass.: 1952).
22. Letter, Arthur MacArthur to the Chief of Staff, Dec. 24, 1904, RG 165, NA.
23. Pershing autobiography, XIV, 11, loc. cit.
24. D. Clayton James, *The Years of MacArthur* (Boston: 1970), I, 91.
25. On MacArthur's activities in Manchuria, see John Greenwood, "American Military Observers in the Russo-Japanese War 1905" (Kansas State Ph.D. dissertation, 1971), 325–326.
26. A. N. Kuropatkin, *The Russian Army and the Japanese War* (London: 1909), I, 307–309. Cf. two excellent recent accounts: Bruce W. Menning, *Bayonets Before Bullets* (Bloomington, Ind.: 1992) and J. N. Westwood, *Russia Against Japan* (Albany, N.Y.: 1986).
27. *Reports of Military Observers Attached to the Armies in Manchuria in the Russo-Japanese War* (Washington, D.C.: 1906), No. 8, Part I, 5–56.
28. Edward Coffman, *The Hilt of the Sword: The Career of Peyton C. March* (New York: 1966), 20.
29. MacArthur, 31.
30. Ibid., 32.
31. The weaknesses of the Army are lucidly set out in Graham Cosmas, *An Army for Empire* (Columbia, Mo.: 1971). Cf. Moseley, "One Soldier's Journey," I, 70, George Van Horn Moseley Papers, MD, LC.
32. Letter, William H. Taft to Elihu Root, Oct. 1, 1900, Elihu Root Papers, MD, LC.
33. "Few officers studied their profession or read anything worth while": Moseley, I, 31, loc. cit.
34. Richard Brown, *The Social Attitudes of American Generals* (Madison, Wis.: 1950), 35.
35. Francis T. Miller, *General Douglas MacArthur* (New York: 1942), 81.

36. William S. Phillips, ed., *The MacArthurs of Milwaukee* (Milwaukee: 1979), 50–51.
37. Moseley, I, 221–222, loc. cit.
38. Poem, "The House of Dreams," MMA.
39. Letter, DM to Fanniebelle V. Stuart, postmarked April 17, 1908, MMA.
40. Frazier Hunt, *The Untold Story of Douglas MacArthur* (New York: 1954), 40–41.
41. David McCullough, *The Path Between the Seas* (New York: 1979).
42. Letters, George H. Cameron, Nov. 16, 1908, and J. B. Kerr, Nov. 23, 1908, in DM 201 File, MMA.
43. Efficiency report extracts for 1906 and 1907, ibid.
44. Efficiency report extract for 1908, ibid.
45. Summary of efficiency reports, 1908, ibid.
46. Letter, E. Eveleth Winslow to chief of engineers, Aug. 7, 1908, ibid.
47. Letter, Mrs. Arthur MacArthur to E. H. Harriman, April 17, 1909, MMA.
48. Letter, D. C. Buell to W. L. Park, July 27, 1909, MMA.
49. "Military Demolitions" (Fort Leavenworth, Kan.: 1909). There are copies in both the MMA and Special Collections at West Point.
50. Letter, Frederick V. Abbot to C. A. Flagler, June 9, 1909, DM 201 File, loc. cit.
51. Mark Clark (Henle interview), 20–21, HHL.
52. Letter, H. Mikkelsen to MacArthur, Feb. 10, 1943, MMA.
53. Hunt, 47.
54. Forrest C. Pogue, *George C. Marshall: The Education of a General* (New York: 1963), 107; Hunt, 42.
55. Letter, C. A. Flagler to president of the Examining Board, June 28, 1910, in DM 201 File, loc. cit.
56. MacArthur, 35.
57. Benjamin Foulois, with Carroll V. Glines, *From the Wright Brothers to the Astronauts* (New York: 1968), 81–82.
58. Hersey, 101; efficiency report extract for 1912, DM 201 File, loc. cit.
59. General orders No. 4, Feb. 21, 1907, HQ, Pacific Division, RG 162, NA.
60. Letters, Arthur MacArthur to William Howard Taft, Feb. 25, March 13, 1907, and the Adjutant General to Arthur MacArthur, March 25, 1907, RG 94, NA.
61. Hersey, 47.
62. *Milwaukee Sentinel,* Sept. 6, 1912.
63. Efficiency report extracts for 1912, DM 201 File, loc. cit.

5. Woodwork

1. Letter, Clarence Thomas to Douglas MacArthur, April 23, 1951, MMA.
2. Jack C. Lane, *Armed Progressive: General Leonard Wood* (San Rafael, Calif.: 1978), 13–14; Fort Wayne Public Library, *Major General Henry W. Lawton* (Fort Wayne, Ind.: 1948), 15–19.
3. Hagood memoir, "Down the Big Road," Johnson Hagood Papers, USAMHI.
4. *New York World,* Aug. 2, 1910.
5. Wood diary, Feb. 5, 1913, and memo, Douglas MacArthur to the Chief of Staff, Dec. 13, 1913, Leonard Wood Papers, MD, LC.
6. Wood diary, October 19, 1913, ibid.
7. Hagood, 352, loc. cit.
8. Wood diary, Nov. 6, 1913, loc. cit.
9. What is unusual about this document is that it is one of the few such interpolations in Wood's extensive and often detailed diary. Also see letter, MacArthur to John Callan O'Laughlin, July 30, 1931, John C. O'Laughlin Papers, MD, LC.

10. Letter, Henry L. Stimson to Louis A. Stimson, Feb. 13, 1913, Stimson Papers, Sterling Library, Yale University.
11. Jack Sweetman, *The Landing at Vera Cruz: 1914* (Annapolis: 1968), 48–49. Cf. Robert Quirk, *An Affair of Honor: Woodrow Wilson and Vera Cruz* (Lexington, Ky.: 1962).
12. Memos, Chief of Staff to chief of the War College Division, Nov. 6, 1913, and Chief of Staff to secretary of war, April 15, 1914, Wood Papers, loc. cit.
13. Quirk, 219–220.
14. Memo, Leonard Wood to the Adjutant General, Nov. 25, 1914, AGO File, RG 94, NA.
15. Douglas MacArthur, *Reminiscences* (New York: 1964), 41–42.
16. Letter, MacArthur to Wood, May 7, 1914; Wood diary, May 15, 1914, loc. cit.
17. See the photograph in *The New York Times,* July 16, 1916.
18. Sweetman, 184.
19. Letter, Frederick Funston to the Adjutant General, Jan. 13, 1915, AGO File, RG 94, NA.
20. "Proceedings of a Board of Officers Convened to Report on the Award of a Medal of Honor to Captain Douglas MacArthur," Feb. 9, 1915, ibid.
21. Frazier Hunt, *The Untold Story of Douglas MacArthur* (New York: 1954), 59.
22. Martin Gilbert, *Winston Churchill* (Boston: 1971), III, 132.
23. Hagood, 183, loc. cit.
24. House diary, Dec. 15, 1915, Edward M. House Papers, Sterling Library, Yale University.
25. Frederick R. Palmer, *Newton D. Baker* (New York: 1931), I, 10.
26. Letter, MacArthur to Wood, March 20, 1916, Wood Papers, loc. cit.
27. *The New York Times,* July 7, 1916; Stephen Vaughn, "Censorship and the News in 1916," *Indiana Military History Journal* (May 1978).
28. Letter, MacArthur to Wood, Nov. 23, 1916, Wood Papers, loc. cit.
29. James M. Goode, *Best Addresses* (Washington, D.C.: 1988), 61.
30. Herbert Molloy Mason, *The Great Pursuit* (New York: 1970), 3–21; Clarence Clendenen, *Blood on the Border* (New York: 1969), 201–210.
31. Mason, 207–210.
32. Donald Smythe, *Guerrilla Warrior* (New York: 1973); Frank Vandiver, *Black Jack* (College Station, Texas: 1977).
33. War Department, *Annual Report of the Secretary of War* (Washington, D.C.: 1916), I, 168.
34. Memo, Army War College Division to the Chief of Staff, Dec. 9, 1916, RG 165, NA.
35. MacArthur, 46–47.
36. Letter, Newton Baker to Frederick Palmer, March 10, 1931, reproduced in Harvey DeWeerd, *President Wilson Fights His War* (New York: 1939), 210n.
37. Joseph P. Tumulty, *Woodrow Wilson as I Know Him* (Garden City, N.Y.: 1921), 259. Tumulty was Wilson's press secretary.
38. Hugh Johnson, *The Blue Eagle from Egg to Earth* (New York: 1935), 75.
39. Mark Sullivan, *Over Here* (New York: 1933), Chapter 5; D. Clayton James, *The Years of MacArthur* (Boston: 1970), I, 130–131.
40. MacArthur, 45.
41. John Hersey, *Men on Bataan* (New York: 1942), 110.
42. Palmer, I, 356.
43. James G. Harbord, *Leaves from a War Diary* (New York: 1925), 201.

6. Soldier's Soldier

1. Letter, Wood to the Adjutant General, May 7, 1917, Leonard Wood Papers, MD, LC; Frederick Palmer, *Newton D. Baker* (New York: 1931), II, 164; Jack C. Lane, *Armed*

Progressive (San Rafael, Calif.: 1978), 203–217; Herman Hagedorn, *Leonard Wood* (New York: 1934), II, 488.

2. Donald Smythe, *Pershing: General of the Armies* (Bloomington, Ind.: 1987), 1–3.
3. Letter, MacArthur to Wood, Aug. 13, 1917, Wood Papers, loc. cit.
4. Thomas T. Handy (Knoff interview), 13, USAMHI.
5. Francis J. Duffy, *Father Duffy's Story* (New York: 1919), 34.
6. Douglas MacArthur, *Reminiscences* (New York: 1964), 52.
7. See Pershing's notebooks, Box 2, John J. Pershing Papers, MD, LC.
8. Palmer, 253.
9. War Department, *The U.S. Army in the World War* [*USAWW*] (Washington, D.C.: 1925), II, 77–79; III, 666–670.
10. Jules Archer, *Front Line General* (New York: 1963), 50; Smythe, 61–62.
11. MacArthur, 53.
12. Frazier Hunt, *The Untold Story of Douglas MacArthur* (New York: 1954), 72.
13. Letter, Alfred Jacobson to Henry Reilly, Jan. 31, 1936. MMA. Jacobson was a French artillery officer assigned to train the 42d Division.
14. Frank Raymond and Cornelius Ryan, *MacArthur: Man of Action* (New York: 1953), 69.
15. Robert Considine, *General Douglas MacArthur* (New York: 1964), 20–21.
16. Hugh Ogden diary, Feb. 21, 1918, 42d Division Papers, USAMHI.
17. Charles T. Menoher, "The Rainbow in Lorraine," *Rainbow Reveille* (Jan. 1952); Raymond and Ryan, 70.
18. General orders, HQ 84th Infantry Brigade, April 7, 1919, RG 120, NA. Some authors have confused the date of the award of the Croix de Guerre, on February 26, with the date of the raid, which occurred nearly a week earlier.
19. VII Corps order No. 218, March 6, 1918, MMA.
20. John Taber, *The Story of the 168th Infantry* (Iowa City: 1925), I, 126.
21. Taber I, 128; unidentified newspaper clipping in Scrapbook No. 1, MMA.
22. Considine, 21.
23. Memo, Major General A. W. Brewster to Major Shannon, April 9, 1918, MMA.
24. Statement by Lieutenant Jasper W. Coghlan, April 18, 1918, 42d Division Records, NA. Coghlan treated MacArthur for nearly two weeks. James Harbord, *An American Army in France* (New York: 1935), 234; Ralph A. Hayes, *Secretary Baker at the Front* (New York: 1918), 89–90.
25. Ogden diary, 199–200, loc. cit.
26. Donovan diary, Feb. 3, 1918, William J. Donovan Papers, USAMHI; Richard Dunlop, *Donovan* (Chicago: 1982), 62–63.
27. Clark Lee and Richard Henschel, *Douglas MacArthur* (New York: 1952), 36.
28. Albert Ettinger, *A Doughboy with the Fighting 69th* (Shippensburg, Pa.: 1990), 88–89.
29. Jean MacArthur interview, Tape 30, MMA.
30. Proceedings of the "Army Day Meeting" at the Union League Club, Chicago, April 6, 1942, MMA.
31. Duffy, 89–90.
32. Donald Smythe, *Guerrilla Warrior* (New York: 1973), 123.
33. Letter, Philippe Pétain to Ferdinand Foch, April 24, 1918, Pershing Papers, loc. cit.; *USAWW,* III, 283; IV, 266.
34. Brewster to Shannon, loc. cit.
35. Ogden diary, 117, loc. cit.
36. John J. Pershing, *My Experiences in the World War* (New York: 1932), I, 363–364.
37. Menoher, op. cit.
38. Pershing diary, July 20, 1917, Pershing Papers, loc. cit.; Babcock memoir, 410, Conrad Babcock Papers, HI.

39. Pershing noted in his diary that he had visited the 42d but made no comment on what he thought of it: diary, June 22, 1918, Pershing Papers, loc. cit. MacArthur's recollection of what occurred is in Hunt, 72–73.

7. The Dominant Feature

1. Billy Mitchell, *Memoirs of World War One* (New York: 1960), 221–222.
2. John Hersey, *Men on Bataan* (New York: 1942), 116.
3. This compilation, now faded and brown, is to be found at the MacArthur Memorial Archives, where it is known as Scrapbook Number 1.
4. Letter, Mary MacArthur to Newton D. Baker, June 7, 1918, John J. Pershing Papers, MD, LC.
5. Letter, Newton D. Baker to Mary MacArthur, June 11, 1918, Newton D. Baker Papers, MD, LC.
6. Letter, Mary MacArthur to Pershing, June 12, 1918, Pershing Papers, loc. cit.
7. Robert Considine, *MacArthur the Magnificent* (New York: 1942), 48.
8. Letter, Peyton C. March to Pershing, July 2, 1918, Pershing Papers, loc. cit.
9. Pershing diary, July 11, 1918, and Aug. 22, 1918, and letter, Pershing to Baker, July 28, 1918, Pershing Papers, loc. cit.; Edward Coffman, *The Hilt of the Sword: The Career of Peyton C. March* (New York: 1966), 48–51; Donald Smythe, *Pershing: General of the Armies* (Bloomington, Ind.: 1986), 167–168.
10. Letter, MacArthur to Pershing, n.d. but evidently July 1918, MMA. His date of rank was July 11.
11. Thomas T. Handy (Knoff interview), 13, USAMHI.
12. Douglas MacArthur, *Reminiscences* (New York: 1964), 57; letter, MacArthur to Harry J. Collins, May 31, 1943, MMA.
13. There are a number of versions of Gouraud's order—e.g., George E. Leach, *War Diary* (n.p.: 1923), 75–76; *Rainbow Reveille* (Oct. 1949); T. Bentley Mott, *Twenty Years a Military Attaché* (New York: 1936), 233–234. Cf. Hersey, 116–117.
14. American Battlefield Monuments Commission [ABMC], *American Armies and Battlefields in Europe* (Washington, D.C.: 1938), 330.
15. Mott, 233–234; William DePuy (Brownlee/Mullen interview), USAMHI.
16. MacArthur, 58.
17. War Department, *The U.S. Army in the World War* [*USAWW*] (Washington, D.C.: 1925), V, 167.
18. Lawrence Stallings, *The Doughboys* (New York: 1962), 87–92.
19. *USAWW,* V, 523–525.
20. Henry J. Reilly, *Americans All* (Columbus, Ohio: 1936), 311–313; Francis J. Duffy, *Father Duffy's Story* (New York: 1919), 163–167.
21. Robert L. Bullard, *American Soldiers Also Fought* (New York: 1936), 71. Cf. letter, MacArthur to Frank E. Lyman, Sept. 16, 1920, MMA.
22. Albert Ettinger, *A Doughboy with the Fighting 69th* (Shippensburg, Pa.: 1990), 121–122.
23. Letter, W. E. Talbot to William B. Ruggles, Oct. 21, 1937, MMA; Frank Raymond and Cornelius Ryan, *MacArthur: Man of Action* (New York: 1953), 72.
24. Duffy, 205–206.
25. Letter, Menoher to Pershing, n.d. but titled "Subject: The distinguished Services of Brigadier General MacArthur," DM 201 File, MMA.
26. Duffy, 206; Bullard, 74.
27. D. Clayton James, *The Years of MacArthur* (Boston: 1970), I, 194.
28. The cigarette case survives to this day. It is on display in Norfolk, Virginia.
29. Considine, 45.

30. Handy, IV, 41a, loc. cit.
31. Pershing diary, Aug. 25 and 29, 1918, Pershing Papers, loc. cit.
32. Richard Goldhurst, *Pipe Clay and Drill* (New York: 1977), 233–234.
33. Leach, 121.
34. John H. Taber, *The Story of the 168th Infantry* (Iowa City: 1925), II, 55–57.
35. Pershing diary, Sept. 7, 1918, Pershing Papers, loc. cit.
36. Leach, 122; Reilly, 540–569.
37. Bullard, 82.
38. Letter, Alfred Jacobson to Henry Reilly, Jan. 31, 1936, MMA; Hersey, 119; undated newspaper, Scrapbook No. 1, MMA.
39. Martin Blumenson, ed., *The Patton Papers* (Boston: 1970), I, 634; Jules Archer, *Front-Line General: Douglas MacArthur* (New York: 1963), 57.
40. George C. Kenney, *The MacArthur I Know* (New York: 1952), 17.
41. MacArthur, 63–64. Cf. Hunter Liggett, *A.E.F.* (New York: 1928), 159–160.
42. B. H. Liddell Hart, *The Real War 1914–1918* (London: 1930), 447.
43. Cf. Hunter Liggett, *Commanding an American Army* (Cambridge, Mass.: 1925).
44. Pershing diary, Oct. 4, 1918, Pershing Papers, loc. cit.
45. Robert L. Bullard, *Personalities and Reminiscences of the War* (Garden City, N.Y.: 1925), 114.
46. Taber, II, 156–166; Reilly, 626–640.
47. MacArthur, 64.
48. Howard G. Smith (Cineworld interview), 4, MMA.
49. Reilly, 659–682; Taber, II, 186.
50. *Berlin* (Wisconsin) *Journal,* March 18, 1943.
51. Frazier Hunt, *The Untold Story of Douglas MacArthur* (New York: 1954), 86. He was the journalist who posed the question.
52. Ibid.; author interview with Roger Cirillo of the U.S. Army Center for Military History, Aug. 10, 1993.
53. Duffy, 276–277; ABMC, *42nd Division—Summary of Operations* (Washington, D.C.: 1930), 53–66.
54. Charles McChord memoir, "I Saved the Life of General MacArthur," n.d., MMA.
55. William Ganoe, *MacArthur Close-Up* (New York: 1955), 143–144.
56. Taber, II, 194–201.
57. ABMC, *American Armies and Battlefields in Europe,* 233–244. In his memoirs Pershing said the importance of what had been achieved on the Romagne Heights "could hardly be overestimated": John J. Pershing, *My Experiences in the World War* (Washington, D.C.: 1932), 340.
58. Cable No. 1805, Pershing to the Adjutant General, Oct. 17, 1918, RG 120; letter, Pershing to MacArthur, Nov. 29, 1918, DM 201 File, loc. cit.
59. Cable, Menoher to Summerall, Oct. 26, 1918, 42d Division records, RG 120, NA.
60. Hunt, 89.
61. Letter, MacArthur to Menoher, Nov. 8, 1918, 42d Division records, RG 120, NA; Reilly, 800–801; Joseph T. Dickman, *The Great Crusade* (New York: 1927), 186. In a later account MacArthur told a somewhat different story, in which he was detained but not treated like a prisoner. See letter, MacArthur to Thomas M. Johnson, March 22, 1939, MMA. This version formed the basis for the account he gave in *Reminiscences.*
62. Message from Commander in Chief, Nov. 5, 1918, RG 120, NA; Pershing diary, Nov. 3, 1918, Pershing Papers, loc. cit.
63. Blumenson, I, 585–586.

64. Letter, C. A. Flagler to Pershing, Dec. 18, 1918; witness statements from Wayne Hill and Reginald H. Weller, both dated Dec. 12, 1918; and memo for record, William N. Hughes, Jr., March 27, 1919, 42d Division records, RG 120, NA.
65. For the kind of feat that Pershing had in mind, see Stallings, 29.
66. Mott, 302.
67. *National Cyclopedia of American Biography,* G, 26–27.
68. Paul Brain, *The Test of Battle* (Wilmington, Del.: 1992), 149.

8. Bon!

1. Francis J. Duffy, *Father Duffy's Story* (New York: 1919), 320–324; Joseph T. Dickman, *The Great Crusade* (New York: 1927), 239–241.
2. Donald Smythe, *Pershing: General of the Armies* (Bloomington, Ind.: 1986), 254.
3. Cable, C. A. Flager to Pershing, Jan. 12, 1919, 42d Division records, RG 120, NA; Douglas MacArthur, *Reminiscences* (New York: 1964), 71; D. Clayton James, *The Years of MacArthur* (Boston: 1970), I, 253.
4. William A. White, *The Autobiography of William Allen White* (New York: 1946), 572–573; letter, White to MacArthur, Dec. 4, 1933, MMA.
5. Pershing diary, March 16, 1919, John J. Pershing Papers, MD, LC. In public Pershing praised the 42d, but in private he persistently criticized it. In fact, it had the distinction of being the only division in the entire Third Army that he did criticize.
6. Letter, S. L. H. Slocum to the Adjutant General, May 15, 1919, AGO File, RG 120, NA.
7. Faubion Bowers, "The Late General MacArthur," *Esquire* (Jan. 1967).
8. Edward Coffman, *The Hilt of the Sword: The Career of Peyton C. March* (New York: 1966), 186. MacArthur makes no reference to his doubts and objections in *Reminiscences.*
9. "Annual Report of the Superintendent of the United States Military Academy," in War Department, *Report of the Secretary of War* (Washington, D.C.: 1919), 63.
10. Maxwell Taylor (Manion interview), 16, USAMHI.
11. William Ganoe, *MacArthur Close-Up* (New York: 1955), 28.
12. Francis T. Miller, *General Douglas MacArthur* (New York: 1942), 115.
13. Ganoe, 47.
14. Letter, MacArthur to Herman Beukema, July 10, 1939, MMA.
15. "Annual Report of the Superintendent of the U.S. Military Academy," in War Department, *Report of the Secretary of War* (Washington, D.C.: 1920), 4–5.
16. Jean Smith, *Lucius D. Clay* (New York: 1991), 39–40.
17. Robert M. Danford (Brower interview), 4, MMA.
18. *Baltimore Sun,* Feb. 1, 1920; Leslie Anders, *Gentle Knight* (Kent, Ohio: 1985), 67.
19. Douglas B. Kendrick, *Memoirs of a 20th Century Army Surgeon* (Manhattan, Kan.: 1992), 198.
20. Earl Blaik, *You Have to Pay the Price* (New York: 1960), 30–31.
21. Smith, 39.
22. Babcock memoir, 819, Conrad S. Babcock Papers, HI.
23. Ganoe, 104–105.
24. Stephen Ambrose, *Duty, Honor, Country* (Baltimore: 1963), 277n.
25. Lyman Lemnitzer (Bideston and Hatch interview), 20, USAMHI; Ganoe, 53–58; Blaik, 25.
26. "A MacArthur Story," n.d. but provisionally dated 1943 and probably written by LeGrande A. Diller, MMA.

27. Ganoe, 76.
28. Remarks by Russell Reeder at dedication of MacArthur statue, Aug. 21, 1970, MMA.
29. Danford, 2–3, loc. cit.
30. Letter, MacArthur to Blaik, Dec. 30, 1929, Earl Blaik Papers, Special Collections, USMA.
31. Blaik, 37 passim.
32. Robert Danford, "USMA's 31st Superintendent," *Assembly* (Spring 1964).
33. Marti Maher, *Bringing Up the Brass* (New York: 1951), 79; Blaik, 36.
34. Letter, MacArthur to Ralph Cannon, April 18, 1939, MMA.
35. Every biography of MacArthur does what Louise would have wanted: takes at least five years off her age. She was born in 1890 and died seventy-five years later. See *The New York Times,* June 1, 1965.
36. There is an undated newspaper clipping from a Baltimore newspaper in Scrapbook No. 1 that dates from the time of Louise's divorce from Brooks and offers an account of their unhappy marriage.
37. Tyler Abell, ed., *Drew Pearson Diaries* (New York: 1974), 412–413.
38. Stephen Roskill, *Admiral of the Fleet Earl Beatty: An Intimate Biography* (London: 1981).
39. Letter, MacArthur to Louise Brooks, Oct. 7, 1921, reproduced in Joseph M. Maddelena, ed., *Profiles in History: The Passionate and Poetic Pen of Douglas MacArthur* (Beverly Hills: 1991), 8.
40. Letter, MacArthur to Louise Brooks, Oct. 25, 1921, ibid.
41. Letters, MacArthur to Louise Brooks, Oct. 27 and Nov. 27, 1921, ibid.
42. Letter, MacArthur to Louise Brooks, Dec. 18, 1921, ibid.
43. Letter, MacArthur to Louise Brooks, Nov. 19, 1921, ibid.; Norman Scott, Jr. (Brower interview), 4–5, MMA.
44. Scrapbook No. 1, MMA.
45. *The New York Times,* Feb. 15, 1922.
46. Robert Considine, *It's All News to Me* (New York: 1956), 342.
47. Smythe, 296–301.
48. Letter, Pershing to MacArthur, Nov. 22, 1921, Pershing Papers, loc. cit.
49. Maddelena, 33–34.
50. Letter, MacArthur to Louise Brooks, Nov. 10, 1921, ibid.
51. Efficiency report on General Officer, Pershing to the Adjutant General, July 1, 1922, DM 201 File, MMA.

9. Americans Don't Quit

1. Alberta M. Snavely (Hasdorff interview), 28–29, HRA.
2. Arthur Vanaman (Ahmann interview), 64, HRA.
3. Wood diary, Oct. 16 and Nov. 3, 1922, Leonard Wood Papers, MD, LC.
4. Lyman Lemnitzer (Bideston and Hutch interview), 17, USAMHI.
5. Frazier Hunt, *The Untold Story of Douglas MacArthur* (New York: 1954), 114.
6. D. Clayton James, *The Years of MacArthur* (Boston: 1970), I, 320.
7. Snavely, 29–30.
8. Clark Lee and Richard Henschel, *Douglas MacArthur* (New York: 1952), 49.
9. Carol Petillo, *Douglas MacArthur: The Philippine Years* (Bloomington, Ind.: 1981), 126.
10. Wood diary, Feb. 26, 1924, Wood Papers, loc. cit.

11. Letter, MacArthur to Louise MacArthur, March 25, 1923, in Joseph M. Maddelena, ed., *Profiles in History: The Passionate and Poetic Pen of Douglas MacArthur* (Beverly Hills: 1993).
12. Letter, MacArthur to Louise MacArthur, April 8, 1923, ibid.
13. Lewis Gleek, Jr., *The Manila Army and Navy Club* (Manila: 1976), 24, 38.
14. Ickes diary, Sept. 25, 1943, Harold E. Ickes Papers, MD, LC.
15. Memo, chief of engineers to Chief of Staff, May 12, 1915, MMA.
16. Edward S. Miller, *War Plan Orange* (Annapolis, Md.: 1991), 54–56.
17. Letter, Wood to Weeks, Sept. 27, 1923, Wood Papers, loc. cit.
18. Miller, 56; Jack Lane, *Armed Progressive: The Life of Leonard Wood* (San Rafael, Calif.: 1978), 257 passim.
19. Philippine Department, "Map Exercise, 1934," 3 vols. (Manila: 1934).
20. Efficiency report on General Officer, George W. Read to the Adjutant General, July 1, 1923; Omar Bundy to the Adjutant General, March 24, 1924, DM 201 File, MMA.
21. Michael P. Onorato, *Leonard Wood and the Philippine Cabinet Crisis of 1923* (Manila: 1967), 43–55; Lane, 254–255, 416–418.
22. Cables, Wood to Weeks, July 12 and July 22, 1924; Wood diary, July 12, Sept. 11 and Sept. 18, 1924, Wood Papers, loc. cit.; James, I, 302–303.
23. Letter, Mary MacArthur to Pershing, n.d. but evidently late 1923 or early 1924, John J. Pershing Papers, MD, LC.
24. Letters, Wood to Weeks, May 9, 1924, and Weeks to Wood, June 13, 1924, Wood Papers, loc. cit.
25. Vanaman, 63, loc. cit.
26. Report of Decoration Board, April 21, 1925, DM 201 File, loc. cit.
27. Rhoades diary, Sept. 19, 1944, Weldon Rhoades Papers, HI.
28. Alfred Hurley, *Billy Mitchell: Crusader for Air Power* (Bloomington, Ind.: 1972), 100–108; Maurer Maurer, *Aviation in the U.S. Army 1919–1939* (Washington, D.C.: 1987), 127–129.
29. *The New York Times,* Sept. 6, 1925.
30. Burke Davis, *The Billy Mitchell Affair* (New York: 1966), 267.
31. Douglas MacArthur, *Reminiscences* (New York: 1964), 85–86; letter, Fred A. Britten to Robert E. Wood, April 17, 1943, Robert E. Wood Papers, HHL; Hurley, Chapter 7.
32. Letters, Louise MacArthur to Pershing, n.d. but late Feb. 1926, and Pershing to Mrs. Douglas MacArthur, March 17, 1926, Pershing Papers, loc. cit.
33. Letter, Katherine Gamble to MacArthur, Feb. 21, 1951, MMA; Lee and Henschel, 51.
34. His speech was published as "The Necessity for Military Forces," *Infantry Journal,* 30 (Fall 1927).
35. Letter, Summerall to MacArthur, Nov. 25, 1927, DM 201 File, loc. cit.
36. Robert Considine, *General Douglas MacArthur* (New York: 1964), 58.
37. Hunt, 121.
38. Letter, Harry Hillman to MacArthur, Feb. 16, 1945, MMA.
39. *Report of the President on the 1928 Olympic Games,* DM 201 File, loc. cit. The poem, titled "The Island Race," is not by MacArthur. It was written by Sir Henry John Newbolt.
40. Calvin Coolidge, *The Autobiography of Calvin Coolidge* (Boston: 1932).
41. The fact that he considered the break with Louise final is indicated by correspondence as early as February 1928 stating that she would not be returning to Manila with him: letters, MacArthur to Summerall, Feb. 14, 1928, and MacArthur to the Adjutant General, Feb. 23, 1928, DM 201 File, loc. cit.

42. Considine, 60.
43. Henry L. Stimson, *On Active Service in Peace and War* (Boston: 1948); Elting E. Morison, *Turmoil and Tradition: The Life of Henry L. Stimson* (New York: 1966), 231–245.
44. General correspondence folder, Feb. 1922–Feb. 1932, John C. O'Laughlin Papers, MD, LC; John Callan O'Laughlin, *Pershing* (New York: 1928).
45. Hagood memoir, "Down the Big Road," 457–458, Johnson Hagood Papers, USAMHI.
46. Ibid., 366–367.
47. Moseley memoir, "One Soldier's Journey," vol. 2, and appendix titled "Historical Notes," George Van Horn Moseley Papers, MD, LC.
48. *The New York Times,* April 21, 1929.
49. Letter, Roy Howard to MacArthur, May 13, 1930, MMA. That was how Hoover described it to Howard.
50. Cables, Summerall to MacArthur, Aug. 23, 1929, and MacArthur to Summerall, Aug. 25, 1925, DM 201 File, loc. cit.
51. Letter, Roy Howard to MacArthur, Aug. 8, 1930, said that for a time the White House "looked with uniform disfavor" on every attempt to advance MacArthur as Chief of Staff. Roy Howard Papers, MD, LC.
52. Moseley, op. cit.
53. Hugh Johnson, *The Blue Eagle from Egg to Earth* (New York: 1935), 372–373.
54. Edward Coffman, *The Hilt of the Sword: The Career of Peyton C. March* (New York: 1966), 242.
55. Letters, Howard to MacArthur, loc. cit., and MacArthur to Howard, Sept. 12, 1930, Howard Papers, loc. cit. MacArthur gave Howard much of the credit for getting this assignment.
56. Moseley, II, 133–134, and "Historical Notes"; letter, Merritte W. Ireland to John Hines, July 8, 1930, John L. Hines Papers, MD, LC.
57. Donald Lohbeck, *Patrick J. Hurley* (Chicago: 1956), 101–102.
58. Herbert Hoover, *Memoirs of Herbert Hoover* (New York: 1952), II, 339. Hoover's anodyne account of why he appointed MacArthur reveals nothing about what actually happened. Nor does MacArthur's *Reminiscences,* 88–89, although he hints that in turning down the post of chief engineer, he knew he was risking his chance of becoming Chief of Staff.
59. He admitted being surprised and apprehensive to one of his closest friends and West Point classmate George Cocheu. See letter, MacArthur to Cocheu, Sept. 10, 1930, MMA.

10. D'Artagnan of the Army

1. Moseley memoir, "One Soldier's Journey," George Van Horn Moseley Papers, vol. 2, MD, LC; Babcock memoir, "From This Generation to the Next," Conrad S. Babcock Papers, HI. Cf. letter, Merritte W. Ireland to John L. Hines, Dec. 12, 1930, John L. Hines Papers, MD, LC. Summerall's blatant favoritism toward one officer, his close friend Stephen Fuqua, had brought Fuqua two stars and appointment as chief of infantry, but it was a move that outraged much of the Army. The Fuqua case was the cover-up that MacArthur had referred to when he told Johnson Hagood to protest against his own assignment. The lid couldn't be kept on indefinitely, and in April 1930 it finally hit the headlines. Summerall was nearly a year away from retirement but chose to step down six months early.

2. Letter, Ireland to Hines, Dec. 12, 1930, Hines Papers, loc. cit.
3. "Report of the Chief of Staff," in War Department, *Annual Report of the Secretary of War* (Washington, D.C.: 1930).
4. *Army and Navy Journal* (Aug. 30, 1930).
5. *New York Herald Tribune,* Nov. 22, 1930.
6. John Hersey, *Men on Bataan* (New York: 1942), 30.
7. W. H. T. Squires, "Norfolk in By-Gone Days," *Norfolk Ledger-Dispatch,* April 2, 1942.
8. Allen P. Julian, *MacArthur: The Life of a General* (New York: 1963), 38.
9. Letter, Ruth Ellen Totten to Madge Mahan, March 23, 1979, MMA.
10. Carol Petillo, *MacArthur: The Philippine Years* (Bloomington, Ind.: 1981), 151.
11. Letters, MacArthur to Isabel Cooper, Sept. 27, 28 and 30, 1929, Morris Ernst Papers, Harry H. Ransome Center, University of Texas.
12. Postcard, MacArthur to Isabel Cooper, n.d. but evidently October 1932, ibid.
13. Dwight D. Eisenhower, "War Policies," *Infantry Journal* (Nov.–Dec. 1931); Eisenhower (Henle interview), 4, HHL.
14. Letter, MacArthur to Eisenhower, Nov. 4, 1931, Dwight D. Eisenhower Papers, EL.
15. Eisenhower diary, Dec. 1, 1931, Eisenhower Papers, loc. cit.
16. Ibid., June 1932.
17. Letter, O'Laughlin to MacArthur, July 21, 1932, John C. O'Laughlin Papers, MD, LC.
18. Frazier Hunt, *The Untold Story of Douglas MacArthur* (New York: 1954), 140; *The New York Times,* Jan. 13, 1933.
19. War Department, *Annual Report of the Secretary of War* (Washington, D.C.: 1931), I, 60–62; Leslie R. Groves (Brower interview), 1–2, MMA.
20. Hunt, 148.
21. Letter, Pershing to MacArthur, Feb. 23, 1933, MMA.
22. "Report of the Chief of Staff," in War Department, *Annual Report of the Secretary of War* (Washington, D.C.: 1932), 56.
23. Moseley, II, 156–157.
24. Hagood memoir, "Down the Big Road," 376–377.
25. Mildred Gillie, *Forging the Thunderbolt* (Harrisburg, Pa.: 1947), 36.
26. Martin Blumenson, ed., *The Patton Papers* (Boston: 1970), I, 866–868.
27. Gillie, 46–47.
28. Shelby Stanton, *U.S. Army Uniforms of World War II* (Harrisburg, Pa.: 1991), 1–2.
29. Evans E. Kerrigan, *American War Medals and Decorations* (New York: 1971), 29.
30. War Department, *Circular No. 6,* Feb. 22, 1932, and general orders No. 3, Feb. 22, 1932.
31. Moseley, II, 138.
32. Donald J. Lisio, *The President and Protest* (Columbia, Mo.: 1974), 51–62; Roger Daniels, *The Bonus March* (Westport, Conn.: 1971), Chapter 5.
33. Letter, Perry K. Heath to Commissioner Herbert B. Crosby, July 20, 1932, HHL.
34. Walter Waters, *The B.E.F.* (New York: 1933), 193–199.
35. Letter, Luther H. Reichelderfer to the attorney general, Aug. 2, 1932, HHL. Reichelderfer was the president of the D.C. Commissioners.
36. Letter, Luther H. Reichelderfer to Hoover, July 28, 1932, HHL.
37. Order, Hurley to MacArthur, July 28, 1932, HHL.
38. Perry L. Miles, *Fallen Leaves* (Berkeley, Calif.: 1964), 307.
39. Letter, Glassford to MacArthur, April 26, 1951, MMA.
40. Edmund W. Starling, *Starling of the White House* (New York: 1948), 296–297.
41. Moseley, II, 144–145.

42. Kenneth G. Crawford, "Moseley Loses His Horse," *The Nation* (June 10, 1939).
43. F. Trubee Davison (Henle interview), 1–3, HHL.
44. Eisenhower (Henle interview), 3, loc. cit.; Eisenhower, *At Ease: Stories I Tell to Friends* (Garden City, N.Y.: 1967), 217–218.
45. Miles, 309.
46. Moseley, II, 146; reports, Perry L. Miles to MacArthur, 1932, RG 98, and Chief of Staff to secretary of war, n.d. but about Aug. 10, 1932, HHL. Eisenhower wrote MacArthur's report.
47. Arthur Curtice (Henle interview), 5, and Davison (Henle interview), 2, HHL; Herbert Hoover, *Memoirs* (New York: 1952), III, 226–227.
48. Ickes diary, Nov. 27, 1943, Harold E. Ickes Papers, MD, LC; *The Washington Post,* Sept. 29, 1932.
49. Letter, Perry L. Miles to MacArthur, Aug. 28, 1952, MMA.

11. The Noblest Development of Mankind

1. Roger Daniels, *The President and Protest* (Westport, Conn.: 1971), 257.
2. Moseley memoir, "One Soldier's Journey," II, 149–151, George Van Horn Moseley Papers, MD, LC; *Washington Herald,* Feb. 23, 1933.
3. Memo, Chief of Staff to the Adjutant General, May 13, 1933, RG 94, NA.
4. John J. McEntee, *Now They Are Men* (Washington, D.C.: 1940), 16.
5. Harold K. Johnson (Jensen interview), 24–26, USAMHI.
6. War Department, *Annual Report of the Secretary of War* (Washington, D.C.: 1933 and 1934).
7. *Army and Navy Journal* (Sept. 2, 1933).
8. Raymond G. Swing, "Take the Army Out of the CCC," *The Nation* (Oct. 23, 1935); "The Militaristic CCC," *World Tomorrow* (Jan. 18, 1934).
9. Letters, MacArthur to John McSwain, Feb. 8, 1935, and George H. Dern to MacArthur, March 8, 1935, RG 94, NA.
10. War Department, *Annual Report of the Secretary of War* (Washington, D.C.: 1934), 53; Gene M. Lyons and John Maslan, *Education and Military Leadership* (Princeton: 1959), 44–48.
11. *The New York Times,* June 9, 1932.
12. Letter, Robert Fechner to MacArthur, Sept. 26, 1935, MMA. Cf. letter, Fechner to Roosevelt, May 31, 1935, FDRL.
13. Letter, MacArthur to Robert Fechner, Sept. 27, 1935, MMA.
14. Ickes diary, July 27, 1933, Harold E. Ickes Papers, MD, LC.
15. Letters, Dern to Roosevelt, July 14, 1933, and Roosevelt to Dern, July 28, 1933, FDRL.
16. Eisenhower diary, Dec. 11, 1930, Dwight D. Eisenhower Papers, EL.
17. Dwight Eisenhower (James interview), 1, MMA.
18. Chynoweth memoir, "Army Recollections," 23, Bradford G. Chynoweth Papers, USAMHI.
19. Letter (unsigned), MacArthur to Isabel Cooper, Sept. 29, 1929, Morris Ernst Papers, Harry H. Ransome Center, University of Texas. I have reconstructed the course of events from Morris Ernst's notes, based on his interviews with Isabel, which are to be found with this correspondence.
20. Ickes diary, Sept. 25, 1943, Ickes Papers, loc. cit.
21. Letters, MacArthur to Louise MacArthur, in Joseph M. Maddelena, ed., *Profiles in History: The Passionate and Poetic Pen of Douglas MacArthur* (Beverly Hills: 1993), 45, 49–50, 53.

22. Jack Anderson, *Confessions of a Muckraker* (New York: 1977), 148.
23. Robert Sherrill, "Drew Pearson: An Interview," *The Nation* (July 7, 1969).
24. The relevant case notes and correspondence between Pearson and the various lawyers involved are in the Ernst Papers, loc. cit.
25. Two affidavits, both dated Dec. 19, 1934, ibid.
26. Ickes diary, May 24, 1942, loc. cit.
27. Carol Petillo, *Douglas MacArthur: The Philippine Years* (Bloomington, Ind.: 1981), 166.
28. F. Trubee Davison (Henle interview), 4, HHL.
29. *Time* (Dec. 3, 1934); Hans Schmidt, *Maverick Marine* (San Rafael, Calif.: 1985), 223–225; Jules Archer, *The Plot to Seize the White House* (New York: 1973).
30. Rexford G. Tugwell, *The Democratic Roosevelt* (Garden City, N.Y.: 1957), 349–350.
31. Army General Staff interviews, "Interview with Major General Irving J. Phillipson," Dec. 2, 1947, USAMHI Archives; John W. Killigrew, "The Impact of the Great Depression on the Army, 1929–1936," Ph.D. dissertation (University of Indiana, 1960), n39, p. 241.
32. *The New York Times,* April 21, 1933.
33. U.S. Congress, "Hearings on National Defense," April 26, 1933 (Washington, D.C.: 1933), 24.
34. Killigrew, 228–229; speech, "Problems of the War Department," May 14, 1933, George Dern Papers, MD, LC.
35. John Hersey, *Men on Bataan* (New York: 1942), 162.
36. Douglas MacArthur, *Reminiscences* (New York: 1964), 101.
37. Memo, MacArthur to George Dern, Oct. 6, 1933, RG 319, NA.
38. Memo, Dern to Roosevelt, Nov. 7, 1933, RG 319, NA.
39. Clark Lee and Richard Henschel, *Douglas MacArthur* (New York: 1952), 60.
40. George C. Kenney, *The MacArthur I Know* (New York: 1952), 25.
41. Lee and Henschel, 60.
42. *Army and Navy Journal* (March 17, 1934).
43. Hagood memoir, "Down the Big Road," 401–403, Johnson Hagood Papers, USAMHI.
44. All these budget figures have been taken from Elias Huzar, *The Purse and the Sword* (Ithaca, N.Y.: 1950), Table III, 141.
45. Ibid., 138–139.
46. Eisenhower (James interview), 3, loc. cit.; letter, Merritte W. Ireland to John L. Hines, May 13, 1931, John L. Hines Papers, MD, LC.
47. Hagood, 119.
48. Benjamin Foulois, with Carroll V. Glines, *From the Wright Brothers to the Astronauts* (New York: 1968), 277.
49. See Lyons and Masland, Table I, 246.
50. Julian Hatcher, *The Book of the Garand* (Washington, D.C.: 1948), 108–111. Cf. letter, MacArthur to Cyril E. Shelvey, Dec. 3, 1940, MMA.
51. Juan Williams, "Marshall's Law," *The Washington Post,* Jan. 7, 1990; Thurgood Marshall, "Report on Korea," n.d., NAACP Legal File, MD, LC.
52. Letters, Charles H. Houston to MacArthur, Aug. 9, 1934, and MacArthur to Houston, Aug. 20, 1934, MMA.
53. William D. Senter (Maryanow and Fuller interview), 17–18, HRA. Senter graduated from West Point in 1933.
54. War Department, *Annual Report of the Secretary of War* (Washington, D.C.: 1933), 49.
55. Letter, MacArthur to John Agnew, Jr., Jan. 7, 1935, MMA.
56. Speech, "Let Us Remember," July 14, 1935, MMA.

57. Moseley II, 156–157; Gerald E. Wheeler, *Admiral William Veazie Pratt, U.S. Navy* (Washington, D.C.: 1974), 356–357.

58. War Department press release, Jan. 9, 1931.

59. James Leutze, *A Different Kind of Victory* (Annapolis, Md.: 1981), 112.

60. Tyler Abell, ed., *The Drew Pearson Diaries* (New York: 1979), 28–29.

61. Robert Considine, *General Douglas MacArthur* (New York: 1964), 36–37.

62. Memo, MacArthur to Hurley, Aug. 14, 1931, HHL. Cf. letter, Dern to McSwain, Feb. 21, 1934, FDRL. Dern's letter to McSwain is an eighteen-page document, single-spaced, almost certainly written by MacArthur and offering an extensive account of his views on the subject of the future role of airpower.

63. Notebooks, Box 2, Henry H. Arnold Papers, MD, LC; Richard Davis, *Spaatz and the Air War in Europe* (Washington, D.C.: 1993), 16.

64. Letters, George H. Dern to John J. McSwain, Feb. 21, 1934, FDRL, and Dwight D. Eisenhower to George Van Horn Moseley, Feb. 21, 1934, EL.

65. Foulois, 238.

66. *The Washington Post*, Feb. 10, 1934.

67. John F. Shiner, *Foulois and the U.S. Army Air Corps 1931–1935* (Washington, D.C.: 1983), 125–149. Cf. Neil Borden, *Air Mail Emergency, 1934* (Freeport, Maine: 1968) and Paul M. Tillett, *The Army Flies the Mails* (Tuscaloosa, Ala.: 1955).

68. Foulois, 254–255.

69. Murray Green, "The Alaskan Flight of 1934," *Aerospace Historian* (March 1977). Two years later, after MacArthur had stepped down as Chief of Staff, his successor awarded the DFC to Arnold for this flight.

70. Maurer Maurer, *Aviation in the U.S. Army 1919–1939* (Washington, D.C.: 1987), 316–322.

71. Memo for the President, June 26, 1935, President's Official File, FDRL; letter, MacArthur to George Van Horn Moseley, June 11, 1950, Moseley Papers, loc. cit.

72. Memo, Dern to Roosevelt, Oct. 25, 1935, FDRL.

73. Draft history of the Philippine Defense Mission, 1, Eisenhower Papers, loc. cit.

74. Ickes diary, Oct. 9, 1937, Ickes Papers, loc. cit. Ickes's source for this story was Roosevelt.

75. Memo, D. C. McDonald to MacArthur, Nov. 12, 1934, MMA.

76. Transcript, President's press conference, Dec. 12, 1934, and memo, Roosevelt to Dern, Dec. 12, 1934, FDRL.

77. Manuel Quezon, *The Good Fight* (New York: 1944), 155–156.

78. MacArthur, 102.

79. Letters, MacArthur to Roosevelt, Sept. 9, 1935, and Roosevelt to MacArthur, Sept. 19, 1935, FDRL. Cf. letter, Quezon to MacArthur, May 21, 1935, MMA.

80. "Memorandum of Terms of the Agreement for Military Adviser to the President of the Philippine Commonwealth Government," Dec. 31, 1935, MMA.

81. Letters, the Adjutant General to MacArthur, Sept. 18, 1935, and Quezon to Dern, Nov. 19, 1934; and memo, Malin Craig to Stephen Early, Aug. 3, 1937, MMA.

82. "Memorandum of the Terms of Agreement Between the President of the Philippine Commonwealth and General MacArthur," n.d. but evidently late 1935, MMA.

12. Sir Boss

1. Cable, Harry H. Woodring to MacArthur, Oct. 2, 1935, DM 201 File, MMA; War Department special orders No. 233, Oct. 2, 1935.

2. War Department special orders No. 220, Sept. 18, 1935, DM 201 File; memo, Roosevelt to George Dern, July 18, 1935, MMA.
3. Cable, Woodring to MacArthur, Oct. 19, 1935, MMA; Dwight Eisenhower, *At Ease: Stories I Tell to Friends* (Garden City, N.Y.: 1967), 223; letter, Dern to Woodring, Oct. 20, 1935, Harry H. Woodring Papers, University of Kansas.
4. Pinky's condition aboard ship is described in a letter from Mary MacArthur to Harry Woodring, the assistant secretary of war. The letter is undated but was evidently mailed from Hawaii and is in Woodring's papers at the University of Kansas.
5. Robert Considine, *General Douglas MacArthur* (New York: 1964), 49.
6. Jean MacArthur interview, Tape 30, MMA.
7. Francis T. Miller, *General Douglas MacArthur* (New York: 1942), 144.
8. Letters, MacArthur to O'Laughlin, Dec. 9 and 18, 1935, John C. O'Laughlin Papers, MD, LC; Eisenhower, 224.
9. *Washington Sunday Star,* April 19, 1964; Joseph Lash, *Franklin and Eleanor* (New York: 1971), 152–155, 160–163.
10. Philip Wylie's famous essay "Common Women" is reprinted in *A Generation of Vipers* (New York: 1948), 194–217.
11. Frank Raymond and Cornelius Ryan, *MacArthur: Man of Action* (New York: 1953), 54.
12. Letter, MacArthur to Pershing, April 23, 1937, John J. Pershing Papers, MD, LC.
13. Jean MacArthur interview, Tape 31, MMA. I have used this quote, from Jean MacArthur, in preference to those used in the newspapers the next day and used by all MacArthur biographers since—viz, "This is going to last a long time." Jean's recollection sounds more like MacArthur to me, with its ring of finality and commitment.
14. Robert Considine, *MacArthur the Magnificent* (New York: 1942), 10.
15. Jean MacArthur interview, Tape 30, MMA.
16. LeGrande A. Diller (Cineworld interview), 7, MMA.
17. Sid Huff, *My Fifteen Years with General MacArthur* (New York: 1964), 23.
18. Raymond and Ryan, 55.
19. Jean MacArthur interview, Tape 30, MMA.
20. William Lee (Hasdorff interview), 48, HRA.
21. Jean Smith, *Lucius D. Clay* (New York: 1991), 78; Huff, 14.
22. Louis Morton, *The Fall of the Philippines* (Washington, D.C.: 1961), 61–65; Edward S. Miller, *War Plan Orange* (New York: 1991), 57–59.
23. Letter, Hines to MacArthur, March 24, 1931, John L. Hines Papers, MD, LC; Hagood memoir, "Down the Big Road," 370, Johnson Hagood Papers, USAMHI.
24. Section 11, Public Law 127, Seventy-third Congress.
25. Letter, MacArthur to Bonner Fellers, June 1, 1939, MMA.
26. Letter, MacArthur to William H. Anderson, March 15, 1938, MMA.
27. J. Lawton Collins (Sperow interview), I, 137, J. Lawton Collins Papers, and William Hoge (Robertson interview), 76, both at USAMHI.
28. "Report on National Defense in the Philippines" (Manila: 1936), 22, MMA.
29. Memo, "Revision of the Cost Estimates of the Defense Plan," Oct. 6, 1937, MMA.
30. Letter, Quezon to Howard, May 15, 1936, Roy Howard Papers, MD, LC.
31. "National Defense in the Philippines," 1, Folder 3, Box 1, RG 1, MMA.
32. "Notes of an Address by Field Marshal Douglas MacArthur Delivered to a Group of Officers Today," Aug. 3, 1936, MMA.
33. Letters, MacArthur to Frederick Payne, Oct. 8, 1936, and MacArthur to George Dern, July 27, 1936, MMA.
34. "Notes of an Interview with General MacArthur Aboard the President Coolidge," MMA.

35. Memo, James B. Ord to MacArthur, Oct. 30, 1937; memo, S. De Jesus to the Adjutant General, Philippine Army, Aug. 25, 1937, MMA.
36. Letter, MacArthur to Quezon, Oct. 14, 1937, MMA.
37. Letter, Paul V. McNutt to Roy Howard, Dec. 11, 1937, Howard Papers, loc. cit.; Stanley Karnow, *In Our Own Image* (New York: 1990), 251–252.
38. Letter, Frank B. Lockhart to Francis B. Sayre, Oct. 18, 1944, Francis Sayre Papers, MD, LC.
39. Speech, "The Philippines," 20, ibid.
40. Memo, "The Political Situation," 1941, ibid.
41. The portrait is reproduced as the frontispiece to Quezon's autobiography, *The Good Fight* (New York: 1944).
42. Memo to the high commissioner, Feb. 21, 1940, Sayre Papers, loc. cit.
43. Letter, Roy Howard to Quezon, Aug. 10, 1936, Howard Papers, loc. cit., is a typical example of the correspondence between the two men—gossipy, frank, revealing, a completely different kind of exchange from that appearing in any of the correspondence between MacArthur and Quezon.
44. J. Woodford Howard, *Mr. Justice Murphy* (Princeton: 1968), 96–100; letter, Dwight Eisenhower to James Ord, Aug. 13, 1937, MMA.
45. Eisenhower (James interview), 8, MMA; Jean MacArthur interview, Tape 31, MMA.
46. Letter, Pershing to O'Laughlin, June 10, 1937, O'Laughlin Papers, loc. cit.
47. Considine, *General Douglas MacArthur,* 53–54.
48. Letter, MacArthur to the editor of the *Times-Dispatch,* Richmond, Feb. 11, 1938; *Our Army* (May 1938).
49. Letter, Arsenio Luz to Howard, June 26, 1936, Howard Papers, loc. cit.; text of Quezon's speech as cabled to the United States on Jan. 21, 1937, FDRL.
50. Ickes diary, Jan. 30, 1937, Harold E. Ickes Papers, MD, LC.
51. Howard, *Mr. Justice Murphy,* 108–109.
52. Forrest C. Pogue, *George C. Marshall: Ordeal and Hope* (New York: 1966), 146–148, 158–159; Mark Watson, *Chief of Staff: Prewar Plans and Preparations* (Washington, D.C.: 1950), 139; Geoffrey Perret, *There's a War to Be Won* (New York: 1991), 121.
53. Memos, Malin Craig to Stephen Early, Aug. 3, 1937; Early to secretary of war, Aug. 5, 1937, DM 201 File, MMA; Eichelberger Dictations, I/26, Robert Eichelberger Papers, Duke University.
54. Letter, Craig to MacArthur, Aug. 6, 1937, DM 201 File, MMA.
55. Cable, MacArthur to Craig, Aug. 22, 1937, ibid.
56. Cable, Craig to MacArthur, Aug. 24, 1937, ibid.
57. Cable, MacArthur to the Adjutant General, Sept. 16, 1927, ibid.; cable, MacArthur to Malin Craig, Sept. 10, 1937, MMA.
58. Letters, J. Tracy Hale, Jr., to MacArthur, Oct. 28, 1937; George D. Haupt to MacArthur, Jan. 4, 1938, MMA.
59. Letter, Theodore Roosevelt to MacArthur, Nov. 11, 1937, MMA.

13. Great Men

1. Press release, "The Cradle of Philippine Defense," 1941, MMA.
2. John Hersey, *Men on Bataan* (New York: 1942), 288.
3. Jean MacArthur interview, Tape 30, MMA; Sid Huff, *My Fifteen Years with General MacArthur* (New York: 1964), 27.
4. Letters, J. C. H. Lee to MacArthur, Dec. 14, 1935; Eisenhower to MacArthur, Sept. 30, 1938; and Garrison Davidson to MacArthur, June 8, 1938, MMA.

5. Draft history of the Philippine Defense Mission, 6, Kevin McCann Papers, EL; William Lee (Hasdorff interview), 101, HRA; William Hoge (Robertson interview), 64, USAMHI.
6. Eisenhower Philippine diary, July 9, 1937, EL.
7. Birthday message, MacArthur to Quezon, Aug. 21, 1939, MMA.
8. "Notes on Men," an undated entry in Eisenhower's diary but evidently March 1933, EL.
9. Eisenhower Philippine diary, May 29, 1936, loc. cit.
10. Letter, MacArthur to John Callan O'Laughlin, Feb. 16, 1936, John C. O'Laughlin Papers, MD, LC.
11. Eisenhower Philippine diary, Sept. 26, 1936, loc. cit.
12. Ibid., Nov. 15, 1936.
13. Letter, Eisenhower to Ord, Aug. 13, 1937, MMA.
14. Dwight Eisenhower, *At Ease: Stories I Tell to Friends* (Garden City, N.Y.: 1967), 225–226; Peter Lyon, *Eisenhower* (Boston: 1974), 79.
15. Letter, Eisenhower to T. J. Davis, Nov. 14, 1940, EL.
16. Letter, Eisenhower to T. J. Spencer, March 26, 1938, EL.
17. Huff, 16.
18. John S. D. Eisenhower, *Strictly Personal* (New York: 1974), 27.
19. Merle Miller, *Ike* (New York: 1983), 293.
20. Efficiency report on Dwight D. Eisenhower, Dec. 31, 1937, MMA.
21. D. Clayton James, *The Years of MacArthur* (Boston: 1970), I, 566.
22. Letter, Eisenhower to L. T. Gerow, Oct. 11, 1939, EL.
23. John Eisenhower, 20–21.
24. Dwight D. Eisenhower (James interview), 5, MMA.
25. Letters, Eisenhower to George Van Horn Moseley, April 26, 1937, and to Ord, July 29, 1937, EL.
26. Ickes diary, Dec. 11, 1943, Harold E. Ickes Papers, MD, LC.
27. Memo, MacArthur to Quezon, Dec. 8, 1939, MMA.
28. Letter, Ord to Eisenhower, July 18, 1937, EL.
29. Eisenhower Philippine diary, June 25, 1937, loc. cit.
30. Jean Smith, *Lucius D. Clay* (New York: 1990), 78.
31. Hoge (Robertson interview), 20, loc. cit.
32. William Hoge, *Engineer Memoirs* (Fort Belvoir, Va.: 1985), 65–66; Lucius D. Clay (Rogers interview), 28–29, USAMHI.
33. Letter, Ord to Eisenhower, Aug. 10, 1937, MMA.
34. Huff, 27–28.
35. Letter, Eisenhower to Ord, Aug. 13, 1937, MMA.
36. Hugh Parker (Burg interview), 12, 28, EL.
37. Ibid., 54.
38. William Lee (Hasdorff interview), 82, loc. cit.; Lee (Gallacher interview), 26, EL.
39. Ickes diary, July 14, 1939, loc. cit.
40. Telegram, MacArthur to Early, July 14, 1939, FDRL.
41. Ricardo Trota José, *The Philippine Army, 1935–1942* (Manila: 1992), 122.
42. *The New York Times,* Nov. 2, 1939.
43. "Memorandum of Conversation Between President Quezon and Mr. Sayre," Jan. 8, 1940, Francis B. Sayre Papers, MD, LC.
44. "Memorandum of Conversation Between High Commissioner Sayre and President Quezon," Feb. 28, 1940, Sayre Papers, loc. cit.; José, 138–141.
45. Theodore Friend, *Between Two Empires* (New Haven: 1965), 193–194.
46. Ibid.

47. Letters, Ickes to Roosevelt, Feb. 15, 1941, Ickes Papers, loc. cit.; Ickes to Roosevelt, April 10, 1941, FDRL.
48. Francis B. Sayre, *Glad Adventure* (New York: 1957). Hart diary, Nov. 12, 1940, Thomas Hart Papers, Naval Historical Center, gives a good account of MacArthur's outspoken hostility to Sayre. On Quezon's conviction that Sayre was a racist, see letter, Joaquín Elizalde to Harold Ickes, April 7, 1941, FDRL.
49. Carol Petillo, *Douglas MacArthur: The Philippine Years* (Bloomington, Ind.: 1981), 195.
50. Letter, Eisenhower to MacArthur, Dec. 8, 1940, MMA.
51. Thomas C. Hart (Mason interview), 92, Butler Library, Columbia University.
52. Hart diary, Feb. 7, 1940, loc. cit.; ibid., 112.
53. Letter, MacArthur to William W. Harts, March 2, 1940, MMA.
54. Hart diary, Jan. 16, 1941, loc. cit.
55. Letter, MacArthur to Stephen Early, March 21, 1941, FDRL.
56. Letter, Edwin P. Watson to MacArthur, April 15, 1941, FDRL.
57. Letter, MacArthur to Watson, May 11, 1941, FDRL.
58. Letters, MacArthur to Marshall, May 29, 1941, and MacArthur to Jorge Vargas, May 29, 1941, and Marshall to MacArthur, June 20, 1941, MMA.
59. Theodore White, *In Search of History* (New York: 1978), 108–109.

14. The Army of the Far East

1. Elliott Thorpe (Griffin interview), 16, USAMHI.
2. Letter, Stimson to Roosevelt, July 25, 1941, FDRL.
3. Cable, Marshall to MacArthur, July 26, 1941, MMA; executive order, July 26, 1941, FDRL.
4. Courtney Whitney, *MacArthur: His Rendezvous with History* (New York: 1955), 8.
5. Robert Considine, *General Douglas MacArthur* (New York: 1964), 55.
6. Sid Huff, *My Fifteen Years with General MacArthur* (New York: 1964), 30.
7. Letter, MacArthur to John C. O'Laughlin, Oct. 6, 1941, John C. O'Laughlin Papers, MD, LC; *Time* (Dec. 29, 1941).
8. Letter, MacArthur to Quezon, n.d. but sometime in July 1940, MMA.
9. John Hersey, *Men on Bataan* (New York: 1942), 15.
10. James Leutze, *A Different Kind of Victory* (Annapolis, Md.: 1981), 164.
11. LeGrande A. Diller, "Douglas MacArthur: Truths and Myths," in William S. Phillips, ed., *The MacArthurs of Milwaukee* (Milwaukee: 1979).
12. Ibid.
13. D. M. Horner, *Crisis of Command* (Canberra: 1982), 125.
14. Letters, Willoughby to MacArthur, 1938, 1940, and MacArthur to Willoughby, May 15, 1940; Charles Willoughby (James interview), 2–3, MMA.
15. Phillips, 35.
16. Cable, MacArthur to Marshall, July 30, 1941, GCMF.
17. Letter, MacArthur to Moseley, Sept. 4, 1941, George Van Horn Moseley Papers, MD, LC.
18. Phillips, 34.
19. Letter, Quezon to Francis Sayre, April 3, 1941, MMA; draft of proposed speech, "The Philippines," Oct. 1944, Francis B. Sayre Papers, MD, LC.
20. *The New York Times,* Nov. 29, 1941.
21. Letter, Sayre to MacArthur, Sept. 30, 1941; report, "Civilian Defense Measures," n.d. but evidently Oct.–Nov. 1941, Sayre Papers, loc. cit.

22. Letter, MacArthur to Quezon, Aug. 16, 1941, MMA.
23. Letter, Arsenio Luz to Roy Howard, July 30, 1941, Roy Howard Papers, MD, LC.
24. Letter, MacArthur to Quezon, Oct. 12, 1940, MMA.
25. Louis Morton, *The Fall of the Philippines* (Washington, D.C.: 1953), 31.
26. Huff, 30.
27. John D. Bulkeley (Cineworld interview), 4, MMA.
28. Duane Schultz, *Hero of Bataan* (New York: 1981), 57.
29. Cables, Marshall to MacArthur, Sept. 5, 1941, and MacArthur to Marshall, Sept. 7, 1941, MMA.
30. Robert Frank Futrell, *Ideas, Concepts, Doctrine: Basic Thinking in the U.S. Air Force 1907–1960* (Maxwell AFB: 1971), 84–88; Henry Stimson, *On Active Service in Peace and War* (Boston: 1948), 388; manuscript of *Global Mission,* XVII, 13–17, Henry H. Arnold Papers, MD, LC.
31. Lucas V. Beau (Green interview), 30–32, Special Collections, USAF Academy.
32. Memo, "Study of the Air Force for USAFFE," Sept. 11, 1941, MMA.
33. *Time* (Feb. 4, 1941).
34. Wilfred Sheed, *Clare Boothe Luce* (New York: 1982), 87.
35. Her papers in the Library of Congress contain two folders of correspondence with Willoughby. The bulk of it is from him and is filled with expressions of devotion. Her letters to him are polite but unrevealing.
36. Clare Boothe, "MacArthur of the Far East," *Life* (Dec. 6, 1941).
37. Hersey, 82.
38. Letter, MacArthur to Clare Boothe Luce, Aug. 20, 1941, MMA.
39. Letter, Luce to MacArthur, Dec. 6, 1941, Clare Boothe Luce Papers, MD, LC.
40. Letter, Willoughby to MacArthur, "Sunday Morning," n.d. but evidently Oct. 1941, MMA; Ralph G. Martin, *Henry and Clare* (New York: 1990), 209.
41. Letter, MacArthur to Marshall, Sept. 9, 1941, MMA.
42. Letter, MacArthur to Grunert, Sept. 7, 1941, MMA.
43. Letter, MacArthur to Marshall, Aug. 30, 1941, MMA.
44. Jonathan Wainwright, with Robert Considine, *General Wainwright's Story* (New York: 1947), 11–12.
45. Chynoweth memoir, "Strange Surrenders," 11, Bradford G. Chynoweth Papers, USAMHI.
46. Ibid., 20.
47. Letter, Marshall to MacArthur, Dec. 1, 1941, MMA.
48. Leutze, 218.
49. Hart diary, Sept. 22, 1941, Thomas Hart Papers, Naval Historical Center.
50. Letter, MacArthur to Marshall, Oct. 28, 1941, MMA.
51. Lewis H. Brereton, *The Brereton Diaries* (New York: 1946), 17–19. There is a problem with Brereton's "diaries." By his own admission, the entries from his time in the Philippines are not based on a diary as most people understand the term. They were written months, possibly years, after his service there, mainly on Brereton's recollection of what he heard, saw and did. It is possible that some entries were written after the war. At all events, they are not, despite the title of the published work, the authentic, contemporaneous account they have generally been taken as being.
52. Ibid., 19.
53. Ibid., 21.
54. Hugh J. Casey, *Engineer Memoirs* (Fort Belvoir, Va.: 1993), 143.
55. Chynoweth memoirs, "Army Recollections," 51–52, and "Strange Surrenders," 6 passim, loc. cit.

56. Letters, Eichelberger to MacArthur, Oct. 20, 1941; cable, MacArthur to Eichelberger, Nov. 11, 1941, MMA. Cf. Earl Blaik, *You Have to Pay the Price* (New York: 1960).

57. Leutze, 225.

58. Letter, MacArthur to Hart, Nov. 7, 1941; memos, Hart to MacArthur, Oct. 23 and Nov. 12, 1941, MMA. Marshall strongly supported MacArthur on this issue. See letter, Marshall to MacArthur, Dec. 5, 1941, MMA.

59. Leutze, 218.

60. Grace Pearson Hayes, *The Joint Chiefs of Staff in World War II* (Annapolis, Md.: 1981), 17–18.

61. Larry Bland and Sharon Ritenour, eds., *Marshall Papers* (Baltimore: 1985), II, 676–679; Hanson Baldwin, *Battles Lost and Won* (New York: 1965), 117.

62. Letter, MacArthur to commanding general, FEAF, Nov. 27, 1941, MMA.

63. Morton, 67.

64. Wainwright, 12–13.

65. Brereton, fn. 20.

66. Morton, 71.

67. Order, MacArthur to commanding general, South Luzon Force, Nov. 28, 1941, MMA.

68. Francis B. Sayre, *Glad Adventure* (New York: 1957), 221.

69. Ibid., fn. 72.

70. USAFFE HQ diary, Dec. 5, 1941; Hersey, 236.

71. Leutze, 225.

72. Report of conference, Dec. 6, 1941, Hart Papers, loc. cit.

73. Order, USAFFE to CG, Harbor Defenses, Dec. 5, 1941, MMA.

74. Letter, MacArthur to Marshall, Nov. 29, 1941, MMA.

75. Chynoweth, 24; Cecil E. Combs (Ahmann interview), 57, and John W. Carpenter (McCants and Thompson interview), 58, HRA.

76. Casey, 150. It was ironic that Brady himself had been urging this step for the past two weeks. See memo, Brady to MacArthur, "Proposed Installations and Facilities for FEAF," Nov. 21, 1941, MMA. This foot-dragging made nonsense of the advice FEAF had itself given MacArthur. Cf. Brereton, 31–35.

77. The excuse Brereton gave for not sending the entire 19th Bomb Group to Del Monte was that the 7th Bomb Group was expected to arrive soon from the United States. The official AAF history accepts this explanation. I find it unconvincing. First, it conflicts with FEAF's own orders and memorandums, which stressed the need to move the B-17s away from Clark for security reasons. Second, it conflicts with Brereton's own claim that he had been opposed to putting B-17s in the Philippines without adequate radar and fighter cover. Third, most of the 7th Bomb Group would not arrive until the end of December or in early January, by which time there would be ample parking space for his bombers at Del Monte. Finally, if necessary, the 7th BG could have been held in northern Australia or the Dutch East Indies until airfields in the central Philippines were ready. There was no compelling need to fly the 7th into the archipelago in December 1941. W. L. Craven and J. L. Cate, eds., *The Army Air Forces in World War II* (Chicago: 1952), I, 188–189.

78. Clark Lee and Richard Henschel, *Douglas MacArthur* (New York: 1952), 70.

79. There are two useful accounts of events at that meeting: Beebe memoir, "Personal Experience Sketches," 1–4, Lewis Beebe Papers, USAMHI, and Casey, 158–161.

80. Cyrus L. Sulzberger, *A Long Row of Candles* (New York: 1969), 672.

81. Eric Larrabee, *Commander in Chief* (New York: 1989), 317.

82. FEAF, "Summary of Activities," Dec. 8, 1941, HRA.

83. Brereton claimed later that he had proposed attacking targets on Formosa, but MacArthur vehemently denied this. *The New York Times,* Sept. 28, 1946. There appears to be some support for Brereton in FEAF's "Summary of Activities," but there are serious doubts about the authenticity of this document. Inspection of it at HRA reveals obvious erasures, crossings out and rewriting, quite possibly at a later date. Both the official Army and AAF histories have cast doubt on it: Craven and Cate, I, 206–209; Morton, 82–83.
84. USAFFE HQ diary, Dec. 8, 1941, MMA.
85. Office diary, Chief of Staff, USAFFE, Dec. 8, 1941, MMA.
86. Transcript, trial of General Masaharu Homma before the War Crimes Commission, 3068, MMA; John Toland, *But Not in Shame* (New York: 1961), 42–43.
87. William Bartsch, *Doomed at the Start* (College Station, Texas: 1992), 55–71.
88. Ronald Spector, ed., *Listening to the Enemy* (Wilmington, Del.: 1988), 51–52.
89. Cables, MacArthur to Adjutant General, Dec. 8, 1941, MMA.
90. Brereton, 50.
91. Francis B. Sayre, *War Days on Corregidor* (New York: 1942), 3.

15. Times When Men Must Die

1. Cable, MacArthur to Arnold, Dec. 10, 1941, MMA.
2. Clark Lee and Richard Henschel, *Douglas MacArthur* (New York: 1952), 139.
3. Lewis Brereton, *The Brereton Diaries* (New York: 1946).
4. USAFFE HQ diary, Dec. 15, 1941, MMA.
5. USAFFE general orders No. 48, Dec. 21, 1941, MMA; W. L. Craven and J. L. Cate, eds., *The Army Air Forces in World War II* (Chicago: 1952), I, 216–217.
6. Hugh J. Casey, *Engineer Memoirs* (Fort Belvoir, Va.: 1993), 160–161.
7. Sid Huff, *My Fifteen Years with General MacArthur* (New York: 1964), 34; Francis Sayre, *Glad Adventure* (New York: 1957), 5.
8. D. Clayton James, *The Years of MacArthur* (Boston: 1975), II, 27–29; Louis Morton, *Fall of the Philippines* (Washington, D.C.: 1953), 122.
9. Cable, MacArthur to Marshall, Dec. 13, 1941, and letters, "Movement of Convoy," MacArthur to Thomas Hart, Dec. 19, 1941, and Hart to MacArthur, Dec. 20, 1941, MMA.
10. Carlos Romulo, *I Saw the Fall of the Philippines* (New York: 1943), 41.
11. Huff, 35.
12. Manuel Quezon, *The Good Fight* (New York: 1944), 198. Quezon says this interview took place on December 12, but Huff places it at December 17. I believe that Huff's version is correct.
13. Hart diary, Dec. 22, 1941, Thomas C. Hart Papers, Naval Historical Research Center, Washington Navy Yard.
14. Courtney Whitney, *MacArthur: His Rendezvous with History* (New York: 1955), 15.
15. Clay Blair, *Silent Victory* (Philadelphia: 1963), 144–151.
16. Huff, 37.
17. Cable, MacArthur to the Adjutant General, Dec. 22, 1941. Although this message is dated the twenty-second, Paul Rogers, MacArthur's clerk, claims it was written on the twenty-second but not sent until the next morning, after news of the collapse of the beach defenses reached USAFFE. See Rogers mss., 4–64, copy of *MacArthur and Sutherland,* Paul Rogers Papers, MMA.
18. USAFFE HQ diary, Dec. 24, 1941, MMA.

19. Quezon, 208; Sayre, 6.
20. USAFFE HQ diary, Dec. 17, 1941, loc. cit.; Orvil A. Anderson (Shaughnessy interview), 53–54, HRA.
21. Brereton, 60–62.
22. Jean MacArthur interview, Tape 31, MMA; Huff, 38.
23. Romulo, 62.
24. Rogers mss., 4–67, loc. cit.
25. Huff, 39; James Leutze, *A Different Kind of Victory* (Annapolis, Md.: 1981), 245–246.
26. Beebe memoir, "Personal Experience Sketches," 6, Lewis Beebe Papers, USAMHI; John Toland, *But Not in Shame* (New York: 1961), 118.
27. Huff, 42.
28. Romulo, 71.
29. Cable, Marshall to MacArthur, Dec. 27, 1941, MMA; *The New York Times,* Dec. 29 and 30, 1941.
30. Memo, Marshall to the Adjutant General, Dec. 30, 1941; John Goodman, *Bataan: Our Last Ditch* (New York: 1991), 9.
31. Message, MacArthur to Parker, Dec. 29, 1941, MMA; Chynoweth memoir, "Strange Surrenders," 40, Bradford G. Chynoweth Papers, USAMHI; Beebe, 10.
32. Romulo, 101; USAFFE general orders No. 10, Jan. 16, 1942, MMA.
33. Huff, 48; Frazier Hunt, *The Untold Story of Douglas MacArthur* (New York: 1954), 227.
34. Romulo, 102.
35. LeGrande A. Diller (Cineworld interview), 7, MMA.
36. Quezon, 244.
37. Beebe, 9; Morton, 254.
38. Jonathan Wainwright, with Robert Considine, *General Wainwright's Story* (Garden City, N.Y.: 1948), 50; Frazier Hunt, *MacArthur and the War Against Japan* (New York: 1945), 52–53.
39. Duane Schultz, *Hero of Bataan* (New York: 1981), 126.
40. Rogers mss., 5/24–25, loc. cit.
41. Romulo, 191.
42. Ibid., 137.
43. Larry Bland and Sharon Ritenour, eds., *Papers of George C. Marshall* (Baltimore: 1991), III, 60.
44. Stimson diary, Jan. 3, 1942, Henry L. Stimson Papers, Sterling Library, Yale University; Peter Lyon, *Eisenhower* (Boston: 1972), 97–98.
45. D. Clayton James, *The Years of MacArthur* (Boston: 1975), II, 53.
46. Edwin Ramsey, *Lieutenant Ramsey's War* (Los Angeles: 1993), 61; James, II, 57.
47. Lee and Henschel, 148.
48. Morton, 281–285; Schultz, 144–146; Goodman, 227–228; Casey, 167–168. Casey had supervised construction of the defenses on Bataan and was present on the spot. He was convinced that Sutherland had blundered and the present line could be held.
49. USAFFE HQ diary, Jan. 27, 1942, MMA.
50. Dwight D. Eisenhower, *Crusade in Europe* (Garden City, N.Y.: 1948), 21–22.
51. Cable, MacArthur to Marshall, Nov. 11, 1941, MMA; Russell D. Buhite, *Patrick J. Hurley* (Ithaca, N.Y.: 1973), 102–103.
52. Eisenhower personal diary, Jan. 1, 1942, passim, Dwight D. Eisenhower Papers, EL.
53. Cable, Eisenhower to MacArthur, Jan. 25, 1942, MMA.
54. Stimson diary, Feb. 2, 1942, loc. cit.
55. Bland and Ritenour, III, 61.
56. Lee and Henschel, 150; Quezon, 264.

57. James MacGregor Burns, *Roosevelt: Soldier of Freedom* (New York: 1970), 206; Morton, 148, 154; *The New York Times,* Dec. 29, 1941.
58. Albert Chandler, ed., *The Papers of Dwight D. Eisenhower* (Baltimore: 1970), I, 97–98.
59. Cable, MacArthur to Marshall, for delivery to Roosevelt, Feb. 9, 1942, MMA; Lee and Henschel, 151–152; Hunt, 230.
60. Morton, 355.
61. Lee and Henschel, 154.
62. Rogers diary, Feb. 13, 1942, Rogers Papers, loc. cit.
63. Cable, Gertrude Algase to LeGrande Diller, April 4, 1942, MMA.
64. Carol Petillo, "Douglas MacArthur and Manuel Quezon: A Note on an Imperial Bond," *Pacific Historical Review* (Feb. 1979); Paul P. Rogers, "MacArthur, Quezon and Executive Order Number One," *Pacific Historical Review* (Oct. 1983). Also see Ickes diary, April 5 and Sept. 5, 1942, Harold Ickes Papers, MD, LC.
65. Letter, the Adjutant General to MacArthur, Sept. 18, 1935; memo, Malin Craig to Stephen Early, Aug. 3, 1937, MMA.
66. Memo for record, June 20, 1942, Dwight D. Eisenhower Papers, EL.
67. Memo, April 5, 1943, PPF 4914, FDRL.
68. Ickes diary, Feb. 15, 1942, loc. cit.
69. Lloyd Ross, *John Curtin* (Melbourne: 1977), 270–273; letter, John Callan O'Laughlin to MacArthur, March 25, 1942, John C. O'Laughlin Papers, MD, LC.
70. Cable, Marshall to MacArthur, Feb. 23, 1942, MMA; Lee and Henschel, 157.
71. Lee and Henschel, 72.
72. Rogers diary, March 7, 1942, loc. cit.
73. John D. Bulkeley (Cineworld interview), 12–13, 23.
74. Romulo, 227.
75. Schultz, 199–200.
76. Lee and Henschel, 72.

16. I Shall Return

1. Douglas MacArthur, *Reminiscences* (New York: 1964), 143.
2. Ibid.
3. William L. White, *They Were Expendable* (New York: 1943), 84; Hugh J. Casey, *Engineer Memoirs* (Fort Belvoir, Va.: 1993), 181–182; Sid Huff, *My Fifteen Years with General MacArthur* (New York: 1964), 61.
4. John D. Bulkeley (Cineworld interview), 3, MMA.
5. Ibid., 20–21; *Baltimore Sun,* Nov. 13, 1993. This copy of the *Sun* contains a recent interview with Bulkeley.
6. Huff, 65.
7. Bulkeley, 23.
8. MacArthur, 144; USAFFE general orders No. 43, March 16, 1942, MMA.
9. Letter, MacArthur to Quezon, March 16, 1942, MMA; William Breuer, with John D. Bulkeley, *Sea Wolf* (San Rafael, Calif.: 1986), 68.
10. Jesus Villamor, *They Never Surrendered* (Quezon City: 1982), 58. Villamor was at Del Monte Field that day.
11. William G. Hipps (Mortensen interview), 24, HRA.
12. Paul Rogers mss., copy of *MacArthur and Sutherland,* 6/78–79, MMA; D. Clayton James, *The Years of MacArthur* (Boston: 1975), II, 103; Clark Lee and Richard Henschel, *Douglas MacArthur* (New York: 1952), 159.

13. Henry Godman, *Supreme Commander* (Harrison, Ark.: 1980), 46.

14. Jean MacArthur interview, Tape 31, MMA.

15. MacArthur, 145.

16. John Toland, *But Not in Shame* (New York: 1961), 275.

17. MacArthur, 145.

18. Jean MacArthur, op. cit.

19. Toland, 275.

20. E. Daniel Potts and Annette Potts, *Yanks down Under* (Melbourne: 1985), 10; Lee and Henschel, 159.

21. Press release, March 21, 1942, MMA. Although the copy of MacArthur's statement is dated March 21, he maintains in his memoirs that it was first issued to journalists at Batchelor Field some days earlier. Whitney, on the other hand, claims it was written on the back of an envelope and handed to journalists when their train reached Alice Springs. There is indirect corroboration of Whitney's version—which MacArthur had the opportunity to correct—in a letter: Patrick J. Hurley to Richard W. O'Neill, Sept. 14, 1949, MMA. James, largely on the basis of a report in *The Times* of London, says the statement was issued in Adelaide.

22. James, II, 107, has the MacArthurs getting out on the C-47, but Jean clearly remembered the B-17 and its pilot, Colonel Richard Carmichael, and the terrifying takeoff from Batchelor Field, as she sprawled facedown in the fuselage: Jean MacArthur interview, Tape 31, MMA.

23. Lee and Henschel, 160.

24. LeGrande A. Diller (Cineworld interview), 12, MMA.

25. Huff, 72.

26. Lee and Henschel, 160–161. Frazier Hunt in *The Untold Story of Douglas MacArthur* claims that MacArthur paced the train all night in distress. This claim, repeated many times since, is more than a little dubious. When MacArthur arrived in Melbourne, Francis Forde, the Australian army minister, thought MacArthur "did not look" his age, which was sixty-two, and was "in the very best physical form." D. M. Horner, *Crisis of Command* (Canberra: 1978), 63.

27. John Hersey, *Men on Bataan* (New York: 1942), 306.

28. *The New York Times,* March 22, 1942.

29. Letter, Johnson to Roy Howard, April 1, 1942, Roy Howard Papers, MD, LC; cf. Horner, 60–61; George H. Johnston, *The Toughest Fighting in the World* (New York: 1944), 51.

30. Huff, 78; Carlos Romulo, *I Saw the Fall of the Philippines* (New York: 1943), 317.

31. MacArthur, 151; Hunt, 251.

32. Horner, 64; Gavin Long, *MacArthur as Military Commander* (London: 1969), 87.

33. Cable, Marshall to Sutherland, Jan. 30, 1942, MMA; Larry Bland and Sharon Ritenour, eds., *The Papers of George C. Marshall* (Baltimore: 1991), III, 147–148; War Department, general orders 16, April 1, 1942; Forrest C. Pogue, *George C. Marshall: Ordeal and Hope* (New York: 1966), II, 353–354.

34. Vorin E. Whan, ed., *A Soldier Speaks: Public Papers and Speeches of General of the Army Douglas MacArthur* (New York: 1965), 117–118.

35. Godman, 51. For some reason Hunt describes MacArthur as making the four-hundred-mile round trip to Canberra by car. Every biographer since has done the same, overlooking the fact that MacArthur had a plane and pilot available. Godman's story is so detailed that I am convinced MacArthur made this trip by air.

36. John Hetherington, *Blamey: Controversial Soldier* (Canberra: 1973).

37. Memo, Marshall to secretary of war, Oct. 29, 1942, RG 165, NA.
38. MacArthur, 152–153.
39. Lloyd Ross, *John Curtin* (Melbourne: 1977), 313 passim; Potts and Potts, 51–52; Horner, 68–74; Long, 93–94; James, II, 114.
40. Beebe memoir, "Some Personal Experiences," 11, Lewis Beebe Papers, USAMHI.
41. James, II, 142–143; Pogue, II, 256–257; Leslie Groves (Brower interview), n.p., MMA.
42. Jonathan Wainwright, with Robert Considine, *General Wainwright's Story* (Garden City, N.Y.: 1948), 75.
43. James, II, 143–144.
44. Morton, 403; Schultz, 227.
45. Cable, MacArthur to Wainwright, April 4, 1942, MMA.
46. Courtney Whitney, *MacArthur: His Rendezvous with History* (New York: 1955), 57–58.
47. Cable, MacArthur to Wainwright, April 14, 1941, MMA.
48. Romulo, 313.

17. These Days of Stress

1. Letters, MacArthur to Roscoe Piety, May 30, 1942, MMA, and MacArthur to Earl Blaik, June 18, 1942, Blaik Papers, Special Collections, USMA.
2. John Hersey, *Men on Bataan* (New York: 1942), 309; Clark Lee and Richard Henschel, *Douglas MacArthur* (New York: 1952), 161.
3. There is a copy of this oration, undated, in the files at the MacArthur Memorial and Archives.
4. George C. Kenney (Hasdorff interview), 107, HRA.
5. Theodore White, *In Search of History* (New York: 1978), 110.
6. Gregory Franzwa and William Ely, *Leif Sverdrup* (Gerald, Mo.: 1980), 112.
7. Louis Morton, *Strategy and Command: The First Two Years* (Washington, D.C.: 1962), 212–217.
8. Edward Drea, *MacArthur's Ultra* (Lawrence, Kan.: 1992), 36; D. M. Horner, *Crisis of Command* (Canberra: 1978), 79.
9. Samuel Eliot Morison, *Coral Sea, Midway and Submarine Actions May 1942–August 1942* (Boston: 1967), Chapter 2.
10. Samuel Milner, *Victory in Papua* (Washington, D.C.: 1957), 39.
11. Cables, Marshall to MacArthur, April 30 and May 1, 1942, RG 165, NA.
12. Cf. cable, MacArthur to Marshall, Aug. 11, 1942, MMA.
13. D. Clayton James, *The Years of MacArthur* (Boston: 1975), II, 166.
14. Morison, 69.
15. Horner, 95.
16. James, II, 188.
17. Cable, MacArthur to Marshall, June 28, 1942, RG 165, NA.
18. Morton, Appendix 11, 619.
19. Dudley McCarthy, *South-west Pacific Area—First Year: Kokoda to Wau* (Canberra: 1959), 120.
20. Milner, 53–55.
21. Cable, MacArthur to Marshall, May 23, 1942, RG 4, NA.
22. Letter, Marshall to Sir John Dill, May 22, 1942, GCMF.
23. Cable, MacArthur to Marshall, Aug. 30, 1942, MMA.

24. Kenney (Hasdorff interview), 112, loc. cit.
25. William D. Breuer, *Sea Wolf* (Novato, Calif.: 1987), 85.
26. Ibid., 88.
27. Samuel Anderson (Ahmann interview), 188, HRA.
28. Ronnie Dugger, *The Politician* (New York: 1964), 245–249; Martin Caidin and Edward Hymoff, *The Mission* (Philadelphia: 1964), 131 passim; Clark Newlon, *L.B.J.—The Man from Johnson City* (New York: 1966), 98–101.
29. Ickes diary, July 26, 1942, Harold Ickes Papers, MD, LC.
30. See unsigned, undated document titled "Report" in Box 73, Lyndon B. Johnson Papers, LBJ Library, University of Texas at Austin; cf. diary for June 1942 in Box 74.
31. Cable, MacArthur to George Cocheu, July 10, 1942, MMA.
32. Horner, 116; cf. George C. Kenney (Green interview), 7, Special Collections, U.S. Air Force Academy.
33. Memo, "Comments of General Brett re Personnel, etc." n.d. but filed with diary for July 1942, George C. Kenney Papers, CAFH.
34. Anderson (Ahmann interview), 186–187, loc. cit.
35. Kenney (Hasdorff interview), 107–108, loc. cit. For a different version, see Thomas Darcy (Green interview), 10, Special Collections, U.S. Air Force Academy.
36. Geoffrey Perret, *Winged Victory* (New York: 1993), 166–167.
37. Kenney diary, July 12, 1942, Kenney Papers, loc. cit. George C. Kenney, *The MacArthur I Know* (New York: 1952), 36.
38. Kenney diary, July 29, 1942, loc. cit.; *The MacArthur I Know*, 41–43.
39. Kenney (Hasdorff interview), 50, loc. cit.
40. Ibid., Aug. 3, 1942; Kenney, *The MacArthur I Know*, 50–51; cable, MacArthur to Marshall, Sept. 30, 1942, MMA.
41. Horner, 104; James, II, 202.
42. Milner, 64–65.
43. John Hetherington, *Blamey: Controversial Soldier* (Canberra: 1973).
44. Cable, MacArthur to Marshall, Oct. 17, 1942, MMA.
45. Letter, MacArthur to Dudley Knox, Aug. 21, 1942, MMA.
46. Drea, 45; Milner, 76–77.
47. Frederic H. Smith, Jr. (Hasdorff interview), 62, HRA. Smith commanded the fighter groups in New Guinea.
48. GHQ SWPA communiqué No. 140, Aug. 31, 1942, MMA.
49. Kenney diary, Sept. 3, 1942, loc. cit.
50. Ibid., Sept. 12, 1942; Kenney (Hasdorff interview), 63, loc. cit.
51. Cable, MacArthur to Marshall, Sept. 21, 1942, MMA.
52. McCarthy, 234–235.

18. You Must Go Forward

1. John Hammond Moore, *Over-Sexed, Over-Paid and Over Here* (St. Lucia, Australia: 1984), 133.
2. Philip La Follette, "With MacArthur in the Pacific," *Wisconsin Magazine of History* (Winter 1980–81).
3. George C. Kenney, *The MacArthur I Know* (New York: 1952), 58–59.
4. E. J. Kahn, *G.I. Jungle* (New York: 1944), 48.
5. Byers diary, Sept. 6, 1942, Clovis Byers Papers, HI; cable, MacArthur to Marshall, Sept. 6, 1942, RG 165, NA.

6. Jay Luvaas, ed., *"Dear Miss Em"* (Westport, Conn.: 1972), 12.
7. Paul Chwialkowski, *In Caesar's Shadow* (Westport, Conn.: 1993), 36; Luvaas, 13.
8. Byers diary, Aug. 26, 1942, loc. cit.
9. Robert L. Eichelberger, *Our Jungle Road to Tokyo* (New York: 1950), 4.
10. Luvaas, 27; Byers diary, Sept. 14, 1942, loc. cit.
11. Byers diary, Sept. 29 and Oct. 1, 1942, loc. cit.
12. Cables, MacArthur to Marshall, Sept. 30 and Oct. 5, 1942, MMA.
13. Kahn, 49.
14. George H. Johnston, *The Toughest Fighting in the World* (New York: 1944), 136–137.
15. Kenney diary, Aug. 13, 1942, George C. Kenney Papers, CAFH.
16. George C. Kenney (Hasdorff interview), 64, HRA.
17. Ibid., Sept. 21, 1942; George C. Kenney, *General Kenney Reports* (New York: 1949), 99.
18. Arnold diary, Sept. 16, 1942, passim, Henry H. Arnold Papers, MD, LC. Cf. Nathan Twining (Green interview), 9–10, Special Collections, USAF Academy.
19. Arnold diary, Sept. 25, 1942, loc. cit.; Arnold to Kenney, July 5, 1943, Kenney Papers, loc. cit.
20. Hugh J. Casey, *Engineer Memories* (Fort Belvoir, Va.: 1993), 194; Gregory Franzwa and William Ely, *Leif Sverdrup* (Gerald, Mo.: 1980), 117.
21. Franzwa and Ely, 129–130.
22. Samuel Milner, *Victory in Papua* (Washington, D.C.: 1957), 135.
23. Cable, Marshall to MacArthur, Oct. 17, 1942, MMA.
24. Kenney diary, Nov. 3, 1942, loc. cit.
25. Ibid., Nov. 7, 1942.
26. Rickenbacker Dictations, Tape 36, Side 1, Edward V. Rickenbacker Papers, MD, LC.
27. La Follette, op. cit.
28. Leslie Anders, *Gentle Knight: The Life and Times of Major General Edward Forrest Harding* (Kent, Ohio: 1985).
29. See Joe Gray Taylor, "The American Experience in the Southwest Pacific," in Benjamin Franklin Cooling, ed., *Close Air Support* (Washington, D.C.: 1990).
30. Lida Mayo, *Bloody Buna* (New York: 1974), 107–113; John F. Shortal, *Forged by Fire* (Columbia, S.C.: 1987), 57.
31. Milner, 189–195.
32. Edward V. Rickenbacker, *Seven Came Through* (New York: 1943), 80.
33. Rickenbacker Dictations, op. cit.
34. Finis Farr, *Rickenbacker's Luck* (Boston: 1978), 241. In his memoir, *Rickenbacker* (Englewood Cliffs, N.J.: 1967), he observed, "I delivered my oral message. Though I remember every word of it to this day, I shall not repeat it. Stimson and MacArthur took it with them to the grave, and so shall I." Farr, however, had access to Rickenbacker's papers, including material not in the Library of Congress, and conducted extensive interviews with Rickenbacker's family. There is also indirect corroboration in Stimson's diary, Oct. 29, 1942, Henry L. Stimson Papers, Sterling Library, Yale University.
35. Kenney diary, Nov. 27, 1942, loc. cit.
36. Richard Frank, *Guadalcanal* (New York: 1990), 462–492.
37. Byers diary, Nov. 30, 1942, loc. cit.; Eichelberger Dictations, I/7, Robert Eichelberger Papers, Duke University; Kenney diary, Nov. 30, 1942, loc. cit.; Luvaas, 32–33.
38. Frazier Hunt, *The Untold Story of Douglas MacArthur* (New York: 1954), 265.
39. Eichelberger Dictations, I/5, loc. cit.; Paul Chwialkowski, *In Caesar's Shadow* (Westport, Conn.: 1993), 58.

40. Mayo, 123 passim; letters, Eichelberger to Sutherland, Dec. 1, 3, 4 and 5, 1942, Eichelberger Papers, loc. cit.
41. Letter, MacArthur to Eichelberger, Dec. 13, 1942, Eichelberger Papers, loc. cit.
42. Letter, MacArthur to Eichelberger, Dec. 25, 1942, MMA.
43. Cable, MacArthur to Marshall, Feb. 9, 1943, MMA.
44. War Department cable No. 353, n.d., MMA. For background on the Marshall-Harding relationship, see my account of the wartime U.S. Army, *There's a War to Be Won* (New York: 1990), 231 passim.
45. Anders, 268; Larry Bland and Sharon Ritenour, eds., *Papers of George C. Marshall* (Baltimore: 1991), III, 553. Forrest Pogue told me that Harding spent many hours in earnest discussion with Samuel Milner, author of the Green Book on the Buna campaign, *Victory in Papua*.
46. Byers diary, Jan. 15, 1943, loc. cit.; cf. letter, Eichelberger to MacArthur, Dec. 24, 1942, MMA.
47. Memo, HQ U.S. Forces, Buna Area, to GHQ Advanced Headquarters, Jan. 16, 1943, MMA; memo, Robert Eichelberger to Emmalina Eichelberger, Oct. 22, 1943, Eichelberger Papers, loc. cit.
48. SWPA GHQ communiqué No. 291, Jan. 28, 1943, MMA.
49. LeGrande A. Diller reminiscence, Aug. 21, 1970, MMA.
50. Luvaas, 32.
51. Cable, MacArthur to Marshall, Aug. 23, 1943, MMA; memo, Eichelberger to Eichelberger, op. cit.

19. The Continuous Application of Airpower

1. Louis Morton, *Strategy and Command: The First Two Years* (Washington, D.C.: 1964), 374–375.
2. SWPA GHQ communiqué No. 271, Jan. 8, 1943, MMA.
3. George H. Johnston, *Pacific Partner* (New York: 1944), 106.
4. SWPA GHQ order of the day, Jan. 9, 1943, MMA.
5. Kenney diary, Jan. 9, 1943, George C. Kenney Papers, CAFH.
6. Cable, MacArthur to Marshall, Jan. 10, 1943, RG 165, NA.
7. D. M. Horner, *Crisis of Command* (Canberra: 1978), 248.
8. Forrest C. Pogue, *George C. Marshall: Organizer of Victory, 1943–1945* (New York: 1973), 21–32; Horner, 249.
9. Morton, 389.
10. Spencer B. Akin, memoir, "MacArthur's Signal Intelligence Service, World War II," MMA; Edward Drea, *MacArthur's Ultra* (Lawrence, Kan.: 1992), 28.
11. Geoffrey Perret, *Winged Victory* (New York: 1993), 161–162.
12. Kenney diary, Jan. 3 and 4, 1943, loc. cit.
13. Ibid., Jan. 7, 1943.
14. Ibid., Feb. 6, 1943; SWPA GHQ communiqué No. 301, Feb. 7, 1943, MMA.
15. Kenney diary, Feb. 28, 1943, loc. cit.
16. George C. Kenney, *General Kenney Reports* (New York: 1949), 205. Cf. Rhoades diary, March 5, 1943, Weldon Rhoades Papers, HI.
17. Kenney diary, March 4, 1943, loc. cit.; undated memo to Ennis Whitehead in Kenney Papers on UN stationery placed within diary pages for March 1943.
18. D. Clayton James, *The Years of MacArthur* (Boston: 1975), II, 295. The number of vessels sunk in the Battle of the Bismarck Sea was the subject of a War Department

inquiry in the summer of 1943. Arnold was horrified when he heard about it and wrote to Kenney to say he was "shocked" that Kenney's figures were questioned. There would have been no investigation, said Arnold, had he not been on a foreign trip at the time it was launched: Letter, Arnold to Kenney, Oct. 11, 1943, Kenney Papers, loc. cit.

19. Larry Bland, ed., *George C. Marshall Reminiscences and Interviews* (New York: 1993).

20. Letters, Arnold to Kenney, Oct. 9, 7, 1943, Kenney Papers, loc. cit.; cf. Kenney, *The MacArthur I Know* (New York: 1951), 90–91.

21. Cables, Marshall to MacArthur, Sept. 6 and 8, 1943, and MacArthur to Marshall, Sept. 7 and 9, 1943, MMA.

22. Courtney Whitney, *MacArthur: His Rendezvous with History* (New York: 1955), 94; cf. the comment by one authority on "MacArthur's willingness to execute scheduled plans despite what ULTRA or other intelligence might reveal about the Japanese." Drea, 59.

23. Drea, 71.

24. SWPA GHQ communiqués, No. 326, March 4, and No. 329, March 7, 1943, MMA.

25. Byers diary, Feb. 6, 1943, Clovis Byers Papers, HI; John Hetherington, *Blamey: Controversial Soldier* (Canberra: 1973), 287; Horner, 248–251.

26. Cable, MacArthur to Marshall, Jan. 11, 1943, MMA.

27. George C. Marshall (Pogue interview), GCMF.

28. Letter, Wood to Krueger, Feb. 24, 1911, Leonard Wood Papers, MD, LC.

29. Letters, Bernard F. Dickman to George H. Dern, June 17, 1933, MacArthur to Dickman, June 19, 1933, and Frank Parker to Krueger, July 8, 1933, Walter Krueger Papers, Special Collections, USMA.

30. Letters, Stimson to Krueger, Oct. 13; Krueger to Stimson, Oct. 27, 1942, Krueger Papers, loc. cit. Days before leaving for Australia, Krueger had lunch with Stimson. Unfortunately neither man left a record of the conversation.

31. Krueger diary, Feb. 8, 1943, Krueger Papers, loc. cit.

32. Memo, Robert Eichelberger to Emmalina Eichelberger, Oct. 22, 1943, Robert Eichelberger Papers, Duke University; Jay Luvaas, ed., *"Dear Miss Em"* (Westport, Conn.: 1972), 68.

33. Letter, Eichelberger to Lesley J. McNair, May 18, 1943, Eichelberger Papers, loc. cit.; Byers diary, May 18, 1943, loc. cit.; cable, MacArthur to Marshall, Aug. 26, 1943, MMA. Cf. Paul Chwialkowski, *In Caesar's Shadow* (Westport, Conn.: 1993), 84.

34. Jules Archer, *The Plot to Seize the White House* (New York: 1966), 241.

35. Byers diary, Sept. 30, 1943, loc. cit.

36. Undated memo, George Brett to Kenney, filed with entries for July 1942, in Kenney's diary, loc. cit.

37. Kenney diary, Feb. 28, 1943, loc. cit.

38. Byers diary, Feb. 5, 1946, loc. cit.

39. Kenney diary, June 17, 1943, loc. cit. Kenney did not include this episode in the typed version of his diary, nor does it appear in *General Kenney Reports*. The clerk who typed the diary was thus not made privy to the most sensitive entries, and most of these holograph contributions were also withheld from the readers of Kenney's book. There is confirmation of Kenney's story, however, in Leslie Groves (Brower interview), 15–16, MMA.

40. Hugh J. Casey, *Engineer Memoirs* (Fort Belvoir, Va.: 1993), 195.

41. Gregory Franzwa and William Ely, *Leif Sverdrup* (Gerald, Mo.: 1980), 184.

42. Kenney, *The MacArthur I Know,* 57.

43. Douglas MacArthur, *Reminiscences* (New York: 1964), 157; "The greatest general the U.S. ever had"—Kenney diary, Sept. 15, 1943, loc. cit.
44. Kenney diary, Jan. 20, 1943, loc. cit.
45. SWPA GHQ press release, Jan. 24, 1943, MMA.
46. Letter, Arnold to MacArthur, July 6, 1943, MMA.
47. Memo, George Dern to John J. McSwain, Feb. 21, 1934, FDRL.
48. Philip Ziegler, *Mountbatten* (London: 1989), 225.
49. Kenney diary, Jan. 31, 1943, loc. cit.

20. Boom! Boom!

1. Courtney Whitney, *MacArthur: His Rendezvous with History* (New York: 1955), 99; Frazier Hunt, "The General and the Sergeant," *Saturday Evening Post* (May 13, 1944).
2. Sid Huff, *My Fifteen Years with General MacArthur* (New York: 1964), 94.
3. Whitney, 98.
4. Ibid., 100; cf. letter, Cornelius Greenway to MacArthur, Nov. 11, 1947, MMA.
5. Huff, 82.
6. Letter, Joe E. Brown to MacArthur, Oct. 28, 1943, MMA.
7. Whitney, 93.
8. Letter, MacArthur to Lord Gowrie, Feb. 18, 1943, MMA.
9. Albert C. Wedemeyer, *Wedemeyer Reports!* (Chicago: 1950), 206–207.
10. Kenney diary, March 17, 1943, George C. Kenney Papers, CAFH; George C. Kenney, *General Kenney Reports* (New York: 1949), 215–216.
11. John Miller, Jr., *Cartwheel: The Reduction of Rabaul* (Washington, D.C.: 1959), 12–16; Louis Morton, *Strategy and Command: The First Two Years* (Washington, D.C.: 1962), 390–399; D. M. Horner, *High Command* (Canberra: 1982), 255.
12. Lloyd Ross, *John Curtin* (Melbourne: 1977), 322; SWPA GHQ press release, April 14, 1943.
13. William F. Halsey and Joseph Bryan III, *Admiral Halsey's Story* (New York: 1947), 154–155; Kenney diary, April 27, 1943, loc. cit.
14. Daniel E. Barbey, *MacArthur's Amphibious Navy* (Annapolis, Md.: 1969), 24.
15. Geoffrey Perret, *There's a War to Be Won* (New York: 1991), 134–135.
16. Arthur Trudeau, *Engineer Memoirs* (Fort Belvoir, Va.: 1983), I, 102; Hugh J. Casey, *Engineer Memoirs* (Fort Belvoir, Va.: 1993), 207; William F. Heavey, *Down Ramp!* (Washington, D.C.: 1947), 48–51.
17. Byers diary, May 27, 1943, Clovis Byers Papers, HI.
18. Miller, 55–59.
19. Kenney diary, June 16, 1943, loc. cit.
20. Jay Luvaas, ed., *"Dear Miss Em"* (Westport, Conn.: 1972), 73; letter, Roosevelt to Kenney, Aug. 15, 1943, Kenney Papers, loc. cit.; cable, Roosevelt to MacArthur, Aug. 20, 1943, FDRL.
21. Letters, Eichelberger to MacArthur, Aug. 26, 1943, and MacArthur to Eichelberger, Aug. 29, 1943, MMA.
22. Kenney diary, Sept. 1, 1943, loc. cit.
23. James A. Huston, *Out of the Blue* (West Lafayette, Ind.: 1972), 220; W. L. Craven and J. L. Cate, eds., *The Army Air Forces in World War II* (Chicago: 1952), IV, 184–186; Gerald Devlin, *Paratrooper!* (New York: 1968), 262–265.
24. Morton, 440–442.
25. Letter, MacArthur to Louis Morton, March 5, 1953, Louis Morton Papers, USAMHI.

26. SWPA GHQ notes of memorandum, Sept. 10, 1943, MMA; letter, Kenney to Ennis C. Whitehead, Nov. 7, 1943, Kenney Papers, loc. cit.

27. Letter, Lewis Douglas to MacArthur, July 22, 1943, MMA; Robert W. Coakley and Richard M. Leighton, *Global Logistics and Strategy 1943–1945* (Washington, D.C.: 1968), 458.

28. Letter, MacArthur to George Van Horn Moseley, Nov. 8, 1943, MMA.

29. Letter, MacArthur to O'Laughlin, Oct. 26, 1943, John C. O'Laughlin Papers, MD, LC.

30. Barbey, 100.

31. George C. Marshall (Larson et al. interview), USAMHI; Geoffrey Perret, *Winged Victory* (New York: 1993), 262–282; Mark Clark, *Calculated Risk* (New York: 1951), 174–177.

32. Letters, Arnold to Kenney, July 5, 1943, Kenney Papers, loc. cit., and Robert E. Wood to MacArthur, Nov. 8, 1943, MMA.

33. Henry Godman, *Supreme Commander* (Harrison, Ark.: 1980), 52.

34. U.S. Strategic Bombing Survey, *The Fifth Air Force in the War Against Japan* (Washington, D.C.: 1946), 59; Lex McAuley, *Into the Dragon's Jaws* (Melbourne: 1990), 97; Edward Drea, *MacArthur's Ultra* (Lawrence, Kan.: 1992), 89–90.

35. Miller, 273–274; Kenney, *General Kenney Reports,* 327.

36. Letter, Kenney to Whitehead, Dec. 10, 1943, Kenney Papers, loc. cit.

37. Miller, 282–289.

38. Forrest C. Pogue, *George C. Marshall: Organizer of Victory 1943–1945* (New York: 1973), 373.

39. Douglas MacArthur, *Reminiscences* (New York: 1964), 183.

40. Kenney diary, Dec. 14, 1943, loc. cit.

41. Letter, Stephen J. Chamberlin to Krueger, Dec. 23, 1943, Walter Krueger Papers, Special Collections, USMA; Barbey, 120.

21. My Ku Klux Klan

1. Rogers mss. copy of *MacArthur and Sutherland,* 17/44, Paul Rogers Papers, MMA; Norman Carlyon (Cineworld interview), 8, MMA; George H. Johnston, *The Toughest Fighting in the World* (New York: 1944), 121–123.

2. Henry Godman, *Supreme Commander* (Harrison, Ark.: 1980), 60.

3. Sid Huff, *My Fifteen Years with General MacArthur* (New York: 1964), 89.

4. Memos, Edward P. Watson to Roosevelt and George C. Marshall to Thomas Handy, Jan. 24, 1944, GCMF; letter, Henry L. Stimson to MacArthur, Jan. 6, 1944.

5. George C. Kenney (Hasdorff interview), 58, HRA.

6. Frederic Smith (Hasdorff interview), 103–104, HRA.

7. John E. Hull (Wurman interview), 12, USAMHI.

8. Roger O. Egeberg, *The General* (New York: 1983), 7.

9. Eric Larrabee, *Commander in Chief* (New York: 1990), 307.

10. Kenney, 98.

11. Rogers memoir, "MacArthur's Clerks," n.p., Rogers Papers, loc. cit.; Philip La Follette, "With MacArthur in the Pacific," *Wisconsin Magazine of History* (Winter 1980–81). It is worth noting that Diller himself never claimed to have written the communiqués, only to have issued them.

12. Kenney diary, Nov. 25, 1942, George C. Kenney Papers, CAFH. In *General Kenney Reports,* 152, this put-down of Sutherland has been changed to "autocrat."

13. Paul Rogers, *MacArthur and Sutherland* (New York: 1989), I, 237; Egeberg, 38.

628 / *Notes*

14. William Manchester, *American Caesar* (Boston: 1978), 349.
15. Letter, Roger Egeberg to Paul Rogers, April 7, 1985, Rogers Papers, loc. cit. Cf. Samuel Anderson (Ahmann interview), 193, HRA.
16. Rogers, *MacArthur and Sutherland,* II, 69.
17. Godman, 62–63.
18. There is a file of correspondence between Diller, Egeberg and Rogers devoted largely to the origins and outcome of this affair in Rogers Papers, loc. cit. Cf. Clyde Eddleman (Smith and Swindler interview), 2, USAMHI.
19. Gregory Franzwa and William J. Ely, *Leif Sverdrup* (Gerald, Mo.: 1980), 107.
20. Edward Drea, *MacArthur's Ultra* (Lawrence, Kan.: 1992), 62; Clay Blair, *Silent Victory* (Philadelphia: 1962), 606.
21. Drea, 59.
22. Elliott Thorpe, *East Wind, Rain* (Boston: 1969), 95; Kenney (Hasdorff interview), 99, loc. cit.
23. Center of Military History, *U.S. Army Signals Intelligence in World War II* (Washington, D.C.: 1994), 214–221; Drea, 28–30; D. M. Horner, *High Command* (Canberra: 1982), 244–245.
24. Cable, MacArthur to Marshall, Aug. 6, 1943, MMA; cf. Anthony Cave Brown, *The Last Hero* (New York: 1986), 512–513; Corey Ford, *Donovan of OSS* (Boston: 1970), 253–254.
25. Courtney Whitney, *MacArthur: His Rendezvous with History* (New York: 1955), 91–92; Allison Ind, *Allied Intelligence Bureau* (New York: 1958), 174.
26. Emidgio Cruz (Brower interview), 2, MMA; Ind, 146–147.
27. William E. Dyess, *The Dyess Story* (New York: 1944), 13–16; Steve E. Mellnik, *Philippine Diary* (New York: 1969), 279–281; Ind, 174.
28. Cables, MacArthur to Marshall, July 28, 1944; Marshall to MacArthur, Oct. 7, 1943, MMA; Stanley Falk, *Bataan: The March of Death* (New York: 1962), 205–206.
29. Carlos Romulo (Cineworld interview), 4–5, MMA; Whitney, 133.
30. John Miller, Jr., *Cartwheel: The Reduction of Rabaul* (Washington, D.C.: 1959), 295–305.
31. Letter, MacArthur to Halsey, Sept. 11, 1943, MMA.
32. Byers diary, Jan. 26, 1944, Clovis Byers Papers, HI.
33. Memo, Robert Eichelberger to Emmalina Eichelberger, Oct. 22, 1943, Robert Eichelberger Papers, Duke University.
34. Byers, Jan. 26, 1944, loc. cit.
35. Louis Morton, *Strategy and Command: The First Two Years* (Washington, D.C.: 1961), 520.
36. Kenney (Hasdorff interview), 115, loc. cit.
37. Stetson Conn et al., *Guarding the United States and Its Outposts* (Washington, D.C.: 1964), Chapter 11.
38. Thomas Buell, *Master of Sea Power: Admiral Ernest King* (Boston: 1980), 319–320.
39. George C. Kenney, *The MacArthur I Know* (New York: 1951), 117.
40. Daniel E. Barbey, *MacArthur's Amphibious Navy* (Annapolis, Md.: 1969), 23–24.
41. Kenney, *The MacArthur I Know,* 98; George H. Decker (Ralls interview), 16, USAMHI.
42. Barbey, 183.
43. Robert Ross Smith, *The Approach to the Philippines* (Washington, D.C.: 1953), 8.
44. Kenney diary, Feb. 24, 1944, loc. cit.
45. Ibid., Feb. 25, 1944.
46. Eddleman, 25. Eddleman was Krueger's G-3. Cf. Barbey, 151.

47. Kenney diary, Feb. 26, 1944, loc. cit.
48. Walter Krueger, *From Down Under to Nippon* (New York: 1950), 49.
49. Eddleman, op. cit.; Krueger diary, Feb. 27, 1944, Walter Krueger Papers, USMA. "Krueger was not the type to voice his objections"—Barbey, 151.
50. Kenney diary, Feb. 26, 1944, loc. cit. This was Kenney's reasoning, and I believe he was right, although, as he remarked, "MacArthur may not even admit that is the way he is thinking to himself, but I have a hunch it applies."
51. Egeberg, 25.
52. Miller, 330–331.
53. *The New York Times,* March 1, 1944.
54. Kenney, *The MacArthur I Know,* 125.
55. D. Clayton James, *The Years of MacArthur* (Boston: 1975), II, 385.
56. SWPA GHQ press release, March 1, 1944.
57. Egeberg, 33.
58. Rhoades diary, March 1–2, 1944, Weldon Rhoades Papers, HI.

22. A New Kind of Warfare

1. William F. Halsey and Joseph Bryan III, *Admiral Halsey's Story* (New York: 1947), 188–189.
2. Letter, Kenney to Whitehead, March 6, 1944, George C. Kenney Papers, CAFH.
3. Letter, MacArthur to A. C. Smith, March 5, 1953, Center for Military History.
4. Douglas MacArthur, *Reminiscences* (New York: 1964), 169.
5. Kenney diary, Dec. 25, 1943, Kenney Papers, loc. cit.; Eichelberger Dictations, I/43, Robert Eichelberger Papers, Duke University.
6. Edward Drea, *MacArthur's Ultra* (Lawrence, Kan.: 1992), 92, 233.
7. Daniel E. Barbey, *MacArthur's Amphibious Navy* (Annapolis, Md.: 1969), 150–151; Hunt memoir, "A Short Biography of Bonner Fellers," Bonner Fellers Papers, HI.
8. Kenney to Whitehead, op. cit.
9. Cable, Marshall to MacArthur, March 9, 1944, GCMF.
10. Kenney diary, March 12 and 28, 1944, loc. cit.
11. Grace Pearson Hayes, *The JCS in World War II* (Annapolis, Md.: 1982), 559–560; D. Clayton James, *The Years of MacArthur* (Boston: 1975), II, 394–395. It is impossible to find out exactly what position the participants took in any JCS meeting, despite the fact that there are extensive records. The records were actually produced sometime after the meeting by the Joint Staff planners but were written to give the appearance of being verbatim accounts: Orvil A. Anderson (Shaughnessy interview), 49–50, HRA.
12. SWPA GHQ press release, March 17, 1944, MMA.
13. Lloyd Ross, *John Curtin* (Melbourne: 1977), 355 passim.
14. D. M. Horner, *High Command* (Canberra: 1982), 309–310.
15. George C. Kenney, *General Kenney Reports* (New York: 1949), 377.
16. Letter, MacArthur to O'Laughlin, Feb. 19, 1944, John C. O'Laughlin Papers, MD, LC.
17. Kenney diary, March 26, 1944, loc. cit.
18. Lewis H. Brown to Albert Bradley, June 24, 1943, Robert E. Wood Papers, HHL.
19. Kenney diary, March 17, 1943, loc. cit.; Kenney (Hasdorff interview), 85, HRA.
20. Arthur S. Vandenberg, Jr., *The Papers of Senator Vandenberg* (Boston: 1952), 79–80.
21. "Scope and Content Note," Wood Papers, loc. cit.; letter, Arthur Vandenberg to Charles Willoughby, Aug. 17, 1943, MMA; letter, Wood to Ernest T. Weir, March 22, 1944, Wood Papers, loc. cit.
22. Ickes diary, Nov. 27, 1943, Harold Ickes Papers, MD, LC.

23. Sid Huff, *My Fifteen Years with General MacArthur* (New York: 1964), 89; Byers diary, May 27, 1943, Clovis Byers Papers, HI; Jay Luvaas, ed., *"Dear Miss Em"* (Westport, Conn.: 1972), 71.
24. Letters, O'Laughlin to MacArthur, Oct. 7 and Dec. 23, 1943, O'Laughlin Papers, loc. cit.
25. Letter, Luce to MacArthur, Oct. 23, 1943, Clare Boothe Luce Papers, MD, LC.
26. Memo, Osborn to Stimson, Jan. 21, 1944, in Stimson diary, Feb. 18, 1944, Henry L. Stimson Papers, Sterling Library, Yale University.
27. Letters, Wood to MacArthur, Dec. 30, 1943; Wood to Philip La Follette, Dec. 30, 1943, Wood Papers, loc. cit.
28. Vandenberg, 83–84; letter, Wood to MacArthur, April 6, 1944, Wood Papers, loc. cit.
29. Letters, Miller to MacArthur, Sept. 18, 1943, MacArthur to Miller, Oct. 2, 1943, MMA.
30. Letter, A. L. Miller to MacArthur, Jan. 27, 1944, MMA.
31. Letter, MacArthur to Miller, Feb. 11, 1944, MMA.
32. James, II, 435–436.
33. Letter, MacArthur to Pershing, n.d. but evidently late July 1918, MMA. In this letter MacArthur thanked Pershing for his promotion to brigadier general and suggested the United States owed it to Pershing to put him into the White House after the war.
34. Letters, O'Laughlin to MacArthur, Oct. 14, 1937, O'Laughlin Papers, loc. cit.; Hugh Drum to MacArthur, June 29, 1936, MMA.
35. *The New York Times,* April 17, 1944.
36. *New York Herald Tribune,* March 12, 1948; letter, Wood to MacArthur, April 29, 1944, Wood Papers, loc. cit.
37. Letter, MacArthur to Perry L. Miles, June 12, 1944, MMA.
38. Maurice Matloff, *Strategic Planning for Coalition Warfare 1943–1945* (Washington, D.C.: 1959), 5.
39. Geoffrey Perret, *There's a War to Be Won* (New York: 1991), 435–436.
40. Kenney diary, April 8, loc. cit.; "History of I Corps," 18, RG 470, NA.
41. Robert Ross Smith, *The Approach to the Philippines* (Washington, D.C.: 1953), 42–48.
42. Barbey, 172.
43. Roger O. Egeberg, *The General* (New York: 1983), 49.
44. Anthony Cave Brown, *The Last Hero* (New York: 1987), 515–517.
45. Kenney diary, April 22, 1944, loc. cit.; Smith, 56–57.
46. Egeberg, 54.
47. Ibid., 53.
48. Eichelberger Dictations, I/18, loc. cit.; Krueger diary, April 22, 1944, Krueger Papers, USMA; SWPA GHQ diary, April 22, 1944, MMA.
49. Barbey, 173; Walter Krueger, *From down Under to Nippon* (Washington, D.C.: 1953), 18.
50. Luvaas, 106, 120.
51. Eichelberger diary, April 22, 1944, loc. cit.; Luvaas, 107, 142.
52. SWPA GHQ communiqué No. 745, April 24, 1944, MMA.

23. I Will Push on That Plan

1. Larry Bland and Sharon Ritenour, eds., *The Papers of George C. Marshall* (Baltimore: 1983), I, 536.
2. Letter, Eichelberger to Marie Byers, Oct. 16, 1943, Clovis Byers Papers, HI.

3. Letter, Marshall to MacArthur, Jan. 6, 1944, MMA.
4. Aubrey S. Newman, "The Power of Words in Messages and Orders," *Army* (April 1973); LeGrande A. Diller (Cineworld interview), 15–16, MMA.
5. Jay Luvaas, ed., *"Dear Miss Em"* (Westport, Conn.: 1972), 87.
6. *The New York Times,* Feb. 27, 1944.
7. SWPA GHQ press release, March 6, 1944, MMA.
8. Barbara Tuchman, *Stilwell and the American Experience in China* (New York: 1971), 463.
9. H. B. Sauvé, "Memoir," 35–37, Sauvé Papers, USAMHI.
10. Elliott Thorpe, *East Wind, Rain* (Boston: 1969), 119.
11. Paul Rogers, *MacArthur and Sutherland* (New York: 1989), I, 11.
12. Robert Ross Smith, *The Approach to the Philippines* (Washington, D.C.: 1959), 101–102.
13. George C. Kenney, *General Kenney Reports* (New York: 1949), 394–397.
14. Smith, 231.
15. Samuel E. Morison, *History of U.S. Naval Operations in World War II* (Boston: 1953), VIII, 107–108, 119–125.
16. SWPA GHQ communiqués, May 28 and June 3, 1944, MMA.
17. Cable, MacArthur to Krueger, June 5, 1944, MMA.
18. George Decker (Ralls interview), 22–23, USAMHI; letter, Krueger to MacArthur, June 8, 1944, Walter Krueger Papers, USMA.
19. Byers diary, June 15, 1944, Clovis Byers Papers, HI; D. Clayton James, *The Years of MacArthur* (Boston: 1975), II, 460.
20. Smith, 323.
21. Cable, MacArthur to Krueger, June 14, 1944, MMA.
22. Letter, Robert Eichelberger to Emmalina Eichelberger, June 16, 1944, Eichelberger Papers, Duke University; Luvaas, 121, 126.
23. Smith, 390–396.
24. SWPA GHQ diary, Aug. 11, 1944, MMA; "Memo of Interview with General MacArthur," Sept. 13, 1944, Eichelberger Papers, loc. cit.
25. Grace Pearson Hayes, *The JCS in World War II* (Annapolis, Md.: 1982), 606–609; Maurice Matloff and Edwin M. Snell, *Strategic Planning for Coalition Warfare, 1943–1945* (Washington, D.C.: 1961), 480–481.
26. Cable, MacArthur to Marshall, June 18, 1944, GCMF.
27. Stimson diary, June 22, 1944, Henry L. Stimson Papers, Sterling Library, Yale University.
28. Cable, Marshall to MacArthur, June 24, 1944, GCMF.
29. Cables, Marshall to MacArthur, July 6, 1944, MacArthur to Marshall, July 18, 1944, Marshall to MacArthur, July 19, 1944, MMA.
30. Rhoades diary, July 26, 1944, Weldon Rhoades Papers, HI.
31. Weldon Rhoades (Cineworld interview), 4–5, MMA.
32. Samuel Rosenman, *Working with Roosevelt* (New York: 1952), 456.
33. Ibid., 457.
34. Byers diary, Dec. 20, 1947, loc. cit.; William Leahy, *I Was There* (New York: 1950), 249–250.
35. Cables, Marshall to Richardson, July 7, 1942, and MacArthur to Richardson, July 8, 1942; letter, Richardson to MacArthur, Aug. 9, 1942, Robert C. Richardson Papers, HI; Eichelberger Dictations, Book 4, VIII-36, Eichelberger Papers, loc. cit.; minutes of conference, July 26, 1942, RG 165, NA.

36. Eichelberger, "Memo of Interview with General MacArthur," Eichelberger Papers, loc. cit.
37. M. Hamlin Cannon, *Leyte: The Return to the Philippines* (Washington, D.C.: 1954), 5.
38. Byers diary, Dec. 20, 1947, loc. cit.
39. Douglas MacArthur, *Reminiscences* (New York: 1964), 197; Byers diary, Dec. 20, 1947, loc. cit. I have also drawn on Marshall's June 24, 1944, letter to MacArthur because it seems to me that it contains much of King's arguments to Marshall, and it seems safe to bet that Nimitz, as King's mouthpiece, put the same arguments to Roosevelt.
40. MacArthur, 198.
41. Ibid.
42. Memo of conversation, May 4–6, 1946, Herbert Hoover Papers, HHL; Byers diary, loc. cit.
43. Eichelberger, "Memo of Interview with General MacArthur," loc. cit.
44. Courtney Whitney, *MacArthur: His Rendezvous with History* (New York: 1955), 125.
45. Letter, Roosevelt to MacArthur, Aug. 9, 1944, FDRL. The White House staff was convinced Roosevelt had been persuaded by MacArthur, and so was Nimitz: Cf. Robert Sherwood, *Roosevelt and Hopkins* (New York: 1950), II, 440–441; Forrest C. Pogue, *George C. Marshall: Organizer of Victory* (New York: 1973), III, 452; letter, John McCormack to MacArthur, July 20, 1945, MMA. Cf. Hayes, 611: "Mr. Roosevelt expressed a preference for the course outlined by General MacArthur and assured him that the Philippines would be taken."
46. W. L. Craven and J. L. Cate, eds., *The Army Air Forces in World War II* (Chicago: 1952), IV, 652–661; Smith, 397–421; Gerald Devlin, *Paratrooper!* (New York: 1979), 423–432.
47. Smith, 420–421.
48. Edward Drea, *MacArthur's Ultra* (Lawrence, Kan.: 1992), 152–153.
49. Daniel E. Barbey, *MacArthur's Amphibious Navy* (Annapolis, Md.: 1969), 227.
50. Cannon, 8–9; William Halsey and Joseph Bryan III, *Admiral Halsey's Story* (New York: 1947), 199–200; Pogue, III, 453–454.
51. Cable, MacArthur to Sutherland, Sept. 16, 1945, MMA.
52. MacArthur, 211.
53. Cable, JCS to MacArthur, Sept. 13, 1944, MMA.
54. Kenney diary, Sept. 16, 1944, Kenney Papers, CAFH; Francis C. Gideon (Cleary interview), 45–46, HRA. The fear of the Navy as the strongest factor behind this decision is spelled out in the diary, but it is not even hinted at in *General Kenney Reports,* 432, or his later account, *The MacArthur I Know,* 158–159, nor is it suggested in MacArthur's *Reminiscences,* 211–212. Cf. Henry H. Arnold, *Global Mission* (New York: 1949), 529–530.
55. James, II, 489.

24. Rally to Me

1. George C. Kenney, *The MacArthur I Know* (New York: 1952), 92.
2. Philip La Follette, "With MacArthur in the Pacific," *Wisconsin Magazine of History* (Winter 1980–81).
3. William Dunn, "The MacArthur Mansion and Other Myths," *Army* (March 1973); Elliott Thorpe (James interview), 5–8, MMA.
4. Daniel E. Barbey, *MacArthur's Amphibious Navy* (Annapolis, Md.: 1969), 232.

5. Kenney diary, Sept. 16, 1944, George C. Kenney Papers, CAFH.
6. Letter, Wood to MacArthur, Oct. 13, 1944, Robert E. Wood Papers, HHL.
7. Lloyd Ross, *John Curtin* (Melbourne: 1977), 274, 293, 306; D. M. Horner, *High Command* (Canberra: 1982), 186–196.
8. Rhoades diary, Sept. 30, 1944, Weldon Rhoades Papers, HI.
9. John E. Hull, memoir, 7–12, Hull Papers, USAMHI; Kenney diary, Aug. 8, 1944, loc. cit.
10. Kenney diary, Sept. 22, 1944, loc. cit.; letter, Richard J. Marshall to MacArthur, Sept. 28, 1944, MMA.
11. Robert W. Coakley and Richard M. Leighton, *Global Logistics and Strategy 1943–1945* (Washington, D.C.: 1968), 414–416; Kenney diary, Oct. 5, 1944, loc. cit.
12. Kenney diary, Sept. 10, 1944, loc. cit.
13. M. Hamlin Cannon, *Leyte: The Return to the Philippines* (Washington, D.C.: 1954), 35–36; Samuel D. Sturgis, "Engineering Operations in the Leyte Campaign," *Military Engineer* (Nov.–Dec. 1947).
14. William Dunn, *Pacific Microphone* (College Station, Texas: 1988), 243.
15. Kenney diary, Oct. 16 and 19, 1944, loc. cit.
16. Courtney Whitney, *MacArthur: His Rendezvous with History* (New York: 1955), 154.
17. Roger O. Egeberg, *The General* (New York: 1983), 66.
18. Letter, MacArthur to Jean MacArthur, Oct. 19, 1944, MMA.
19. Kenney diary, Oct. 19, 1944, loc. cit.
20. Douglas MacArthur, *Reminiscences* (New York: 1964), 215.
21. Whitney, 155.
22. Dunn, 5.
23. Gregory Franzwa and William Ely, *Leif Sverdrup* (Gerald, Mo.: 1980), 197–198; Egeberg, 80–81.
24. Eichelberger Dictations, I/54, Robert Eichelberger Papers, Duke University.
25. Dunn, 6.
26. Jean MacArthur interview, Tape 30, MMA; William Dunn (Cineworld interview), 4, MMA.
27. Whitney, 158.
28. Kenney, *The MacArthur I Know,* 164–165.
29. Kenney diary, Oct. 20, 1944, loc. cit.
30. Dunn, 9.
31. Proclamation, "To the People of the Philippines," Oct. 20, 1944, MMA.
32. Rhoades diary, Oct. 20, 1944, loc. cit.
33. Letter, MacArthur to Roosevelt, Oct. 20, 1944, FDRL.
34. Kenney diary, Oct. 20, 1944, loc. cit.
35. Dunn, 11.
36. Kenney, loc. cit.
37. SWPA GHQ special communiqué, Oct. 20, 1944, MMA.
38. Kenney diary, Oct. 21, 1944, loc. cit.
39. Rhoades diary, Oct. 21, 1944, loc. cit.
40. Egeberg, 70.
41. Kenney, *The MacArthur I Know,* 165–166.
42. Kenney diary, Oct. 22, 1944, loc. cit.
43. D. Clayton James, *The Years of MacArthur* (Boston: 1975), II, 560–561; Rhoades diary, Oct. 23, 1944, loc. cit.; Dunn, 245–246.
44. Kenney, *The MacArthur I Know,* 167.

45. Kenney diary, Oct. 23, 1944, loc. cit.
46. Whitney, 162.
47. Clark Reynolds, *The Fast Carriers* (New York: 1968), 275.
48. Egeberg, 74.
49. The most recent authoritative account is Thomas Cutler, *The Battle of Leyte Gulf* (New York: 1994). Still useful, however, are Samuel E. Morison, *Leyte: June 1944–January 1945* (Boston: 1958), and C. Vann Woodward, *The Battle for Leyte Gulf* (New York: 1947).
50. Kenney, *The MacArthur I Know,* 170.
51. Kenney diary, Oct. 25, 1944, loc. cit.
52. Ibid., Oct. 27, 1944; Kenney, *The MacArthur I Know,* 173.
53. James, II, 586; Jean MacArthur interview, Tape 30, MMA.
54. Letter, Charles Willoughby to Luce, Oct. 29, 1944, Clare Boothe Luce Papers, MD, LC; Franzwa and Ely, 195, 201; Jay Luvaas, ed., *"Dear Miss Em"* (Westport, Conn.: 1972), 172.
55. Letter, MacArthur to Arthur MacArthur, n.d. but approximately Nov. 5, 1944, MMA; Whitney, 161; Egeberg, 82. The MacArthur Memorial staff has dated this as "Probably Oct. 20, 1944," but this date is wrong by about two weeks.
56. Cannon, 92–96; Stanley Falk, *Decision at Leyte* (New York: 1966), 53–55, 104–108.
57. Walter Krueger, *From down Under to Nippon* (New York: 1950), 168–181; Cannon, 245–247.
58. Memo, MacArthur to Krueger, Nov. 20, 1944, Walter Krueger Papers, USMA.
59. Cannon, 283–287.
60. Luvaas, 176–177.
61. Byers diary, Feb. 5, 1946, Clovis Byers Papers, HI; Weldon Rhoades, *Flying MacArthur to Victory* (College Station, Texas: 1990), 285; Egeberg, 59.
62. Egeberg, 92–93.
63. Paul Rogers, *MacArthur and Sutherland* (New York: 1990), II, 211.
64. Rhoades diary, Dec. 18, 1944, loc. cit.; Luvaas, 179; La Follette, op. cit.
65. George C. Kenney, *Dick Bong: Ace of Aces* (New York: 1955), 86; Kenney diary, Dec. 12, 1944, loc. cit. MacArthur wrote out a longer speech in advance, which he reproduces in *Reminiscences,* 238, but Kenney says he did not use it.
66. Cable, MacArthur to Jean MacArthur, Dec. 25, 1944, MMA.

25. Go to Manila

1. A. E. Schanze, memoir, "This Is the Army," 21, Schanze Papers, USAMHI. Schanze was Eichelberger's aide.
2. M. Hamlin Cannon, *Leyte: The Return to the Philippines* (Washington, D.C.: 1954), 367.
3. Wesley F. Craven and James L. Cate, eds., *The Army Air Forces in World War II* (Chicago: 1952), V, 407–408.
4. Kenney diary, Nov. 30, 1944, George C. Kenney Papers, CAFH.
5. D. Clayton James, *The Years of MacArthur* (Boston: 1975), II, 606–607.
6. Robert Ross Smith, *Triumph in the Philippines* (Washington, D.C.: 1963), 52.
7. Ibid., 94.
8. Vincent L. Powers, "Reprints: Stories from GHQ Advance Echelon, Leyte-Luzon," 24–26, HSTL.
9. Letter, MacArthur to Jean MacArthur, Jan. 8, 1945, MMA; Roger O. Egeberg, *The General* (New York: 1983), 99–100.
10. Egeberg, 104.

11. Douglas MacArthur, *Reminiscences* (New York: 1964), 240.
12. Ibid., 238; letter, Krueger to Frank Kowalski, Jr., March 27, 1957, Walter Krueger Papers, USMA.
13. Clyde Eddleman (Smith and Swindler interview), 12, USAMHI.
14. James, II, 621.
15. Cable, MacArthur to Marshall, Jan. 17, 1945, MMA.
16. Gregory M. Franzwa and William J. Ely, *Leif Sverdrup* (Gerald, Mo.: 1980), 209–214; Egeberg, 105–106; Craven and Cate, V, 417–418.
17. Cables, Marshall to MacArthur, Jan. 16, 1945, GCMF; MacArthur to Kenney, January 18, 1944, Kenney Papers, loc. cit.; Krueger diary, Jan. 18, 1944, loc. cit.
18. Egeberg, 112–113.
19. Smith, 167–179, 202–206.
20. Memo, "Comments on 'Triumph in the Philippines,' " n.d., Krueger to the chief of military history, and "Douglas MacArthur," n.d., both in Krueger Papers, loc. cit.
21. Smith, 192–201.
22. Egeberg, 115; Jay Luvaas, ed., *"Dear Miss Em"* (Westport, Conn.: 1972), 198.
23. George Decker (Ralls interview), 16, USAMHI.
24. Kenney diary, Jan. 23, 1945, loc. cit.; letter, Robert Eichelberger to Emmalina Eichelberger, Jan. 23, 1945, Robert Eichelberger Papers, Duke University.
25. Kenney diary, Jan. 24, 1945, loc. cit. The plan consisted of having the parachute regiment drop in late afternoon to grab the airstrip. The glider regiments would have been flown in early on the second day, along with artillery.
26. Luvaas, 203–204.
27. Paul Chwialkowski, *In Caesar's Shadow* (Westport, Conn.: 1993), 115–117.
28. Kenney diary, Jan. 23, 1944, loc. cit.
29. Smith, 216–229; Gerald M. Devlin, *Paratrooper!* (New York: 1979), 690–694.
30. Memo, "The 11th Airborne Division's Dash to Manila and Facts Pertaining Thereto," Jan. 2, 1953, Eichelberger Papers, loc. cit.; MacArthur, 245; Smith, 266–269.
31. William Dunn, *Pacific Microphone* (College Station, Texas: 1992), 289.
32. Egeberg, 122–123.
33. Bertram C. Wright, *The 1st Cavalry Division in World War II* (Tokyo: 1947), 125–126; memo, Russell Brines, Jan. 4, 1948, MMA. The Brines memo consists of notes of conversations with MacArthur.
34. William C. Chase, *Front Line General* (Houston: 1975), 81–89. Chase commanded the 1st Cavalry's flying column.
35. James, II, 642–643; Philip La Follette, "With MacArthur in the Pacific," *Wisconsin Magazine of History* (Winter 1981–82); Courtney Whitney, *MacArthur: His Rendezvous with History* (New York: 1955), 188–189.
36. Paul L. Freeman (Ellis interview), 73–74, USAMHI; Egeberg, 131–132.
37. SWPA GHQ communiqué No. 1035, Feb. 6, 1945, MMA.
38. Egeberg, 135–136; MacArthur, 248.
39. MacArthur, 246.
40. SWPA GHQ diary, Feb. 7, 1945, MMA.
41. Egeberg, 143.
42. Smith, 266–269. In his *Reminiscences* MacArthur claimed he reached the hotel that day, but it was not regained by American troops until February 22. MacArthur's recollection of what happened when he reached Manila on February 7 consists of the events of a two-week period packed into a single day.
43. Charles Willoughby, ed., *The Reports of General MacArthur* (Washington, D.C.: 1966), I, 277–280.

44. Egeberg, 150.
45. Ibid.; James, II, 649–650.
46. Kenney diary, Feb. 7, 1945, loc. cit.
47. Letter, Krueger to Kowalski, op. cit.
48. Kenney diary, Feb. 19, 1945, loc. cit.; Craven and Cate, V, 431–434; Daniel E. Barbey, *MacArthur's Amphibious Navy* (Annapolis, Md.: 1969), 307.
49. Smith, 348–350.
50. Edward M. Flanagan, *The Los Baños Raid* (New York: 1987), 186–199.
51. Smith, 240.
52. George C. Kenney, *The MacArthur I Know* (New York: 1952), 98–99.
53. Byers diary, Feb. 5, 1945, Clovis Byers Papers, HI; Chase, 95.
54. Memo, LeGrande Diller to Paul Rogers, n.d., Rogers Papers, MMA.
55. MacArthur, 247; letter, Charles Willoughby to Luce, Feb. 23, 1945, Clare Boothe Luce Papers, MD, LC. Cf. Luvaas, 225—"The Big Chief has been in a very bad mood for a while. . . ."
56. Kenney diary, Feb. 19, 1945, loc. cit.; Smith, 300–301; Willoughby, I, 271–276; cf. Rafael Steinberg, *Return to the Philippines* (Alexandria, Va.: 1979), 106–149.
57. MacArthur, 251–252; Whitney, 191–192; James, II, 646–648.
58. Vorin E. Whan, ed., *A Soldier Speaks: Public Papers and Speeches of General of the Army Douglas MacArthur* (New York: 1965), 136; Barbey, 308.

26. It Will Terminate This Year

1. D. Clayton James, *The Years of MacArthur* (Boston: 1975), II, 659.
2. Letter, George D. Sears to MacArthur, Feb. 14, 1945, MMA; Jean MacArthur interview, Tape 31, MMA.
3. James, II, 659.
4. George C. Kenney, *The MacArthur I Know* (New York: 1952), 128.
5. Sid Huff, *My Fifteen Years with General MacArthur* (New York: 1964), 100.
6. Letter to the author from James Halsema, Nov. 19, 1993. Halsema was a prisoner at Bilibid: "Jean astonished us by her white gloves." Huff mistakenly says this happened at Santo Tomas.
7. Letters, Walter M. Harrison to Krueger, Dec. 18, 1945, George Decker Papers, USAMHI; Lee Caine to Jean MacArthur, March 25, 1945, and Robert L. Gillian to Jean MacArthur, March 25, 1945, MMA.
8. Roger O. Egeberg, *The General* (New York: 1983), 191.
9. Letter, Jean MacArthur to Douglas MacArthur, Jan. 26, 1945, MMA.
10. Egeberg, 168–170.
11. Clark Lee and Richard Henschel, *Douglas MacArthur* (New York: 1952), 75.
12. Frazier Hunt, "The General and the Sergeant," *Saturday Evening Post* (May 13, 1944).
13. Memo, Douglas Aircraft to director, Air Technical Services Command, Nov. 28, 1944, MMA; Donald Douglas (Shaughnessy interview), 34, Butler Library, Columbia University; letter, Victor Bertrandais to MacArthur, Jan. 4, 1945, MMA; Rhoades diary, April 19, 1945, Weldon Rhoades Papers, HI.
14. Rhoades diary, May 9, May 11, June 15, 1945, loc. cit.; Egeberg, 163.
15. Elliott Thorpe, *East Wind, Rain* (Boston: 1969), 151–153; Elliott Thorpe (Griffin interview), 60–61, Thorpe Papers, USAMHI.
16. Thorpe, *East Wind, Rain*, 164.
17. "Report of General Arthur MacArthur," *War Department Annual Report* (Washington, D.C.: 1901).

18. Affidavit sworn by Roy Howard, Oct. 29, 1945, Roy Howard Papers, MD, LC; Jesus Villamor, *Against All Odds* (Quezon City: 1989), 226–227.
19. David J. Steinberg, *Philippine Collaboration in World War II* (Ann Arbor: 1967), 32–33.
20. Rhoades diary, July 16, 1945, loc. cit.
21. Villamor, 134–135, 244–251; James, II, 598.
22. James, II, 692.
23. Edwin J. Ramsey, *Lieutenant Ramsey's War* (New York: 1992), 321–322; cf. Egeberg, 172.
24. Cable, Marshall to MacArthur, April 4, 1945, GCMF.
25. Forrestal diary, Feb. 28, 1945, James Forrestal Papers, Mudd Library, Princeton University.
26. Cornelius Vanderbilt Whitney, *The Lone and Level Sands* (New York: 1951), 312; letter, Willoughby to Luce, July 24, 1945, Clare Boothe Luce Papers, MD, LC.
27. Robert Ross Smith, *Triumph in the Philippines* (Washington, D.C.: 1963), 692; William H. Gill (War College interview), USAMHI.
28. SWPA GHQ proclamation, Oct. 23, 1944, MMA.
29. William Manchester, *American Caesar* (Boston: 1978), 428–429.
30. *The New York Times,* Dec. 29, 1941.
31. Roosevelt and Marshall explicitly sanctioned a liberation campaign in messages to MacArthur during the advance on Manila: cables, Roosevelt to MacArthur, Feb. 2, 1945, and Marshall to MacArthur, Feb. 7, 1945, MMA. Cf. Joseph Forbes, "General Douglas MacArthur and the Implementation of American and Australian Civilian Policy Decisions in 1944 and 1945," *Military Affairs* (Jan. 1985).
32. Jay Luvaas, ed., *"Dear Miss Em"* (Westport, Conn.: 1972), 260.
33. William H. Arnold (Stampe interview), 24, William H. Arnold Papers, USAMHI.
34. Letters, Curtin to MacArthur, Feb. 27, 1945; MacArthur to Curtin, March 5, 1945, MMA; Gavin Long, *The Final Campaigns* (Canberra: 1963), 42–43; D. M. Horner, *High Command* (Canberra: 1982), 394–395, 407–409; Kenney diary, Feb. 25, 1945, loc. cit.; Lloyd Ross, *John Curtin* (Melbourne: 1977), 376–377.
35. Kenney diary, March 16 and April 11, 1945, loc. cit.
36. Ibid., June 2, 1945.
37. Egeberg, 171; Walter A. Luszki, *A Rape of Justice* (Lanham, Md.: 1993), 115.
38. Luvaas, 278.
39. Kenney diary, June 10, 1945, loc. cit.
40. Kenney, *The MacArthur I Know,* 133–134; Courtney Whitney, *MacArthur: His Rendezvous with History* (New York: 1955), 196.
41. Egeberg, 177.
42. Whitney, 197; Egeberg, 178.
43. Daniel E. Barbey, *MacArthur's Amphibious Navy* (Annapolis, Md.: 1969), 319.
44. Whitney, op. cit.; Egeberg, op. cit.
45. Cable, Marshall to MacArthur, July 4, 1945, MMA; Kenney diary, July 5, 1945, loc. cit.
46. Edward J. Drea, *MacArthur's Ultra* (Lawrence, Kan.: 1992), 209–210. Cf. memo, "Sixth Army G-2 Estimate of the Enemy Situation with Respect to Olympic Operation," Aug. 1, 1945, Walter Krueger Papers, USMA.
47. Weldon Rhoades, *Flying MacArthur to Victory* (College Station, Texas: 1990), 386.
48. Robert Considine, *It's All News to Me* (New York: 1967), 343; Vincent C. Jones, *Manhattan: The Army and the Atomic Bomb* (Washington, D.C.: 1985), 534–535.
49. Leslie Groves (Brower interview), 6–7, MMA.

50. Halsema letter, op. cit.
51. Robert J. C. Butow, *Japan's Decision to Surrender* (Palo Alto, Calif.: 1954), 210–223.
52. Theodore White, *In Search of History* (New York: 1979), 224.
53. George C. Kenney (Stanley interview), 42, HRA.
54. Thorpe (Griffin interview), 61, loc. cit.

27. Big Number One

1. Truman diary, June 17, 1945, Harry S. Truman Papers, HSTL. Truman was not high-mindedly indifferent to medals. He told Wainwright and other recipients of the Medal of Honor that he would rather have that decoration than be president of the United States. He had also sought a Purple Heart for his service in World War I, even though there was no record of his ever having been wounded. See memo, AGO to Burdette M. Fitch, Aug. 25, 1939, RG 407, NA.
2. Truman diary, Aug. 10, 1945, loc. cit.
3. "Directive to the Supreme Commander for the Allied Powers," Aug. 14, 1945, MMA.
4. Jay Luvaas, ed., *"Dear Miss Em"* (Westport, Conn.: 1972), 301.
5. Memo, B. W. Davenport to Harry Vaughan, June 20, 1945, HSTL.
6. LeGrande A. Diller (Cineworld interview), 19, MMA; Philip Ziegler, *Mountbatten* (London: 1991), 302.
7. William D. Senter (Maryanow and Fuller interview), 116–118, HRA.
8. George C. Kenney, *The MacArthur I Know* (New York: 1952), 180.
9. Sid Huff, *My Fifteen Years with General MacArthur* (New York: 1964), 104–105.
10. Robert Eichelberger, *Our Jungle Road to Tokyo* (New York: 1955), 262; William Dunn, *Pacific Microphone* (College Station, Texas: 1988), 350.
11. Roger O. Egeberg, *The General* (New York: 1983), 202.
12. Ziegler, 301. The idea of having Wainwright participate in the surrender originated not with MacArthur but with Marshall. See cable, Marshall to MacArthur, Aug. 20, 1945, MMA. It appears that having Percival participate too was MacArthur's suggestion once it became clear that Wainwright was strong enough to travel to Tokyo.
13. Douglas MacArthur, *Reminiscences* (New York: 1964), 272; Egeberg, 205–206; Jonathan Wainwright, with Robert Considine, *General Wainwright's Story* (Garden City, N.Y.: 1946) 277; Elliott Thorpe, *East Wind, Rain* (Boston: 1969), 185–186; Dunn, 355.
14. Cable, MacArthur to Marshall, Aug. 1, 1942, GCMF; Stimson diary, Sept. 8, 1942, Henry L. Stimson Papers, Sterling Library, Yale University; Forrest C. Pogue, *George C. Marshall: Ordeal and Hope* (New York: 1966), 258–259; Duane Schultz, *Hero of Bataan* (New York: 1981), 332–336, 427–428.
15. Gordon Newell, *Mighty Mo* (Seattle: 1969), 45.
16. Jean MacArthur interview, Tape 30, MMA; Egeberg, 212, diplomatically calls it "a severe migraine."
17. Weldon Rhoades, *Flying MacArthur to Victory* (College Station, Texas: 1990), 452.
18. Dunn, 361.
19. Stilwell diary, Sept. 2, 1945, Joseph Stilwell Papers, HI.
20. Charles Willoughby, ed., *The Reports of General MacArthur* (Washington, D.C.: 1966), I, 455.
21. Kenney, 188.
22. Rhoades, 454.
23. *The New York Times,* Sept. 3, 1945.

24. Theodore White, *In Search of History* (New York: 1979), 230.

25. State Department, *The Axis in Defeat: A Collection of Documents on American Policy Toward Germany and Japan* (Washington, D.C.: 1945), 27–28. The surrender document was largely the work of John J. McCloy; see Kai Bird, *The Chairman* (New York: 1993), 260–262.

26. Mamoru Shigemitsu, *Japan and Her Destiny* (London: 1958), 375–377; SCAP, *Political Reorientation of Japan* (Washington, D.C.: 1949), II, 427; presidential press statement, Sept. 24, 1945, HSTL.

27. SCAP, *Political Reorganization of Japan* (Tokyo: 1949), I, 11–13.

28. Theodore Cohen and Herbert Passin, *Remaking Japan* (New York: 1987), 10–11. D. Clayton James, *The Years of MacArthur* (Boston: 1985), III, 11–12, claims that the crucial directive was "U.S. Initial Post-Surrender Policy for Japan," which was largely the work of the State Department. But Cohen, who served as a high-level official at GHQ SCAP from 1946 to 1949, firmly rejects this assertion—e.g., "I cannot remember anyone in GHQ ever referring to the State Department's policy paper."

29. William Sebald, *With MacArthur in Japan* (New York: 1965), 98.

30. MacArthur, 287.

31. Shigeru Yoshida, *The Yoshida Memoirs* (New York: 1960), 50–51; Richard Finn, *Winners in Peace: Yoshida and MacArthur* (Berkeley and Los Angeles: 1992), 23.

32. Faubion Bowers (Cineworld interview), 10, MMA.

33. Egeberg, 224–227; Rhoades diary, Sept. 27, 1945, Weldon Rhoades Papers, HI.

34. MacArthur, 288.

35. Finn, 24–25.

36. Katherine Sansome, *Sir George Sansome* (Tallahassee: 1972), 167; David Bergamini, *Japan's Imperial Conspiracy* (New York: 1971), 830; David Anson Titus, *Palace and Politics* (New York: 1974), 315–324.

37. Egeberg, 227.

38. Gaetano Faillace (Cineworld interview), 9, MMA.

39. Faubion Bowers, "The Late General MacArthur," *Esquire* (Jan. 1967).

40. Akira Matsui (Cineworld interview), 6–7, MMA.

41. Letter, Charles Willoughby to Luce, July 24, 1945, Clare Boothe Luce Papers, MD, LC.

42. Memo, Fellers to MacArthur, Oct. 2, 1945, MMA. In his memoirs MacArthur claimed the Soviets and the British were demanding that Hirohito be charged with war crimes. This is misleading in that neither the Soviet nor British government formally made such a demand. It came from people, like Mountbatten, who were expressing a personal view.

43. Finn, 189–190; Yoshida, 51. MacArthur later claimed that the pressure to try Hirohito came from the Soviets and the British, but the documentary record does not indicate that they did so. What seems to have happened is that individual Britons and Russians, such as Mountbatten and Derevyanko, expressed this view, but their governments did not.

44. Letter, Bonner Fellers to Arthur MacArthur, Sept. 8, 1945, MMA. Arthur was given two threads from this flag before it was sent back to the United States; cf. memo, Eichelberger to MacArthur, Sept. 7, 1945, MMA.

45. Byers diary, Sept. 8, 1945, Clovis Byers Papers, HI; Eichelberger, 264–265; William C. Chase, *Front Line General* (Houston: 1975), 130–131; Dunn, 367.

46. Courtney Whitney, *MacArthur: His Rendezvous with History* (New York: 1955), 226.

47. Jean MacArthur interview, Tape 30, 29–30, MMA.

48. Huff, 113; Whitney, 229.

49. Huff, 114; Bowers, "The Late General MacArthur."
50. Frank Sackton, "The Gentle Conqueror," *Army* (Sept. 1990).
51. Thorpe, 211; Elliott Thorpe (Griffin interview), 77, MMA.
52. Douglas B. Kendrick, *Memories of a 20th Century Army Surgeon* (Manhattan, Kan.: 1992), 132; Jean MacArthur interview, Tape 30, MMA.
53. Frank A. Sackton, remarks made during dedication of MacArthur statue, Aug. 21, 1970, MMA.
54. Letters, MacArthur to Blaik, April 28, 1945, and MacArthur to William L. Knapp, Sept. 6, 1949, Earl Blaik Papers, USMA.
55. Whitney, 236, presents a completely different picture, but John Gunther, *The Riddle of MacArthur* (New York: 1951), 47, is much closer to the truth: "Arthur has few playmates." Cf. Kenney, 256.
56. Kathryn Hardy (Brower interview), 4, Sept. 13, 1966, MMA.
57. Kendrick, 128–129; Huff, 128–129; Frank Sackton (Cineworld interview), 10, MMA; Gunther, 47.

28. Let History Decide

1. Letter, Willoughby to Luce, May 4, 1946, Clare Boothe Luce Papers, MD, LC.
2. James H. Polk (Tausch interview), 26, USAMHI.
3. Letters, Robert Eichelberger to Emmalina Eichelberger, Oct. 9 and 20, 1945, Robert Eichelberger Papers, Duke University.
4. Letter, Eisenhower to Bradford Chynoweth, March 7, 1946, Eisenhower Papers, EL; Stephen Ambrose, *Eisenhower* (New York: 1983), I, 430–432. Eichelberger was due to retire when he reached sixty-four, in March 1950. He could, like Ike, have been Chief of Staff for two years, after serving two years as deputy. That was what John Hines, Pershing's successor, had done in the 1920s. This would not have done any harm to the Marshall protégés Bradley and Collins, who were only fifty-two and forty-nine respectively when the war ended. Indeed, an extra couple of years might have made them better prepared to head the Army.
5. Cables, Handy to MacArthur, Nov. 21, 1945, MacArthur to Eisenhower, Nov. 22, 1945, Eichelberger to Eisenhower, Nov. 23, 1945, MMA.
6. Paul Chwialkowski, *In Caesar's Shadow* (Westport, Conn.: 1993), 159–160.
7. Memoir, "General MacArthur Coming and Going," 55, A. E. Schanze Papers, USAMHI; U. Alexis Johnson (Cineworld interview), 2, MMA.
8. Chwialkowski, 159.
9. Letter, "Chas" to Marne, Jan. 27, 1946, Walter Krueger Papers, USMA.
10. Memo, Byers to Eichelberger, Dec. 4, 1945, Clovis Byers Papers, HI; Weldon Rhoades, *Flying MacArthur to Victory* (College Station, Texas: 1990), 523.
11. Frank A. Sackton, remarks during dedication of MacArthur statue, Aug. 21, 1970, MMA.
12. Letter, Karl Compton to Truman, Oct. 4, 1945, Truman Papers, HSTL.
13. Charles Willoughby, ed., *The Reports of General MacArthur: MacArthur in Japan* (Washington, D.C.: 1966), IV, 174–187. Cf. Meirion and Susie Harries, *Sheathing the Sword* (New York: 1987).
14. Courtney Whitney, *MacArthur: His Rendezvous with History* (New York: 1955), 231.
15. Douglas MacArthur, *Reminiscences* (New York: 1964), 282.
16. D. Clayton James, *The Years of MacArthur* (Boston: 1985), III, 17. Where James is wrong is in the importance he gives to the "Initial Post-Surrender Policy for Japan,"

which was largely a State Department production. The directive MacArthur actually followed was JCS 1580/5, which was worded as a direct order from his military superiors and was considerably more detailed in its instructions.

17. Jim Bishop, *FDR's Last Year* (New York: 1974), 518.
18. SCAP, *Political Reorientation of Japan* (Washington, D.C.: 1949), I, 427, 796–806.
19. Gregory Franzwa and William Ely, *Leif Sverdrup* (Gerald, Mo.: 1980), 233; Roger O. Egeberg, *The General* (New York: 1983), 196.
20. MacArthur, 275–276.
21. Letters, Robert E. Wood to MacArthur, Sept. 4, 1945, and Bonner Fellers to Wood, Oct. 1, 1945; cable, MacArthur to Wood, Sept. 14, 1945, Robert E. Wood Papers, HHL.
22. Memo, Samuel Rosenman to Truman, Sept. 19, 1945, HSTL; Robert J. Donovan, ed., *The Diary of Eben Ayers* (New York: 1984), 81; *The New York Times*, Sept. 18 and 23, 1945; Dean Acheson, *Present at the Creation* (New York: 1969), 126.
23. State Department, *Foreign Relations of the United States, 1945* (Washington, D.C.: 1969), VI, 715–720.
24. Cable, Marshall to MacArthur, Sept. 17, 1945, MMA; Harry S. Truman, *Memoirs* (Garden City, N.Y.: 1956), II, 520–521; MacArthur had no doubts that the message to return home had really come from the President: Eichelberger diary, Feb. 5, 1946, Robert Eichelberger Papers, loc. cit.
25. John Gunther, *The Riddle of MacArthur* (New York: 1951), 6.
26. James, III, 23.
27. Ickes diary, March 30, 1942, Harold Ickes Papers, MD, LC.
28. Walter Isaacson and Evan Thomas, *The Wise Men* (New York: 1986), 333; Faubion Bowers, "The Late General MacArthur," *Esquire* (Jan. 1967); Thomas T. Handy (Knoff interview), IV, 37–40, Thomas T. Handy Papers, USAMHI.
29. Letter, Harry H. Vaughan to MacArthur, Nov. 15, 1946, MMA; Vaughan (Henle interview), 29, HHL.
30. Letters and cables, Eisenhower to MacArthur, Jan. 2, Jan. 28, Feb. 12, Oct. 25, Nov. 8, 1946, May 13, 1947, Dwight D. Eisenhower Papers, EL.
31. Letter, Lucius Holbrook to MacArthur, Aug. 7, 1949, and cables, Eisenhower to MacArthur and MacArthur to Eisenhower, both dated Aug. 13, 1946, MMA.
32. Letter, Eisenhower to Jean MacArthur, Feb. 8, 1946, Eisenhower Papers, loc. cit.
33. Memo, MacArthur to Eisenhower, n.d. but Oct. 1946; letter, May 13, 1947, MMA.
34. Bowers, op. cit.; cable, MacArthur to Eisenhower, May 4, 1946, MMA.
35. Peter Lyon, *Eisenhower the Hero* (Boston: 1977), 372–373; James, III, 194–195.
36. Letter, Eisenhower to MacArthur, Dec. 7, 1948, Eisenhower Papers, loc. cit.; cf. cable, Eisenhower to MacArthur, May 19, 1946, MMA: "I shall always treasure [the] old friendships with you and your family."
37. Bowers, op. cit.
38. James, III, 43.
39. Justin Williams, *Japan's Political Revolution Under MacArthur* (Athens, Ga.: 1979), 89.
40. Justin Williams (Cineworld interview), 10, MMA; Edward Almond (Fergusson interview), II, 73, USAMHI.
41. Williams, *Japan's Political Revolution*, 75.
42. The official Army history, Harry L. Coles and Albert K. Weinberg, *Soldiers Become Governors* (Washington, D.C.: 1966), does not even attempt to deal with the occupation of Japan, a reflection of how thoroughly MacArthur froze out the civil affairs personnel.

43. Theodore Cohen, *Remaking Japan* (New York: 1987), 79.

44. Shigeru Yoshida, *The Yoshida Memoirs* (New Haven: 1960), 6; John Dower, *Empire and Aftermath* (Cambridge, Mass.: 1979), 323; Richard Finn, *Winners in Peace: Yoshida and MacArthur* (Berkeley and Los Angeles: 1992), 23; Akira Matsui (Cineworld interview), 8, MMA.

45. State-War-Navy Coordinating Committee [SWNCC], "Reform of the Japanese Governmental System," in State Department, *Foreign Relations of the United States, 1945* (Washington, D.C.: 1946), VIII, 99–101; Finn, 90–92; Charles Kades (Cineworld interview), 5, MMA.

46. SCAP, I, 622–623.

47. Ibid., 102, 750.

48. Yoshida, 137; cf. Williams, 42, and Whitney, 257–258.

49. Kyoko Inoue, *MacArthur's Japanese Constitution* (Chicago: 1991), 266–270.

50. Dower, 320–321; Finn, 114–115.

51. MacArthur, 301.

52. "U.S. Initial Post-Surrender Policy for Japan," State Department *Bulletin* (13) (1945), 423–427; memo, Leahy to JCS, Sept. 6, 1945, RG 218, NA.

53. Meirion and Susie Harries, *Soldiers of the Sun* (New York: 1991), 463; James, III, 97–98.

54. Richard Lael, *The Yamashita Precedent* (Wilmington, Del.: 1982), 116.

55. Finn, 339.

56. *In Re Yamashita,* 327 U.S. Reports 1 (1946), 28.

57. SCAP press release, Feb. 5, 1946, MMA.

58. MacArthur, 296. According to Paul Rogers, MacArthur had told Sutherland, "I'm going to try Homma, and then I will hang him," but Sutherland offered no evidence to support this assertion. Paul P. Rogers, *MacArthur and Sutherland* (New York: 1988), II, 14.

59. Averell Harriman, *Special Envoy* (New York: 1984), 554.

60. Elliott Thorpe, *East Wind, Rain* (Boston: 1969), 197.

61. Elliott Thorpe (Griffin interview), 65–66, USAMHI.

62. SCAP press release, Nov. 24, 1948, MMA; William Sebald, *With MacArthur in Japan* (New York: 1965), 167–172.

63. Cf. Richard H. Minear, *Victor's Justice* (Princeton: 1971); Lawrence Taylor, *A Trial of Generals* (South Bend, Ind.: 1981).

64. Letter, Stone to Sterling Carr, Dec. 4, 1945, Harlan Fiske Stone Papers, MD, LC.

29. Ten Thousand Angels

1. Elliott Thorpe, *East Wind, Rain* (Boston: 1969), 164.

2. David Joel Steinberg, *Philippine Collaboration in World War II* (Ann Arbor: 1967), 146.

3. Cable, Paul Steindorf to Truman, June 25, 1946, HSTL.

4. Douglas B. Kendrick, *Memoirs of a 20th Century Army Surgeon* (Manhattan, Kan.: 1992), 143.

5. John Gunther, *The Riddle of MacArthur* (New York: 1951), 46; William Sebald, *With MacArthur in Japan* (New York: 1965), 107–108; John M. Allison, *Ambassador from the Prairie* (Boston: 1975), 168.

6. Courtney Whitney, *MacArthur: His Rendezvous with History* (New York: 1955), 234; Edward Almond (Brower interview), 7–8, MMA.

7. Frank Sackton (Cineworld interview), 8–9, MMA.

8. "Clinical Records, 1900–1952," in DM 201 File, MMA.
9. Hugh J. Casey, *Engineer Memoirs* (Fort Belvoir, Va.: 1993), 274; Carl Mydans (Cineworld interview), 10.
10. Russell Brines, *MacArthur's Japan* (Philadelphia: 1948), 65.
11. Kendrick, 157–158.
12. Memos, W. S. Paul to Burdette M. Fitch, Oct. 3, 1946, MMA; Kenneth S. Royall to Truman, July 8, 1948, HSTL.
13. Letter, MacArthur to J. Lawton Collins, March 7, 1950, MMA.
14. SCAP press statement, March 15, 1947, MMA.
15. Theodore Cohen, *Remaking Japan* (New York: 1987), 68.
16. Brines, 63.
17. George C. Kenney, *The MacArthur I Know* (New York: 1952), 252.
18. SCAP, *History of Non-Military Activities* (Tokyo: 1950), XIV, 8.
19. Kenney, 245.
20. Shigeru Yoshida, *The Yoshida Memoirs* (New Haven: 1960), 148–155; John Dower, *Empire and Aftermath* (Cambridge, Mass.: 1979), 294.
21. Letter, MacArthur to Wood, Jan. 12, 1948, Robert E. Wood Papers, HHL; Richard Finn, *Winners in Peace: MacArthur and Yoshida* (Berkeley and Los Angeles: 1992), 83; Charles Kades (Cineworld interview), 6, MMA. Cf. SCAP, *The Purge 1945–1951* (Tokyo: 1952) and Hans H. Baerwald, *The Purge of Japanese Leaders* (Berkeley and Los Angeles: 1959), 80.
22. Letter, MacArthur to the Adjutant General, Nov. 19, 1946; cables, MacArthur to the Adjutant General, Jan. 24, 1947, the Adjutant General to MacArthur, Jan. 28 and March 1, 1947, MMA.
23. Roger Baldwin, "MacArthur: Man and Mission," *The Progressive* (May 1951).
24. Peggy Lamson, *Roger Baldwin* (Boston: 1976), 246.
25. Ibid., 247.
26. Letter, MacArthur to John Haynes Holmes, Dec. 30, 1949, Roger Baldwin Papers, Mudd Library, Princeton University.
27. Letter, MacArthur to Paul Marella, March 3, 1947, MMA.
28. Cable, MacArthur to American Bible Society, Nov. 27, 1947; letter, MacArthur to Howard H. Hamlin, May 31, 1950, MMA.
29. Brines, 69.
30. Elliott Thorpe (Griffin interview), 70–71, USAMHI.
31. Memo, Hoover to MacArthur, Nov. 12, 1945, HHL.
32. Yoshida, 80; Finn, 51.
33. Douglas MacArthur, *Reminiscences* (New York: 1964), 307; cable, MacArthur to Eisenhower, May 21, 1946, MMA.
34. Jon Halliday, *A Political History of Japanese Capitalism* (New York: 1975), 192.
35. Finn, 131.
36. Cohen, 71.
37. Letters, Matthew Woll to MacArthur, Dec. 11, 1946, and Jan. 24, 1947; MacArthur to Woll, Jan. 7, 1947. Woll was a vice-president of the AFL.
38. SCAP, *Missions and Accomplishments in the Economic and Scientific Fields* (Tokyo: 1950), 41–43.
39. Cohen, 288–295; Finn, 141–142; MacArthur, 308–309; Yoshida, 81.
40. George Kennan, *Memoirs* (Boston: 1967), I, 190.
41. Letters, Irvin R. Kuenzli to MacArthur, May 19, 1949, MacArthur to Kuenzli, June 5, 1949, MMA.
42. Quoted in Finn, 57.

43. Sebald, 72–74; Finn, 37.
44. *Newsweek* (Jan. 27, 1947); *Fortune* (April 1949).
45. Letter, MacArthur to Hoover, Oct. 7, 1947, HHL; SCAP press release, Jan. 1, 1948, MMA.
46. SCAP, *Political Reorientation of Japan* (Tokyo: 1949), I, 765–766.
47. Forrestal diary, Oct. 21, 1947, James Forrestal Papers, Mudd Library, Princeton University.
48. Kennan, I, 376, 389.
49. State Department, *Foreign Relations of the United States, 1948* (Washington, D.C.: 1973), VI, 638–642. For criticisms of MacArthur's "insubordination" see Finn, 206, and Schaller, 137–139.
50. Memo of conversations, May 4–6, 1946, Herbert Hoover Papers, HHL.
51. Letters, Hoover to MacArthur, Oct. 17, 1946, and MacArthur to Hoover, Oct. 31, 1946, HHL.
52. Gunther, 53; Faubion Bowers (Cineworld interview), 9, MMA.
53. Carl Mydans (Cineworld interview), 19–20, MMA.
54. Cyrus L. Sulzberger, *A Long Row of Candles* (New York: 1967), 560–562, 610. Sulzberger thought him "earnest, decent, hopeful . . . [with] a certain amount of rather long-range thinking and a good deal of highly impractical poppycock."
55. John Bright Holmes, ed., *Like It Was: The Diaries of Malcolm Muggeridge* (London: 1981), 234–235; Ian Hunter, *Malcolm Muggeridge* (Nashville, Tenn.: 1981), 161.
56. Weldon Rhoades, *Flying MacArthur to Victory* (College Station, Texas: 1990), 526.
57. Letter, Frayne Baker to Edward R. Murrow, April 26, 1947, MMA; Gunther, 67.
58. Sebald, 111. See Justin Williams, *Japan's Political Revolution Under MacArthur* (Athens, Ga.: 1979), 267–268, and William Coughlin, *Conquered Press* (Palo Alto, Calif.: 1952), 111–145.
59. Cable, MacArthur to War Department, July 24, 1957, MMA.
60. Letter, MacArthur to Wood, Wood Papers, loc. cit.
61. *The New York Times,* Jan. 24, 1948.
62. Finn, 159.
63. *The New York Times,* March 9, 1948.
64. Richard Norton Smith, *Thomas E. Dewey and His Times* (New York: 1989), 349.
65. Sebald, 106.
66. Letter, MacArthur to Wood, April 29, 1948, Wood Papers, loc. cit.
67. Letter, Philip F. La Follette to Jean MacArthur, Sept. 3, 1948, MMA.
68. Memo, Norbert Bogdan to MacArthur, April 1, 1948, MMA.
69. Jean Smith, *Lucius D. Clay* (New York: 1991), 525.

30. With One Arm Tied Behind My Back

1. William Sebald, *With MacArthur in Japan* (New York: 1965), 45–46.
2. Elliott Thorpe (Griffin interview), 72, USAMHI; Douglas MacArthur, *Reminiscences* (New York: 1964), 285.
3. Harry S. Truman, *Memoirs* (Garden City, N.Y.: 1956), I, 439–457, 457–458.
4. D. M. Horner, *High Command* (Canberra: 1982), 422–432.
5. Forrestal diary, Oct. 26, 1945, James Forrestal Papers, Mudd Library, Princeton University.
6. Letter, John J. McCloy to MacArthur, Nov. 15, 1945, MMA.
7. Truman, I, 600.
8. John Gunther, *The Riddle of MacArthur* (New York: 1951), 21.

9. Verne Newton, *The Cambridge Spies* (Lanham, Md.: 1991), 274; Andrew Boyle, *The Climate of Treason* (London: 1979), 358–359; Sebald, 147–150. Sebald, a Japanese-speaking diplomat on assignment from the State Department, was MacArthur's political adviser and chairman of the ACJ.

10. Douglas B. Kendrick, *Memoirs of a 20th Century Army Surgeon* (Manhattan, Kan.: 1992), 229.

11. Courtney Whitney, *MacArthur: His Rendezvous with History* (New York: 1955), 306.

12. Gunther, 22.

13. D. Clayton James, *The Years of MacArthur* (Boston: 1985), III, 268–270.

14. Letter, Bradley to MacArthur, June 3, 1949, MMA.

15. Letter, MacArthur to Bradley, June 16, 1949, MMA; Omar Bradley, with Clay Blair, *A General's Life* (New York: 1982), 526.

16. Letters, MacArthur to Tracy Voorhees, June 16, 1949, Voorhees to MacArthur, Aug. 3, 1949; and MacArthur to Acheson, June 16, 1949, Acheson to MacArthur, Sept. 9, 1949, J. Lawton Collins to MacArthur, Sept. 16, 1949, MMA.

17. Memo of conversations between General MacArthur and W. A. Harriman, Aug. 6, 1950, HSTL.

18. Dean Rusk, *As I Saw It* (New York: 1984), 124.

19. Edward Almond (Fergusson interview), II, 11, USAMHI; J. Lawton Collins, *War in Peacetime* (New York: 1969), 28. Almond personally delivered this message to Forrestal and the JCS.

20. Dean Acheson, *Present at the Creation* (New York: 1969), 356–357.

21. Cyrus L. Sulzberger, *A Long Row of Candles* (New York: 1967), 562–563.

22. Letter, Bradley to MacArthur, May 20, 1948, MMA.

23. Letter, Bradley to MacArthur, Feb. 13, 1950, MMA; Bradley, with Blair, 529; Almond (Fergusson interview), 15–16, loc. cit.; Earl Partridge (Sturm and Ahmann interview), 548–549, HRA.

24. Jack Anderson, *Confessions of a Muckraker* (New York: 1979), 141–144. Even Anderson, Pearson's assistant, conceded that Pearson played a major role in driving Forrestal to suicide.

25. Letter, Bradley to MacArthur, Feb. 13, 1950, MMA; Bradley, with Blair, 529; Almond, op. cit.

26. *Time* (June 5, 1950).

27. James, III, 419–420; Whitney, 315–316.

28. See Philip Meilinger, *Hoyt S. Vandenberg* (Bloomington, Ind.: 1989), an admiring biography but one that makes no claims for Vandenberg the strategic thinker.

29. Earl Partridge (Reynolds interview), 44–45, HRA.

30. Roy E. Appleman, *South to the Naktong, North to the Yalu* (Washington, D.C.: 1961), 17–18.

31. John Allison, *Ambassador from the Prairie* (Boston: 1973), 136.

32. State Department memo of conversation, June 25, 1950, HSTL.

33. Allison, 137.

34. Truman, II, 383.

35. Partridge (Reynolds interview), 39, loc. cit. Partridge commanded the Fifth Air Force and was in the teleprinter room at the time. There is confirmation of his story in Clyde Eddleman (Smith and Swindler interview), 2, Eddleman Papers, USAMHI.

36. Sebald, 189n.; Marguerite Higgins, *War in Korea* (New York: 1952), 31–32.

37. U.S. Senate, Judiciary Committee, *Interlocking Subversion in Government Departments,* Eighty-third Congress, Second Session (Washington, D.C.: 1954), XXV, 2060–2061; Almond (Fergusson interview), 13–14, loc. cit.

38. J. Lawton Collins, *Lightning Joe* (Baton Rouge: 1973), 360–361; Almond, op. cit.
39. Truman diary, June 30, 1950, Harry S. Truman Papers, HSTL.
40. Barton J. Bernstein, "New Light on the Korean War," *International History Review* (April 1981).
41. D. Clayton James, *Refighting the Last War* (New York: 1991), 33–34.
42. Collins, *War in Peacetime,* 81–84; Sebald, 191.
43. Otto P. Weyland (Hasdorff interview), 191, HRA; Bradley, with Blair, 539, 543.
44. Garrison Davidson, memoir, "Grandpa Gar," 118–119, Garrison Davidson Papers, USMA.
45. Almond (Fergusson interview), 21–22, loc. cit. Almond was with Walker and MacArthur during this meeting. No one else was present.
46. Appleman, 207–208.
47. Cable, MacArthur to Marshall, Dec. 10, 1941, MMA.
48. Lemuel C. Shepherd (Heinl and Frank interview), 140, Marine Corps Historical Center; Robert Heinl, *Victory at High Tide* (New York: 1964), 19.
49. Letter, Truman to Gordon L. McDonough, Aug. 29, 1950, HSTL.
50. Rudy Abramson, *Spanning the Century* (New York: 1992), 451; MacArthur, 340.
51. Vernon Walters, *Silent Missions* (Boston: 1992), 197. Walters was present, as Harriman's note taker.
52. Memo, "Conference in the Office of CINCFE," Aug. 8, 1950, and "Memorandum of Conversations—General MacArthur and W. A. Harriman," n.d., HSTL.
53. Heinl, 24.
54. Collins, *War in Peacetime,* 123.
55. MacArthur, 350.
56. Heinl, 42.
57. Cable, JCS to MacArthur, Aug. 28, 1950, MMA.
58. Lemuel Shepherd (Brower interview), 12, MMA.
59. Shepherd (Heinl and Frank interview), 160–161, loc. cit.

31. We're Going Home

1. Robert Ferrell, ed., *Off the Record: The Private Papers of Harry S. Truman* (New York: 1980), 108 passim.
2. James F. Schnabel and Robert J. Watson, *History of the Joint Chiefs of Staff: The Korean War* (Wilmington, Del.: 1979), I, 551.
3. Edward Almond (Fergusson interview), 65–67, Almond Papers, USAMHI.
4. William Sebald, *With MacArthur in Japan* (New York: 1965), 122.
5. Harry S. Truman, *Memoirs* (Garden City, N.Y.: 1956), I, 353–354.
6. State Department memo of conversation, Aug. 4–6, HSTL; George C. Kenney (Hasdorff interview), 119, HRA; Sebald, 189.
7. D. Clayton James, *The Years of MacArthur* (Boston: 1985), III, 458.
8. *The New York Times,* Aug. 29, 1950.
9. Truman diary, April 6, 1951, Harry S. Truman Papers, HSTL.
10. Truman, *Memoirs,* II, 355–356; Douglas MacArthur, *Reminiscences* (New York: 1964), 351–352.
11. Cable, MacArthur to Louis Johnson, Aug. 27, 1950, HSTL.
12. David McCullough, *Truman* (New York: 1993), 800–801; Omar Bradley, with Clay Blair, *A General's Life* (New York: 1983), 572; Cabell Phillips, *The Truman Presidency* (New York: 1966), 318–322; Robert J. Donovan, *Tumultuous Years* (New York: 1977), 284.

13. Dean Acheson, *Present at the Creation* (New York: 1969), 456.
14. Cable, Marshall to MacArthur, n.d. but about Oct. 8, 1951, marked "War Department message 93678," MMA; Harry S. Truman, *Public Papers, 1950* (Washington, D.C.: 1965), 665–666.
15. Courtney Whitney, *MacArthur: His Rendezvous with History* (New York: 1955), 385; William Manchester, *American Caesar* (Boston: 1978), 588–596.
16. Merle Miller, *Plain Speaking: An Oral Biography of Harry S. Truman* (New York: 1973), 294–295.
17. John Edward Wiltz, "Truman and MacArthur: The Wake Island Meeting," *Military Affairs* (Dec. 1978).
18. Elmer F. Smith (Hasdorff interview), 58–59, HRA; "Log of President Truman's Trip to Wake Island, Oct. 11–18, 1951," HSTL. Smith was Truman's pilot.
19. Memo for record, "Wake Island," April 6, 1951, HSTL; Vernon Walters, *Silent Missions* (New York: 1983), 204–205.
20. Truman, *Memoirs,* II, 365; MacArthur, 361.
21. Whitney, 387.
22. Walters, 206.
23. Memo, "Substance of Statements Made at Wake Island Conference on Oct. 15, 1950," compiled by Omar Bradley, HSTL.
24. K. M. Pannikar, *In Two Chinas* (London: 1955), 109–110.
25. Truman, *Memoirs,* II, 363.
26. Dean Rusk, *As I Saw It* (New York: 1984), 168–169.
27. Philip C. Jessup, "The Record of Wake Island—A Correction," *Journal of American History* (March 1981).
28. Whitney, 395; Manchester, 590; Truman, *Memoirs,* II, 365.
29. Vernice Anderson (Hess interview), 10–11, HSTL.
30. *The Washington Post,* May 4, 1951.
31. Truman, *Memoirs,* II, 398.
32. State Department, *Foreign Relations of the United States, 1950* (Washington, D.C.: 1976), VII, 781–782.
33. J. Lawton Collins, *War in Peacetime* (Boston: 1969), 367–370; Bradley, with Blair, 568.
34. Cables, Marshall to MacArthur, Sept. 29, 1950, and MacArthur to Marshall, Sept. 30, 1950, MMA.
35. Barton J. Bernstein, "New Light on the Korean War," *International History Review* (April 1981).
36. Truman, *Memoirs,* II, 362.
37. Schnabel and Watson, I, 274.
38. Cable, JCS to MacArthur, Oct. 21, 1950, MMA.
39. Cable, MacArthur to JCS, Oct. 24, 1950, MMA.
40. Roy Appleman, *Disaster in Korea* (College Station, Texas: 1992), 13–14.
41. James, III, 519.
42. MacArthur, 369–370.
43. FEC GHQ special communiqué, Nov. 6, 1950, MMA.
44. Appleman, 57.
45. MacArthur, 373.
46. Billy C. Mossman, *Ebb and Flow: November 1950–July 1951* (Washington, D.C.: 1990), 61–104.
47. State Department, *Foreign Relations of the United States, 1950,* VII, 1237–1238.
48. Collins, 232.

49. Robert F. Futrell, *The U.S. Air Force in Korea 1950–1953* (Washington, D.C.: 1983), 271 passim.
50. Cable, Ridgway to MacArthur, Feb. 2, 1951, MMA; Clay Blair, *The Forgotten War* (New York: 1987), 553.
51. Matthew B. Ridgway (Blair interview), III, 84, USAMHI.
52. Truman diary, Nov. 25, 1950, loc. cit.
53. *U.S. News & World Report* (Dec. 1, 1951); cable, JCS to MacArthur, Dec. 8, 1951, MMA; Truman, *Memoirs,* II, 435–437.
54. Sebald, 221.
55. Truman, *Memoirs,* II, 493–495.
56. Schnabel and Watson, I, 439–440.
57. MacArthur, 383; Robert Smith, *MacArthur and the Korean War* (New York: 1982), 125–126; cf. Ridgway (Blair interview), III, 79, loc. cit.
58. *The New York Times* (March 24, 1951). The message sent to MacArthur by Truman after this event was remarkable for its blandness. He was merely reminded of the existing "gag" order: cable, JCS to MacArthur, March 24, 1951, HSTL.
59. Whitney, 468, hints as much in his account of this affair. Even if MacArthur had known he would be fired, says Whitney, "he still would not have been deterred."
60. Memo for record, "The MacArthur Dismissal," April 28, 1951, HSTL.
61. Letter, MacArthur to Martin, March 20, 1951, MMA.
62. Truman diary, April 5, 1951, loc. cit. Cf. Truman, *Memoirs,* II, 447–448; Dean Acheson, *Among Friends: Personal Letters of Dean Acheson* (New York: 1980), 105–106; Bradley, with Blair, 631–636.
63. James, III, 591–592.
64. Almond (Fergusson interview), 43, loc. cit.
65. Miller, 305. Cf. letter, J. Salter to Bonner Fellers, June 5, 1964, post-presidential file, HHL.
66. Robert Considine, *It's All News to Me* (New York: 1967), 349.
67. Sid Huff, *My Fifteen Years with General MacArthur* (New York: 1964) 6–7, 137; MacArthur, 395.

32. I Bid You Goodbye

1. Memo, Hoover to MacArthur, April 13, 1951, HHL; Bonner Fellers (Henle interview), 14–15, Bonner Fellers Papers, HI; Richard Norton Smith, *An Uncommon Man* (New York: 1989), 394–395.
2. William Sebald, *With MacArthur in Japan* (New York: 1965), 229; Douglas MacArthur, *Reminiscences* (New York: 1964), 295.
3. Letter, Margaret Almond to Edward Almond, April 12, 1951, Edward Almond Papers, USAMHI.
4. *The New York Times,* April 17, 1951; Courtney Whitney, *MacArthur: His Rendezvous with History* (New York: 1955), 480.
5. Lemuel C. Shepherd (Brower interview), 18, MMA.
6. Norman H. Scott, Jr. (Cineworld interview), Tape 2, MMA.
7. *The New York Times,* April 19, 1951.
8. Whitney, 483, says "the irony of the situation did not escape him," but I believe this is merely a euphemistic way of expressing what MacArthur really felt.
9. MacArthur, 401–405.
10. Robert J. Donovan (Cineworld interview), 11, MMA.

11. Cable, MacArthur to JCS, Dec. 30, 1950, Matthew B. Ridgway Papers, USAMHI; Earl Partridge (Reynolds interview), 55, Otto P. Weyland (Hasdorff interview), 128–129, HRA.

12. Truman diary, Jan. 27 and May 18, 1952, Harry S. Truman Papers, HSTL; State Department memo of conversation, Jan. 7, 1952, Dean Acheson Papers, MD, LC.

13. MacArthur, 404.

14. Omar Bradley, with Clay Blair, *A General's Life* (New York: 1983), 640.

15. Forrest C. Pogue, *George C. Marshall: Statesman* (New York: 1987), 489–490. Direct communications between MacArthur and McCarthy seem to consist of just two letters, McCarthy to MacArthur, Oct. 18, 1951, and MacArthur to McCarthy, Oct. 22, 1951, MMA; MacArthur's letter is little more than an acknowledgment of McCarthy's.

16. Richard Norton Smith, *Thomas E. Dewey and His Times* (New York: 1989), 567–568.

17. William S. Phillips, ed., *The MacArthurs of Milwaukee* (Milwaukee: 1979), 45.

18. Letter, George O. Wilson to Truman, June 16, 1951, HSTL.

19. Bonner Fellers (Henle interview), 14–16, loc. cit.; letters, Frank E. Gannett to Robert E. Wood, Sept. 24, 1951, Wood to Gannett, Feb. 6, 1952, Wood to MacArthur, May 2, 1952, MacArthur to Wood, June 17, 1952, Robert E. Wood Papers, HHL.

20. Albert C. Wedemeyer (Henle interview), 25–27, HHL; James T. Patterson, *Mr. Republican* (Boston: 1972), 280–284; Cyrus L. Sulzberger, *A Long Row of Candles* (New York: 1967), 771.

21. Letters, Wedemeyer to MacArthur, Oct. 21, 1952, MMA; James E. Rand to Robert E. Wood, Oct. 8, 1953, Wood Papers, loc. cit.

22. Letter, Bradley to MacArthur, Dec. 16, 1951, MMA; memo of conversation, Dec. 14, 1952, Ann Whitman File, and Eisenhower (Crowl interview), 8–9, EL.

23. Memo, Albert C. Wedemeyer to MacArthur, n.d. but evidently Jan. 1952, MMA.

24. Clark Lee and Richard Henschel, *Douglas MacArthur* (New York: 1952), 77; Robert Considine, *It's All News to Me* (New York: 1967), 353.

25. William Ganoe, *MacArthur Close-Up* (New York: 1961), 162.

26. James Farley (Henle interview), 14–15, HHL.

27. Kiera Huff (Cineworld interview), 3–4, MMA.

28. Ty Cobb, *My Life in Baseball* (Garden City, N.Y.: 1961), 7.

29. There are dozens of letters between MacArthur and Blaik in Blaik's papers, which are housed in the Special Collections at West Point. Also see Earl Blaik, *You Have to Pay the Price* (New York: 1960); Blaik (Mattox interview), 3–4, MMA.

30. Louis Sullivan (Cineworld interview), 5, 7, MMA. Sullivan was a retired New York Police Department detective and MacArthur's bodyguard.

31. Jean MacArthur interview, Tape 30, MMA.

32. Averell Harriman, memo of conversation, Aug. 6, 1950, HSTL; *Chicago Daily News,* Jan. 26, 1950.

33. Jean MacArthur, op. cit.

34. Leslie R. Groves (Brower interview), 8–9, MMA.

35. Letter, Milton Hill to MacArthur, June 2, 1946, MMA.

36. Letters, Courtney Whitney to Charles R. Lehner, Aug. 30, 1955, Courtney Whitney Papers, HI; Edward K. Thompson to Robert E. Wood, Oct. 19, 1954, Nov. 13, 1954, March 31, 1955, and Wood to Whitney, Dec. 1, 1954, Wood Papers, loc. cit.; cable, Thompson to Wood, Nov. 26, 1954; Laurence E. Bunker (Zobriski interview), 6, HSTL.

37. Robert J. Donovan, ed., *Off the Record: The Private Papers of Harry S. Truman* (New York: 1982), 322–323; *Life* (Feb. 13, 1956); letter, MacArthur to Edward Almond, April 28, 1958, MMA.

38. Letter (with enclosures), MacArthur to R. W. Stephens, Nov. 15, 1957, Whitney Papers, loc. cit.
39. Author interview with Brigadier General Edward H. Simmons, Aug. 20, 1994.
40. Jean MacArthur interview, Tape 31, loc. cit.
41. Letters, Sverdrup to Hoover, Sept. 4, 1959, and Jan. 13, 1960, HHL.
42. Letter, Eisenhower to MacArthur, Jan. 18, 1960, MMA.
43. MacArthur had written to an old friend, "It is no secret that the present administration is as hostile to me as was the past," which was completely untrue: letter, MacArthur to George W. Cocheu, Oct. 11, 1954, MMA. Cf. Eisenhower to MacArthur, April 15, 1959, MMA, which invited MacArthur to come and have dinner at the White House with Winston Churchill. Ike's only conceivable motive in extending this invitation was friendship.
44. Weldon Rhoades, *Flying MacArthur to Victory* (College Station, Texas: 1990), 516.
45. *New York Post,* Jan. 27, 1960. MacArthur had requested that no reporters or photographers be present, but Gene Smith, an enterprising young journalist, managed to pass himself off as a Waldorf employee and helped the guests as they struggled out of their coats, then helped them to get back into them after the party broke up.
46. Robert H. White (Cineworld interview), 4, MMA.
47. Kenneth P. O'Donnell et al., *"Johnny, We Hardly Knew Ye"* (New York: 1973), 13–14, 320; Earl Blaik, *The Earl Blaik Story* (New York: 1969), 498–499.
48. Jean MacArthur interview, Tape 30, loc. cit.
49. Letter, Whitney to John K. Swensson, March 18, 1965, Whitney Papers, loc. cit.
50. MacArthur, 426.
51. Norman Scott (Alexander interview), 4, 9; "Medical Records—Final Illness," DM 201 File, MMA.
52. Cable, MacArthur to Quezon, Aug. 11, 1939, MMA.
53. Letter, MacArthur to Louise Brooks Cromwell, Nov. 16, 1920, in Joseph M. Maddelena, ed., *Profiles in History: The Passionate and Poetic Pen of Douglas MacArthur* (Beverly Hills: 1993), 12.
54. Francis Trevelyan Miller, *General Douglas MacArthur* (New York: 1942), 116.
55. Joseph Choate, *Douglas MacArthur as I Knew Him* (Los Angeles: 1986), 24.

Index

ABOUT THE AUTHOR

GEOFFREY PERRET was born into an Anglo-American family and reared as a transatlantic commuter. He served in the U.S. Army from 1959 to 1961, and attended the University of Southern California, Harvard, and the University of California at Berkeley, where he was elected Phi Beta Kappa. His first book was an award-winning account of the American World War II home front, *Days of Sadness, Years of Triumph*. Perret is also the author of *A Country Made by War*, a military history of the United States; *There's a War to Be Won*, a chronicle of the United States Army in World War II; and *Winged Victory*, a history of the Army Air Forces in World War II.

ABOUT THE TYPE

This book was set in Times Roman, designed by Stanley Morison specifically for *The Times* of London. The typeface was introduced in the newspaper in 1932. Times Roman has had its greatest success in the United States as a book and commercial typeface, rather than one used in newspapers.